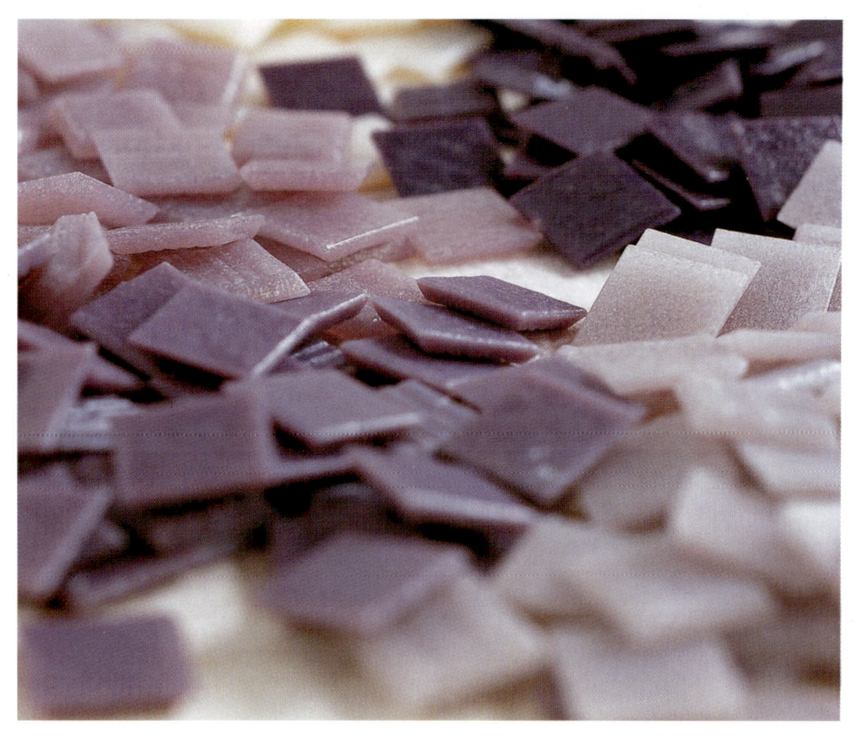

THE COMPLETE PRACTICAL GUIDE TO

MOSAICS

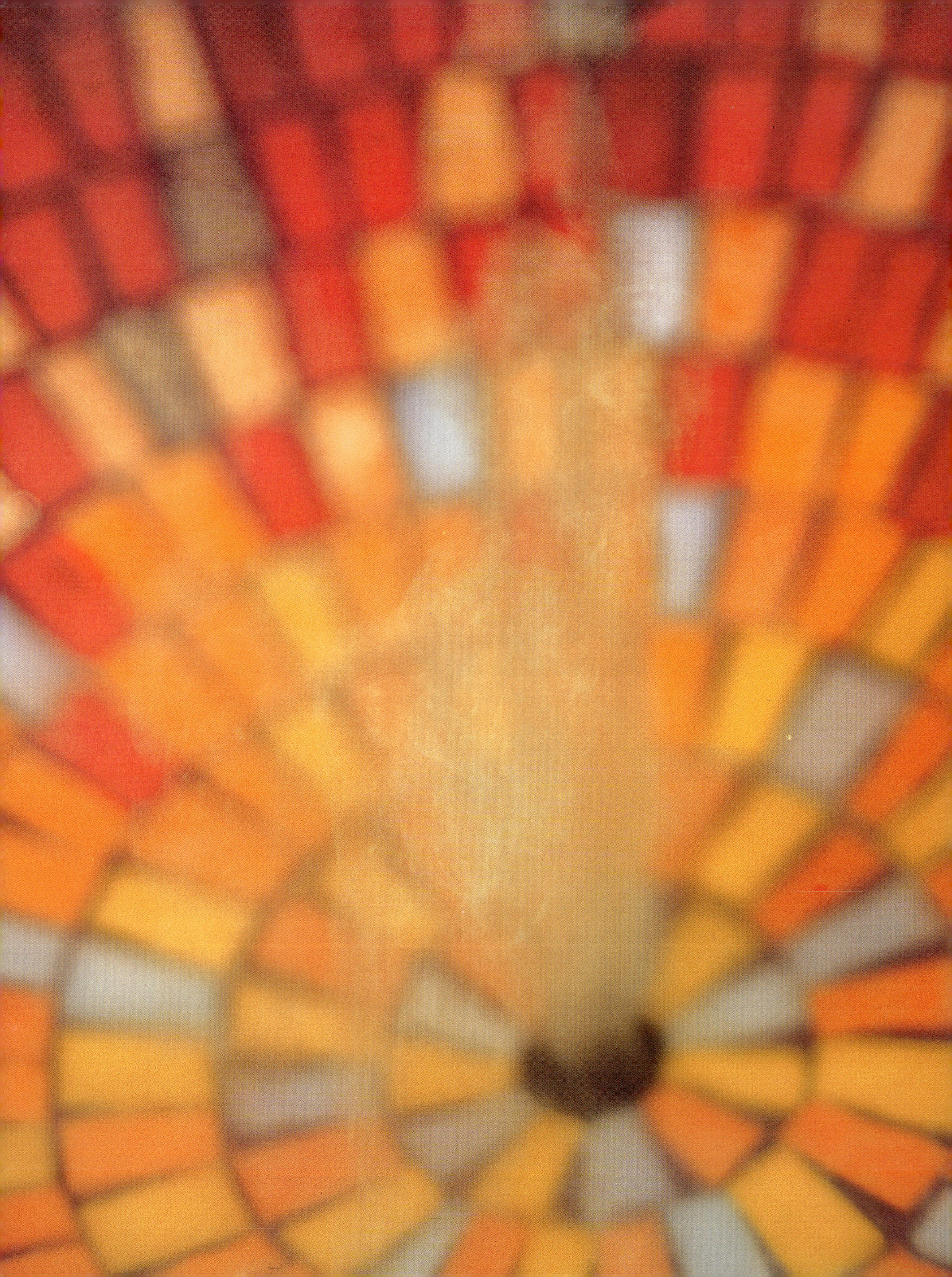

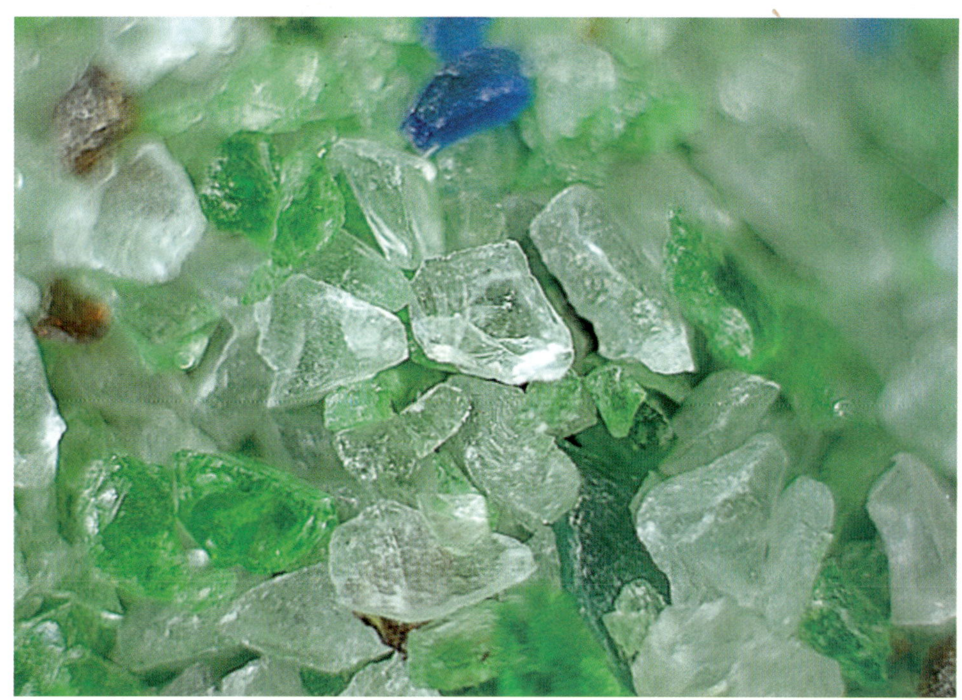

HELEN BAIRD

THE COMPLETE PRACTICAL GUIDE TO MOSAICS

WITH OVER 60 STEP-BY-STEP TECHNIQUES AND PROJECTS FOR EVERY HOME AND GARDEN

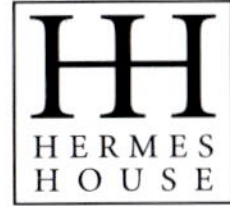

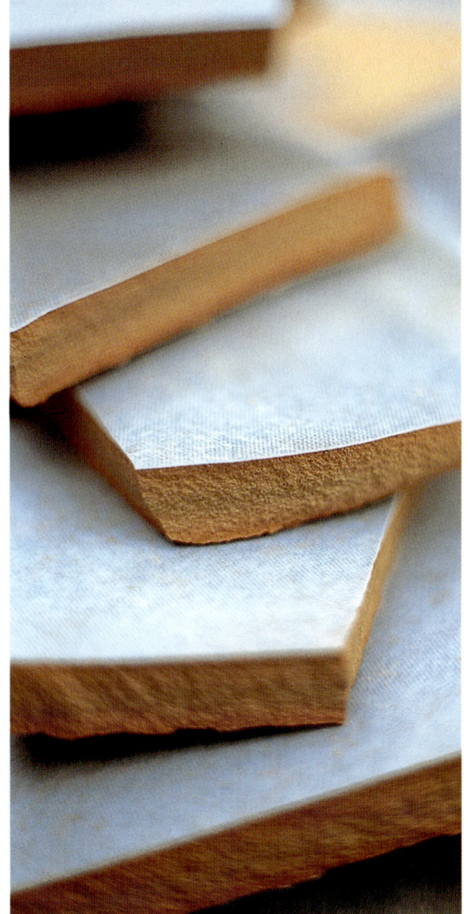

This edition is published by Hermes House

Hermes House is an imprint of Anness Publishing Ltd
Hermes House, 88–89 Blackfriars Road, London SE1 8HA
tel. 020 7401 2077; fax 020 7633 9499; info@anness.com

A CIP catalogue record for this book is available from the British Library.

Publisher Joanna Lorenz
Editorial Director Judith Simons
Project Editor Katy Bevan
Text Editor Alison Bolus
Designer Adelle Morris
Editorial Reader Jay Thundercliffe
Production Controller Pedro Nelson
Additional text Caroline Suter, Celia Gregory, Mary Maguire, Cleo Mussi, Marion Elliot
Photography Polly Eltes, Debbi Treloar, Rodney Forte, Spike Powell, TIm Imrie,
Adrian Taylor, Debbie Patterson, Zul Mukhida

10 9 8 7 6 5 4 3 2

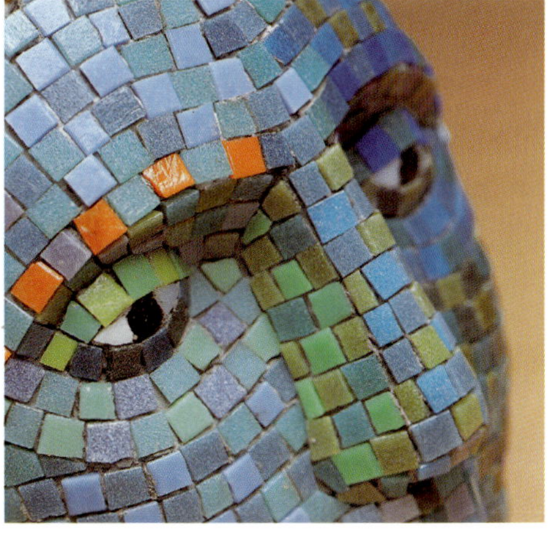

Publisher's note

Projects are graded for difficulty from 1–5 indicated by this brush symbol.

The authors and the publisher have made every effort to ensure that all the instructions contained in this book are accurate and that the safest methods are recommended. Readers should follow all recommended safety procedures and wear protective goggles, gloves and clothing at all times during the making of mosaics. You should know how to use all your tools and equipment safely and make sure you are confident about what you are doing. The publisher and author cannot accept liability for any resulting injury, damage or loss to persons or property as a result of using any equipment in this book or carrying out any of the projects.

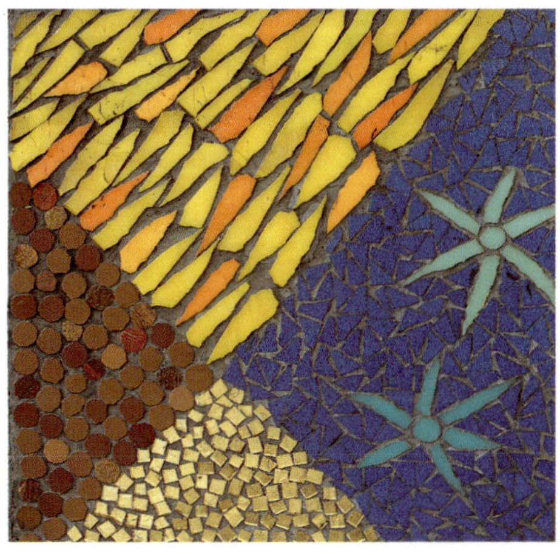

Contents

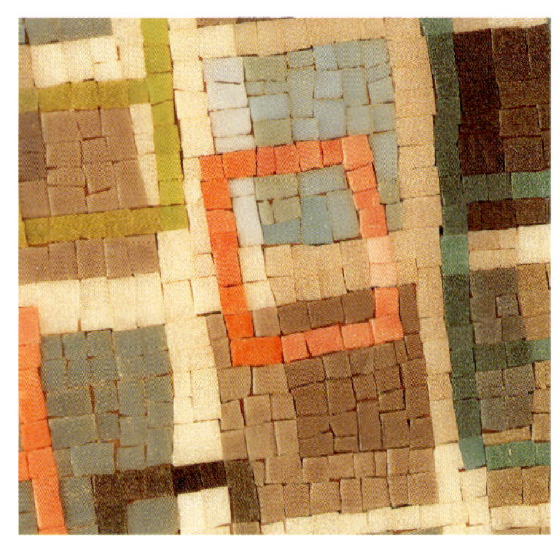

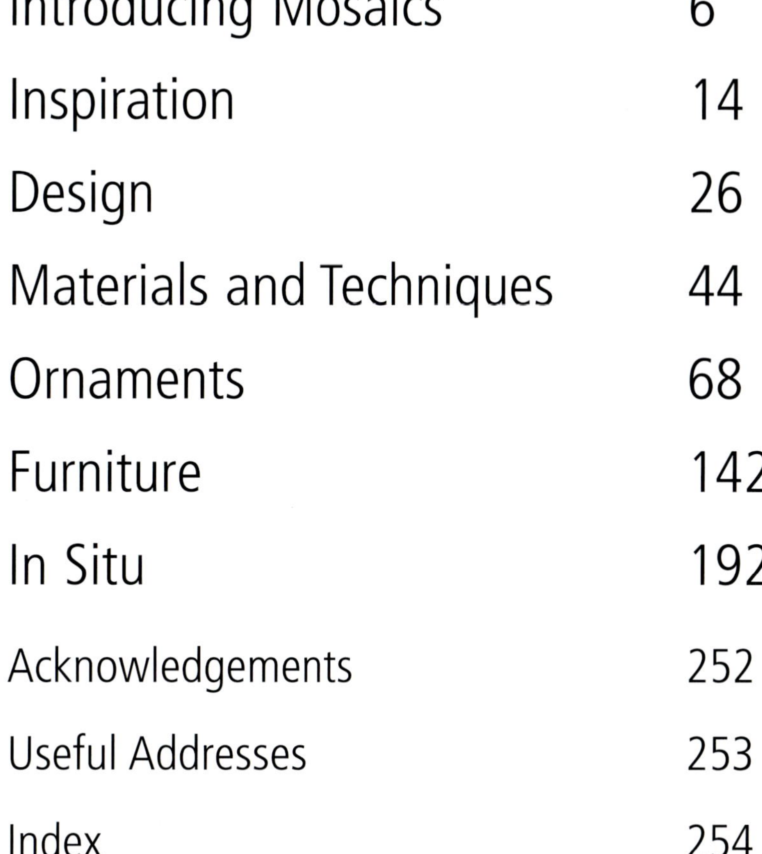

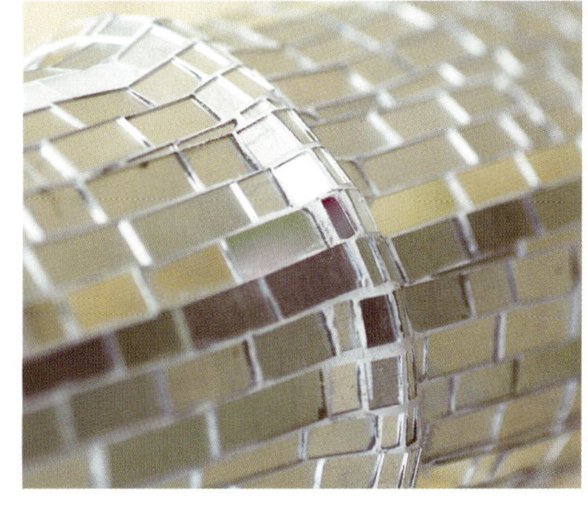

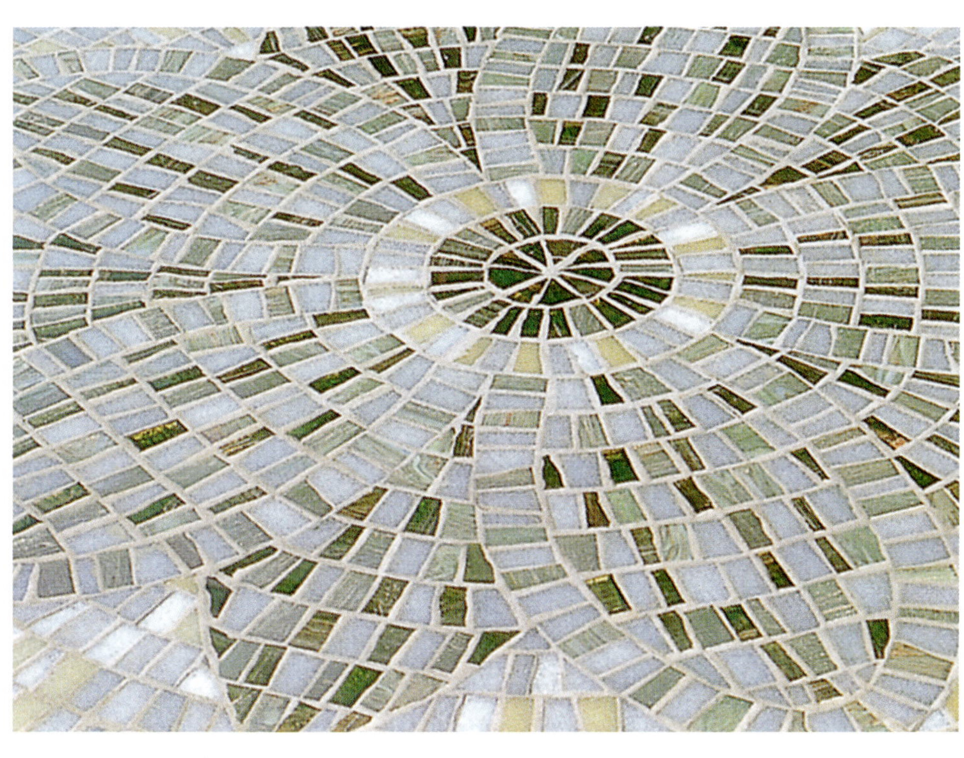

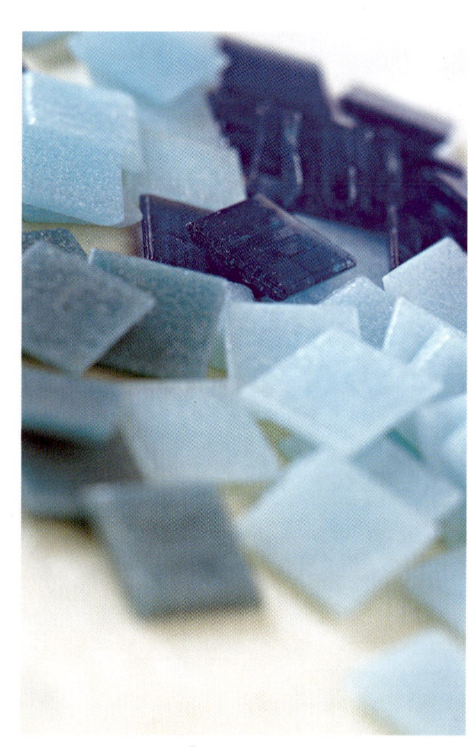

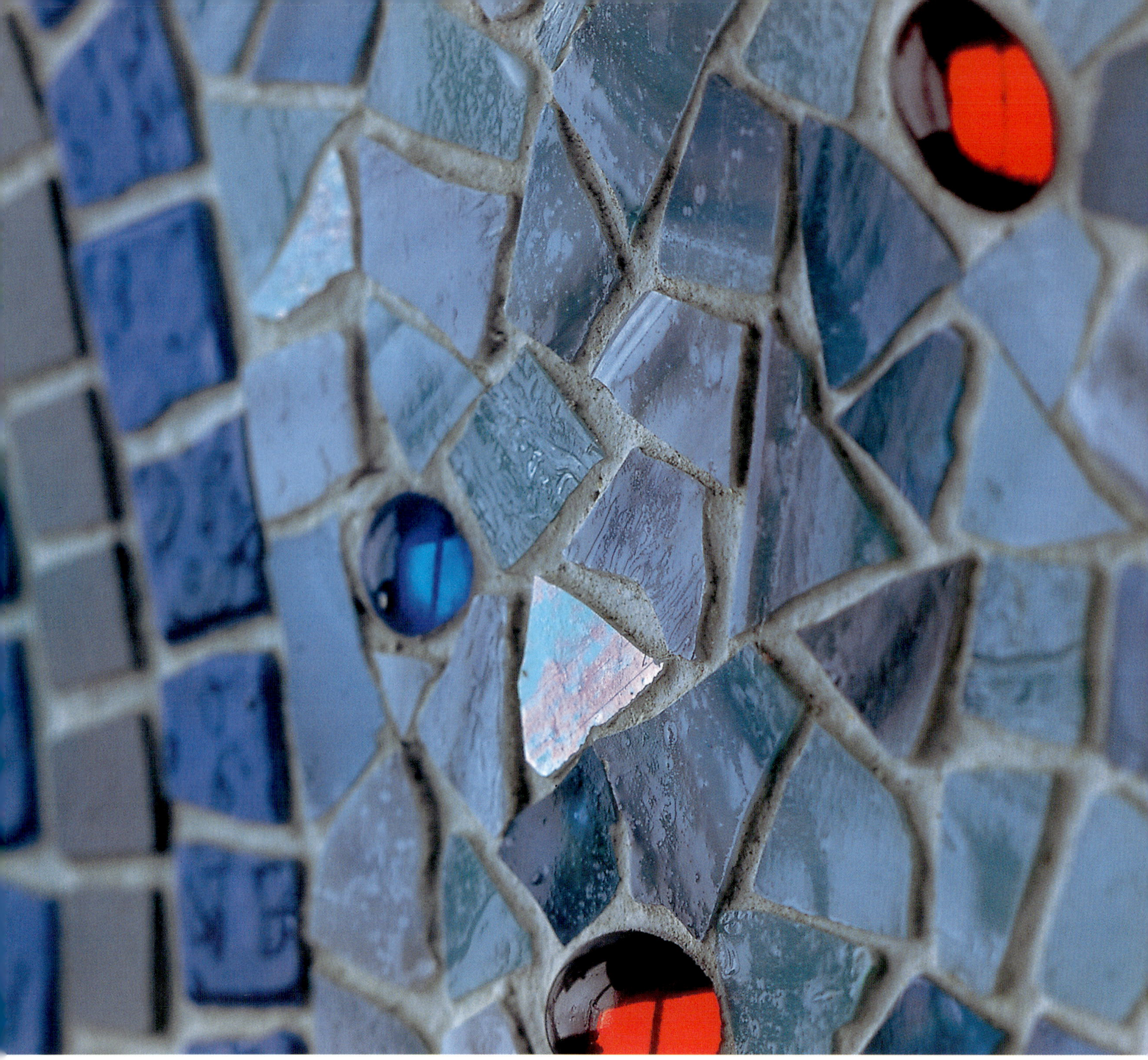

Introducing Mosaics

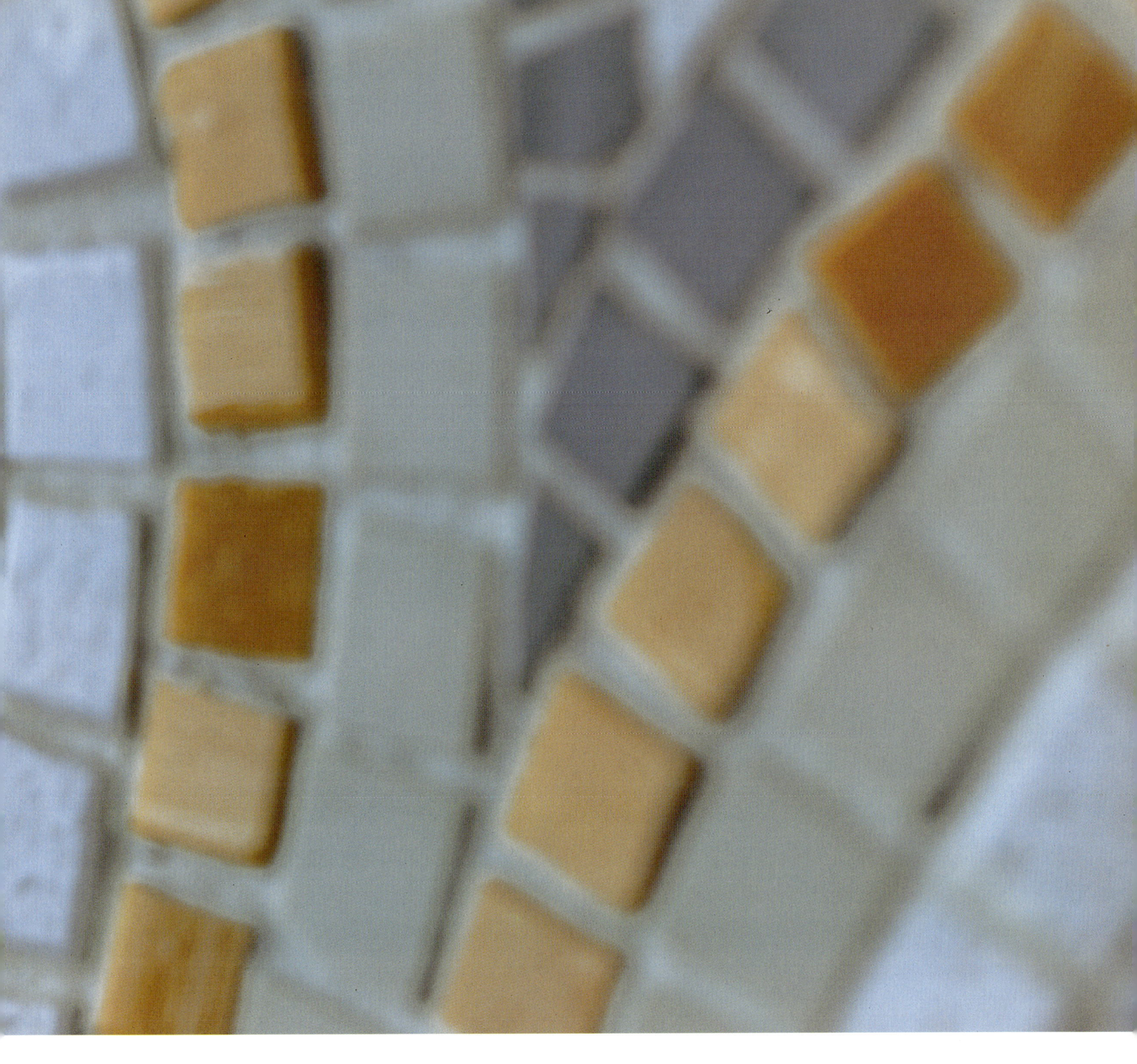

We know that the ancient art of mosaic was practised extensively throughout history because so many impressive examples have survived. It is a remarkably durable and versatile medium – in public places, on the outside of buildings in the playground or park, and in more domestic situations in private homes and gardens. Also beautiful and decorative, mosaics that are created for our enjoyment now are a legacy for the future.

Mosaics have been made by many civilizations who discovered the technique independently of each other. They are unusual in having survived long enough for us to enjoy hundreds of years later.

A History of Mosaic

Most of us will be very familiar with mosaic as an art form, and perhaps the image most often conjured up is that of Roman floors and walls. However, although the term "mosaic" originates from Italy, the art form itself certainly existed long before Roman times and has been practised in various ways by subsequent cultures and civilizations.

Today we have access to a huge variety of work from a multitude of sources, to which we can look for our inspiration. Perhaps the reason we so often associate mosaic with the past is the durability of the materials used to make them, for example stone, glass or ceramics. Consequently, many ancient examples have survived centuries of upheaval, and can still be seen today.

Western Europe

The earliest surviving mosaics were made in about 3000BC by the Sumerians in ancient Mesopotamia, now known as Iraq. These consisted of arrangements of coloured clay pegs that were pressed into wall surfaces. Later, the Egyptians used fragments of coloured materials and semi-precious stones to decorate walls and to inlay furniture, decorative objects and items of jewellery.

Ancient Greece is the earliest civilization known to have used natural stones and pebbles in varying colours to create permanent designs, and it was probably the originator of what we today think of as "mosaic".

The Romans built on this technique, standardizing practices by cutting natural stone into regular cubes. They also used fired clay and some glass for special effects. Another Roman innovation was the use of cements and mortars. These made their mosaics astonishingly durable, and as a result there are many surviving examples of floor and wall mosaics throughout countries that were once part of the Roman Empire.

In their mosaics the Romans used an extraordinarily varied range of styles and subjects – from realistic, observed studies of everyday life to naïve garden mosaics, and from classical depictions of the gods to purely decorative designs and geometric borders. These early mosaics were executed in the

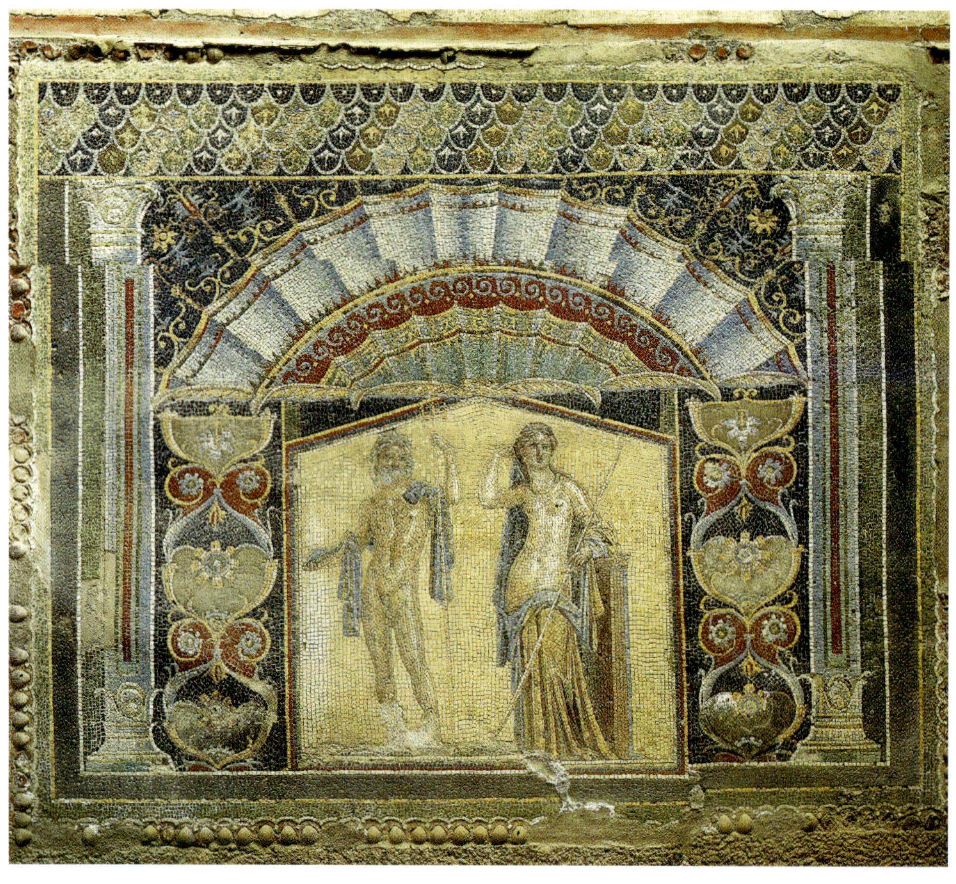

Left: This image of Neptune and Amphitrite is from a house in Herculaneum and has survived a volcano in AD79, and all the subsequent years.

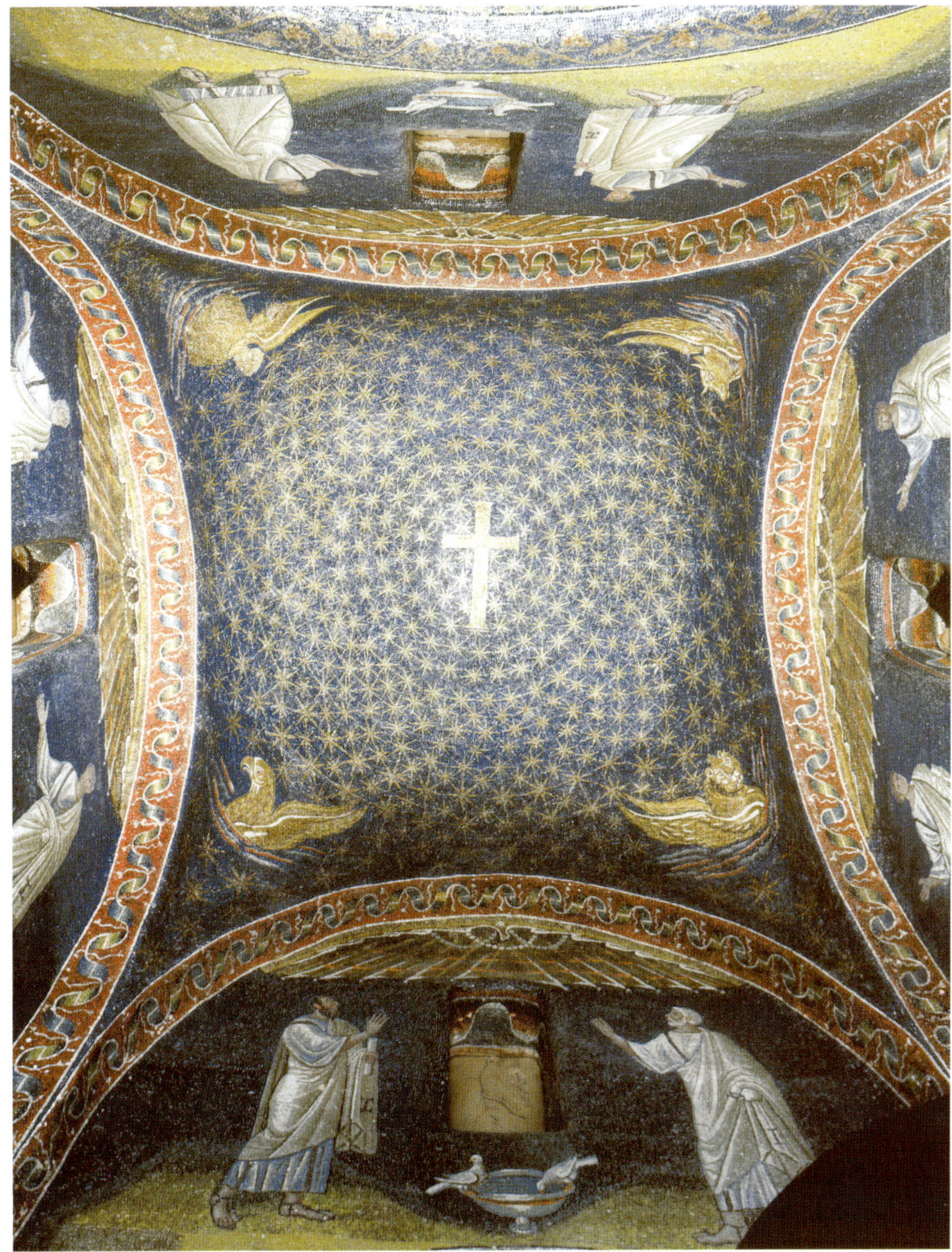

Right: The stars in this Byzantine vaulted roof in the Mausoleum of Galla Placidia, Ravenna, Italy, still shine as brightly as when they were created, 5th century AD.

natural colours of the materials they were made from: greys, terracotta, ochre, white, dull blues and greens.

The growth of Christianity introduced new subject matter, but techniques and colours remained broadly unchanged until the Byzantine era, usually dated as beginning with the reign of the Emperor Justinian in Ravenna, about AD527. This was to be a very rich and innovative period in the history of mosaic, exemplified by the beautiful, luminous creations adorning Byzantine churches.

At this time, Ravenna was a wealthy imperial town and the main trading link between East and West. It is here that the best examples of Byzantine mosaic can be found, and the influence of Eastern art is apparent in the designs, such as the large Egyptian eyes, flattened shapes and ordered poses. This iconoclastic style was rendered with a new kind of tessera, or mosaic tile – glass "smalti". Glass, which previously had been used sparingly for highlights, now became the main component of mosaics. It was fired with metallic oxides, copper and marble, or had gold and silver leaf sandwiched between layers of glass. This new material gave mosaic artists access to a large palette of luminous colours. The technique of setting the pieces into the mortar bed at varying angles achieved wonderful effects with the reflective qualities of glass.

During this period, the art of mosaic making was superseded by fresco painting. The mosaics that did continue to be created tended to be copies of paintings – a tendency that persisted right up to the 20th century. As a result, the mosaicist had become a master craftworker and copyist rather than an original artist, which meant that mosaic did not develop as an art form in Western Europe for a long time.

At the beginning of the 20th century, however, the Art Nouveau movement gave artists a new direction, and mosaic began to be seen again as an artistic medium that could be celebrated for its own qualities. Pure pattern re-emerged and forms were simplified and stylized.

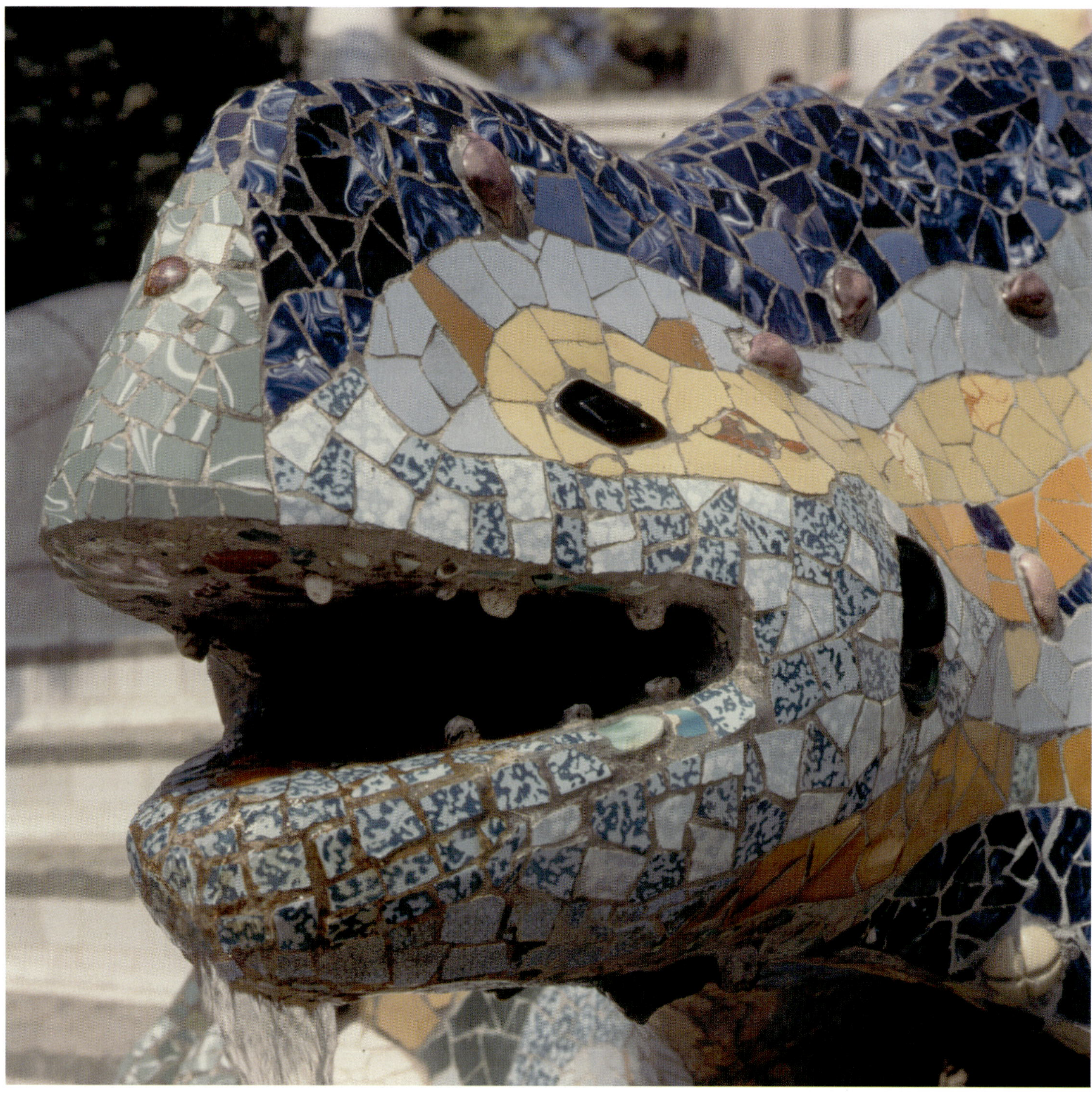

Mosaic was given a further boost with the onset of modernism. The best-known exponent of mosaic in this era was the architect Antonio Gaudí (1852–1926). He covered the large exterior surfaces of his buildings, both plain and formed, with irregularly shaped coloured tiles. He also commissioned prominent modern artists of the time, such as Kokoschka, Klimt and Chagall, to make designs for the mosaics that clad his buildings. Examples of his mosaics in Barcelona, Spain, include the façade of Casa Batlló, the spires of the (unfinished) Sagrada Família cathedral, and the serpentine benches on the terrace of the extraordinary Parc Güell.

Above: This undulating mosaic-covered lizard is a fountain designed by Antonio Gaudí, Parc Güell, Barcelona, Spain.

Josep Maria Jujol, a collaborator of Gaudí, is also interesting for the ceramic medallions that he made for the ceiling of the Hypostyle Hall in Parc Güell. He set brilliantly coloured

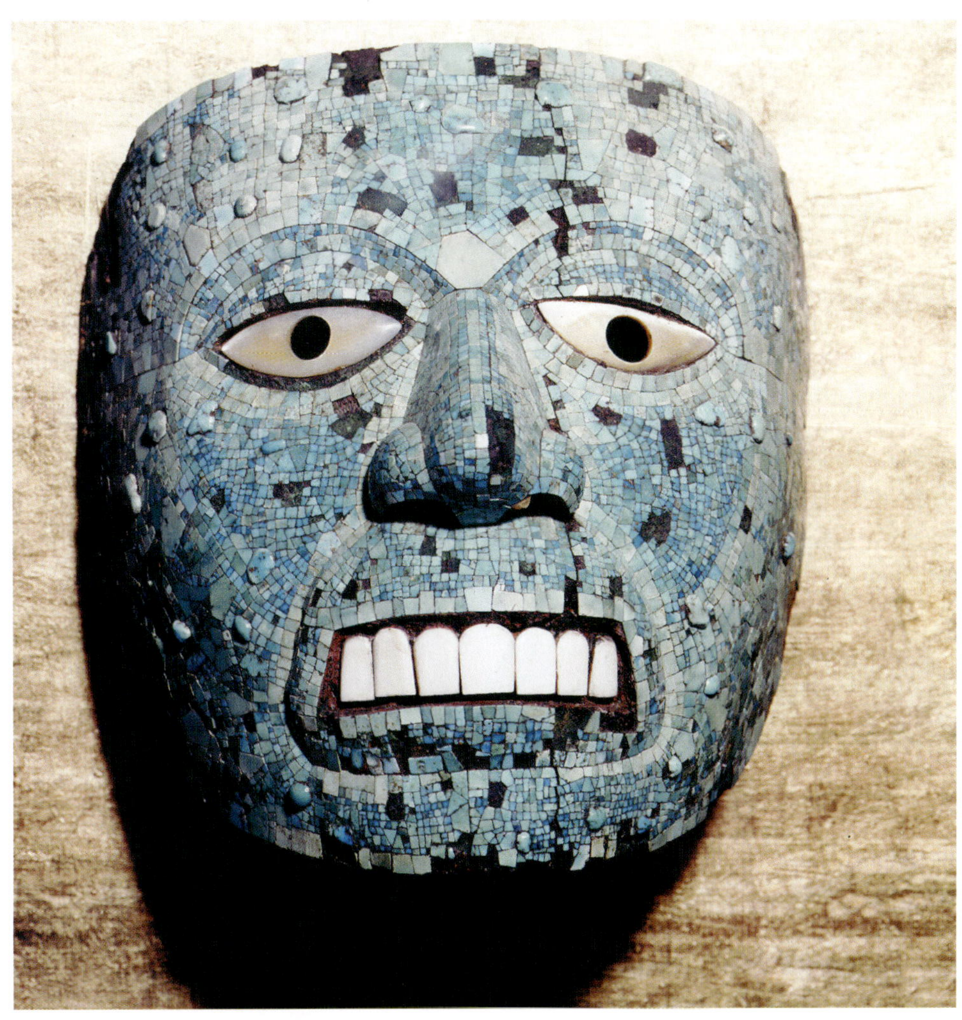

Right: This turquoise mosaic mask represents Quetzalcoatl, the feathered serpent god of ancient Mexico, c.1500. The pieces of precious stone would have been attached to a carved wooden base.

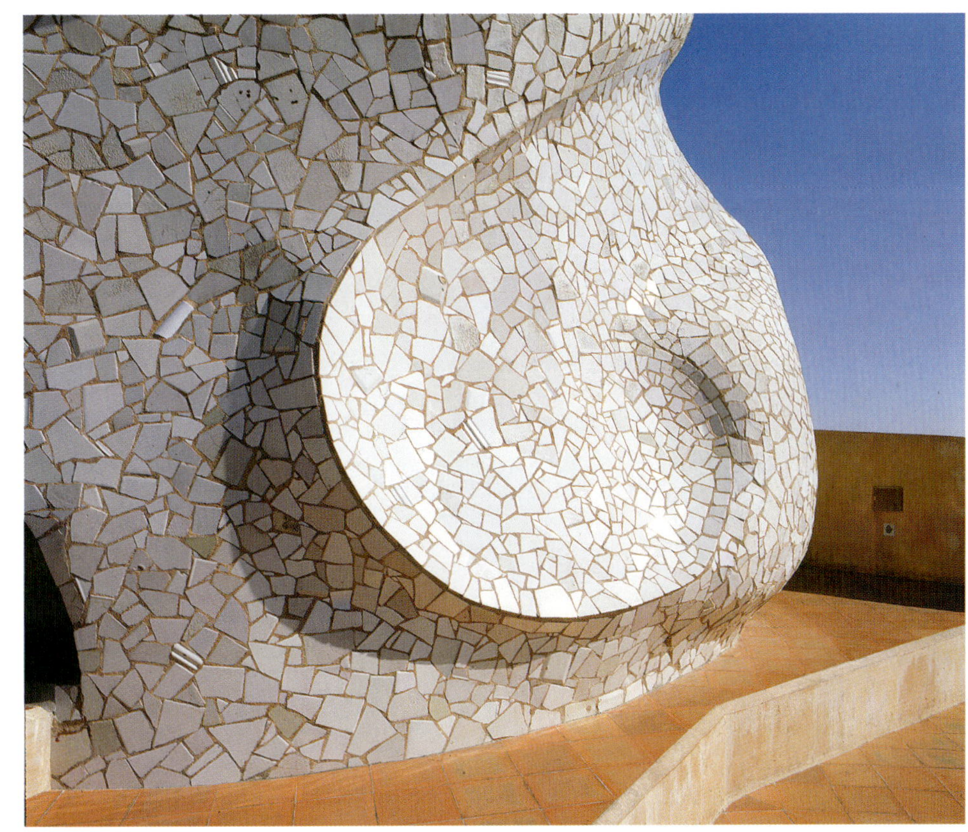

Below right: Roof of Casa Milà, La Pedrera, Barcelona, Spain, showing chimney pots and ceramic structures designed 1906–10 by Antonio Gaudí.

mosaic pieces (tesserae) against ceramic fragments, such as bases of bottles, cups and dishes, all arranged in patterns of stars and spirals.

Central America

The history of mosaics is not confined to Western Europe. Long before the arrival of Europeans in Central America, the Aztecs and Mayas had developed mosaic techniques separately from the rest of the world. There, mosaic was not used to convey images or systematic patterns, as was the tradition in Europe. Rather, it was used simply to embellish three-dimensional forms, very beautifully, using tesserae made from fragments of precious materials, most often coral and turquoise. These objects were often of a votive or ceremonial nature, such as skulls, weapons and carved snakes, and were encrusted with a variety of precious materials to give them beauty and importance.

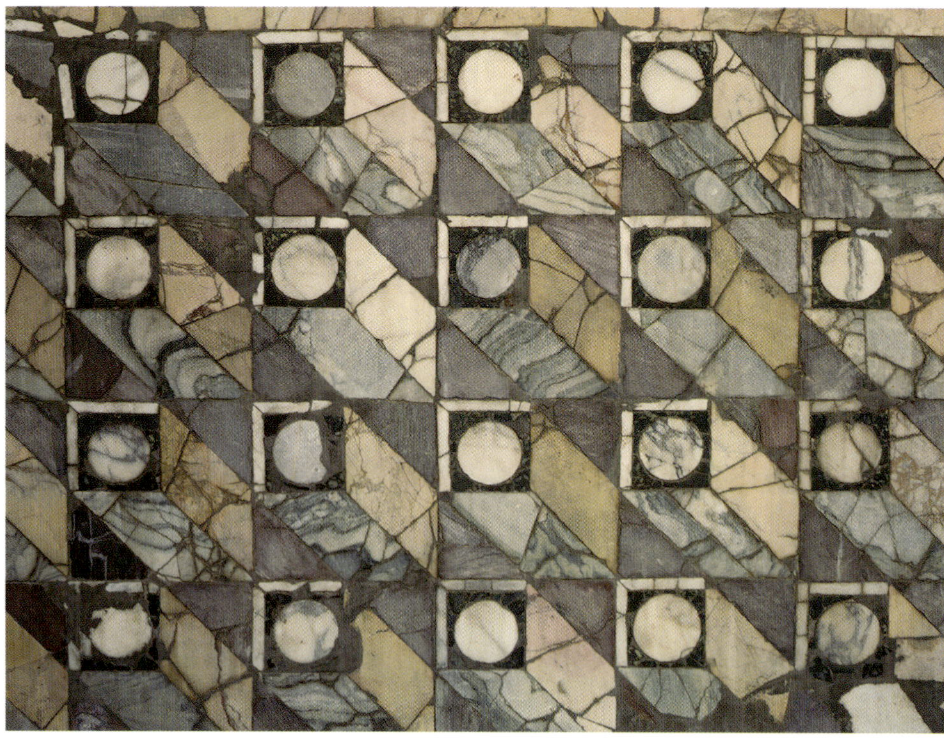

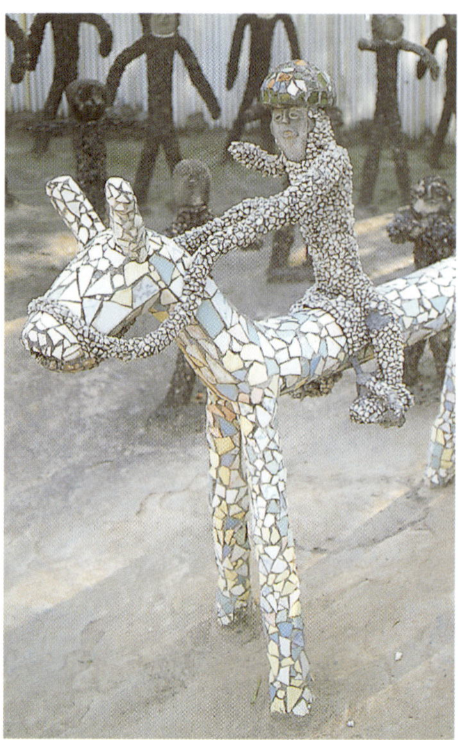

Islamic mosaic

Mosaic is also an important component of Islamic art. The designs are closely related to the buildings in which they are set and seem to rise naturally from the architecture. A fine example of the Islamic mosaic tradition can be seen in the 14th century palace of the Alhambra in Granada, Spain. Muslim craftspeople still construct complicated geometric mosaics today.

Other influences

Many cultures use mosaic-like effects to adorn buildings and objects. In African art, for example, everyday objects are often studded with tacks or covered in coloured beads. The effect is that of mosaic, although the method by which the pieces are attached differs from the traditional technique.

The handwoven carpets of India and Turkey are in many ways comparable to the medium of mosaic. The patterns are made up of individual units of colour, and these can be very useful as inspiration for designs.

Today, mosaic artists draw their inspiration from many different cultures and traditions, combining these influences with techniques and ideas that have developed in Europe.

Interesting exponents

Some of the most amazing examples of mosaic have, however, been made by people who had no formal arts training and who developed their work away from the public eye, often begging their materials from anywhere they could. Raymond Isidore, a manual worker in Chartres, France, covered his entire house and garden with intricate mosaics made from broken crockery.

His nickname, *Picassiette* (the French for "scrounger"), is now the name used for this style of mosaic. One of the best examples of this type of art is Nek Chand's rock garden in Northern India. Like Raymond Isidore, Nek Chand had a humble day job: he was a transport official in the nearby city of Chandigarh. Over the course of 18 years, however, he worked in secret on a clearing he made in the jungle. He built structures and sculpted figures, covering everything in a mosaic made from the city's discarded urban debris and from stones found on nearby hillsides. Forty years on, his incredible garden covers more than 11 hectares (27 acres) and attracts over 5,000 visitors a day.

Above left: Coloured stone mosaic, 9th–10th century AD, from the palace at Divanyolu, Istanbul, Turkey.

Above: Some of Nek Chand's creations, The Rock Garden of Chandigarh, India.

Opposite: Dancing – part of an installation by Nek Chand in India.

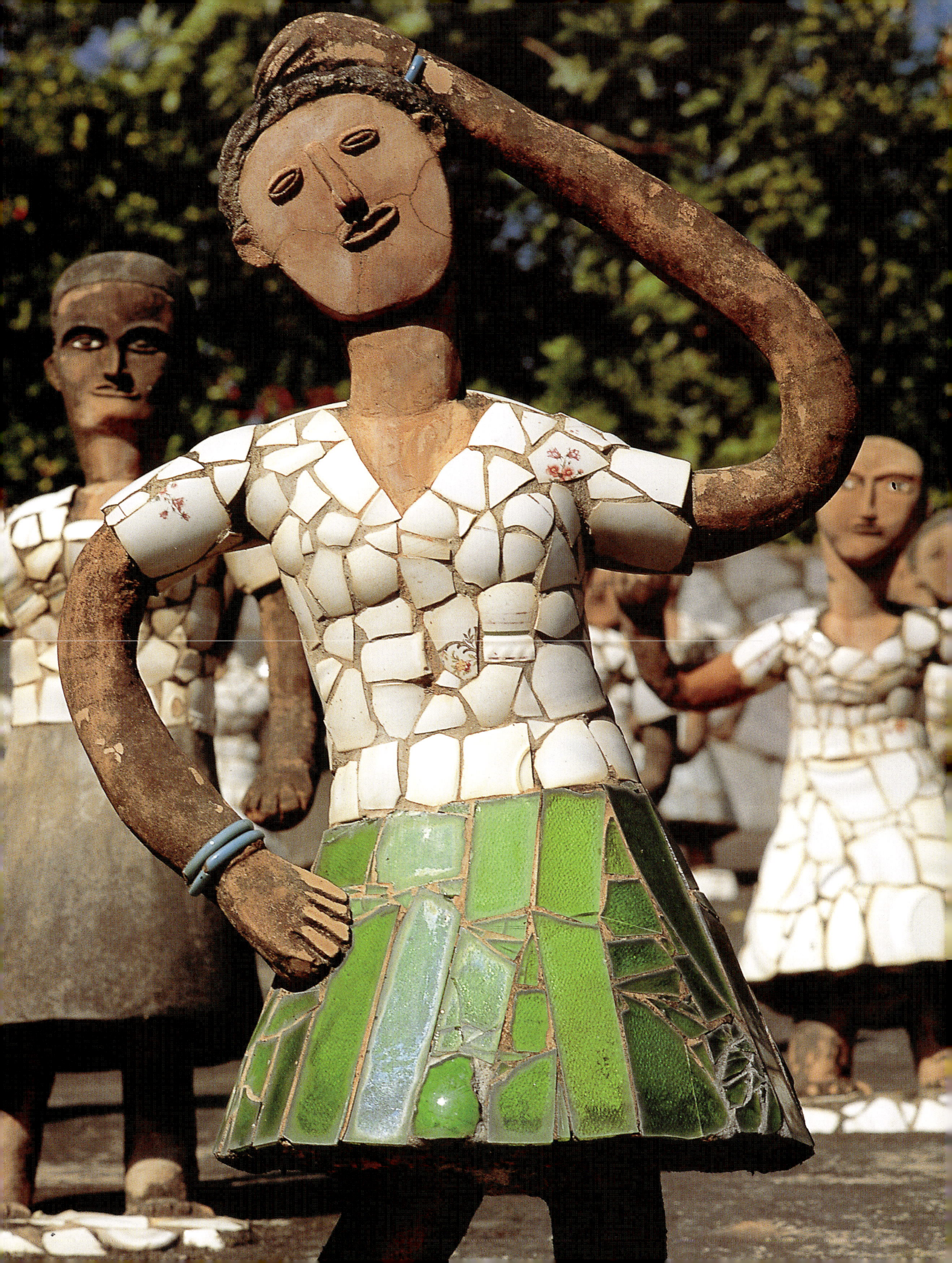

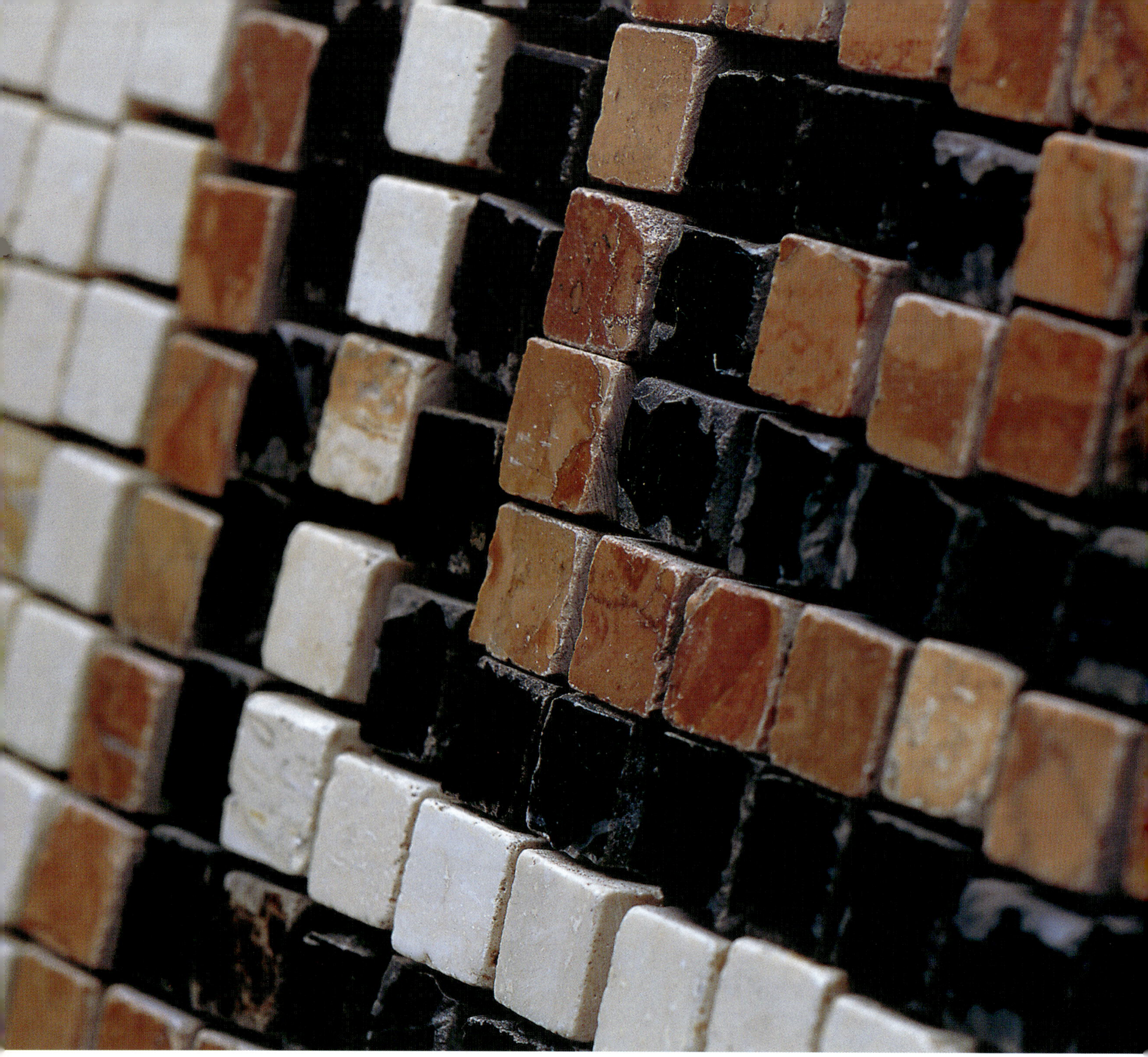

Inspiration

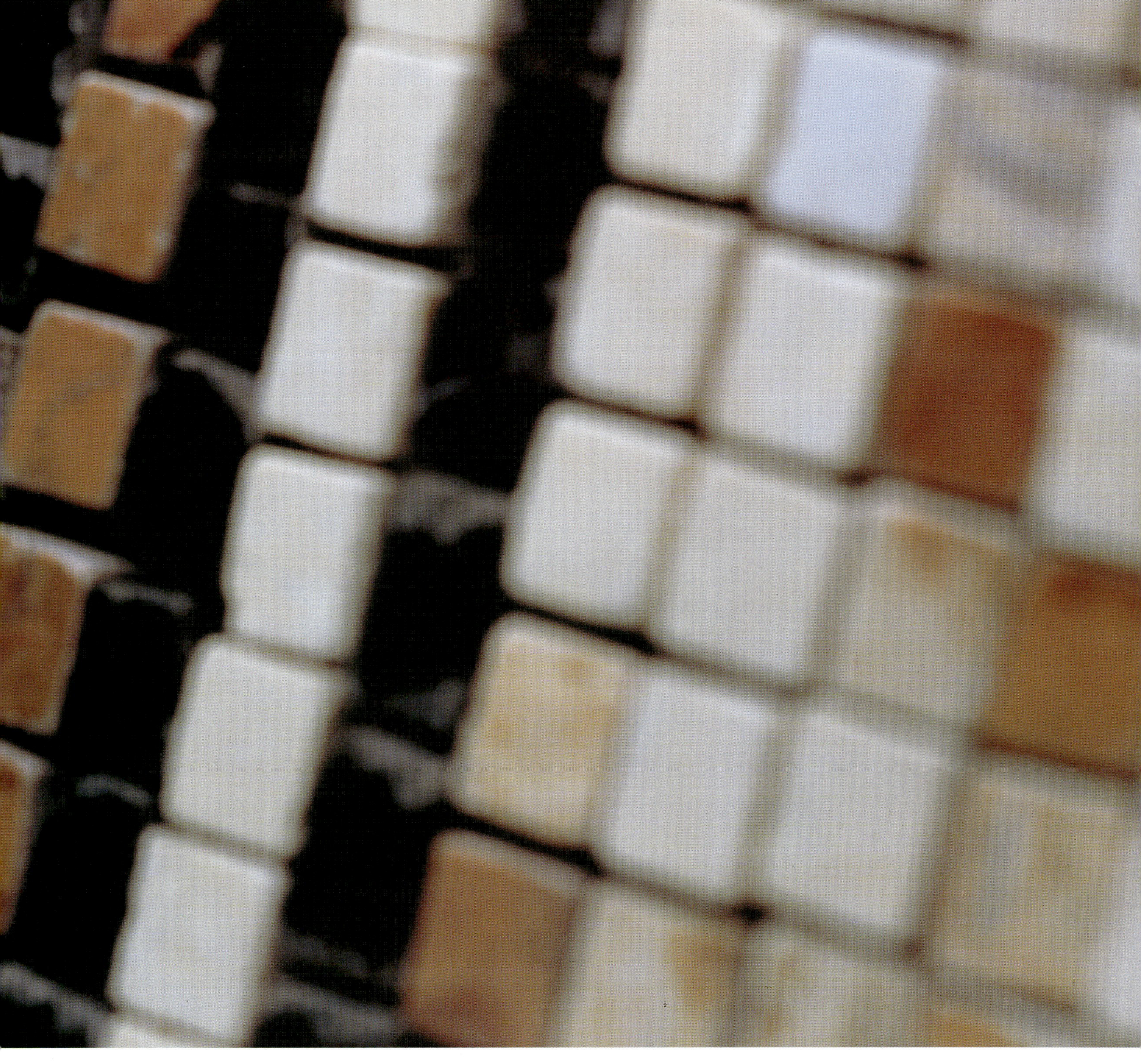

Mosaics may have a history that reaches back before Roman times, but the inspiration behind the designs can come from the everyday world around us. Designs can be influenced by our surroundings, from people and animal life, to landscapes and art. These influences can affect not just the motifs but also the choice of colour and texture, and the type of materials to be used. All these things will affect the movement and feel of the final piece of mosaic.

Modern mosaicists work in all manner of styles and bring immense flair to the art. Some draw on traditional influences and methods, while others forge new ground in their use of size, shape and materials.

Contemporary Mosaic

There has been a renewed interest in mosaic among the general public, and mosaic is now being applied to all kinds of objects in the decorative arts and sculpture, for private enjoyment, and to decorate public places. You can see the effectiveness of mosaic as a hard-wearing design element in locations as varied as railway stations, swimming pools, bars and shopping centres, as well as private homes.

Mosaic artists all around the world derive inspiration from many sources, including nature, animal and plant forms, as well as from the repeating or geometric patterns typical of Roman, Celtic and Cubist art. The bold and abstract art of 20th century artists, such as Picasso and Matisse, has also influenced the work of many current mosaic artists. Some employ traditional materials in exciting new ways and others incorporate more unusual materials and textures in their work.

The scale of work varies from small portable panels and accessories to patios and large expanses of floor as well as murals and immense sculptures. French artist Niki de Saint Phalle (b.1930) spent 1979–96 creating a fabulous mosaic Tarot Garden in Garavicchio, Tuscany, Italy, which unites sculpture and mosaic in fantastical figures, using brightly coloured tiles, glass and mirror. Sculptural mosaics are currently popular among young artists, but many prolific mosaic makers work on panels, murals and indoor pieces.

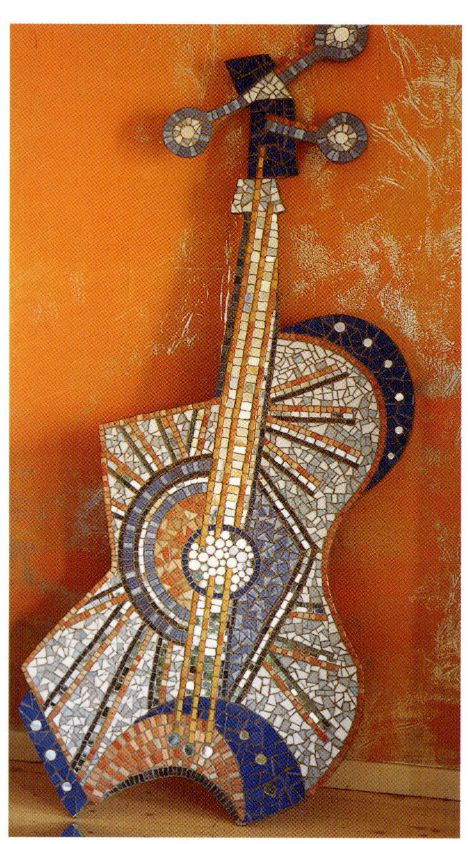

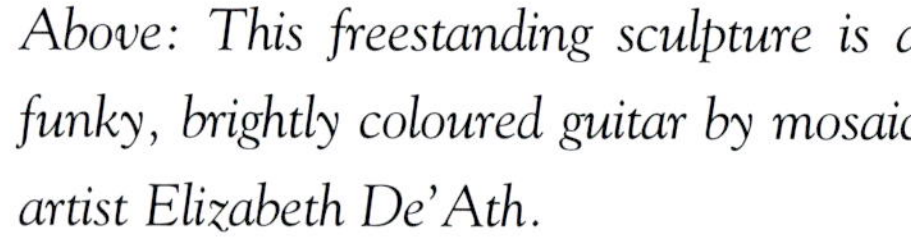

Above: This freestanding sculpture is a funky, brightly coloured guitar by mosaic artist Elizabeth De'Ath.

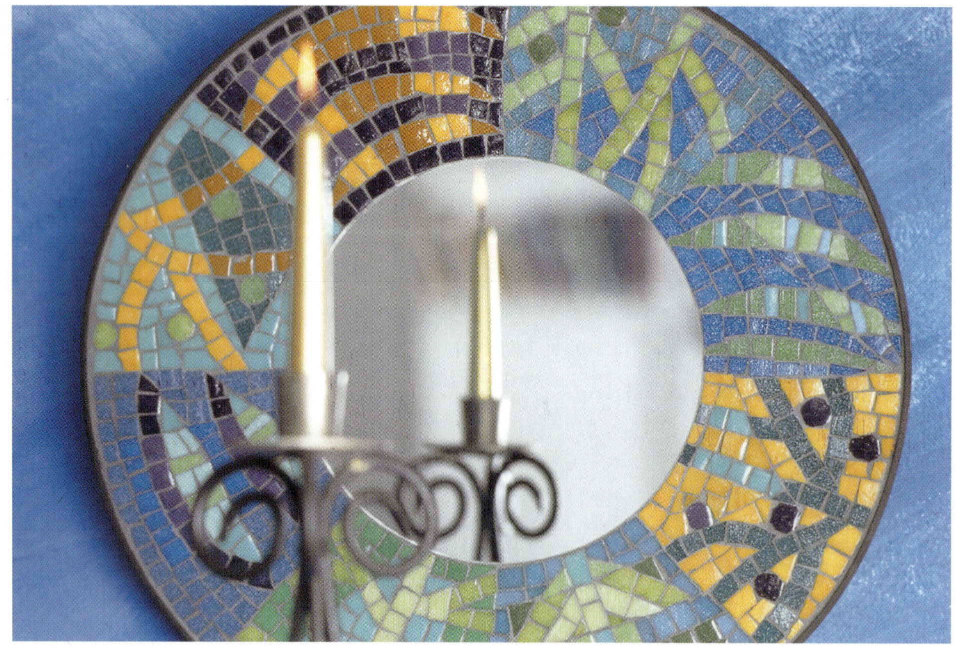

Left: Mosaic is an applied art that can complement contemporary interiors. This design for a mirror frame was worked out on paper first, before committing to the final design.

Opposite: A pyramid sculpture created with chicken wire and cement by artist Celia Gregory. The mosaic is made from small pieces of rectangular mirror and stained glass.

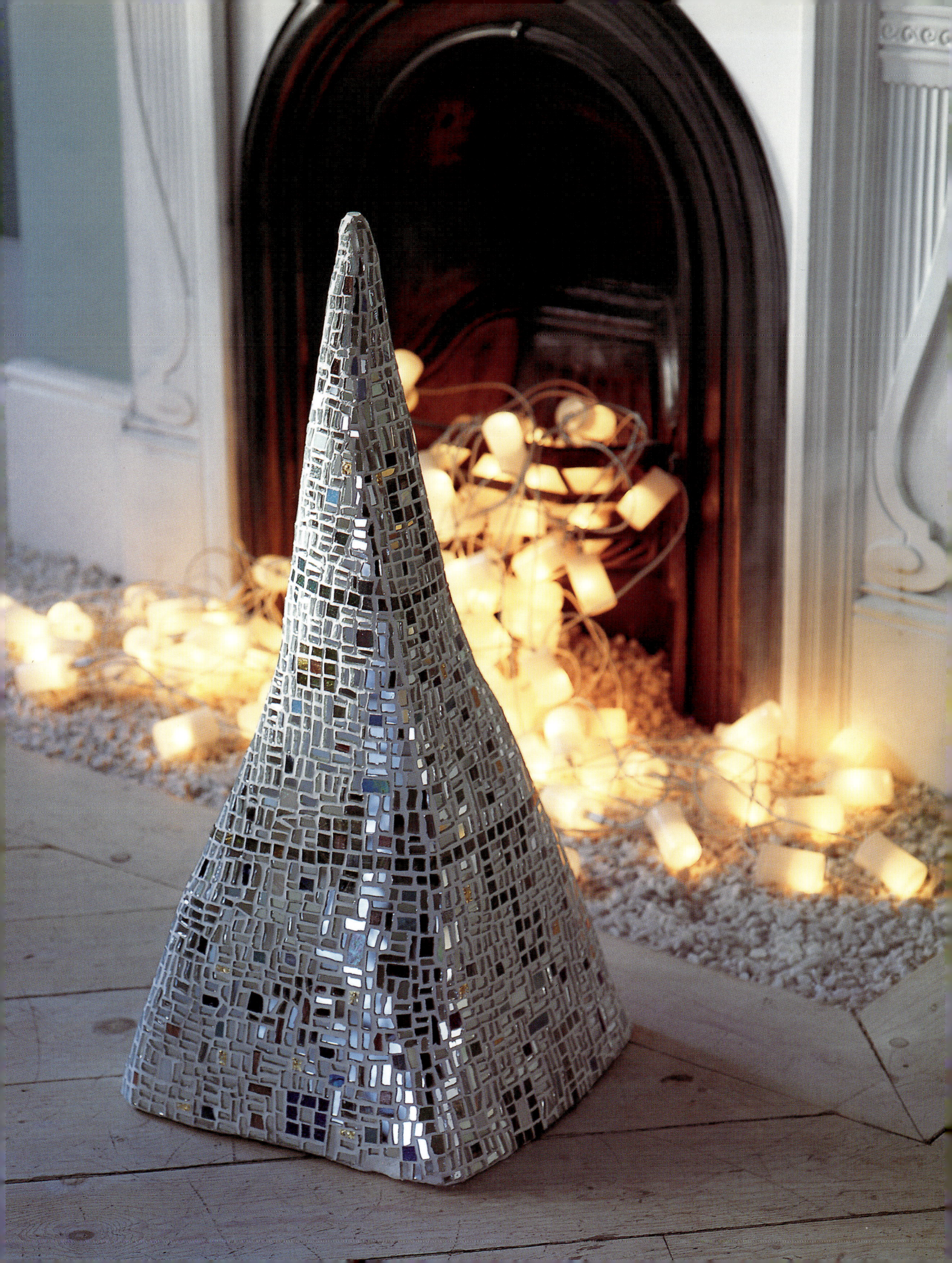

The depiction of the human form can take several guises. It can be realistic, as the Romans chose, or it can be more abstract. Likewise, birds, animals and fish can be shown naturalistically or allegorically.

Humans and Animals

Figurative mosaic in the hands of an expert may lend itself to great detail and intricacy. In such mosaics, the contours of the face and body are skilfully rendered through the way in which the tesserae are cut to size and positioned for their shape – notably to show the jut of the chin, cheekbones and brow. Tesserae are chosen to suggest the modelling of the features, for their gradations of colour and tone and to show the way light and shade fall on the face or body.

Ancient Roman images of the living world are mostly realistic, though sometimes they convey a quirky sense of humour. Animals in art have often served a symbolic purpose, for example dogs can indicate fidelity. Birds were a common Roman subject, especially doves at a fountain, which suggested harmony and peace.

In Byzantine times, mosaic was largely confined to religious or imperial subjects and was concerned to show figures such as emperors, Christ, God, the Virgin Mary and the saints in an idealized, and therefore essentially stylized, way. Forms were made slender, elongated and more elegant, faces became regular and expressionless, and gestures and rituals (such as benediction) were formalized and ritualized. It is a style that continues to inspire mosaicists today.

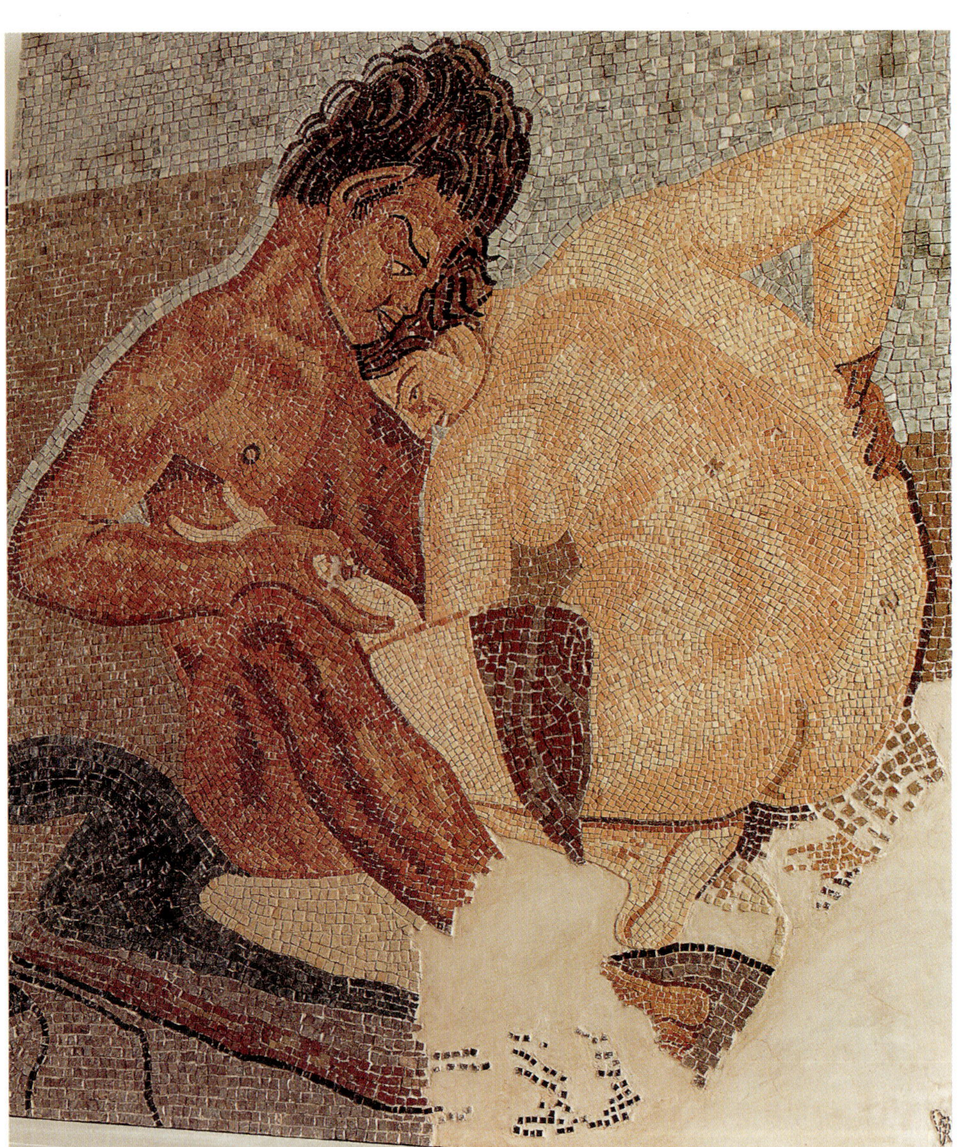

Above: Satyr and Maenad *– a highly detailed replication by Salvatore Raeli of a 2nd century mosaic panel from the House of the Faun, Pompeii, Italy.*

Moving with the times

In later centuries, including the Renaissance and Victorian eras, mosaics remained largely classical and representational in inspiration.

During the 20th century, however, there was a move towards the abstract representation of human figures. This style of depicting people was practised by many artists, including Pablo Picasso, Matisse and Chagall, whose styles and superb workmanship lent themselves well to mosaic, with the emphasis on outline and colour rather than detail, and the free rendition of line and form.

Modern depiction

The current revival of interest in mosaic often displays a more naturalistic approach, revelling in the beauty and detail of the natural world. Nature can be depicted in numerous ways. For example, a bird could be the main focus within a panel or roundel, or be a stand-alone image on a plain background, such as a garden wall. How the mosaic is executed will depend on the artist's own style. Animals and birds can be treated in a symbolic manner, or they can be allegorical or humorous, realistic or naturalistic. They can appear in outline against a one- or two-colour background, or in silhouette, or have two- or three-dimensional effects. More unusual materials can be added to give detail, texture and depth.

Often animals, birds and insects will form part of a larger mosaic; when they do there needs to be enough tonal contrast in the work to allow the images to stand out, and colours must be chosen carefully. Birds and insects are challenging subjects, but the potential for using vibrant colour is endless, especially with bright plumage. With regard to the human form, today's mosaic artists can choose to depict this in many ways, varying from ethnic art to the vibrant, contemporary approach of the strip cartoon.

Below far left and centre: Takako Shimizu's cobweb and spider brilliantly convey the delicacy and transparency of the web. The well-camouflaged mosaic bat has texture and a three-dimensional quality.

Below: A rabbit panel by Claire Stewart shows the broad outlines of the animal's body against a simple background.

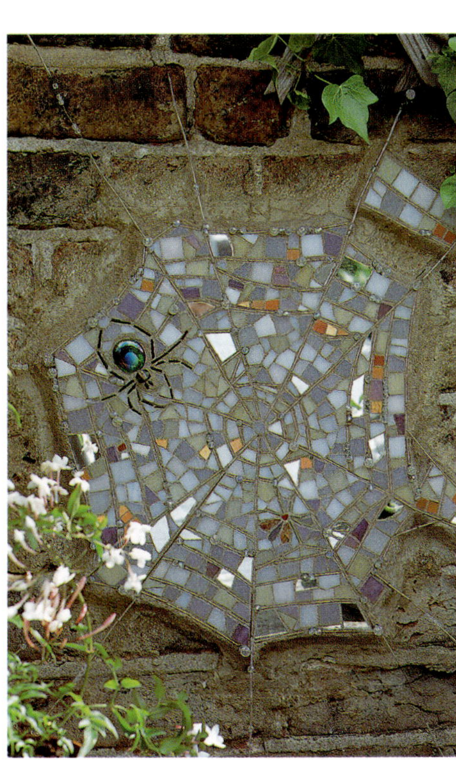

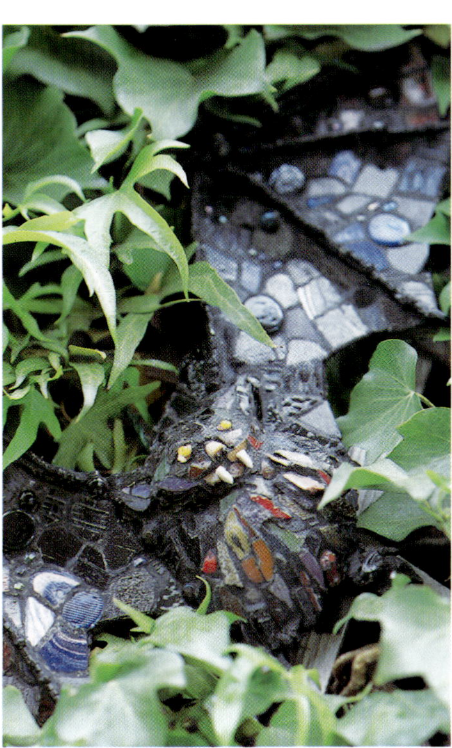

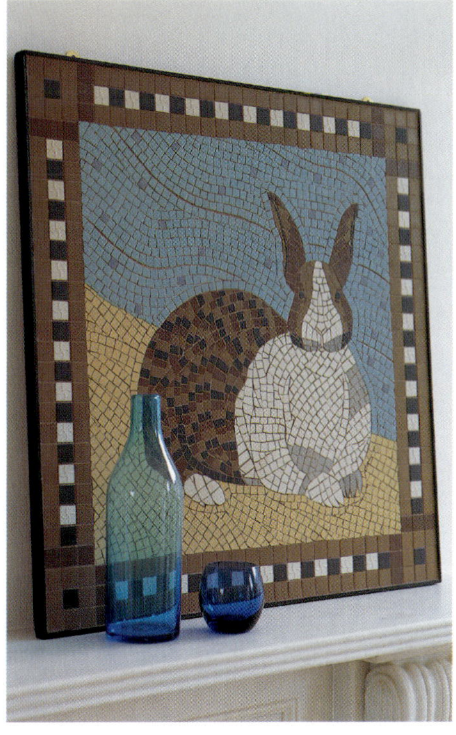

The ocean and the teeming variety of life found in it have provided the mosaic artist with a rich source of inspiration for centuries. Likewise, landscapes, whether naturalistic or abstract, appear often in mosaic.

The Natural World

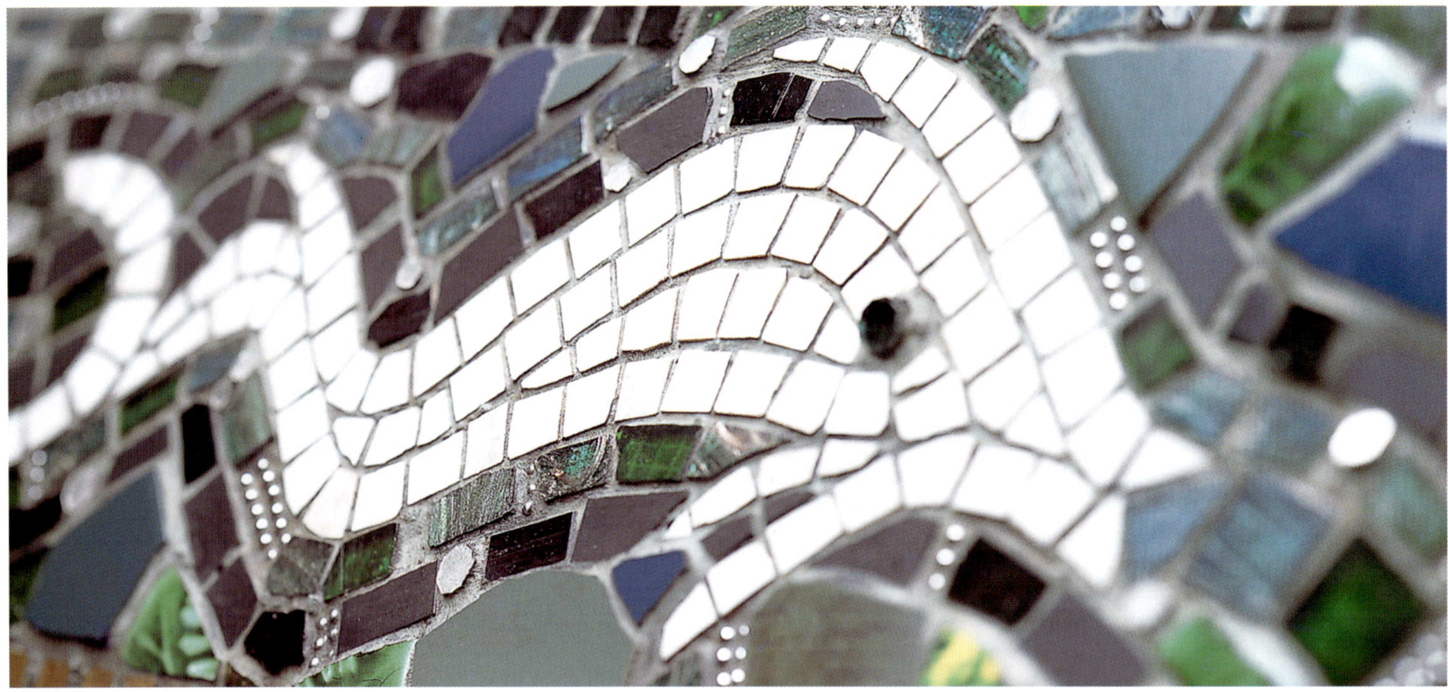

Marine themes are popular choices for bathroom mosaics. Splashbacks, tiled panels, floors and walls can all be decorated with dolphins, fish and shells. The recreation of landscapes will tend to be seen in large-scale mosaics, such as wall panels, or even whole walls.

Marine life

Many mosaic materials, especially the intense and vibrant material smalti, are wonderful for recreating the beautiful colours of fish and the many shades of the ocean – azure, emerald, turquoise and aquamarine. Marine themes offer wonderful opportunities for mosaic artists to experiment with exciting and vivid colour.

Marine life, including dolphins, fish, octopuses, starfish and seaweed, can create a flowing mosaic design, full of action and energy. The impression of water, light and movement can be conveyed effectively and with surprising economy in the way in which the tesserae are laid. Artists can also intersperse the mosaic with iridescent and reflective materials, such as mirror, to highlight certain areas and create a glistening scene.

Mosaics inspired by sea life are often very graphic and highly patterned. In fact, the scales on fish often look like mosaics themselves, and mosaic artists can depict this natural patterning with intricate detail.

Above: A detail from a picture frame by Norma Vondee, showing a classical-style dolphin. The white tiles highlight an area of the body, making it appear to glisten.

Landscapes

As with any painting, the creation of a landscape begins with the composition. It needs to be planned and sketched out, and the order of work and colours and tones of the tesserae need to be considered in advance.

Landscapes can, at first glance, appear to be faithful to reality, but most will involve a certain amount of stylization, of tidying up, of selecting particular subjects for the foreground and background, of highlighting

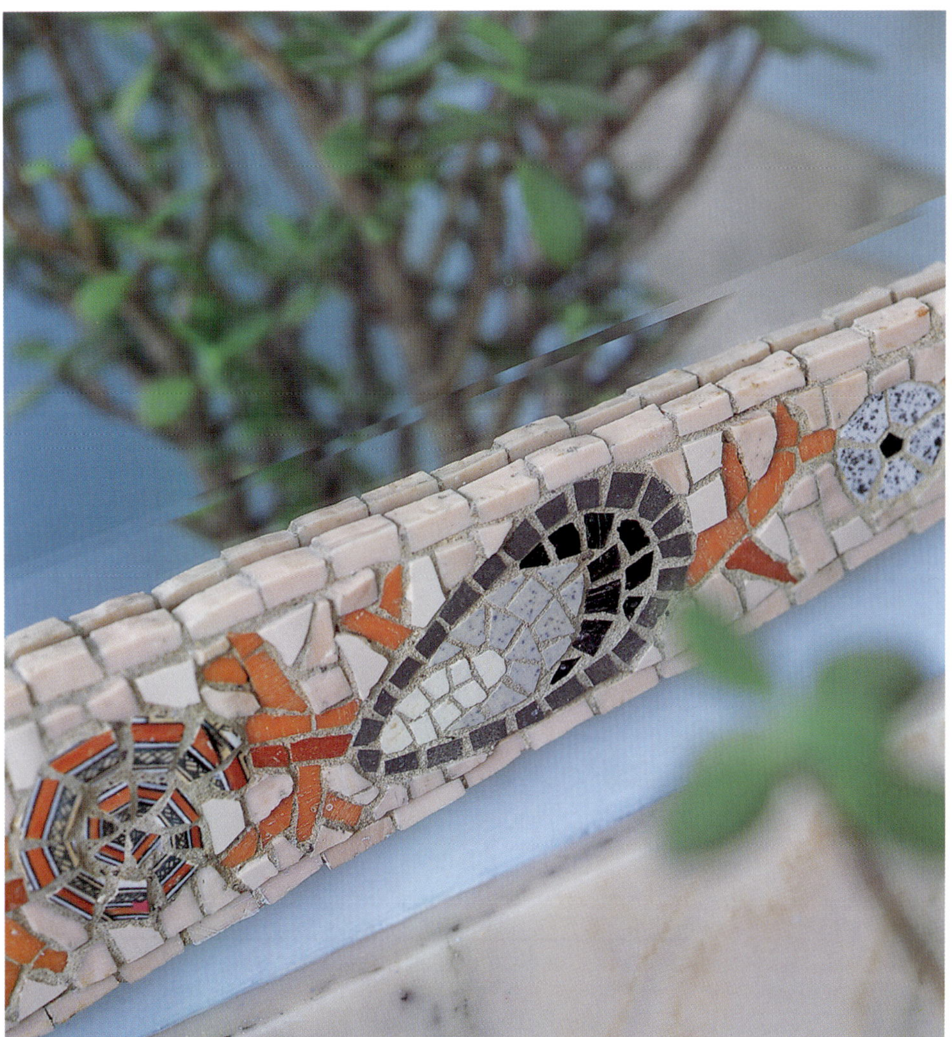

Right: A close-up of a soft coral smalti mirror frame decorated with sea creatures, by Norma Vondee.

Below right: Roman mosaic provided great inspiration for artists throughout the last millennium. This reproduction, using tiny pieces of marble and stone, depicts sea creatures that were intended to look as if they were swimming around a classical water feature.

details and of trying to create a feeling of distance and three-dimensional space. Images are built up by laying lines of regular or cut tesserae around images such as trees or hills, and backgrounds can include other patterns. A mosaic landscape is like a pixellated image that has to be viewed from a certain distance for it to be in focus.

Mosaic landscapes in earlier centuries were often very detailed, showing the subtle undulations of hills, the movement of water and the gradations of blue in the sky, but images do not have to be naturalistic to be effective. Some contemporary mosaic artists take inspiration from naive art and the surreal landscapes of de Chirico, and they have produced scenes that make full use of mosaic's textural and graphic qualities. Such works suggest a complete landscape rather than showing highly detailed images and objects.

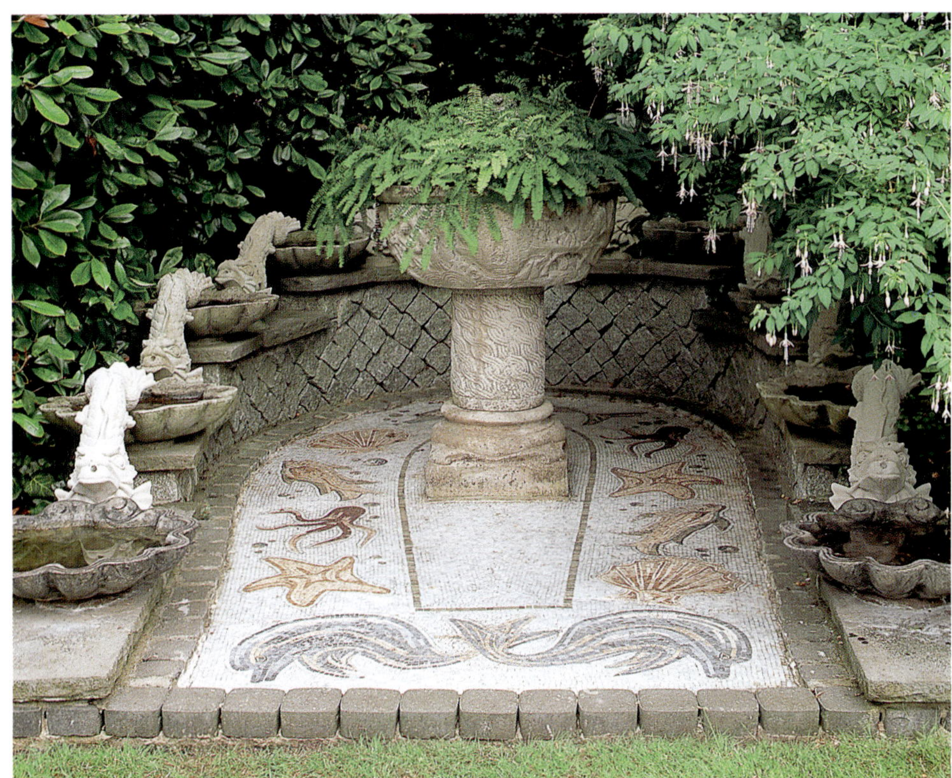

For the mosaic maker, plants and flowers are appealing subjects. They soothe the senses, are easy to look at, are universally popular and valued, and can be depicted in many different artistic styles.

Plants and Flowers

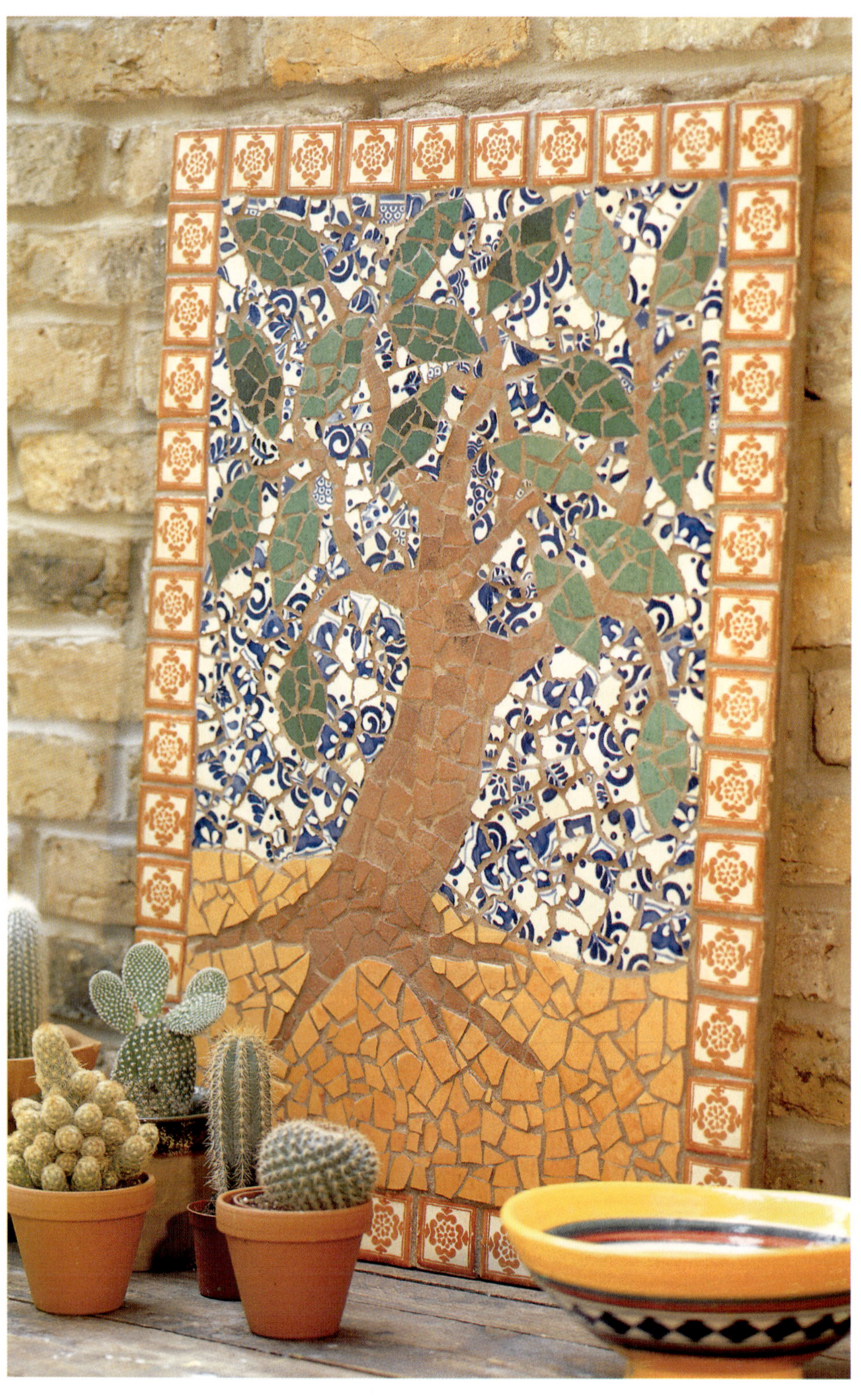

Natural plant forms are a very popular theme in mosaic, and plants are often woven into the designs of mosaic borders. They can flow around a panel or large mural, creating wonderful rhythm and activity, which adds interest and depth to a design. Plant forms can be depicted in a very elegant and stylized manner.

Contemporary mosaicists often use the medium's graphic qualities to produce remarkable work based on natural forms. Bold colours and chunky textures can combine to create vivid three-dimensional images. Plants and flowers are also excellent individual images, perhaps best for table tops and panels, as the petals, leaves and stems lend themselves well to flowing ornamentation. Trees, especially the tree of life, are a common theme in mosaic.

The images could be depicted in subtle materials, such as marble, and have delicate, soft-toned flowers, or they could be bold and graphic and less representational, using funkier colours and materials, such as vitreous glass and mirror. Ceramic tiles can give a warm, earthy feel to mosaic pictures of plants.

Left: Tree of Life *– a panel with a border of hand-painted Mexican tiles by Helen Baird. Trees are a popular source of inspiration in mosaic.*

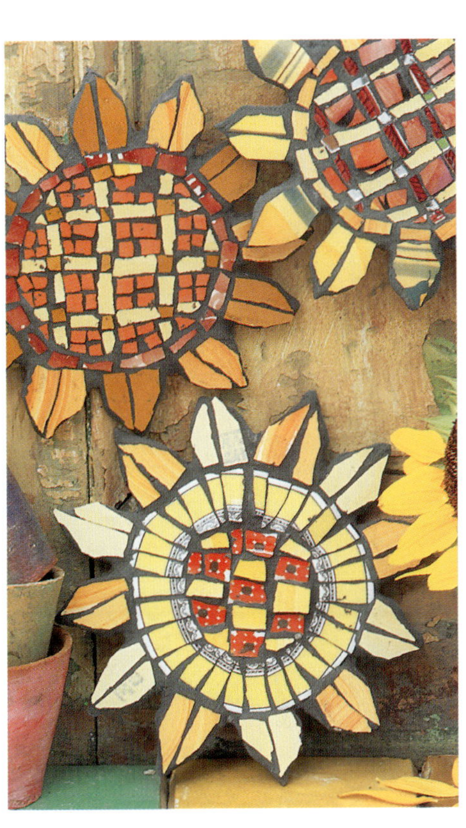

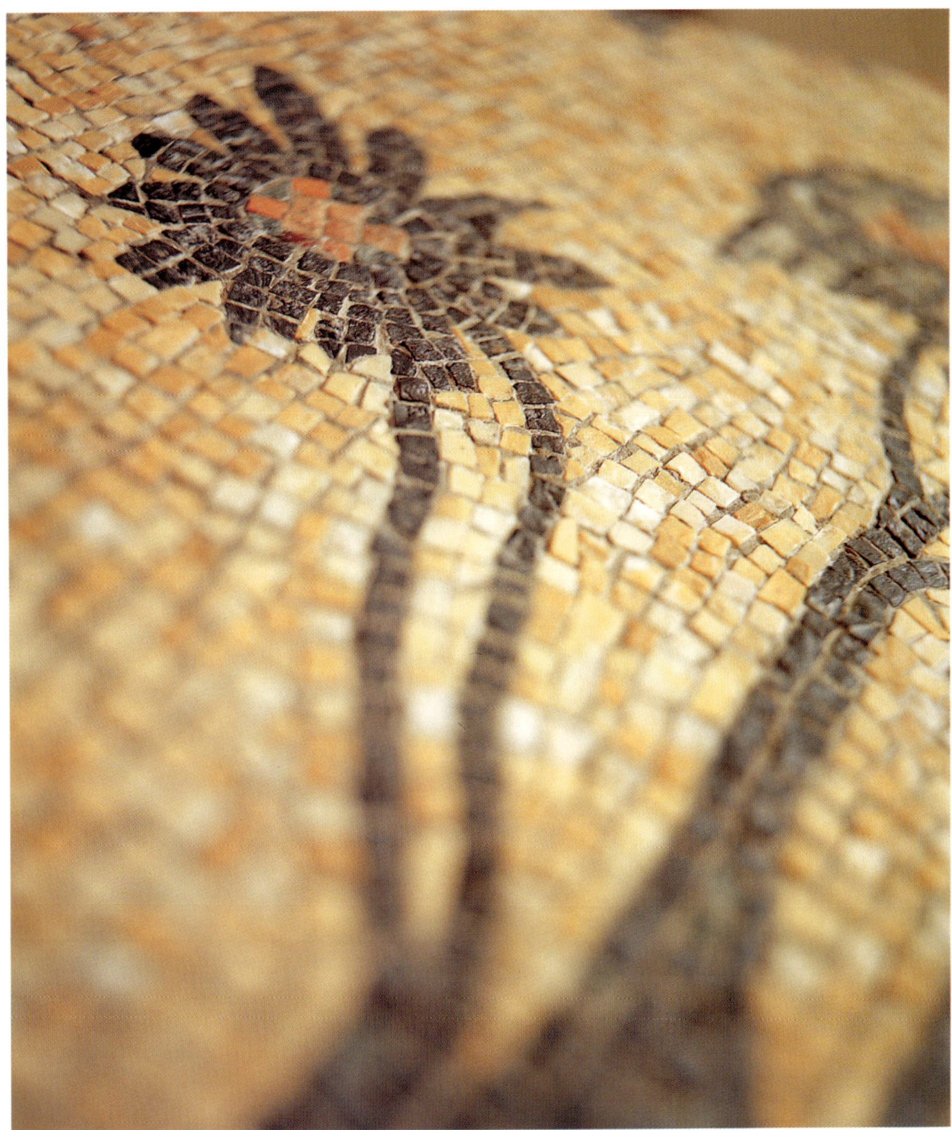

Above: These simple tiles take their inspiration, colour and shape from the bright sunflower.

Above right: Detail of part of the bush from Bird on a Bush*, a marble mosaic using soft, warm variegated tones, by Salvatore Raeli.*

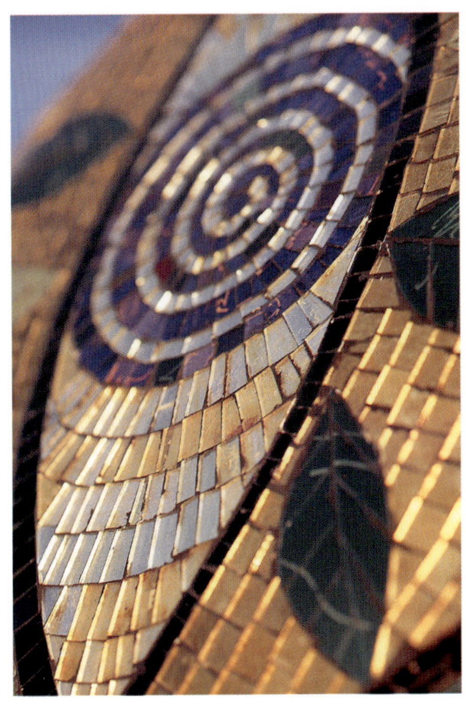

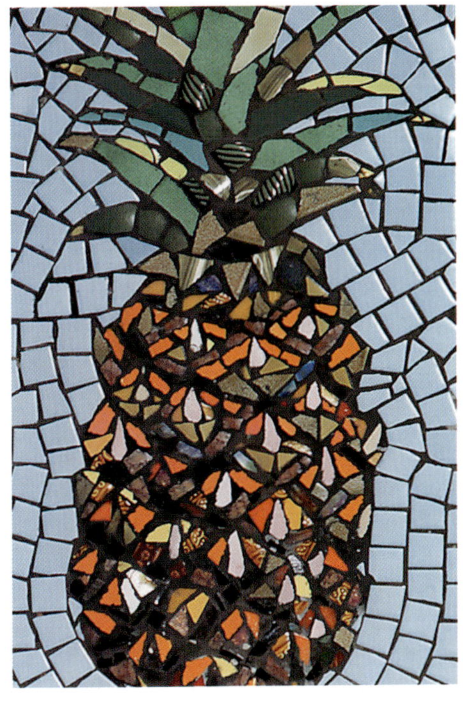

Right: This garden ornament by Rebecca Newnham shows how well natural plant forms can be expressed abstractly.

Far right: The knobbly textured surface of a pineapple is vividly conveyed by Norma Vondee.

Many mosaics make use of non-representational geometric and abstract patterns of one form or another. The range of motifs is almost limitless, and designs with repeated patterns are ideal for borders.

Geometric and Abstract

By their nature, geometric patterns are very well suited to the art of mosaic. The basic outline is simple and ideal for the shape of tesserae, and shapes can be repeated as often as is needed. The repetition is not monotonous; quite the opposite. The effect can be soothing and pleasing to the eye, and variations can be achieved through different colourways.

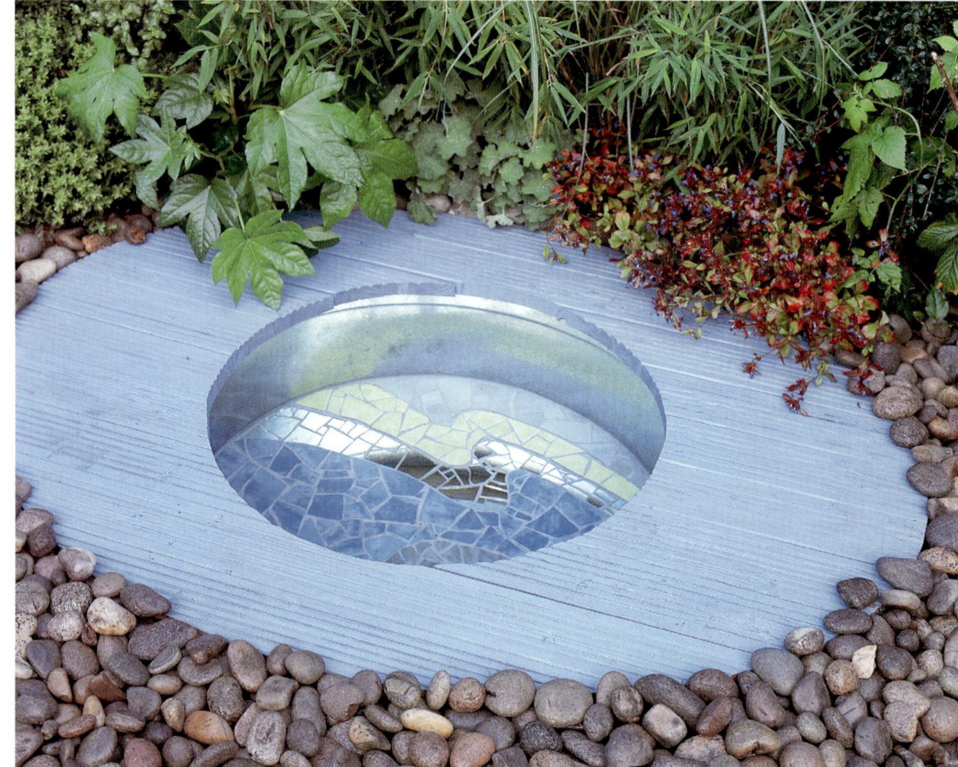

Pattern

A repeated pattern is an effective way of linking spaces: for instance, a path and hall floor could both be in a simple chequerboard pattern, the path in, say, black and white, and the hallway in blue and white. The transition from outdoors to indoors is conveyed by the change in colourway. Although the two areas are relatively small, a continuity of pattern makes the overall space seem larger.

There are many standard geometric patterns to choose from, such as the Greek key, which remains ever popular, the intertwining, flowing rope designs of Celtic art, or the sinuous calligraphic motifs of Islamic or Arabic art. Geometric shapes frequently occur in 20th century art, and the blocks of colour of Mondrian, for example, would translate well into a mosaic project.

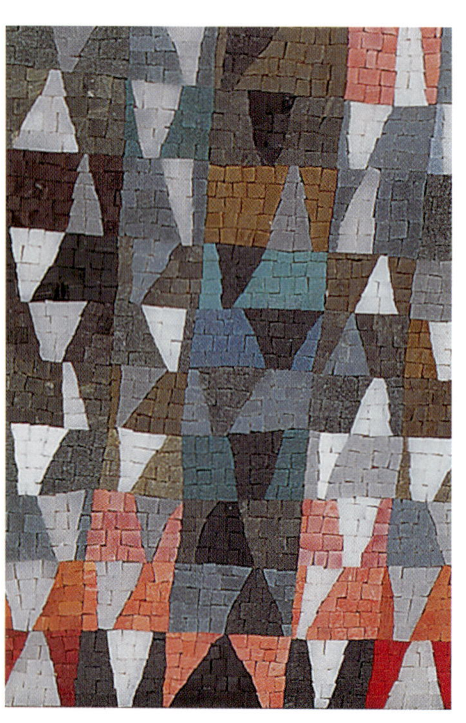

Above: Patchwork mosaic is reflected in the sides of this sunken pond feature. Patterns in ponds are best kept simple because of the constant movement of the light playing on the water.

Left: Triangles *– an ungrouted mosaic in vitreous glass by Emma Biggs. Irregular and asymmetrical in design, the black and white triangles give intensity to the subject of colour and form.*

Opposite: Echoes of the art of Paul Klee are visible in this geometric birdbath in tones of blue. The grid effect is offset by the changes in colour.

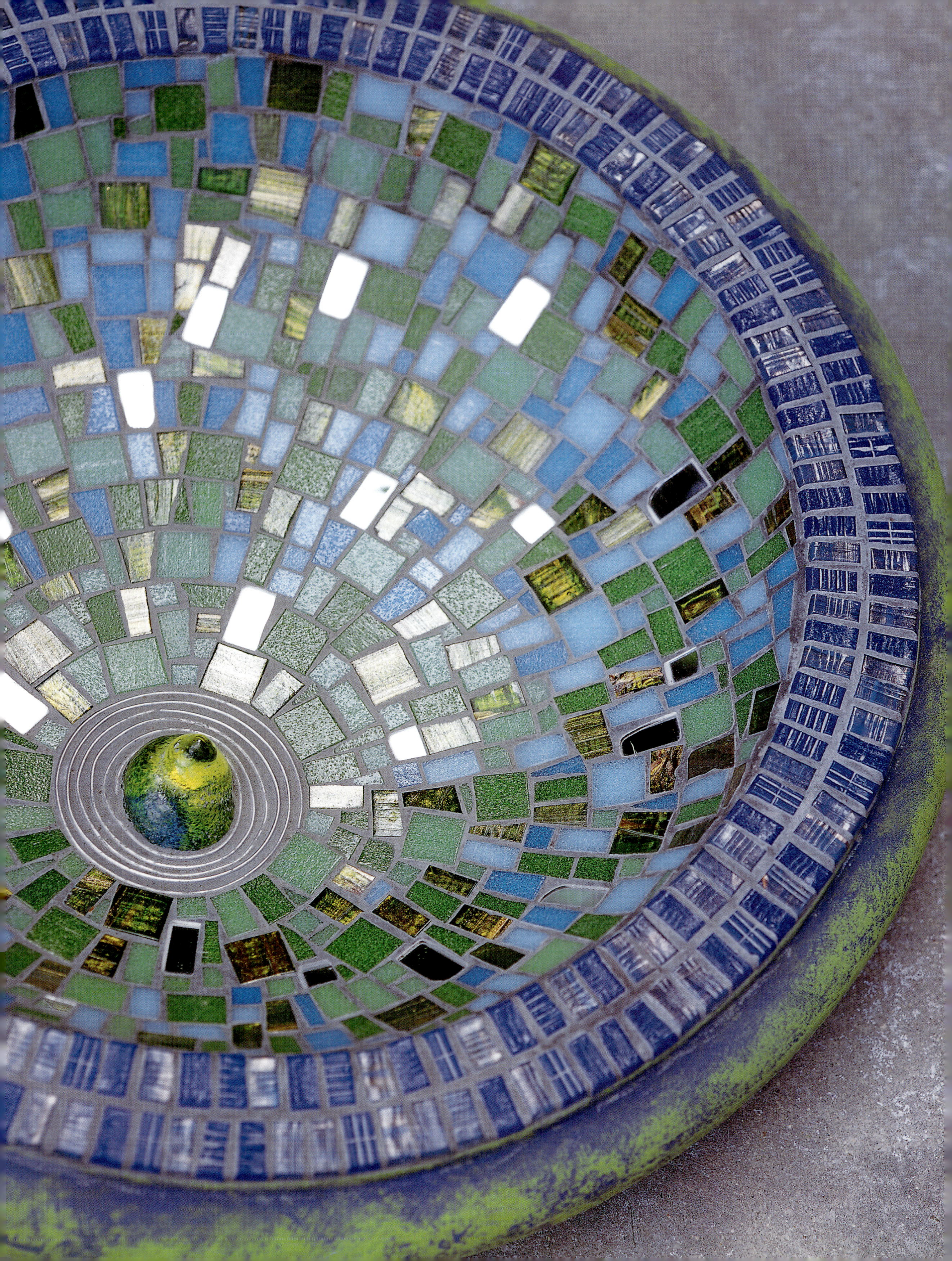

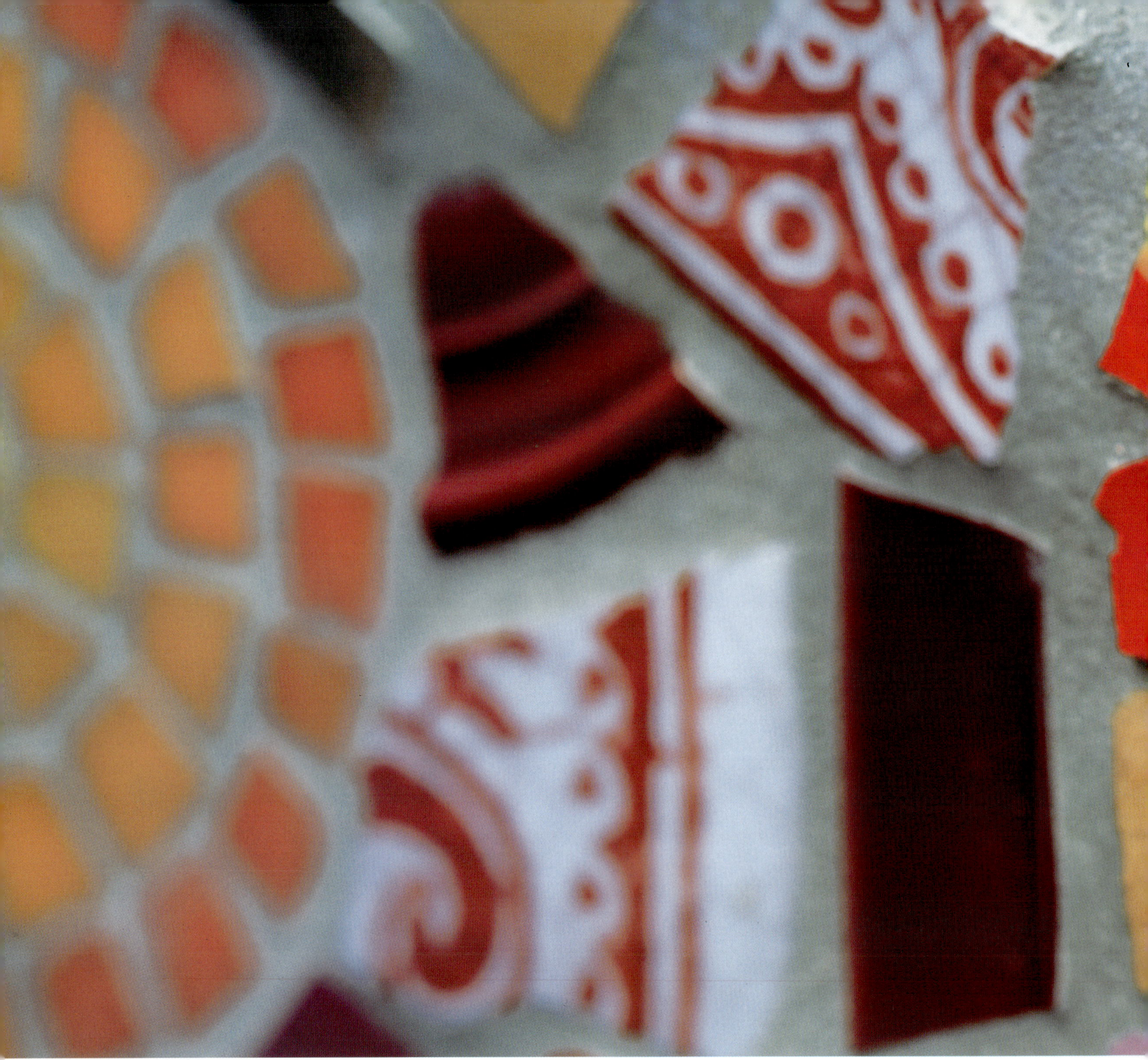

Design

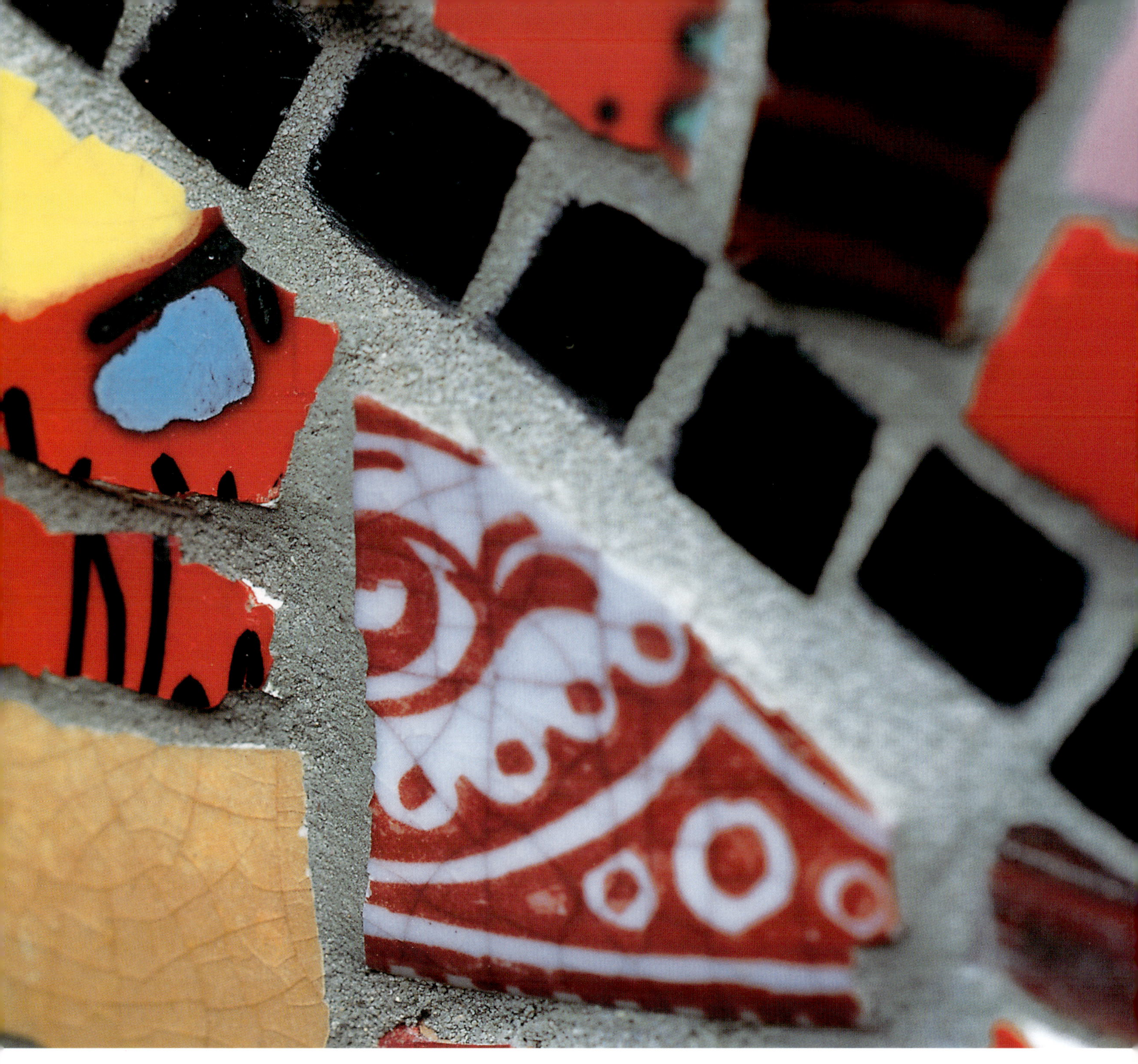

Once you have your inspiration, next comes the practical part of the design. Before embarking on a project consider its situation and the materials to use in order to make it durable enough to survive. Also the intended use should be taken into account. For instance, a mosaic designed as a flooring will need to be smooth and without edges to trip up on and waterproof so it can be cleaned. All these elements will affect the final design that you decide upon.

The wide choice of materials available means that designing a mosaic is a highly personal process. You need to consider such aspects as size, location, function and colour before starting work.

Practicalities

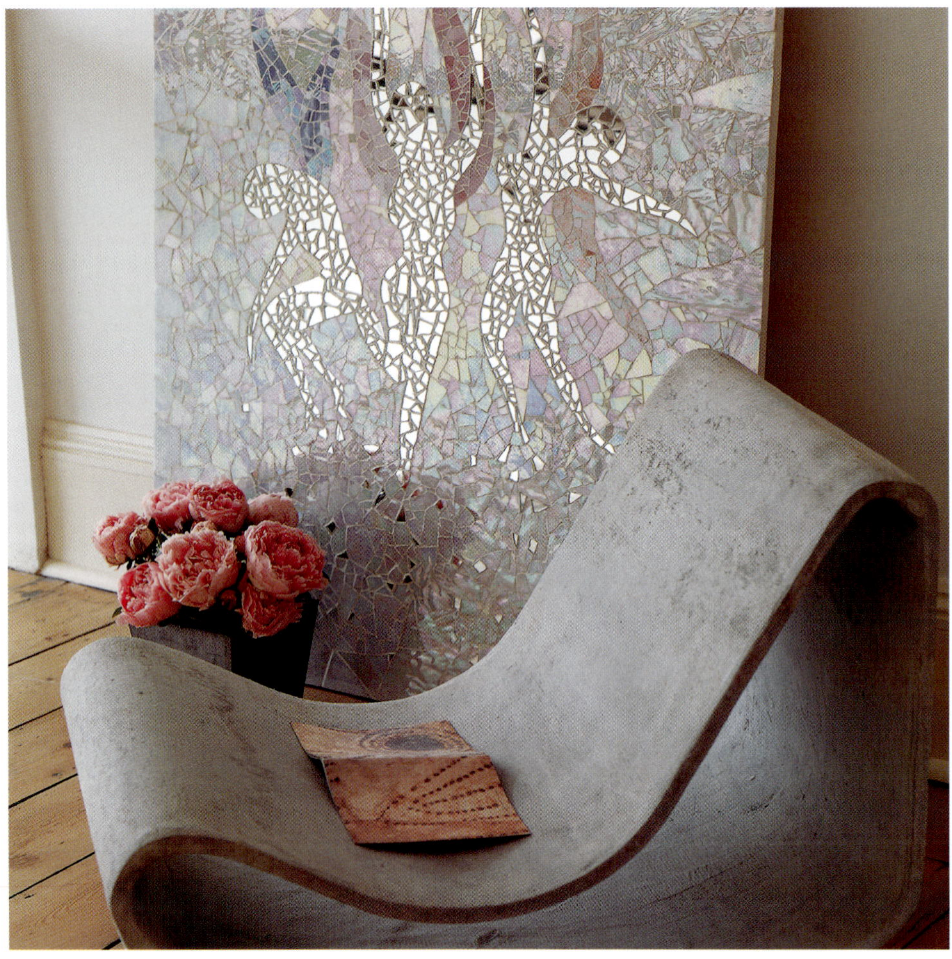

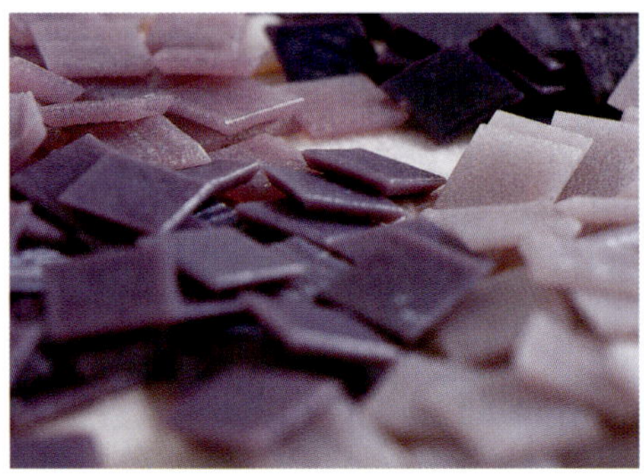

Above: Square tiles are the basis of most mosaic work and can be laid whole or clipped into tesserae of the desired shape and laid in a variety of ways.

Left: Fairies *– a beautiful abstract image of three fairies made from mirror and iridescent stained glass by Celia Gregory.*

When you are designing with mosaic, you have the liberty to use just one material, such as smalti, or to combine as many as you wish. Sometimes, this freedom can make it harder to reach decisions. Of course, no object exists in a vacuum and there will be other factors to consider when creating your designs.

Your mosaic may be intended for a predetermined place within a room or open-air space, surrounded by other objects. It may also be used for a specific purpose, such as to contain water. Your designs should also take into account the fact that mosaic is long-lasting and the colours virtually permanent. Unlike textile, paper or even paint, stone, glass and ceramic do not disintegrate; nor do they break easily or fade. Once the setting medium is hard, changes cannot be made. These qualities are the great strengths of mosaic, but they also mean you cannot go over your work and cover it up.

All you need to do is be clear about what you want to achieve and how you want to realize it. Do this, and materials, colour and style will marry happily with setting, mood and size to give you a mosaic of which you are proud. Before committing tesserae to adhesive, consider the following points.

Function

Always consider the main function of the mosaic: is it to be practical or decorative? Most mosaic is hardwearing and water-resistant, which makes it quite safe to use for items such as splashbacks behind the bathroom basin or kitchen sink, or for the floor of a hallway,

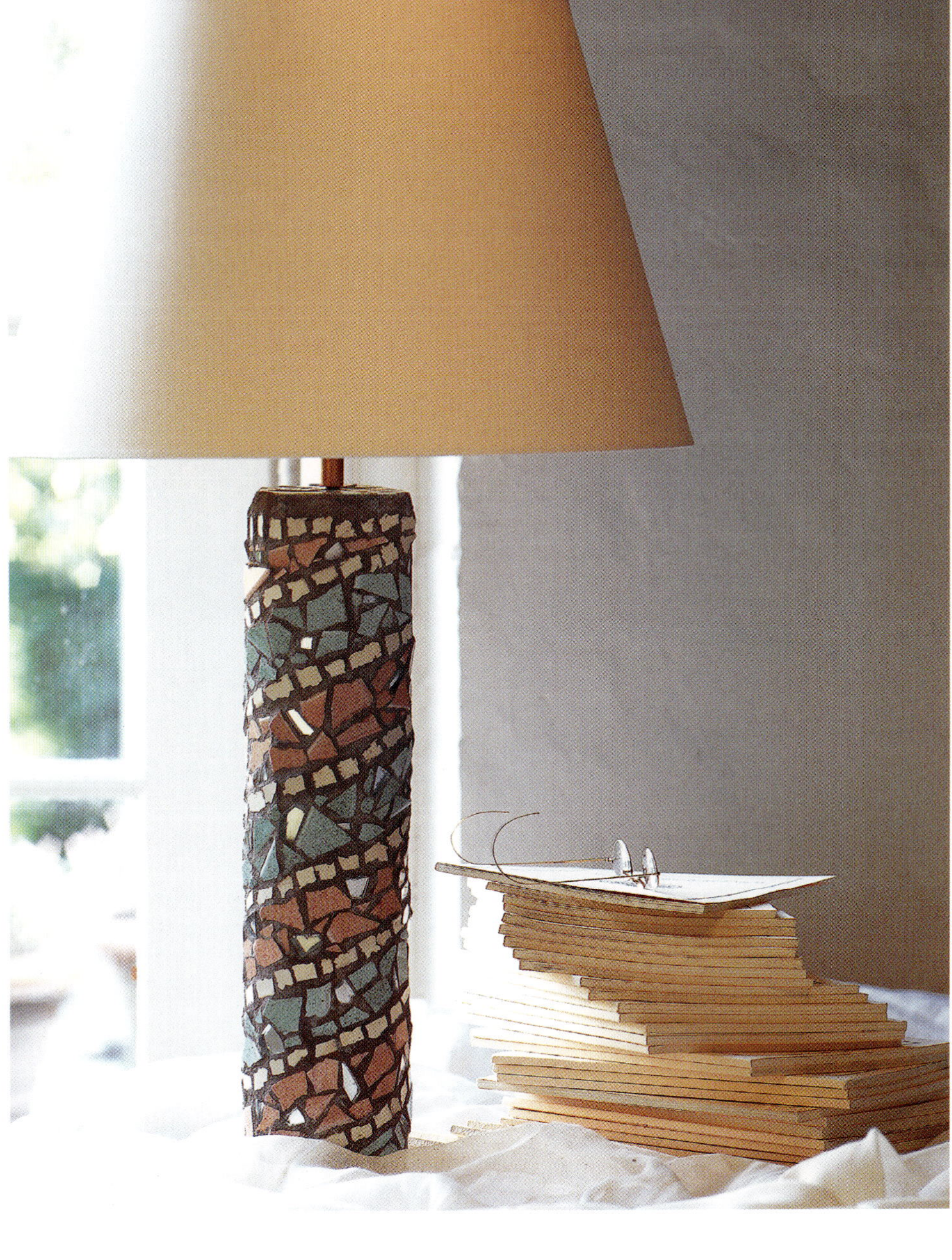

garden room or patio. If the work is to withstand wear and tear from feet or soap and water, think about which materials will be best suited to your needs: glass, for example, is not so suitable for the passage of feet, bikes and perhaps the odd piece of garden equipment. However, if a purely decorative effect is what you are after, clearly these considerations do not apply and your choice is wider.

Location

Consider where the mosaic is to be positioned. Every aspect of the design – whether it is simple or complex, abstract or representational, the size, the colours to be used and the materials – is influenced by which room of the house the mosaic is intended for, or its position in the garden.

Focal point

Decide whether the mosaic is to stand out from or blend in with its surroundings. Will it be the focal point of a decorative or planting scheme, or is it to go with established furniture or features? Your answers will determine how strong the design needs to be.

Mood

Consider the impact and mood the mosaic is to create. It is worth being clear at an early stage just how much of a centrepiece you want your mosaic to be, as it is a strong medium that can easily upstage its surroundings. The mosaic can be as bold as you like, but its style should have a link with its situation. For example, a bright geometric mirror frame will jar in a guest bedroom that is decorated in soft florals; likewise a large panel in bright folk art reds and oranges might swamp a tiny but sophisticated all-white courtyard garden.

Above: The earthy tones of this lamp stand complement the dusky yellow lampshade. Its spiral design is eye-catching, yet soothing, so it does not dominate the room.

Size

You need to decide on the size of the mosaic. Ensure that the design is in scale with the overall size: a tiny pattern will look out of place in a large mural, while a big pattern will look just as wrong in a tiny space.

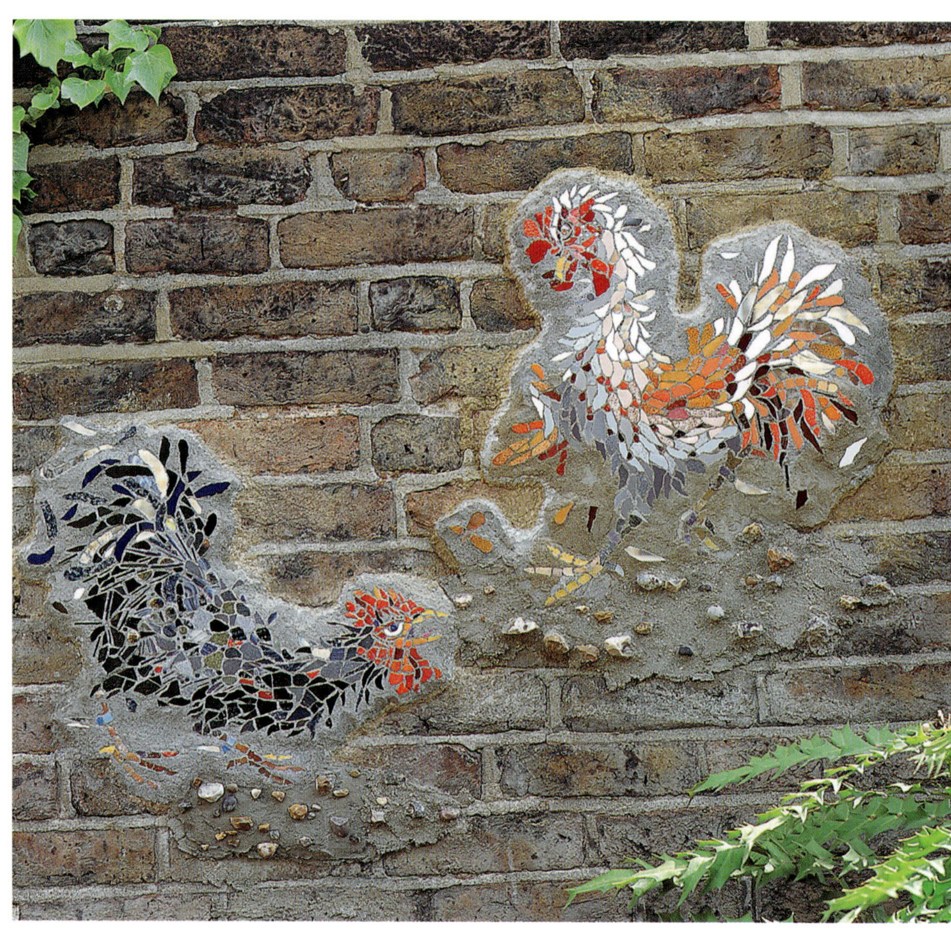

Remember, too, that patterns or designs look larger the closer they are to your eye level. Look at one of the illustrations in this book at eye level, then put the same page on the floor; you will see how much detail is lost. Operate on a "less is more" principle and take out superfluous detail for smaller-scale pieces or those that will be viewed only from afar.

When designing a mosaic for either an interior or exterior space, there are some important factors to consider.

Above: A dull brick wall is enlivened by an impressionistic mosaic of two cockerels by Takako Shimizu.

To aid you in your planning and preparation and to help you avoid making time-consuming mistakes, there are some questions in the boxes to consider. These will help you to be clear about the purpose of your design, taking into consideration if it is a purely decorative or practical mosaic.

Mosaic is a bold medium and you can cover large areas with it and create dramatic effects. Indoors, especially, it will be a strong feature. You want it to be striking but, if it is large, not to overpower its surroundings. Bear these considerations in mind when beginning to plan work on design, colour, materials and size.

points to consider for EXTERIORS

- What is the mosaic for?
- Where is it going to be sited?
- Do you want it to blend in with established plants and garden features, or will it be the centrepiece from which all else flows?
- Are the colours suitable for its purpose, size and location?
- Is the mosaic the right size for its specific purpose: not so small that it is lost, nor so big that it dominates the space?
- If it is to convey information, such as a house name or number, is the design clear enough and uncluttered with detail to enable it to be viewed from a distance?

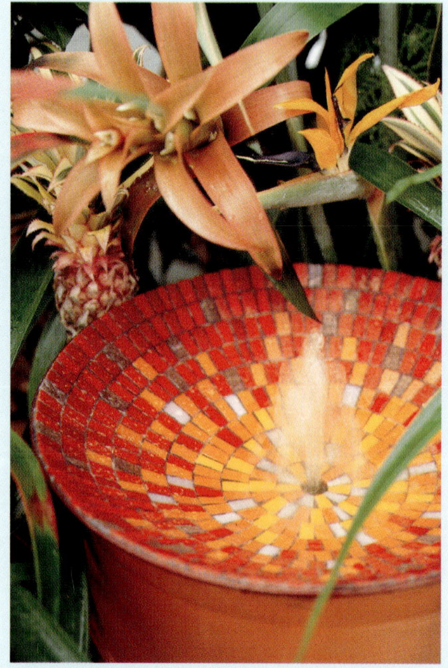

Above: The hot colours of this small water feature by Tabby Riley suit the exotic planting around it.

Being so durable means that mosaic is ideal for out-of-doors, where wind, rain and frost would quickly see off a less hardwearing medium. When considering your initial design, make sure your mosaic fits within its environment.

Light

Bear in mind the nature of daylight where you live: essentially blue in temperate areas and more red in tropical parts. Take some tesserae outside to see how natural light alters their colours.

There is no reason why you cannot use strong, hot colours in temperate areas, but be aware of how vibrant they can look. Mosaics in brilliant reds and oranges need to be carefully placed in temperate gardens. If allowed to peep from under lavish green planting, they can add a touch of drama and humour, and are good for shady areas, dark courtyard gardens or a particular "room" in a large garden, perhaps set among hot-toned flowers. Using cool blues and greens in warmer settings can, conversely, create an area of calmness and tranquillity.

Siting

Clever positioning is part of a successful mosaic, where all aspects of its design (subject, pattern, framing, colour, texture and size) come together in the right setting. You might like to choose a design that is appropriate for the site, for example food in the kitchen, or vines in the dining room.

When you are working in a room on a ceiling or floor, consider the viewing lines. If the mosaic is to be seen at an angle, make sure it gives the best view. If the piece is in an architectural setting, make sure that the design is sympathetic to its surroundings.

Mosaic-framed mirrors should be sited adjacent to windows, not opposite them, to achieve the best effects. Subtle colours should be positioned with care so the colours are enhanced, not lost by glare or bright light.

points to consider for INTERIORS

- What is the mosaic's function?
- Which room is it going in?
- Is the room's colour scheme being built around the mosaic?
- If not, does the mosaic fit in with the existing scheme?
- Is the design you like appropriate to the room where you intend to place the mosaic?
- Are the weight of the object and the material used appropriate to its function and position?
- What happens if you decide to redecorate your home?
- Is the mosaic portable (wall-mounted, for instance, or on furniture)?
- If not, what will happen if you later want to move it to another place, or take it with you when you move into different accommodation?

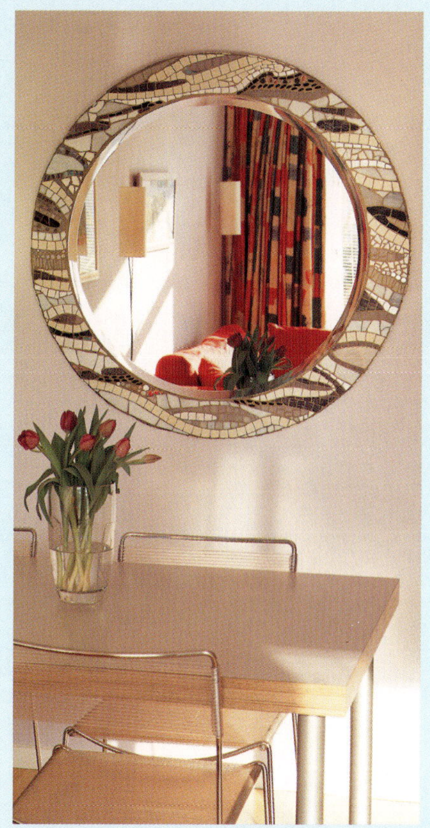

Above: In a restrained modern setting this very striking mirror frame, designed by Marion Lynch, is all the ornamentation you need.

Scale

The size of your design is important, so this must be borne in mind when planning, and detail that will be lost at a distance must be eliminated.

The importance of size applies equally to the actual size of the tesserae you are working with. Choose sizes that will look right for their intended position: they must not be so large that they cannot cope with the design or pattern you want; neither should they be too small or they will tend to look untidy and ineffective, reducing a strong design to something weaker and with less impact.

Colour is one of the most fundamental elements of any mosaic design and has a profound effect on our response to the work. In addition, the way light, real or artificial, falls on these colours is hugely important.

Using Colour

When deciding which colours to use, you should have some samples to place in the setting you have in mind. Here you can see how the natural light falls on them. The closer to the window they are, the stronger the colours will look. If they are set on a wall between two windows and against the glare of daylight, however, quite the opposite happens and they will appear darker. What is more, the same shade of red will look slightly different when placed flat on the floor and when hung vertically on the wall. Also, as anyone who has tried to match colours under fluorescent lighting or has caught sight of themselves in an elevator mirror will know, the light source can profoundly affect some colours. For this reason, colour samples should be viewed in all the types of light in which they will be seen (daylight, tungsten bulb, halogen, neon and so on), and consideration should be given to how the light changes at different times of the day.

Hot and cool colours

What we perceive as colourless white light is divided into the colours of the spectrum – red, orange, yellow, green, blue, indigo and violet. These divide broadly into hot colours (red, orange and yellow) and cold (green, blue and indigo). The shades that centre around violet (a mixture of red and blue) tend to be cooler or warmer, depending on the proportion of red to blue: mauve and lilac incline to cool, maroon and purple to warm.

In addition, colours are either predominant or recessive: in other words, some catch the eye more than others. It is a question not just of light and dark, but of which colours attract the eye first, and which colours are seen second. If you glance casually at a selection of colour images you will notice that your eye instinctively goes to some colours first. You will probably find that it alights immediately on any reds, oranges or yellows, or any strong, clear colours (in an all-blue room, for instance, the eye goes first to the brightest shade of blue). Only after that does it move to the more recessive tones, the blues (or softer shades of blue in our all-blue room), the greens and the browns.

So, when deciding which colours to use, you need to bear in mind the visual effect they will have. A palette of

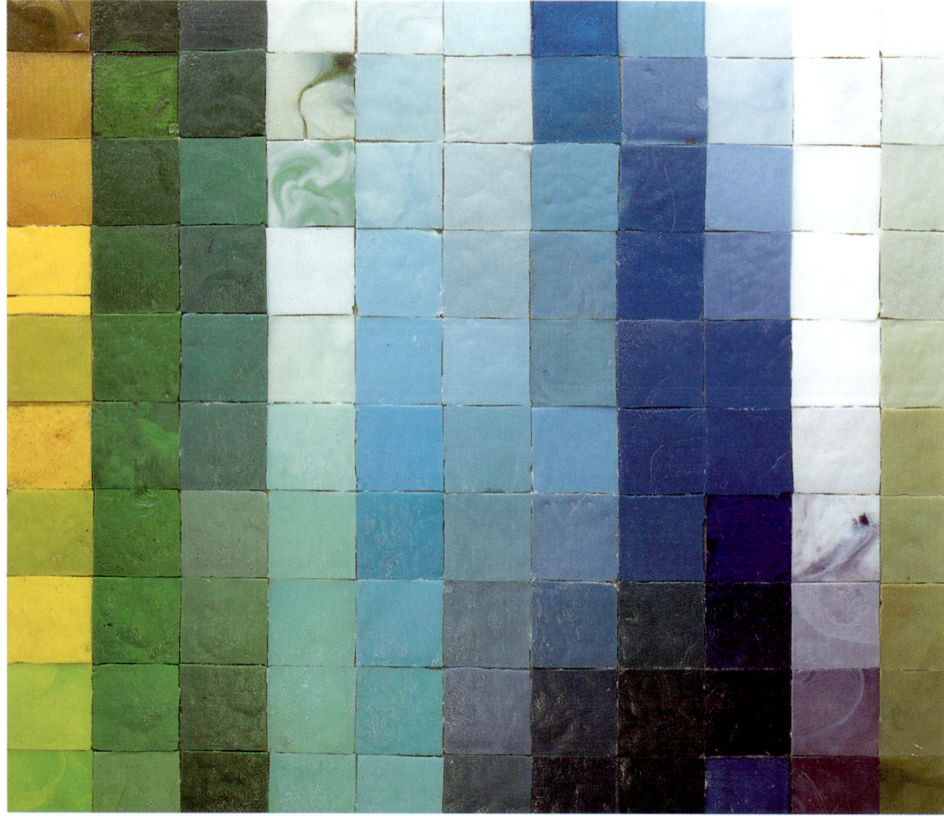

Left: This is a small indication of the vast range of colours and hues of smalti that are now widely available to the mosaic artist.

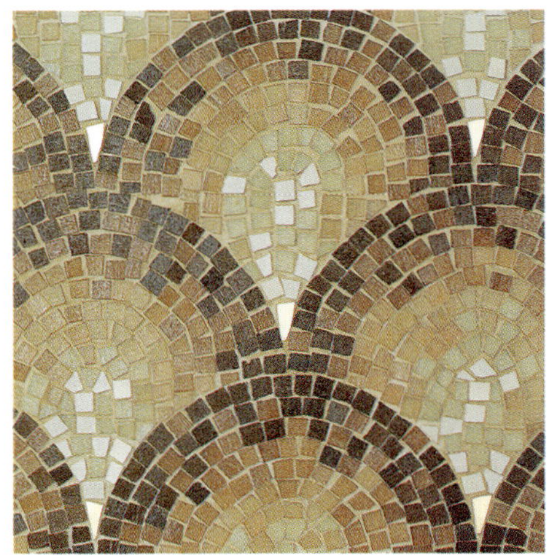

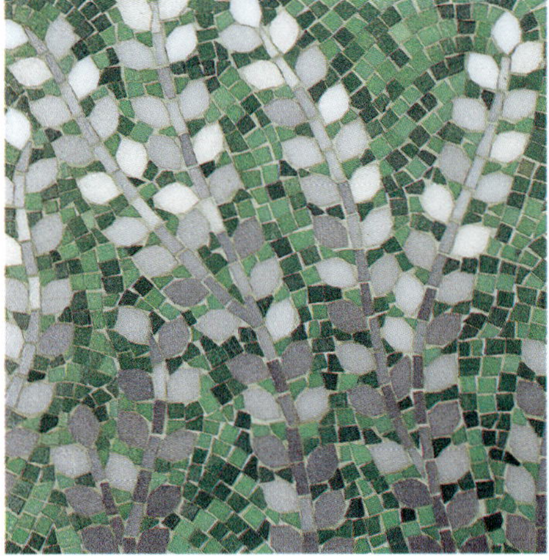

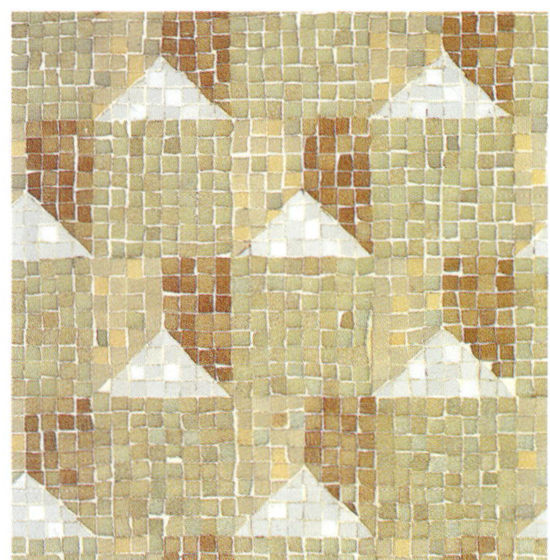

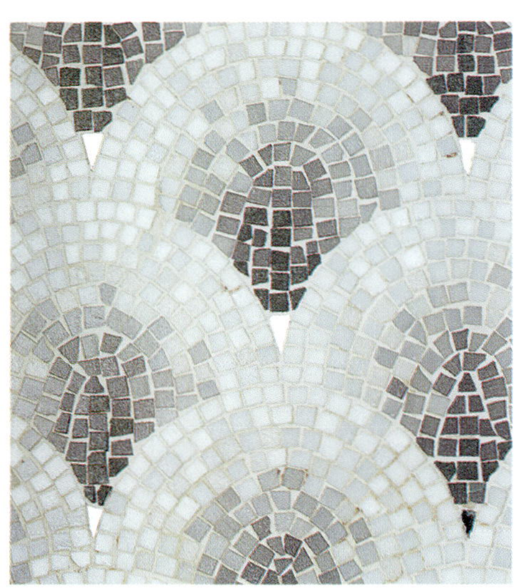

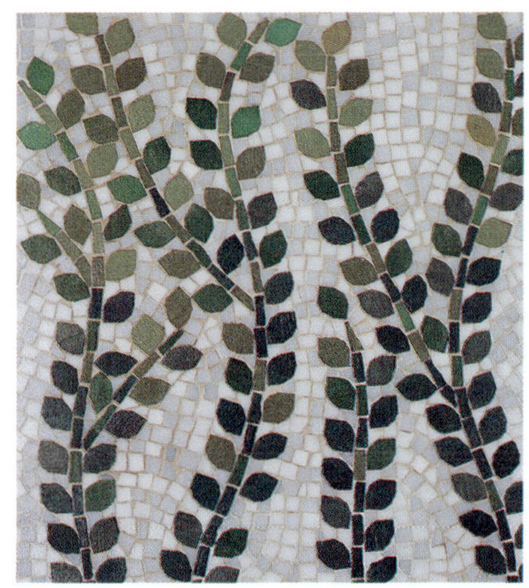

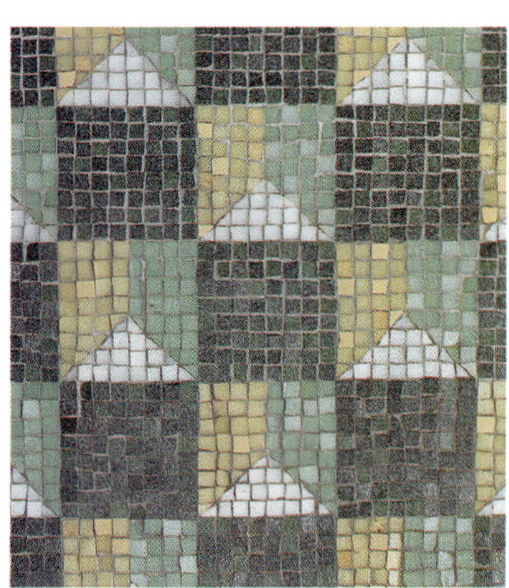

Above: Using darker and lighter colours throws different elements of a design into relief and brings others to prominence.

Above: A strong colour used against a light background stands out more clearly than white on a coloured background.

Above: The use of colour alone can produce entirely different results from the same pattern.

warm colours – reds, oranges and yellows – will create a warm impression. They will also be strong, dominating their surroundings. And because they draw the eye, they will make spaces seem smaller. This need not be a disadvantage – an entrance hall in warm tones will seem extra-welcoming on a cold winter's night, and a north-facing bathroom can have the chill taken off it and be made to feel cosy and inviting by using colours from the warm end of the spectrum – but they could make a small room seem cramped.

The cool colours of blues, greens and indigos, coupled with the "hard" effect of mosaic, may make a cold room seem more so. Along with browns, they are also recessive, so they will be well suited to making small spaces seem larger, provided you do not opt for too many dark tones, which will make areas seem more confined. So, soft blues, greens and lilacs would be a good choice for a mosaic at the end of a small garden.

When it comes to dark and light colours, received wisdom is that a dark area stands out more when surrounded by light-toned colours. This will happen if the colours are not too bland (too much magnolia, cream or beige can be dull). However, it can often be as successful to play up the dark aspect by choosing a similar tone of another colour. The secret is to make the colour deep but rich, such as dark scarlet, blackcurrant, peacock blue, racing green or chocolate brown. Boldness pays off. Whichever colour you do choose, note that if using large areas of the same colour, varying the tone and sizes of the mosaic pieces adds interest.

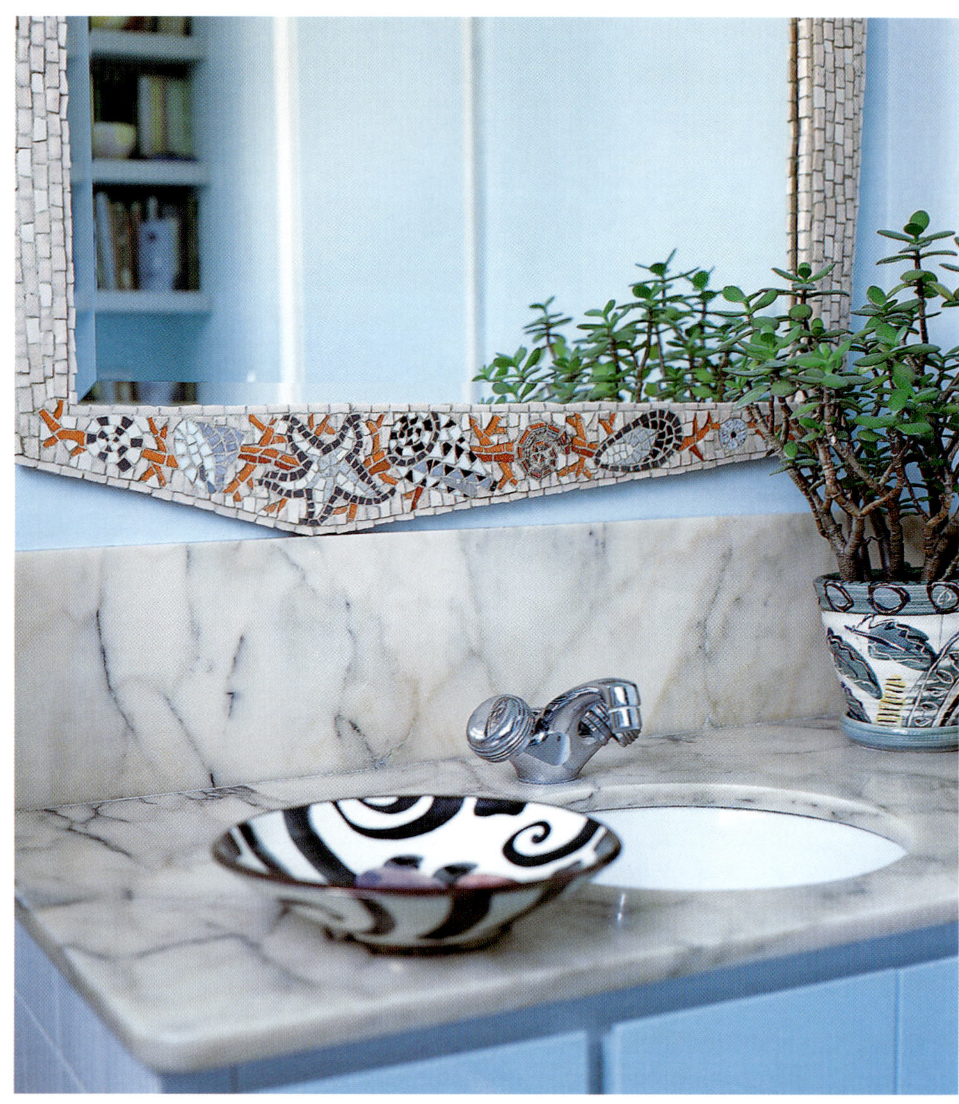

Matching colour to style

Another very important aspect of colour is that the palette you choose must match the style of the design if the whole is not to look incongruous. For example, a folk art pattern would not suit a combination of chrome yellow, black and silver, while an Art Deco design would work less well in primary blue, red and yellow. Similarly, a realistic floral mosaic will be most successful executed in colours as close as possible to the real plant, while a piece inspired by the work of Tiffany asks for his characteristic delicate turquoises, lavenders, chartreuse greens and soft pinkish whites.

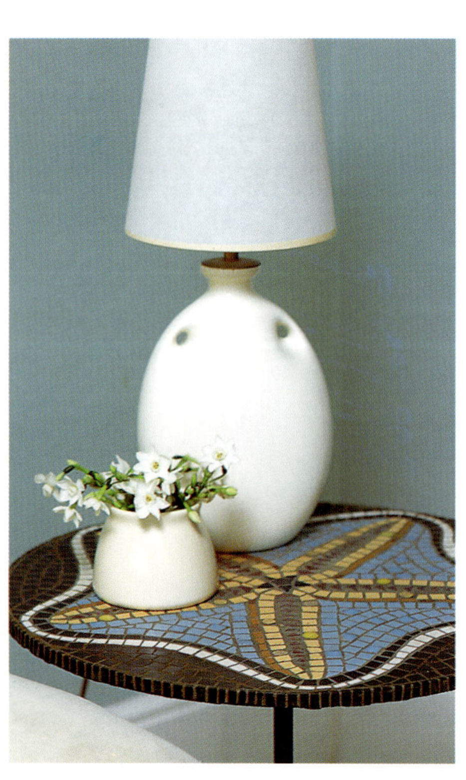

Matching colour to surroundings

You will need to take into consideration the items that will surround your mosaic. However much you may want it to provide a focal point, it needs to bear some relation to the existing colour scheme in the room or it will simply look out of place.

By studying the furniture, walls, and fabrics in the room you can tell if there is an overall colour scheme. You can then blend your mosaic with it, perhaps picking up on some of the colours in a particular item.

Whether it is to go on the wall, be placed on the floor, or sit on another item, a mosaic panel needs to relate to the wall or floor colour. Perhaps the background colour could be one or two tones lighter or darker than the walls or floors. Perhaps its design could echo the colour of the tiles in a tiled hall, or its frame could replicate other picture frames in the room.

Above: Decorative mosaics can be used as accessories to coordinate with existing schemes and fittings. For example, this marine-inspired mirror frame echoes the coral marble sink unit.

Left: Ideas and designs derived from the sea, such as this starfish, often look best in blues, greens and sandy shades.

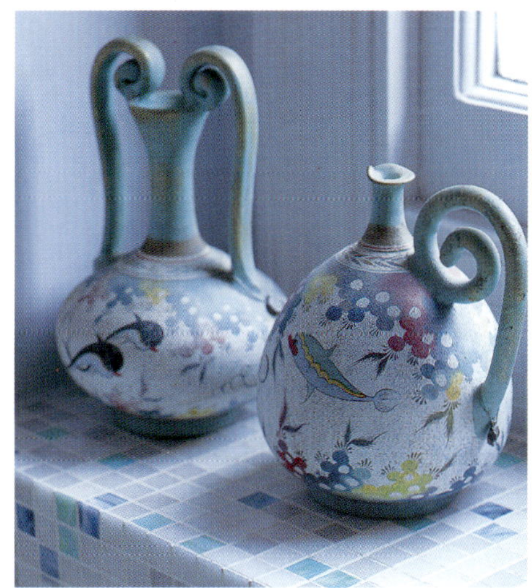

Right: The colours of the mosaic tiles have been carefully chosen to echo the vases on the windowsill.

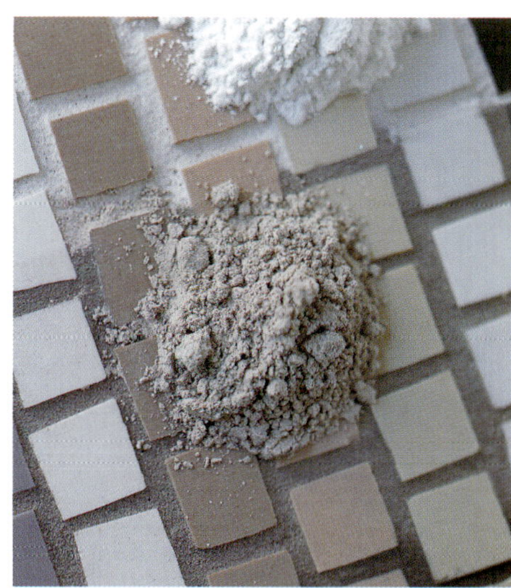

Above: The choice between white or dark grouting will affect the overall appearance of the mosaic.

Below: Soft, earthy, rain-washed colours suit the quality of light in temperate gardens and match their surroundings well.

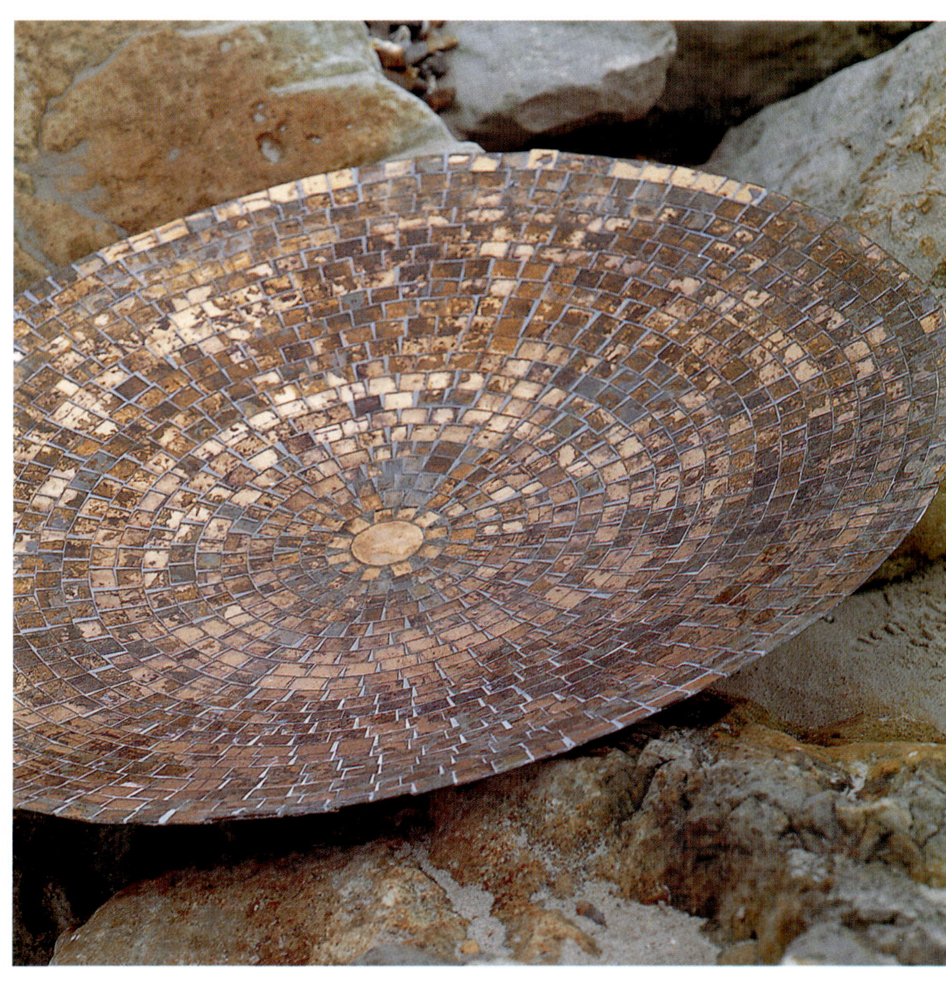

Cool and warm light

The fact that the quality of light varies depending on which country you live in becomes particularly relevant when considering the garden. In temperate latitudes, the light, even in midsummer, tends to be blue.

In the Mediterranean and tropical parts of the world, the light is significantly warmer and redder. This explains why the colours of Provence, Italy or Santa Fe in New Mexico – ochres, terracottas and earth tones with splashes of cobalt blues and rust reds – look so right there but do not always translate so well in temperate zones. By contrast, the soft greens, browns and grey-blues that suit cloudy skies can look too subdued and washed-out in stronger sunlight.

White and dark grout

In mosaic, the gaps between the pieces are as much a part of the design as the tesserae themselves, and these gaps are filled by a grouting medium. The effect of the mosaic varies dramatically depending on the colour of grout chosen: a white grout will make the overall effect very much lighter; a dark grout is deep and sombre but can create contrast. It is well worth testing out a small sample to decide which effect you want. See the section on grouting, on page 64 for four examples of the same tiles finished with different coloured grouts.

The element of contrast adds drama and movement to a design, and is necessary to satisfy the eye and keep it interested. It can be introduced in many different ways, not just in the choices of colour.

Using Contrast

In mosaics, creating contrast ensures that a design remains attractive and intriguing. It is easily achieved by mixing materials and varying their texture, changing the colours and sizes of the pieces, and by introducing elements of surprise, such as gold or silver, glass, mirror and strangely shaped pieces. The fall of light and the opacity of the work also have effects.

You can also achieve contrast by making a soft, sinuous design out of an intrinsically hard material. Mixed media mosaics create the vital element of contrast simply through their mixture of materials.

Size and shape

Tiles are usually cut into quarters, but they can, in fact, be cut into numerous shapes, including squares, rectangles, triangles, and, with practice, even semi-circles and wedge shapes. Varying tile sizes and shapes within patterns and various areas of the design is a way of creating contrast.

For example, a round table top could have a circular central section of large, unstructured, broken household tiles, and a contrasting border of neatly laid tiles in a more formal design, or with distinct shapes, such as triangles or repeating squares.

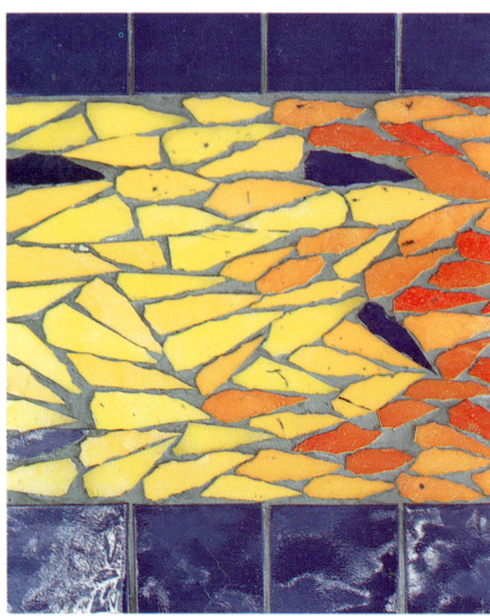

Shaping mosaic

Their usually square shape and hard texture means that mosaic tesserae are well suited to geometric or angular design. However, there is no reason at all why you cannot deliberately play up the visual differences between squares of clay or glass and sensuous curves and arcs. On some of Antonio Gaudí's extraordinary houses in Barcelona, Spain, the undulating walls and roofs flow like ocean waves, covered in gleaming tiles and mosaic.

Left: Shape and colour both give contrast here, as a river of pointed shards flows between a retaining border of square tiles.

Right: Within this soft natural colour palette, contrast comes from the juxtaposition of the star with the circle and the black and white unglazed tiles.

Colour

Using colour is a simple but effective way of providing contrast. An obvious example would be a floral mosaic in which the flower is brilliantly coloured and the background is plain, perhaps palest green.

Using just black and white is the most extreme contrast, or you could limit yourself to one or two dark and light colours to focus on how the tiles are cut and laid, and experiment with patterns in individual areas.

If a bright, vibrant look is desired, you could use combinations from opposite sides of the colour wheel, such as scarlet with blue or purple with yellow. However, contrasts do not have to be extreme to work; shades of the same colour, or a palette of related tones, can be just as effective.

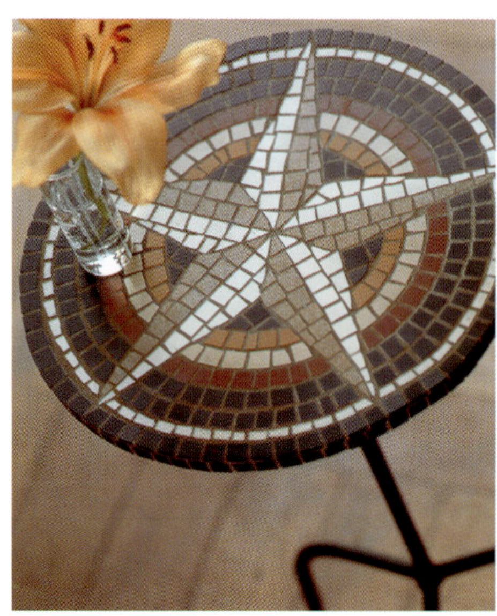

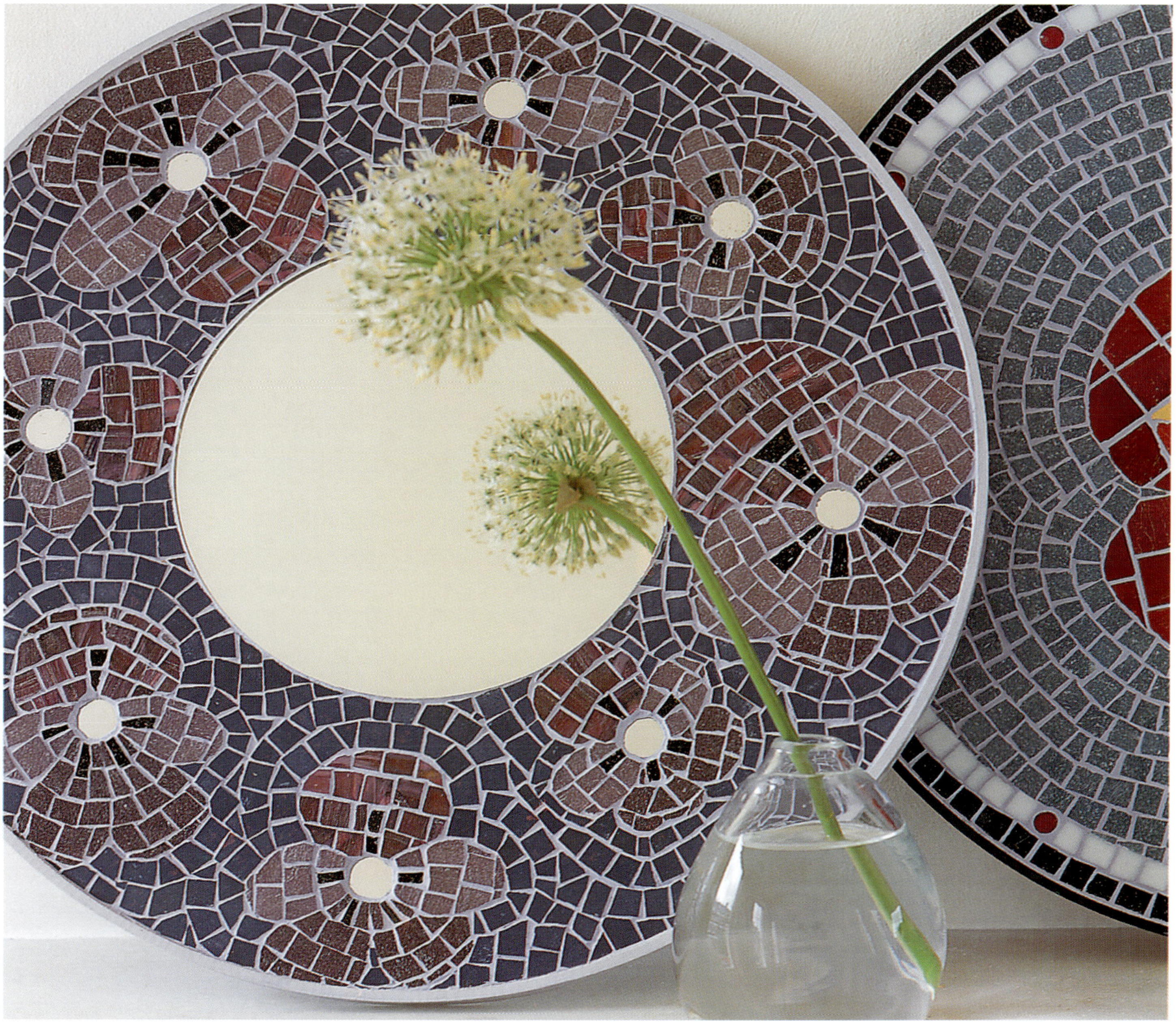

Varying materials

A touch of the unexpected is an ideal way of enlivening a design. A matt chequerboard in black and white can be transformed by silver or glass tesserae placed at random intervals, while a pebble pool surround may be brought to life with a few beautifully shaped shells. Similarly, a monochrome mosaic can be changed beyond recognition by the addition of a panel made of broken patterned china in either the same or a contrasting colour.

Above: The mirror juxtaposes a swirling pattern with the plain mirrored centre, while the small table top contrasts a plain surround with a vibrantly coloured centre.

Right: This elegant alcove was created using rectangular stone mosaic by Robert Grace. The side wall contrasts with the other surfaces as the tesserae are laid in a more haphazard manner. The gold mosaic panels are of the Madonna, a Byzantine replica, and the Young Patrician, *both by Salvatore Raeli.*

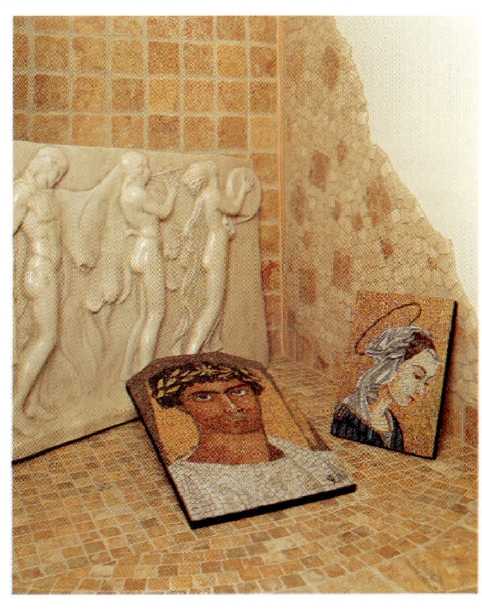

You can create almost any pattern or shape you want with mosaic, once you have gained some experience of cutting and working with the medium. Outlines, rhythm and variety, and shading are all vital elements.

Using Pattern

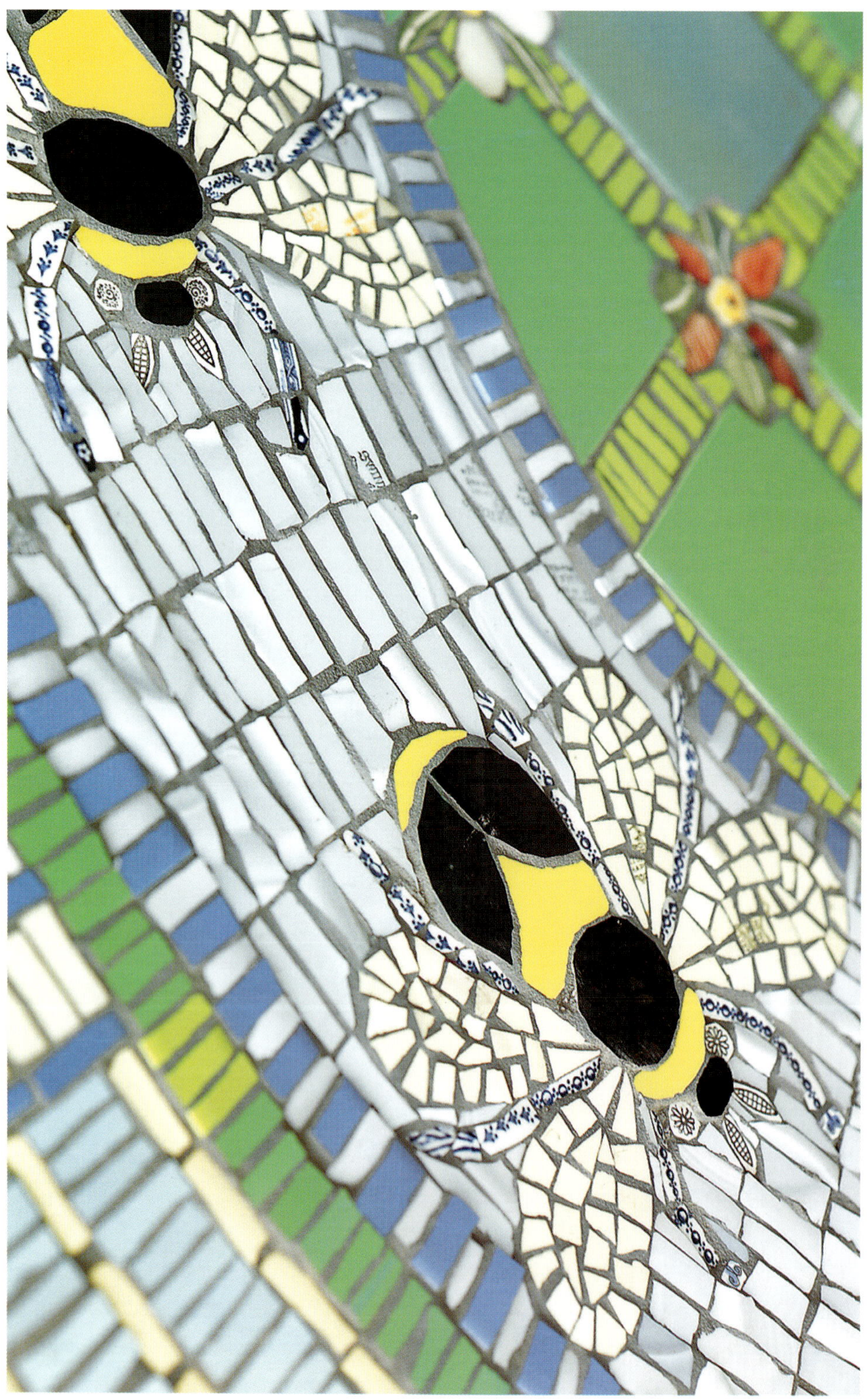

If you are a beginner, it is sometimes better to think of mosaic as a medium that is most effective in broader outline rather than fine detail. Unlike drawing or painting, mosaic can become less effective the more it is weighed down with detail; instead, a few bold outlines can be filled in with patterns and shapes. Pattern alone can be the focus of a mosaic.

Simple outlines

If you are a good draughtsperson and you can draw or paint, you may find that your initial attempts at design may not be quite right for mosaic, as you will be tempted to add too much detail by way of shading, moulding and modelling.

To start with, you may like to study the work of cartoonists, who can evoke people, places and whole landscapes with a few lines of the pen. A facial expression may be conveyed with single strokes for eyes, brows, mouth and so on; movement is also minimally expressed. Equally, you could examine the cut-outs in the late work of Matisse to see how brilliantly he captured the contours of the human body

Left: Arch Air Condensed – *detail of a bee from a recycled china mosaic by Cleo Mussi. The background patterns are as vivid as the bees.*

Top: This detail shows various ways of changing direction and outlining movement.

Below: This mosaic table top by Salvatore Raeli shows how the pattern dictates the direction of the tiles.

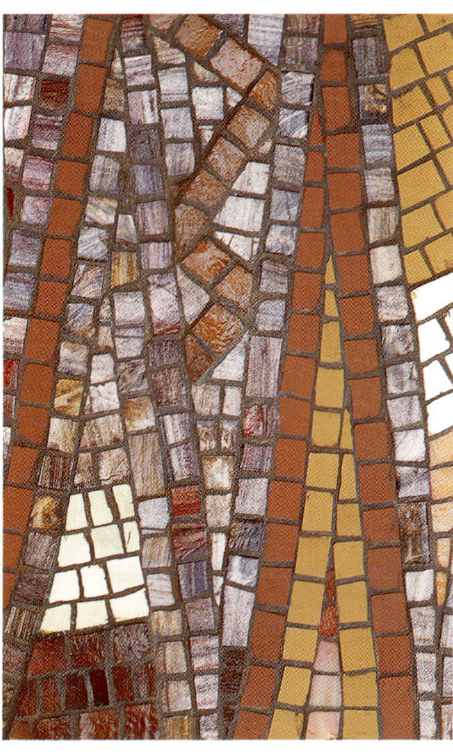

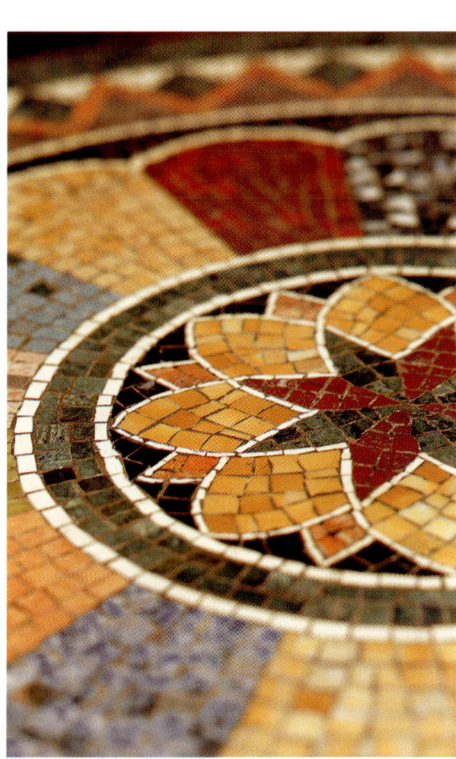

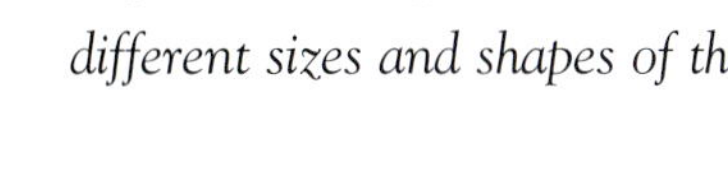

Top: Here the pattern is created by the different sizes and shapes of the pieces.

Below: Bold, strong patterns can be made by using larger, clipped pieces of tiles – shape and pattern become one.

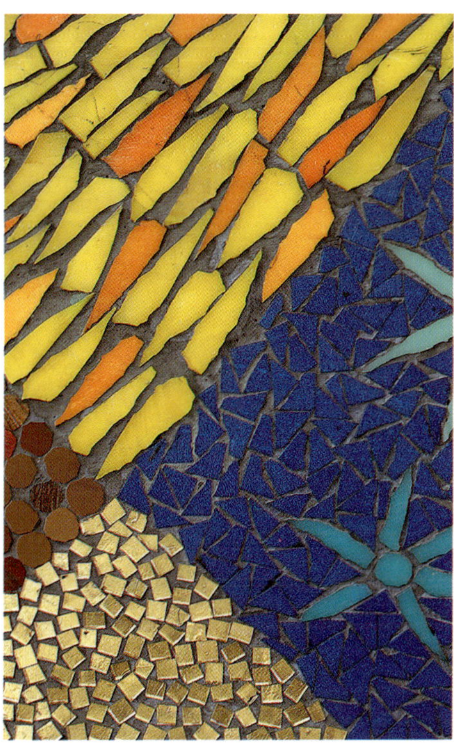

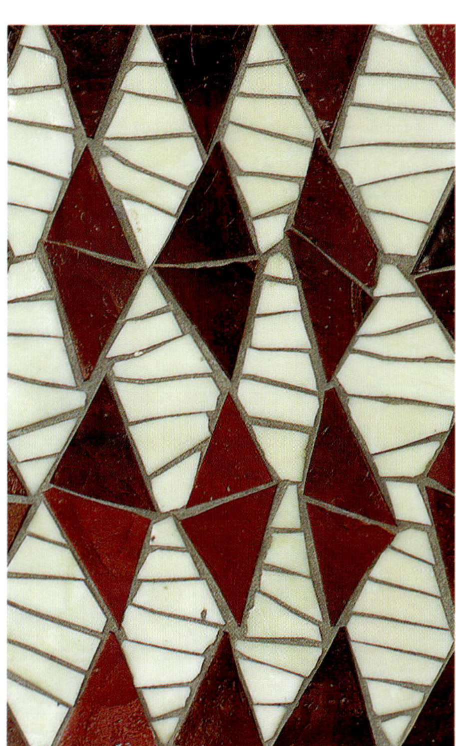

Top: The lines here are laid in curves, to give a sense of movement.

Below: This intricate design by Cleo Mussi uses the direction of the pieces to emphasize the pattern.

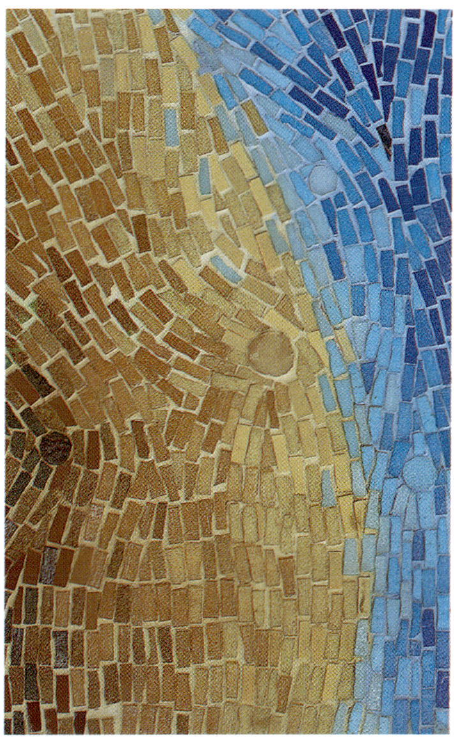

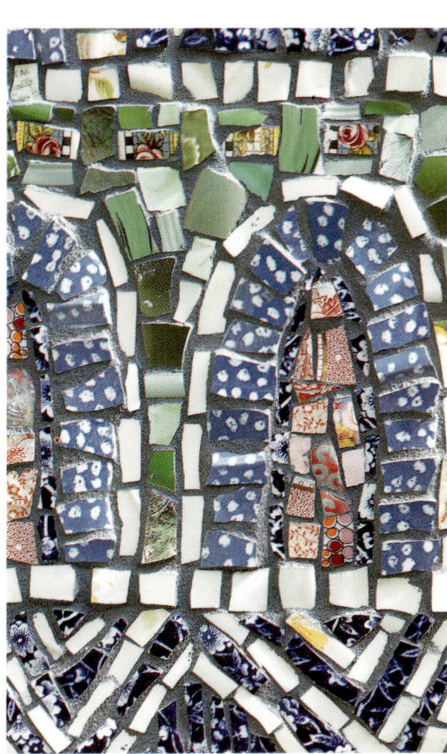

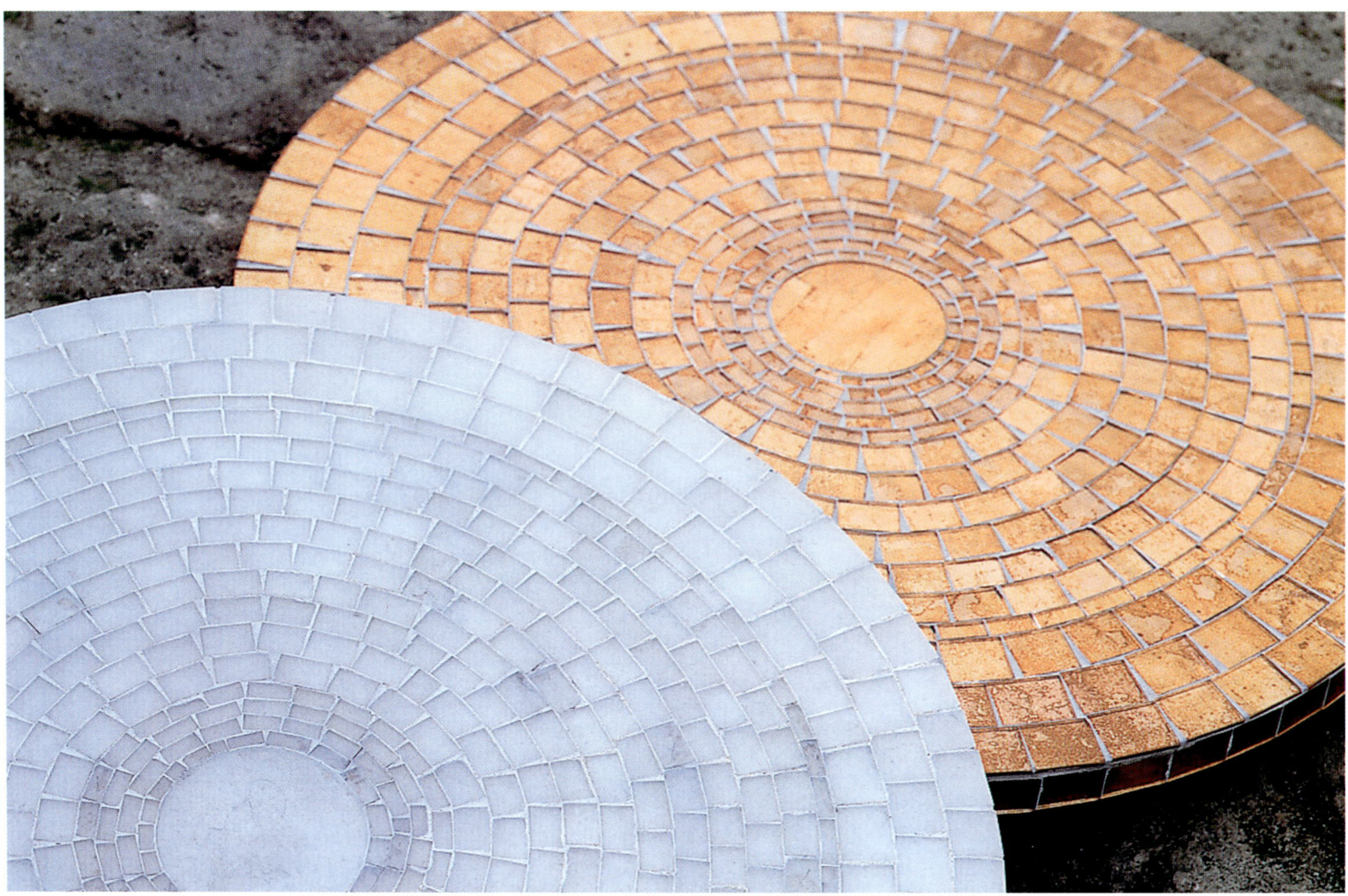

in movement with pieces of coloured tissue paper. It is worth experimenting with this "less is more" principle.

If you prefer to adapt an existing design, all you need to do is trace the basic shape, hold it away from your original to make sure the outlines are sufficient to show what you want to portray, then make your outlines the right size. This is easy with modern photocopiers that enlarge or reduce.

Forming patterns

The art of laying tesserae to form images and patterns is called *opus* (*opera* is the plural). There are no strict rules to adhere to, as each artist develops his or her own style, but there are a few things to consider. A fan shape is frequently seen in mosaic, and this gives pattern and interest to a background, especially if you are laying just one colour. A pair of compasses will help to draw the curves. Rows of straight square tesserae laid like brickwork can also fill large areas.

When laying circular mosaics, guidelines should be drawn with a large pair of compasses. If the design comes to a central point, then tesserae cut at angles will be needed to work the centre. This can be fiddly and involve using tiny pieces. Alternatively, you could cover the central point with a large piece of tile and work around it.

Rhythm and variety

These are essential elements of pattern. When the lines of tesserae flow around a particular subject or group of subjects and create rhythm and movement, it is called *opus vermiculatum*. Images can also be outlined in the background colour or in a distinct colour to help emphasize them and define their shape and pattern. Laying two or three lines of tiles around a shape will also add clarity to the design. Lines of tesserae can be laid to flow in directional lines, leading the eye to or around a design: this is called *andamento*.

Random patterns of tiles can be used to add variety to a mosaic. Sometimes this is necessary to fill

Above: The simple, but elegant, circular design of these table tops by Rebecca Newnham echoes the shape of the objects and focuses the eye on the material.

awkward or asymmetrical shapes. You can vary the interstices, or spaces between the tesserae, depending on the effect you require.

Geometric shapes are ideal for creating rhythm in mosaics and they will not become monotonous. Squares or oblongs, checks, chevrons, circles, swirls or spirals, Greek key, interlocking or separated – all are intrinsically pleasing to the eye and have an inbuilt sense of movement. This is why these motifs have remained so popular across the world and through the ages.

Shading with pattern

Often, you will need to convey some variation in shading and change of colour in a mosaic. You may stagger lines of colour in alternate rows to create fingers of colour or introduce some tonal shading so the change is not too abrupt. This often occurs in patterns using subtle colours. Some degree of moulding or shading is vital in representational mosaics, and this can be achieved by varying the size and/or the shape of the mosaic pieces, as well as their colour, to suggest the contours of a face (nose, eyes, chin, brow), the body and limbs, or the shape of a flower.

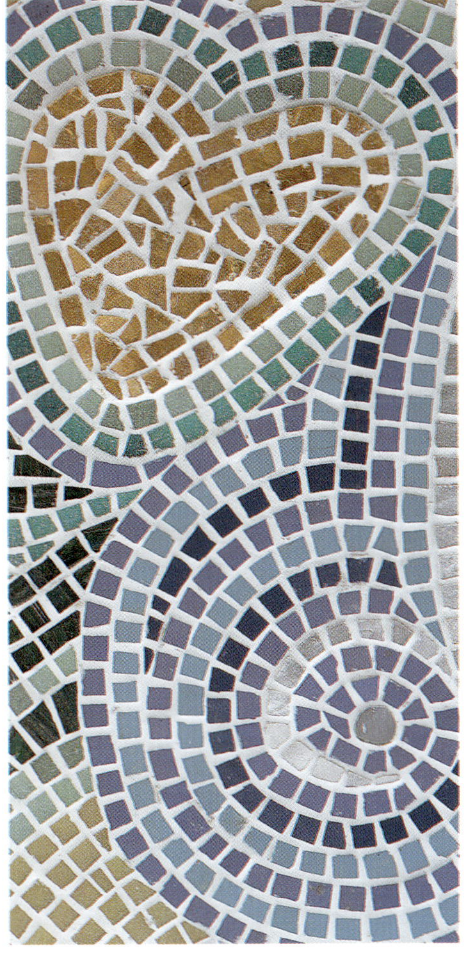

Left: It is possible to create wonderful patterns with square mosaic tessarae. The lines in this piece are laid in curves that give a great sense of movement.

This is a skilled procedure. Be sure to practise carefully beforehand, laying out your pieces like a jigsaw puzzle on a piece of cardboard, well away from any setting medium, until every piece is in the right place.

Grout lines also play a part in helping the rhythm and flow of a design. Straight lines give a more formal, structured effect and curved lines help to give a feeling of movement. The widths and colours of the lines can vary.

Below: Here, light falls on the eyes and nose – facial features that are skilfully conveyed through a varied use of pattern and colour.

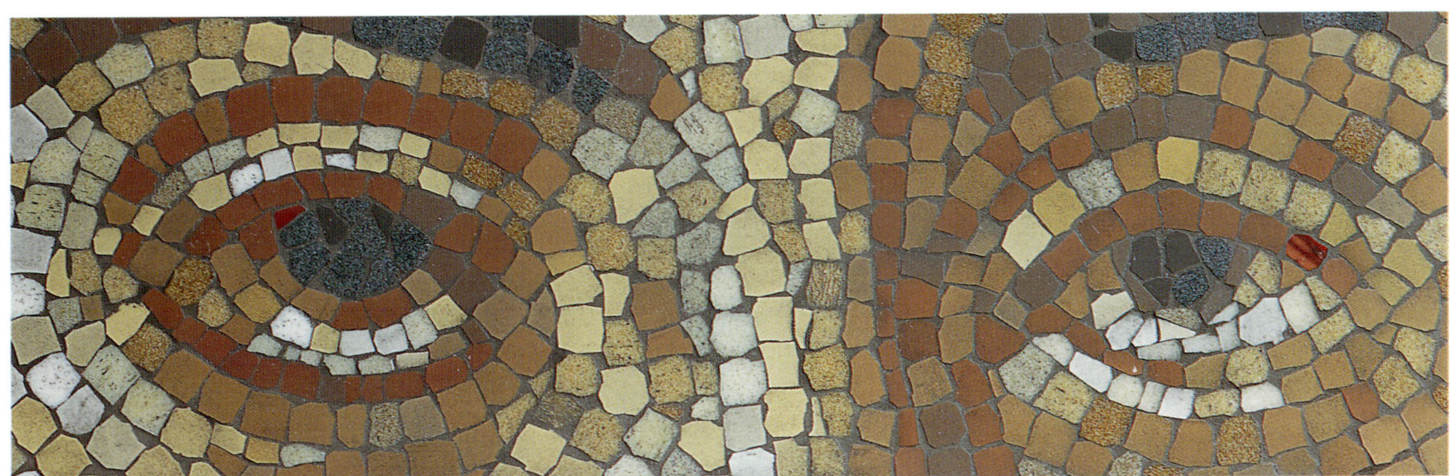

Texture can be one of the most interesting, exciting aspects of mosaic. Even on a flat panel, the depth of tile can vary and many materials can be used to vary the surface and create sparkling shapes and textural schemes.

Using Texture

Different materials have their own inherent qualities. Clay or ceramic have an even surface but have a slight organic roughness. Metal is hard and angular. Wood is rough but warm to the touch. Stone is smoother and cooler in its effect, while smalti and glass are the most responsive to light.

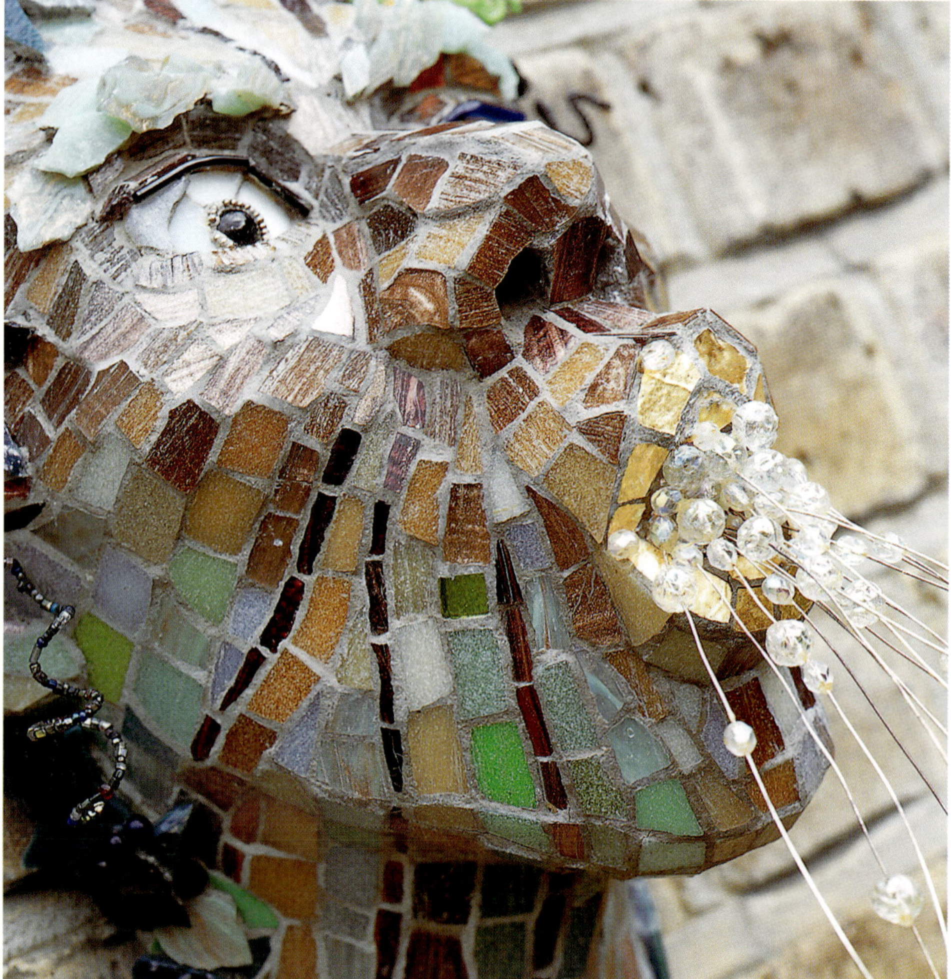

Mixed media

Combining two or more different materials is a way of adding drama, pattern and variety. Mixed media can achieve all kinds of exciting textural effects. Inserting pieces of broken china in an otherwise plain design adds not just colour and pattern: the broken pieces have a different texture and the fractured edges add spots of roughness to the even surface. You can contrast ceramic, which is slightly textured, with glass, which is smooth, or metal with stone. If you experiment with combinations of various textures, however, do not overload the mosaic with too many at the expense of clarity.

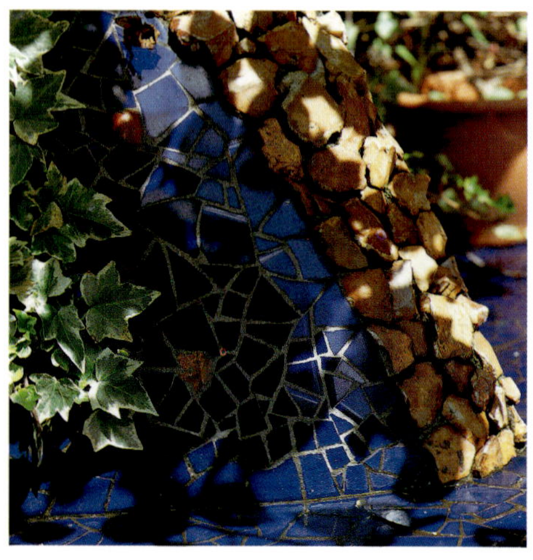

Above: Iridescent, multi-faceted beads, shells and glass all contribute to the varied texture of this dramatic, sculptural garden wall head by Takako Shimizu.

Left: A detail of a mosaiced garden seat, which provides durable external seating, designed by Celia Gregory. The stones make rough, textured breaks in the smoother blue and gold sections of the seating area.

Setting

The texture should be chosen according to the purpose of the mosaic. A splashback, kitchen countertop or cabinet door needs to throw off grease and water, not hold them. A floor or garden path should not be slippery underfoot, nor should it be so uneven that people risk tripping when they walk on it. There is also an aesthetic aspect to choice of texture, so that it suits its setting. A rougher texture might look right in a farmhouse kitchen, but smoothness looks better in a more classical setting. The hardness of metal is ideal in a contemporary loft-style interior, while stone and pebbles are a natural choice for a garden.

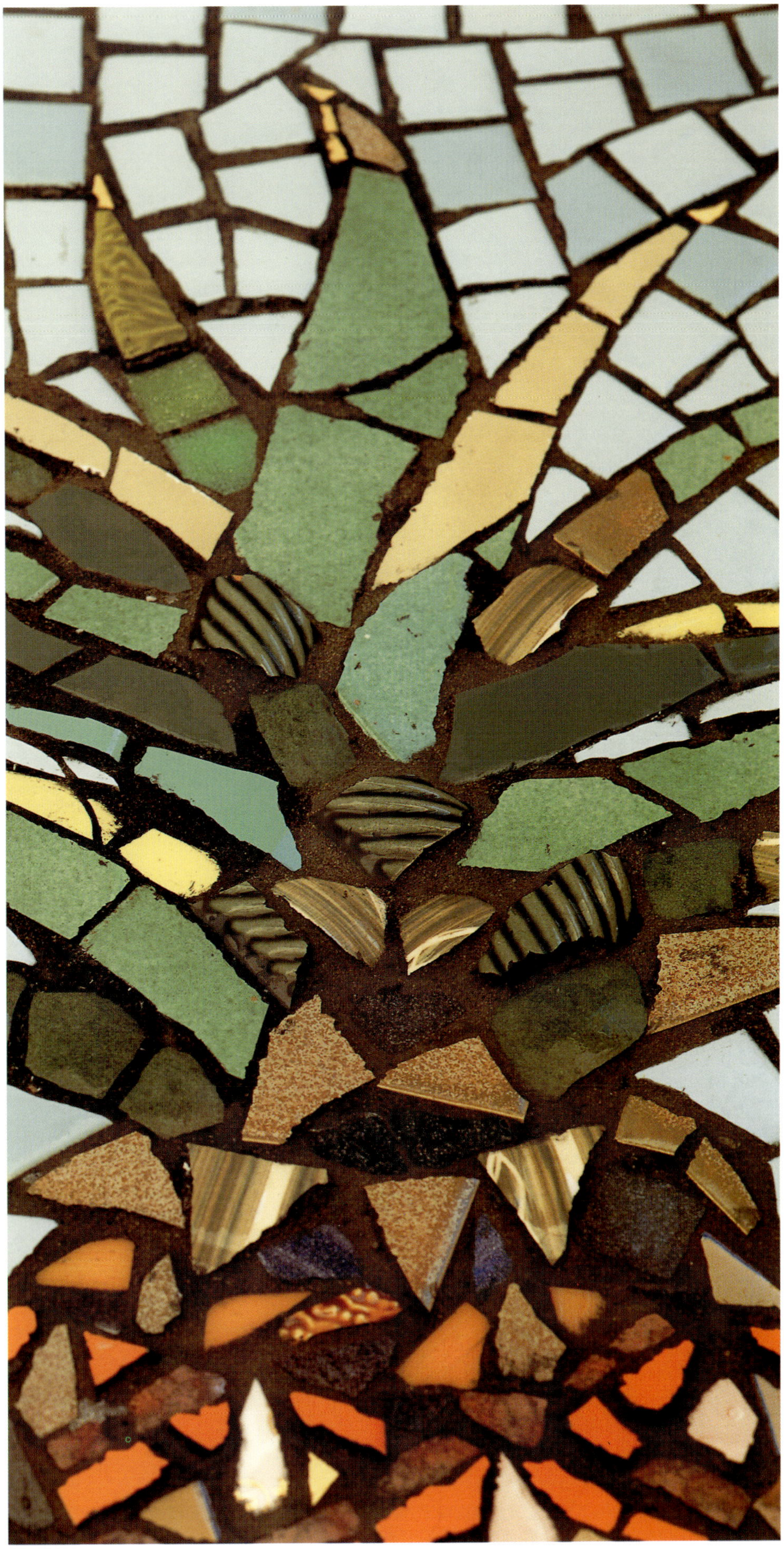

Right: A close-up of Norma Vondee's beautiful panel shows how the artist has depicted the sharp, spiky texture of a pineapple and included ridged glass along with rough and smooth ceramic pieces.

Below: The uneven qualities of river-washed glass are very subtle in this mirror frame by Celia Gregory. Within the mosaic are trinkets of china, some of which come from pieces of Tudor pottery.

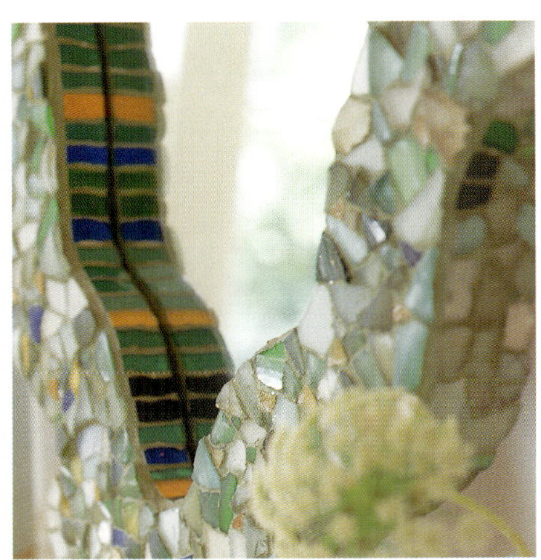

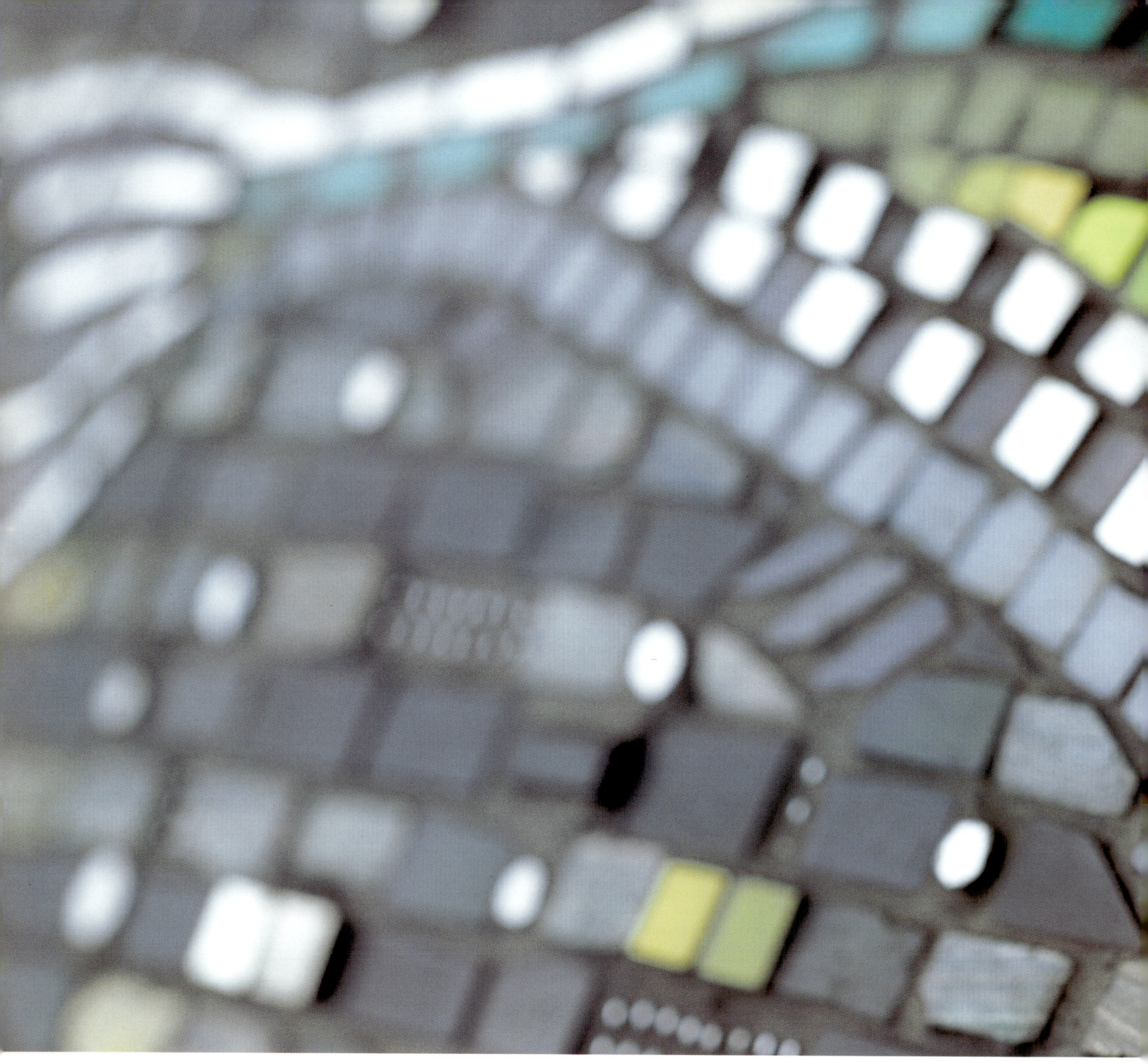

Materials and Techniques

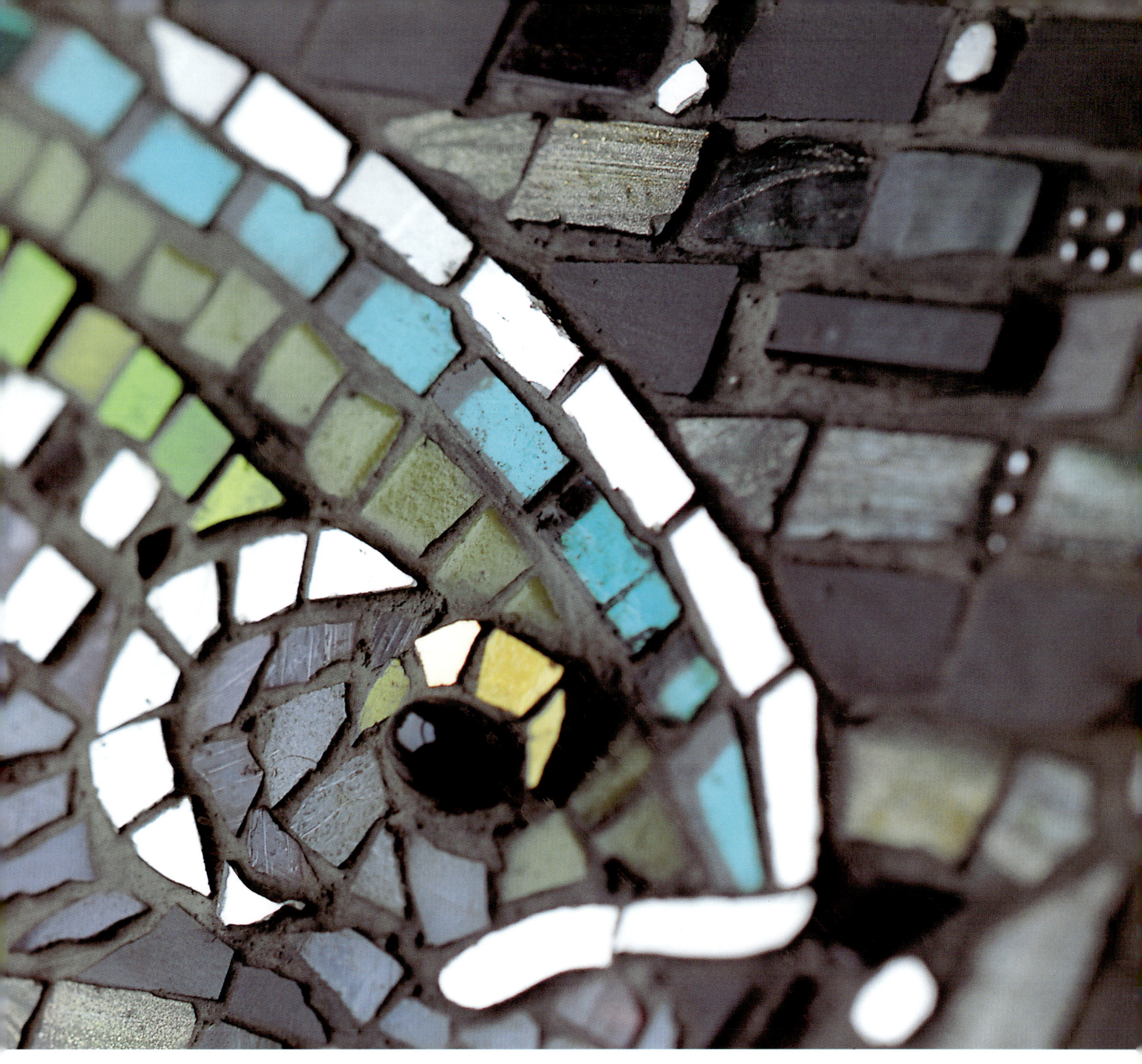

Mosaic is a versatile art form with great potential for personal creativity, and the range of materials available is visually exciting, colourful and tactile. And, as mosaic becomes more popular, the choice of material continues to grow. Planning projects and preparing the materials carefully enables you to create the mosaics you want, and this is followed by the vital grouting and cleaning stages, after which your mosaic is ready to be displayed.

The subtle colours of marble, the opacity of smalti and the sheer opulence of gold leaf make these invaluable materials. These three types of material give a luxurious appearance to any mosaic.

Marble, Smalti and Gold Leaf

Each mosaic material has its own qualities that will influence the colour, style, look and texture of the finished piece. You can choose to work in just one medium or mix materials to create interesting texture and variety. Marble, smalti and gold leaf can work together to produce sumptuous results.

Marble

This is a natural material; it was used in Graeco-Roman times and is still associated with the luxurious qualities of modern Italian mosaics. Its hard and durable qualities make it excellent for use on floors. Marble is also a subtle material: it represents sheer beauty and natural elegance, and has a depth and timeless quality beyond any other material.

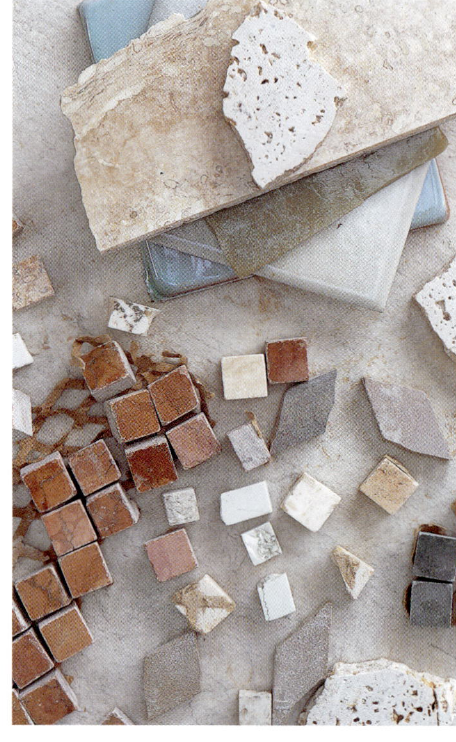

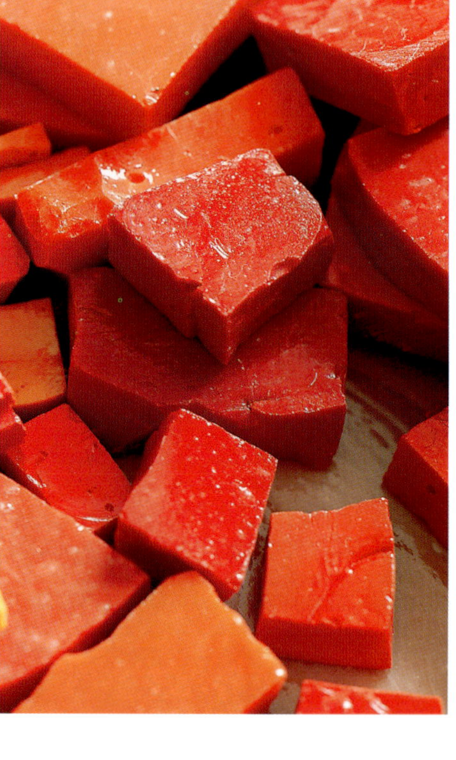

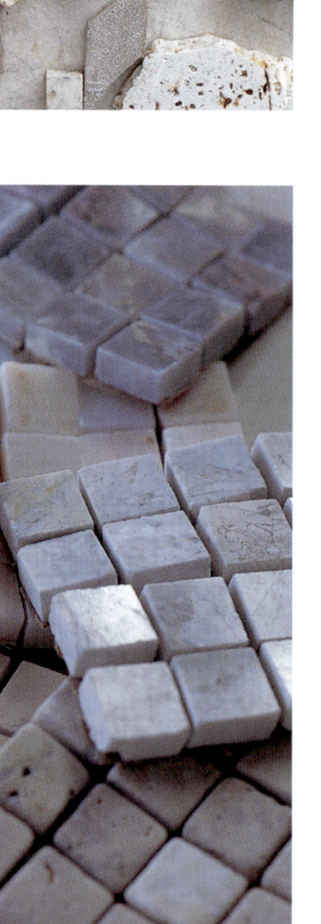

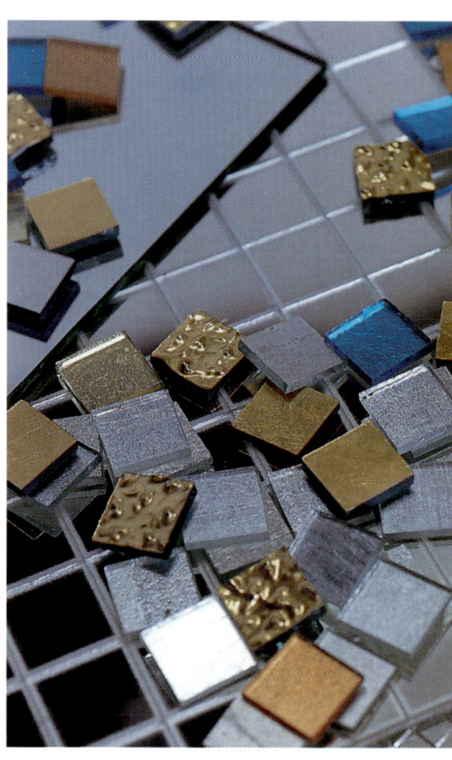

Above right: Marble comes in large slabs that can be cut into squares by hand to produce a more authentic style of mosaic.

Above far right: Smalti has been made for over 2,000 years. It is opaque and creates a wonderfully textural finish to mosaic.

Right: Machine-cut marble in regular squares on mesh or paper backing is effective for covering large areas.

Far right: A selection of tiles with gold and silver leaf twinkle with luxury and magic.

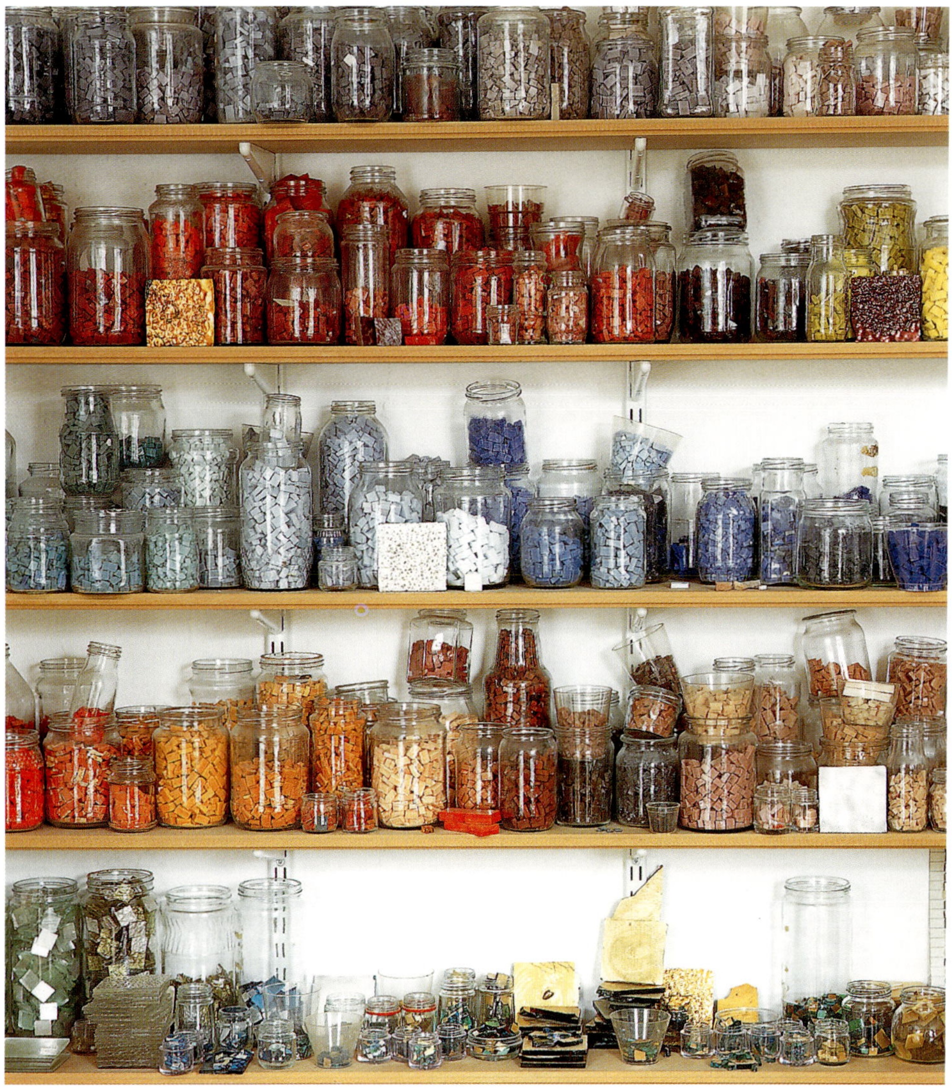

The colours are soft and the variations in tone are subtle: white, chalky pinks and rose, through to delicate greens, blues and blacks. Polishing intensifes the colours. When marble is cut, it has a crystalline appearance and the grains vary according to which part of the world the stone has come from.

For use in mosaics, marble is generally cut from rods with a hammer and hardie (a type of anvil). It is an expensive material, and this limits its use to the finest quality of mosaic.

You can also buy marble that has been machine-cut into regular squares. These squares are laid on to a paper backing, which can be soaked off. The handmade characteristic of the mosaic is lost in this form, but its quality is not impaired, and this is a cheaper form that can be used to cover large areas quickly.

Smalti

Traditionally made in Italy, smalti is opaque glass that is available in a great variety of colours. It is individually made, and the thickness, colour and size vary slightly each time. Each round slab, called a *pizze*, is made from molten glass fired with oxides, metals and powdered marble. Once it has cooled, it is cut into tesserae. It is often sold by the half kilo (1¼lb). *Smalti filati* are threads of glass rods of smalti used for micro-mosaics.

Designs made from smalti have a slightly uneven characteristic that creates a brilliant reflective surface. This bumpiness means that smalti mosaics are often not grouted and cannot be used on floors. Smalti comes in a superb range of colours, and any irregularities create character.

Gold leaf

This is the most opulent tile available to the mosaic artist. It is expensive, yet irresistible, and nothing can surpass its reflective quality. It can be used sparsely in a mosaic and still have a great impact and effect. The tesserae have a backing glass, which is usually turquoise, yellow or green. Then there is a layer of 24-carat gold leaf, which is protected with a thin layer of clear or coloured glass called the *cartellina*. The gold tesserae can have a smooth or bumpy surface.

Different variations are available with silver or copper leaf, a thin film of gold alloy or other metals. The colours of tile, ranging from deepest gold to vivid blues and greens, are formed when either the *cartellina* or the backing glass is altered.

Above: Storing tiles in glass jars is a colourful and practical way to see what you have in stock.

With their luminous quality, wide range of colours and great choice of surface texture, glass tiles are invaluable to the mosaic artist. Ceramic tiles, which are widely available, offer additional textural variation.

Glass and Ceramic Tiles

These are usually made from vitreous glass and glazed and unglazed clay or porcelain, and come in small, regular tiles. They are laid on to mesh or brown paper to make up sheets measuring approximately 30 x 30cm (12 x 12in), which can be used to cover large areas without the tiles having to be laid individually. The range of materials is always expanding and there is a huge variety of colours and shapes to choose from.

Glass tiles

Vitreous glass is the most commonly used mosaic glass. Its production has been standardized, and it is therefore cheaper than smalti and more accessible to the amateur. It comes in sheets, and the individual tile is a regular square about 2 x 2cm (¾ x ¾in). The

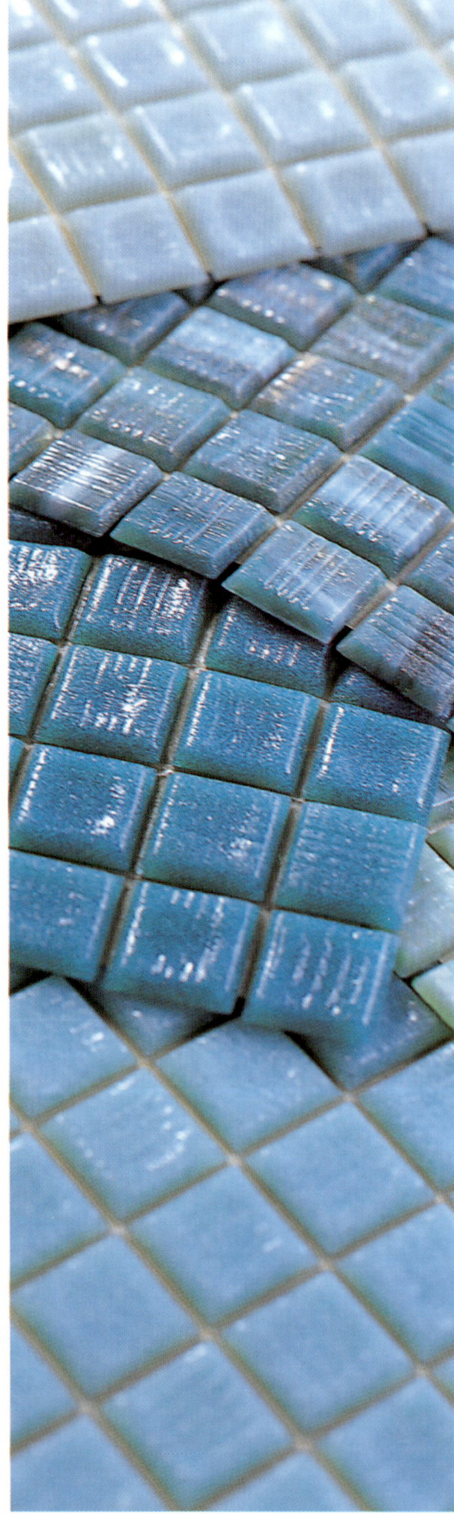

Right: Vitreous glass tiles come on sheets of mesh or brown paper, which are soaked off in warm water. The individual tiles can be clipped into smaller squares.

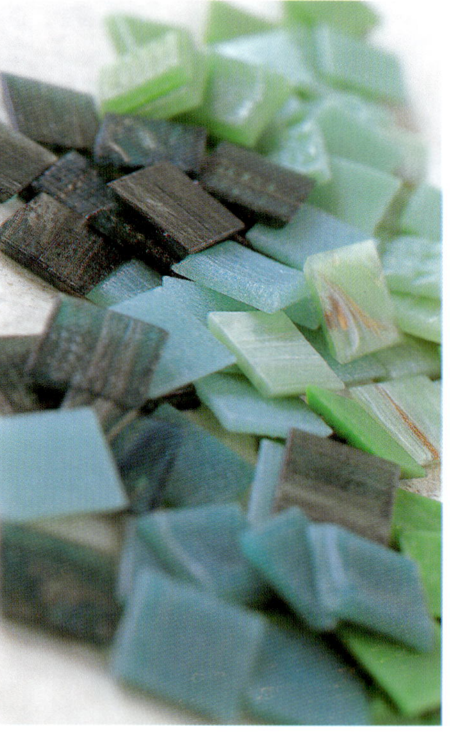

Above far right: Vitreous glass is a commonly used material; there is a lovely selection of colours. They are easy to clip with mosaic tile nippers.

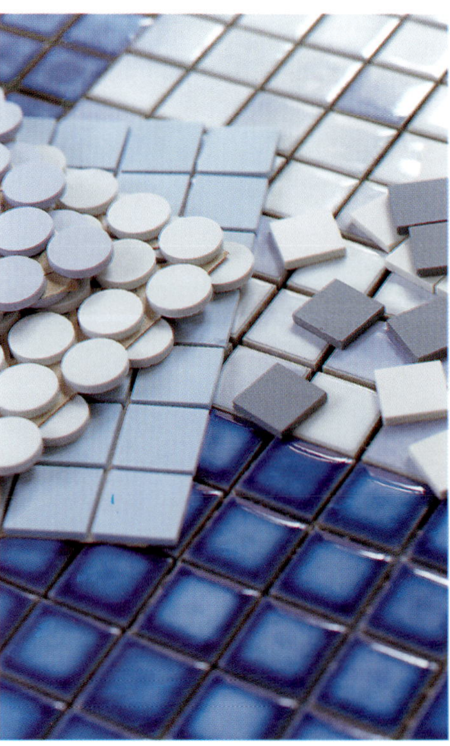

Far right: Ceramic mosaic tiles come in many shapes and colours, and different kinds of textures.

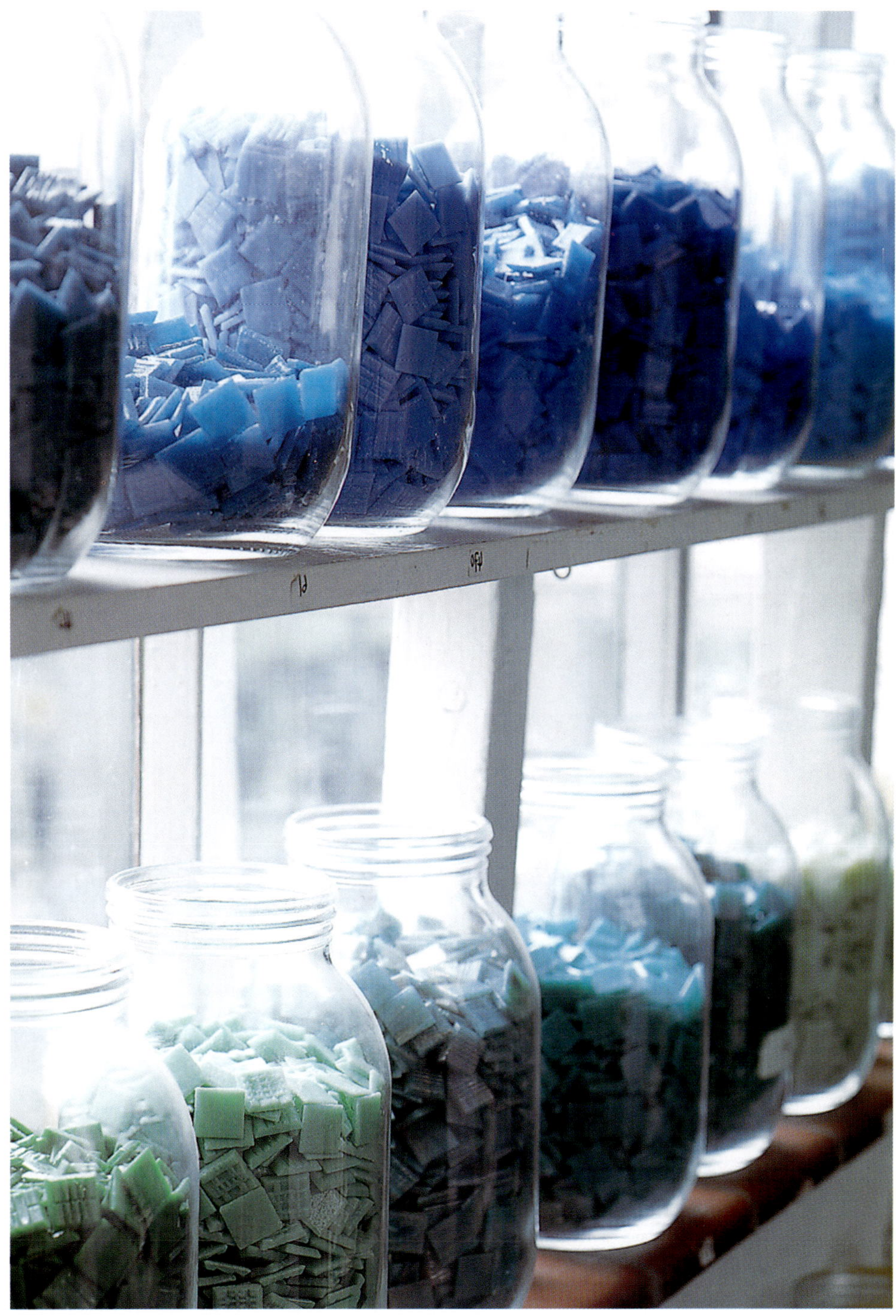

sheets can be used whole to cover large areas or split into sections for individual mosaics.

Glass is available in a wide variety of colours. The famous Bizzaria range has a grainy quality to the glass and offers a beautiful selection of tiles that have copper blended into the glass, creating a reflective quality that the other tiles can lack. Cutting the individual tiles into four creates the classic square tesserae; the glass is easy to clip and offers extensive potential for intricate design.

There is a now also a new range of glass mosaic made in France. The colours are more rustic than Bizzaria. The glass is smooth and the concentration of the colour is even throughout, appearing like plastic. When these glass tiles are blended with the other glass ranges, they provide the mosaicist with a beautiful palette.

Glass is liable to chip or crack, so tile manufacturers have developed several types of sheet mosaic that are suitable for floors: these are non-slip and non-absorbent and meet many of the regulations associated with commercial properties.

Glass tiles can be shiny, round, square, bumpy, thick, thin, smooth or textured, and come in many different colours. Tiles for mosaic artists are like sweets for children: it is difficult to know which ones to choose. Stored in clear glass jars, the colourful array can be quite spectacular.

Above: Display your mosaic tesserae in groups of colours in clear glass jars. You can easily see what you have available to use, and the gradations of tone and shade.

Ceramic tiles

Mosaic ceramic tesserae are round or square and are made from porcelain. They are good for creating texture, as they can be glazed or unglazed: a combination of the two creates surface interest. The colour is uniform in unglazed tiles, and the surface is likely to be matt and more porous than glazed tiles. Ceramic tiles are inexpensive and widely available.

All the materials mentioned so far build an image using mainly squares. Broken-up household tiles, smashed china and mirror and pieces of stained glass, however, create mosaic pictures in a very different style.

Tiles, China, Mirror and Glass

Shiny household tiles, broken pieces of china, in all colours and shapes, pieces of reflective mirror and shimmering stained glass all bring a new creative freedom to mosaic making.

Household tiles

Glazes on household tiles can be shiny, which enables you to play with the reflection of light in the design. When smashed up into irregular shapes, they are fantastic for working into abstract designs. The random shapes of the pieces also make them excellent for covering three-dimensional and sculptured surfaces. They are easy to handle and allow a freedom in expression that some regular square tiles lack, especially when working over curves.

Household tiles can reflect the contemporary aspect of mosaic. They offer enormous variety and versatility to the mosaic artist and it is possible to cover large areas cheaply with them.

China

The use of broken china is a wonderful way to recycle and make something beautiful out of otherwise useless items. A mosaic created with broken china is completely individual because no two pieces are likely to be the same.

China and crockery are not really suitable for intricate designs, but are wonderful for working with patterns and texture. The curving nature of the material gives the final mosaic a textured finish. Odd pieces of pottery with quirky handles, lids and patterns can add some humour to a mosaic.

Mirror

You can buy mirror in sheets made up of small squares, or rectangles, or in large sheets that need to be smashed up. Mirror works very well scattered through a coloured mosaic. It also produces a fantastic effect when covering entire surfaces, especially sculptured forms. You can generally get offcuts from a glazier for free.

Stained glass

Walking into a stained glass supplier is like walking into an Aladdin's cave. Not only is there the most beautiful array of colours, but the glass has a wonderful shimmering quality to it, rather like beautiful jewels. There is even a stained glass that is iridescent and reflects light like mother-of-pearl.

Some types of stained glass are pieces of art in themselves. They can be used to cover whole surfaces for a luxurious finish or used in small areas to highlight details in a picture or an abstract pattern. Using stained glass in a mosaic design will create something extra special.

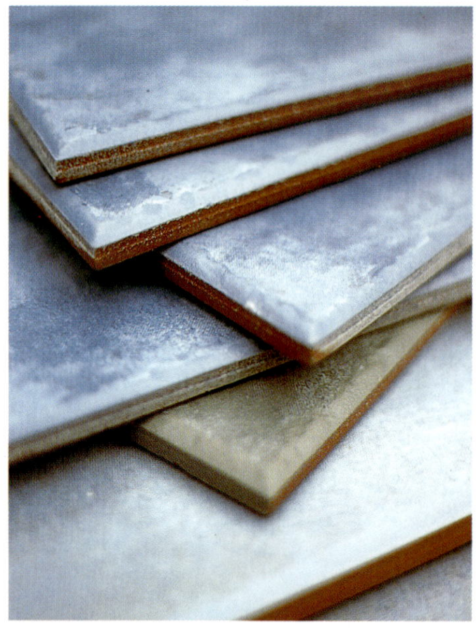

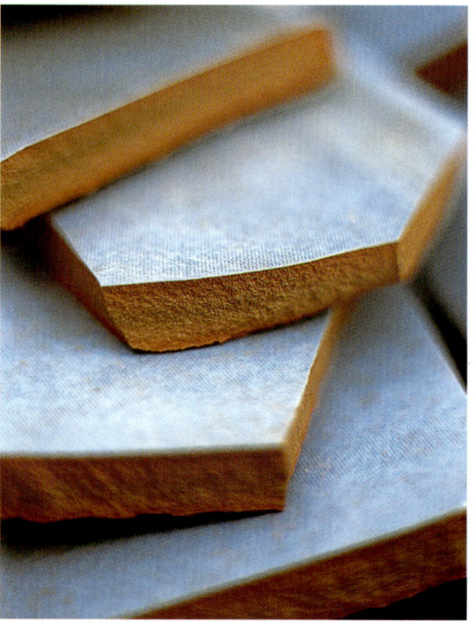

Above and above left: Plain household tiles are easy and cheap to obtain and can be easily cut to shape. They are good for sculptures and can be useful when you require the mosaic to be water-resistant.

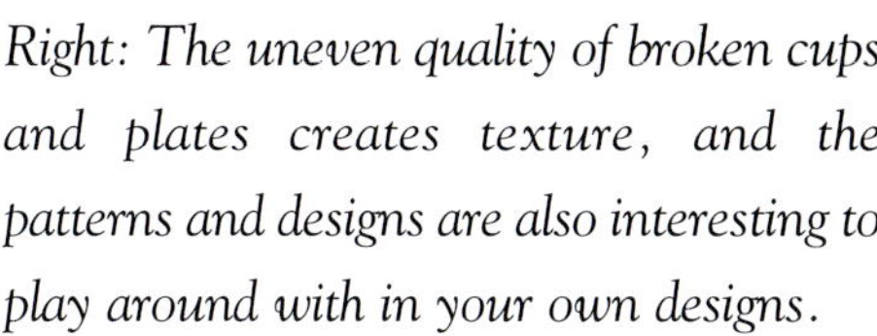

Right: The uneven quality of broken cups and plates creates texture, and the patterns and designs are also interesting to play around with in your own designs.

Below and below centre: Stained glass offers a beautiful array of colours and textures, and possesses wonderful reflective qualities. Each sheet of glass could be a piece of art in itself, and when it is broken up into small fragments provides a fantastic mosaic material.

Below far right: Recycling broken crockery to use in mosaic is an inventive and cheap source of materials. Collect pieces, and sort them by colour and pattern.

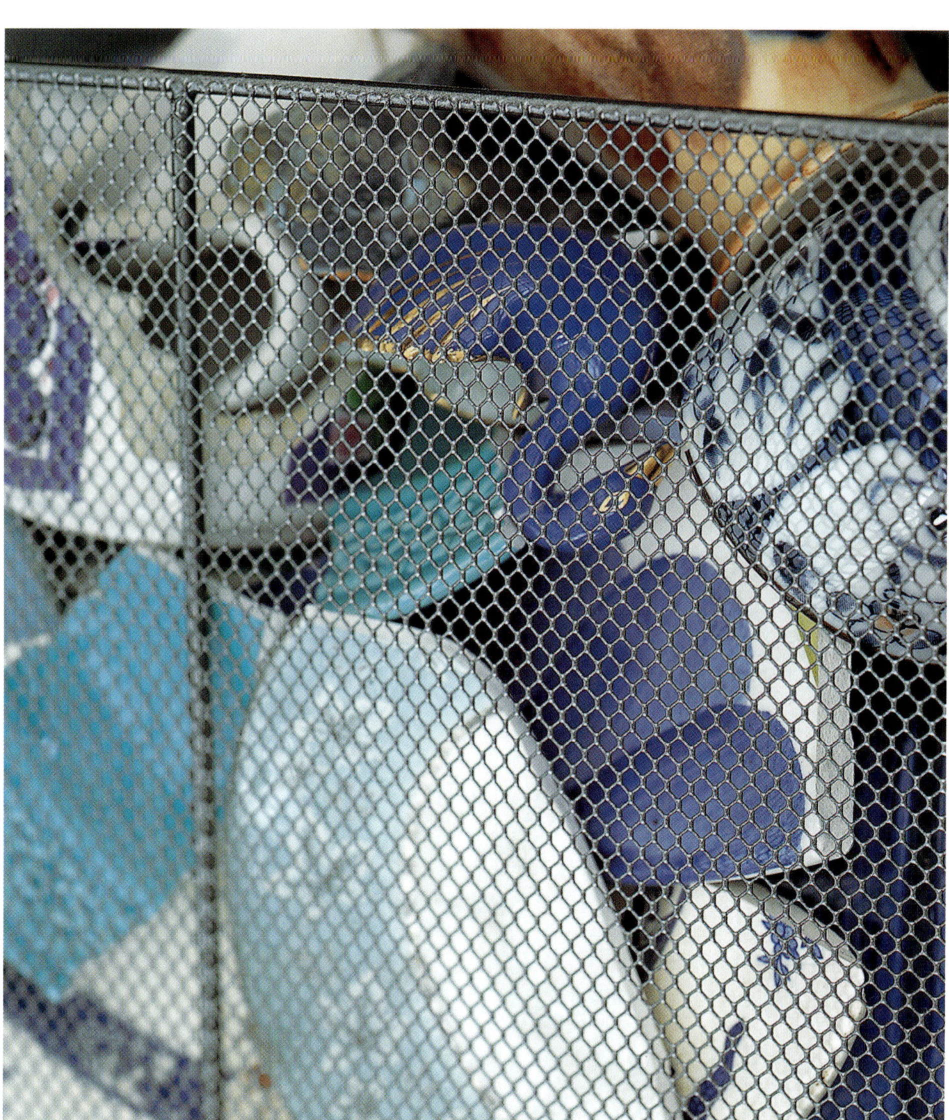

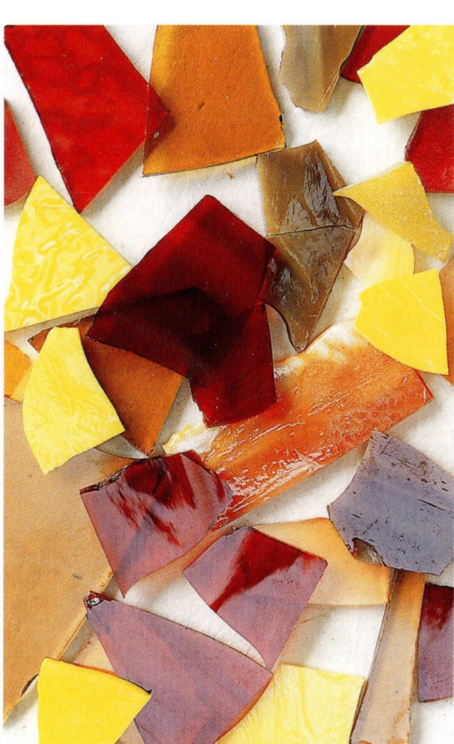

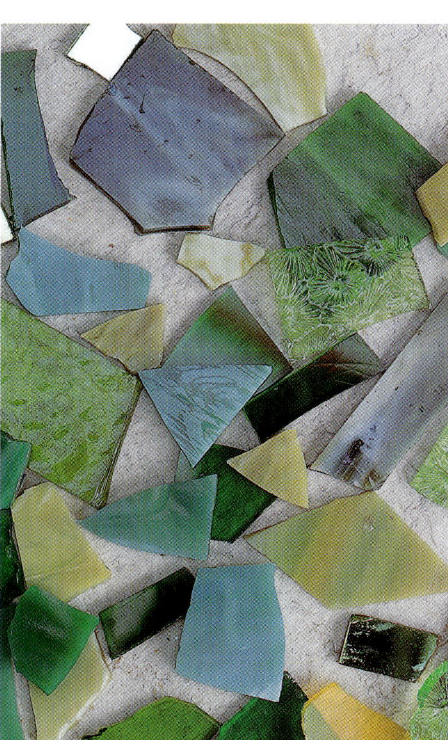

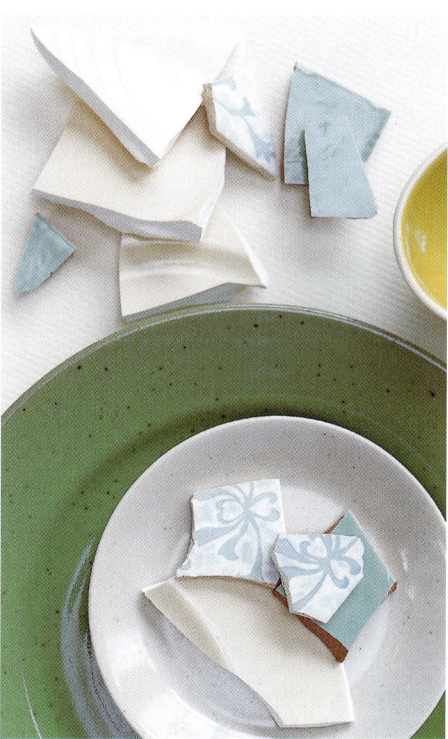

When making decorative mosaics, you can use both traditional materials and more unusual found and collected objects, ranging from shells and washed glass from beaches, to glass jewels and semi-precious stones.

Mixed Media

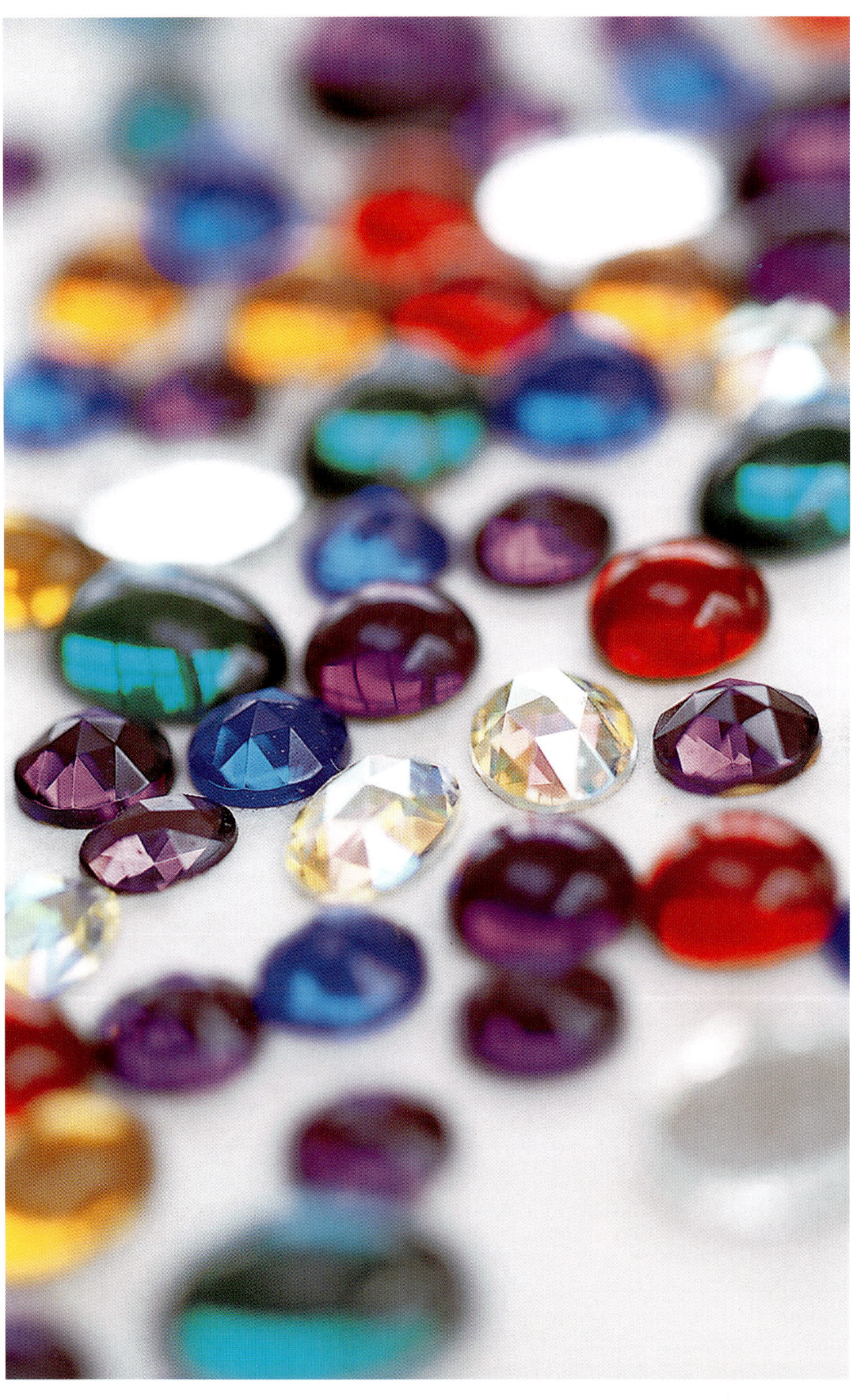

Using a variety of materials can bring personality and originality to mosaic designs. Mixed materials are particularly effective in sculptural mosaics and for creating a variety of textures and depth in two-dimensional work. It is also fun to gather a collection, such as natural materials from beaches or rivers, or old china from second-hand or thrift stores. There are no boundaries to what can be used, and it can be challenging to experiment with new methods and new materials.

Pebbles

Some of the earliest known mosaics were made from pebbles, and there is still a strong tradition in making pebble mosaics in Greece. In Lindos, Rhodes, you can find many pebble doorsteps and pavements.

Pebbles from the sea or rivers can be found in many subtle colour variations. They have a certain simplicity that is easy on the eye. They are long-lasting and it is possible to seal them, which makes them appear wet and the colours richer. Pebbles are traditionally used to cover large areas in gardens. They offer good drainage, and the simple designs look good without being overpowering.

Left: Glass beads with a flat metallic back used for making jewellery are brilliant for bringing a sparkle to mosaics.

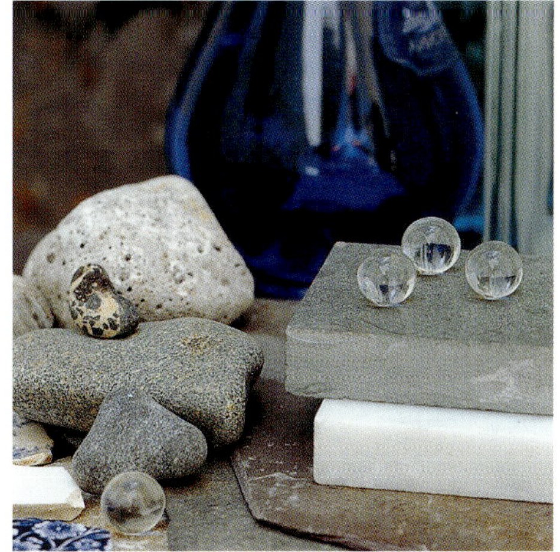

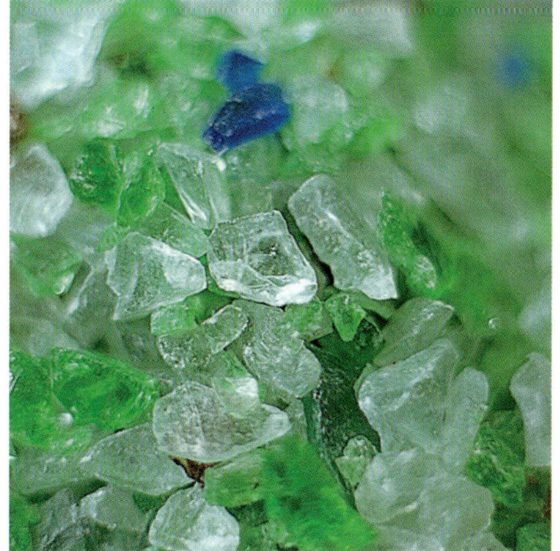

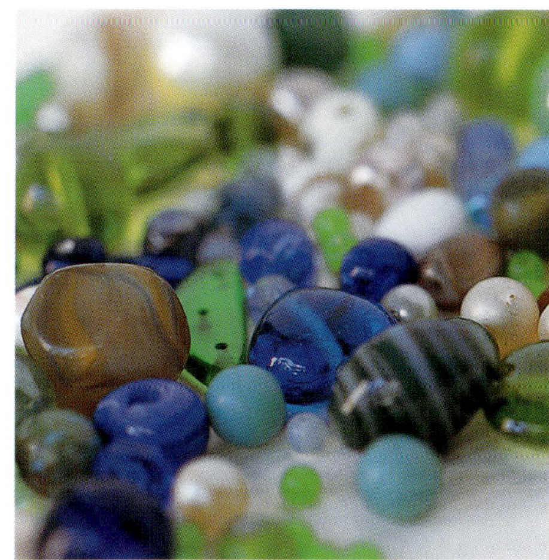

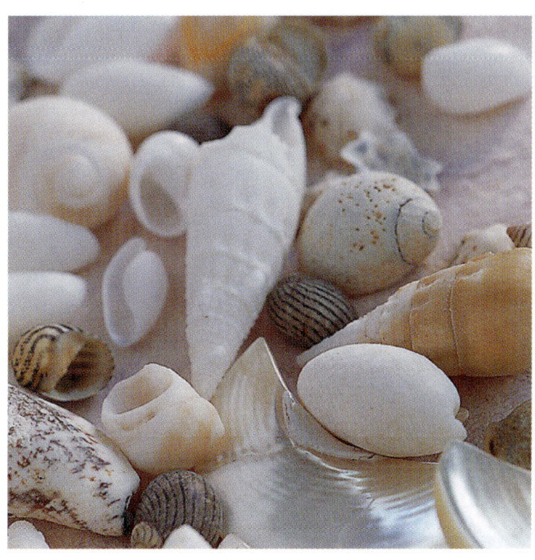

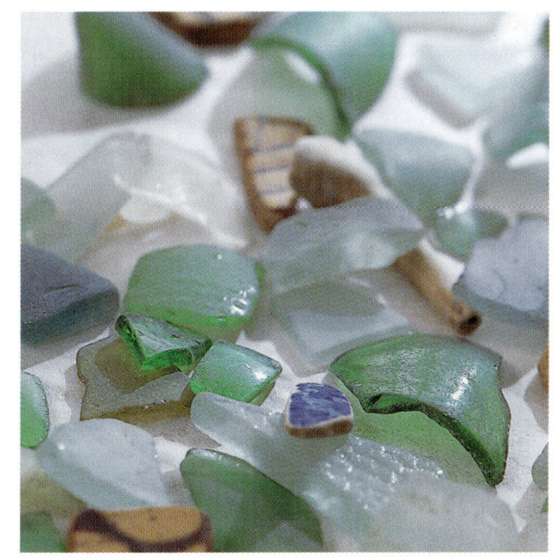

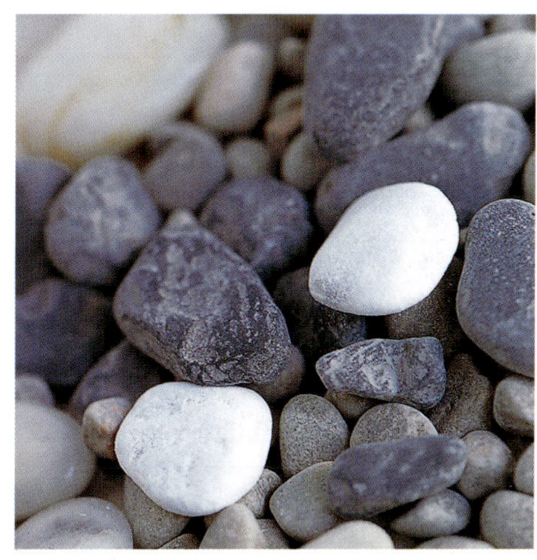

Top: Stone, marble and slate can be cut into small pieces to create natural, subtle yet textural, mosaics.

Above: Shells come in beautiful soft colours and are traditionally used in grottoes or garden follies.

Top: Small pieces of washed glass can be added to mosaics for effect. Their soft colours give a gentle look.

Above: Washed glass and old pottery can often be found on a riverbank. Both will add character to a mosaic.

Top: Glass, plastic and antique beads all work well in mosaics, adding texture and colour to the work.

Above: Pebbles are good for creating simple, lasting designs and have natural muted tones and textural qualities.

Shells

Seashells, in their teeming variety of shapes and colours, have provided inspiration for craftspeople for centuries. The Chinese used mother-of-pearl for inlaying. Shells bedded into lime cement line the grottoes of Italian Renaissance gardens, and 18th-century European country house owners adorned their garden follies with them.

Salvaged materials

The edges of washed glass and pottery that have been smoothed and rounded by years of erosion in the water can be found on beaches and riverbanks. The effect of the water also softens the colours to create a gentle mosaic material. Collected or salvaged materials could include anything from old coins to forks and spoons. Metal foil, building blocks or even dice can be used.

Beads and jewels

Glass beads and jewels catch the light and twinkle. Their unevenness creates texture, which emphasizes the detail in a mosaic. Antique beads often have peculiarities within the glass that make them distinctive. You can buy jewels created for jewellery making that have a flat back, which makes them easier to lay, and placed in a mosaic they will add glints of colour.

Creating a design is fun, and collecting ideas in a scrapbook will be very useful for inspiring your projects. The design will affect your choice of materials, colours and style and the most suitable method of application.

Planning Projects

Take inspiration for your designs from books, magazines, other artists, nature or any other source that stimulates you. Keep any pictures or images that grab your attention for reference later. Stick them in a scrapbook and make notes about what you liked.

Drawings

The initial drawing will be only a guideline for your mosaic. Keep it simple and clear, with strong lines. If you cannot draw, trace an image or cut out a photocopy, and enlarge or adjust it to a suitable size and draw around it. It may be a good idea to make a few copies, so that you can try out different colour schemes before buying the tiles.

When you start applying the tesserae, your ideas may change as you work. This is all part of the evolutionary process of responding to the materials and their colour and texture.

It is not usually necessary to make all the design decisions at the beginning of the project. Creativity is a journey; allow the space during the process for new ideas and additions to unfold. When thinking about your design, bear in mind the colours, textures and contrast of the materials. Also, bear in mind how much time you want to spend on your mosaic, as this may influence the intricacy and complexity of the design.

Starting out

If the task is site specific, make an accurate template with graph paper or brown paper and/or take measurements before you start the detailed planning and work. Make clear notes while you are on site so it is easy to decipher the figures and information gathered when you are in your studio. It may help to photograph the site, too.

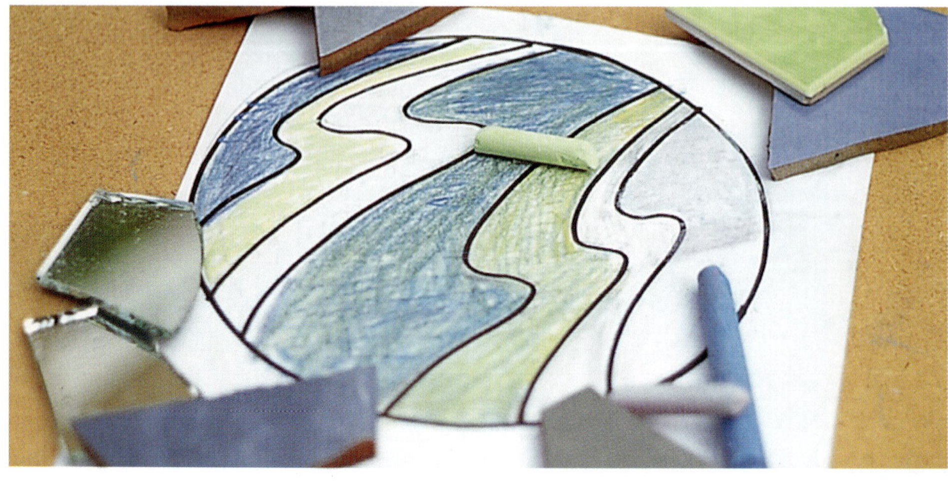

If you are a beginner, it is best to start with basic techniques and a small project, such as a pot stand, terracotta pot or small wall panel. As you become more confident, you can be more ambitious and explore your creativity.

Choosing tiles

The appearance of the mosaic is totally dependent on the materials you use. The design may even revolve around using a certain tile, the unique quality of which is your source of inspiration. Discovering how different materials work alone and with each other is an exciting aspect of mosaic artistry that takes time to master.

There is a fantastic range of tiles from all over the world in different colours, glazes and textures. You can use stone, with its soft colours, or choose from a lavish range of stained glass. There is no shortage of choice.

Aside from aesthetic decisions, there are various factors to take into account when choosing. The cost could be a consideration; for example marble is a very beautiful and durable material, but it is very expensive, while porcelain is a much cheaper alternative.

Left: It is useful to make a simple line drawing first using a soft pencil, then emphasize the lines with a black pen and shade in the colours to be mosaiced.

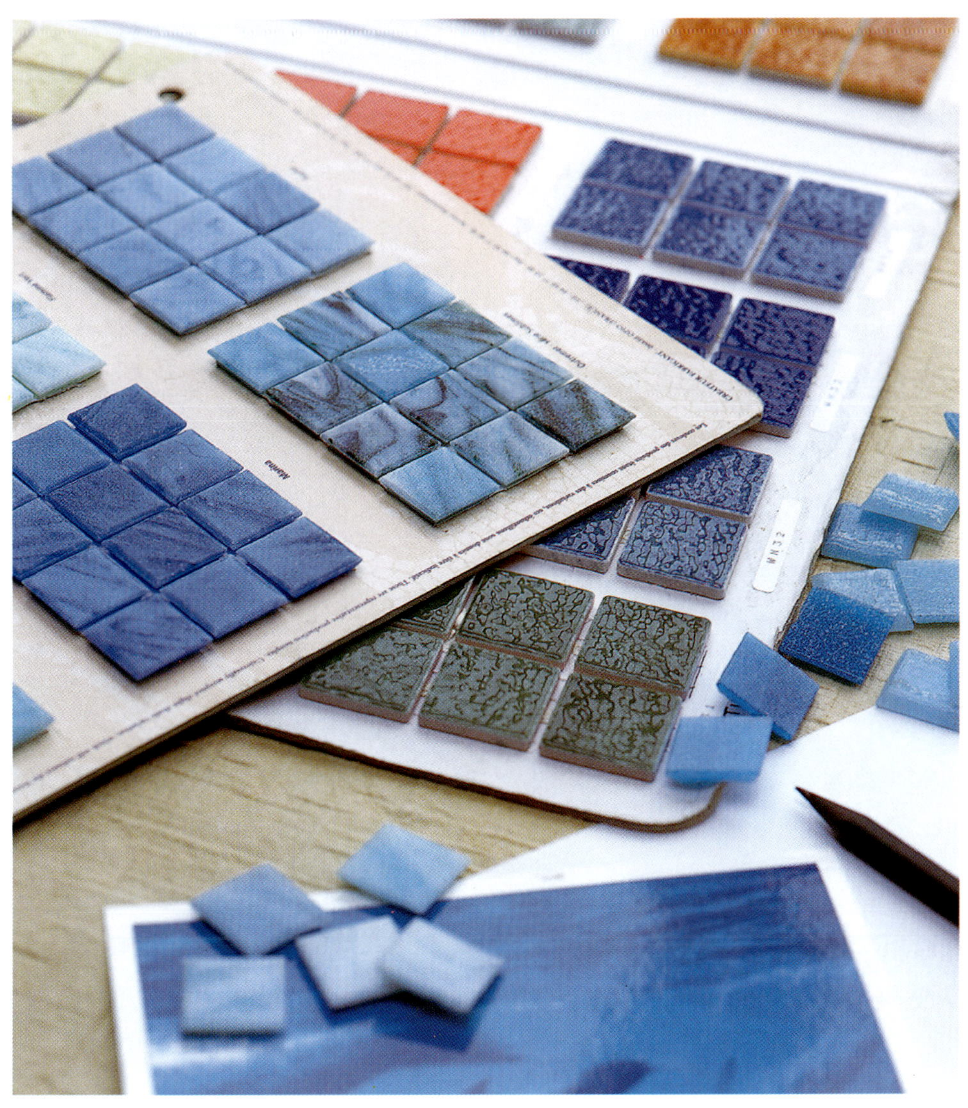

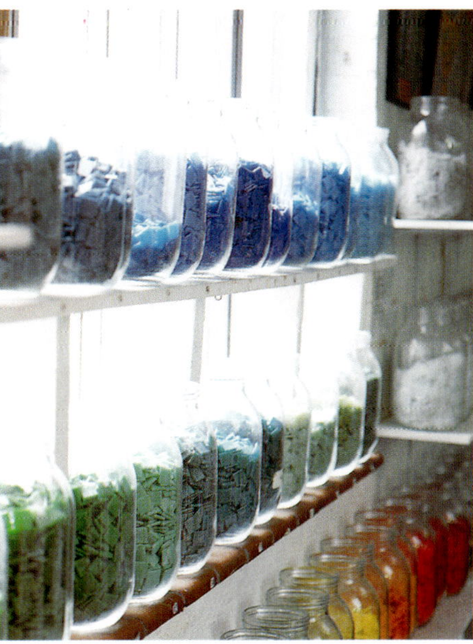

Above: There is a huge range of mosaic tiles to choose from. Vitreous glass tiles, shown here, are best suited to indoor work.

Left: Tile sample boards are a useful way of choosing colours and tiles for a project. Tile suppliers have a wealth of knowledge, and it is important to check with them that the tiles you choose suit the project you are undertaking.

Qualities of tiles

Not all tiles are suitable for all situations, so it is vital to make the right choice if your mosaic is to last. Each tile and material varies, so check their qualities and uses when you buy them.

Glass tiles or stained glass would be damaged quickly if positioned on a floor and exposed to high heels. Glazes also come in varying levels of hardness; a soft glaze would restrict the tile use to inside. A harder glaze can be used on the floor, and a frost-proof tile can be used outside. The fired clay that lies under the glaze also has its own individual qualities, such as absorbency, which can affect whether the tiles are suitable for a shower or bathroom.

choosing the right technique

Each project is different and no task is approached in exactly the same way. You need to decide which technique to use and the suitable fixing agents that are required. Here are some questions that you should consider before starting:

- Where is the piece to be finally positioned?
- Will you work directly, for example on to the pot?
- Will you choose a semi-indirect method, for example on to mesh, which is good for a floor panel?
- Is the site accessible, or is it easier to make the mosaic off-site?
- How durable does the mosaic need to be?
- Does the mosaic need to be water-resistant, waterproof, weather- or frost-proof?

While a small project could be made in the kitchen, it is advisable to allocate a special space in which to work, giving you a clean area for drawing and a workbench or table for doing the mosaic.

Creating a Workspace

The workspace is your own creative environment, so some wall space should be allocated for displaying your finished mosaics and any images that inspire you. Shelving will be needed, to store books, files, tools and materials, and a water supply is essential.

Posture

The most comfortable way to mosaic is definitely working at an easel or a table. It is important to have the seat or stool at a suitable height. It is worth spending time getting this right so that a good posture can be maintained and you can avoid shoulder and back strain.

Lighting

Ideally, the table or workbench should be placed near a natural source of light. Daylight is the best way to see true colour. When light is limited or when you are working at night, daylight bulbs are ideal. It is best to have more than one light source to avoid shadows.

Storage

When organizing materials, it is a good idea to build shelving and store tiles in glass or clear plastic jars, so it is easy to see how much stock you have and all the different colours. Tools are expensive and rust easily, so keep them clean and dry. Adhesives and grouts solidify if they get wet, so they must all be stored in a damp-free area, preferably in sealed containers. Most chemicals have a limited shelf life and can go off, so should be checked regularly.

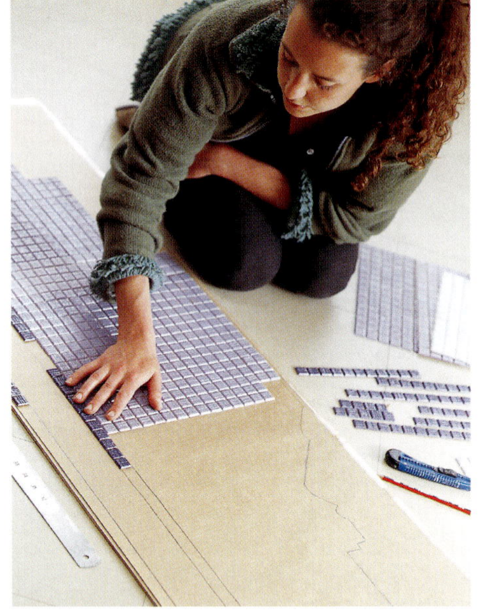

Large mosaics

When working on a mosaic that is too big for a table or easel, you should work on, or at least prepare the design on, the floor. You will need a hard

Left: Larger projects can be planned on the floor or in an area where it is possible to see the whole design.

safety

These are sensible precautions you can take to avoid injuring yourself:

- Wear goggles when cutting materials to avoid getting fragments in your eyes. Hold the mosaic tile nippers away from your face.
- Wear a face mask when cutting wood or mixing powder to avoid inhaling fine powder into sinuses and lungs.
- Wear hardwearing gloves when cutting wire and use rubber or latex gloves when mixing up powders, and also when grouting, cleaning or sculpting. Your hands will get dry and sore if they come into contact with water and adhesives for too long. It is also recommended to wear thin latex gloves when making mosaics. Take care, and keep antiseptic cream, plasters and hand cream on your shelving.
- Hold mosaic tile nippers at the far end of the handle to avoid hand blisters.
- Always clean and vacuum the work area regularly to avoid an unnecessary build-up of dust.
- Create your mosaic with awareness to the safety of those around you, as well as yourself.

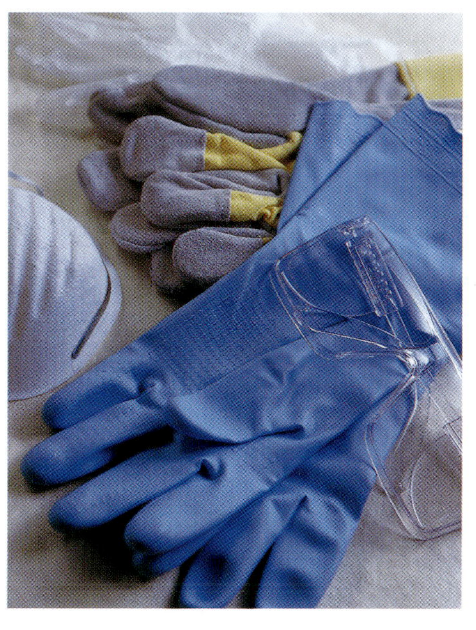

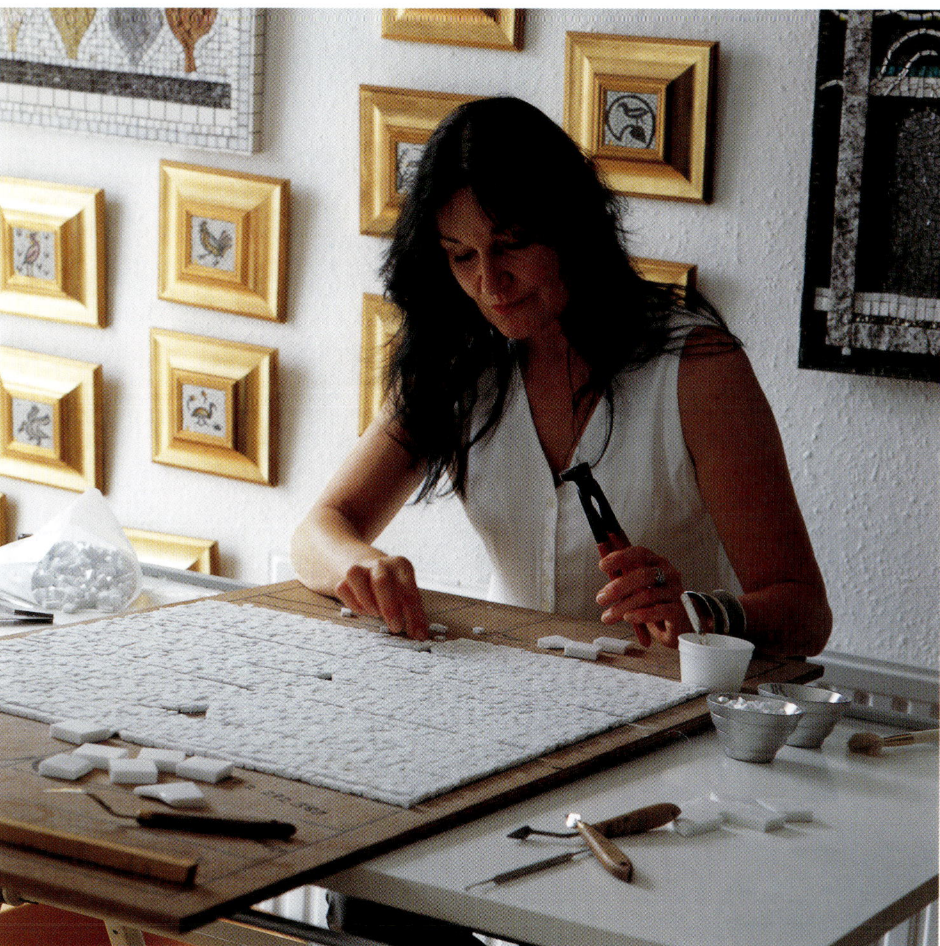

surface, so if the floor is carpeted, use a large piece of wood. If you are using mesh or brown paper, you should draw up the design and get a clear understanding of the whole image. Then you can cut the image into fragments and work in sections on the workbench.

If you need to see the whole design develop, it is best to work on the floor and protect the surrounding surfaces with plastic sheeting. This can be hard on the back, so you should take regular breaks and have a good stretch.

Preparing for work

Once you have chosen where and how to work and what to mosaic, you should gather all the required tools and materials together, mix enough fixing agents for the immediate work and prepare a good range of tiles before commencing.

Keep the work area clean, sweeping away loose fragments regularly. It also makes good sense to keep coloured tiles in some kind of order, placing different tiles, colours and shapes in separate small piles, for ease of use. When working with cement-based adhesive, clean off any excess while it is damp; if left overnight, the cement will harden and become very difficult to remove from the surface it is on.

Cleaning up

Sweep up or vacuum at the end of each session, as fragments get everywhere and can be sharp. Cleaning and reorganizing will also make the next day's work much easier. If different cement-based adhesives and grouts are allowed to mix in the drains, this can cause serious blockages and endless problems. When cleaning mixing bowls that held these materials, therefore, always scrape out and throw away as much excess as possible, before washing away the residue. Placing gauze over the plug can avoid the need to clean the drains regularly.

Above: Good light, a work surface and seating at the right height for good posture are essential for comfortable and productive mosaic making.

Above left: Gloves, goggles and face masks should be worn to protect against any injury or harmful inhalation caused by sharp chips or ground glass or tile.

The materials for a mosaic usually need some form of preparation for the work. Tiles can be smashed, nipped or sawn, glass cut and marble or smalti reduced to the correct size pieces by a hammer and hardie.

Preparing Materials

By preparing and clipping the materials you will be using before you start the mosaic – in the same way as a painter would mix a palette of paints – you will be free to concentrate on laying the mosaic design.

Sheet mosaic

Many mosaic tiles come on sheets, either on fibreglass mesh or on brown paper; the tiles are about 2cm (¾in) square and the sheets are approximately 30cm (12in) square. These are useful for laying a large area.

When making smaller mosaics using sheet mosaic, you should take the tiles off their backing. To remove the tiles from sheets formed with brown paper or mesh, soak the whole sheets in clean warm water. When the glue has dissolved, the tiles will slip off the backing material easily.

Smashed ceramic tiles

Antonio Gaudí is famous for his extensive use of mosaic in his fairytale buildings in Barcelona. They are very colourful and predominantly use ceramic tiles smashed into small fragments. Ceramic tiles come in an enormous range of colours, tones, textures and glazes, and are suitable for both interior and exterior use, as many are frost-proof. They are fun and easy to work with.

Clipping tiles

Mosaic tile nippers are the essential tool for any mosaicist, and are good for clipping most materials. With practice, intricate shapes can be achieved.

The mosaic nippers should be held at the end of the handles for the best possible leverage. The rounded side of the head is placed over the tile, which need be inserted only a few millimetres. To cut the tile in half, the nippers are positioned in the centre of the tile with the head pointing in the direction the cut is needed. Holding the opposite edge of the tile between thumb, forefinger and index finger will stabilize it. The ends of the handles are then presssed together.

Goggles are essential, as initially the tiles seem to fly all over the place. With practice, however, it becomes possible to control the cuts, and the fingers support the bits in place. If the cut goes astray, the excess can be nibbled away on the edge of the tile.

Cutting and sawing tiles

A hand tile cutter is the tool traditionally used for cutting tiles, and it is available from do-it-yourself stores. It

smashing ceramic tiles

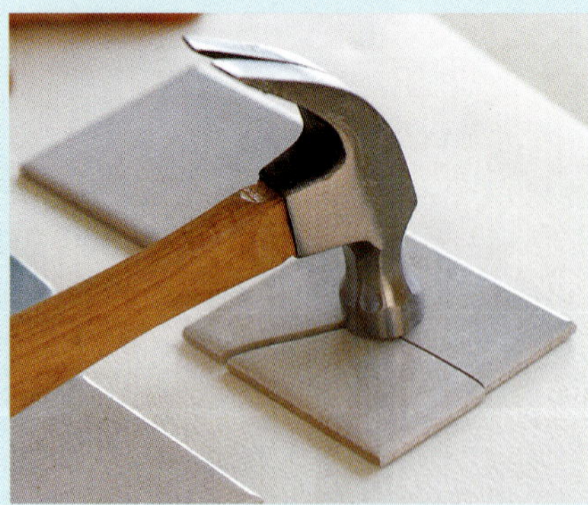

1 Wearing goggles and protective gloves, smash the tiles with a small hammer, aiming at the centre of the tile. To make these fragments smaller, gently smash with a hammer in the centre of each fragment.

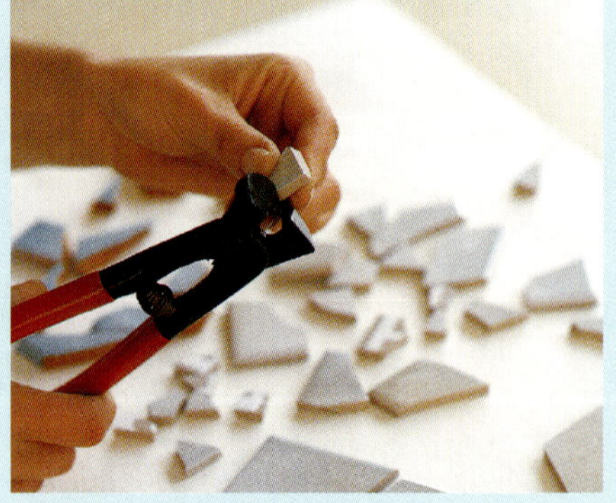

2 Pieces can fly all over the place if you hit the tile too hard, so for protection, cover the tiles with a cloth and wear goggles. Use the mosaic nippers to shape the ceramics into the size and style required.

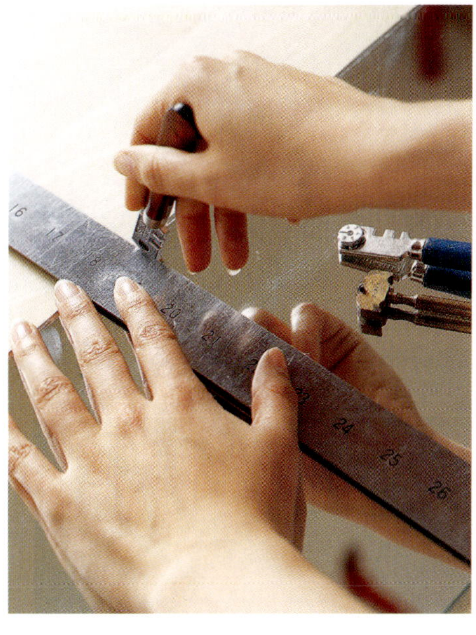

Right: Glass and mirror can be cut with a glass cutter. The surface is scored lightly, using a metal rule as a guide, then broken.

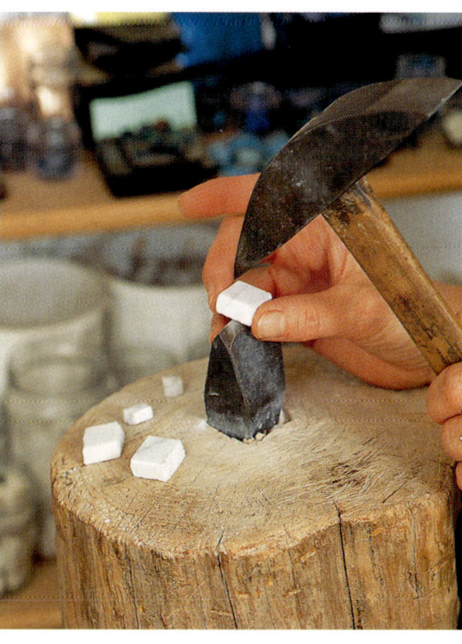

Far right: A hammer and hardie are used to break thick materials, such as stone and smalti, into pieces.

will cut straight lines on tiles, though its use is limited to ceramic tiles with a soft clay base.

Hard floor tiles or stone need to be cut with a wet tile saw. This specialized piece of equipment is essential for certain tasks, such as cutting thin strips of marble, which are then made into the correct size for mosaicing with a hammer and hardie. It is possible to hire wet tile saws.

The saw cuts the material with a metal disc that is revolved by a motor and kept cool with water. As the tile hits the blade, the water can spray out, making this quite a messy but effective technique needing protective clothing.

Cutting glass

A glass cutter is used for cutting straight lines or large shapes in stained glass and mirror.

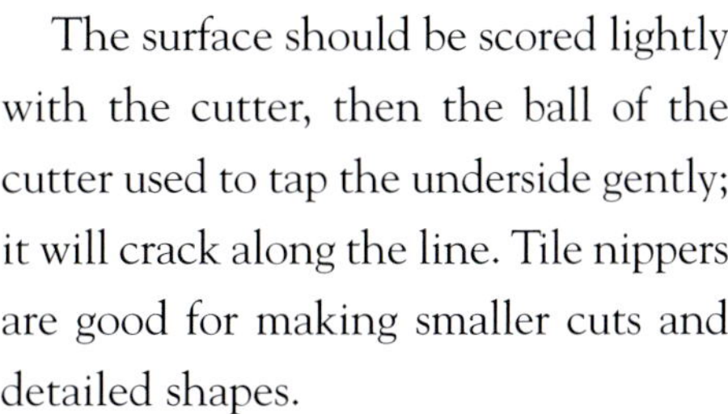

The surface should be scored lightly with the cutter, then the ball of the cutter used to tap the underside gently; it will crack along the line. Tile nippers are good for making smaller cuts and detailed shapes.

Goggles and gloves should be worn when handling glass and mirror, since even the smallest splinters cut easily.

Cutting stone and smalti

A hammer and hardie are the traditional tools for cutting stone and smalti, both of which are too thick for modern tile clippers. The material is held over the chisel between the thumb and forefinger and the hammer swung down on to this point. With practice, accurate cutting is obtained.

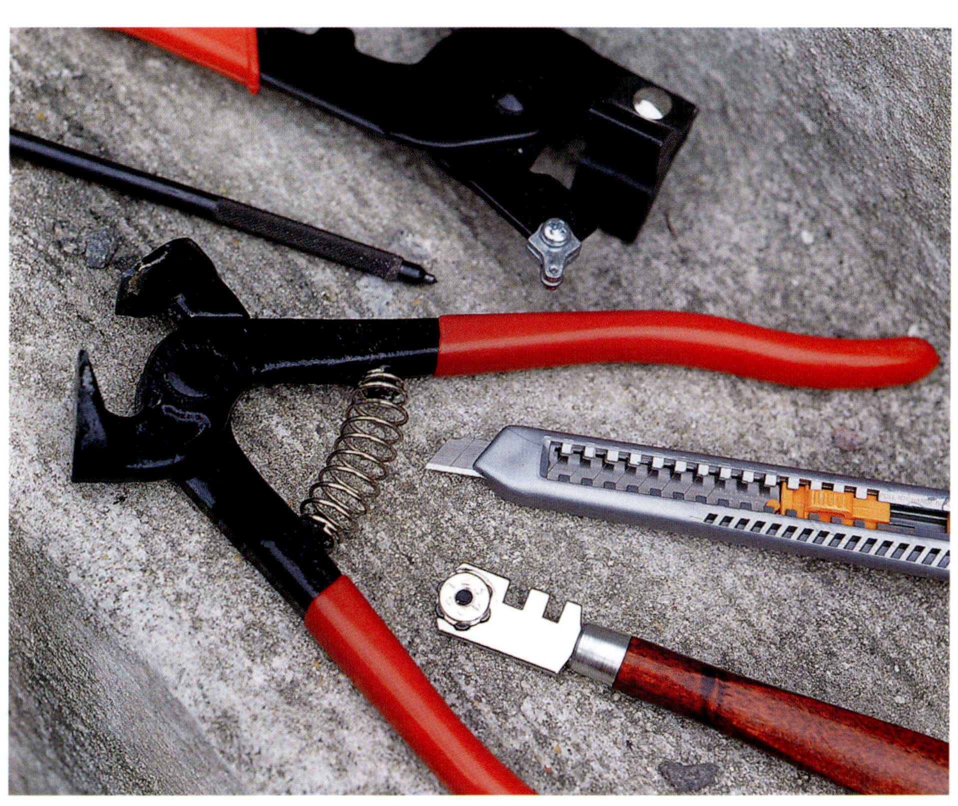

Right: (from the top) Tile cutters, for cutting straight lines; a tile scorer; mosaic tile nippers, for cutting tiles into shapes; a craft (utility) knife; and a glass cutter for cutting glass and mirror.

Mosaics can be laid on to a variety of different surfaces, and, as long as the correct procedures are followed, they will be hardwearing and waterproof and have a professional-quality finish.

Preparation and Fixing

Traditional mosaics were laid on to a cement bed. Now, we can also mosaic on to all sorts of different surfaces, such as wood, old furniture, plaster, ceramic, terracotta or fibreglass.

Bases

Unless working with a sculptured form, you should work on to a flat, even surface for a professional-quality mosaic. Uneven surfaces should be sanded down. If working on to cement, a new surface should be laid; self-levelling cement is an easy option.

The base or surface should be rigid. For example, floorboards are flexible, and any mosaic laid on them will lift if there is movement. So a thin layer of wood should be cut to fit and screwed in evenly to cover the entire surface.

Wood is a very good base, but if the mosaic is going outside or will come into contact with water, the wood must be exterior grade, such as marine ply.

Priming surfaces

Most working surfaces, such as wood, concrete, terracotta urns, old furniture or plaster, are porous, so the surface must be sealed with diluted PVA (white) glue (see box below). This greatly improves the sticking power of adhesive and makes the final mosaic more hardwearing and waterproof.

Before sealing, it is important to ensure that the surface is clean of all loose debris and hair. Smooth surfaces, such as wood or fine plaster, should be scored with a sharp implement, such as a bradawl or craft (utility) knife. On more slippery surfaces, such as plastics or existing tiles, a special two-part resin primer can be brushed on to provide a key. It creates a surface to which an adhesive can easily attach.

Diluted PVA glue can also be used to coat terracotta pots in order to make them frost-resistant.

Fixing methods

Once the surface has been properly prepared, there are various ways to fix the tiles. Choosing which technique to use depends partly on where the mosaic is situated and partly on personal preference. The direct method involves placing the material straight on to the working surface. The indirect method involves creating the mosaic off-site, then installing it. Two semi-indirect methods are worked on to paper or mesh off-site and then fitted into the cement on-site, so combining aspects of both methods.

Traditional stone and smalti mosaics were laid straight on to a bed of cement. Modern materials, however, are often much thinner, and need to be stuck as well as embedded.

priming wood

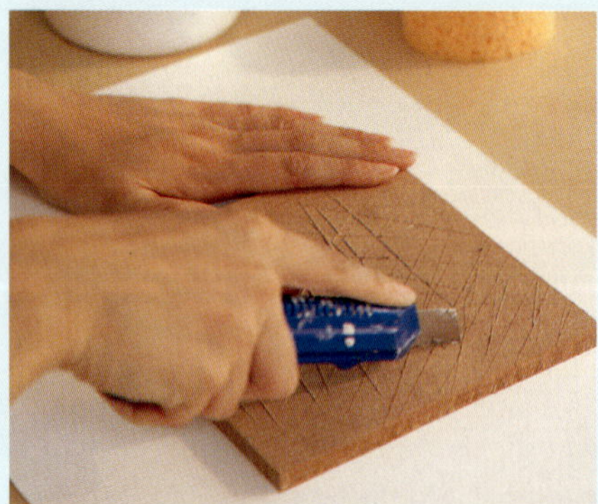

1 Take a craft (utility) knife and score the surface of the wood, creating a key. This improves the grip between the tiles and the adhesive.

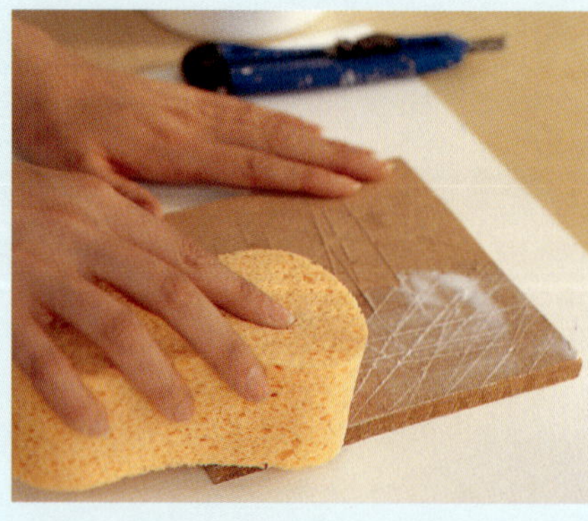

2 Mix up PVA (white) glue with water in a ratio of 1 part glue to 3 parts water. Apply this evenly with a dense sponge or a paintbrush.

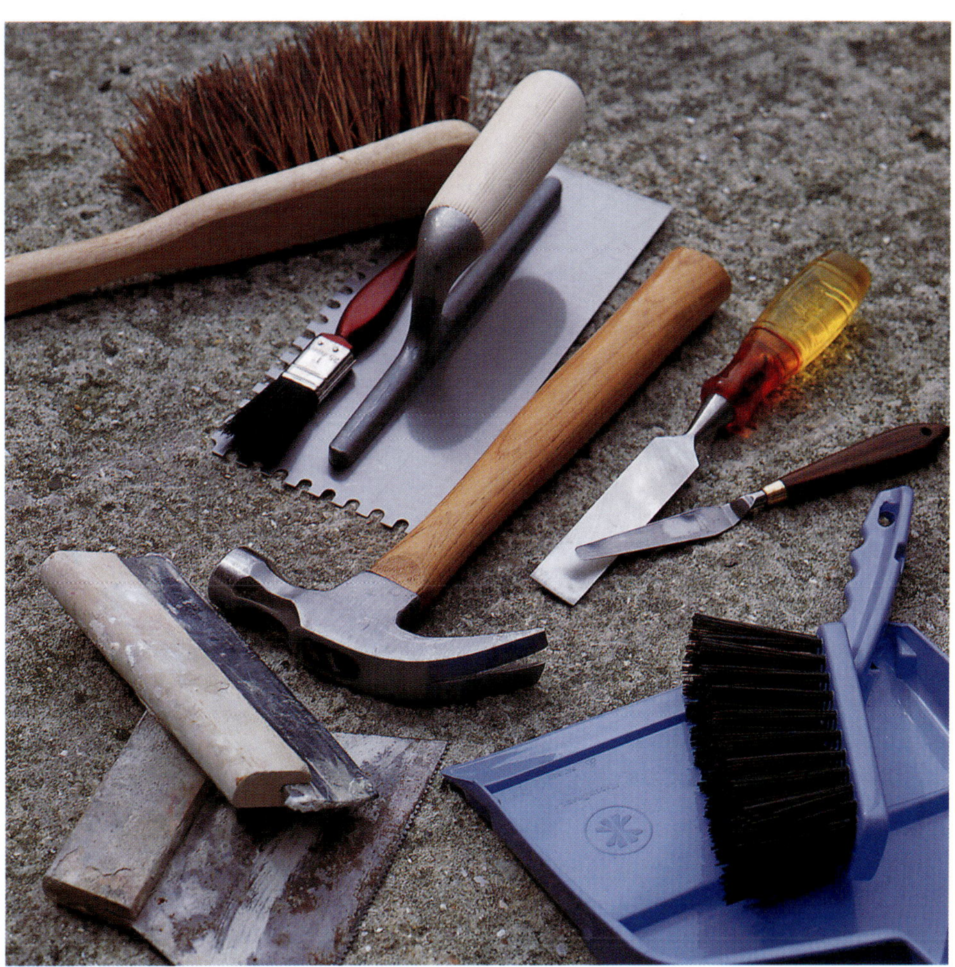

Right: You will need some, if not all, of these tools to prepare surfaces and apply adhesive. Clockwise from top left: hard bristle brush, paintbrush for glue, notched trowel, hammer, chisel, flexible knife, dustpan and brush, rubber spreader and adhesive applicator.

Direct method

This method involves simply sticking the tesserae, face up, on to the base, which has been covered with a layer of cement-based tile adhesive. It is good for working on to wood or sculptured forms, when working with smashed ceramic tiles, washed glass, tiles of different heights, or when covering large areas. It is also good to work directly into adhesive because it avoids having to spend extra time fitting and allows the design to develop in the environment where the mosaic is situated.

The direct method is easiest to start with and recommended for beginners.

Indirect method

Originally, this technique was devised as a way of making large-scale mosaics off-site, so that they could be moved ready-made, then laid in position. The design would be sectioned into manageable areas, and each area made into a slab. It is equally useful, however, for mosaics that cannot be laid directly due to an awkward location.

working with cement-based tile adhesive

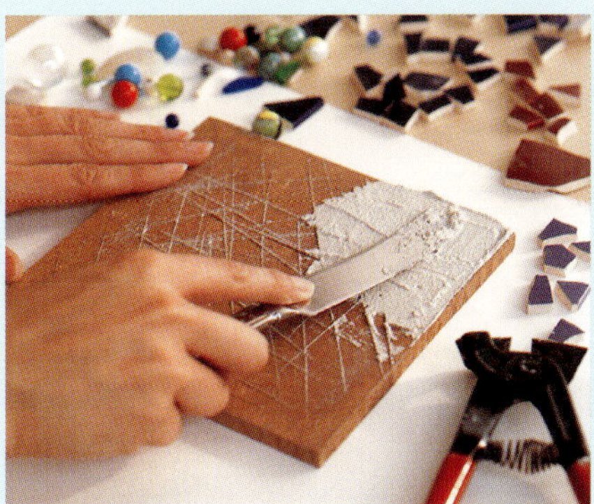

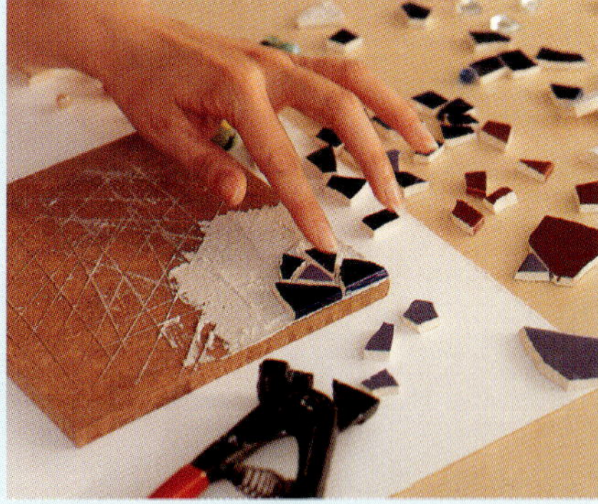

1 Mix white cement-based tile adhesive with water in the ratio of 2½ parts powder to 1 part water, until you have a smooth consistency. Choose and prepare the tiles you are going to use. Apply adhesive to the base with a flexible knife.

2 Stick the tesserae into the adhesive, ensuring good contact by pushing them in with your fingertips. If you use too much adhesive, the excess will squeeze through the gaps and get messy, but if you use too little, the tesserae will fall off.

A wooden frame is made to the size of the finished slab, and greased internally with petroleum jelly. The mosaic is appplied to a piece of brown paper marked with the dimensions of the slab, using the semi-indirect brown paper method (see right).

When the tesserae are dry, the frame is placed over the paper and dry sand sprinkled over the design and nudged into the crevices with a soft brush. The frame is then filled with mortar. The surface is smoothed, then covered with damp newspaper and polythene (polyethylene) sheeting and left to dry slowly for five to six days.

When the mortar is dry, the slab and frame are turned over and the brown paper dampened with a wet sponge, then peeled away. The frame is unscrewed and the slab removed.

Brown paper method

This reverse technique involves gluing the tesserae into position off-site, then setting them into adhesive on-site, cutting up the sheets of mosaic if needed.

When using this technique, the tesserae are glued face down on brown paper with PVA (white) glue; if they are uneven in any way, the irregularity will occur on the underside of the mosaic, making this method ideal for mosaics requiring a smooth surface.

The front of the mosaic is invisible during the design process, so this method is limited to tesserae that are coloured right through.

Once the mosaic sheet is pressed into the waiting adhesive, and been left to dry for 24 hours, the brown paper is soaked off with a wet sponge.

Mesh method

In this second semi-indirect method, fine-weave fibreglass mesh acts as a perfect base for the mosaic. The tesserae are stuck face up on to the mesh, so it

the direct method using PVA glue

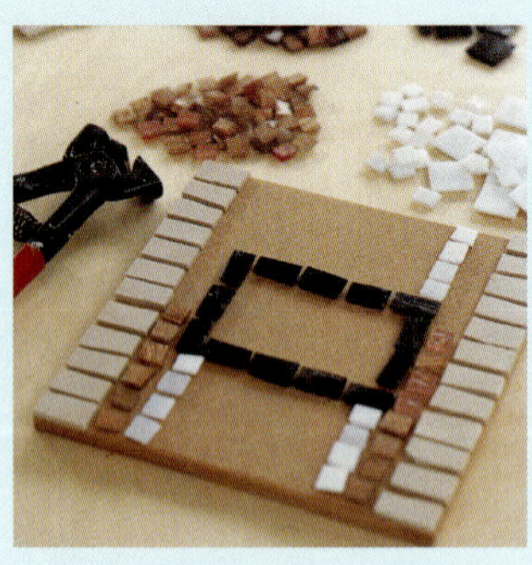

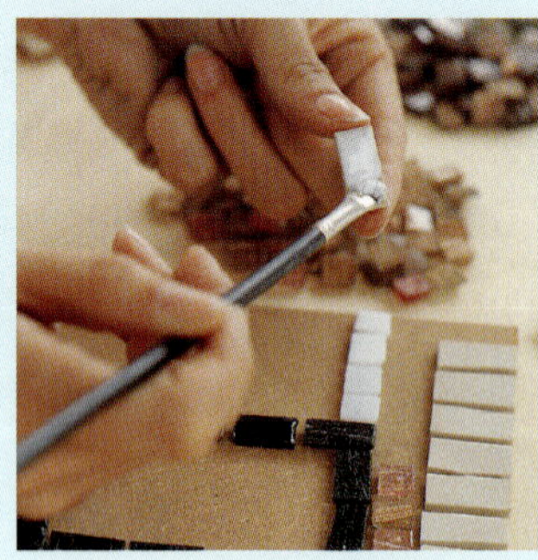

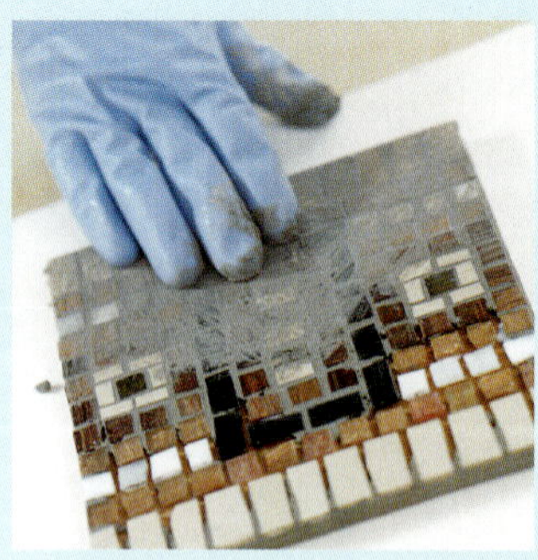

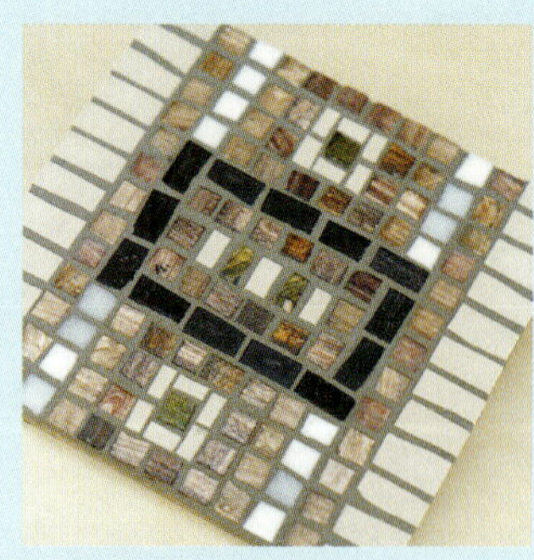

1 Cut a piece of wood to the desired size. Clip a selection of tiles into quarters and halves. Experiment with the tesserae; the design does not need to be complicated.

2 Once you are happy with the design, use a small brush to apply the PVA (white) glue to the back of the tesserae, and stick them in place and leave to dry.

3 Mix up some grey powder grout with water in the ratio of 3½ parts grout to 1 part water. Apply with your fingertips, wearing rubber (latex) gloves.

4 Wipe down the surface with a damp sponge to remove all traces of grout on the tesserae. Once the grout is dry, polish the tiles with a dry, soft cloth.

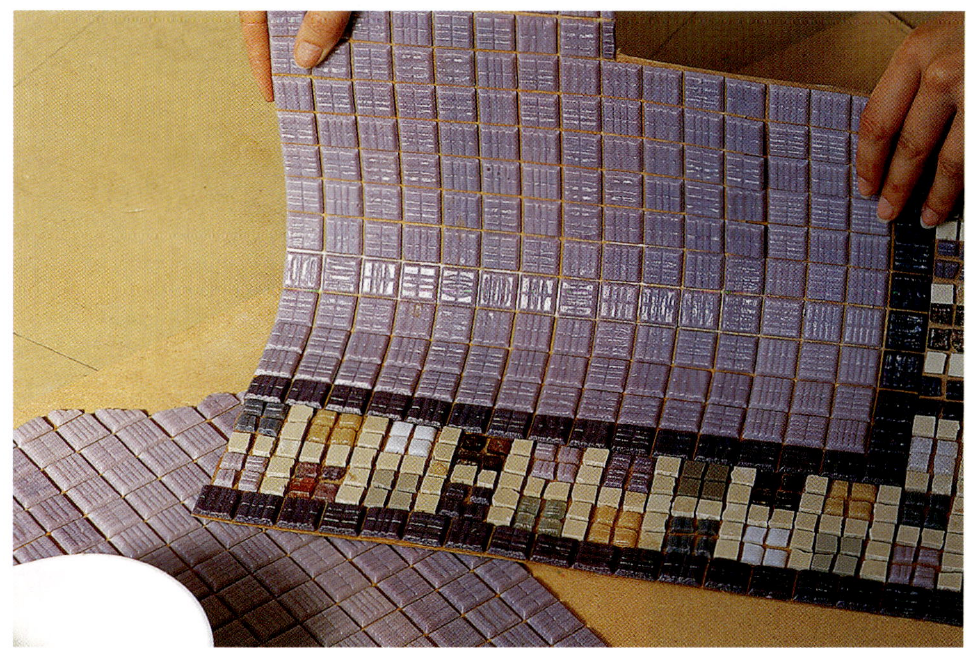

Left: The completed mosaic, on its brown paper base, needs to be cut into sections that can be handled easily.

is possible to see the mosaic design developing and taking shape. If the mosaic is large, it can be cut up and transported easily. When the tesserae are secure on the mesh, it is pressed, face up, into the adhesive and left to dry.

Cement-based tile adhesives

There is a vast range of modern cement-based tile adhesives for use on both direct and indirect mosaics. They come in a variety of shades, mainly white and grey. Your choice of colour will be influenced by what colour you want to grout in: grey for grey, black or dark colours; white for lighter shades.

Medium-strength adhesive comes in tubs ready-mixed, which is fine for decorative pieces or if the mosaic does not need to be particularly waterproof.

Most large tile companies have their recommended range of cement-based adhesive and additives. It is worth asking which materials are most suitable for the job you are undertaking. There is a variety of products for all situations, from exterior frost-proof, cement-based adhesives through to flexible liquid additives, such as admix, which can be added for extra protection against movement or to make the adhesive suitable for a shower.

PVA glue

This is good for sticking tiles directly on to wood, when it should be used undiluted. For priming or sealing, dilute PVA (white) glue 3:1 with water. It is water-based, so its use is limited to internal use only. It dries slowly, so tiles may be repositioned.

Epoxy resin glue

This is a strong glue made up of two separate components: the hardener and the resin. It is good for use in underwater locations or in damp places, but it has a limited working time and is sticky and toxic, so a face mask should be worn. Epoxy resin glue is useful when working with the direct method as it sets in just four hours, reducing drying times drastically.

Right: This soft mesh is used for subtle relief work, while chicken wire is more effective for larger-scale sculpting. Big exterior sculpting can be formed with bricks or breezeblocks (cinderblocks) then covered with a layer of tile adhesive.

Far right: In the mesh method, the mosaic pieces are glued, face up, straight on to the fibreglass mesh.

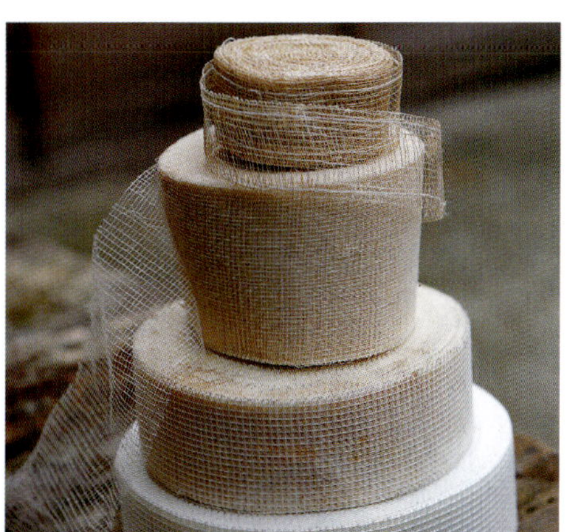

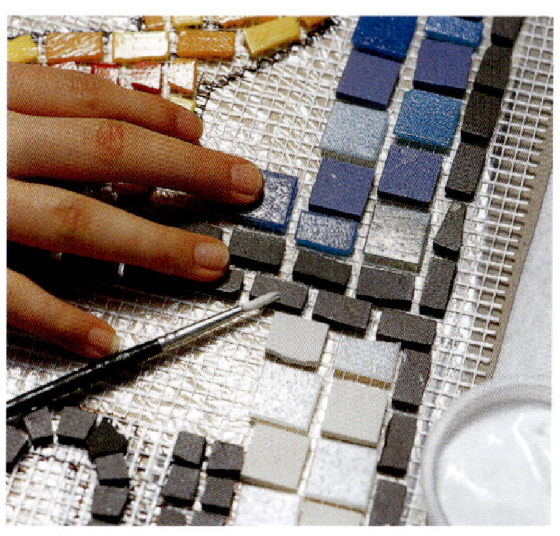

Grouting is incredibly satisfying: it unifies the mosaic and blends the images and colours. Designs that felt garish or too busy are softened, and patterns that work with movement come to life.

Grouting

On a practical level, grouting is when the gaps between the tiles are filled with a cement mortar that has a different quality to the adhesives. The process strengthens the mosaic and makes it waterproof. Grouting ensures that mosaic can be a functional art form that can be used in swimming pools, showers, water features, external wall murals or lavish floors.

Grout comes either ready-mixed or in a powder and in a variety of colours. There are also powdered stains that you can add to create almost any colour you want. The colour you choose will have a profound effect on the colours and look of the finished mosaic. Some of these differences can be seen in the four panels below. The grid of grey grout overpowers the neutral tiles, and the white grout is also very strong. The cream grout works well with the white tiles, as there is balance, while the beige grout warms the white tiles.

Note that white grout will blend with pale tiles, lighten darker colours and contrast blacks, while black grout will deepen blacks and blues, make reds and greens really rich and contrast with white. The qualities and varieties are endless, giving you great scope for creativity.

Grouting is a messy job, especially if stains are used, so clothes and surroundings should be well protected and rubber (latex) gloves should be worn to protect the hands.

When to grout

The finished mosaic should be grouted when the tile adhesive is dry. Before

Right: These four panels of neutral vitreous glass mosaic were grouted in four different shades: clockwise from top left, beige, grey, cream and white.

Below: Grout comes in different colours, which can dramatically alter the finished look of the mosaic.

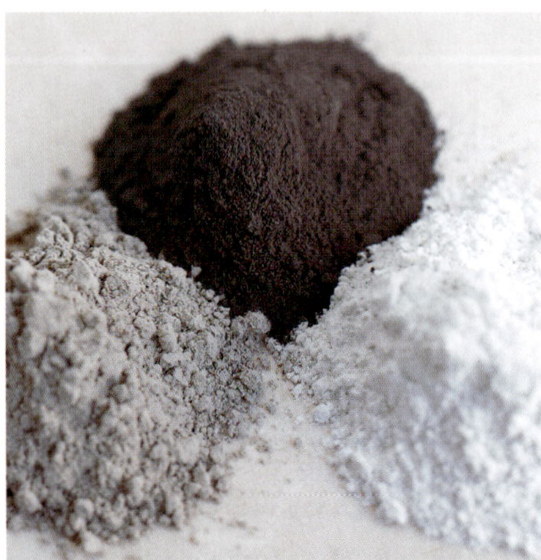

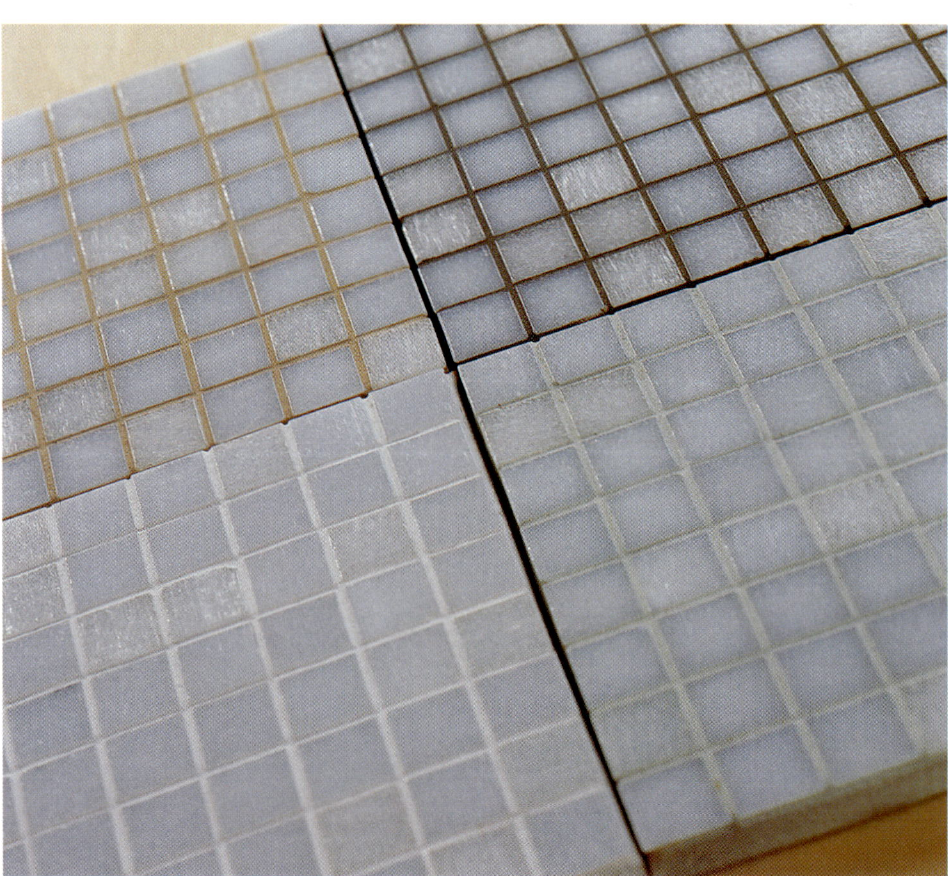

being grouted, small mosaics can be gently shaken to remove loose adhesive, and any loose tiles can be re-adhered. On larger-scale mosaics, light vacuuming can be effective.

On a large-scale project, the whole surface should not be grouted in one go, because when you start to clean off the grout, the first areas may have already dried. One section should be grouted at a time, then cleaned off before the next section is begun. The grout should be left to dry for 24 hours until it is completely hard.

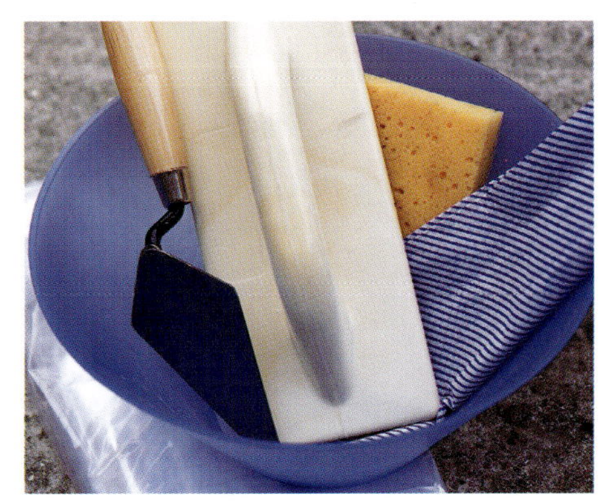

Above: For grouting and cleaning your mosaics, you will need a mixing trowel, a grout spreader, some cleaning cloths, a sponge, a bowl and protective sheeting.

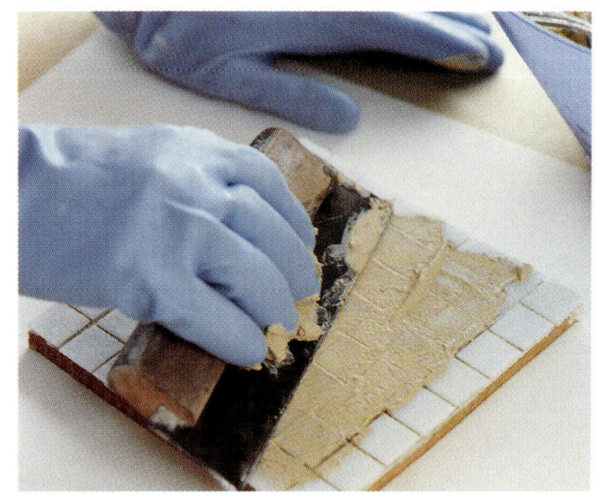

Above: Wear rubber (latex) gloves and grout your mosaic using a rubber spreader. Rub the grout into any gaps using your fingertips.

grouting and cleaning

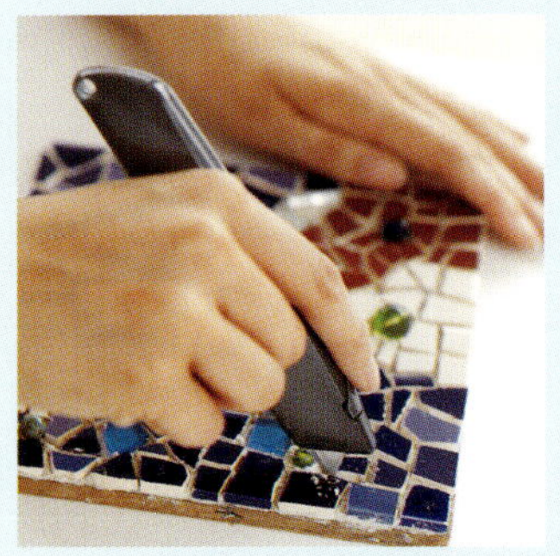

1 When the mosaic is being laid, adhesive can squeeze through the gaps between the tesserae. Scrape this away with a blade or craft (utility) knife. Then ensure that the mosaic is clean.

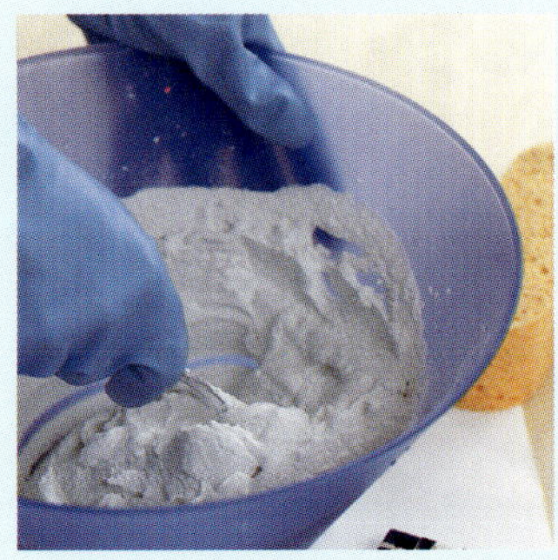

2 Wearing rubber (latex) gloves, mix together the powdered grout and clean water in a bowl. Follow the manufacturer's instructions to achieve the right consistency.

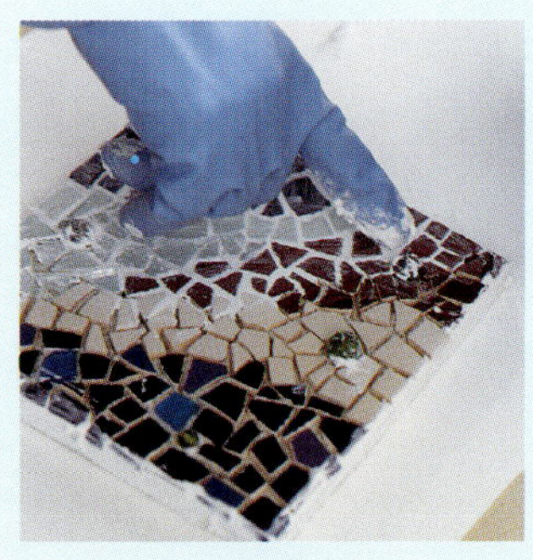

3 Apply the grout over the mosaic, using your fingers, a grout spreader or a rubber spreader. Push the paste into the gaps and smooth it evenly over the whole surface.

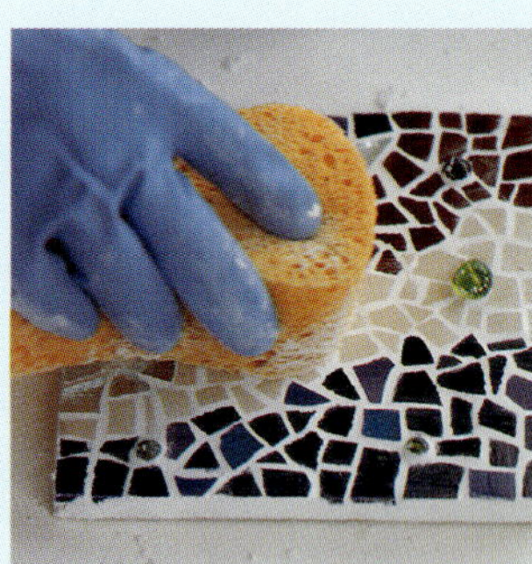

4 Wipe away any excess grout with a damp sponge. After 10 minutes, any remaining excess grout can be rubbed away easily with a dry cloth. (If left much longer, remove with a nail-brush or paint scraper.)

Once the colours and the design of the mosaic have been revealed by the cleaning process, attention must be paid to where and how to present the finished work, how to light it and how to maintain its beauty.

Finishing Your Work

If the tesserae of the mosaic have a shiny glaze, the grout will have come off easily with the sponging process. Matt porcelain, however, holds the grout, making it harder to clean.

It is possible to buy an acid called patio cleaner, used by builders for cleaning cement off brickwork. When diluted with warm water, it is very effective for removing resilient grout. If sponged or poured on to the mosaic, it will make a fizzing noise as it eats away at the grout left on the surface of the tiles. After a few minutes, the dirty water can be sponged away. Resistant areas can be removed with a paint-scraper or abrasive paper (sandpaper), before being polished with clean cloths.

Sealing

Stone and pebbles look richer when sealed, appearing slightly wet and retaining their subtlety of tone without the addition of a varnish or shine to the surface. Sealants come in matt or shiny varieties.

Beeswax can be rubbed on to matt tiles to give them a deeper colour. Terracotta tiles need to be treated with linseed oil. This is flammable, so always dispose of cloths that the oil comes into contact with carefully.

Siting

There are no hard-and-fast rules about where to site your mosaic; it is a matter of judgement and common sense, which you must learn to trust. Asking someone to hold the mosaic in place so you can have a look is always wise. You can usually tell when the site is right. If you are unsure, you can swap with your helper to ask their opinion.

Aside from the positioning of the mosaic, the colour of the surrounding walls must be taken into consideration. You do not want the walls to clash with the mosaic, or for them to overpower it.

Hanging

A small mosaic can be hung like a picture, using wire and picture hooks. Hanging a larger, heavier mosaic, however, requires more thought.

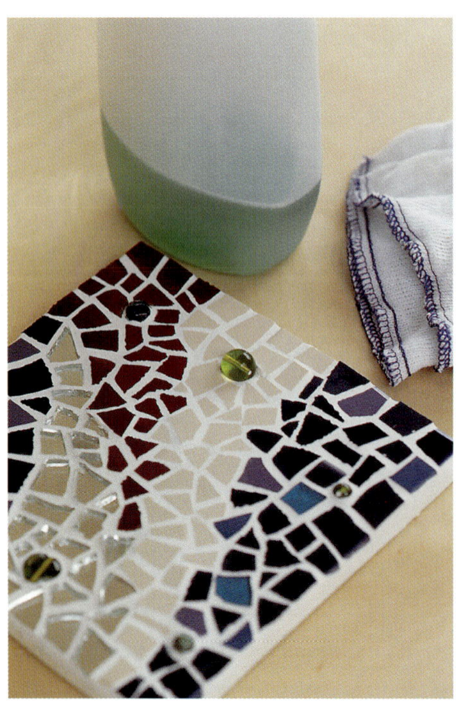

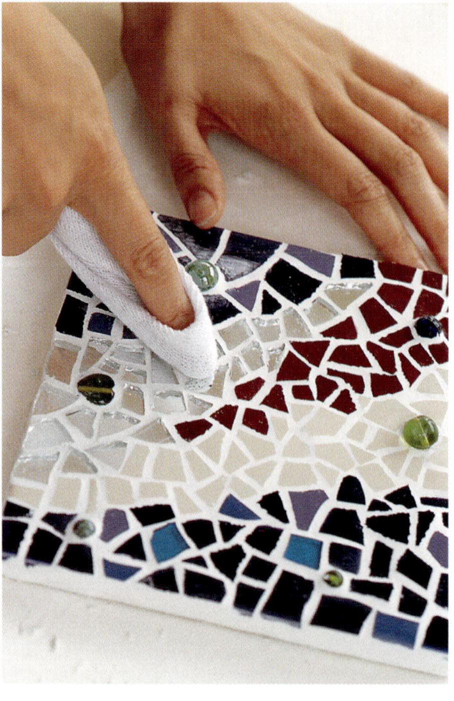

Far left: This colourful panel is lightened by the white grout, and the glazed tiles laid in a Gaudí-style mosaic have a fresh flowing feel. To clean, first spray the mosaic with glass cleaner. Any proprietary window cleaner will do. If you do not have this, use some water with vinegar added to reduce smearing.

Left: Polish with a clean dry cloth, preferably a lint-free one, and you should achieve a good shine on the glass and the glazed ceramic tiles. The colours weave into each other, while the mirror and glass balls make shimmering focal points within the mosaic.

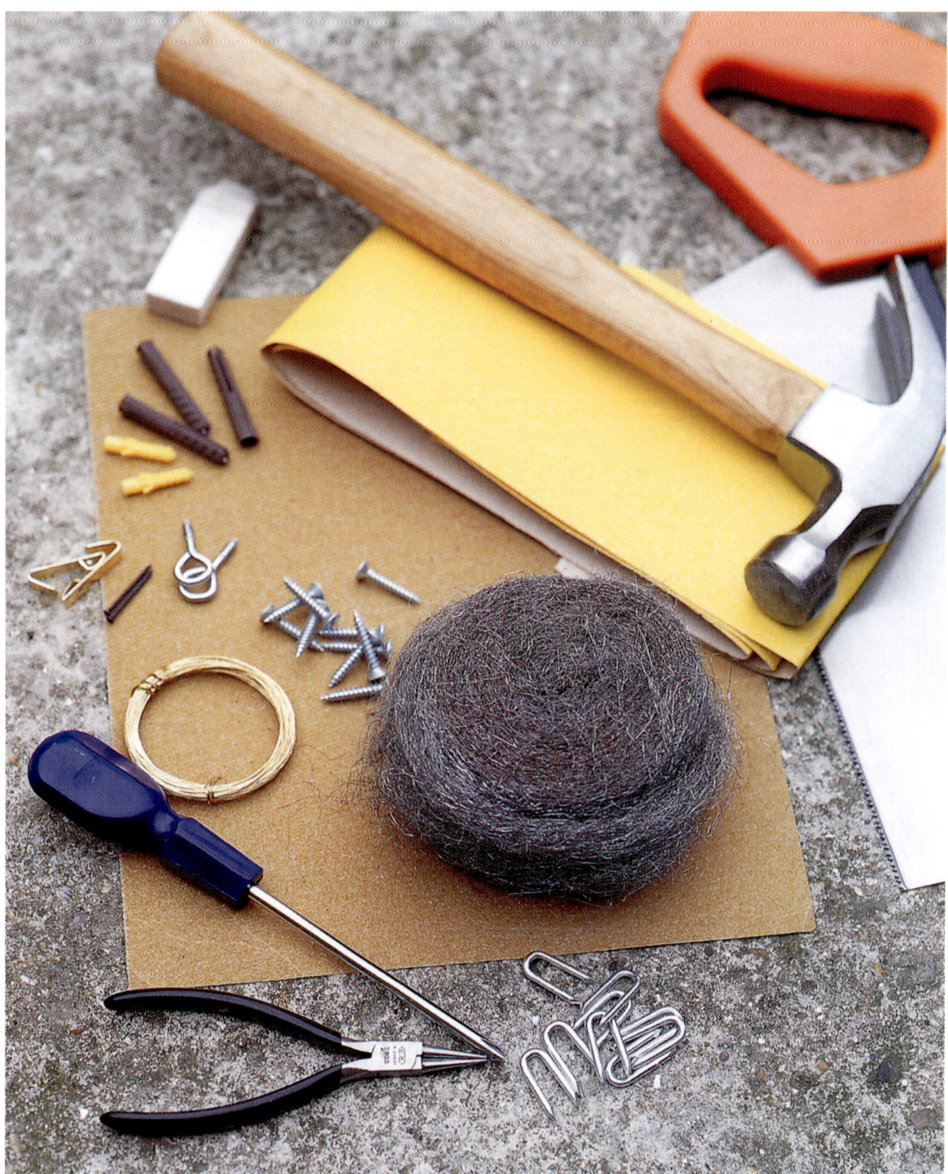

It is important to find out whether the wall you intend to fix the mosaic to can hold the weight. Plasterboard (gypsum board) will not, so if it is a partition wall, the mosaic must be fixed to a supporting strut.

When fixing into brick or plaster, you will need to drill holes, using a drill bit that is compatible with the size of screw you have chosen. The correct position for the fixings should be marked on the wall with a pen. Wall plugs (plastic anchors) should be placed in the drilled holes to give the screws something to grip on to, then the mosaic can be hung in place.

Mosaic panels can also be fixed to the wall with mirror plates. Protruding mirror plates are fitted to the wood at the edge of the panel and then the mirror plates are screwed to the wall. Those with a keyhole opening are fitted to the back; they then slot over screws inserted into the wall.

Lighting

Mosaics nearly always look their best in natural light, with its soft tones. Yet the night-time light is important and needs consideration.

A mosaic could be lit with a spotlight fixed on the ceiling or a traditional picture light. It is important not to over-light and bleach out the colours and subtle reflective quality of the tiles. Different colours and wattages of bulb, as well as different angles and distances, should all be tried.

Maintenance

The best way to maintain a mosaic is to clean it regularly, so avoiding the build-up of resilient dirt. A floor mosaic should be swept and mopped with a gentle cleaning agent, making sure the dirty water is removed properly. Decorative mosaics should be dusted and cleaned using glass cleaner and a dry cloth. Bathroom mosaics should be cleaned as any other tile.

Above: These are some of the tools you may need when siting and installing your mosaic. Clockwise, from top right: saw, hammer, abrasive paper (sandpaper), wire (steel) wool, U-shaped hooks, pliers, screwdriver, picture wire, picture hooks, hanging hooks, screw eyes, screws, wall plugs (plastic anchors) and eraser.

If the mosaic has got really dirty, the patio cleaner referred to opposite should be used, though it may be necessary to re-grout after cleaning. If the correct maintenance steps are taken, the mosaic could last for a millennium.

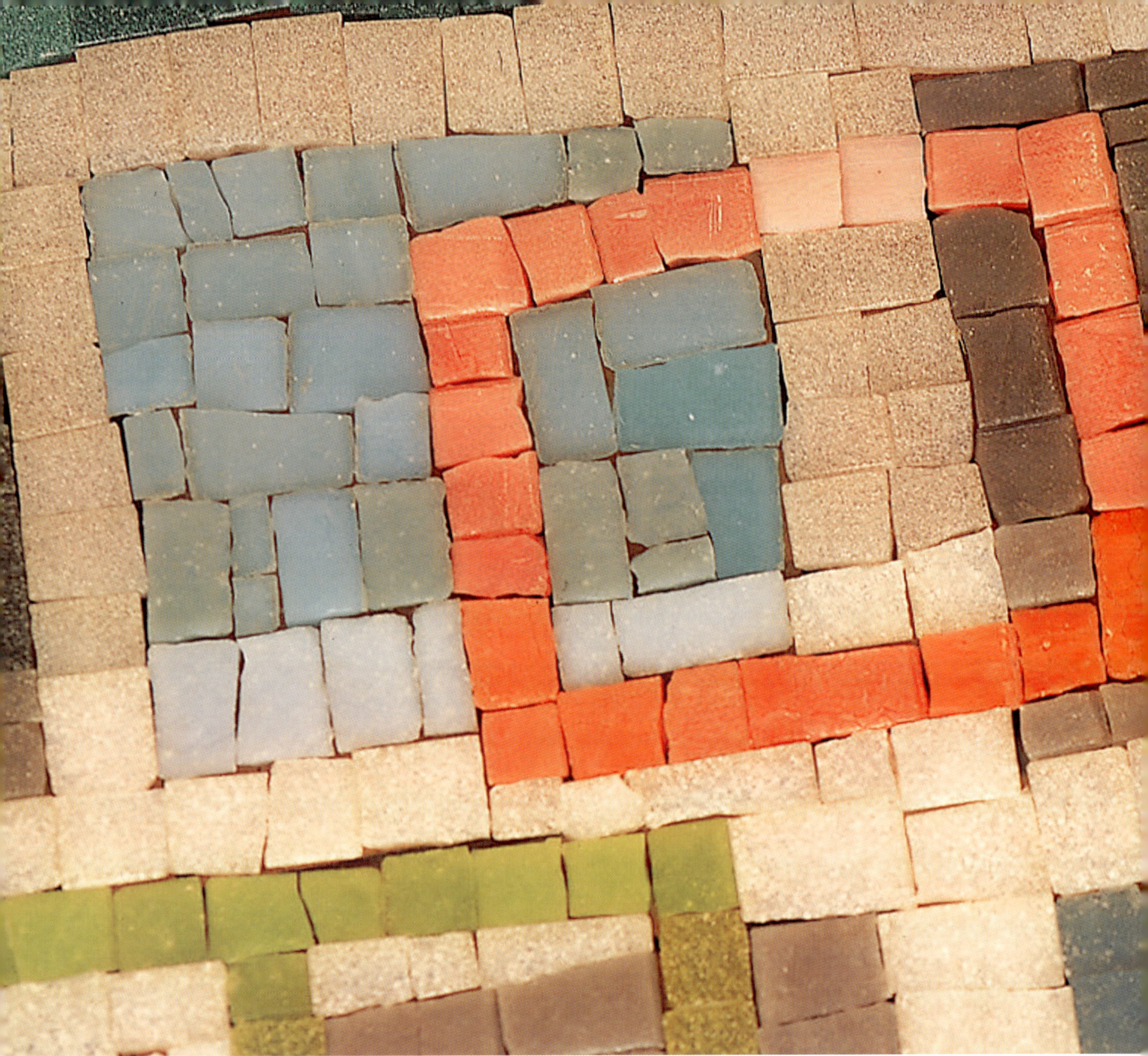

Ornaments

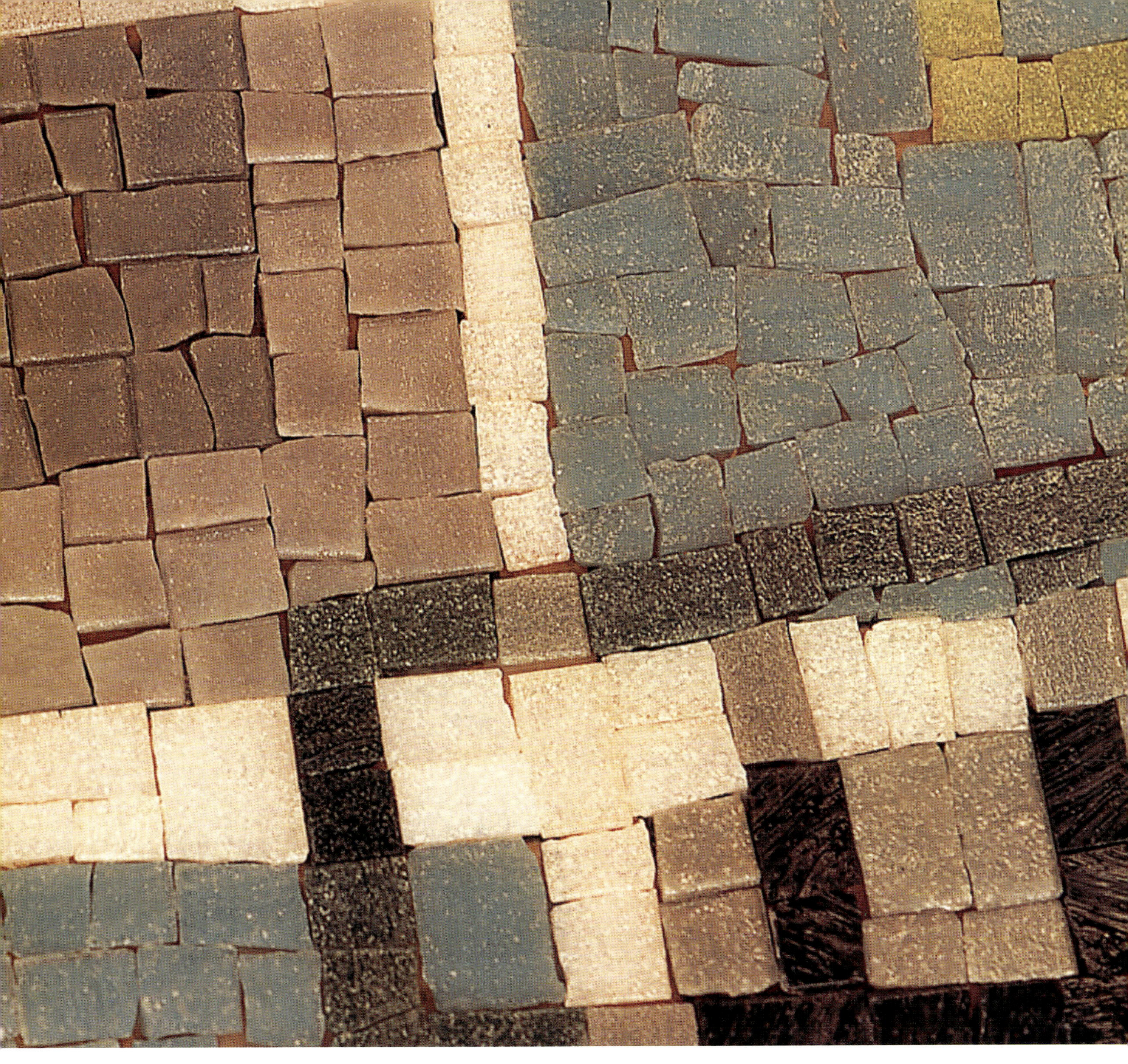

Ornaments are not just the frippery that they are made out to be. Often they are useful objects that we need to have around the house or garden, but that can be disguised or decorated in such a way as to make them a pleasure to have around. Even those objects which are solely decorative do perform a psychological function in brightening up our everyday lives. All the projects have been graded from one to five, one being the easiest.

Ornamental items offer a limitless supply of design opportunities for the mosaicist: from simple objects, such as a plant pot or letter rack, to more advanced items, such as a lamp base, vase or fire screen.

Indoor Ornaments

Mosaic is an effective disguise for many everyday objects, transforming the mundane or mass-produced into something original. Containers, in particular, make excellent subjects for mosaic decoration. Plant pots, terracotta urns, candle-holders, vases and bowls are just a few suggestions.

Smaller ornaments

Excellent hunting grounds for objects to mosaic – such as picture frames, plain wooden boxes, old pots and bowls – are car-boot sales, junk (curio) shops and even house clearance auctions. "Job lot" boxes of assorted odds and ends can be picked up extremely cheaply. These do not require a huge commitment in terms of time, effort or cost of materials, making them good items on which to practise your ideas and techniques. The objects can be functional or purely decorative.

A letter rack, house number plaque, pot stand or a china tile would be ideal choices to start with, since they are regular in shape, can be laid flat and are easy to work with. A set of mats or coasters would be an easy way of experimenting with colour and patterns before embarking on larger projects. Some decorative spheres, in a wide range of patterns and colours, a

Below left: Gentle spiralling bands of mosaic cover this tall terracotta urn.

Below centre: Pots of fresh herbs in the kitchen become decorative objects in their own right.

Below right: Squares of textured coloured glass cast beautiful patterns when a candle is lit in this mosaic candle-holder.

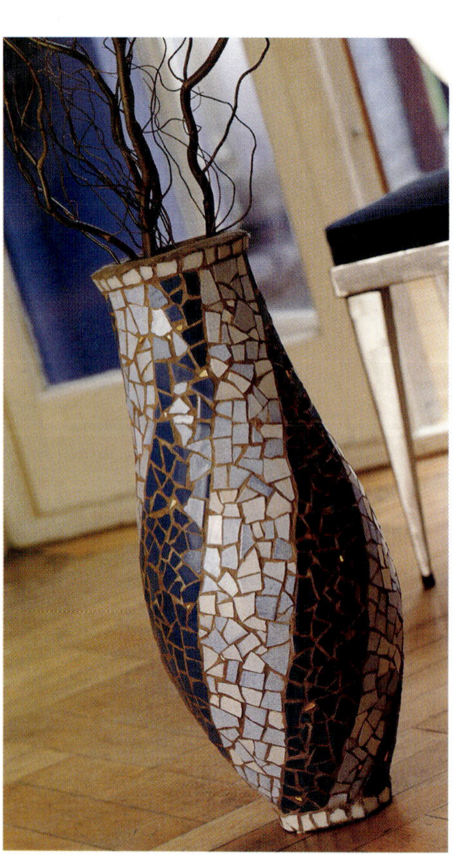

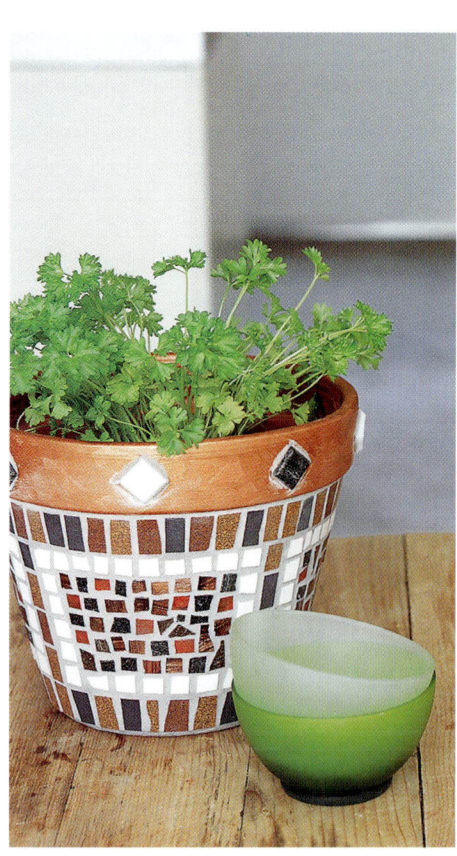

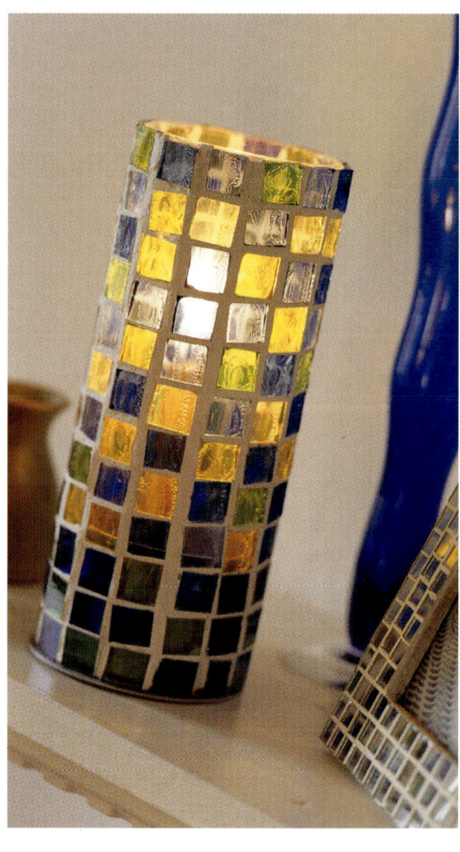

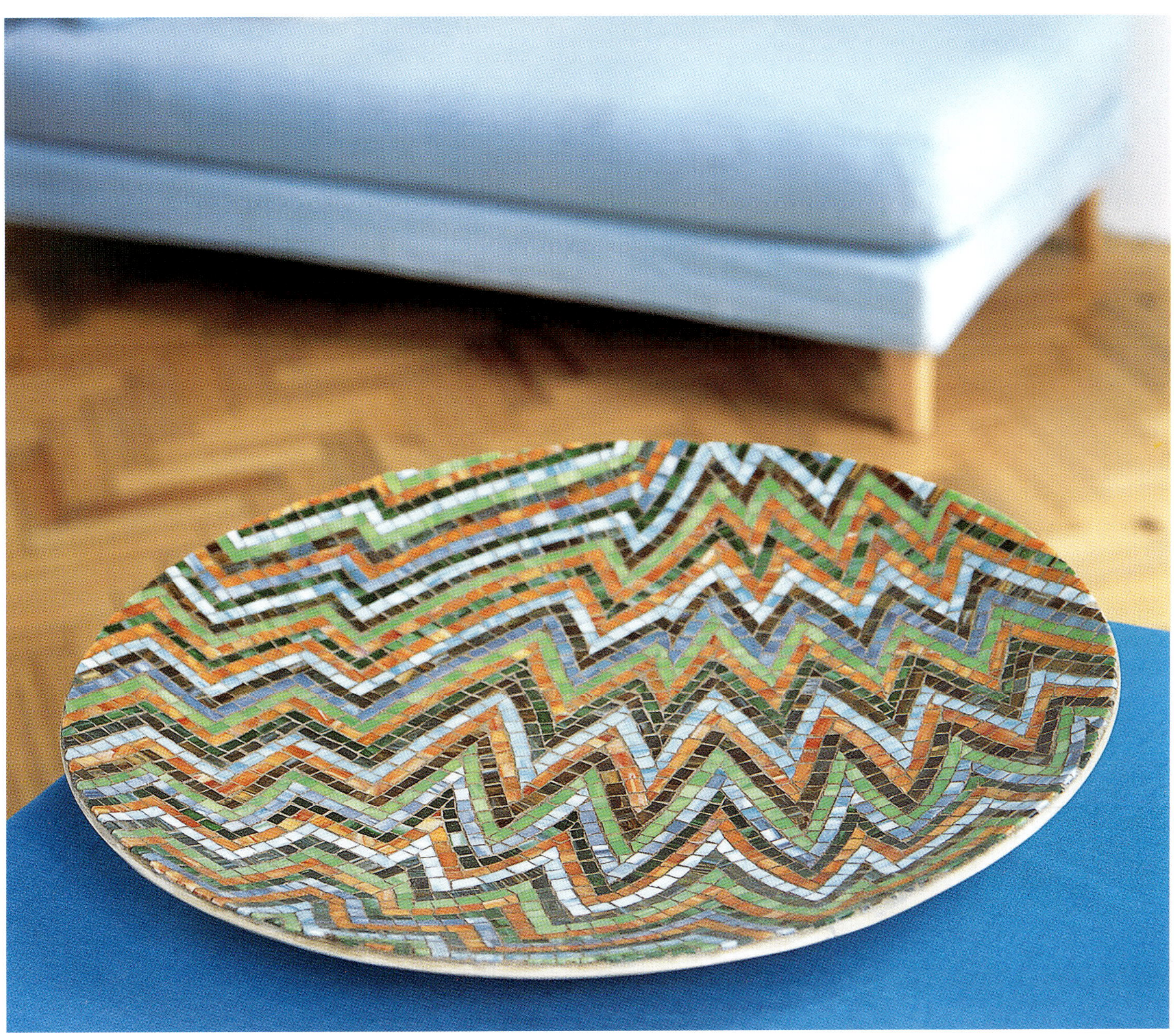

Above: This large, striped, stained-glass mosaic bowl was made by Martin Cohen.

group of cheerful plant pots and simple mirror frame would expand your repertoire a little, while still being fairly simple projects that are easy to work.

A contemporary mosaic bowl can be made by buying a shallow, light, wooden, metal or plastic shape to which you can adhere mosaic on the inside only. This will give you a stable base on to which to add your pattern.

Larger ornaments

Once you have gained confidence, you may feel ready to try some items that are more ambitious in terms of scale or complexity.

A tray for the kitchen gives scope for quite a large design, with a ready-made border formed by the sides. A floral lamp base for the sitting room worked on a breezeblock (cinderblock) combines both artistry and some basic wiring, while a spiral lamp stand makes use of an old carpet tube.

The cosmic clock – at home in any room – could be an inspiration for many different clock designs. A hole must always to drilled to allow for the spindle to be pushed through to the front, and the mosaic design must avoid tiling over this hole. The surface decoration needs to be designed to allow for the function of the clock and the movement of the hands.

Looking to the bedroom, the floral trinket box transforms a plain wooden box into a work of great beauty.

One of the most popular subjects for mosaic is the mirror frame, and the variety of effects shown in this chapter gives an indication why. Mirrors are useful objects both for practical reasons and decorative ones.

Mirror Frames

Mirror frames can be bought ready made, or they can be made from many diverse materials that can be customized with mosaic. They can be flat or include three-dimensional or sculptural elements. They can also be as extravagant or simple as you want. They provide an excellent platform for self-expression, and you can explore combinations of colour and texture to create collage-like effects.

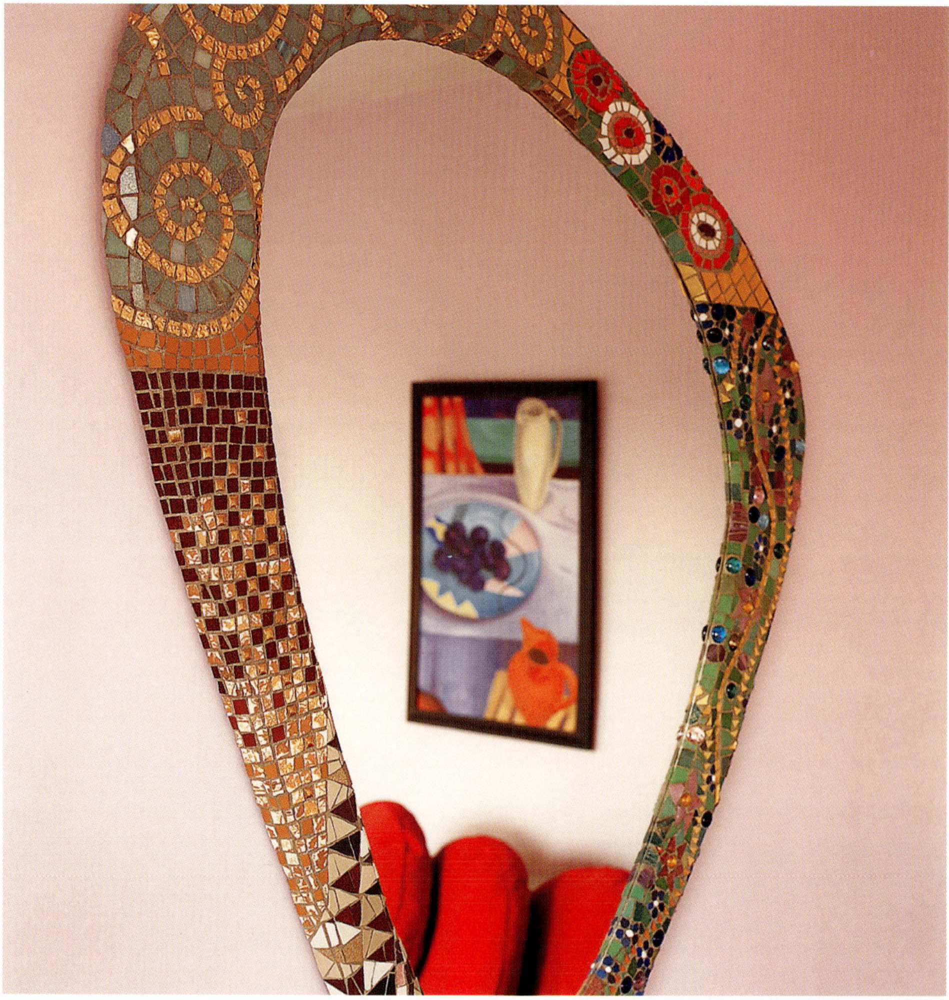

Right: This large, curved mirror was inspired by a Gustav Klimt painting, reflected in the shape of the design. Its use of flowing lines of gold smalti, broken up in a rhythmic pattern, makes a very decorative and individual piece, designed by Norma Vondee.

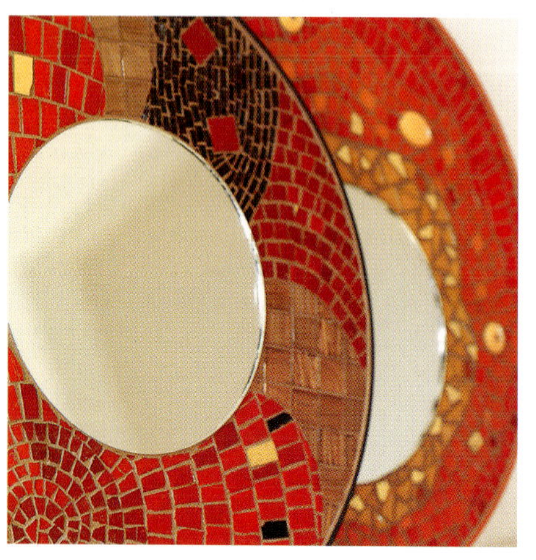

Below: A pair of complementary circular mirrors are given extra interest by having the mirrors placed off-centre.

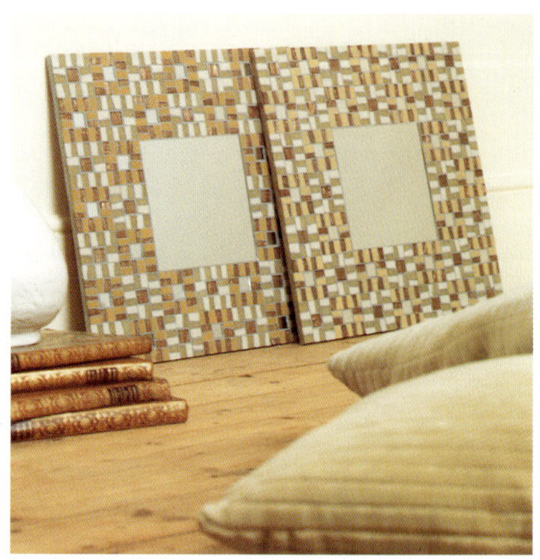

Left: Two differently toned variations of the same style mirror echoing the soft, warm tones of the wooden floor.

Opposite: This large, curvaceous mirror by Celia Gregory was made from washed glass collected from the banks of the River Thames, and contrasts with the angular shape of the fireplace. The soft greens beautifully complement the whites and neutral tones of the room.

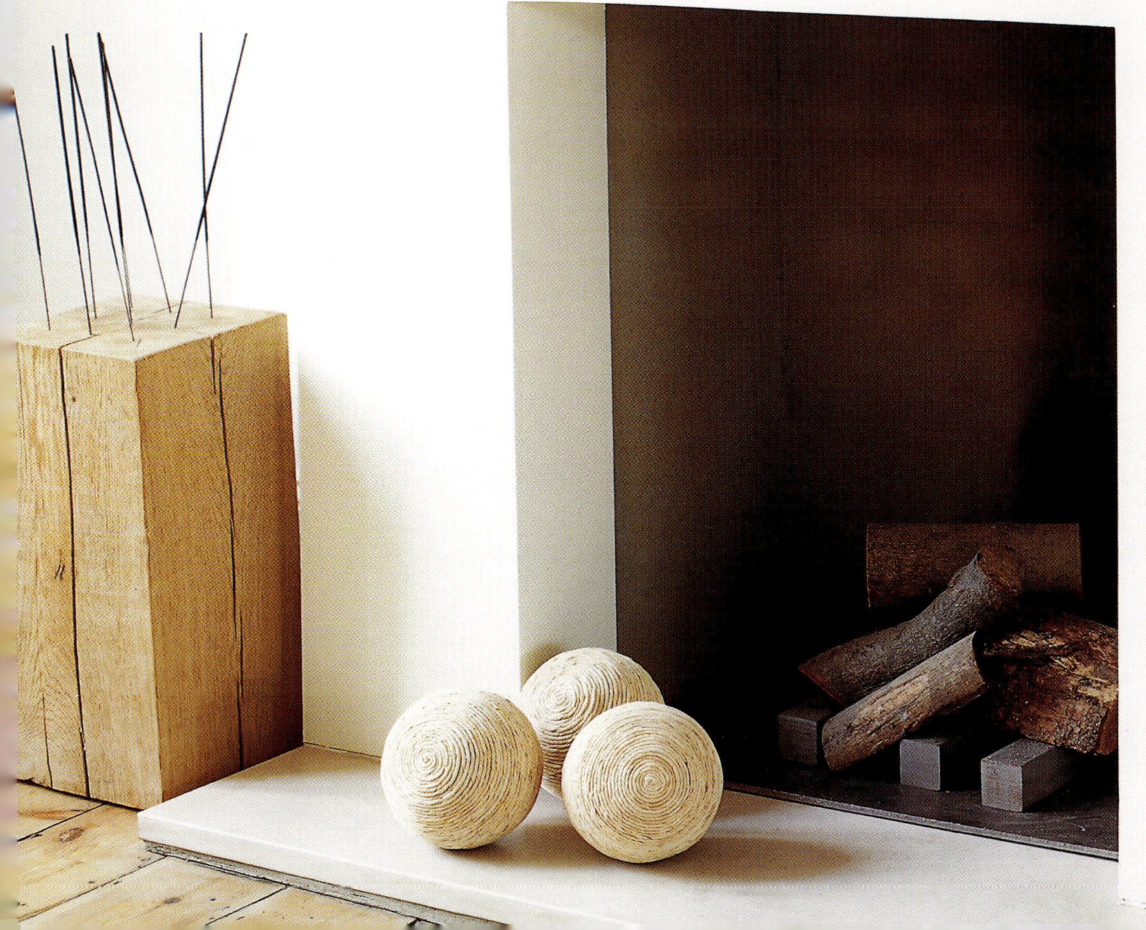

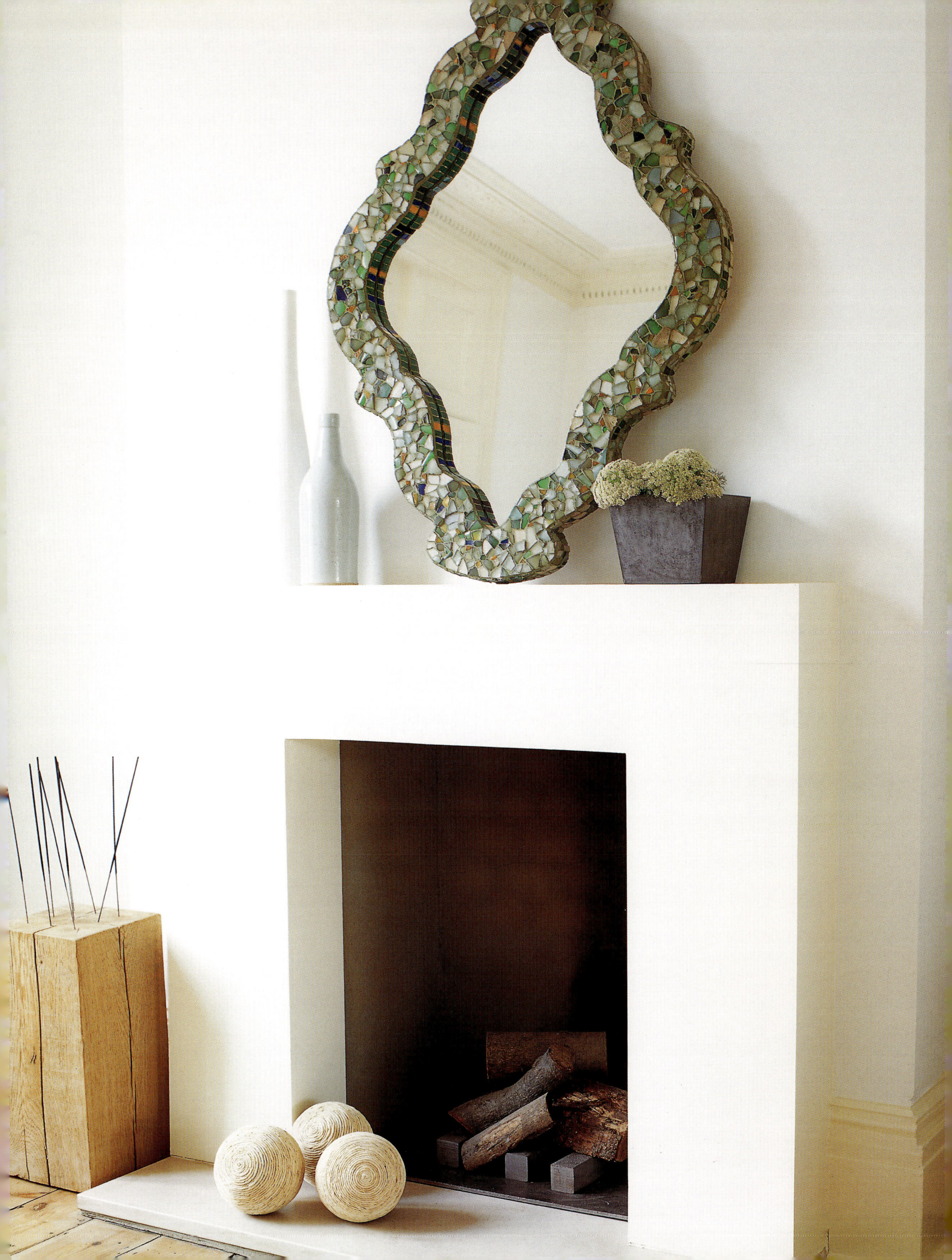

Only the most minimalist of gardeners wishes to exclude any suggestion of ornament from their garden. Containers, in particular, are an ideal choice for mosaic and provide a welcome splash of colour in any garden.

Garden Ornaments

Mosaic seems quite at home in a garden, adding a touch of colour to a dull area, or providing a dramatic focal point. Blue colour schemes are ideal to complement the surrounding green.

Pots and containers

Mosaic can be applied to many kinds of garden containers, from night lights, window boxes and chimney pots to the largest urn. The most commonly covered containers are, however, ceramic pots. Use a frost-resistant terracotta pot as a base where you can, and if it is not glazed, you must varnish the inside to stop moisture seeping through from the inside and pushing off the tesserae. This is important if the pot is to be used for plants that are left outside. It is also advisable to use water- and frost-resistant cements and grouts.

There is also a wide range of excellent plastic containers available that accurately replicate almost any kind of finish you care to name, from verdigris, terracotta and copper to stone, but have the advantage of being lightweight. Mosaic can be applied to add detail and personalize any of these types of pot. Once a pot is covered in mosaic, no one will know that the base is plastic rather than terracotta.

An elaborately carved or shaped antique-style container, in real or simulated stone, may need a different treatment to simple plant pots. Large urns look good partially covered with mosaic, as it highlights the contrast between the pot and mosaic, but tesserae should be chosen to enhance the base colour. Urns make stunning focal points and add a sculptural feel to any garden.

Considerations to take into account concern the appearance of not only the container but also the plants. Your design and chosen colour palette should complement the environment. For example, a restrained geometric design would suit a clipped topiary box tree, but a more vibrant, abstract design would harmonize with bright red geraniums.

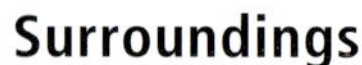

Surroundings

In any garden, the plants must be the first feature. You do not want any decoration to "shout" at the plants or detract from their beauty. When planning your design, therefore, you must make the surrounding plants your first consideration, so that your mosaic design echoes their beauty.

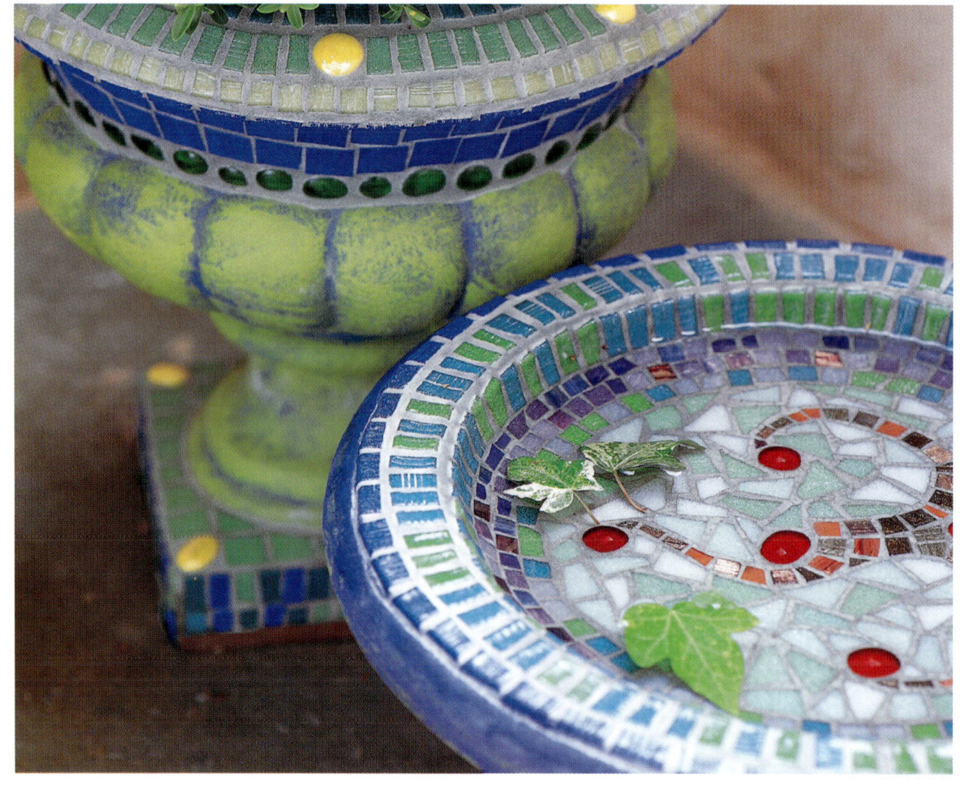

Left: A bright urn, and accompanying birdbath, with strong colours and designs are ideal for dark or shady courtyards.

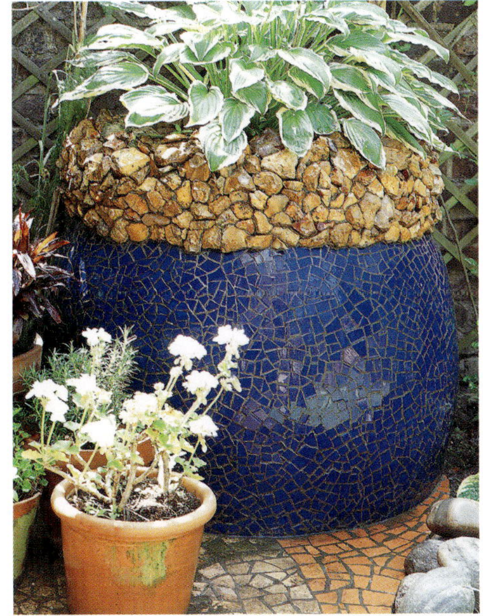

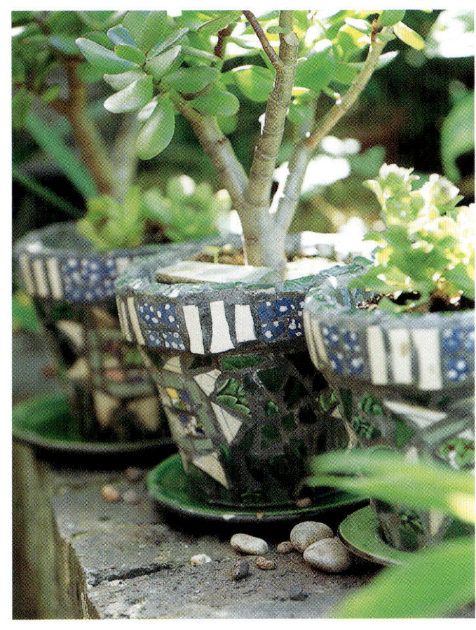

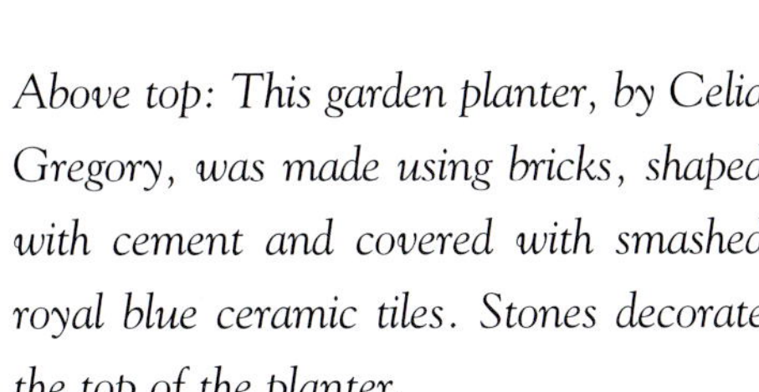

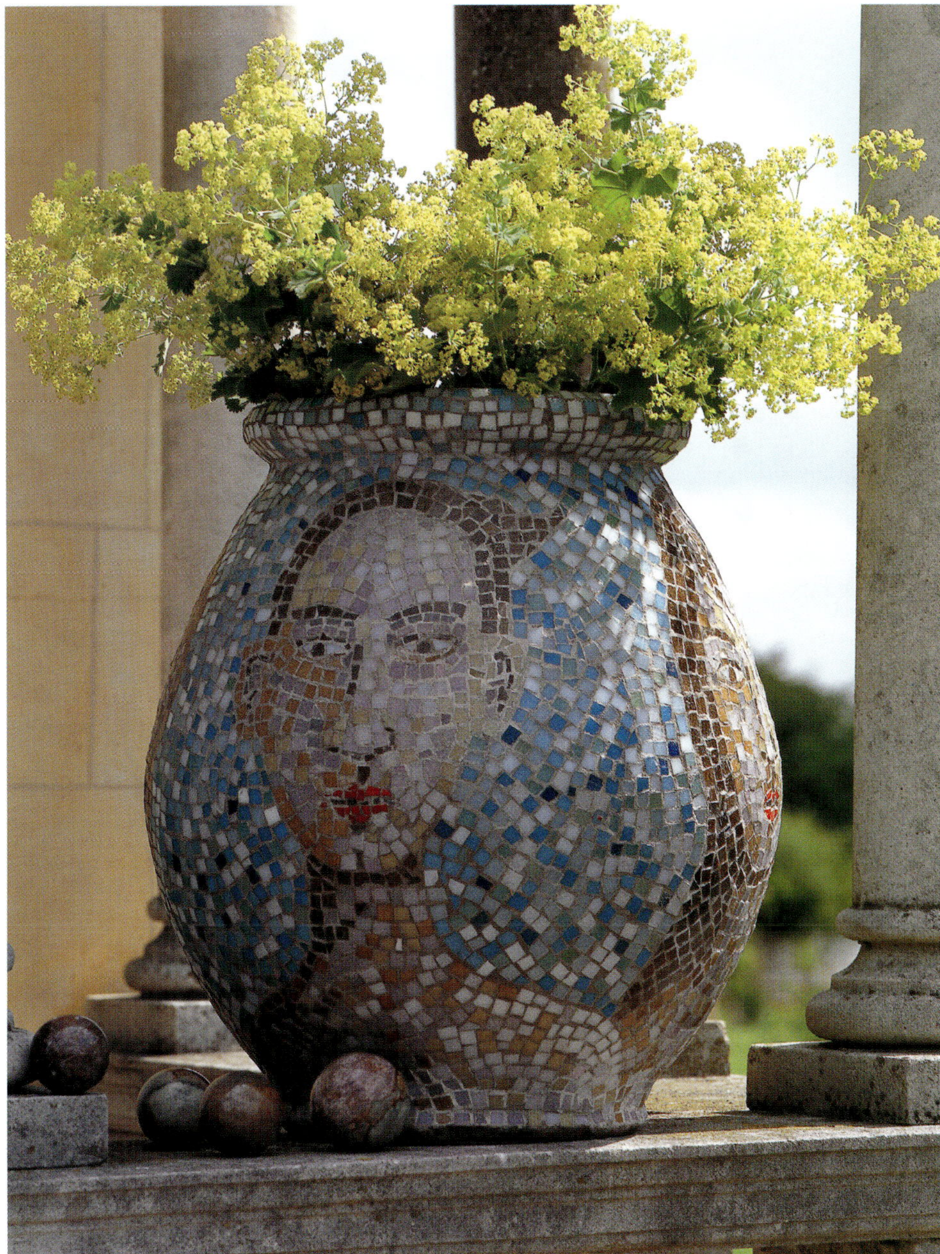

Above top: This garden planter, by Celia Gregory, was made using bricks, shaped with cement and covered with smashed royal blue ceramic tiles. Stones decorate the top of the planter.

Above: In a predominantly green space, brightly patterned ceramic pots by Cleo Mussi add interest.

Above right: This traditional garden urn is decorated with unusual modern faces in subtle, muted tones.

Which plants are going to be nearby and what colours are their leaves or flowers? The leaves may change colour when young in spring, at their peak in summer and when they turn in autumn. If leaves drop, what other plant will then be thrown into prominence? In winter, how does your garden change? Or perhaps your colour scheme is subdued, with grasses and low-maintenance shrubs or evergreens. In this case, do you want ornaments to blend in or stand out?

Out of doors, even under cloudy skies, light is ever-changing and so very important. Will your mosaic be in shade, dappled shade or full sun? What does it look like under different weather conditions, from bright sun to rain?

For all these considerations, you need to choose whether you want to keep to gentle shades and natural tones or opt for bold, bright colours that have impact. Either way, mosaic will complement the natural surroundings and allow your plants to shine.

Made with tesserae cut from brightly coloured tiles and small pieces of mirror, this striking number plaque should be clearly visible from a distance. A larger plaque could be made to display a house name.

House Number Plaque

You will need
12mm (1/2in) thick chipboard (particle board)
Saw
Felt-tipped pen
PVA (white) glue
Paintbrushes
Ceramic household tiles: yellow, mid-blue and dark blue
Mirror
Tile nippers
Tile adhesive
Flexible knife
Black tile grout
Grout spreader
Sponge
Waterproof exterior paint
Wall fastening
Screws
Screwdriver
Soft cloth
Clear glass polish

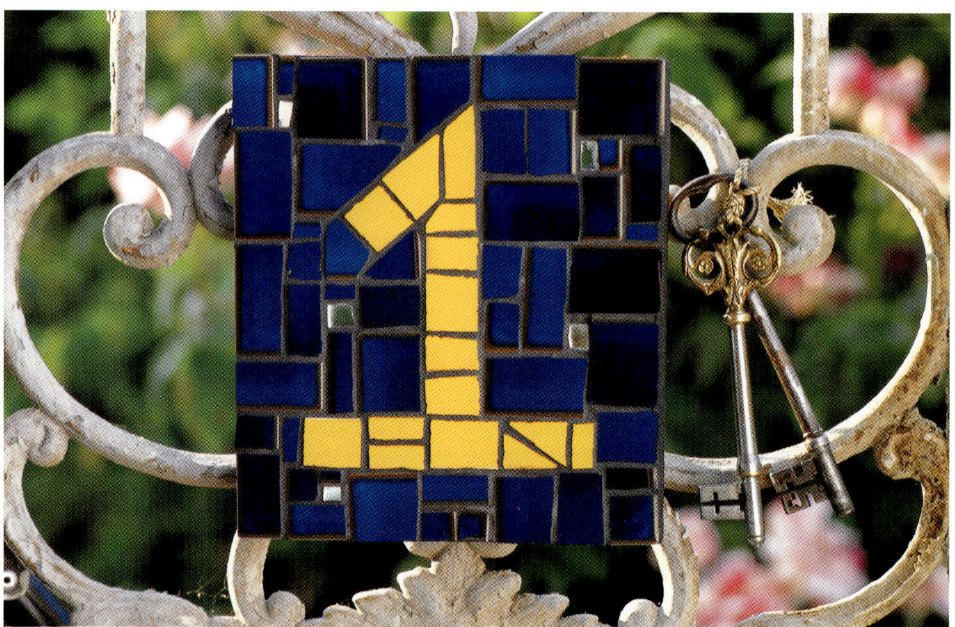

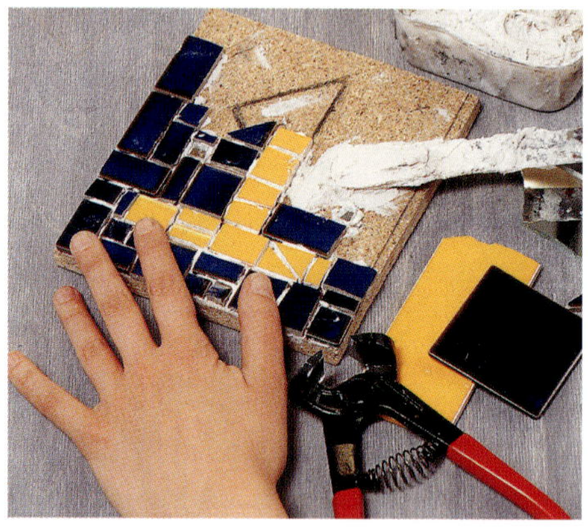

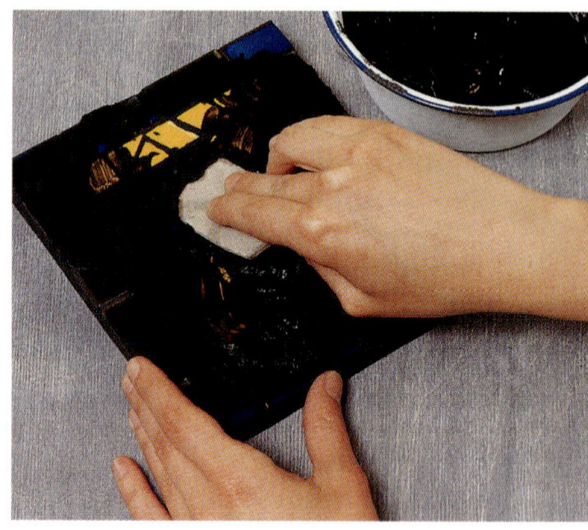

1 Cut a piece of chipboard (particle board) to size, depending on the length of the house number required. The one used here is 18 x 15cm (7 x 6in). Draw the house number on the chipboard, making sure it is at least 1.5cm (⅝in) wide. If you wish, you can also mark the intended positions of the mirror. Paint the chipboard – front, back and sides – with diluted PVA (white) glue. Leave to dry thoroughly.

2 Cut the tiles and mirror into small pieces using tile nippers. First tile the number with the yellow tesserae you have cut, sticking them on the base, a small area at a time, with tile adhesive. Then tile the area around the number in both shades of blue, cutting and applying small pieces of mirror to the marked positions. Wipe off any excess tile adhesive and leave the plaque to dry for 24 hours.

3 Cover the surface with black tile grout, filling all the gaps between the tesserae so no moisture can penetrate to the chipboard base. Spread the grout along the edges of the plaque, then leave to dry for about 10 minutes. Sponge off the excess grout and leave to dry for a further 24 hours. Paint the back with an exterior paint and fix a clip for hanging. Polish the plaque with a soft cloth and clear glass polish.

As well as protecting your table top, this mosaic pot stand will brighten up any meal time. The geometric shape is integral to the pattern in which the brightly coloured tesserae are laid.

Pot Stand

You will need

12mm (½in) thick chipboard (particle board), 30 x 30cm (12 x 12in)
Pencil
Ruler
PVA (white) glue
Paintbrush
Jigsaw (saber saw)
Abrasive paper (sandpaper)
Ceramic household tiles: yellow, dark blue and lilac
Tile nippers
Mirror
Tile adhesive
Flexible knife
Black tile grout
Grout spreader
Sponge
Felt
Scissors
Soft cloth
Clear glass polish

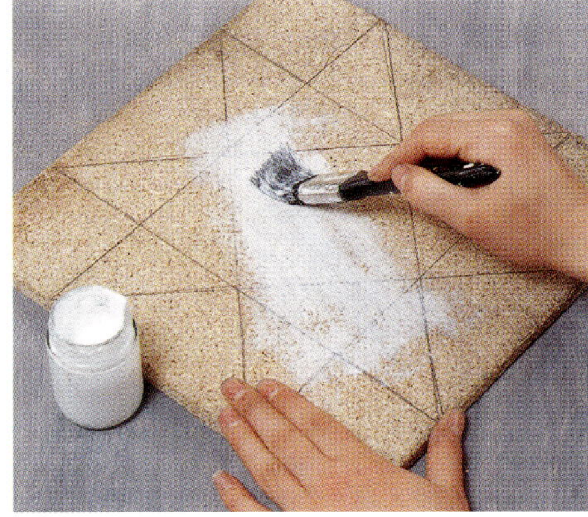

1 Carefully mark the proportions of the pot stand on to the piece of chipboard (particle board); use a ruler to make sure the lines are straight.

Prime both sides of the chipboard with diluted PVA (white) glue and leave to dry. Cut around the outline of the design using a jigsaw (saber saw). Sand down any rough edges and prime with diluted PVA glue. Leave to dry.

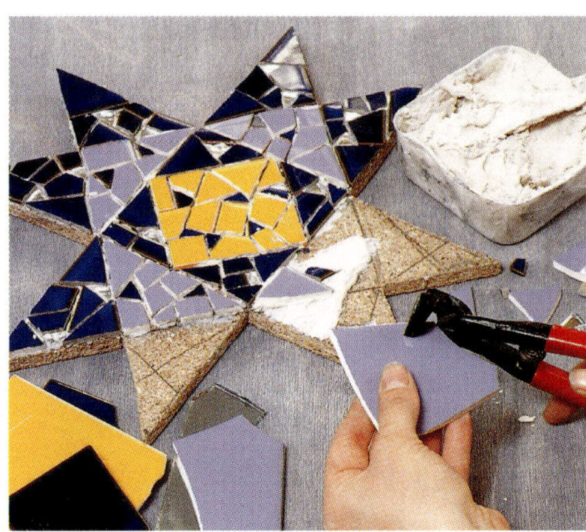

2 Using tile nippers, cut the tiles into small pieces that will fit inside the shapes you have drawn. Here, small pieces of mirror have been added to the dark blue sections, and small pieces of the dark blue tiles have been included in the lighter areas. Fix them in position with tile adhesive, using a flexible knife. When the surface is covered, sponge off any excess adhesive and leave to dry for 24 hours.

3 Fill the gaps between the tesserae with black tile grout. Rub the grout into the sides of the stand as well, then leave to dry for about 10 minutes. Wipe off any excess grout with a sponge, then leave to dry for 24 hours. Paint the sides of the pot stand with diluted PVA glue. Cut felt to size and stick it to the back of the stand with PVA glue. Finish by polishing the top with a soft cloth and clear glass polish.

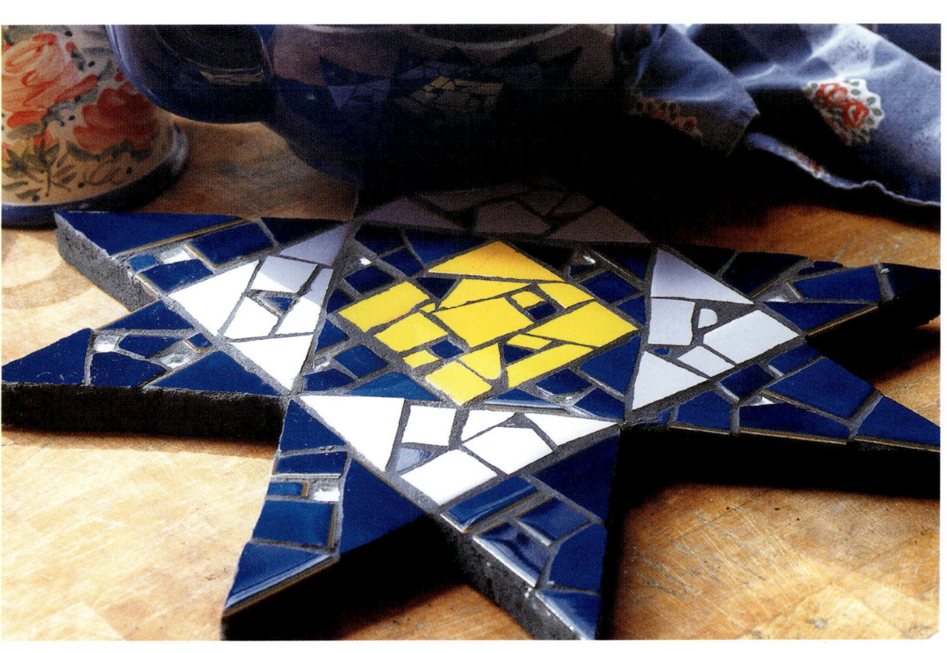

If you would like to introduce mosaic to an outdoor setting but are daunted by a large project, these tiles are the perfect solution. They can be left freestanding or be fixed to a wall as an interesting feature.

China Tiles

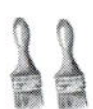

You will need

Plain white ceramic household tiles
PVA (white) glue
Paintbrush
Pencil
Selection of china
Tile nippers
Tile adhesive
Acrylic paint or cement stain
Tile grout
Nailbrush
Soft cloth

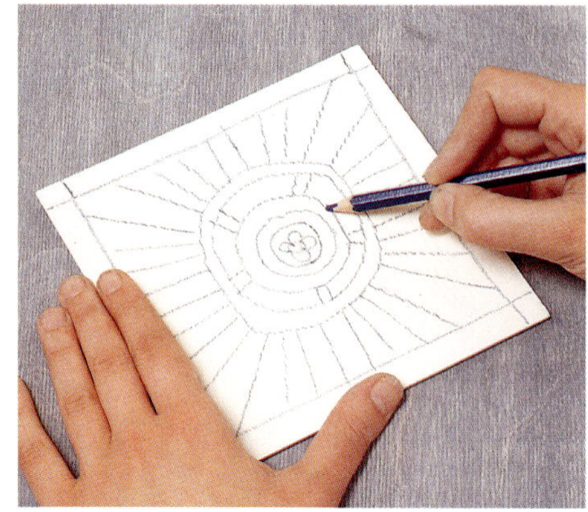

1 Prime the back of a plain tile with diluted PVA (white) glue using a paintbrush and leave to dry. Draw a simple, rough design on the back of the tile using a soft pencil.

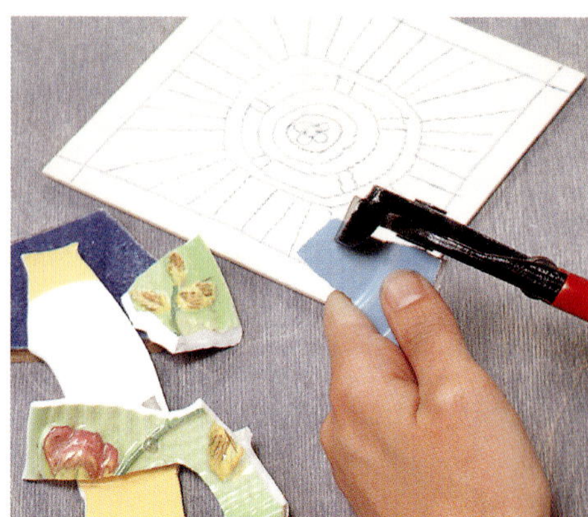

2 Using tile nippers, cut a selection of china into small pieces that will fit into your design and arrange these in groups according to their colour and shape.

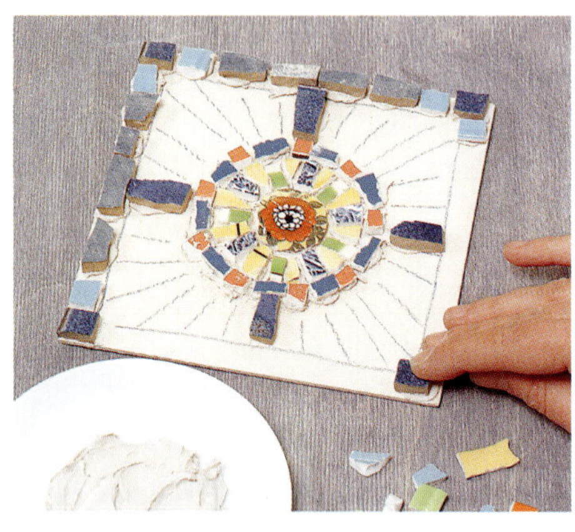

3 Dip the tesserae into tile adhesive and press them, one by one, on to the tile, using the drawing as a guide. Make sure there is enough adhesive on the tesserae; when they are pressed on the tile, glue should ooze out around them. When the tile is covered, leave it to dry overnight.

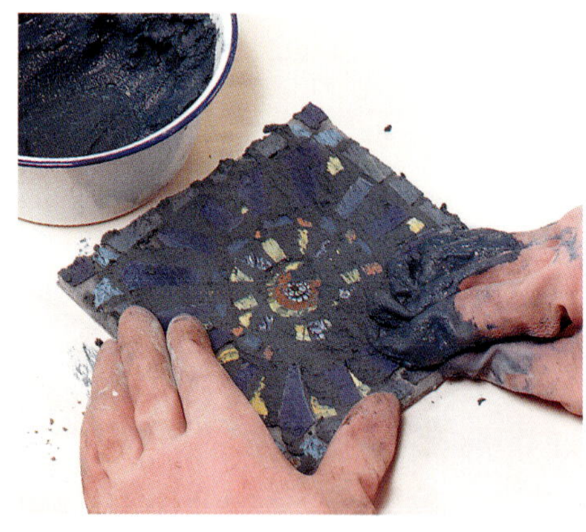

4 Mix acrylic paint or cement stain with the tile grout. Rub the grout into the surface of the mosaic with your fingers, making sure all the gaps between the tesserae are filled. Leave to dry for 10 minutes.

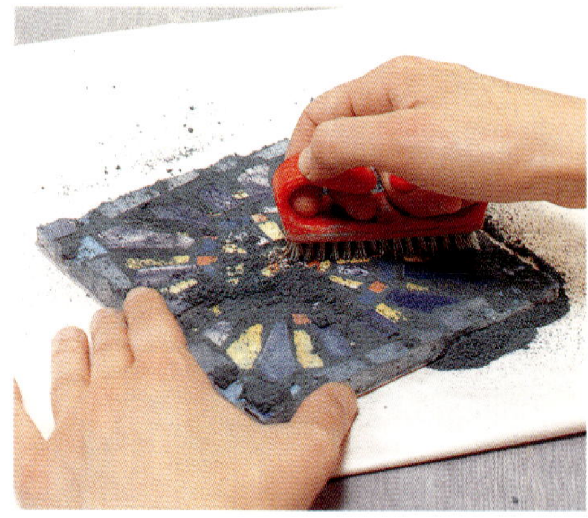

5 Scrub the surface of the tile with a stiff nailbrush to remove all the excess grout, which should come away as powder. When clean, leave the tile to dry for 24 hours. Finish by polishing it with a dry, soft cloth. Repeat for any other tiles you want to make.

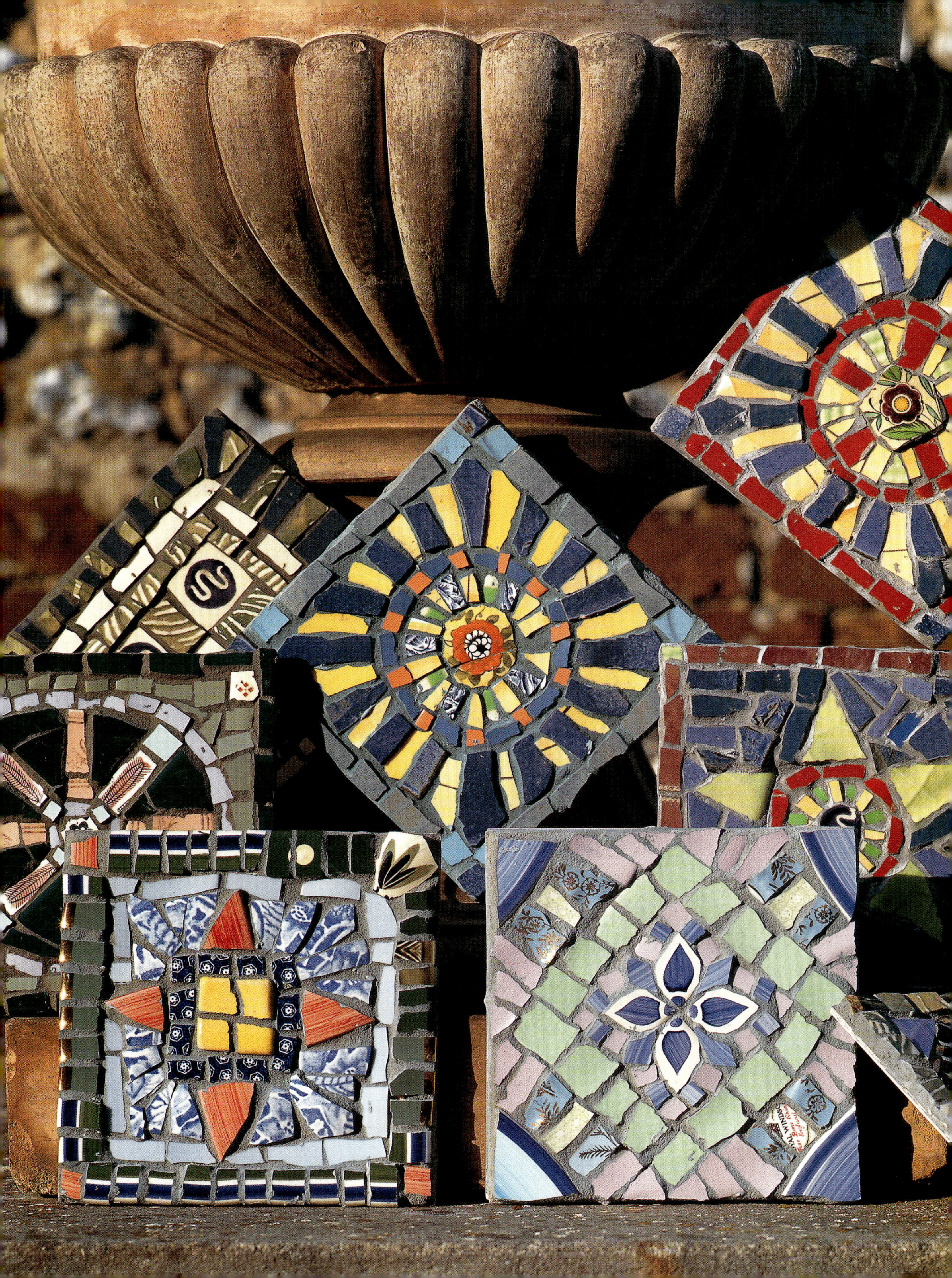

Personal letters and correspondence often have a tendency to be lost or misplaced in a busy household. This simple design for a boldly coloured letter rack could be a decorative solution.

Love Letter Rack

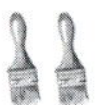

You will need

3mm (⅛in) and 12mm (½in) thick MDF (medium-density fiberboard) or plywood sheet
Pencil
Jigsaw (saber saw)
PVA (white) glue
Paintbrushes
Wood glue
Panel pins (brads)
Pin hammer
Vitreous glass mosaic tiles
Tile nippers
White cellulose filler (Spackle)
Grout spreader
Sponge
Abrasive paper (sandpaper)
Red acrylic paint

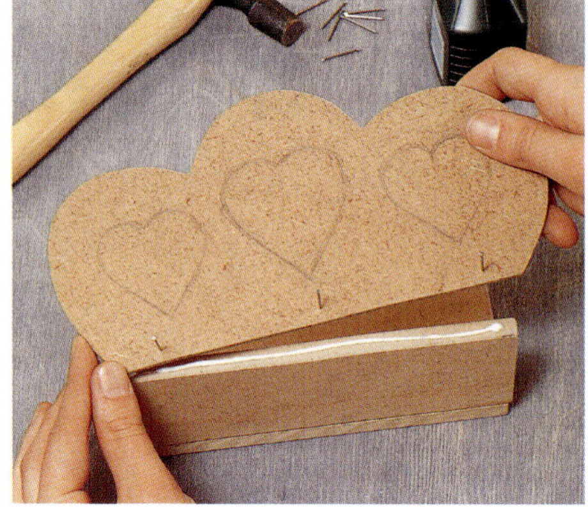

1 Draw shapes for the front and back pieces on the thinner piece of MDF (medium-density fiberboard) or plywood. Then draw a base on the thicker piece. Cut them out with a jigsaw (saber saw). Prime the surfaces with diluted PVA (white) glue. When dry, draw three hearts on to the front panel. Stick the pieces together with wood glue and secure with panel pins (brads).

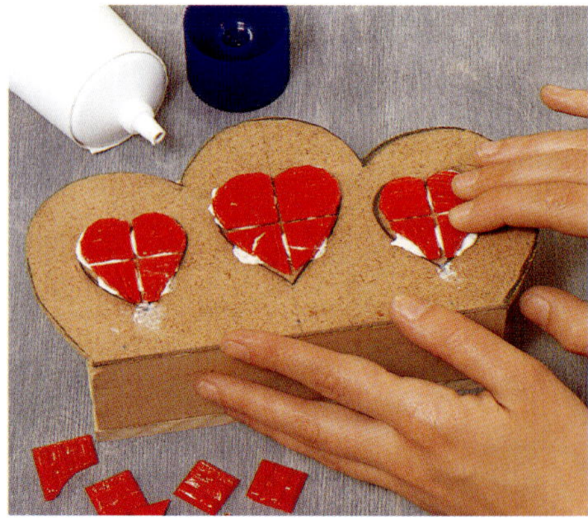

2 When the glue is dry, select two slightly different tones of red vitreous glass tiles for the heart motifs. Using tile nippers, nibble the tiles into precise shapes to fit your design. Fix the tesserae in position on the front panel of the letter rack with white cellulose filler (Spackle).

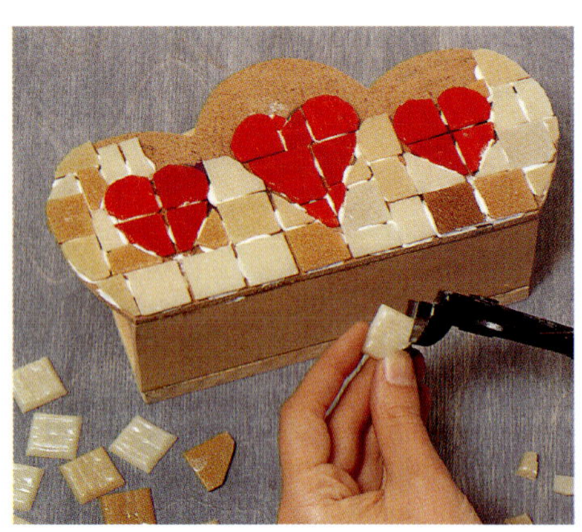

3 Select the colours of vitreous glass for the background. Trim the tiles to fit snugly around the heart motifs and within the edges of the letter rack. Fix them to the base as before. Leave the rack to dry overnight.

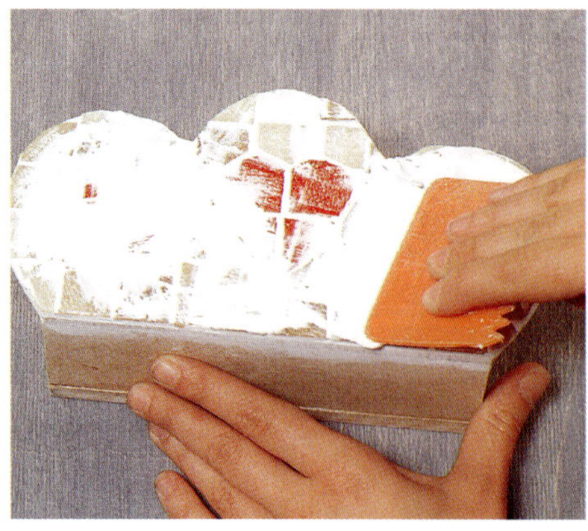

4 Smooth more filler over the mosaic using a grout spreader. Rub the filler into all of the gaps with your fingers. Rub off any excess filler with a damp sponge and leave to dry.

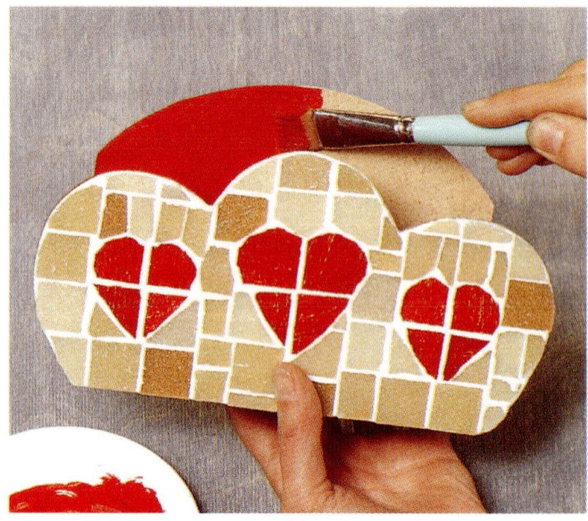

5 Use abrasive paper (sandpaper) to remove any filler that has dried on the surface of the mosaic and to neaten the edges. Paint the parts of the letter rack that are not covered with mosaic with red acrylic paint. Leave to dry.

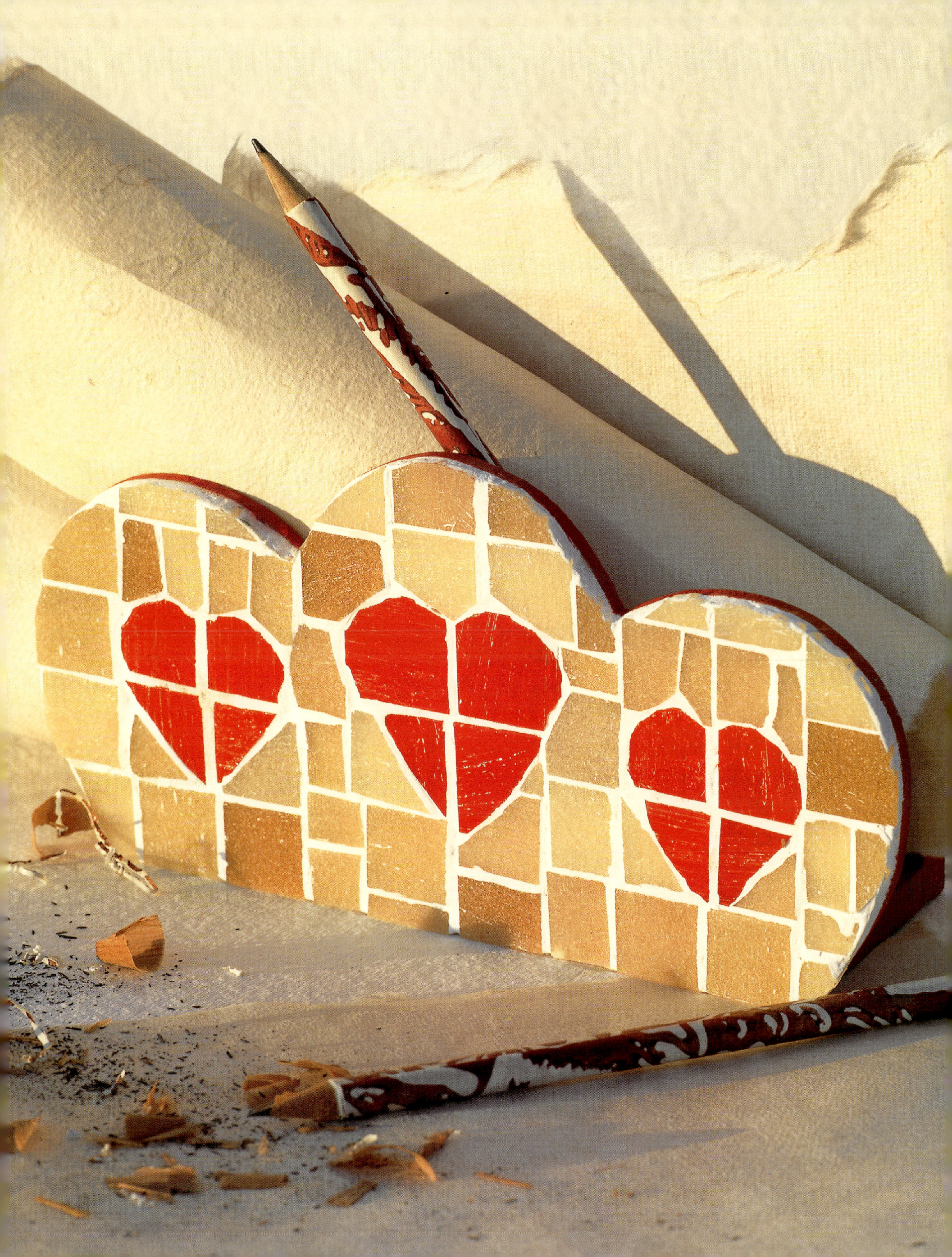

Fragments of plain and patterned broken tiles have been incorporated into the design of these plant pots. Collect your materials by looking in junk shops for old china in contrasting and complementary patterns.

Plant Pots

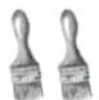

You will need

Terracotta flower pots
PVA (white) glue and brush (optional)
Acrylic paint
Paintbrush
Chalk or wax crayon
Plain and patterned ceramic tiles
Tile nippers
Tile adhesive
Flexible knife
Tile grout
Cement stain
Cloth
Nailbrush
Soft cloth

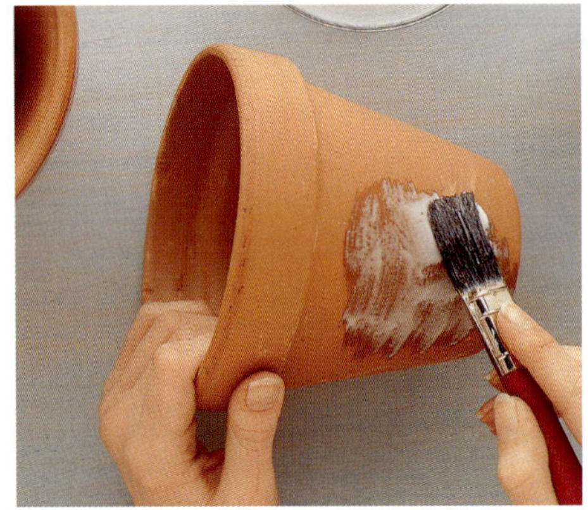

1 If the plant pots are not frost-resistant and are intended for outdoor use, seal them inside and out with a coat of diluted PVA (white) glue. This will help to keep out any water that might seep into the pourous pot, making it vulnerable to frost damage. Allow to dry.

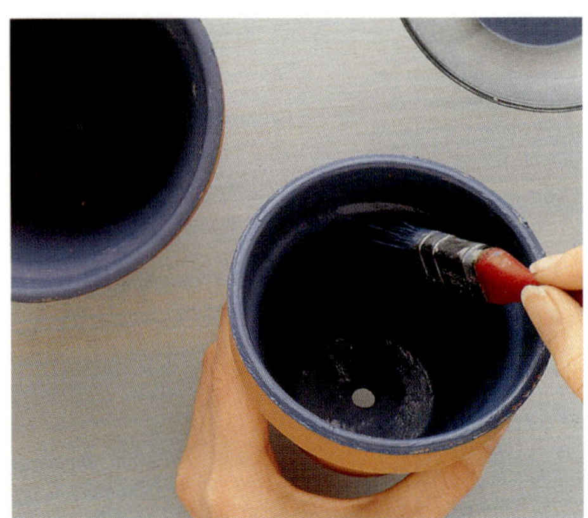

2 Paint the inside of the pots with acrylic paint in your chosen colour. Leave to dry. Using chalk or a wax crayon, roughly sketch out the design for the tile pieces on the unpainted outside of the pot. Keep your designs as simple as possible and in keeping with this small scale.

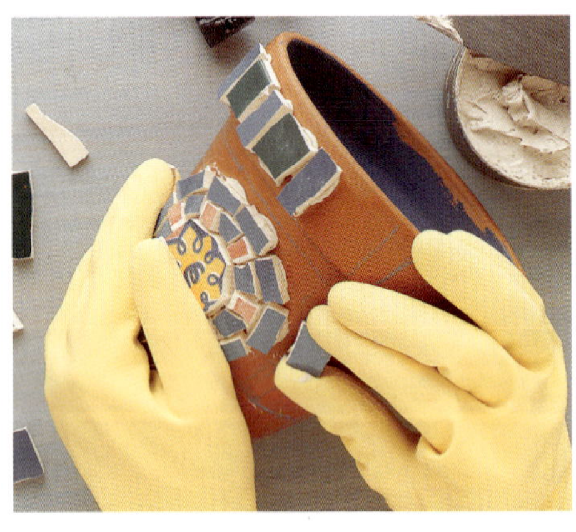

3 Using tile nippers, snip small pieces of tile to fit within your design. Using a flexible knife, spread tile adhesive on to small areas of the design at a time. Wearing rubber (latex) gloves, press the tesserae in place, working on the outlines first, then the background. Leave for 24 hours.

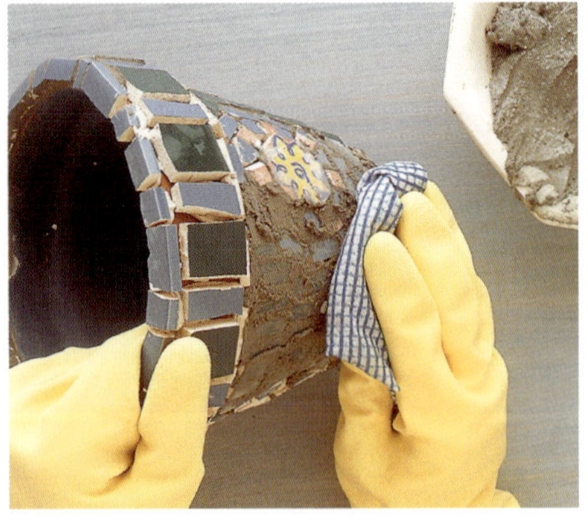

4 Mix the tile grout with a little cement stain. Spread the grout over the pot with a cloth, filling all the cracks between the tesserae. Wipe off any excess grout. Allow the surface to dry thoroughly.

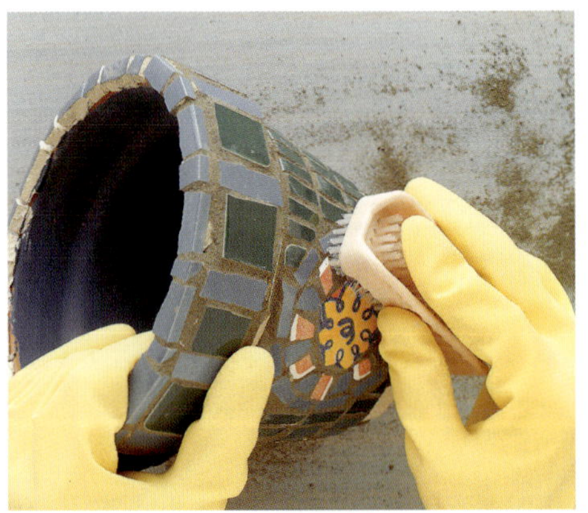

5 Brush off any dried-on grout with a nailbrush. If there are stubborn parts of grout that will not come off at first, you might try wire (steel) wool, a paint scraper, or patio-cleaner. Allow the mosaic to dry thoroughly for at least 48 hours, then polish with a dry, soft cloth.

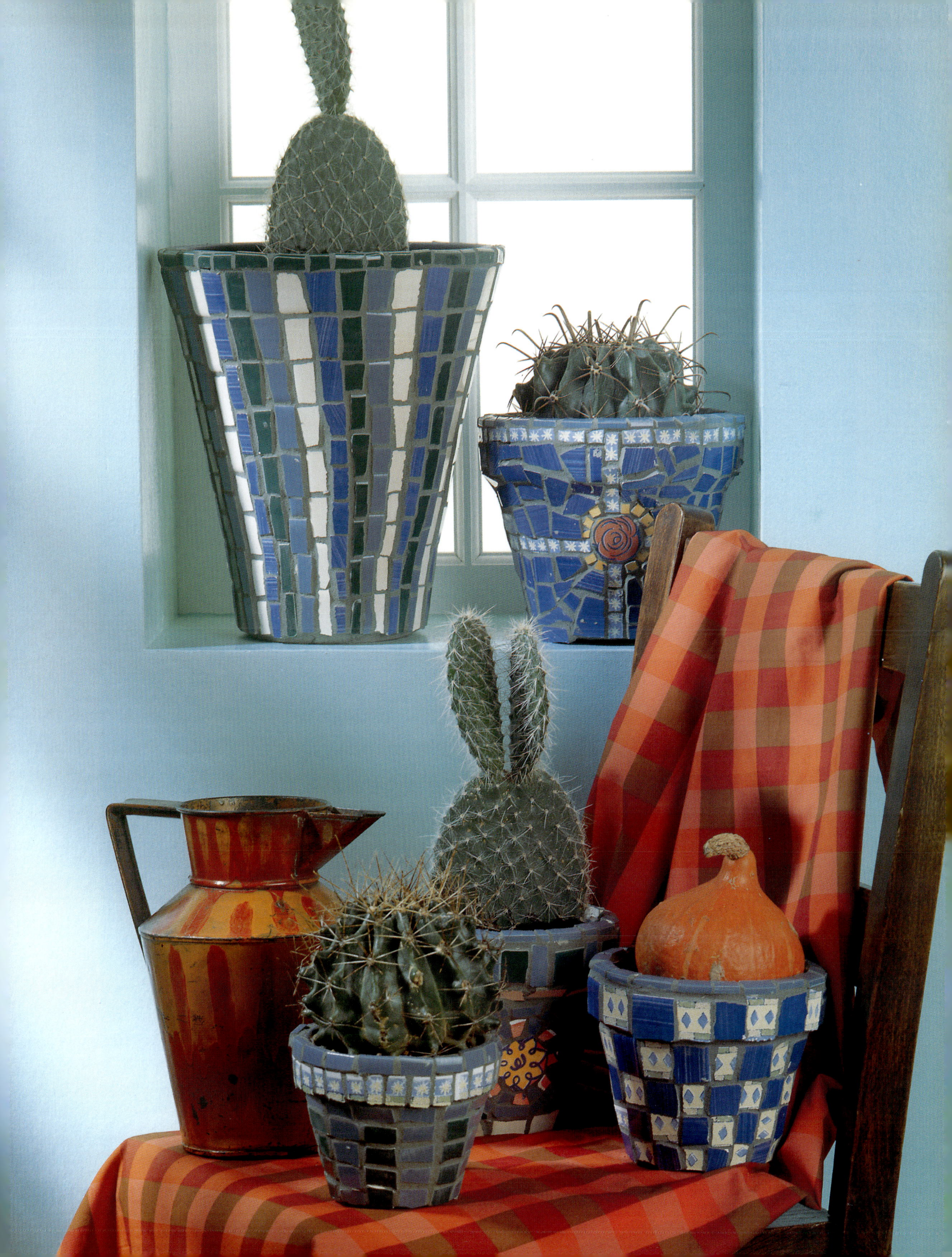

Squares of coloured glass cast beautiful patterns at night, when the candle is lit in a darkened room. Practise the glass-cutting technique first on scraps of clear glass.

Stained-glass Candle-holder

You will need
Pencil
Ruler
Graph paper
Sheets of textured coloured glass
Glass cutter
Pliers
Clear all-purpose adhesive
Clear glass candle-holder
Tile grout
Flexible knife
Sponge or soft cloth

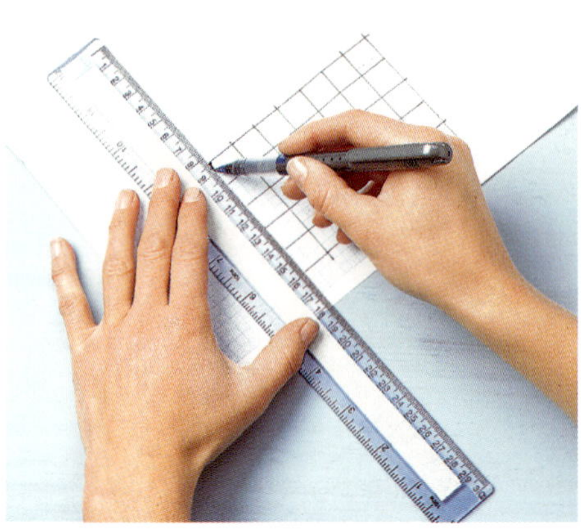

1 Using a pencil and ruler, draw a grid of 4cm (1½in) squares on graph paper.

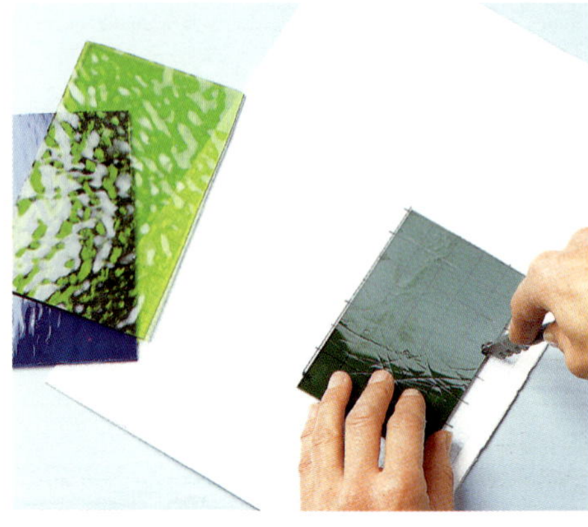

2 Place each sheet of coloured glass over the grid. Following your drawn lines, score vertical lines with a glass cutter (see Materials and Techniques).

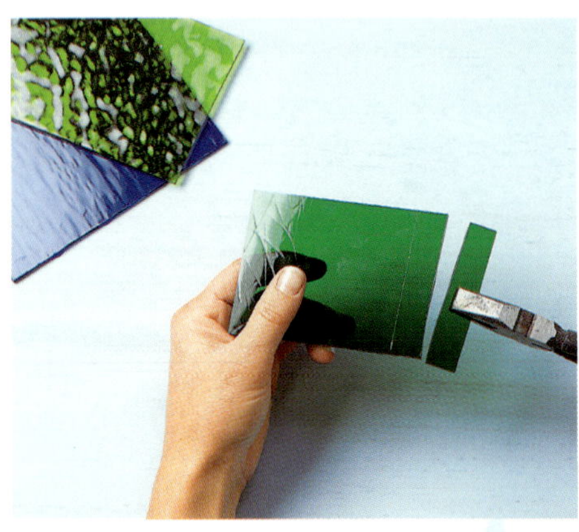

3 Using pliers, and holding the glass carefully, snap the glass along the scored lines into neat, evenly sized pieces.

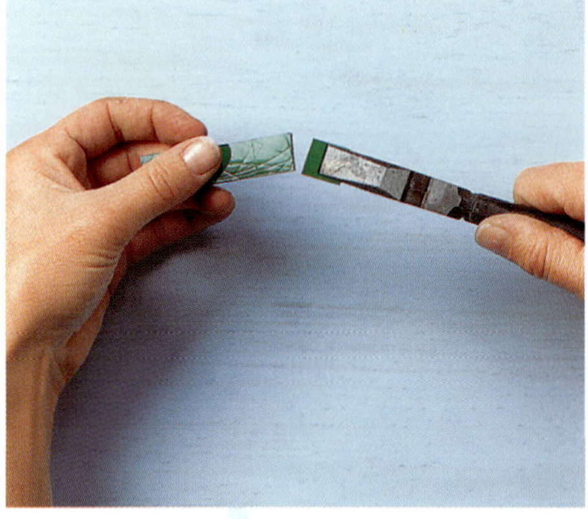

4 Place each strip of glass over the paper grid, score horizontal lines and snap off the squares with the pliers, until you have enough squares to cover the candle-holder.

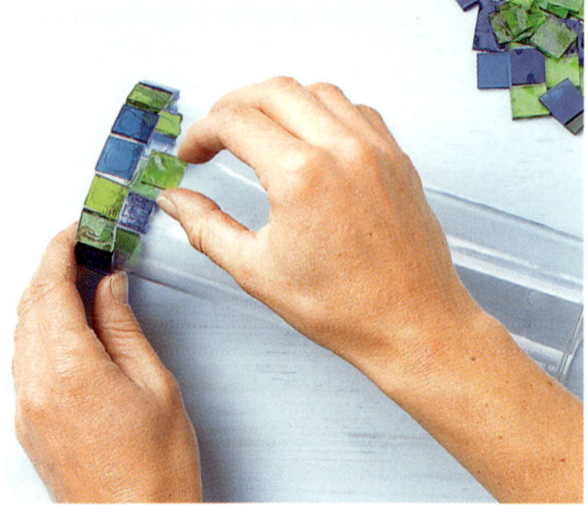

5 Stick the squares of glass in neat rows around the candle-holder with clear adhesive, alternating the colours, and leaving a tiny gap between each tile. Using a flexible knife, spread the tile grout over the mosaic, filling all the gaps. Rub the excess grout off with a damp sponge or soft cloth. Leave to dry completely before using.

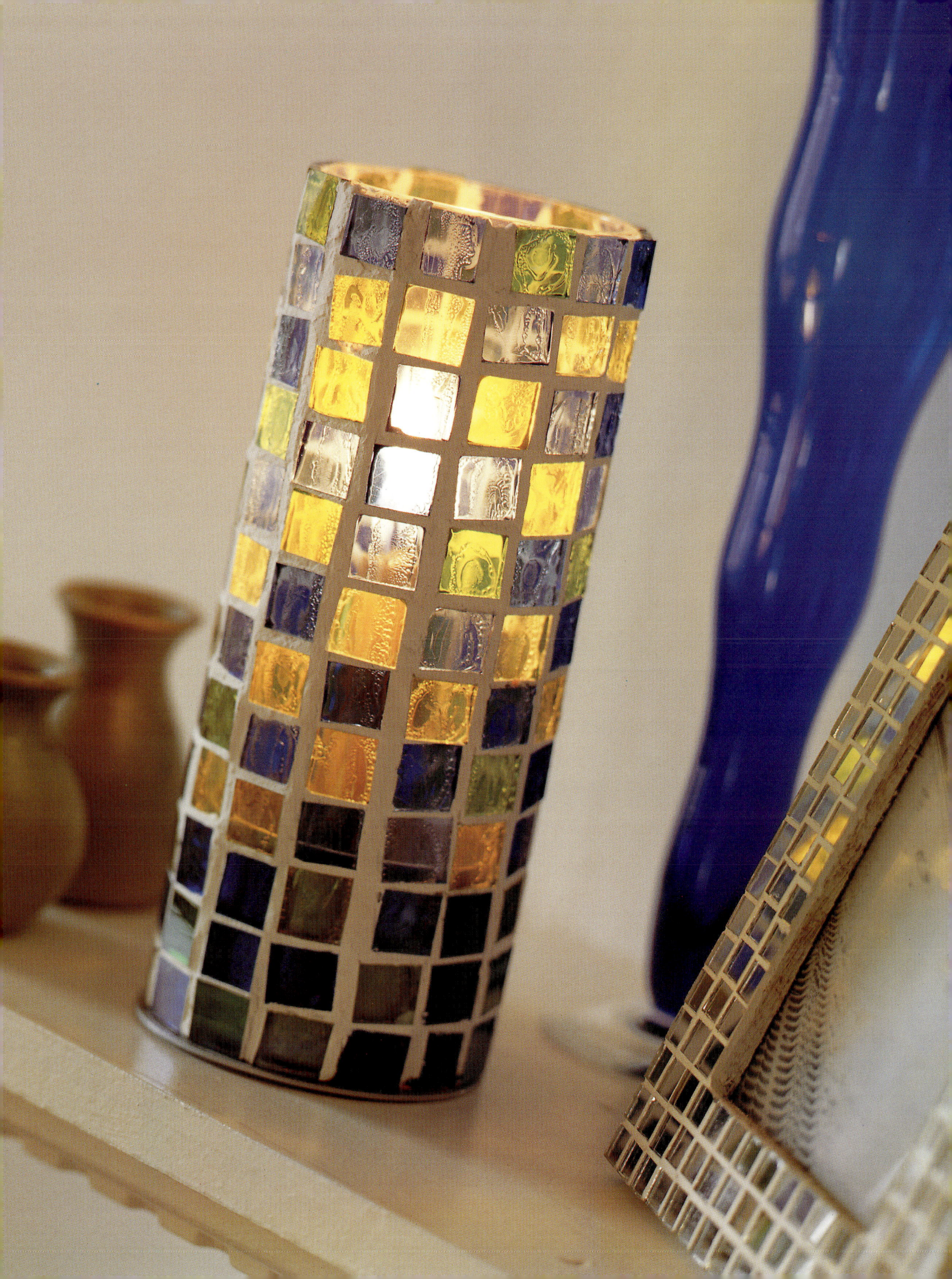

These mosaic spheres can be used as unusual garden ornaments, or a bowlful could make a striking table centrepiece. Select fragments of china to complement your tableware or garden.

Decorative Spheres

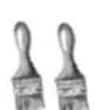

You will need

- 10 polystyrene (Styrofoam) balls or wooden spheres
- PVA (white) glue
- Paintbrush
- Pencil
- Selection of china
- Mirror
- Tile nippers
- Tile adhesive
- Vinyl matt emulsion (flat latex) or acrylic paint
- Tile grout
- Nailbrush
- Soft cloth

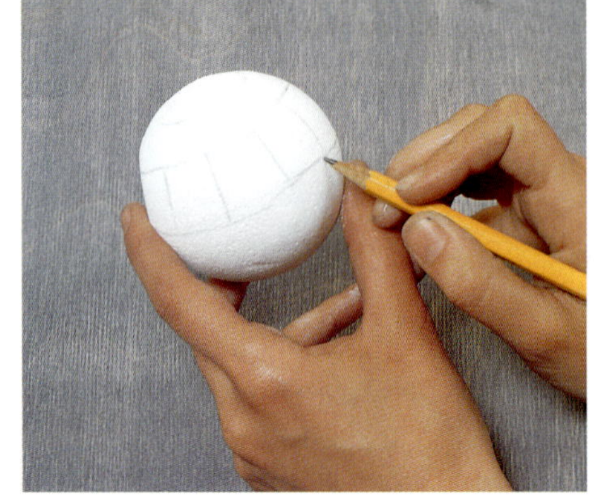

1 Seal the polystyrene (Styrofoam) or wooden spheres with diluted PVA (white) glue. Leave to dry. Roughly draw a simple design on to each sphere using a pencil. A combination of circular motifs and stripes works well, but you can experiment with other geometric shapes and abstract designs.

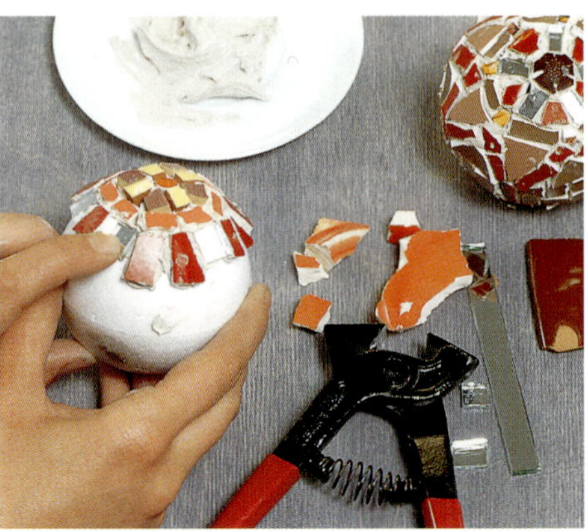

2 Cut the china and mirror into pieces using the tile nippers. Combine different sizes of tesserae to fit the design. Stick them to the spheres with tile adhesive. Leave to dry overnight.

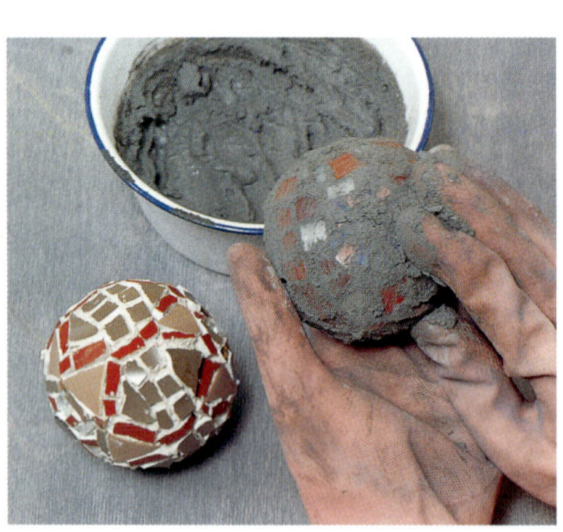

3 Add a little coloured vinyl matt emulsion (flat latex) or acrylic paint to the tile grout. Wearing rubber (latex) gloves, rub the grout into the surface of each sphere, filling all the cracks between the tesserae.

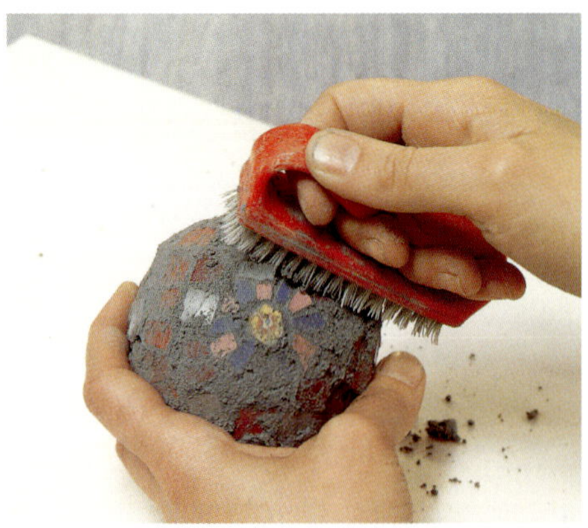

4 Leave for a few minutes until the surface has dried, then brush off any excess grout using a stiff nailbrush.

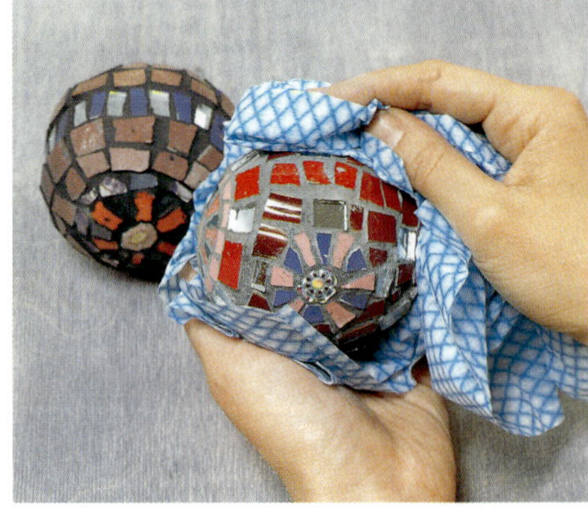

5 Leave to dry overnight, then polish with a dry, soft cloth. Allow the spheres to air for a few days before you arrange them.

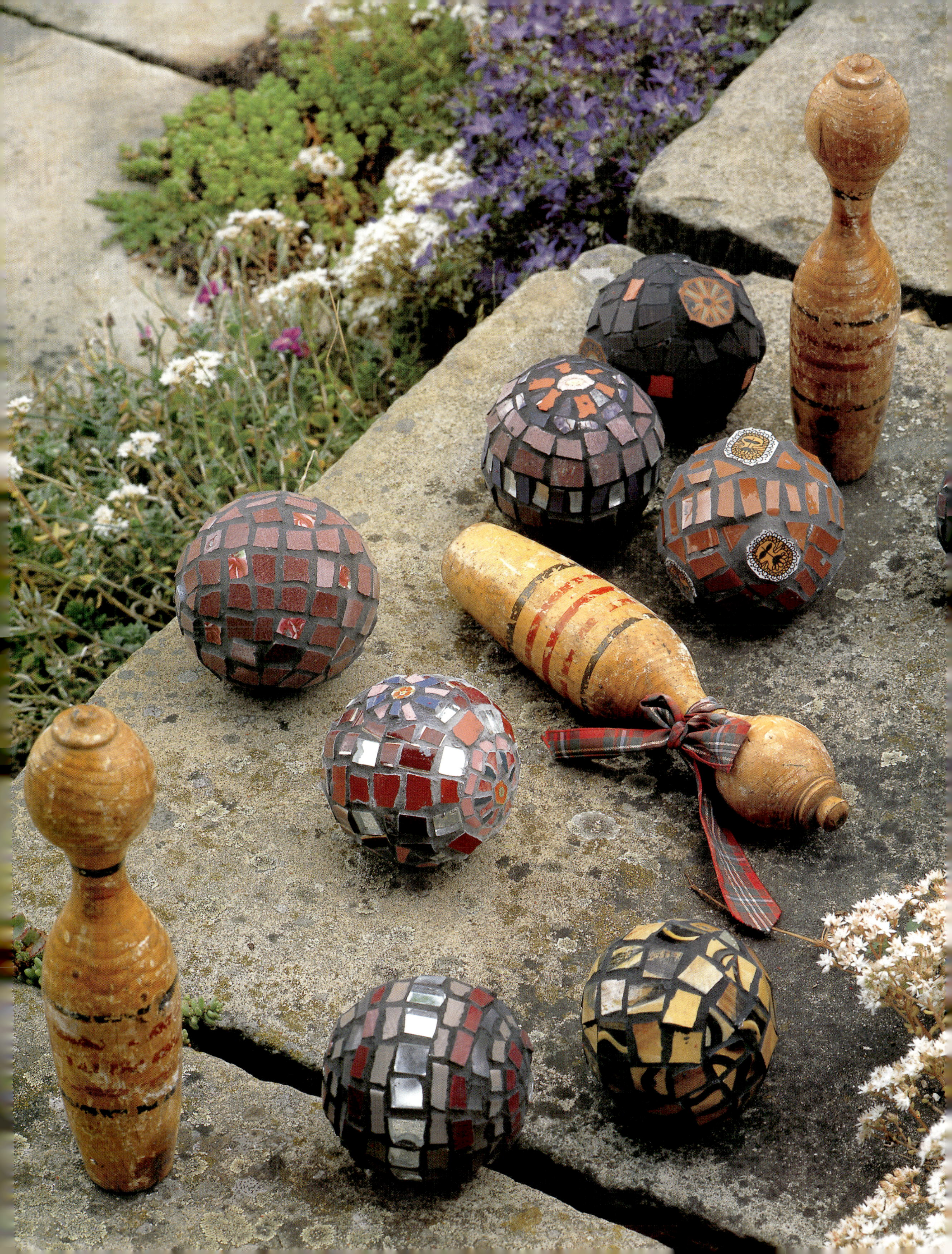

A plain terracotta pot is decorated with squares of brightly coloured tesserae and mirror glass, set in white tile adhesive. This project is simple but effective – you could decorate several matching pots.

Jazzy Plant Pot

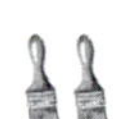

You will need

Small terracotta plant pot
Yacht varnish
Paintbrush
Vitreous glass mosaic tiles
Tile nippers
Mirror
Tile adhesive
Flexible knife
Sponge
Abrasive paper (sandpaper)
Soft cloth

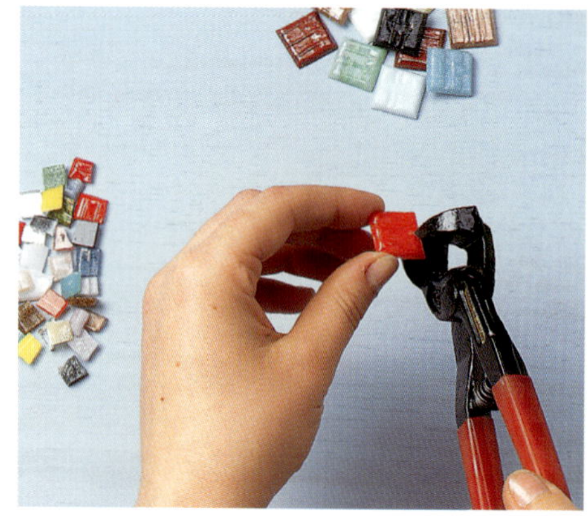

1 Paint the inside of the terracotta plant pot with yacht varnish. Leave to dry. Cut the glass tiles into neat quarters using tile nippers. Cut small squares of mirror to the same size, also with tile nippers. Continue cutting the tiles until you have enough tesserae, in a variety of colours, to cover your pot completely.

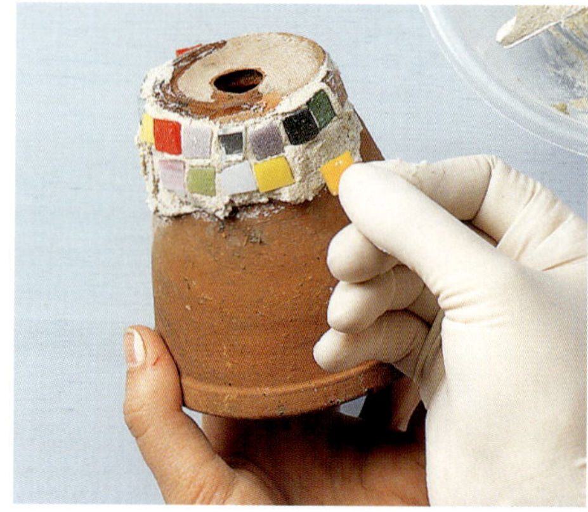

2 Working from the bottom of the pot, spread a thick layer of tile adhesive over a small area at a time using a flexible knife. Press the tesserae into the tile adhesive in rows, including the pieces of mirror. Leave to dry overnight.

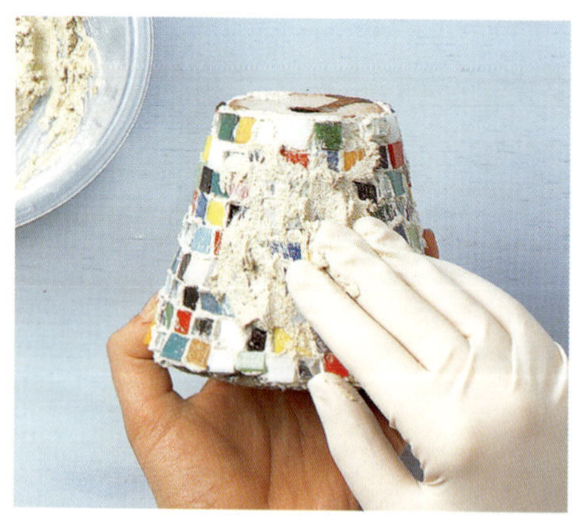

3 Rub some more tile adhesive all over the surface of the mosaic. Fill any gaps in between the tesserae, then wipe off the excess adhesive with a damp sponge before it dries. Again, leave to dry overnight.

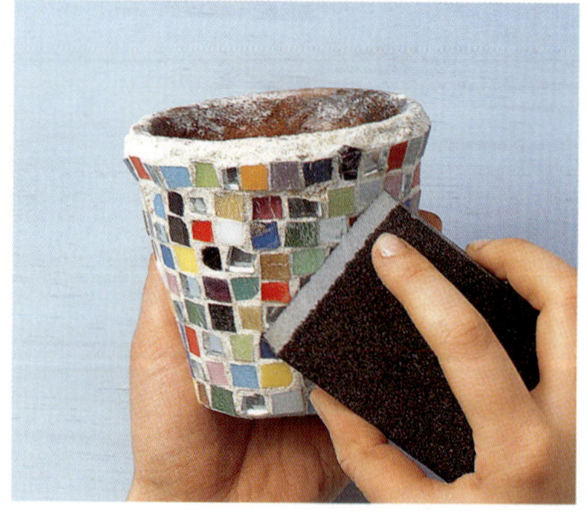

4 Use abrasive paper (sandpaper) to remove any lumps of tile adhesive that may have dried on to the surface of the tesserae, and to neaten the bottom edge of the pot.

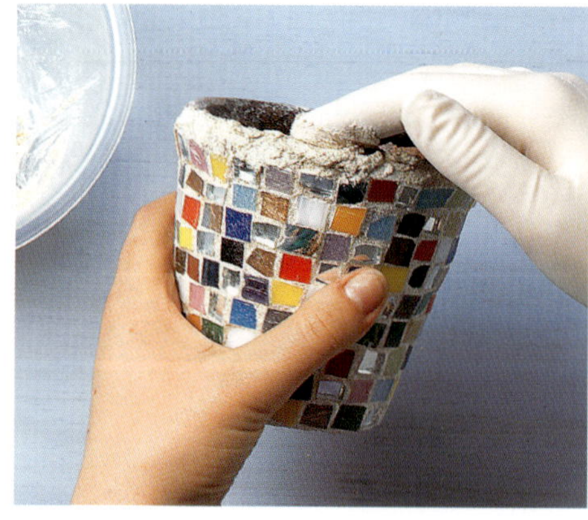

5 Smooth some more tile adhesive all over the rim of the pot. Leave until completely dry, and then polish the finished mosaic with a dry, soft cloth.

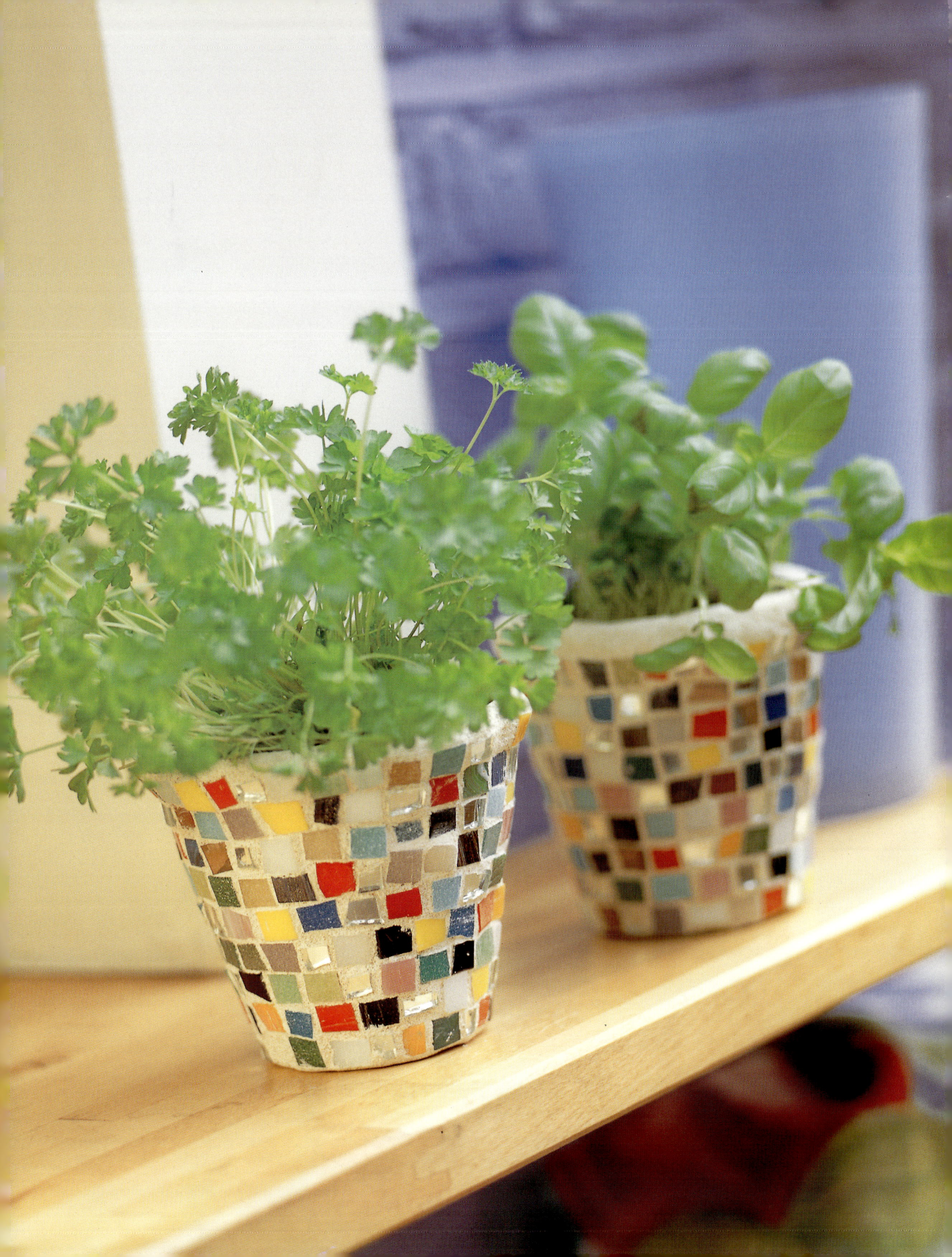

A terracotta planter can be embellished with pieces of tile, which are further enhanced by being grouted in a colour chosen to complement them. If the planter is frost-resistant, it can safely be used outdoors.

Decorative Planter

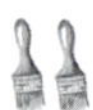

You will need

Ceramic mosaic tiles in several colours
Tile nippers
Notched trowel
Tile adhesive
Terracotta planter
Putty knife
Tile grout
Cement stain
Rubber spreader
Nailbrush
Soft cloth

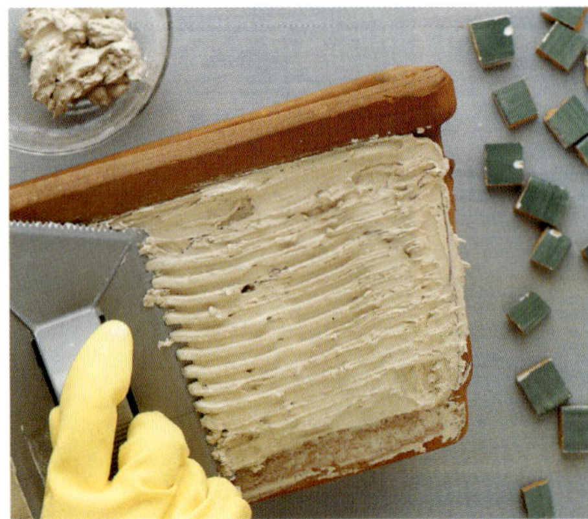

1 Snip the tiles into small pieces with tile nippers. You will need a selection of small squares of a single colour to create the borders, and random shapes in several different colours to fill the space between them. Use the notched trowel to apply tile adhesive generously to the sides of the planter.

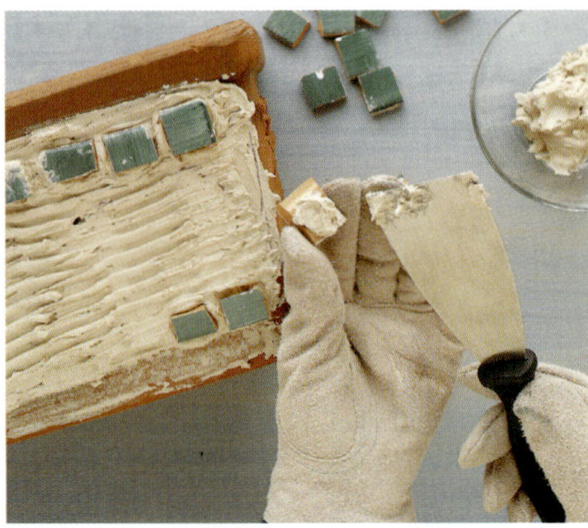

2 Using a putty knife, apply a small amount of tile adhesive to the back of the single-coloured square tesserae. Position them on the planter to form two straight lines parallel with the horizontal sides of the planter, making a border at the top and bottom edges of your pot.

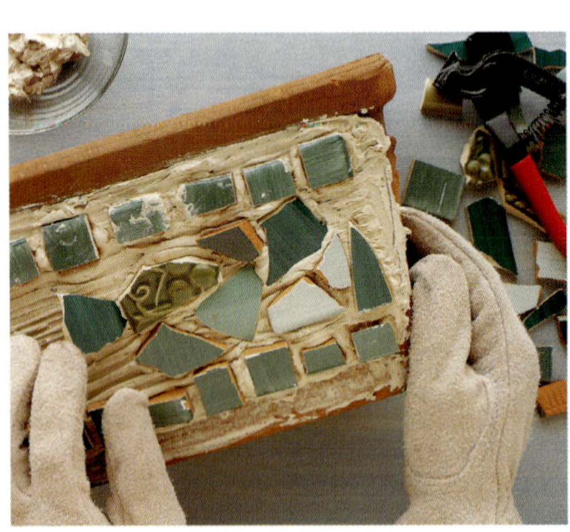

3 Fill in the central design in the same way with the randomly cut tesserae, mixing the colours to make an abstract design. Leave fairly large gaps of a consistent size between the tile pieces, as thick bands of coloured grout are part of the final design. Leave to dry for 24 hours.

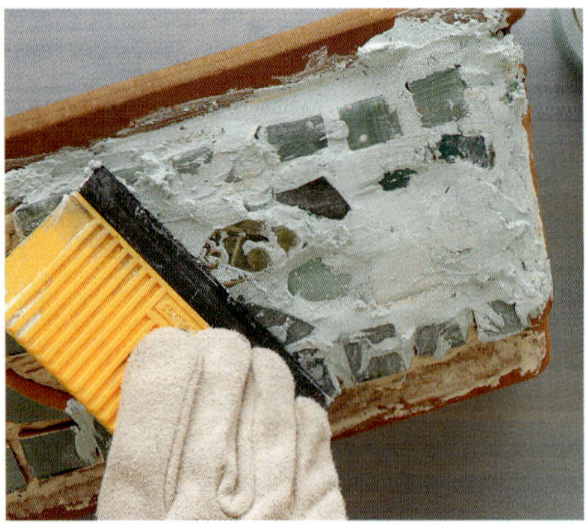

4 Mix the tile grout with a little cement stain. Using the rubber spreader, apply grout all over the surface of the planter, pressing right down between the tesserae. Wipe the spreader over the surface of the planter to make sure the grout is evenly applied. Allow the surface to dry.

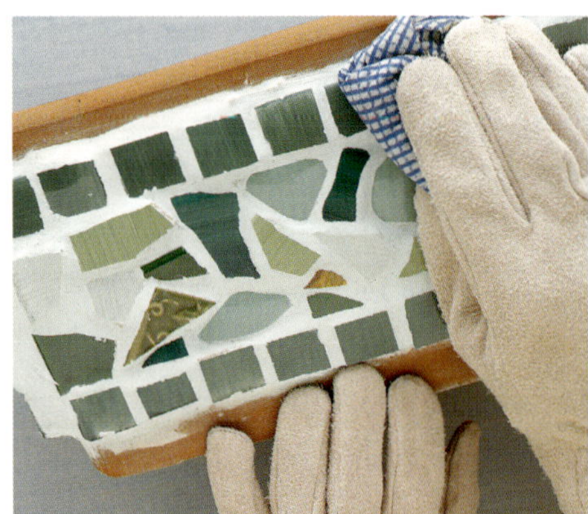

5 Brush off any excess grout with a nailbrush, then leave to dry for 48 hours. Polish with a dry, soft cloth.

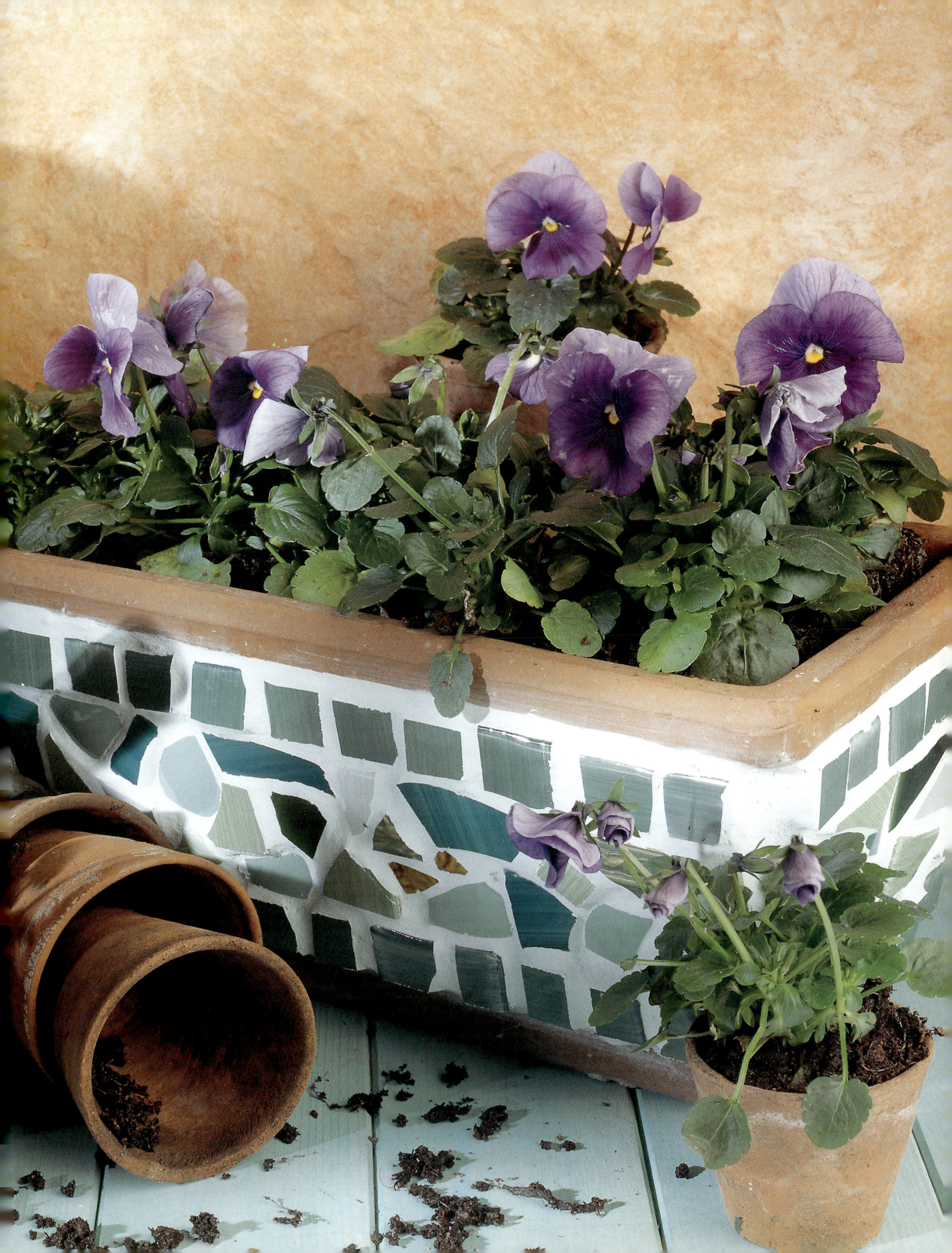

For this flowerpot, which combines both the functional and decorative qualities of mosaic, Cleo Mussi has chosen a design and colours that reflect the flowers to be planted in it. Squares of mirror add reflections.

Part-tiled Flowerpot

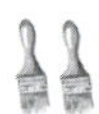

You will need

Ready-glazed, high-fired terracotta flowerpot
Chalk or wax crayon
Selection of china
Tile nippers
Tile adhesive
Flexible knife
Tile grout
Cement stain
Nailbrush
Soft cloth

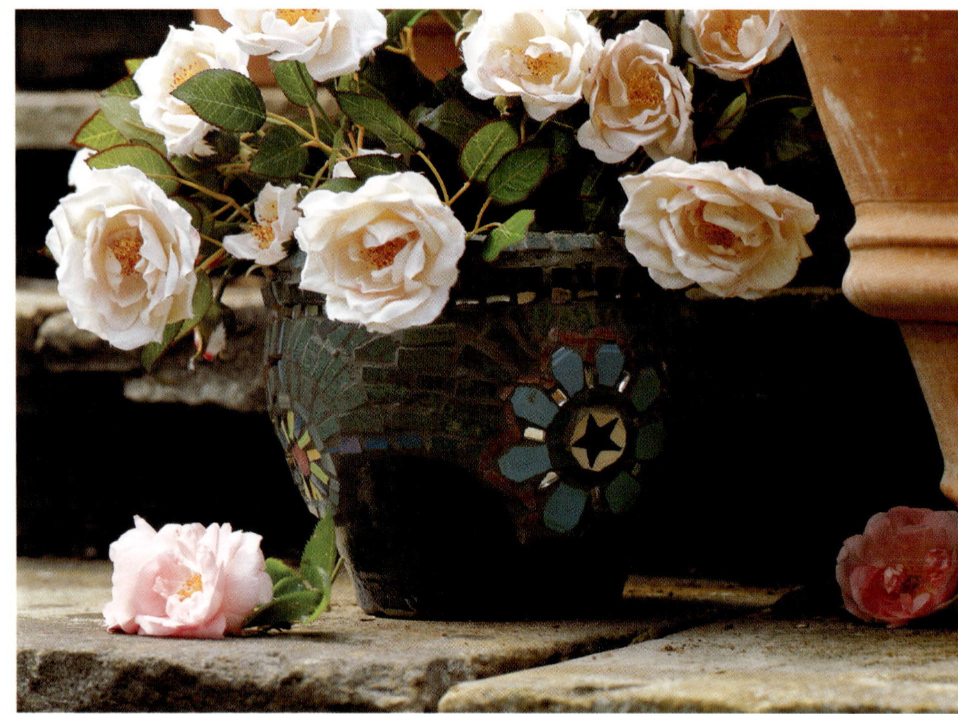

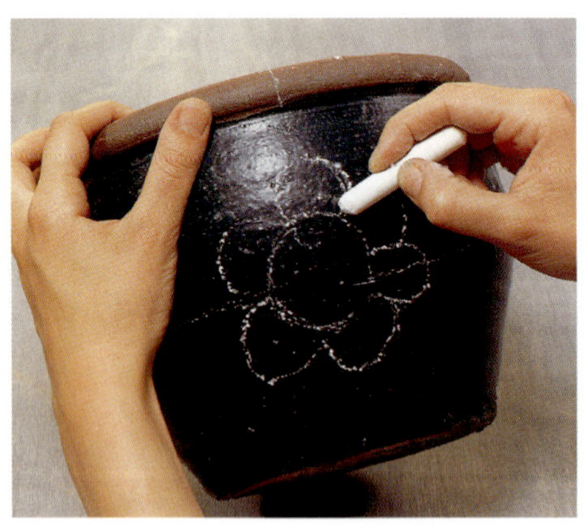

1 Draw a simple design on the pot, using chalk or a wax crayon. Cut appropriate shapes from the china using tile nippers. Use tile adhesive to fix the tesserae to the pot, spreading it with a flexible knife. Work first on the main lines and detailed areas, applying the adhesive to small areas at a time so you can follow the lines of the design.

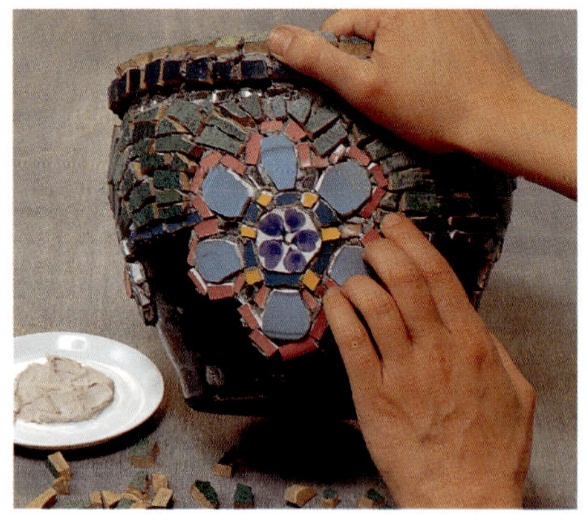

2 Fill in the larger areas of the design using tesserae in a plain colour. When these areas are complete, leave the pot to dry for 24 hours.

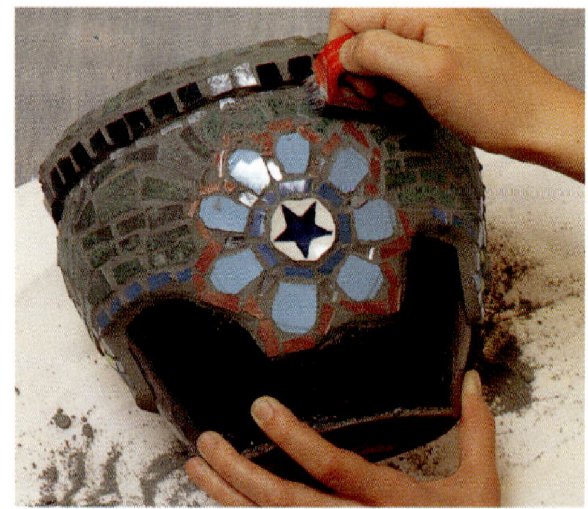

3 Mix the tile grout with a little cement stain, then spread the grout over the pot with your fingers, filling all the cracks between the tesserae. Allow the surface to dry, then brush off any excess grout with a nailbrush. After the pot has dried for about 48 hours polish it with a dry, soft cloth.

This sunflower mosaic is simple to make, and, if you have enough china, you could make several plaques to brighten up an outdoor wall using bright fragments of china in a harmonious blend of colours.

Sunflower Mosaic

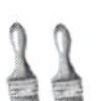

You will need

5mm (¼in) thick plywood sheet
Pencil
Coping saw or electric scroll saw
Abrasive paper (sandpaper)
Bradawl
Electric cable
Wire cutters
Masking tape
PVA (white) glue
Paintbrushes
White undercoat
China fragments
Mirror strips
Tile nippers
Tile adhesive
Tile grout
Cement stain
Nailbrush
Soft cloth

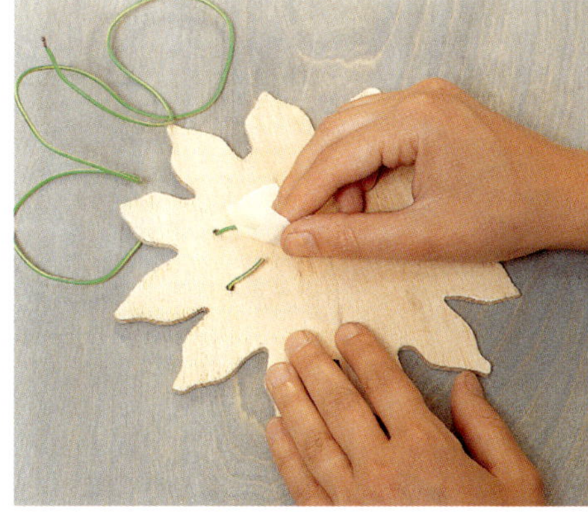

1 Draw a sunflower on the plywood. Cut it out with a saw and sand any rough edges. Make two holes in the plywood with a bradawl. Strip the cable and cut a short length of wire. Push the ends of the wire through the holes from the back and fix the ends with masking tape at the front. Seal the front with diluted PVA (white) glue and the back with white undercoat.

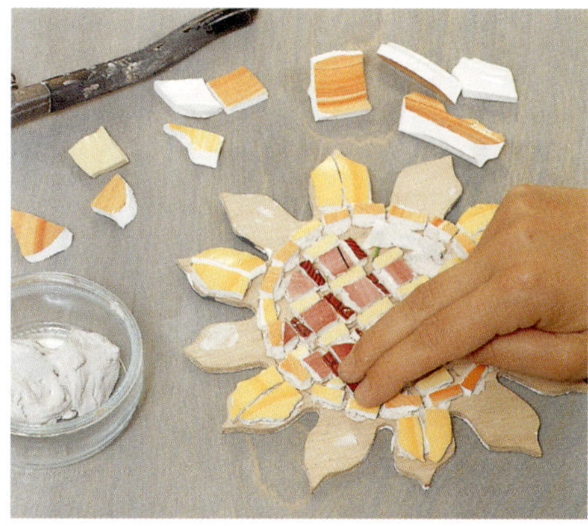

2 Using tile nippers, cut the china and mirror strips into irregular shapes. Dip each fragment in the tile adhesive and stick them to the plywood. Scoop up enough of it to cover the sticking surface; the tile adhesive needs to squelch out around the edge of the mosaic to make sure that it adheres securely. Leave the adhesive to dry thoroughly overnight.

3 Mix some cement stain with the grout. Press small amounts of grout into the gaps on the mosaic with your fingers. Leave to dry for about 5 minutes, then brush off any excess with a nailbrush. Leave again for 5 minutes and then polish well with a dry, soft cloth. Leave overnight to dry.

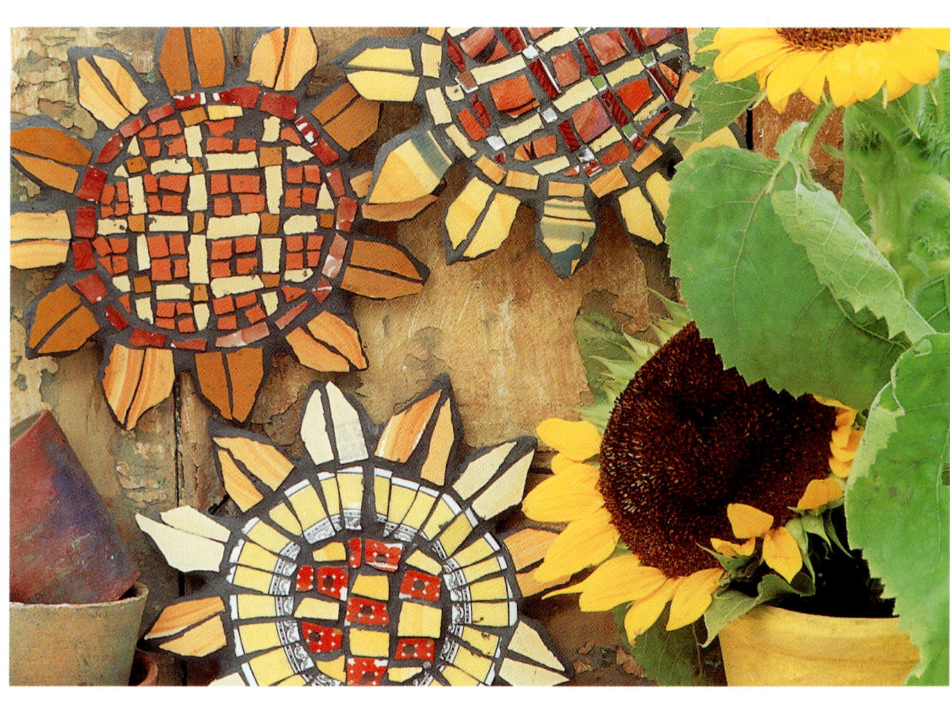

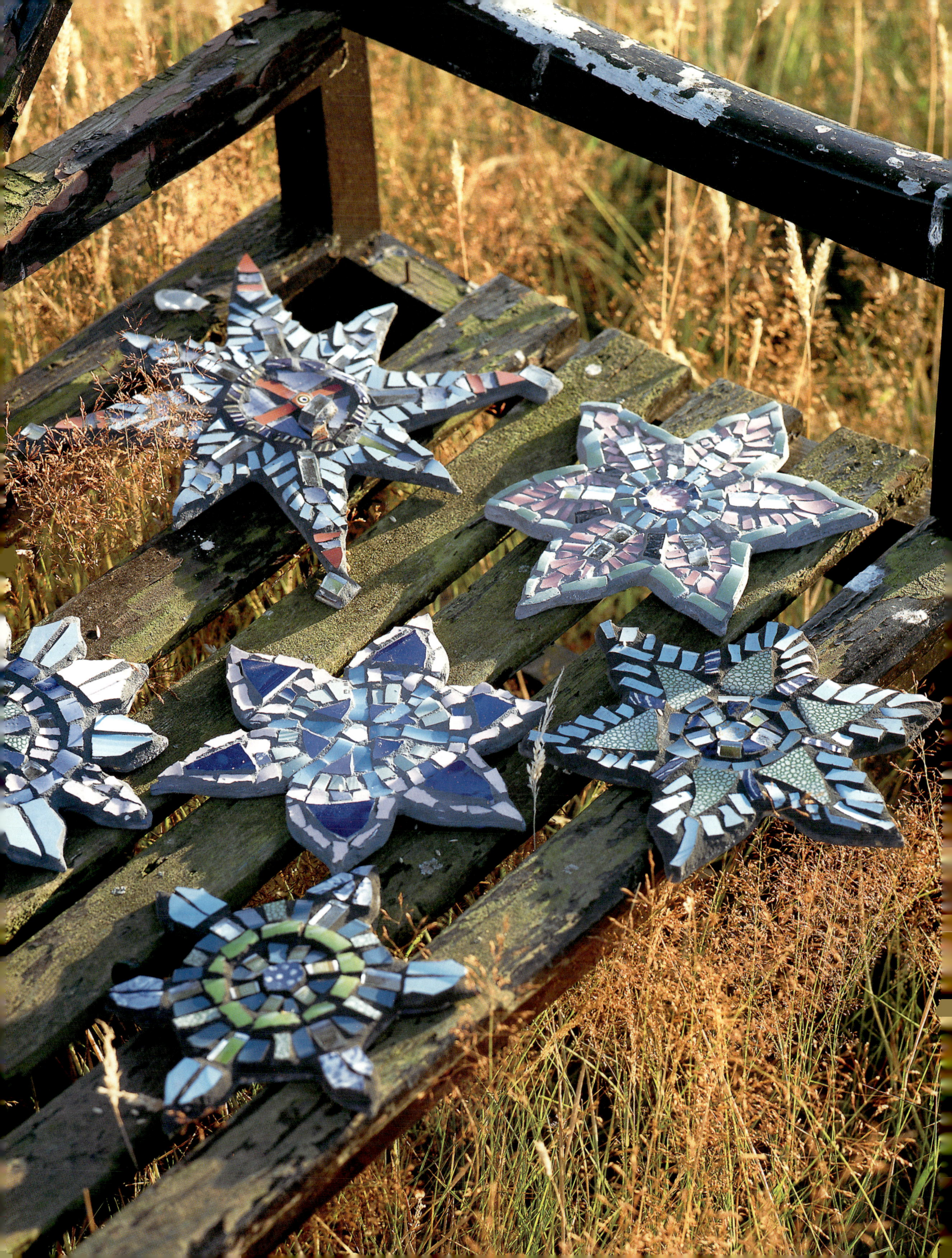

These little star-shaped wall motifs have been created by Cleo Mussi to add sparkling focal points to a garden. They are particularly effective when displayed in clusters or surrounded by lush foliage.

Star Wall Motifs

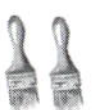

You will need

- 3mm (⅛in) thick plywood sheet
- Pencil
- Set square (triangle)
- Ruler
- Pair of compasses
- Coping saw or electric scroll saw
- Abrasive paper (sandpaper)
- PVA (white) glue
- Paintbrushes
- Bradawl
- Wood primer
- White undercoat paint
- Gloss or matt (flat) paint
- Wire
- Wire cutters
- Adhesive tape
- Selection of china
- Mirror
- Tile nippers
- Tile adhesive
- Tile grout
- Cement stain
- Nailbrush
- Soft cloth

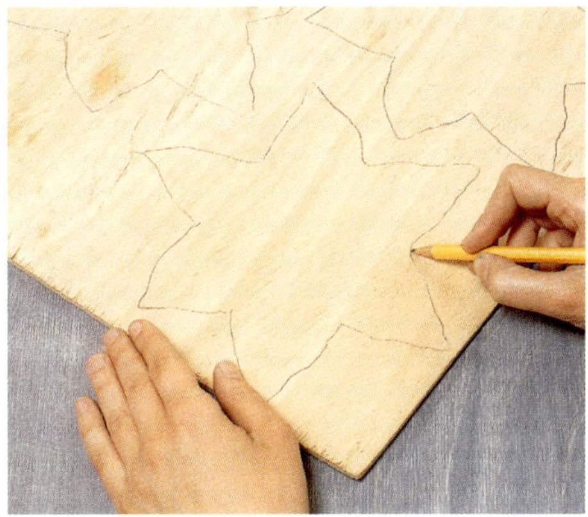

1 Draw a star motif on a sheet of plywood, using a pencil, set square (triangle), ruler and pair of compasses.

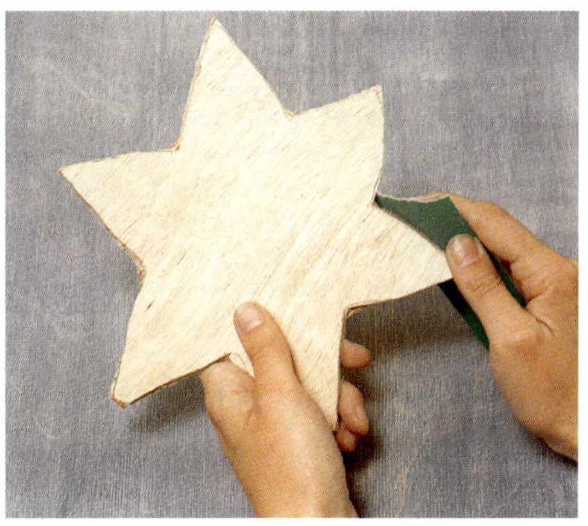

2 Cut out the star using a coping saw or an electric scroll saw. Sand down any rough edges, then seal one side with diluted PVA (white) glue.

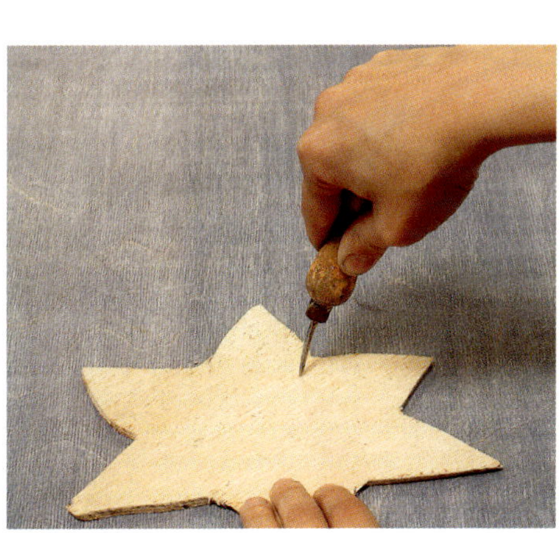

3 Make two small holes through the star using a bradawl.

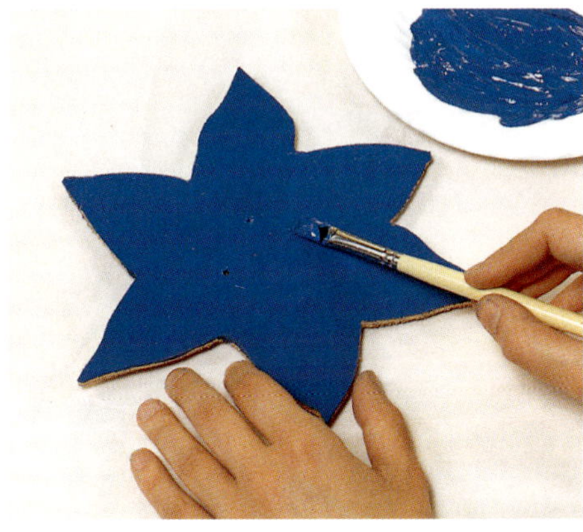

4 Paint the unsealed side with wood primer, then undercoat and finish with a coat of gloss or matt (flat) paint. Allow each coat to dry before applying the next.

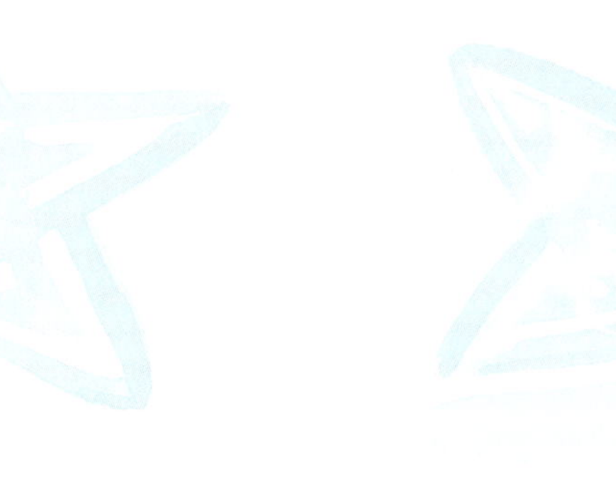

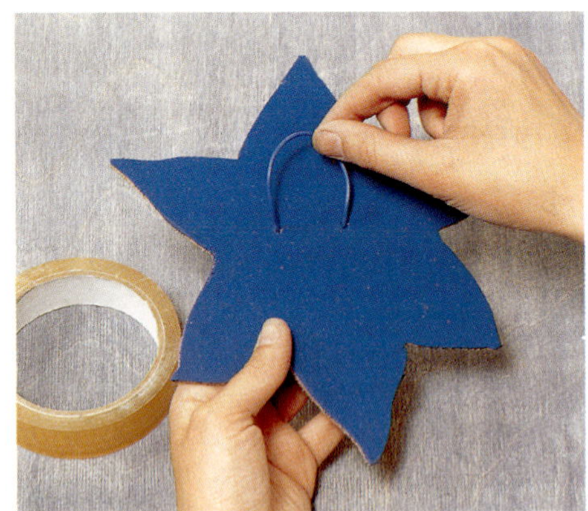

5 Cut a short length of wire and bend it into a loop for hanging the star. Push the ends through the holes in the star from the painted side and secure them to the front with adhesive tape.

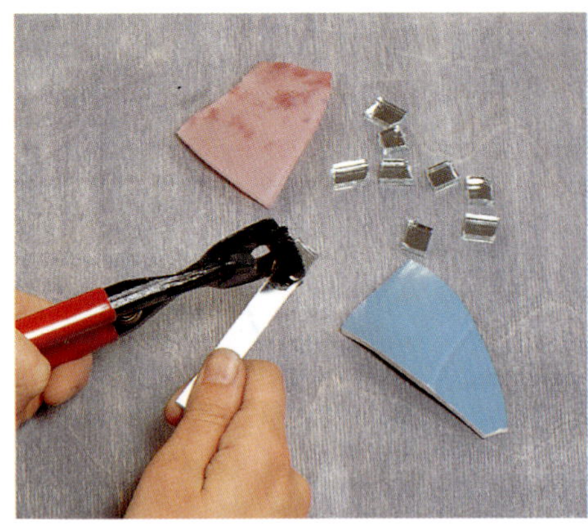

6 Snip the china and mirror into small pieces using the tile nippers, then arrange these tesserae into groups according to colour and shape.

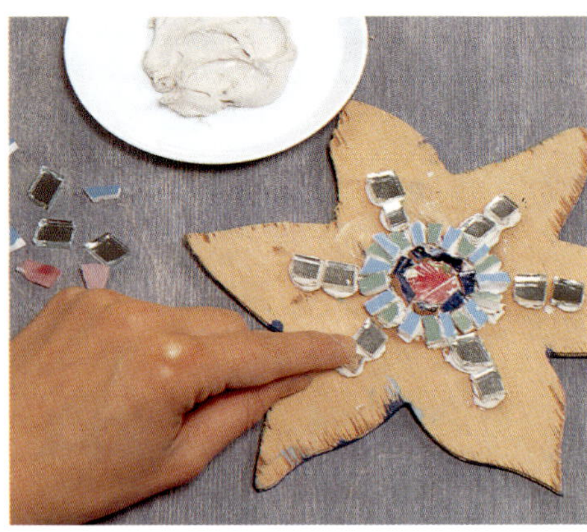

7 Stick the china and mirror tesserae to the surface of the star, one piece at a time. Take each tessera and dip it into the tile adhesive, or paint some on with a brush, making sure enough is on the tessera to ooze a little from under its edges when pressed on to the base. Cover the surface of the star in this way, then leave overnight to dry.

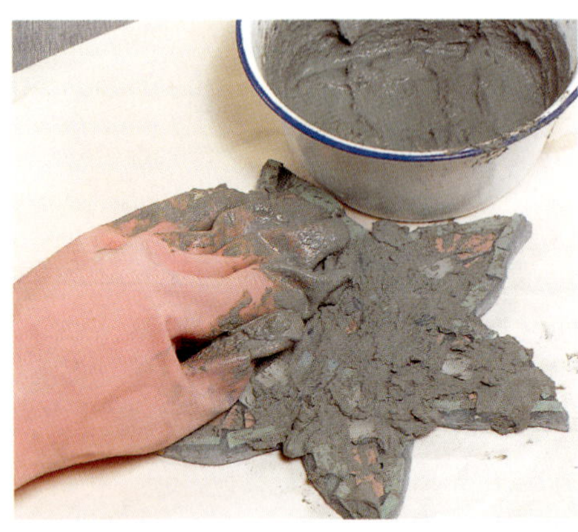

8 Mix the desired quantity of grout with some cement stain. Wearing rubber (latex) gloves, rub the grout into all the gaps between the tesserae. Leave to dry for a few minutes.

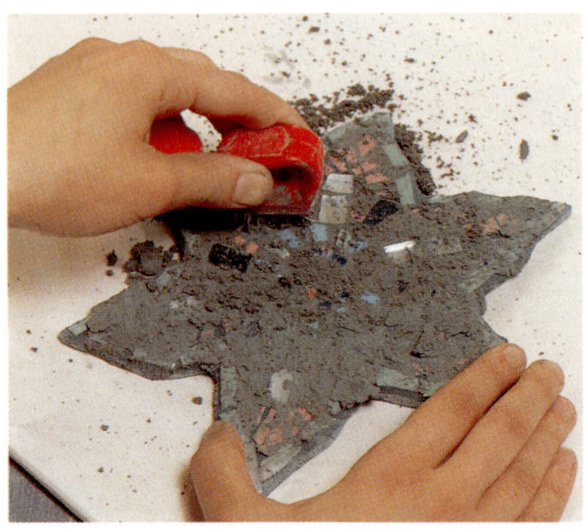

9 Using a nailbrush, gently remove all the excess grout. This should brush away as powder; if it does not, the grout is still too damp, so leave to dry for a few more minutes before brushing again.

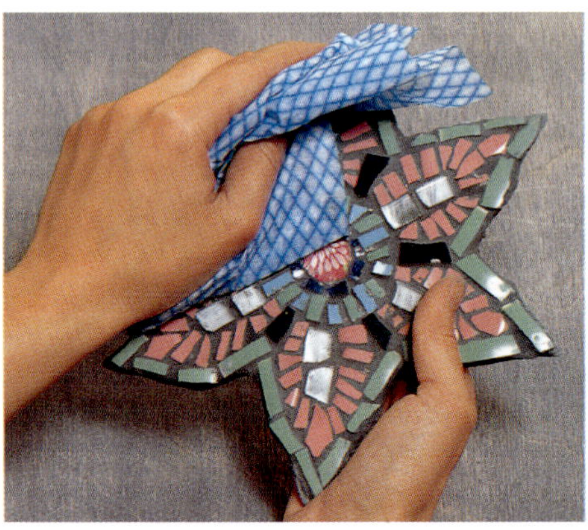

10 Polish the surface with a soft, dry cloth, then leave to dry for 24 hours before hanging outside.

In this unusual modern design, the coloured grout forms a major feature, with untiled areas left to show it off. Within this design, the tesserae appear as separate decorative elements, rather than parts of a whole.

Funky Fruit Bowl

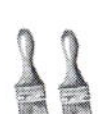

You will need

Soft dark pencil
Terracotta bowl
Vitreous glass mosaic tiles: yellow, turquoise and white
Tile nippers
PVA (white) glue
Paintbrush
White glazed ceramic household tiles
Matt (flat) coloured glass nuggets
Fabric stain
Flexible knife
Tile grout
Rubber spreader
Sponge
Soft cloth

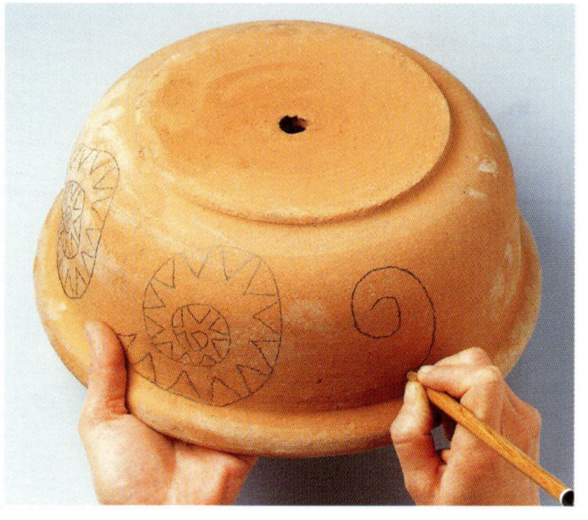

1 Using a soft pencil, draw freehand spirals on the outside of the bowl, as shown. Each spiral should be about the same depth as the pot. Mark a row of triangles along the edges of each spiral.

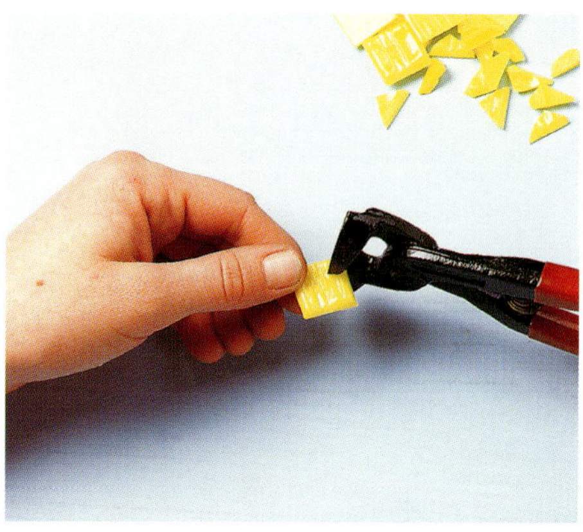

2 Using tile nippers, cut the glass tiles into small, equal-sized triangles, to fit the triangles drawn on the bowl.

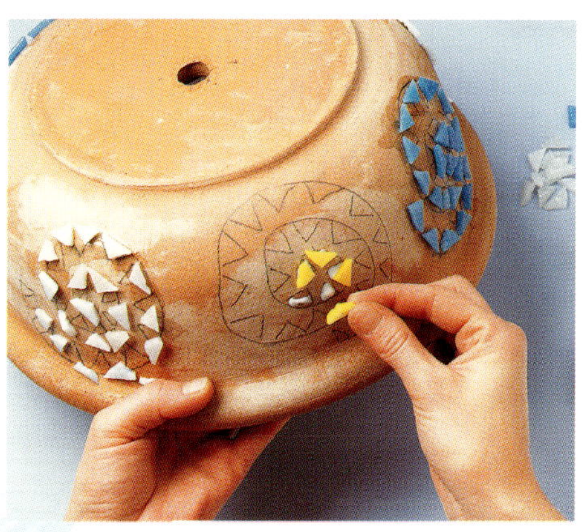

3 Place a small blob of PVA (white) glue on each pencilled triangle, then press on a glass triangle. Hold the tesserae in place until they stick.

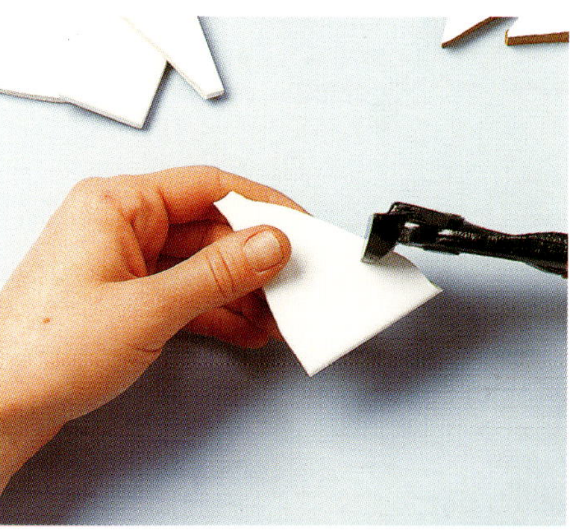

4 Using tile nippers, cut the white ceramic tiles into large triangles of equal size.

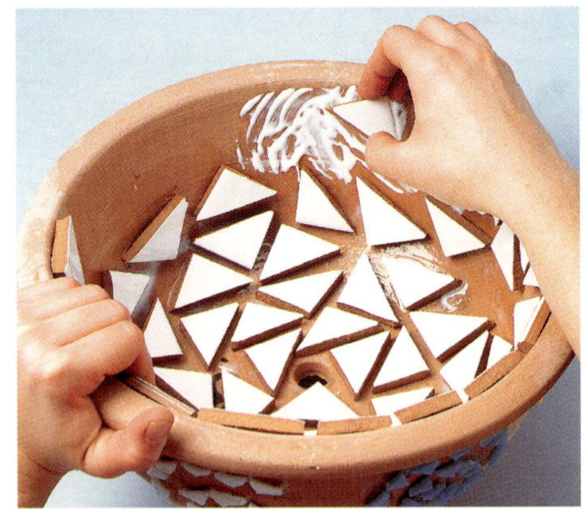

5 Apply a thick layer of glue over the inside of the bowl and over the back of each triangle. Press the triangles in place, leaving large gaps between them.

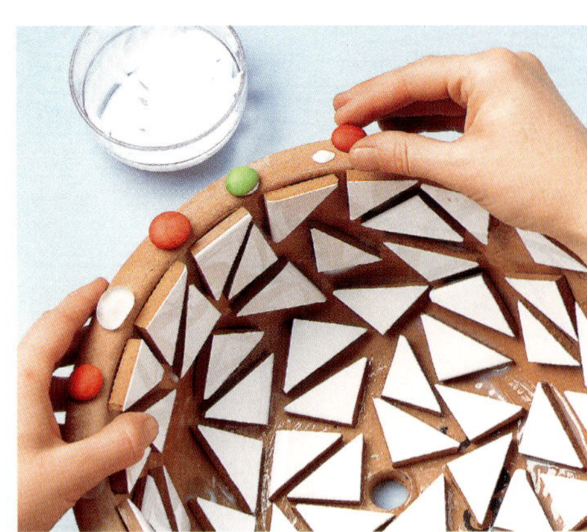

6 Dot blobs of glue at regular intervals around the rim of the bowl and press in the glass nuggets. Leave to dry overnight.

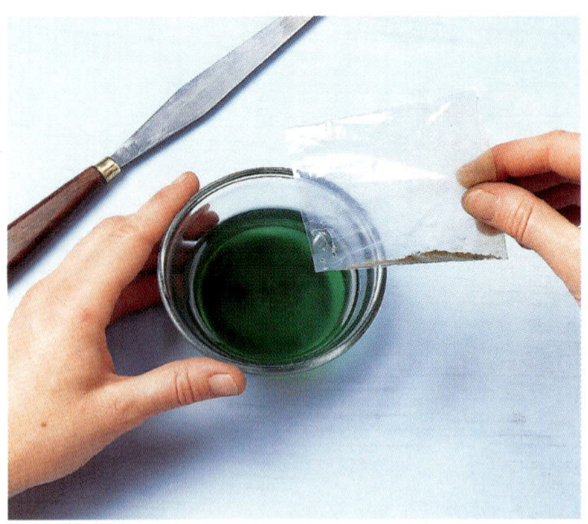

7 Mix the fabric stain with water. You can choose any of the many colours available. Bright primary colours will work well with this design.

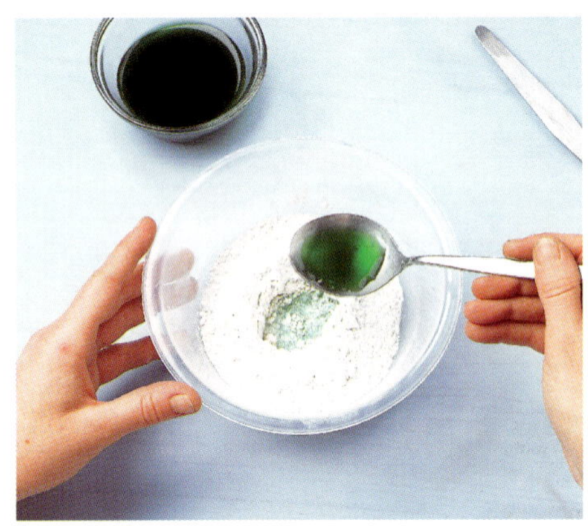

8 Gradually add the stain to the tile grout, a spoonful at a time, and mix thoroughly. The final colour of the grout once it has dried will be slightly lighter than its colour when wet.

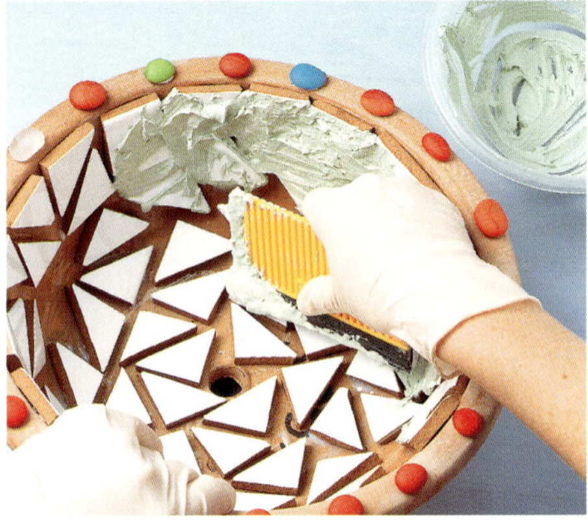

9 Using a rubber spreader, spread the coloured grout over the entire bowl, evening out the surface. Gently smooth it all over the bowl with your hands. Wipe off the excess grout with a damp sponge. Leave to dry for 1 hour.

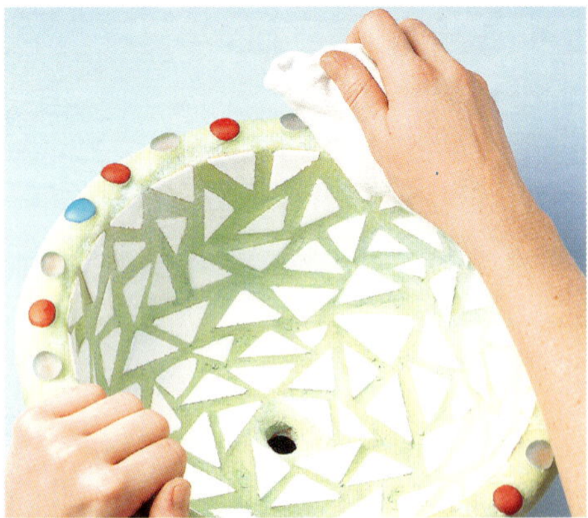

10 Polish the surface of the bowl with a dry, soft cloth, removing any residual tile grout.

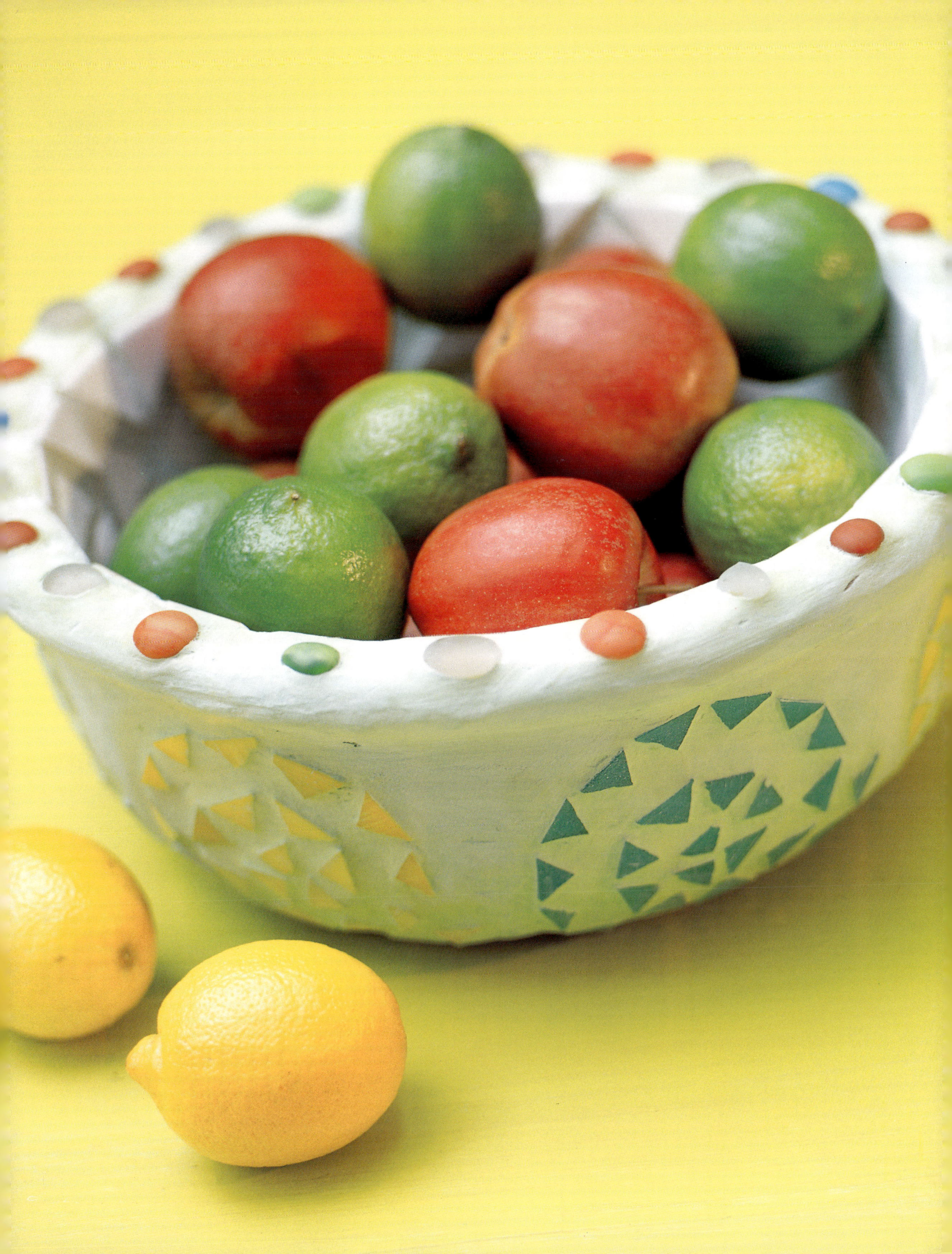

This unusual design is shown here as a mirror frame, but a similar frame could just as easily be used to frame a photograph or favourite picture. Only two colours are used, although the grouting is a third element.

Squiggle Frame

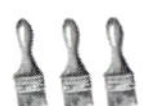

You will need

9mm (⅜in) thick plywood
Jigsaw (saber saw)
PVA (white) glue
Paintbrush
Glazed ceramic household tiles:
6 blue, 10 black
Dishtowel
Hammer
Pencils
Tracing paper
Tape measure
Carbon paper
Thick felt-tipped pen
Tile adhesive
Admix
Tile grout
Rubber spreader
Sponge
Soft cloth
Mirror

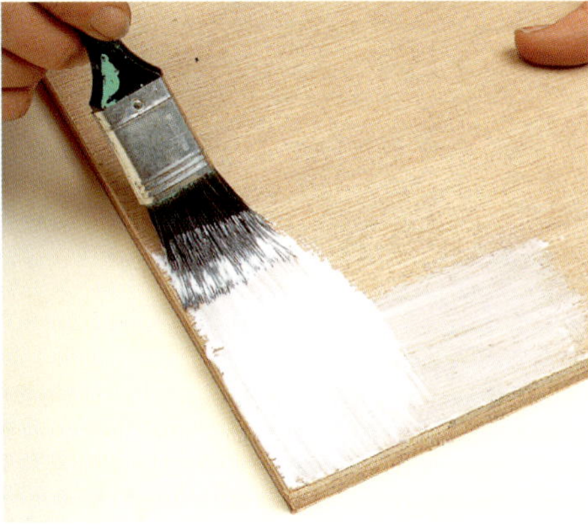

1 Cut a sheet of plywood measuring 50 x 70cm (20 x 28in) with a jigsaw (saber saw). Using a large brush, prime the wood by coating it all over with diluted PVA (white) glue. Leave it to dry for 24 hours.

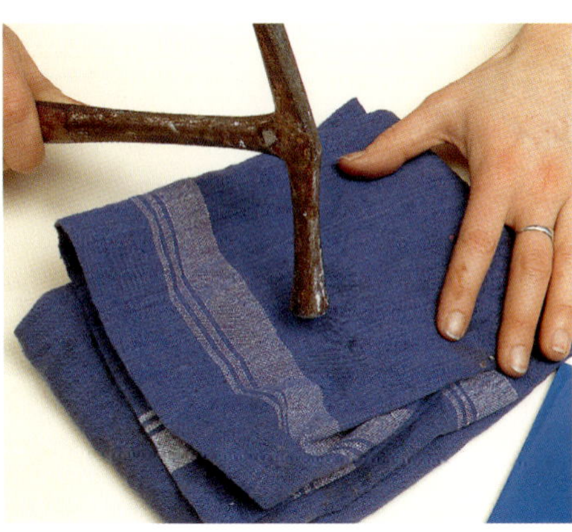

2 Place two blue tiles face down on a dishtowel and fold over the edges. Using a hammer, smash the tiles repeatedly, checking from time to time until they are roughly broken into manageable fragments, keeping the blue and black pieces in separate piles.

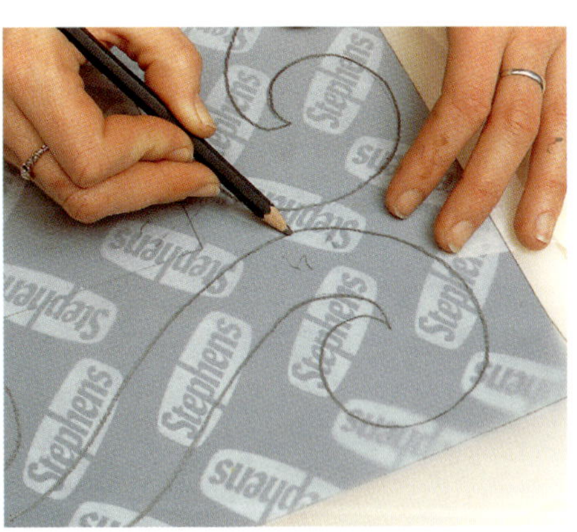

3 Draw around the plywood sheet on a large sheet of tracing paper, then draw an inner rectangle of 39 x 60cm (16 x 24in). Sketch one scroll design on the tracing paper, then use sheets of carbon paper to transfer your design onto the plywood, flipping the tracing paper to repeat a mirror image another five times. Go over with a thick pen.

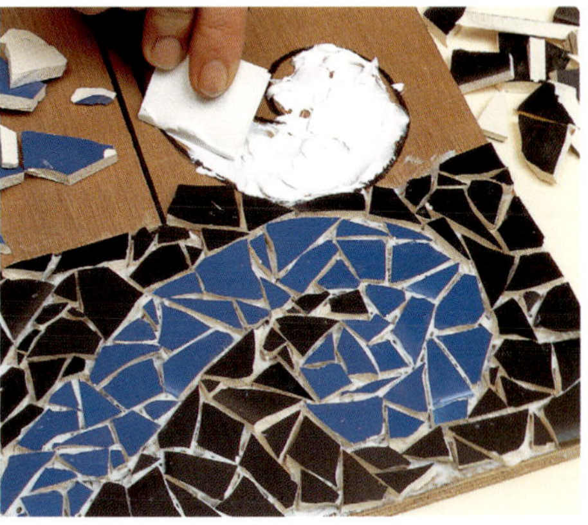

4 Mix some tile adhesive with admix, then spread it 3mm (⅛in) thick over a small section of one of the scrolls, removing any excess. Working from the scroll edge out, fill in the blue tiles, and repeat until the frame is covered. Allow 24 hours for the adhesive to dry.

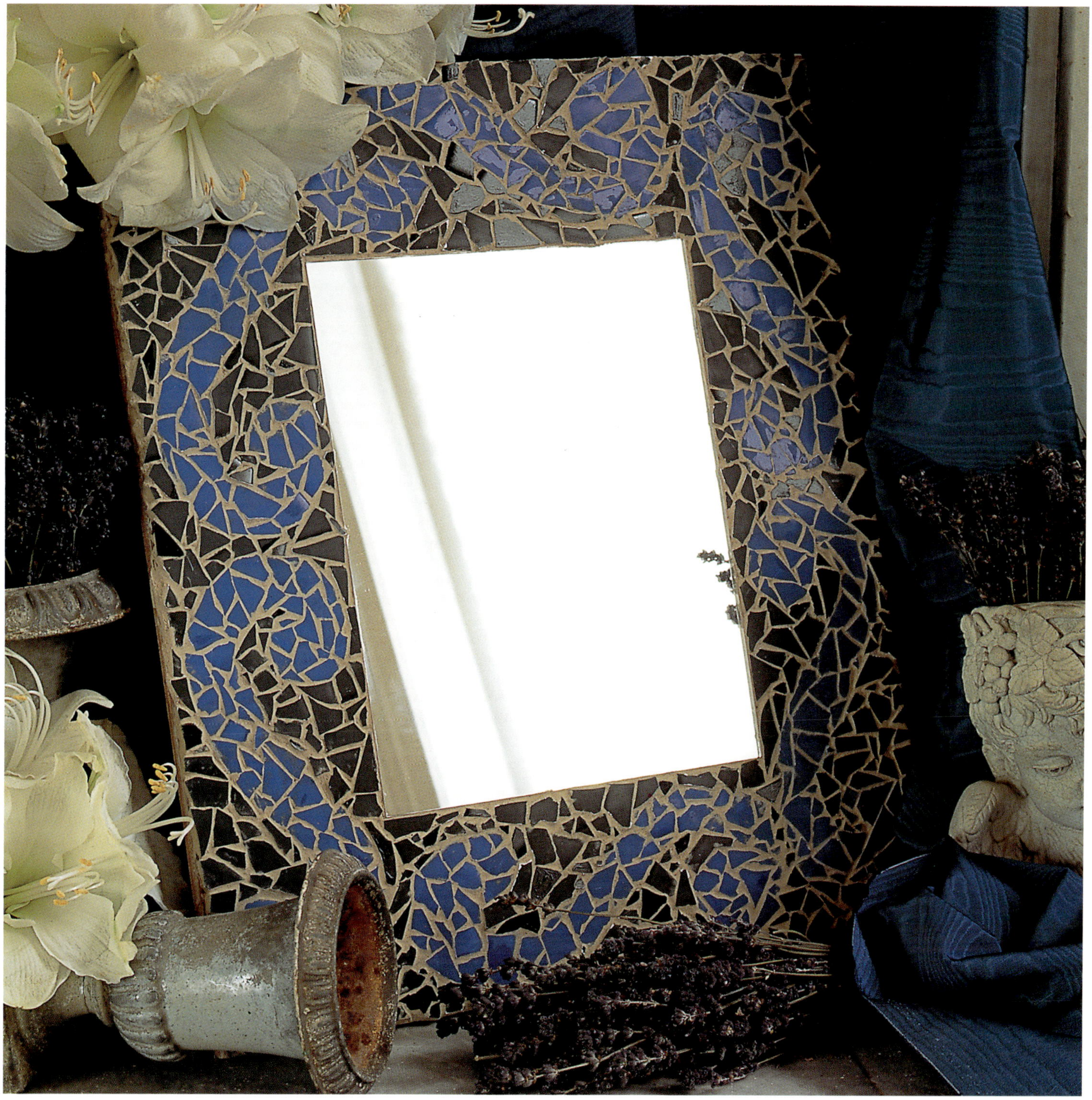

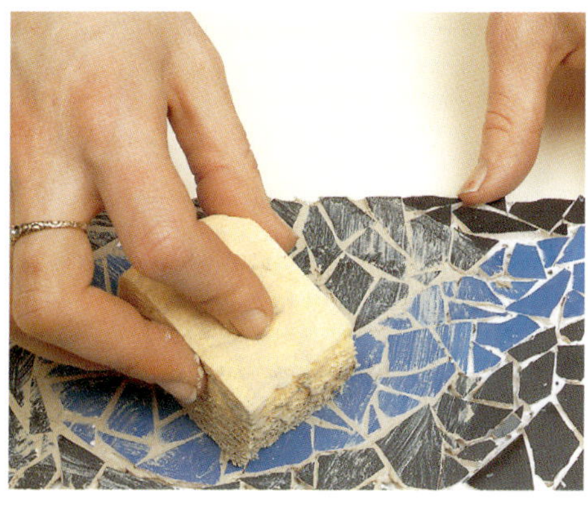

5 Spread some tile grout over the mosaic with a rubber spreader, using a circular motion. Continue until the grout fills all the gaps and is level with the tesserae. Sponge away any surface grout with a damp sponge. Allow to dry for 1 hour, then polish with a dry, soft cloth to rub off any residual grout. Glue the mirror in place.

Small mosaic tiles make an attractive Mediterranean-style frame. To keep the project simple, plan the dimensions of the frame to suit the size of the tiles, so avoiding having to cut and fit odd-shaped pieces.

Mediterranean Mirror

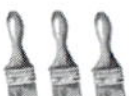

You will need

2cm (¾in) thick MDF (medium-density fiberboard)
Pencil
Saw
Drill
Jigsaw (saber saw)
Wood glue
White acrylic primer
Paintbrush
Tile adhesive
Grout spreader
Vitreous glass mosaic tiles: blues, greens, and yellows
Tile grout
Soft cloth
Mirror
Narrow frame moulding
2 ring screws and brass picture wire

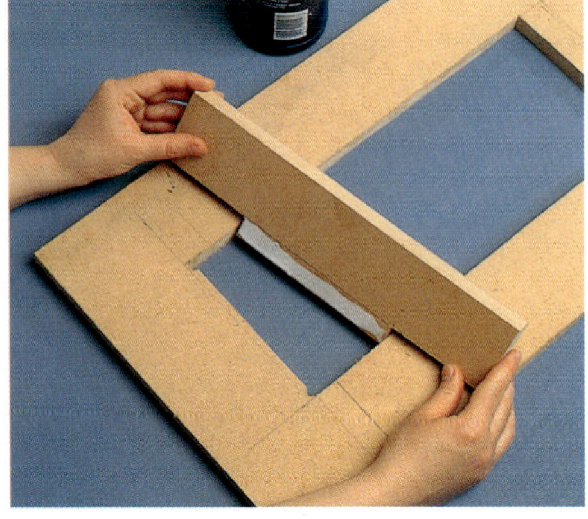

1 Draw a rectangular frame on MDF (medium-density fiberboard). Cut it out using a saw. Drill corner holes for the centre and cut this out with a jigsaw (saber saw). Cut out a shelf and glue it to the frame with wood glue. Allow to dry.

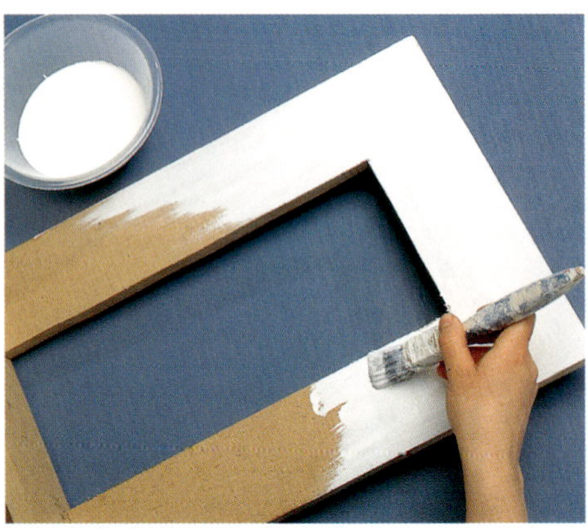

2 Prime both sides of the frame and shelf with white acrylic primer to seal it. Allow to dry. Apply tile adhesive to a small area of the frame, using the fine-notched side of a grout spreader.

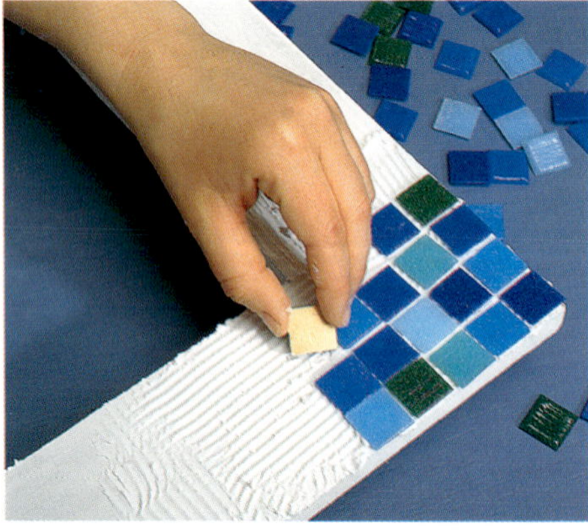

3 Apply a random selection of tiles, leaving a 2mm (1/16in) gap between them. Complete the frame, working on a small area at a time. Tile the edges with a single row of tiles.

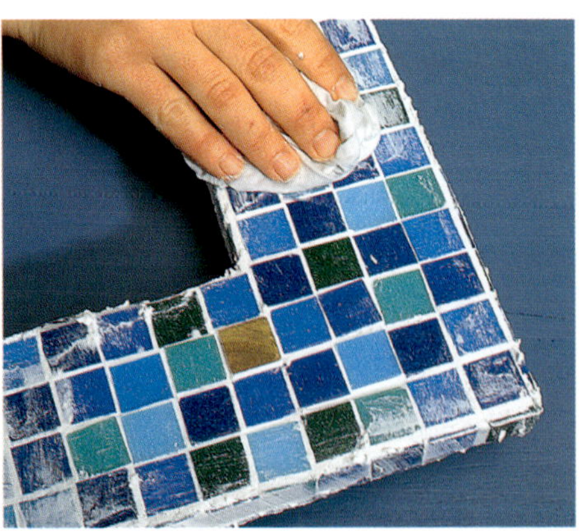

4 Allow the tile adhesive to dry. Wearing rubber (latex) gloves, spread grout over the surface of the tiles with the grout spreader. Scrape off the excess with the spreader and clean off any remaining grout with a soft cloth. Leave to dry thoroughly.

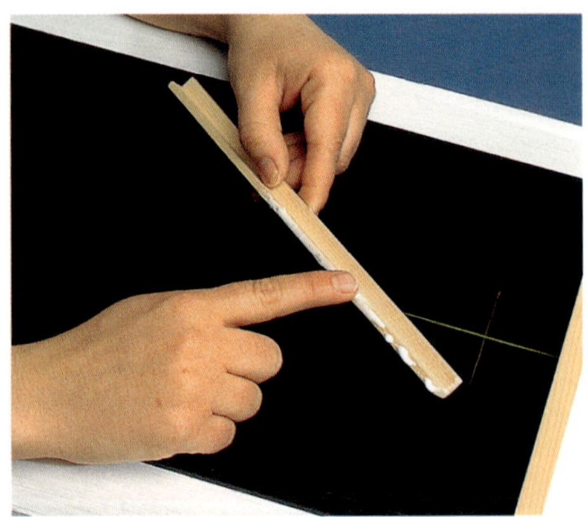

5 Place the mirror face down on the back of the frame and secure it with narrow frame moulding, glued in place with wood glue. Allow to dry.

Screw two ring screws in place on the back of the mirror, more than halfway up the side towards the top, and tie on picture wire securely, to hang it on a wall.

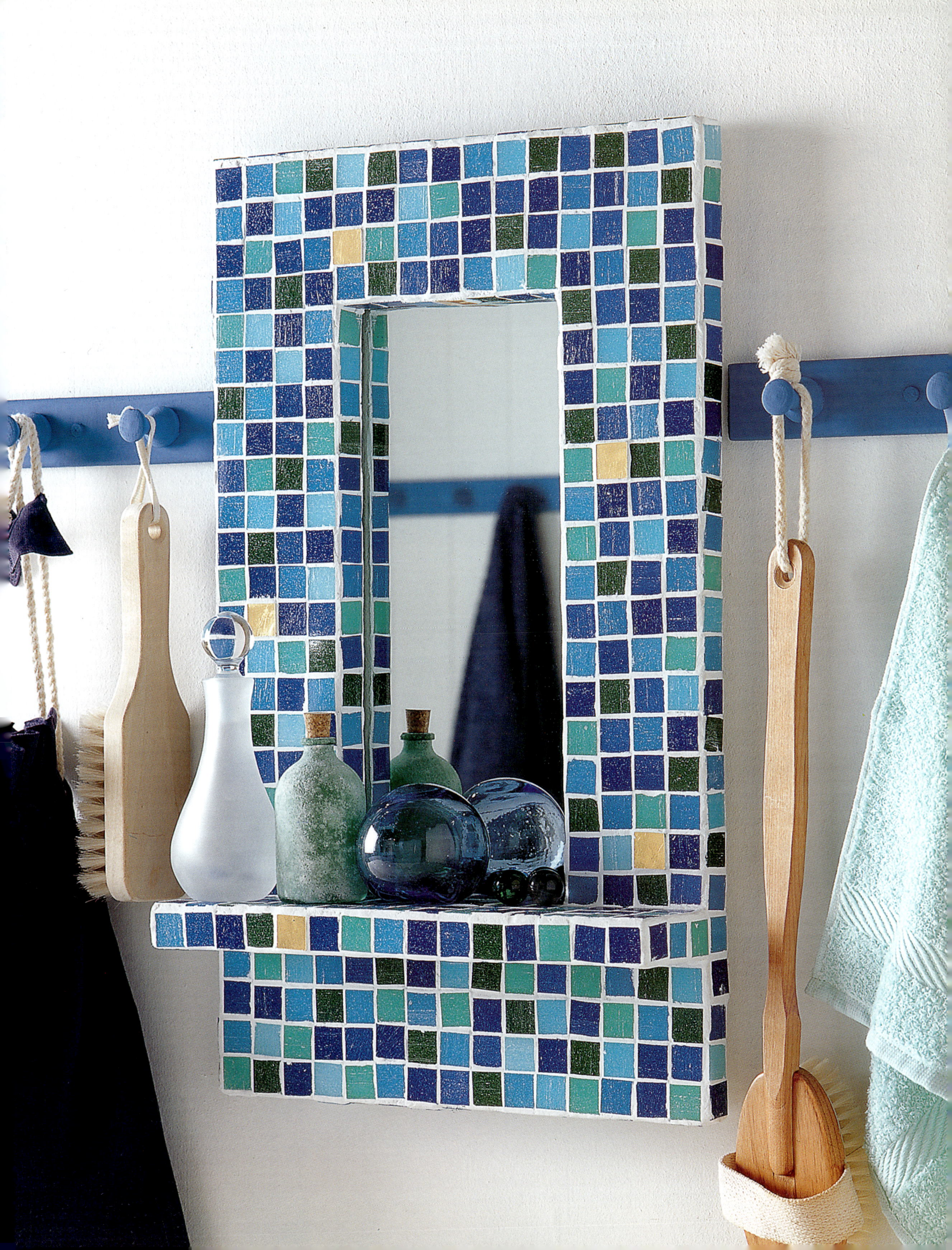

Gently spiralling bands of mosaic look very effective on a tall, elegantly shaped vase. The top and base of the vase are given a marble finish to enclose the rest of the mosaic.

Spiral Vase

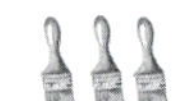

You will need

Tall vase
Yacht varnish and paintbrush (optional)
White chalk
Marble tile
Piece of sacking (heavy cloth)
Hammer
Tile adhesive
Flexible knife
Glazed ceramic household tiles:
pale blue and royal blue
Gold smalti
Tile nippers
Notched spreader or cloth pad
Sponge
Abrasive paper (sandpaper)
Soft cloth

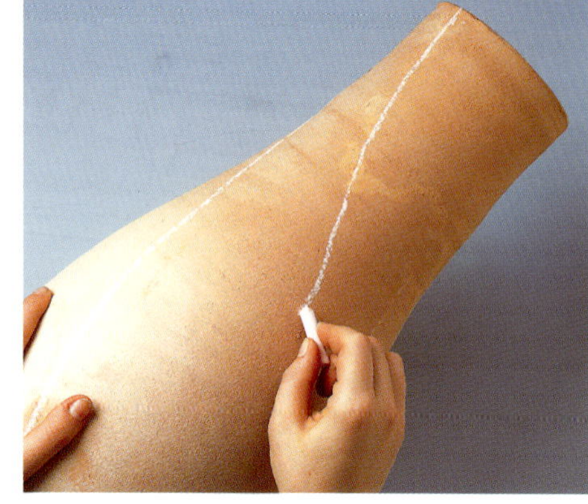

1 If your vase is unglazed, seal it by painting all around the inside top lip with yacht varnish. Using a piece of white chalk, draw lines spiralling gently from the rim of the vase to the base. Make sure you have an even number of bands and that they are regularly spaced.

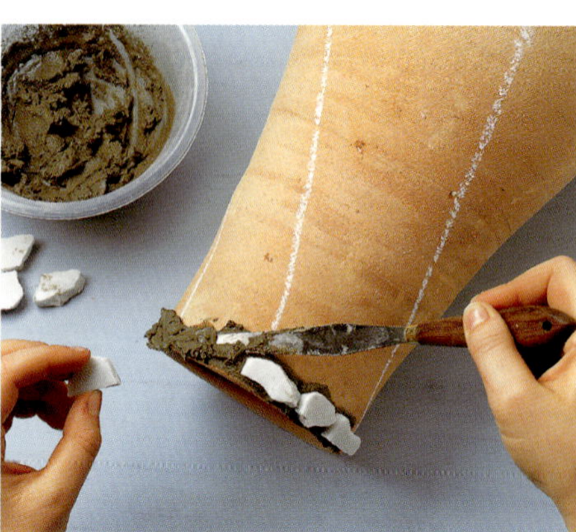

2 Wrap the marble tile in sacking (heavy cloth), then break it up using a hammer. Using a flexible knife, spread a thin band of tile adhesive around the top and bottom of the vase, press in the marble pieces and leave to dry overnight.

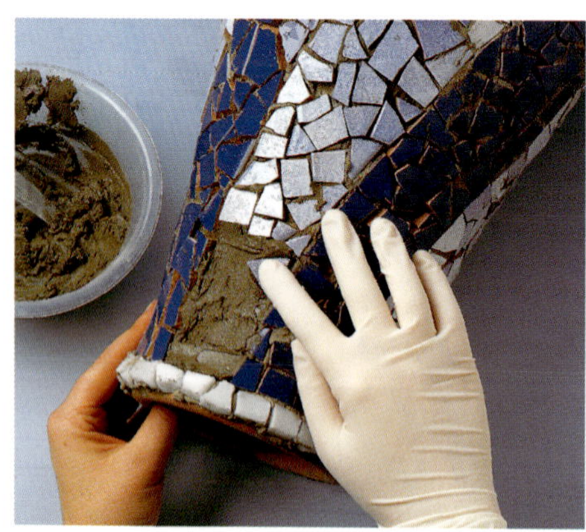

3 Using a hammer and a piece of sacking, break up all the pale blue and royal blue tiles. Spread tile adhesive over the vase, a band at a time, and press in the tesserae, alternating the two colours. Leave to dry, preferably overnight.

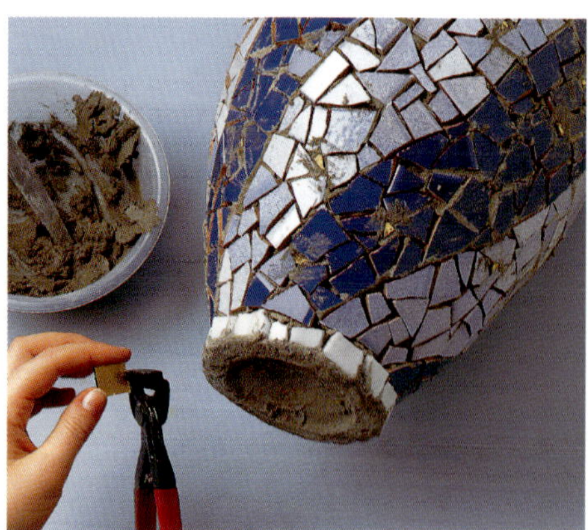

4 Use the tile nippers to cut the gold smalti into small pieces. Using the flexible knife, place blobs of adhesive in the larger gaps between the blue tesserae. Press the gold smalti pieces at random over the blue spirals, checking that they are all level with the rest of the tiles. Leave to dry overnight.

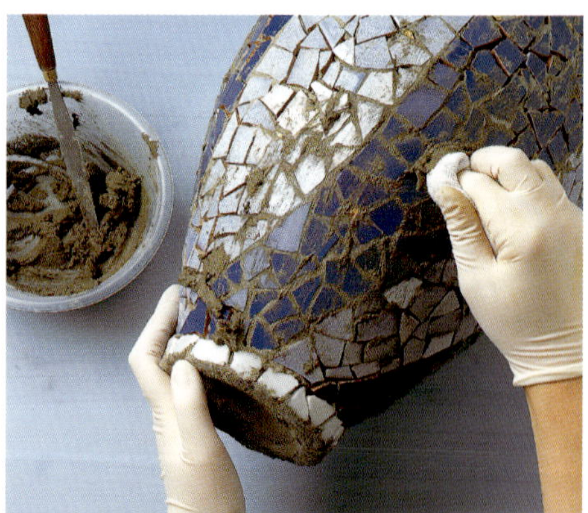

5 Using a notched spreader or cloth pad, rub more tile adhesive in the colour of your choice over the surface of the mosaic, carefully filling all the gaps. Wipe off the excess with a damp sponge and leave to dry overnight. Sand off any adhesive dried on the surface, then polish with a dry, soft cloth.

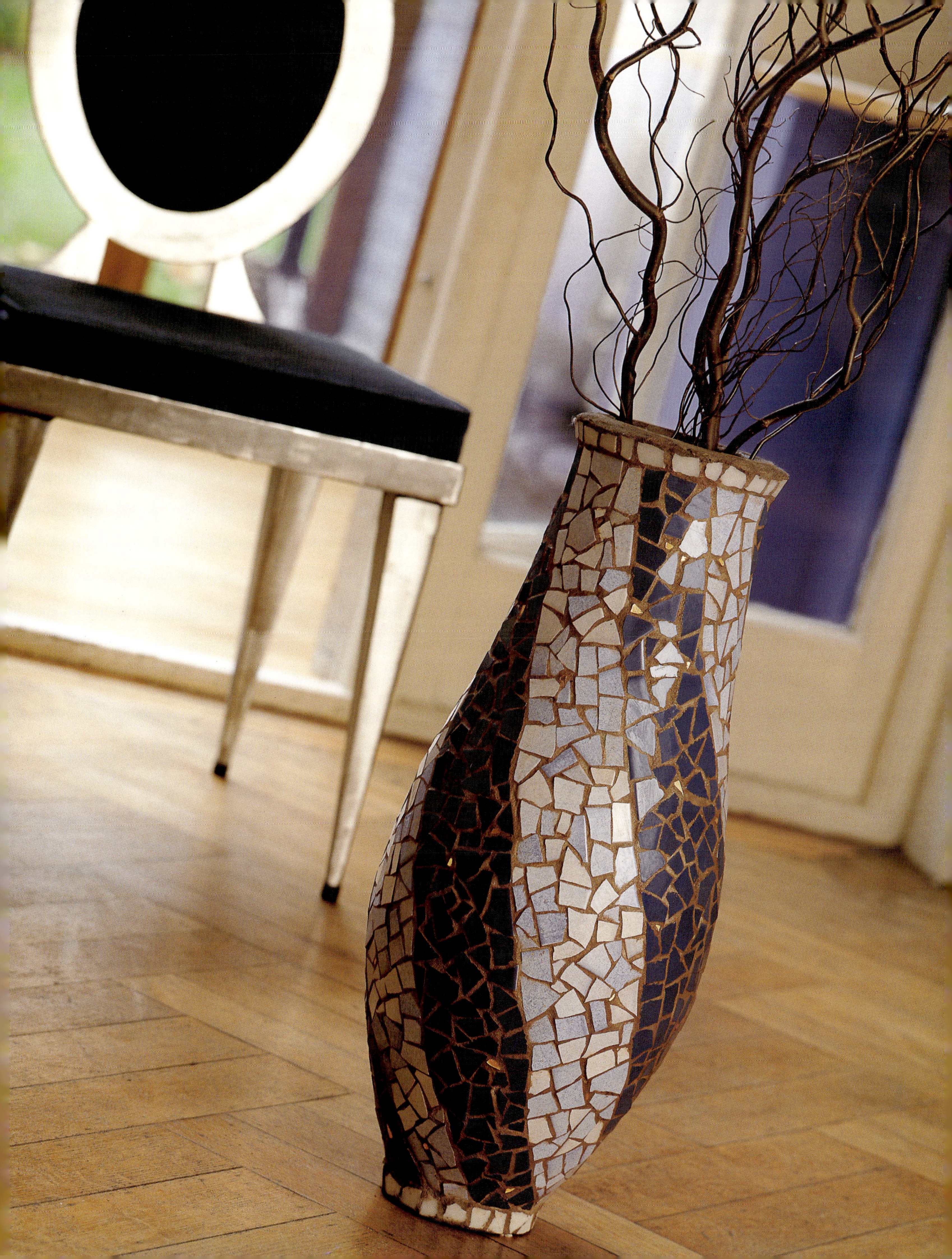

This design is simple to execute and adds a naïve charm to a plain wooden tray. The semi-indirect method of laying the tiles used here helps to keep the surface of the mosaic smooth and flat.

Country Cottage Tray

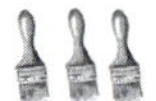

You will need

Wooden tray
Scissors
Brown paper
Pencil
Vitreous glass mosaic tiles in various colours
Tile nippers
Water-soluble glue
White spirit (paint thinner)
PVA (white) glue
Paintbrush
Bradawl
Masking tape
Tile adhesive
Notched spreader
Sponge
Soft cloth

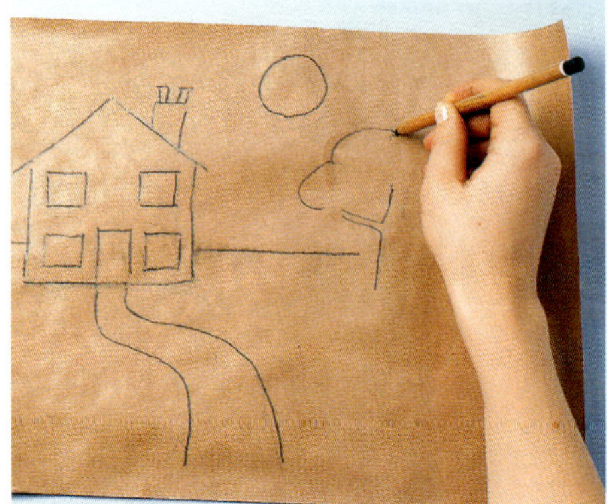

1 Cut a piece of brown paper to fit the bottom of the wooden tray. Draw a country cottage scene in pencil. Plan out the colour scheme for the picture, then, using the tile nippers, cut all of the vitreous glass tiles into quarters.

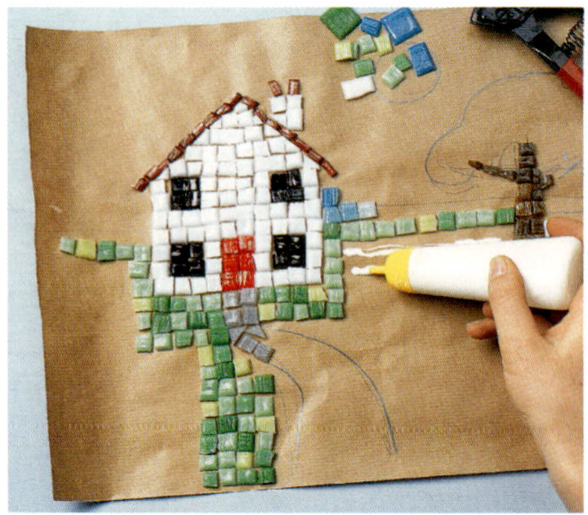

2 Position the tesserae on to the paper to check your design before going any further. Once you are satisfied with the design, apply water-soluble glue on to the paper in small areas, and stick the tesserae on, face down. Take care to obscure any pencil marks. Trim the tesserae to fit if necessary.

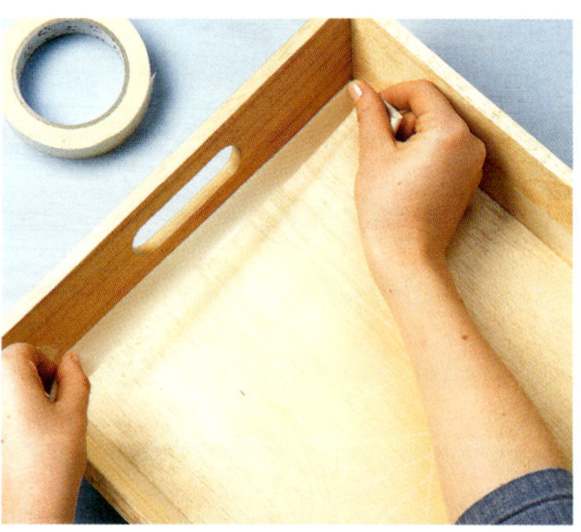

3 Prepare the bottom of the tray by removing any varnish or polish with white spirit (paint thinner). Prime with diluted PVA (white) glue, leave it to dry, then score it with a sharp instrument such as a bradawl. Protect the sides with masking tape.

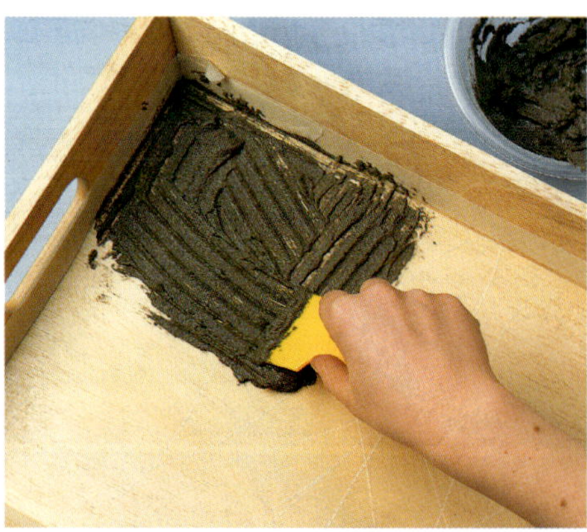

4 Spread an even layer of tile adhesive over the bottom of the tray, using a notched spreader. Cover the tray completely and spread the adhesive well into the corners.

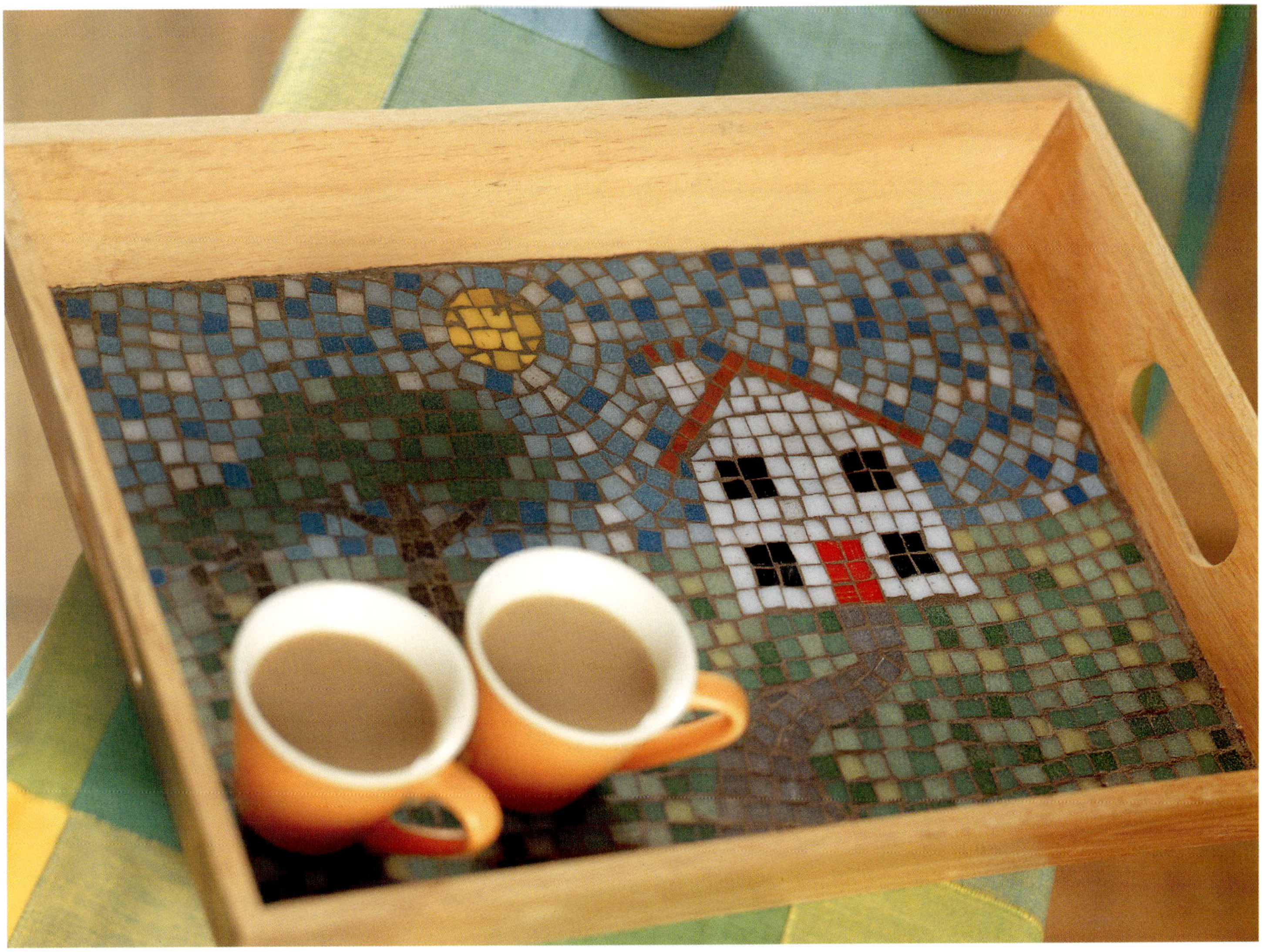

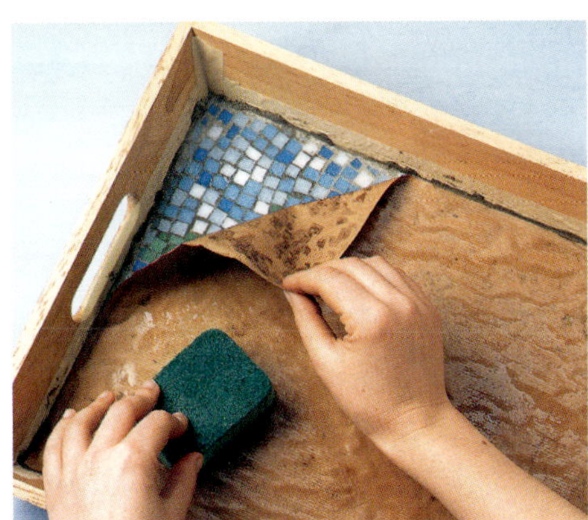

5 Place the mosaic carefully on the freshly applied tile adhesive, paper side up. Press down firmly over the whole surface, then leave for about 30 minutes. Moisten the paper with a damp sponge and peel off. Leave the tile adhesive to dry overnight.

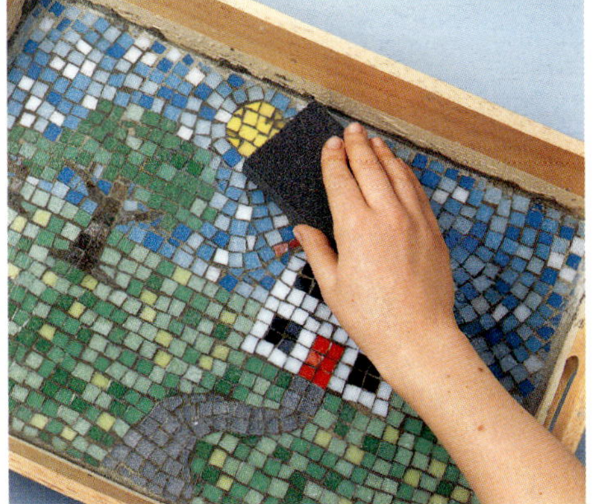

6 Some parts of the mosaic may need to be grouted with extra tile adhesive. Leave it to dry, then clean off any of the adhesive that may have dried on the surface with a sponge. Remove the pieces of masking tape and then polish the mosaic with a dry, soft cloth.

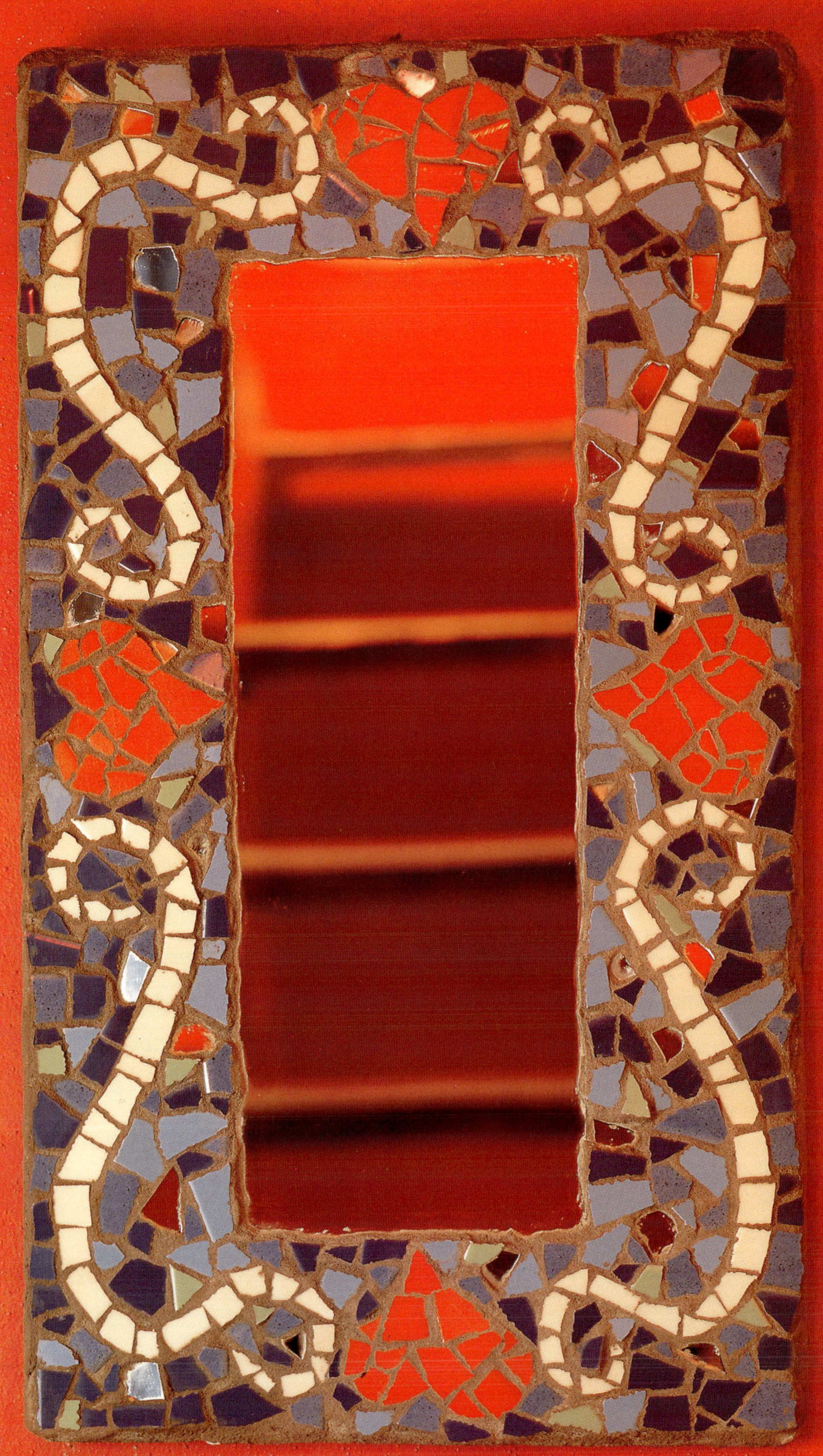

In this lovely hallway mirror, romantic red hearts and scrolling white lines are beautifully set off by the rich blue background, which sparkles from the inset chunks of mirror glass.

Valentine Mirror

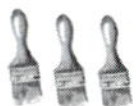

You will need

12mm (½in) thick plywood sheet, to size of mirror frame required
PVA (white) glue
Paintbrush
Bradawl
Drill and rebate (rabbet) bit
Mirror plate, with keyhole opening
Screwdriver
2 x 12mm (½in) screws
Mirror
Brown paper
Scissors
Masking tape
Ruler
Soft dark pencil
Tile adhesive
Thin-glazed ceramic household tiles: red, white and several rich shades of blue
Tile nippers
Flexible knife
Hammer
Mirror tiles
Piece of sacking (heavy cloth)
Notched spreader
Rubber spreader
Fine abrasive paper (sandpaper)

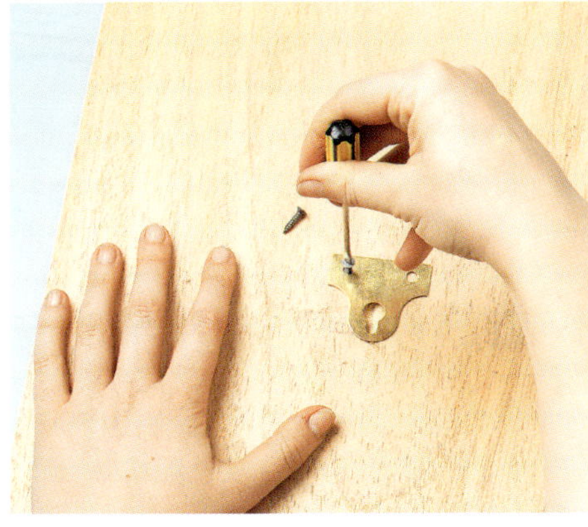

1 Prime both sides of the plywood with diluted PVA (white) glue and leave to dry. Score one side (the front) with a bradawl. Turn the board over and make a dent in the centre about a third of the way down, using a drill. Screw the mirror plate over the dent.

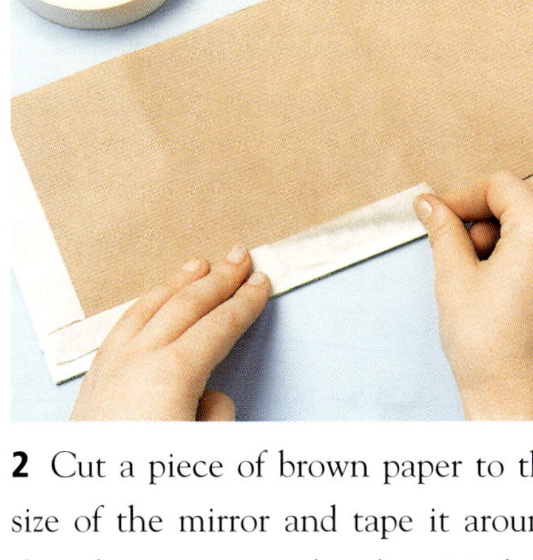

2 Cut a piece of brown paper to the size of the mirror and tape it around the edge to protect the glass. Mark its position in the centre front of the plywood board with a ruler and pencil, and stick it in place with tile adhesive.

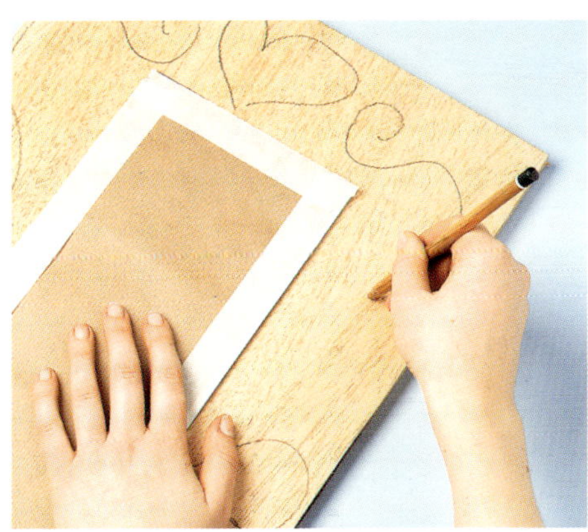

3 Draw a small heart in the centre of each border and scrolling lines to connect the four hearts.

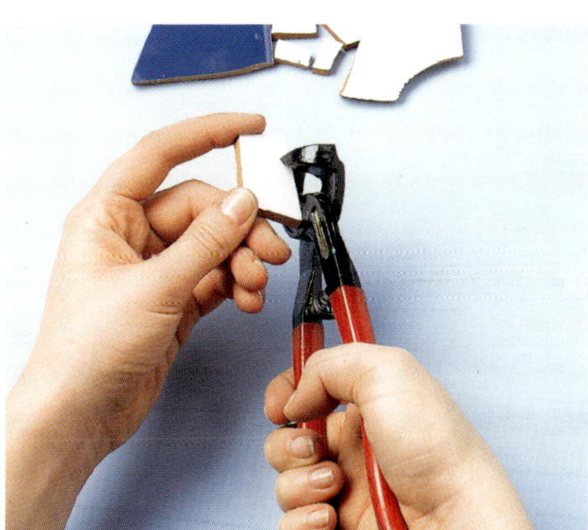

4 Using tile nippers, cut the red tiles into small, irregular pieces and the white tiles into regular-sized squares.

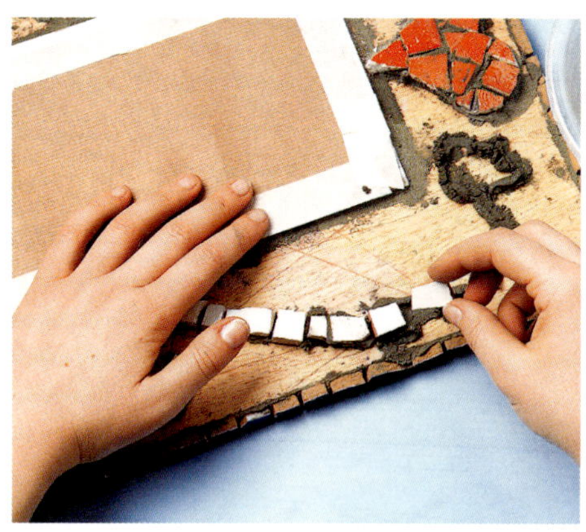

5 Spread the tile adhesive over the pencilled heart shapes with a flexible knife and press in the red tile pieces. Repeat for the scroll lines using the white tiles. Scrape off any excess adhesive and leave to dry overnight.

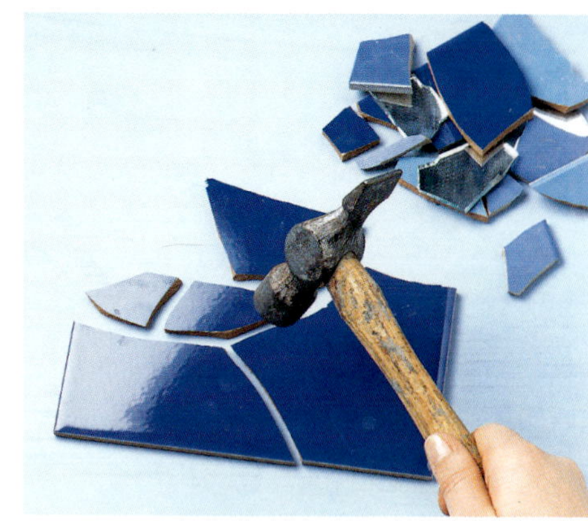

6 Using a hammer, carefully break up the blue ceramic tiles and the mirror tiles into small pieces. It is advisable to wrap each tile in a piece of sacking (heavy cloth) before breaking up, to avoid the tile shattering or splintering.

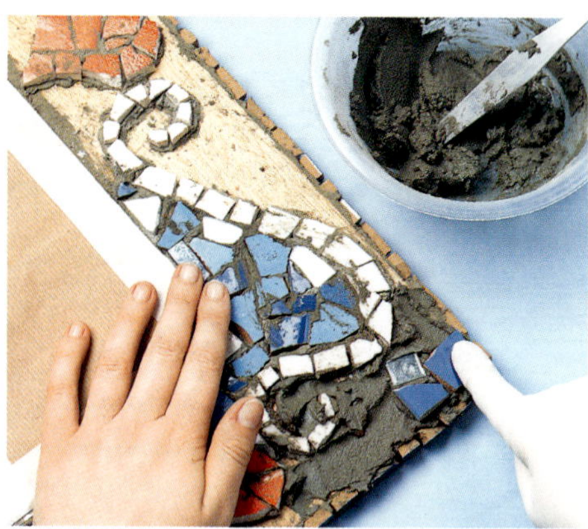

7 Working on a small area at a time, spread tile adhesive over the background areas with a notched spreader, then press in the blue and mirror pieces. Leave to dry overnight.

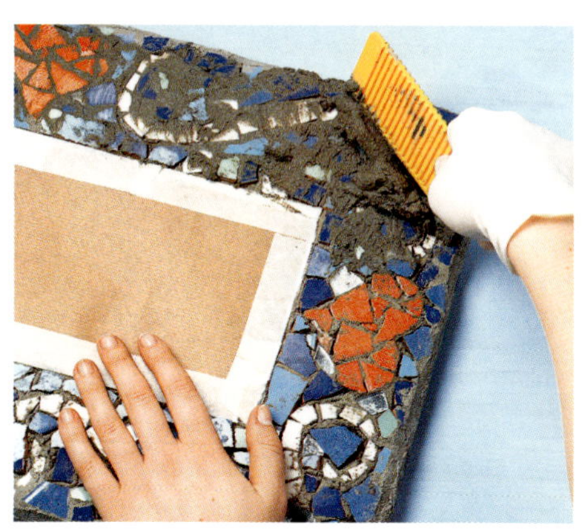

8 Grout the mosaic with tile adhesive, using a rubber spreader to distribute the adhesive over the flat surface and your fingers for the edges.

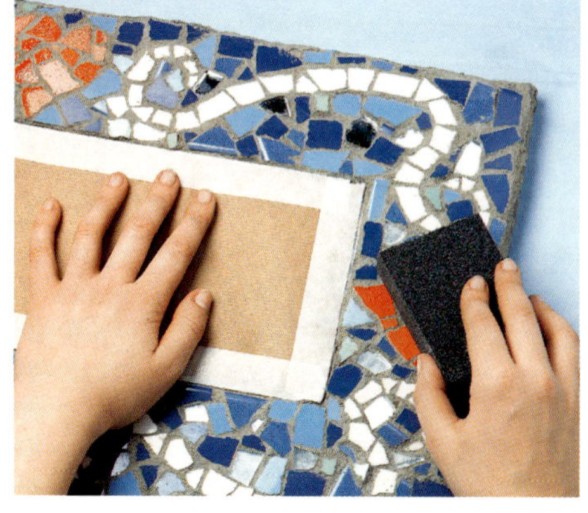

9 Carefully sand off any lumps of remaining adhesive that may have dried on the surface of the mosaic, using fine abrasive paper (sandpaper).

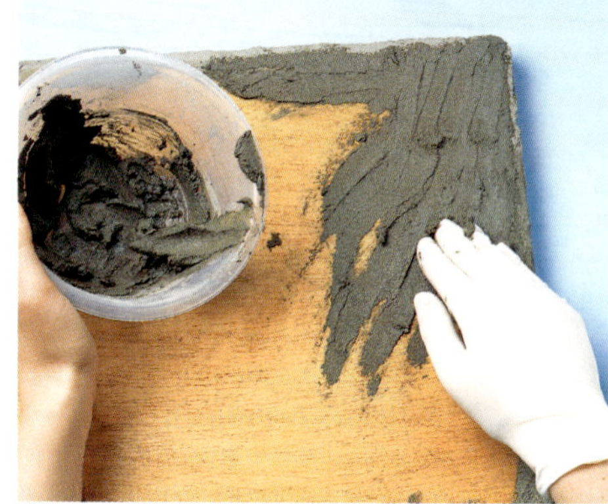

10 For a professional finish, rub tile adhesive into the back of the plywood board. Remove the protective brown paper from the mirror.

This geometric mosaic uses contrasting colours of glass and ceramic tiles to create a stunning wall panel. Mirror and gold-leaf tiles add an opulent feel. Hang this mosaic where it can be a dramatic focal point.

Mirror Mosaic

You will need

Pencil
Ruler
9mm (3/8in) thick MDF (medium-density fiberboard), cut to 46 x 46cm (18 x 18in)
Paintbrushes
PVA (white) glue
Tile adhesive
Mirror, cut to 19.5 x 19.5cm (7 3/4 x 7 3/4in)
Gold vitreous glass tiles in a light and dark shade
Matt (flat) ceramic mosaic tiles in light and dark shades
Tile nippers
Mirror tiles
Tile grout
Rubber spreader
Sponge
Soft cloth

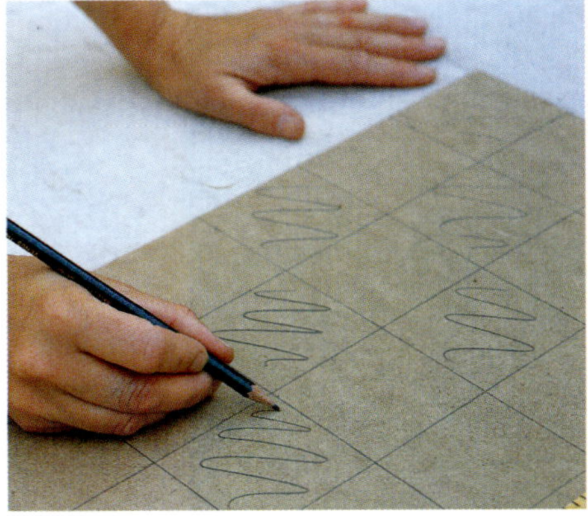

1 Using a pencil and ruler, divide the board so that there are seven equal spaces along each edge. Join up your marks carefully to form a grid of squares. Mark the alternate squares with a pencil squiggle to show where the different squares of tones will be mosaiced.

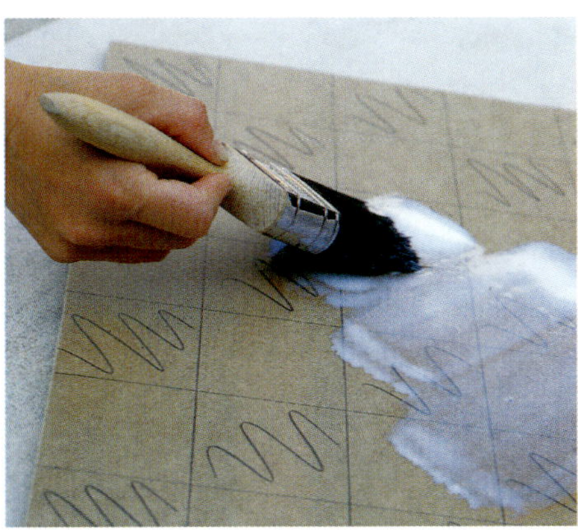

2 Using a large paintbrush, seal the board with a coat of PVA (white) glue diluted 1:1 with water. Allow to dry thoroughly. The PVA will dry clear, so the design will still be visible.

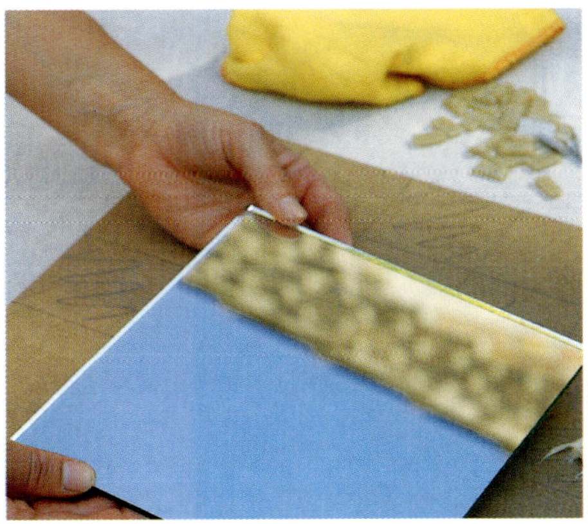

3 Using tile adhesive, stick the main mirror on to the centre of the board so that there are even borders all around it. Leave it to dry.

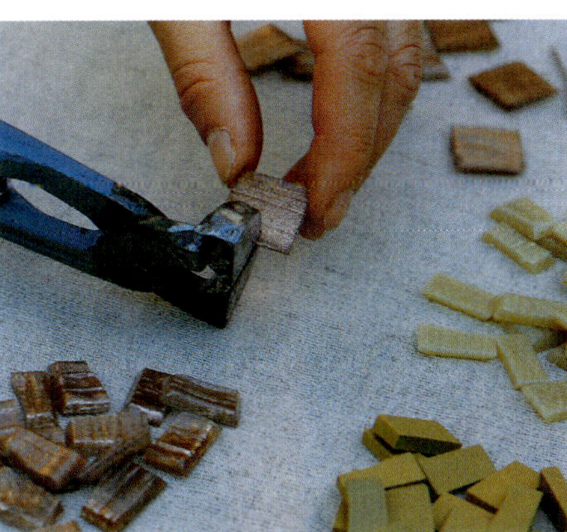

4 Cut the gold vitreous glass and the two shades of ceramic mosaic tiles in half with the tile nippers. Squeeze the nippers firmly for a clean cut.

▶

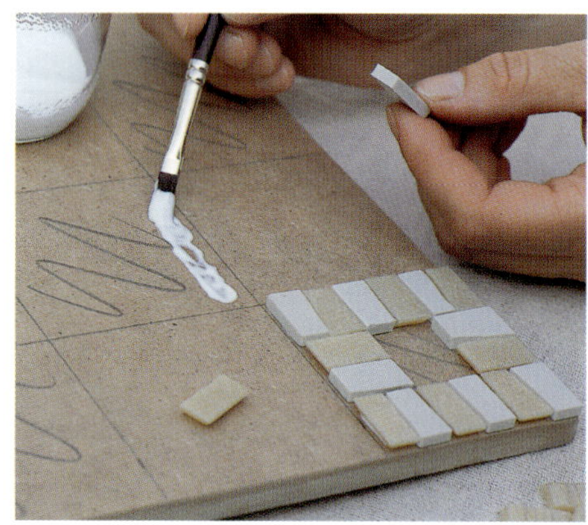

5 Starting on the squares marked with the pencil squiggles, stick the tiles in position, alternating between a light shade of vitreous glass and a light shade of matt (flat) ceramic. Leave a slight gap between each piece. Paint undiluted PVA glue on to each square and stick the tiles to fit within the pencil guidelines.

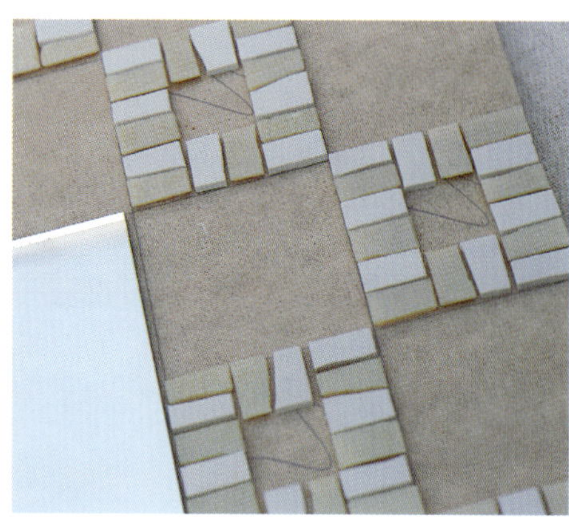

6 Finish sticking these lighter squares over the entire board, working carefully to ensure the gaps between each piece remain even.

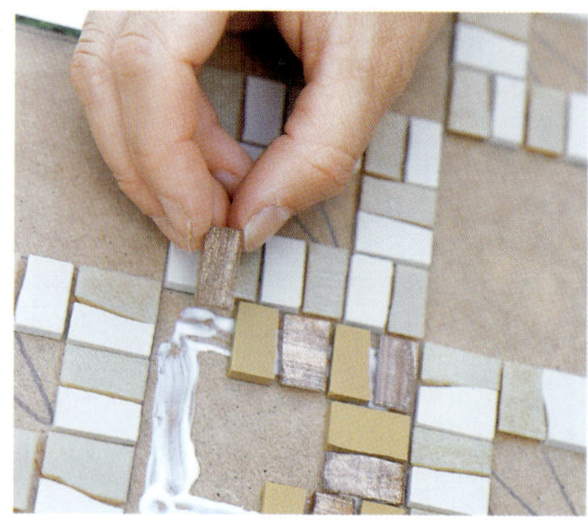

7 Cover the alternate squares over the entire board with two darker colours, one of the matt ceramic, and the other of the vitreous glass, sticking them in position as before and keeping the spacing even throughout.

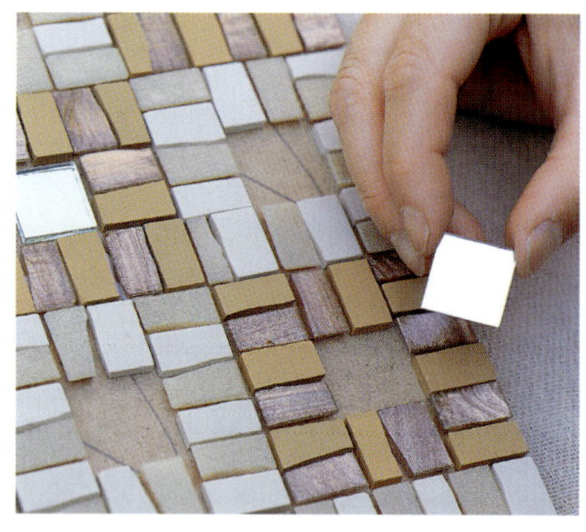

8 Stick the mirror tiles in the centre of the darker squares using PVA glue as before to create a dark square with a centre of light.

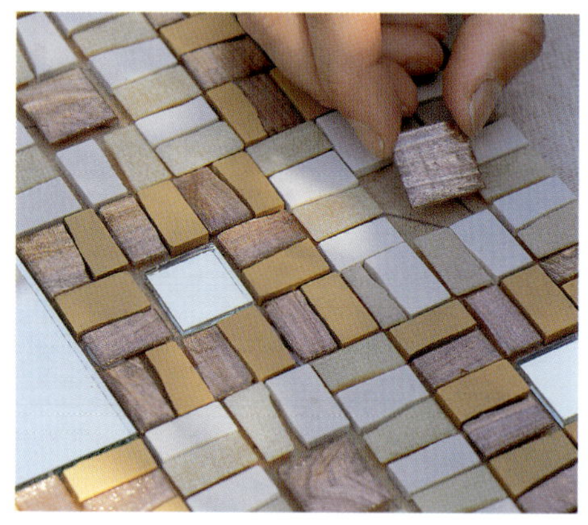

9 Stick squares of the darker vitreous glass tiles in the centre of the lighter squares to create lighter squares with a dark centre. Allow to dry.

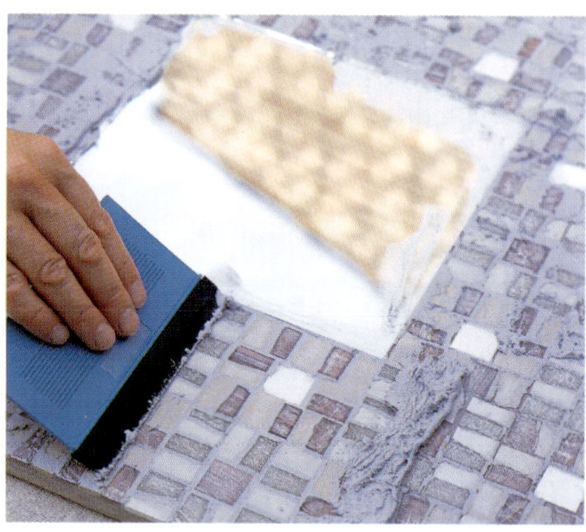

10 Spread tile grout evenly over the board with a rubber spreader, making sure the gaps between the tiles have been filled. Smooth a little grout around the edge of the board. With a slightly damp sponge, wipe away any excess grout from the surface and the edge of the board. Leave to dry. Polish with a dry, soft cloth.

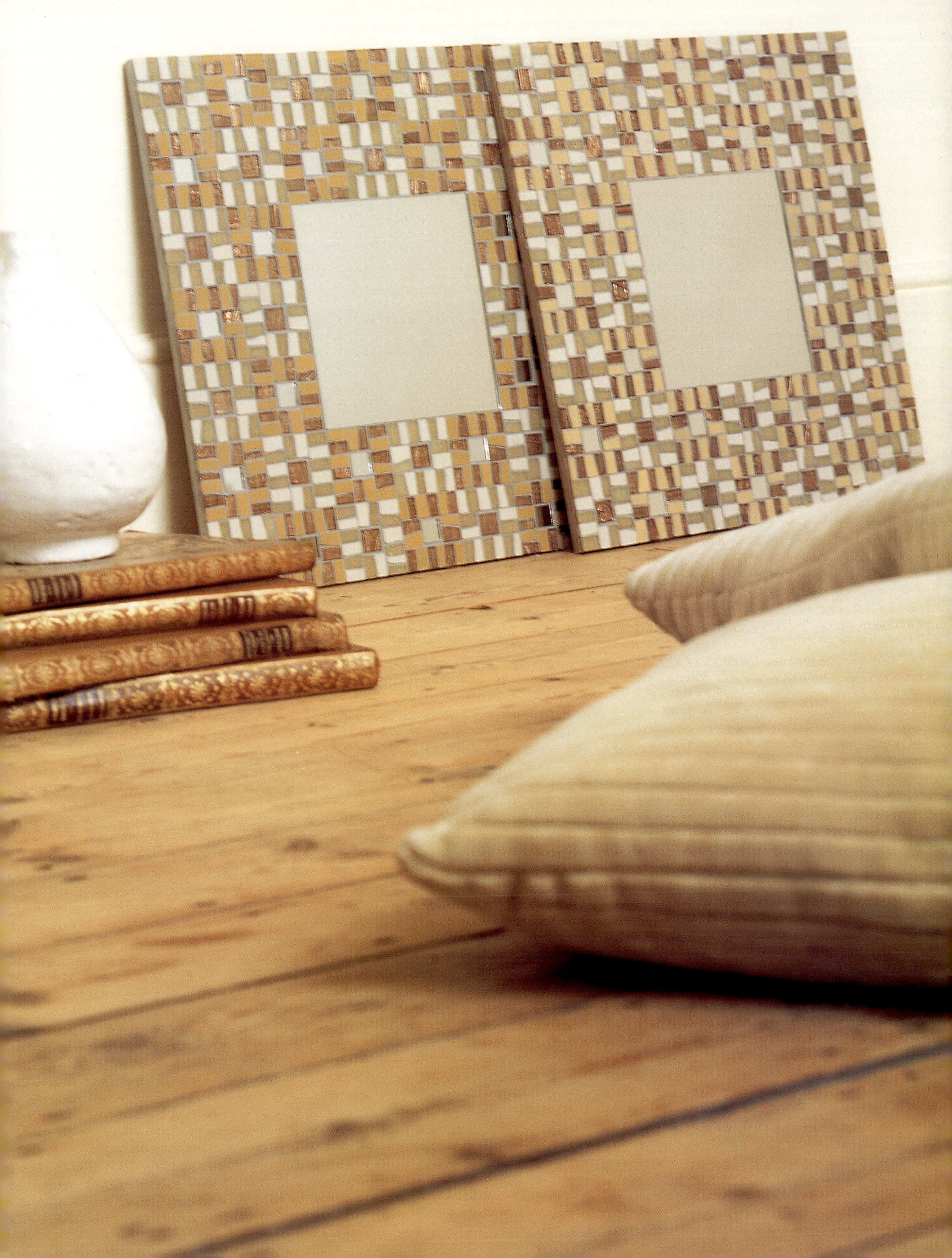

In this vivid mosaic, it is important that the tesserae are accurately shaped, with no gaps between them. They are left ungrouted so that tile adhesive dust will not disturb the workings of the clock.

Cosmic Clock

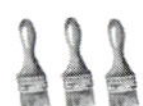

You will need

40cm (16in) diameter circle of wood
Strip of plywood, 5mm (3/16in) deeper than the circle of wood and 130cm (52in) long
Hammer
Tacks
Black paint
Paintbrush
Brown paper
Scissors
Drill
Charcoal or black felt-tipped pen
Vitreous glass mosaic tiles
PVA (white) glue and brush
Tile nippers
Tile adhesive
Admix
Grout spreader
Piece of flat wood
Sponge
Craft (utility) knife
Soft cloth
Double-sided tape
Clock mechanism and hands
Picture-hanging hook

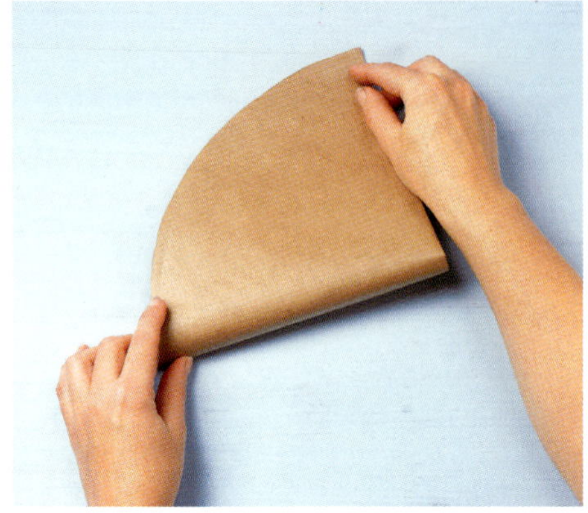

1 Position the strip of plywood around the circumference of the circle of wood, and, using a hammer and tacks, cover the edge of the circle to make a neat rim. Paint the rim black and leave to dry. Cut a circle of brown paper to fit inside the rim. Fold it in quarters to find the centre, and make a small hole.

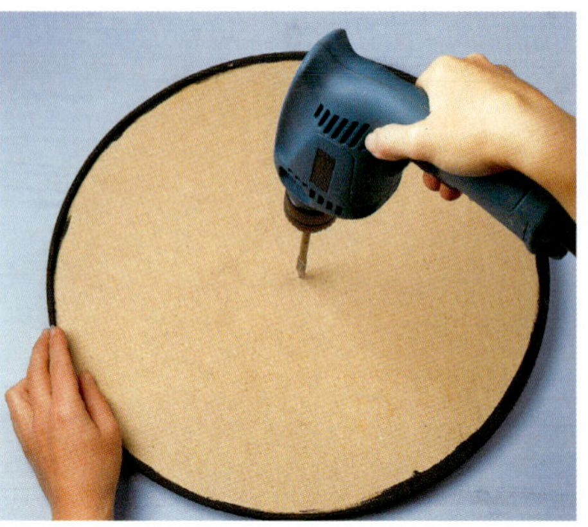

2 Place the paper over the circle of wood and mark the centre through the hole on to the wood. Remove the paper and then drill a hole through the centre of the wood, large enough to allow the spindle of the clock mechanism to rotate freely.

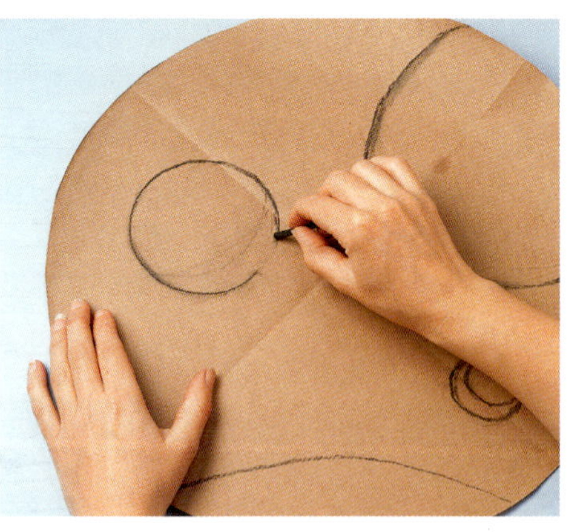

3 Draw a cosmic design on the brown paper circle, using a stick of charcoal or a felt-tipped pen. (Charcoal is easier to correct.)

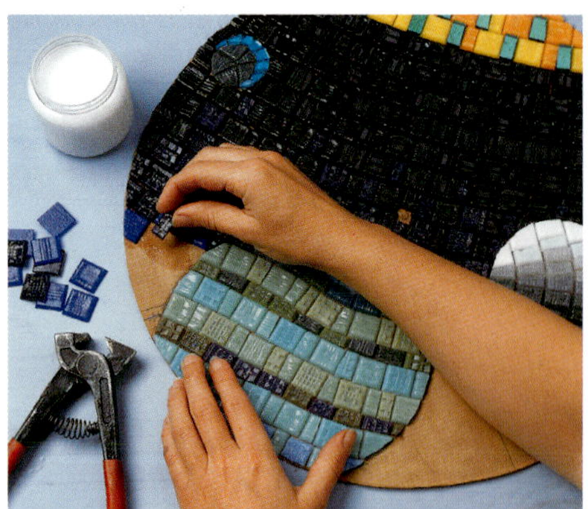

4 Snip the glass tiles into tesserae using tile nippers, then stick the tesserae face down on the paper, using PVA (white) glue. Place them as close together as possible, without any gaps in between. Make any further cuts necessary to allow them to fit around the curves in your design.

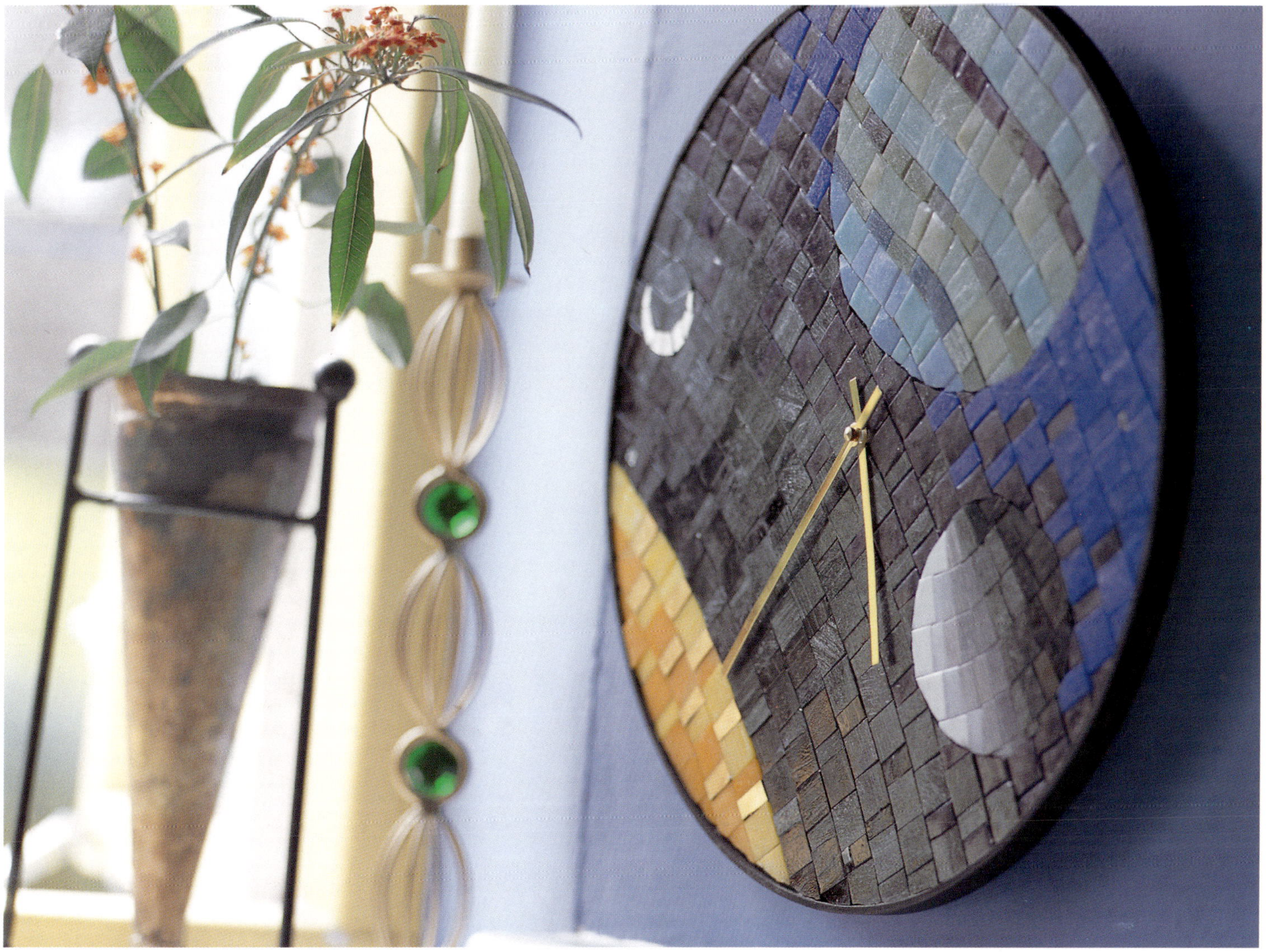

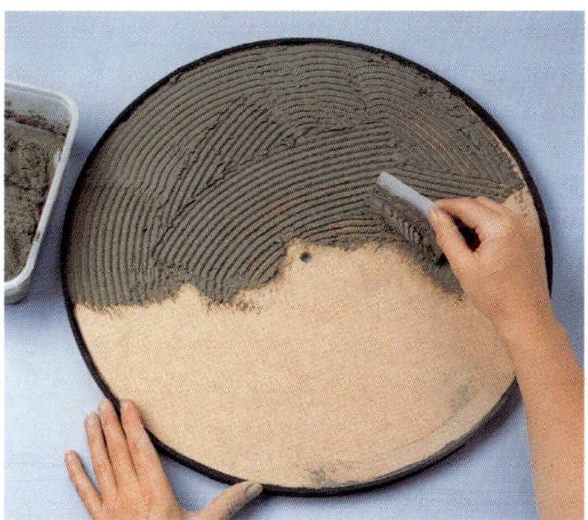

5 Mix the tile adhesive and admix according to the manufacturer's instructions. Using the fine-notched edge of a grout spreader, spread this over the whole of the board, right up to the edge. Lower the mosaic on to the adhesive and press flat.

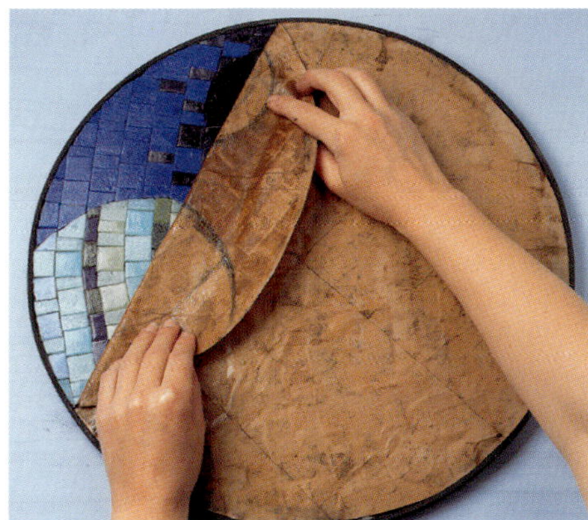

6 Smooth over the paper with a flat piece of wood, using small, circular movements. Leave for 20 minutes, then dampen the paper and gently pull it away from the mosaic. Scrape away any adhesive that has come through the tesserae with a craft (utility) knife. Leave to dry for at least 2 hours.

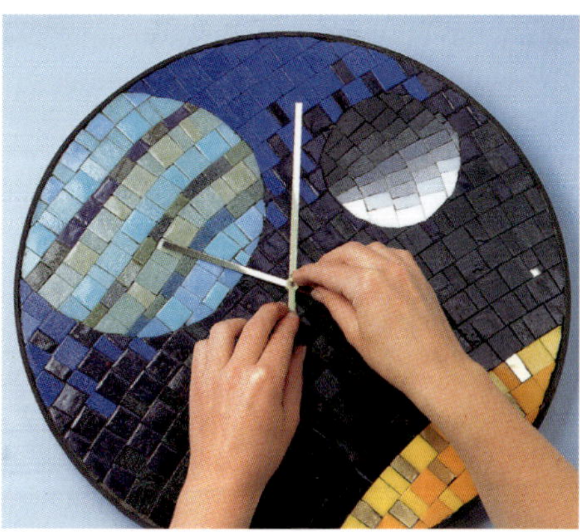

7 Carefully wipe any remaining glue from the surface of the mosaic with the sponge and polish with a dry, soft cloth. Using double-sided tape, attach the clock mechanism to the back of the board. Insert the spindle through the hole in the centre and fit on the hands. Fit a picture hook to the back.

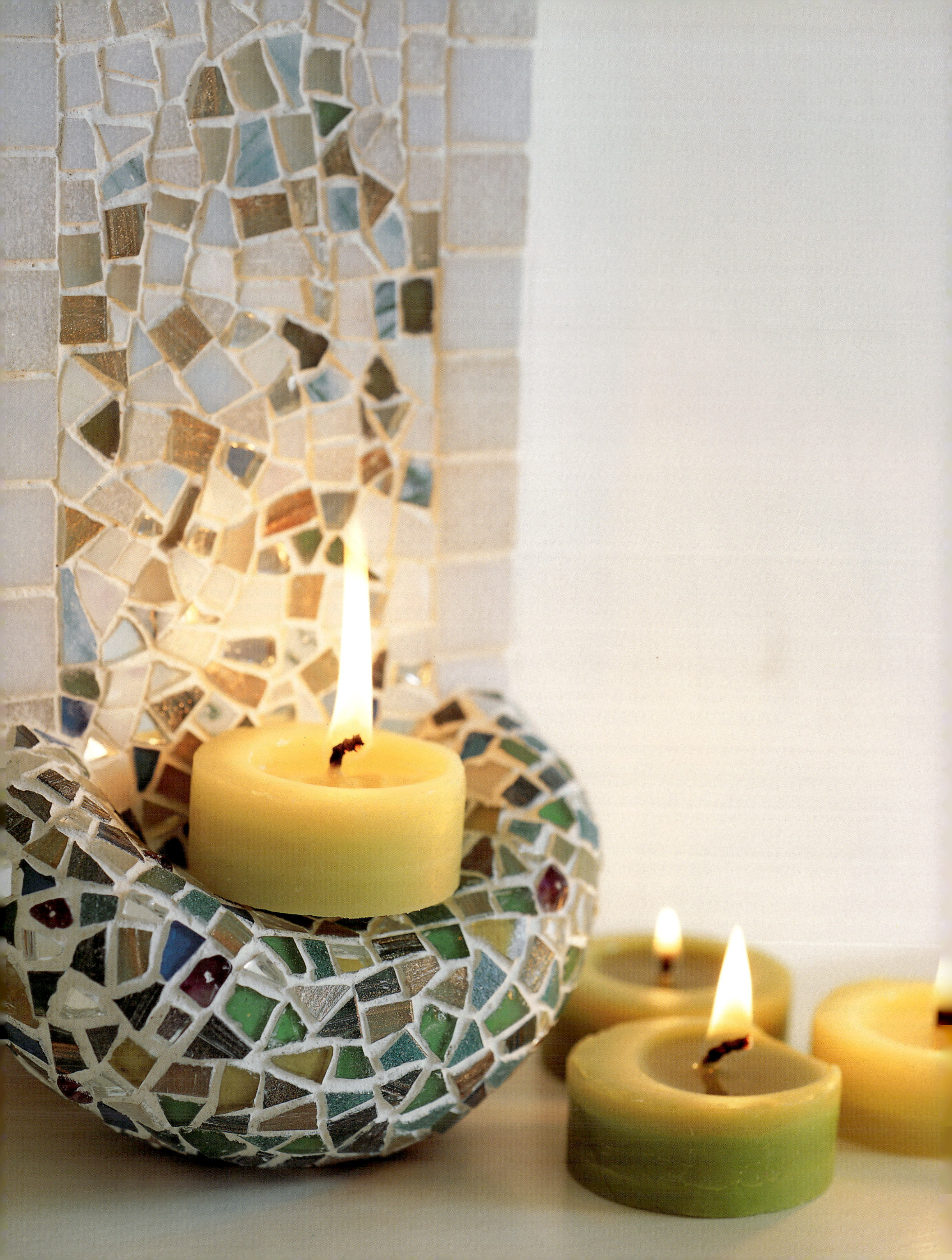

This candle sconce looks beautiful hung on a bathroom wall or in a bedroom. The mirror reflects the candlelight and, together with the small pieces of coloured tile, this gives the mosaic a magical quality.

Candle Sconce

You will need

Tape measure
2cm (¾in) thick plywood sheet
Pencil
Ruler
Vitreous glass mosaic tiles
Jigsaw (saber saw)
Abrasive paper (sandpaper)
Wire cutters
Chicken wire
Hammer
U-shaped nails
Picture hooks
Bonding plaster
PVA (white) glue
Sponge
Tile adhesive
Knife
Vitreous glass mosaic tiles, mirror, washed glass, stained glass, and amethyst
Tile nippers
Craft (utility) knife
Tile grout
Soft cloths
Old sheet
Drill with rebate (rabbet) bit
Mirror plate, with keyhole opening
Screwgun or screwdriver
Small screws

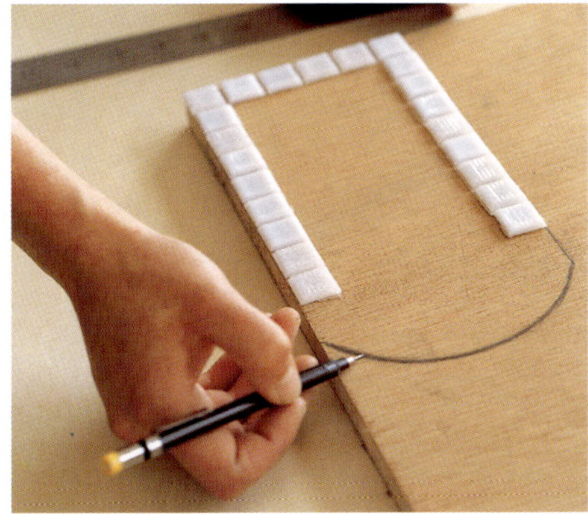

1 Measure and mark out the plywood to a width to fit six whole glass tiles (13cm/5¼in) and length to fit 10 whole tiles (22cm/9in). Use a ruler, working from the corner of the wood and the two straight edges. At the end of this rectangle, draw a semicircle.

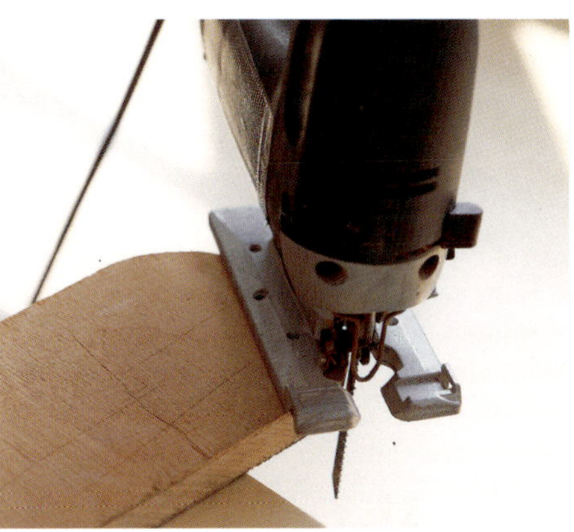

2 Clamp the wood on to the edge of a workbench. Using a jigsaw (saber saw), cut out the shape. Sand the edges of the wood lightly.

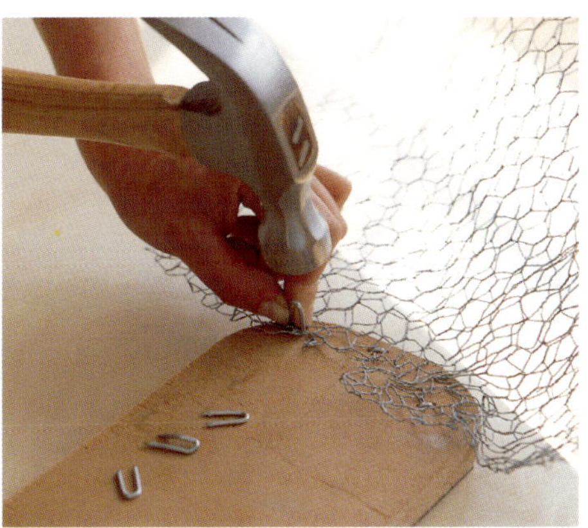

3 Using wire cutters, cut out a piece of chicken wire 20 x 50cm (8 x 20in). With a hammer and U-shaped nails, attach one end of the wire to the semicircle to create a curve. Remove the excess wire using wire cutters or pliers.

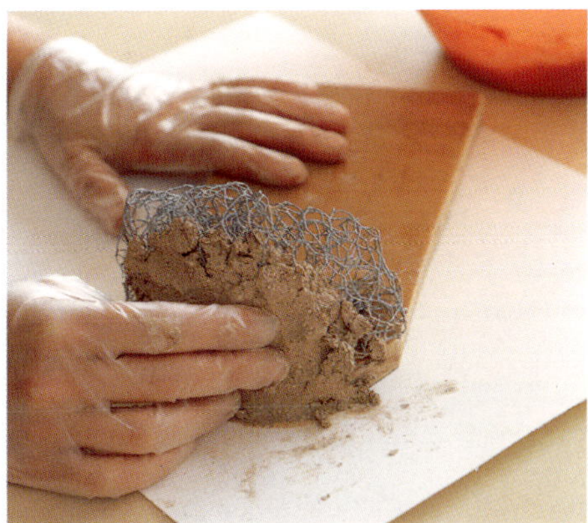

4 Fold the wire over and compress it to create the basic shape, fixing the top end to the wood with picture hooks. Mix up some bonding plaster in a bucket into a soft but firm consistency. Pack this into the chicken wire until the structure is filled. Start to create the shape by applying small lumps where there are uneven dips.

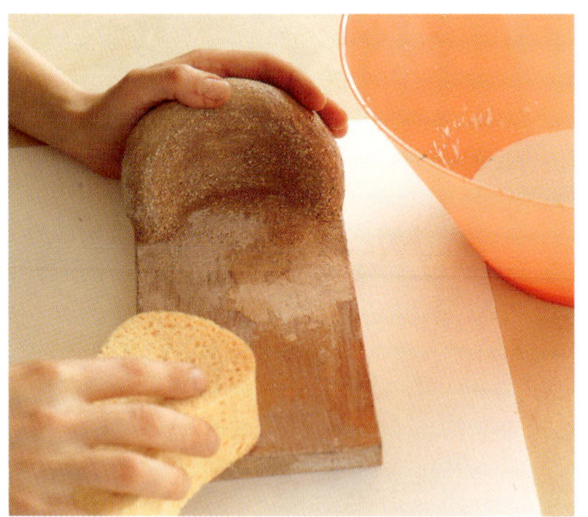

5 When the shape is complete, dip your fingers into water and run them over the surfaces until there is a smooth finish. Leave the plaster to dry for 24 hours, then seal the surface with a thin film of diluted PVA (white) glue, applied with a sponge.

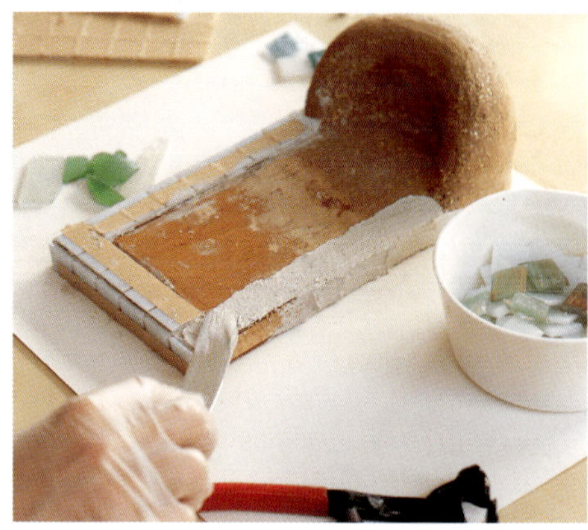

6 Using a knife, apply an even layer of tile adhesive to the outer edges, or border, of the candle sconce. Stick strips of whole vitreous glass tiles (paper side up) on to the border, clipping the last tile to fit and meet the curve at the top of the sculptured holder. Stick further strips of glass tiles on to the sides of the sconce, continuing around the base. Clip the remaining glass tiles and all the other tiles into small pieces.

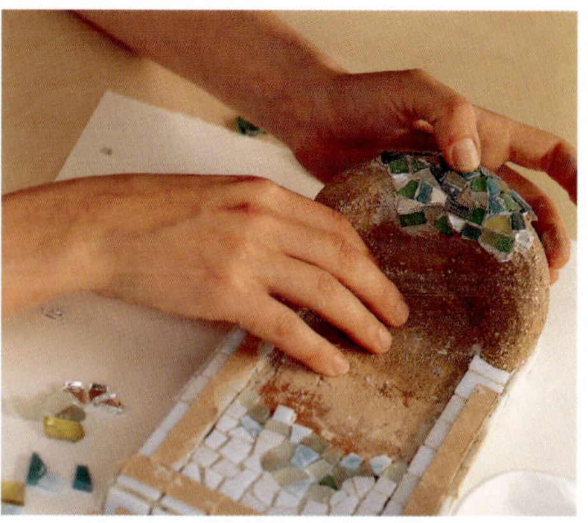

7 Starting from the top, within the border created from whole tiles, apply tile adhesive and place small, clipped pieces of white tile next to the whole tiles. As the space fills, introduce light pieces of pale blue and green washed glass, working downwards. On the shaped holder, work with richer greens and blues, and include pieces of stained glass and amethyst. Place pieces of mirror randomly to reflect the light.

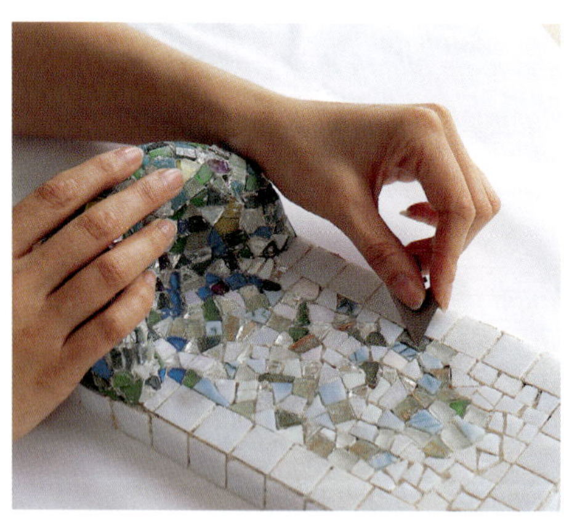

8 When the mosaic is finished, remove the brown paper on the whole tiles, having moistened it with a damp sponge. Clean the surfaces of the tiles and remove any excess adhesive in the gaps with a craft (utility) knife.

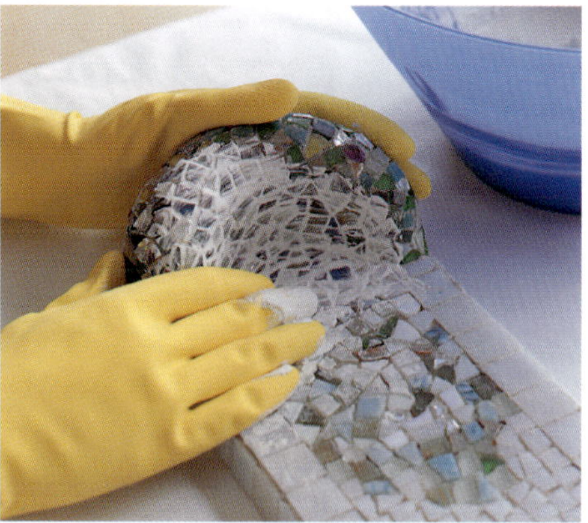

9 Apply tile grout over the mosaic, working it into the gaps with your fingers. Gently clean off any excess grout with a damp sponge. After about 10 minutes, use a dry cloth to rub away any excess grout. If it is still wet, leave it for a little while then try again.

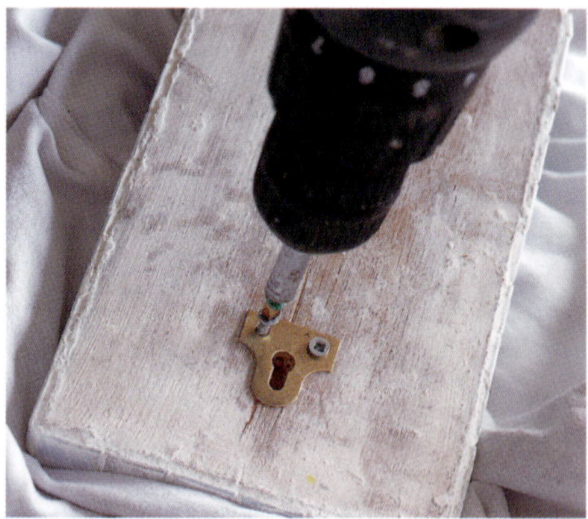

10 Place the completed candle sconce face down on an old sheet. Place the mirror plate in position, then mark with a pencil the area under the keyhole-shaped opening. Drill this area so that it is large enough to take a screw head, then screw the mirror plate in position.

A breezeblock makes a safe, solid base for a large lamp. It is covered in a chunky floral design made of floor tiles and marble, with tiny pieces of mirror set into the gaps to catch the light from the lamp.

Floral Lamp Base

You will need

Breezeblock (cinderblock)
Ruler
Soft pencil
Drill with a long bit (at least half the length of the block and just wider than the metal rod)
Chisel
Hammer
Lamp power cord
Hollow metal rod with a screw thread, cut to the height required for the lamp
Tile adhesive
Piece of chalk
Ceramic floor tiles: shades of yellow for the petals
Piece of sacking (heavy cloth)
Flexible knife
White marble tiles
Mirror
Tile nippers
Rubber spreader
Sponge
Dust mask
Abrasive paper (sandpaper)
Soft cloth
Copper pipe
Hacksaw
Lamp fittings
Plug
Screwdriver
Lampshade

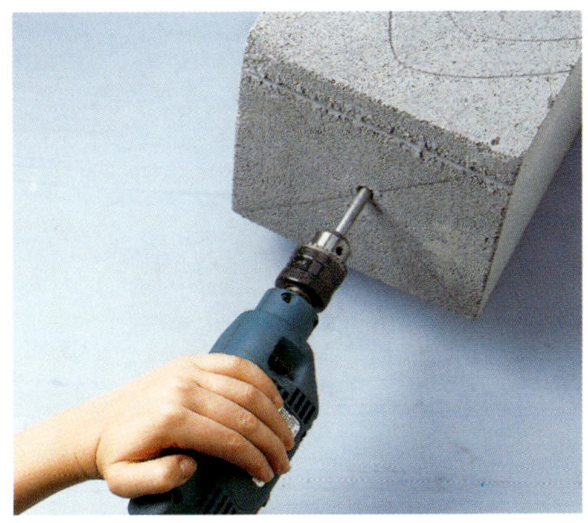

1 On one end of the breezeblock (cinderblock), mark diagonal lines to find the centre. Drill a hole right through, turning the block over if necessary to drill from the other end.

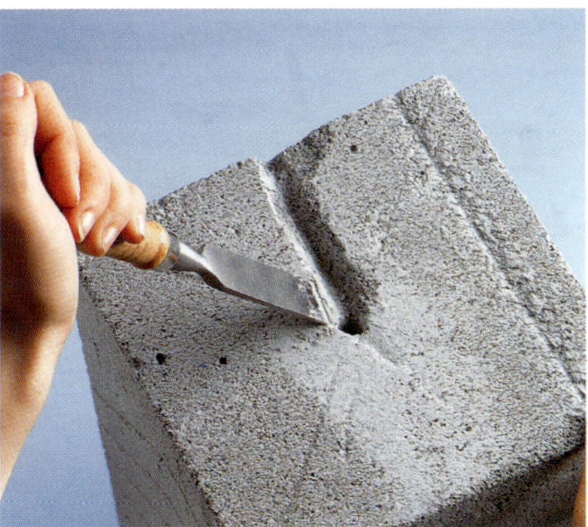

2 On one end, use a chisel to cut a deep groove from the centre hole to one edge to contain the lamp power cord. This will be the bottom of the lamp base.

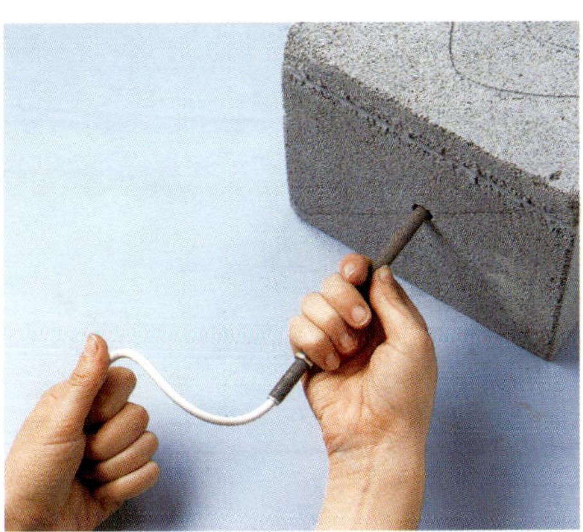

3 Pass the metal rod through the centre hole, with the screw thread at the top, then thread the cord through the rod, leaving a long length at the bottom. Tuck the cord into its groove, leaving enough length to reach an electrical socket. Fill in the groove with tile adhesive to secure the flex. Leave to dry.

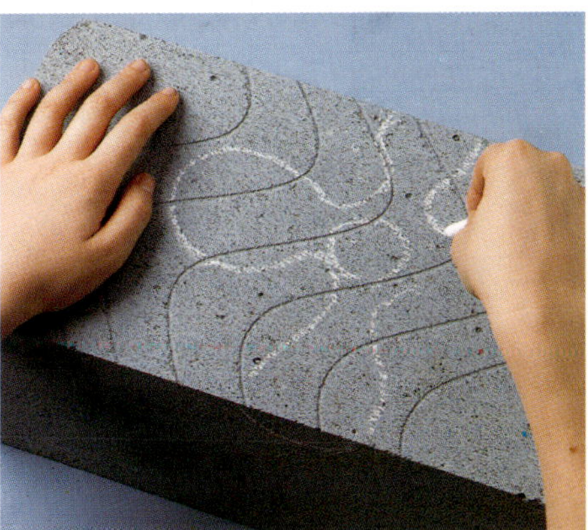

4 Using a piece of chalk, draw a large, simple flower design on the sides of the breezeblock. Exclude the bottom of the block. Plan out the colour scheme for your petals, keeping the yellow for the flower centres and white for the background.

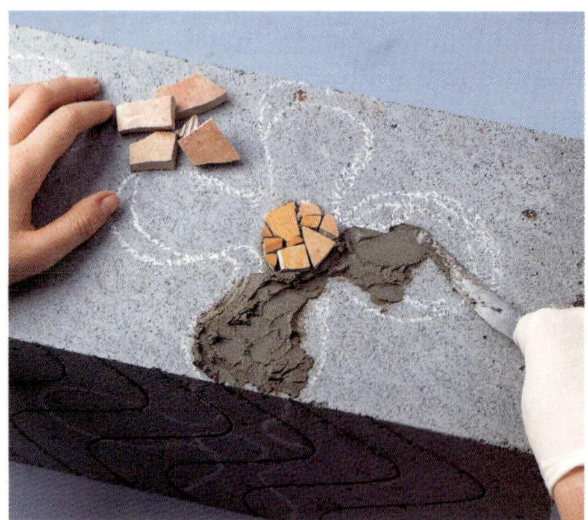

5 Wrap each floor tile in sacking (heavy cloth) and break it up into pieces with a hammer. Using a flexible knife, spread tile adhesive over each flower shape. Press the yellow tesserae into the adhesive and build up the flower centres. Now start work on the petals, using the other tiles, and continue until they are all covered.

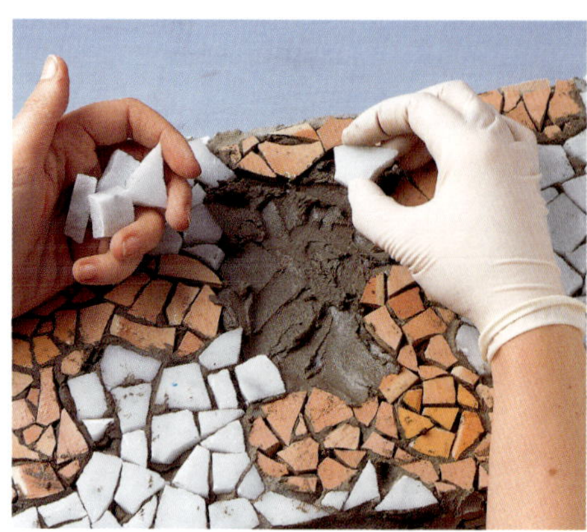

6 Break up each white marble tile in the same way. Working on a small area at a time, spread tile adhesive over the background and press in the marble pieces. Don't worry if your pieces don't butt up to each other. Leave to dry for 12 hours or overnight.

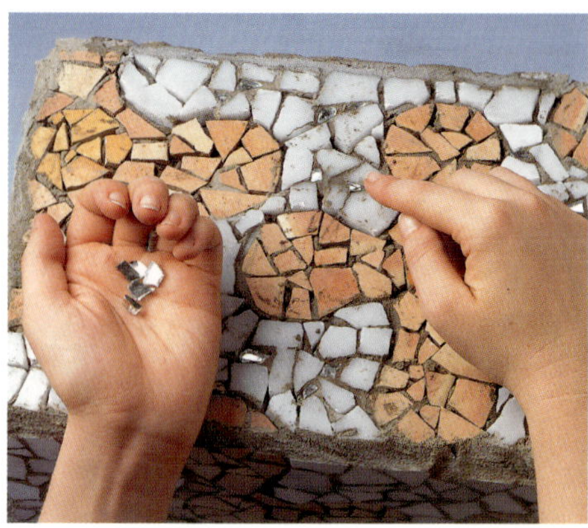

7 Using tile nippers, cut the mirror into small fragments. Insert blobs of tile adhesive into the larger gaps between the tesserae. Then push in the mirror fragments, checking they are level with the rest. Continue inserting mirrored pieces over the base until covered. Leave to dry overnight.

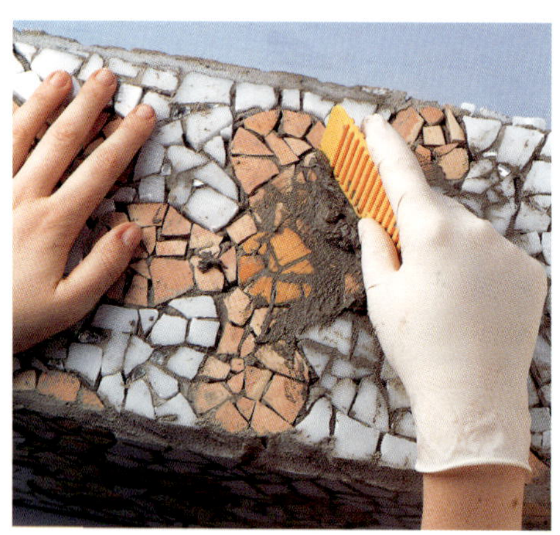

8 Grout the lamp base by scraping tile adhesive over the surface with a rubber spreader. This will bind all the pieces of tesserae together firmly. Use your fingers to smooth it right into the fissures and along the sides of the block. Wipe off the excess tile adhesive with a damp sponge and leave to dry overnight.

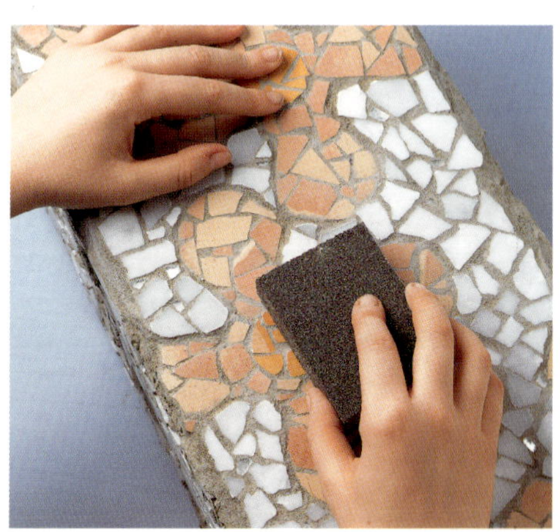

9 Wearing a dust mask, sand off any adhesive that may have dried on the surface. Polish with a soft, dry cloth. Finish off by slipping the copper pipe, cut to size, over the hollow rod, so that the screw end is exposed. Attach the lamp fittings, bulb, plug and chosen lampshade.

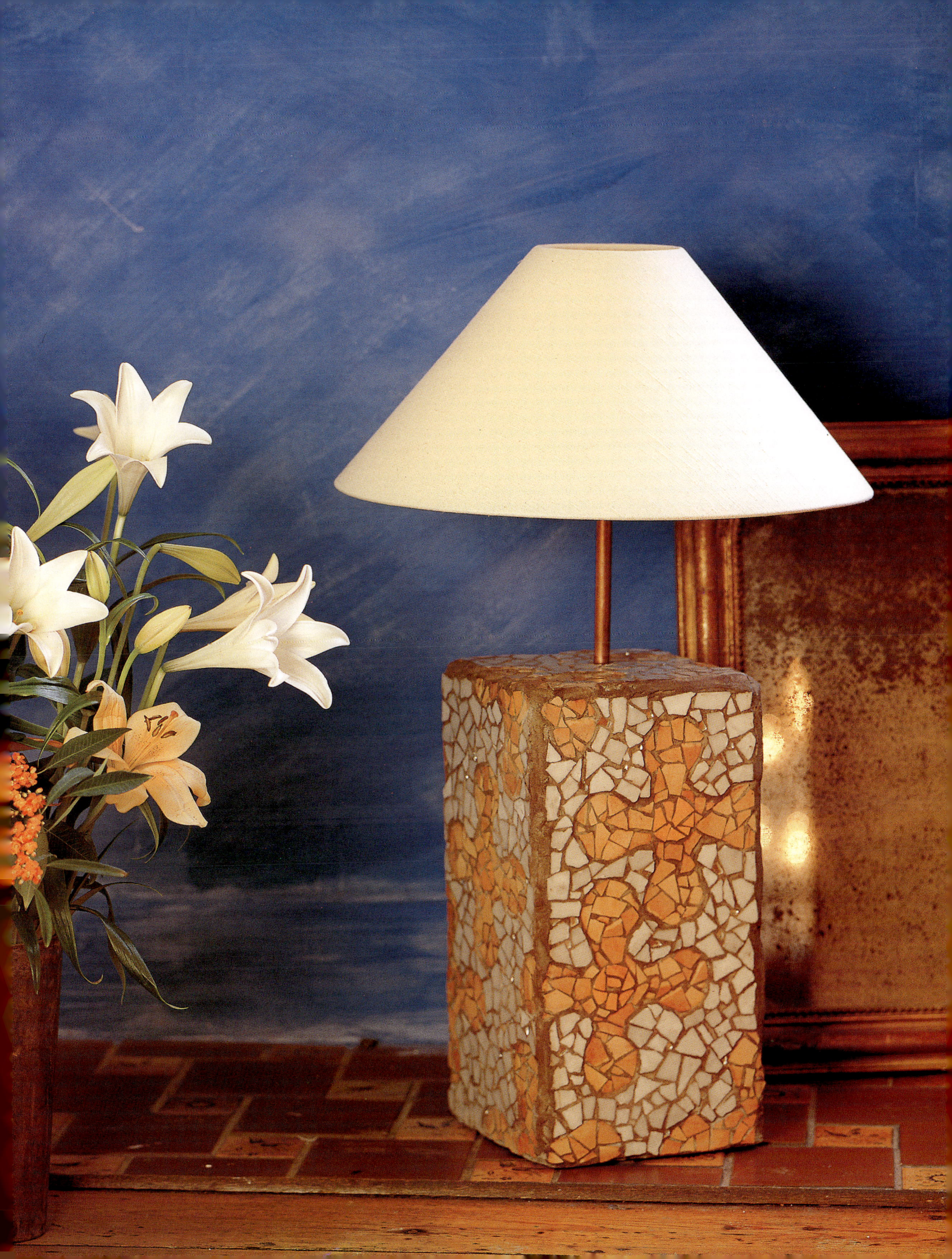

In this project, vitreous glass mosaic tiles in striking colours are used to decorate a ready-made fire screen. Most of this design uses whole tiles, cut diagonally into triangles.

Mosaic Fire Screen

You will need

Ready-made fire-screen base
Pencil
Ruler
Craft (utility) knife
PVA (white) glue
Paintbrushes
Vitreous glass mosaic tiles
Tile nippers
Tile grout
Nailbrush
Wood primer
White undercoat paint
Gloss paint
Soft cloth

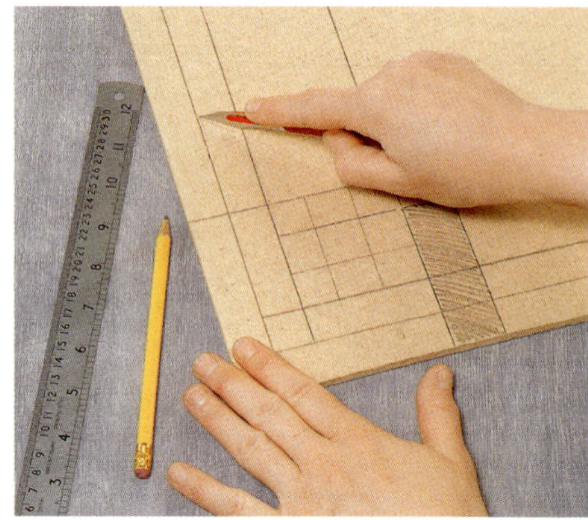

1 Draw the design on to the surface of the screen and its feet. Calculate the space needed to accommodate the tiles required and mark the main areas with a ruler. Score the whole of the surface with a craft (utility) knife, then prime with diluted PVA (white) glue and leave to dry completely.

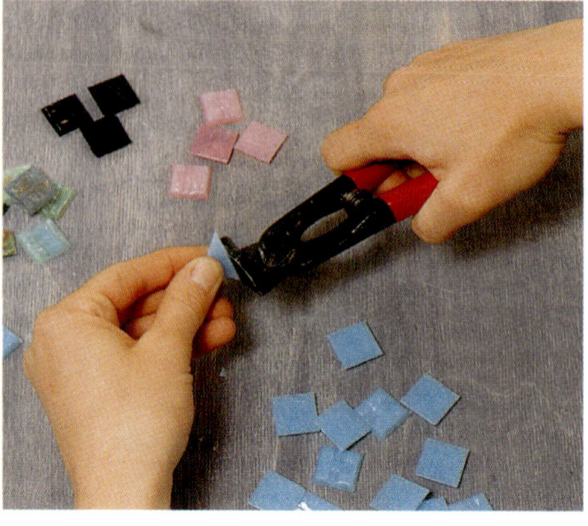

2 Select a range of vitreous glass tiles in the colours you require. Use tile nippers to cut some of the tiles into right-angled triangles for use in the inner border design.

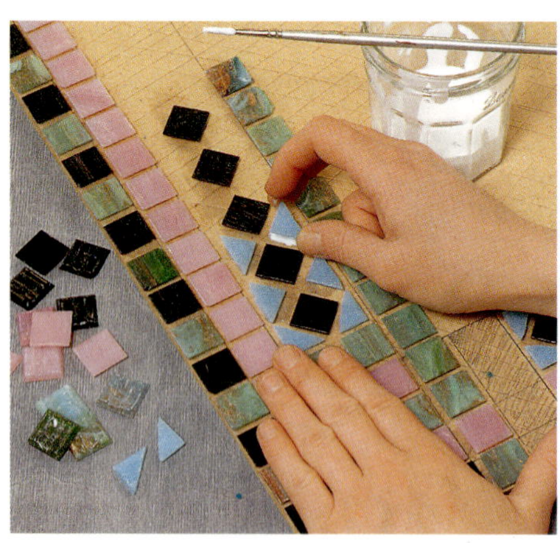

3 Stick the tiles and half-tiles to the base with undiluted PVA glue. Try to make all the gaps between the tiles equal and leave the area that will be slotted into the feet untiled.

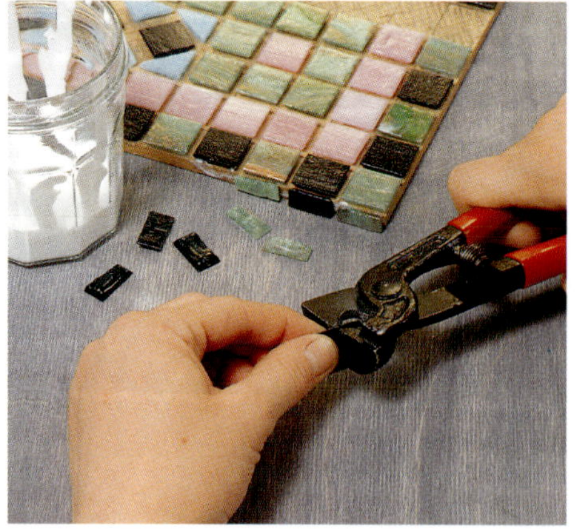

4 Tile the edge, then the feet, making sure that they will still slot on to the screen. Leave overnight to dry. Rub tile grout into the entire surface of the mosaic with your fingers, making sure that all the gaps between the tesserae are filled.

5 Leave the grout to dry for about 10 minutes, then remove any excess with a nailbrush. Allow to dry for a further 12 hours, then paint the back of the screen with wood primer, then undercoat paint and finally gloss paint, allowing each coat to dry before you apply the next. Finally, polish the mosaic with a dry, soft cloth and slot on the feet.

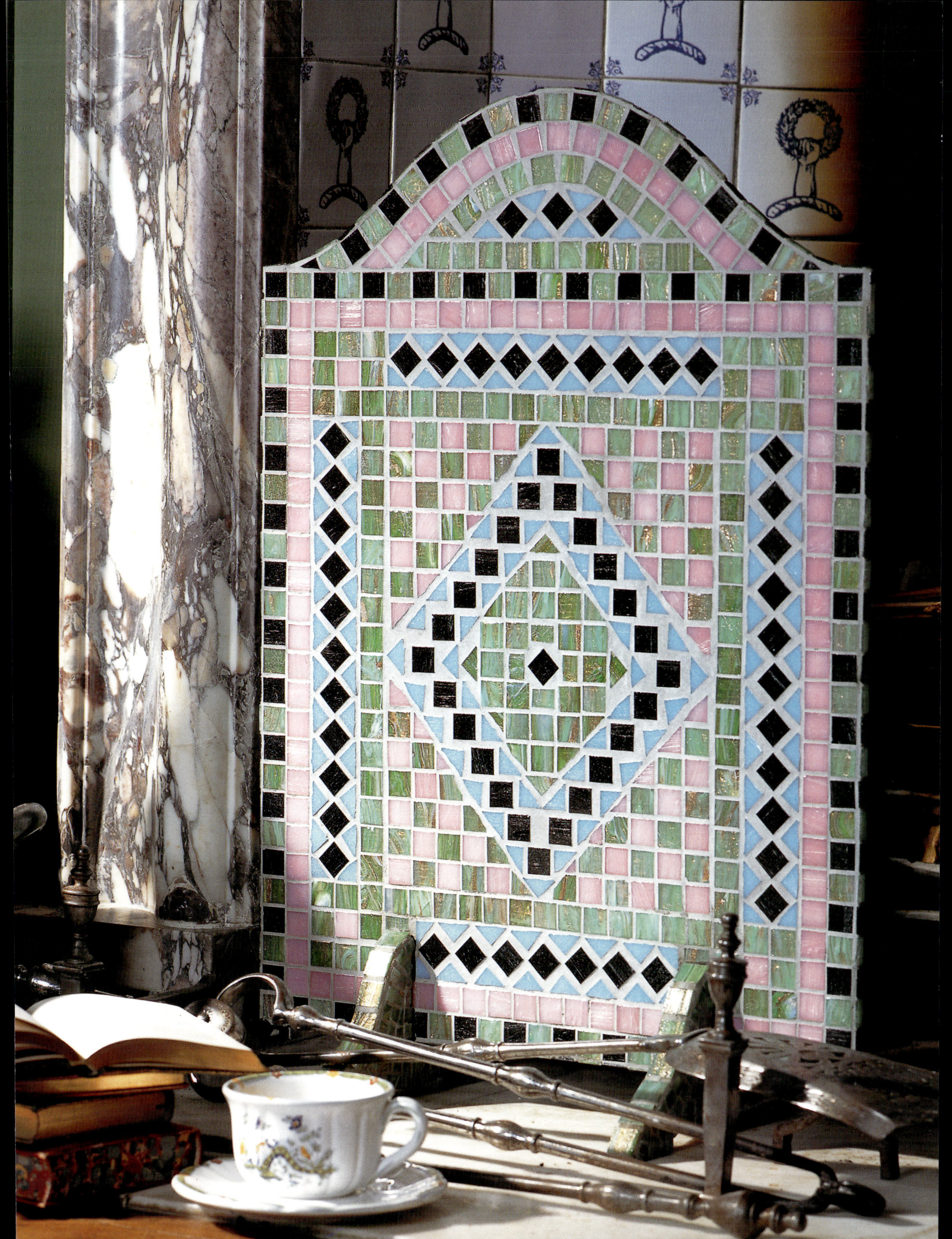

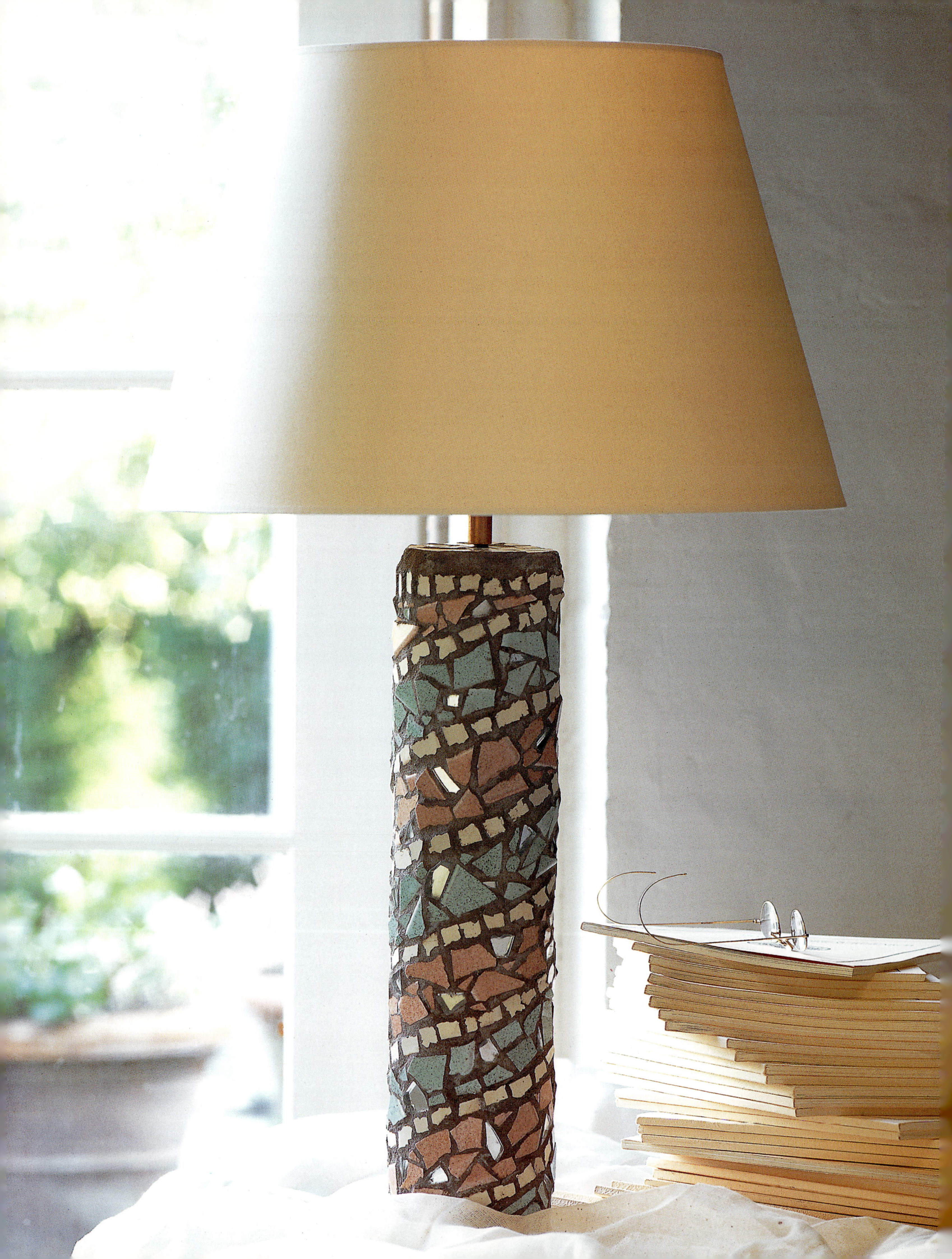

A simple spiral was the inspiration for this tall, elegant lamp base. Pieces of mirror have been added to catch the light, and they sparkle when the lamp is switched on.

Spiral Lamp Stand

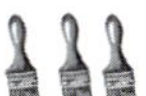

You will need

- Cardboard carpet roll tube
- 5mm (¼in) thick plywood sheet
- Pencil
- Jigsaw (saber saw)
- Drill with a bit just larger than the metal rod
- Bradawl or awl
- Wood glue
- Shellac
- Paintbrushes
- Lamp power cord
- Hollow metal rod with a screw thread, cut to the height required
- Plaster of Paris
- Ceramic household tiles in three colours
- Tile nippers
- Tile adhesive
- Sponge
- Mirror
- Flexible knife
- Abasive paper (sandpaper)
- Soft cloth
- Copper pipe
- Hacksaw
- Lamp fittings
- Plug
- Screwdriver
- Lampshade

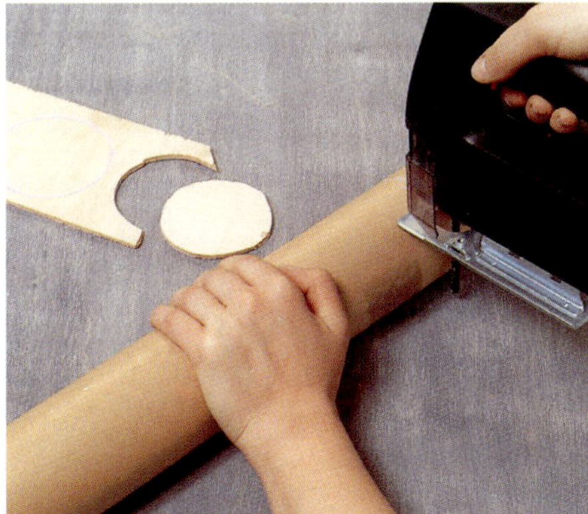

1 Draw twice around the circular end of the cardboard tube on to the plywood. Cut around these circles using a jigsaw (saber saw) and cut the cardboard tube to the length required. Drill a hole through the centre of one of the plywood circles. Use a bradawl to make a hole in the cardboard tube 2cm (¾in) in from one end and large enough to take the lamp power cord.

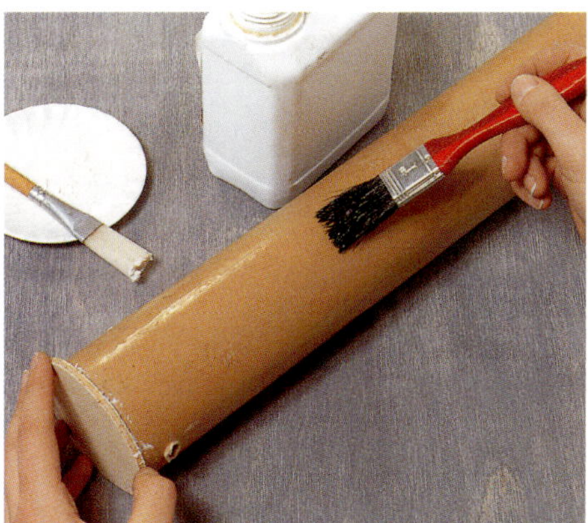

2 Use wood glue to stick the plywood circle without the drilled hole to the end of the tube near the cord hole. Leave to dry overnight, then paint the cardboard tube with shellac. Thread the cord in through the hole in the tube and then through the hollow metal rod. Stand the metal rod inside the tube with the screw thread at the top.

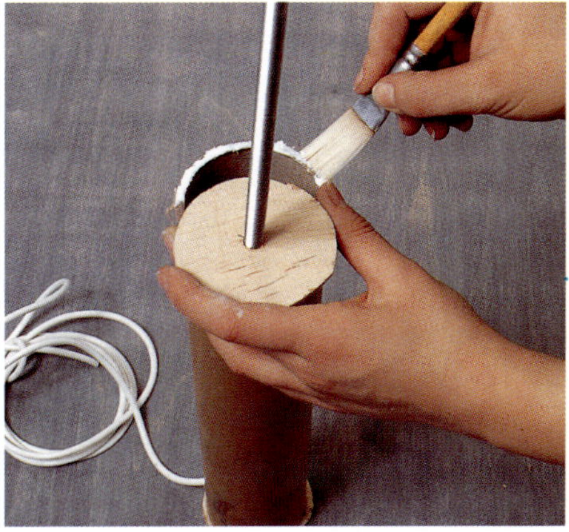

3 Mix some plaster of Paris with water and quickly pour it into the tube. Slip the second plywood circle over the metal rod and secure it with wood glue to the top of the cardboard tube. As soon as you have poured the plaster of Paris into the tube, you must work quickly to secure the top, as it is very important that the plaster dries with the rod in an upright position.

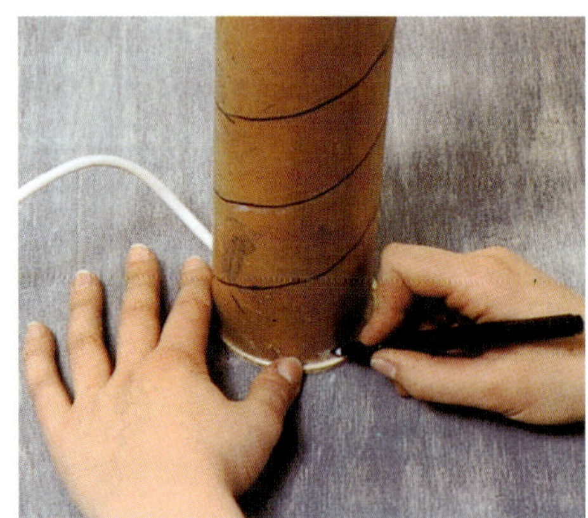

4 With a pencil, draw the design on to the tube, following the spiral lines already present on the cardboard tube. You can add variations and embellishments at this stage.

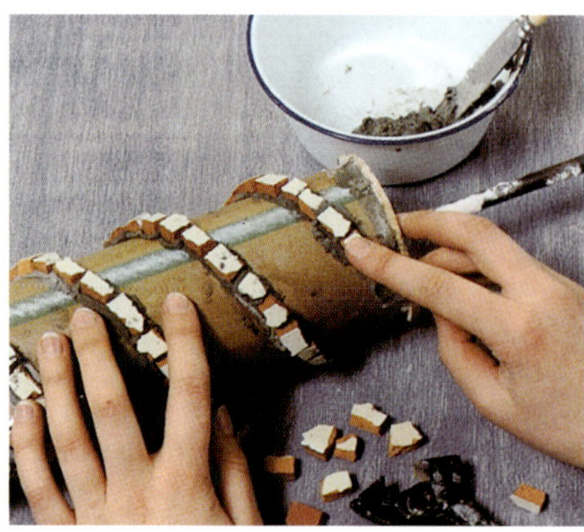

5 Cut the tiles for the outline colour into small pieces using tile nippers. Stick these to the lines of your design using tile adhesive. Use a sponge to wipe away any large blobs of adhesive that seep out from under the tesserae, then leave to dry overnight.

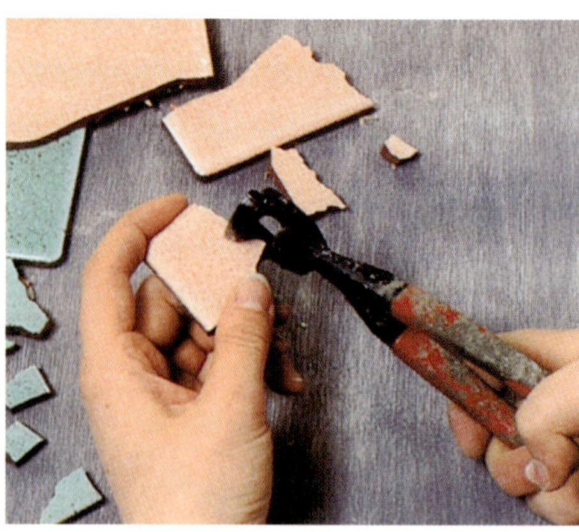

6 Select two colours of tile to fill the areas between the spiralling lines. Use the tile nippers to cut the tiles into various shapes and sizes, then cut the mirror into various shapes and sizes.

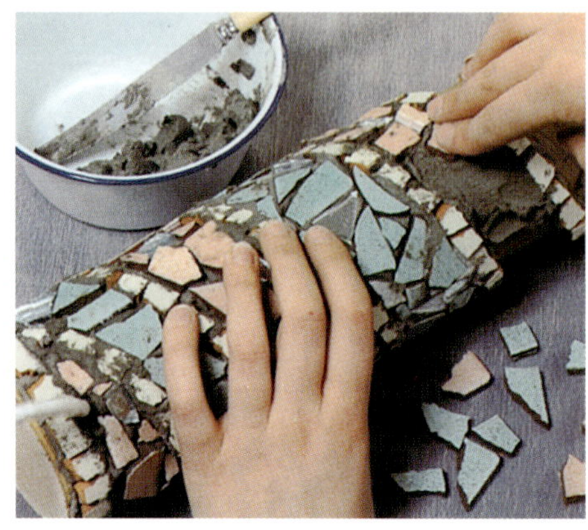

7 Spread tile adhesive on to the remaining cardboard area with a flexible knife, and apply the tesserae in separate bands of colour. Work on a small area at a time, so that the surface does not become too messy. Intersperse the coloured tesserae with pieces of mirror as you work. Cover the whole surface of the cardboard tube, then leave it to dry overnight.

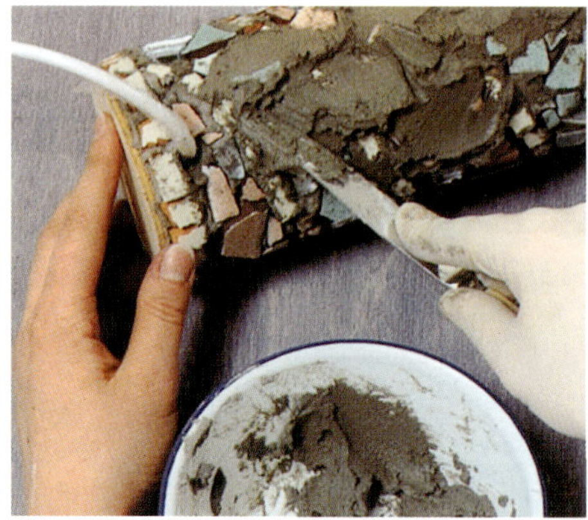

8 Apply more tile adhesive over the whole area of the lamp stand, taking care to press it down between all the tesserae. Wipe off the excess adhesive with a damp sponge and leave the stand to dry overnight. Rub off any excess surface adhesive with abrasive paper (sandpaper), and polish with a dry, soft cloth.

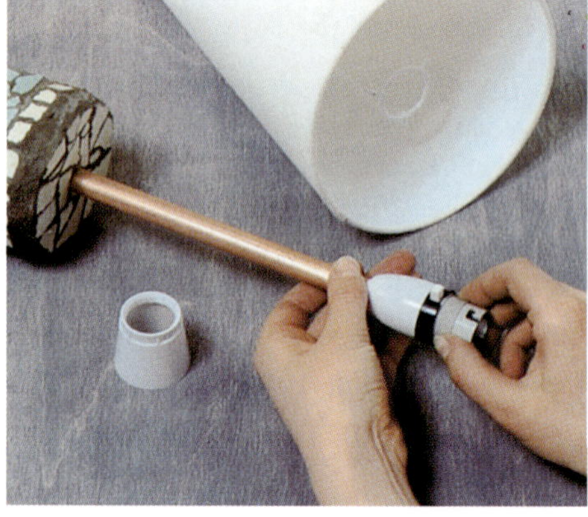

9 Finish off by attaching all the fittings. Slip the copper pipe, cut to size, over the central rod, leaving the screw end exposed. Attach the lamp fittings, plug and lampshade.

Mosaic forms a very effective surround to a mirror: the undulating, fractured surface perfectly sets off the smooth, reflective plane of the glass, used here with china, delicate patterns and touches of gold.

Bathroom Mirror

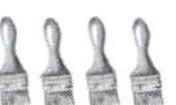

You will need

2cm (¾in) thick plywood sheet, cut to size required
Pencil
Ruler
Jigsaw (saber saw)
Abrasive paper (sandpaper)
PVA (white) glue
Paintbrushes
Wood primer
White undercoat paint
Gloss paint
Drill with rebate (rabbet) bit
Mirror plate, with keyhole opening
2 x 2cm (¾in) screws
Screwdriver
Thick card (stock)
3mm (⅛in) thick foil-backed mirror
Tile adhesive
Flexible knife
Masking tape
Tracing paper (optional)
Selection of china
Tile nippers
Tile grout
Vinyl matt emulsion (flat latex) or acrylic paint (optional)
Rubber spreader
Nailbrush
Soft cloth

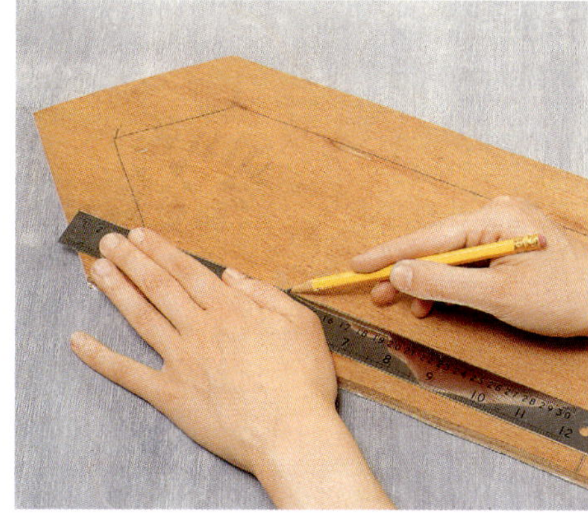

1 Draw the outer shape of the mirror frame on to the piece of plywood. Cut around this shape using a jigsaw (saber saw), then sand down the rough edges. On to this base panel, draw the desired shape of the mirror. Here, the shape of the mirror echoes the shape of the panel, but it could be a completely different shape if desired. Make sure it is a shape that the glass supplier will be able to reproduce.

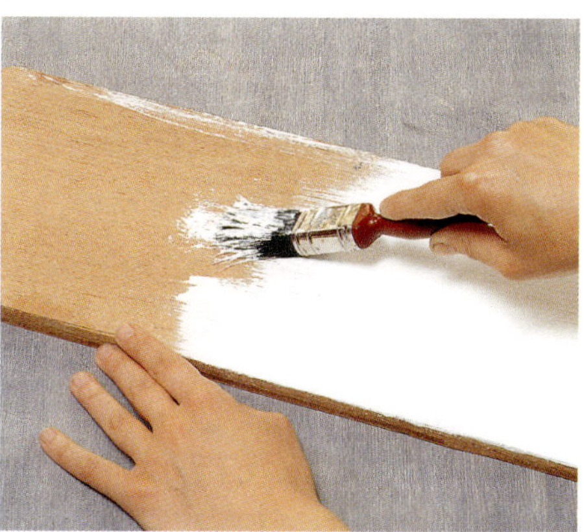

2 Seal the sides and front of the base panel with diluted PVA (white) glue, and paint the back, first with wood primer, then undercoat paint and finally gloss paint. Mark the position of the mirror plate on the back of the panel. Using a rebate (rabbet) bit, drill the area that will be under the keyhole-shaped opening so that it is large enough to take a screw head, then screw the mirror plate in position.

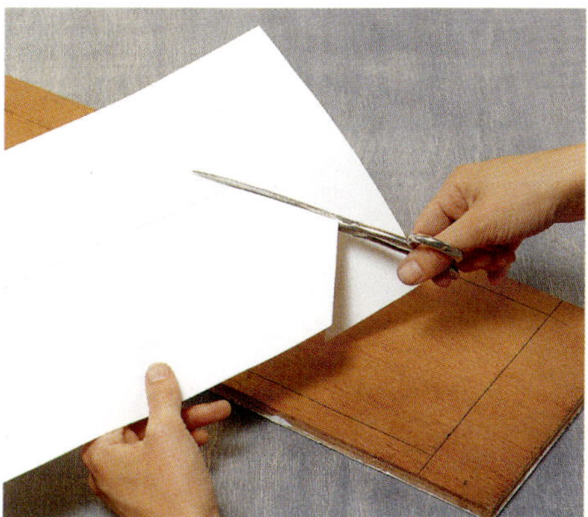

3 Make a card (stock) template in the exact dimensions of the mirror shape you have drawn on the base. Ask your supplier to cut a piece of 3mm (⅛in) foil-backed mirror using the template.

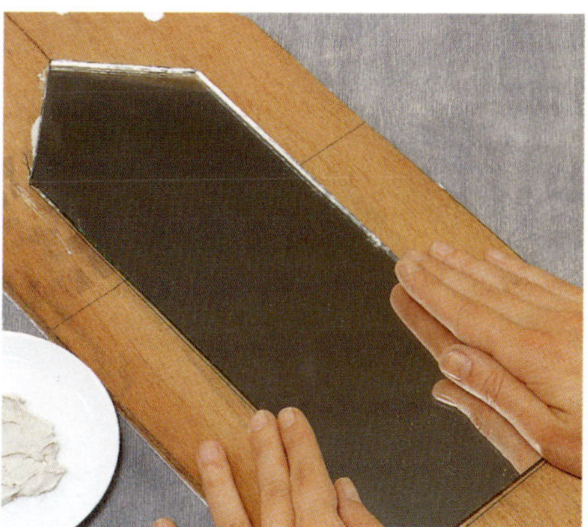

4 Stick the mirror in position using tile adhesive spread with a flexible knife. Leave to dry overnight.

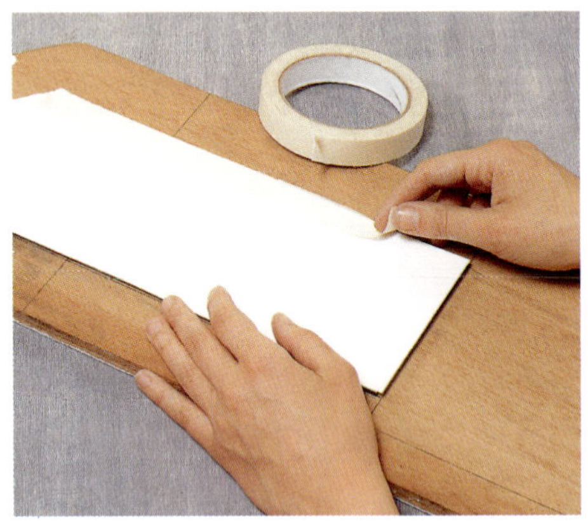

5 Trim 2mm (1/16in) from the card template all around the edge and cover the mirror with it, securing it in place with masking tape; this should prevent the mirror from being scratched or covered with adhesive. The mosaic will eventually overlap this 2mm (1/16in) of uncovered mirror.

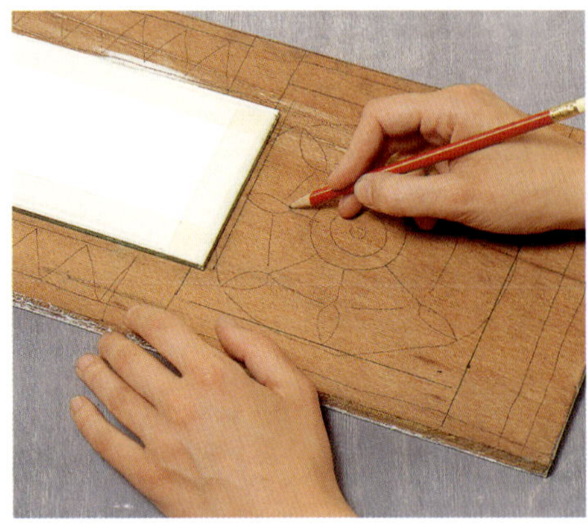

6 Draw the design for the frame on the dry, sealed surface surrounding the mirror; use tracing paper and a soft pencil to copy and transfer your original plan, if you wish.

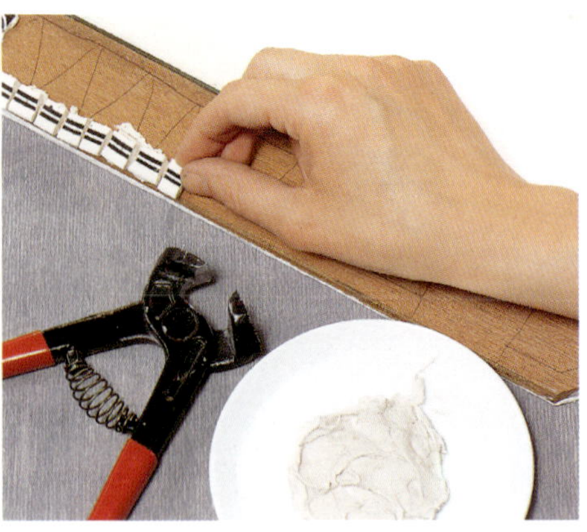

7 Using tile nippers, snip the smooth edges from the cups and plates you have collected. Use these to tile the outside edge of the base panel and to overlap the 2mm (1/16in) edges of the mirror, sticking them down with tile adhesive. Cut the remainder of the china into small pieces and stick these along the structural lines of your design.

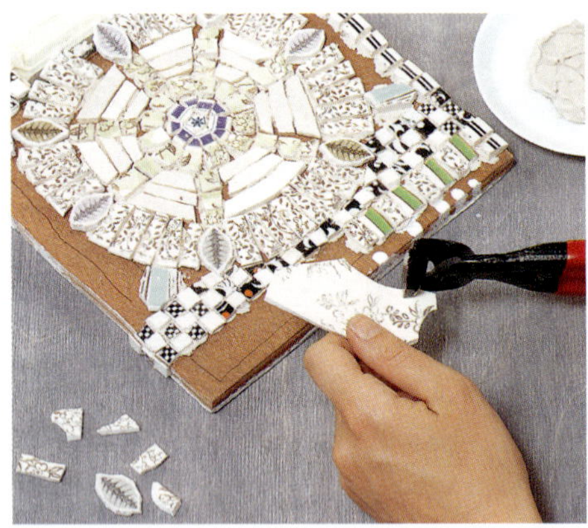

8 Fill in the areas of detail between the outlining tesserae. When the mirror frame is completely tiled, leave to dry for 24 hours.

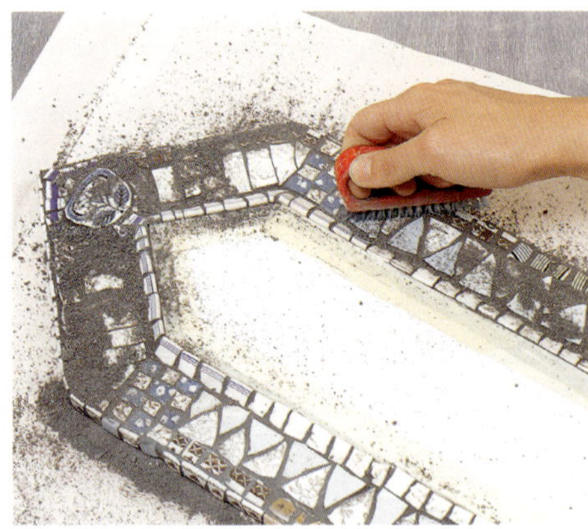

9 Mix tile grout with vinyl matt emulsion (flat latex) or acrylic paint, if colour is desired. Spread this over the surface of the tesserae using a rubber spreader, and rub it in by hand, making sure all the gaps are filled. Allow the surface to dry for 10 minutes, then brush off the excess grout with a stiff-bristled nailbrush. Wipe clean with a dry, soft cloth.

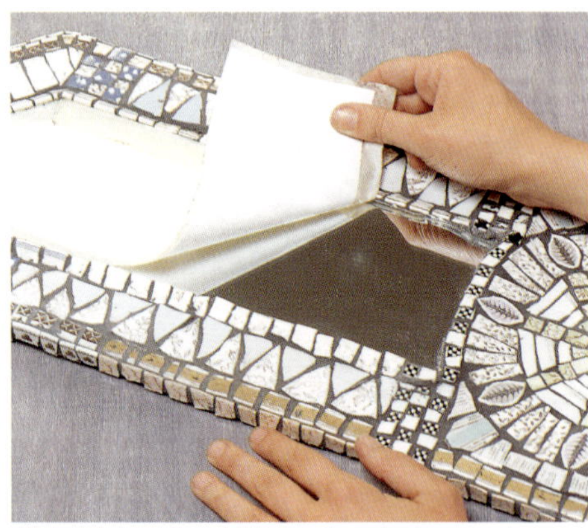

10 Leave the mirror overnight to dry thoroughly, then remove the protective card from the mirror. Finally, hang the mirror in position using the mirror plate on the back of the panel.

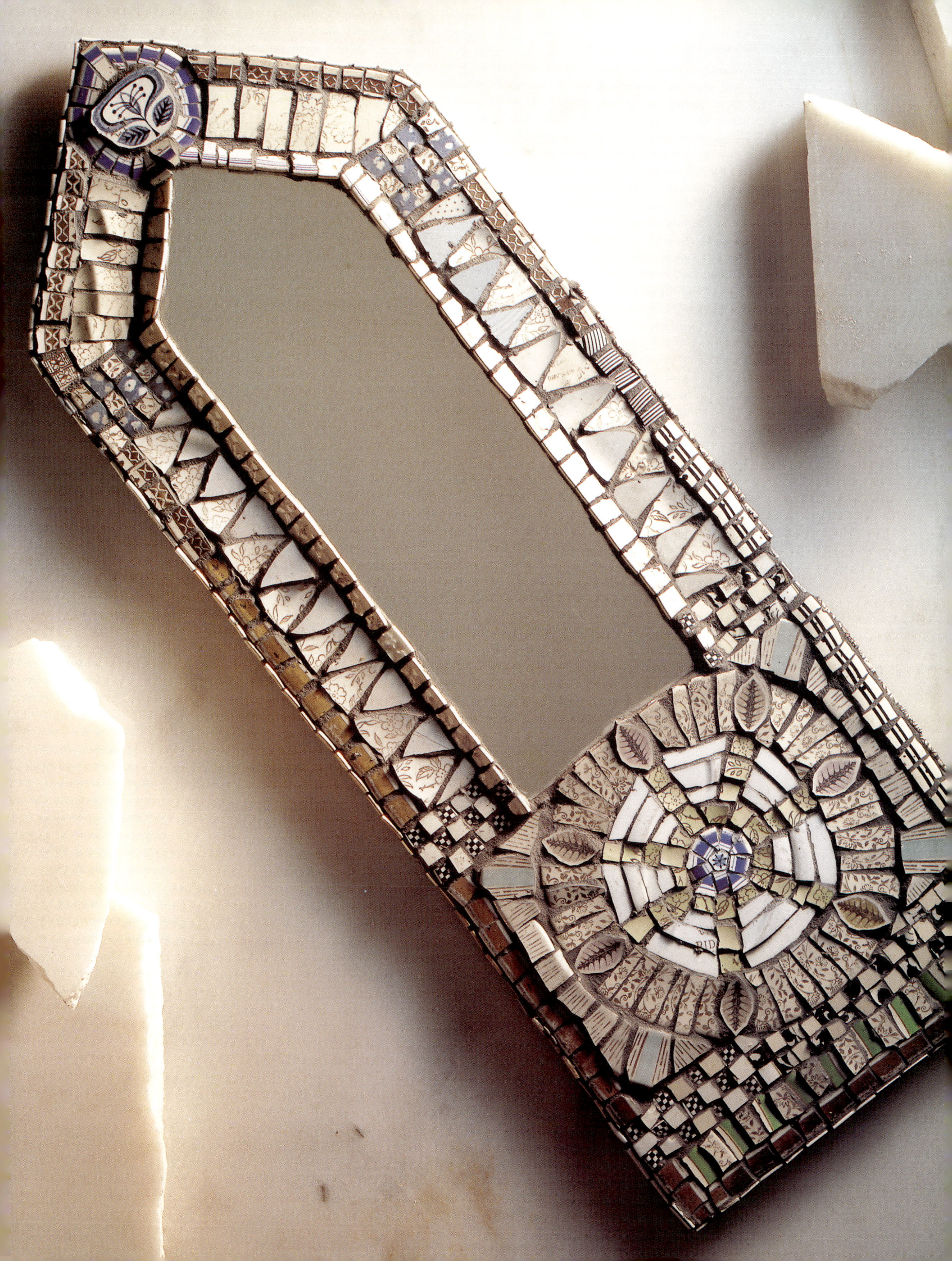

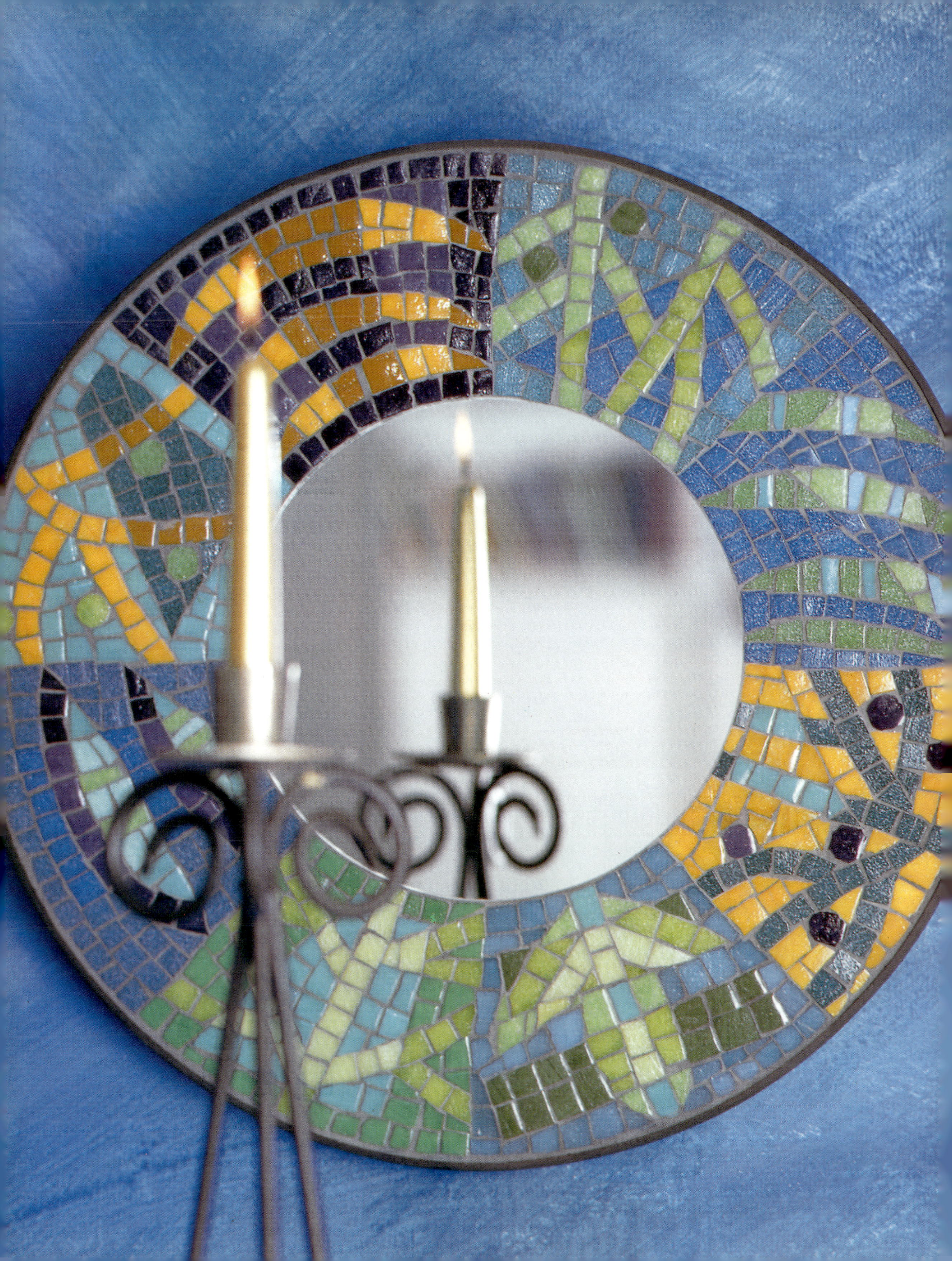

This abstract frame, with its glowing colours, was created using the semi-indirect method of mosaics. In this way, you can arrange the tesserae on paper first, before committing yourself to the final design.

Abstract Mirror

You will need

40cm (16in) diameter circle of wood
Brown paper
Pair of compasses
Pencil
Scissors
20cm (8in) diameter circle of mirror
Black felt-tipped pen
Masking tape
Vitreous glass mosaic tiles
Tile nippers
PVA (white) glue and brush
Strip of plywood, 5mm (¼in) deeper than the circle of wood and 130cm (52in) long, painted black
Hammer
Tacks
Craft (utility) knife
Tile grout
Sponge
Tile adhesive
Grout spreader

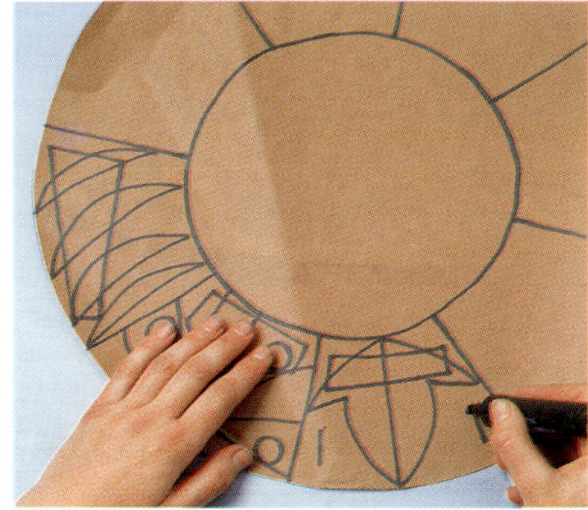

1 Using a pair of compasses, draw a circle on brown paper 2mm (1/16in) smaller than the wooden circle. Cut it out. Place the mirror in the centre and draw around it in black pen. Divide the border into eight equal sections. Draw a design clearly in each section.

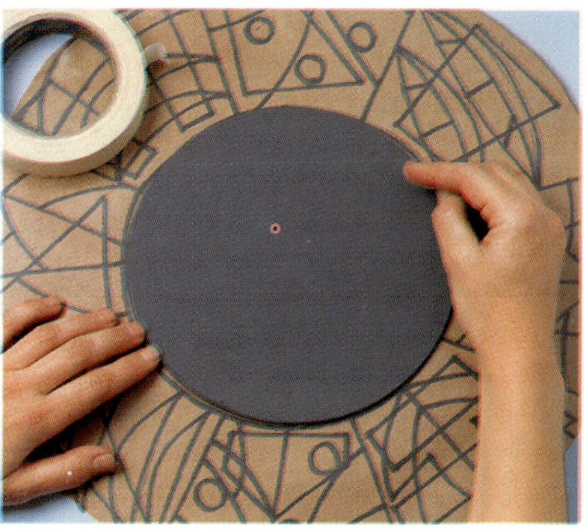

2 Place the mirror face down in the centre of the paper and attach it from underneath with masking tape.

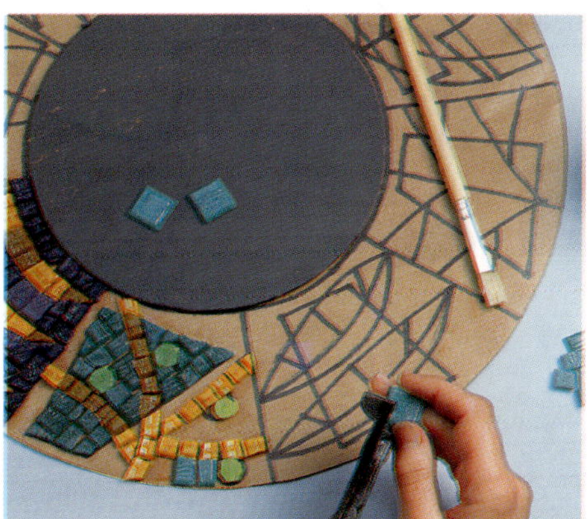

3 Cut the tiles into tesserae of the right size with tile nippers. Stick them face down on the paper design, using PVA (white) glue. Keep the gaps between them as even as possible.

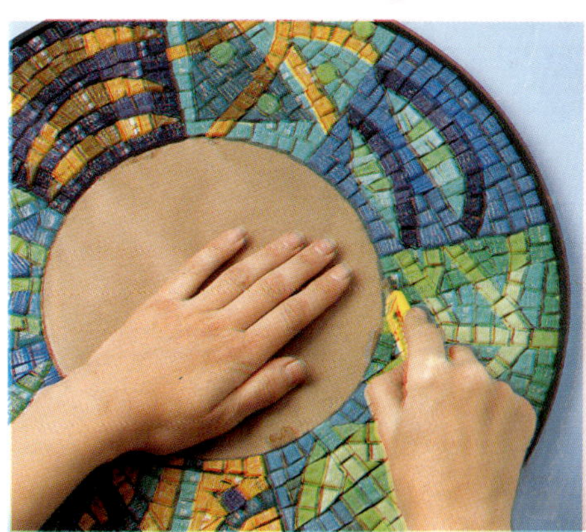

4 When the design is complete, carefully lower the mosaic on to the board. Position the strip of plywood around the edge of the circle and attach it using a hammer and tacks to form a rim. Remove the mirror and cut away the brown paper underneath, using a craft (utility) knife.

▶

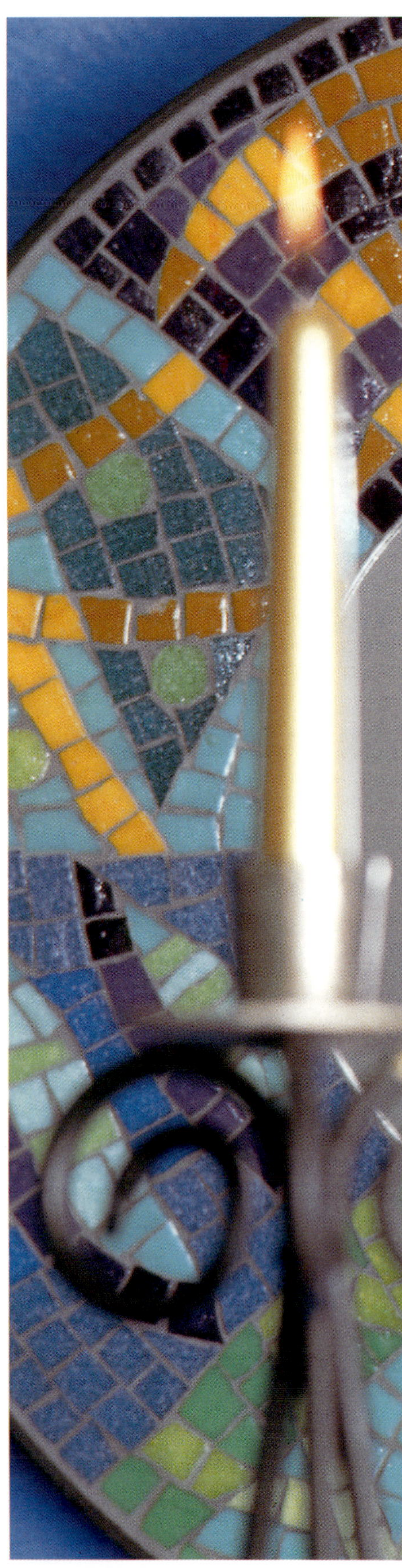

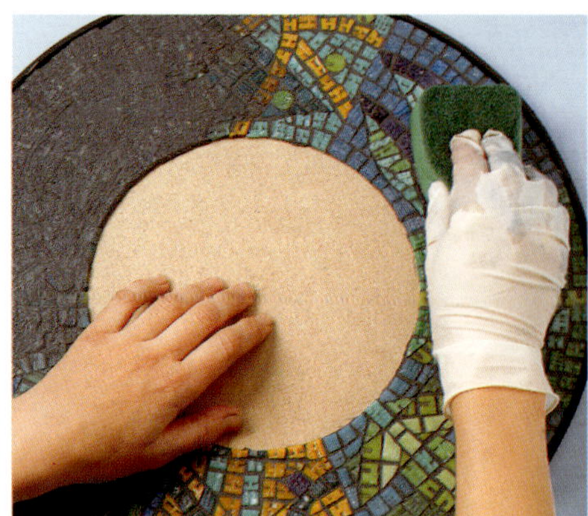

5 Rub a small amount of tile grout into the mosaic with your fingers, then wipe off the excess with a damp sponge. This will bind the tesserae together. Leave until almost dry.

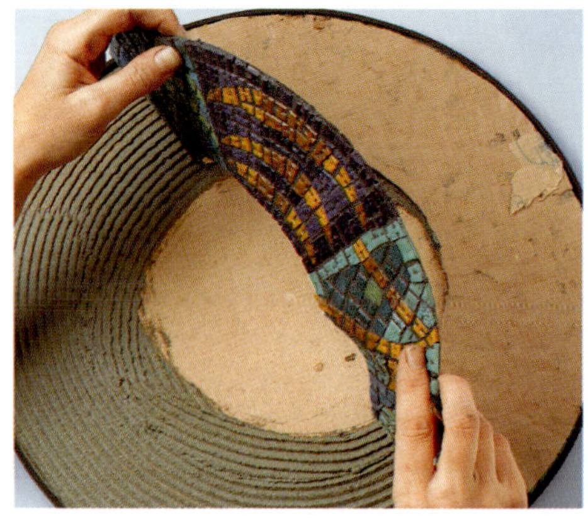

6 Gently remove the mosaic from the board by turning it upside down. Using the fine-notched side of a grout spreader, spread the outer area of the board with tile adhesive. Lower the mosaic down into the adhesive, mosaic side down, and press firmly.

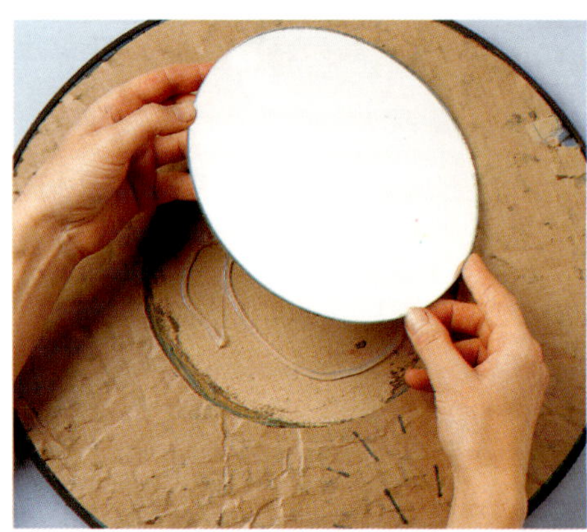

7 Coat the back of the mirror with tile adhesive and stick it in the centre. Leave to set for 20 minutes.

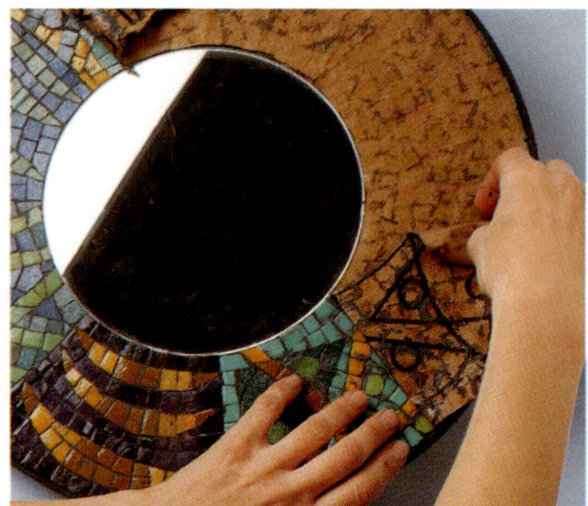

8 Dampen the paper with a wet sponge, wait for 10 minutes until the glue has dissolved, then gently peel it off the mosaic. Clean away any protruding lumps of adhesive with a damp sponge. Leave to dry, then re-grout, filling in any cracks, and sponge clean.

This delicate mosaic is made entirely from old cups and plates. The pretty trinket box is ideal for displaying on a dressing table, and can be used for storing jewellery, letters and other treasures.

Floral Trinket Box

You will need

- Wooden box
- PVA (white) glue
- Paintbrush
- Bradawl or awl
- Soft dark pencil
- Selection of china: white and patterned
- Tile nippers
- Tile adhesive
- Admix
- Flexible knife
- Sponge
- Paint scraper
- Soft cloth

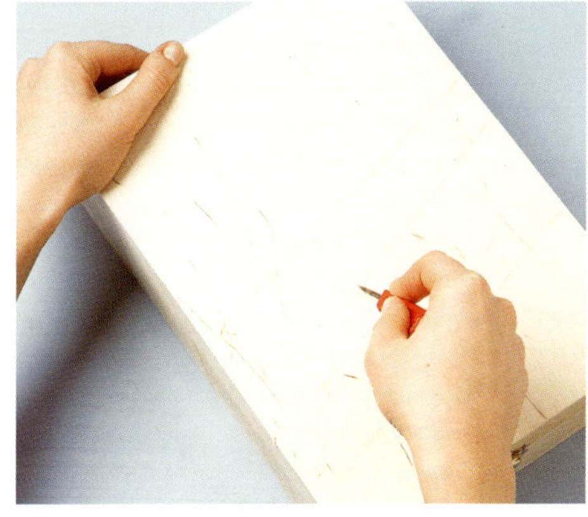

1 Prime the top and sides of the wooden box with diluted PVA (white) glue. Leave to dry, then score at random with a bradawl or awl to provide a good key.

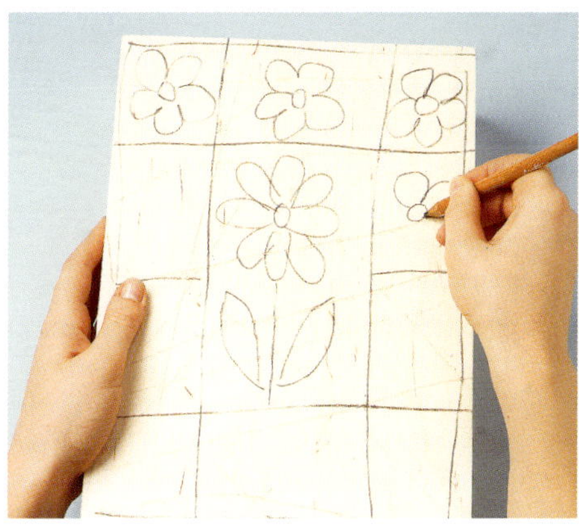

2 Using a soft pencil, draw a grid on the box. Freehand, draw a flower in each square, and a large flower in the centre. Keep the design simple for the best effect.

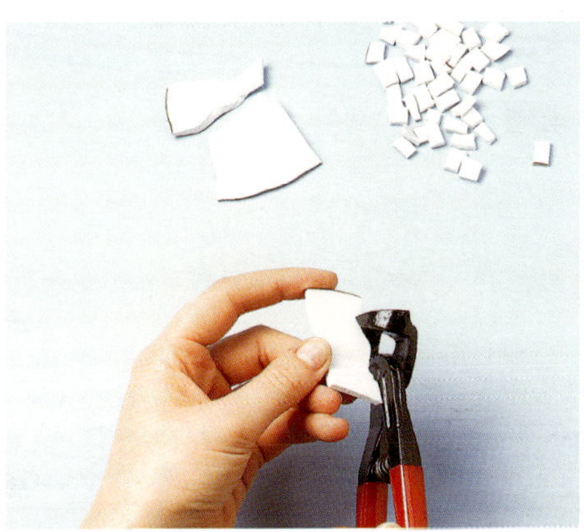

3 Using tile nippers, cut white pieces of china into small squares. Mix the tile adhesive with admix following the manufacturer's instructions. Using a flexible knife, spread this along the grid lines, a small area at a time.

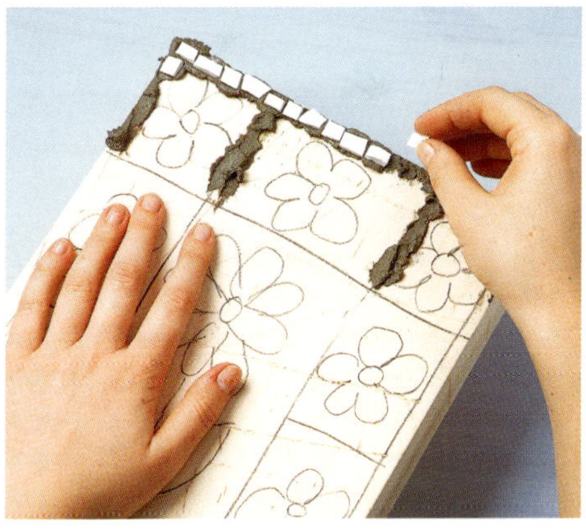

4 Press the white tesserae into the adhesive in neat, close-fitting rows. Cover all the grid lines on both the top and sides of the box. Leave to dry overnight.

▶

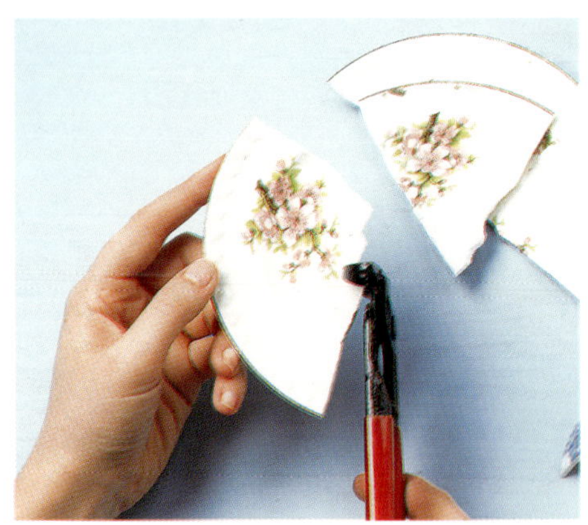

5 Using tile nippers, cut out small patterned pieces from the china and sort them into colours. Position the tesserae on the box and plan out the colour scheme for the mosaic before committing to the design.

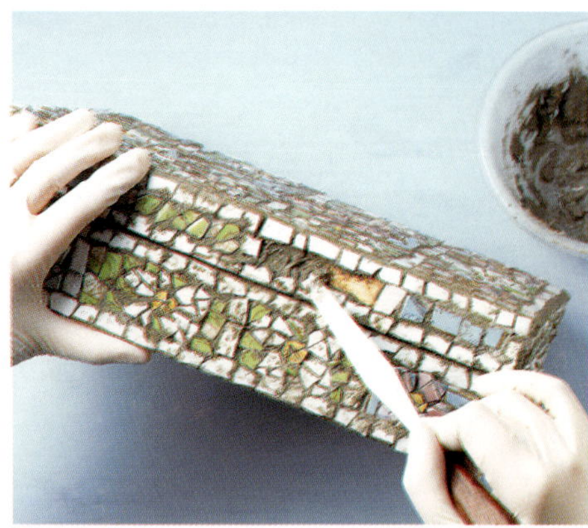

6 Spread the tile adhesive and admix mixture over each square of the top and sides in turn. Press in the tesserae to make each flower and use a contrasting, plain colour in the background. Leave to dry.

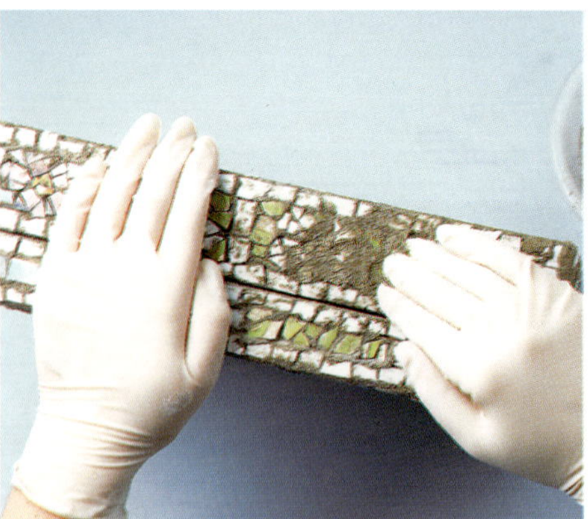

7 Using your fingers, spread tile adhesive all over the surface of the mosaic, getting right into the crevices. Wipe off any excess adhesive with a damp cloth or sponge.

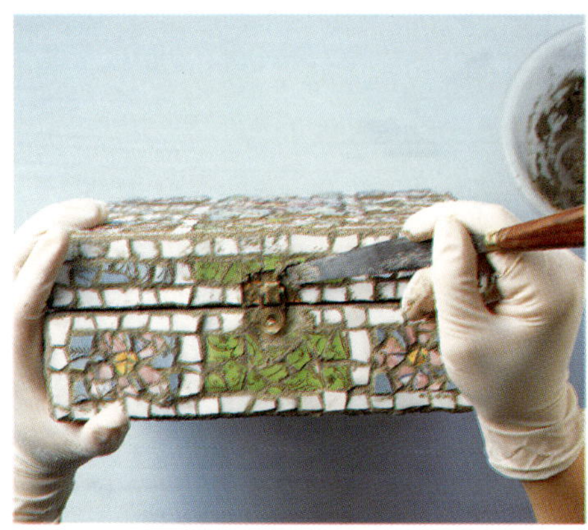

8 Using a flexible knife, smooth the tile adhesive around the hinges and clasp, if there is one. Remove any excess adhesive immediately with a sponge before it dries. Leave to dry.

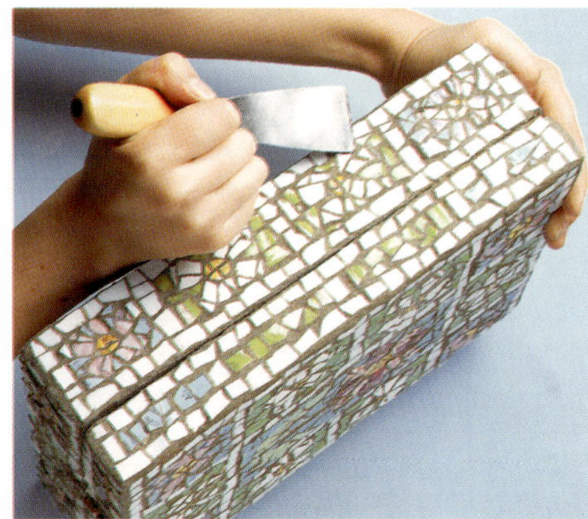

9 Carefully scrape off any tile adhesive that may have dried on the surface of the mosaic with a paint scraper. Take care not to scratch the surface of the tiles.

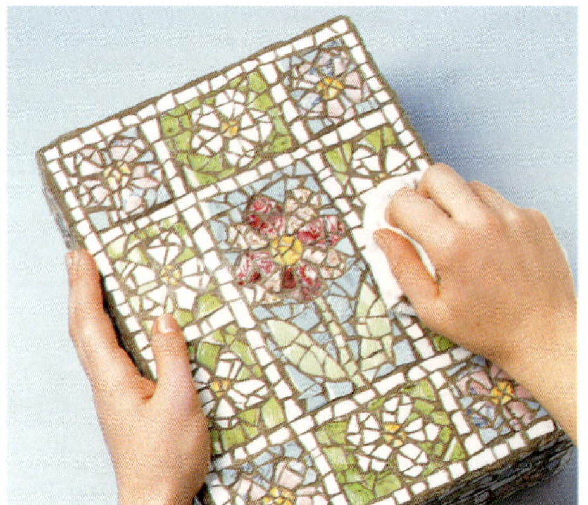

10 When all the excess grout has been removed, polish the surface of the box with a dry, soft cloth, rubbing each tile fragment to a high shine.

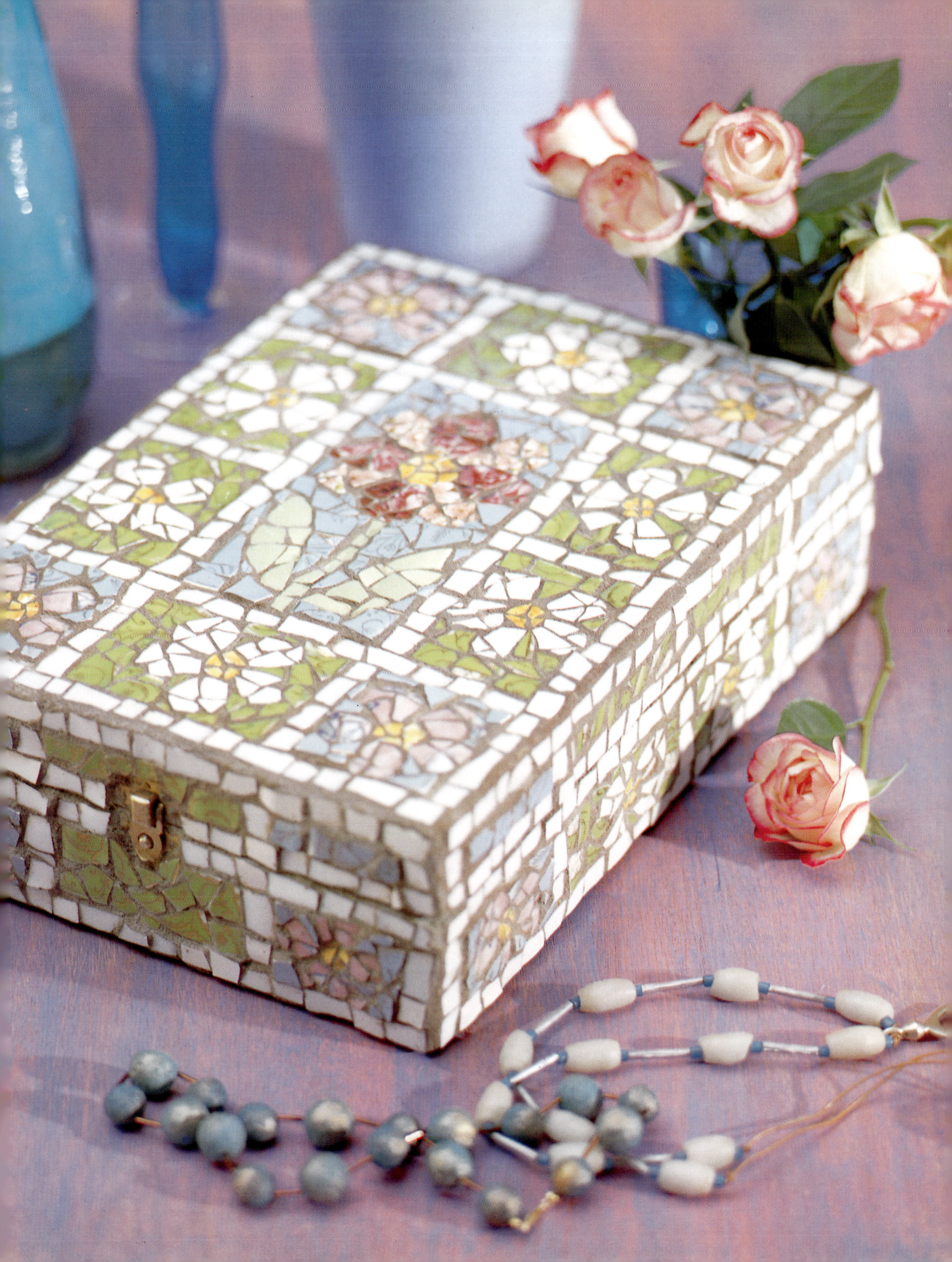

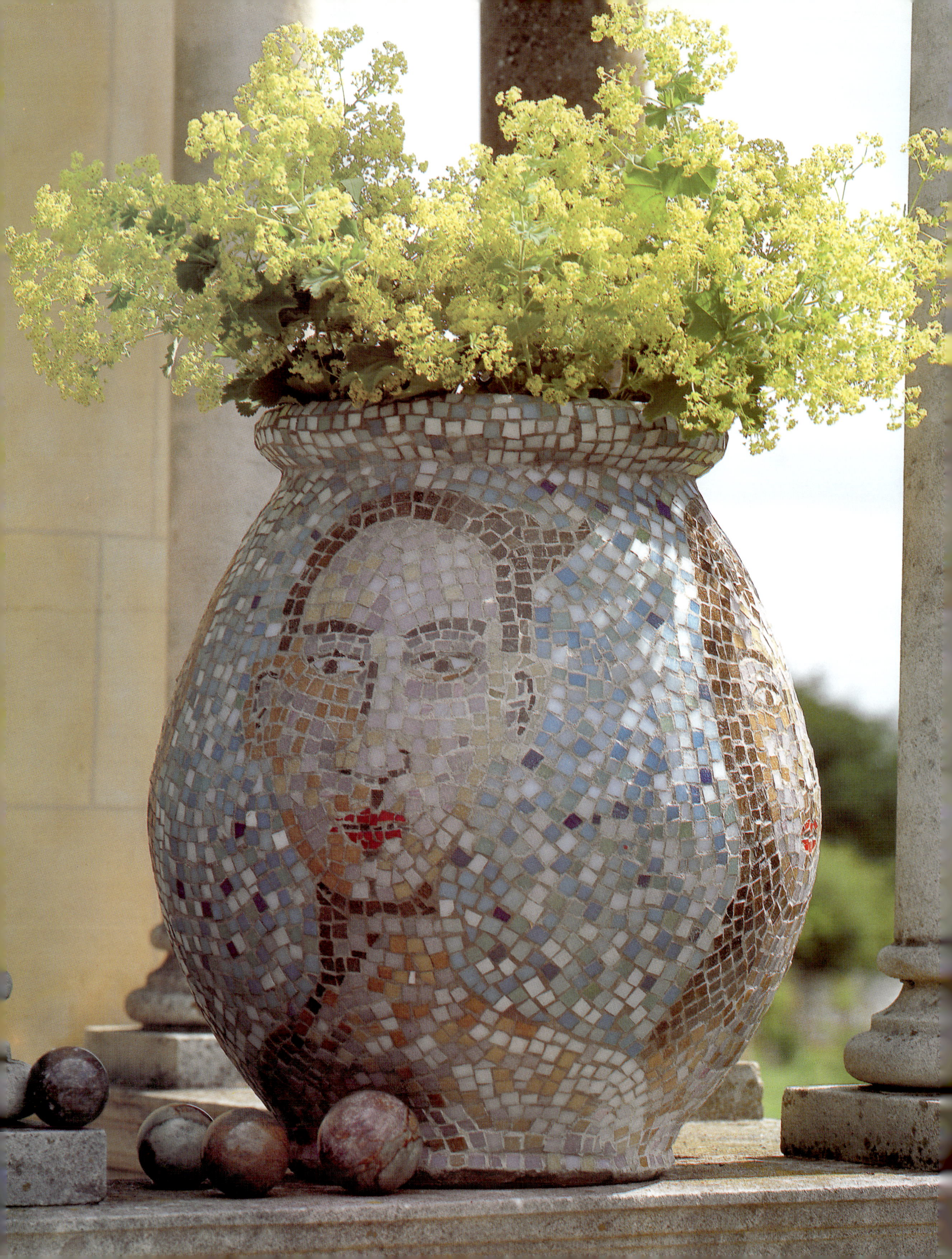

This unusual garden urn is decorated with modern faces but has a look reminiscent of Byzantine icons. Many people shy away from attempting to draw the human form, but such a simple, naïve drawing is worth a try.

Garden Urn

You will need

- Large frost-resistant urn
- Yacht varnish and paintbrush (optional)
- Chalk
- Vitreous glass mosaic tiles in various colours
- Tile nippers
- Tile adhesive
- Flexible knife
- Sponge
- Abrasive paper (sandpaper)
- Dilute hydrochloric acid, safety goggles and rubber (latex) gloves (optional)
- Soft cloth

1 If the urn is not glazed and it is to stand outdoors, paint the inside with yacht varnish to stop moisture seeping through from the inside and pushing the tesserae off. Leave to dry.

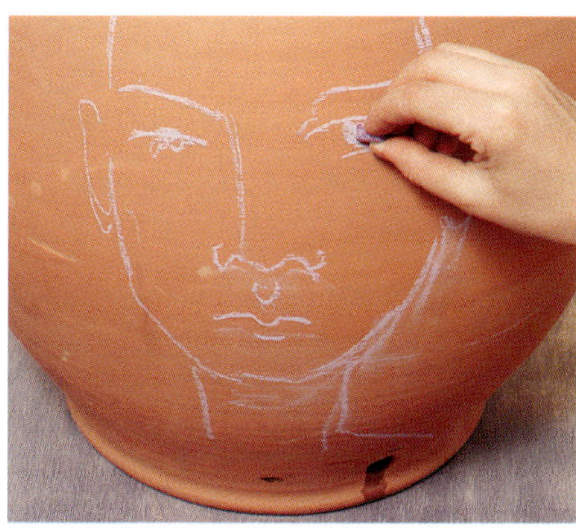

2 Divide the pot into quarters and draw your design on each quarter with chalk. The design used here depicts four different heads and shoulders. Keep the drawing very simple, sketching just the basic elements of the face.

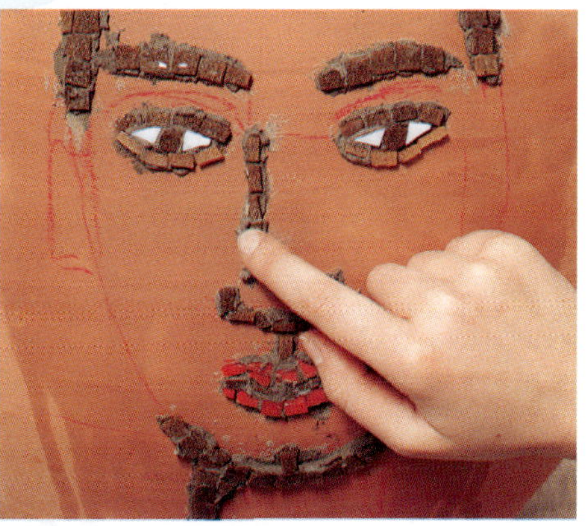

3 Choose a dark colour from the range of vitreous glass tiles for the main outlines and details such as eyes and lips. Snip the tiles into eighths using tile nippers. Spread tile adhesive with a flexible knife and stick the tesserae to the lines of your drawing.

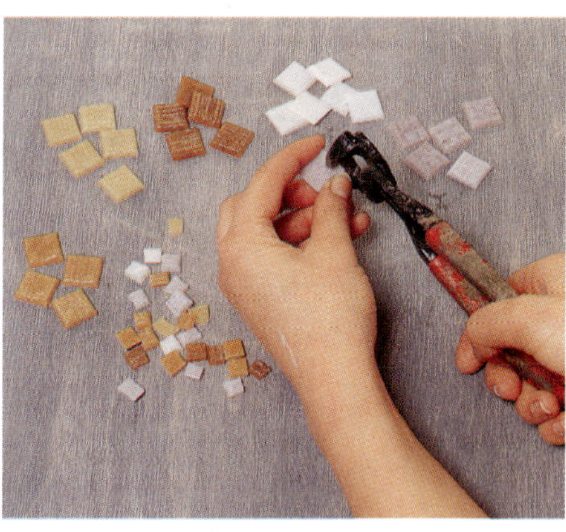

4 Select tiles in a range of colours for the flesh tones, and snip them into quarters.

▶

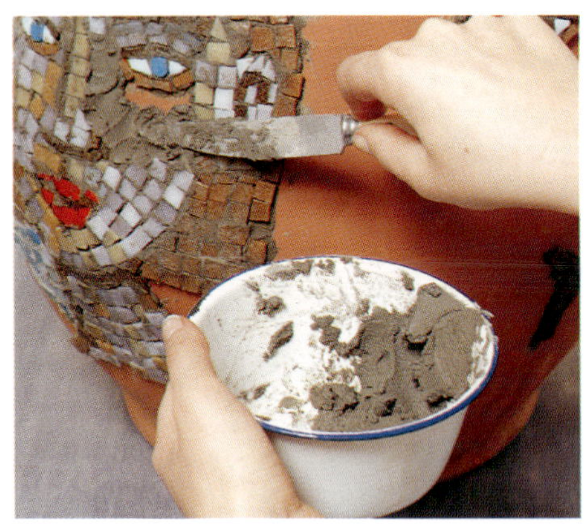

5 Working on a small area at a time, apply tile adhesive to one of the heads and shoulders and press the tesserae into it. Use a mixture of all the colours, but in areas of shade use more of the darker tesserae, and in highlighted areas use the lighter ones.

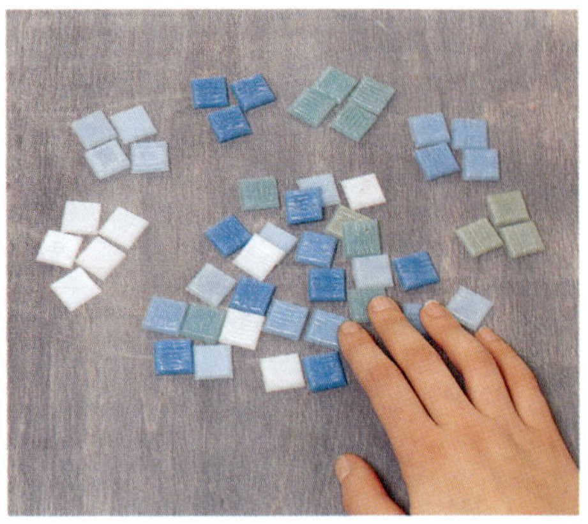

6 Repeat step 5 for the other heads, then choose colours for the area surrounding the heads. Spread these out on a clean table to see if they work together. A mixture of blues and whites with a little green was chosen here. Snip the pieces into quarters.

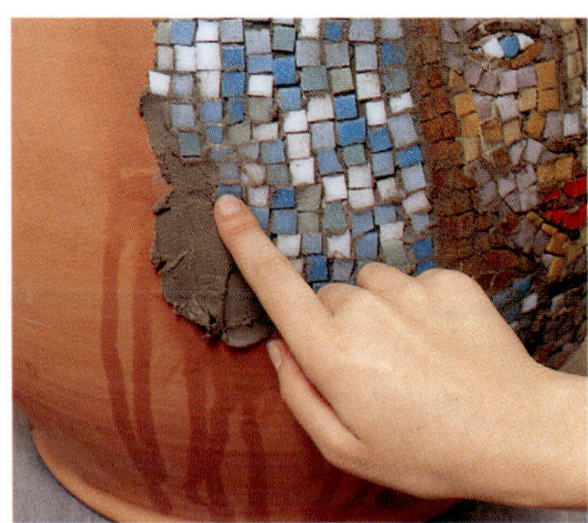

7 Working on a small area at a time, spread tile adhesive on to the surface and press the glass tesserae into it, making sure the colours are arranged randomly. Cover the entire outer surface of the urn, then leave to dry for 24 hours.

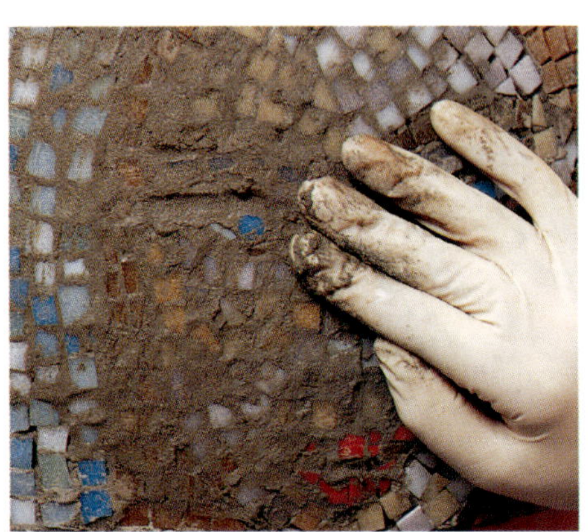

8 Mix up more tile adhesive and spread it over the surface of the mosaic with your fingers. Do this very thoroughly, making sure you fill all the gaps between the tesserae. This is especially important if the urn is going to be situated outside. Wipe off any excess adhesive with a sponge, then leave to dry for 24 hours.

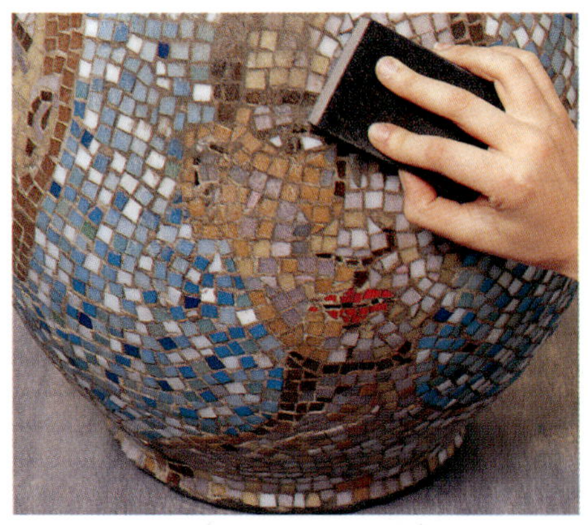

9 Use abrasive paper (sandpaper) to remove any adhesive that has dried on the surface of the mosaic. If the adhesive is proving hard to remove, dilute hydrochloric acid can be used, but you must wear goggles and rubber (latex) gloves and apply it outside or where there is good ventilation. Wash any acid residue from the surface with plenty of water. Leave to dry. Polish with a dry, soft cloth.

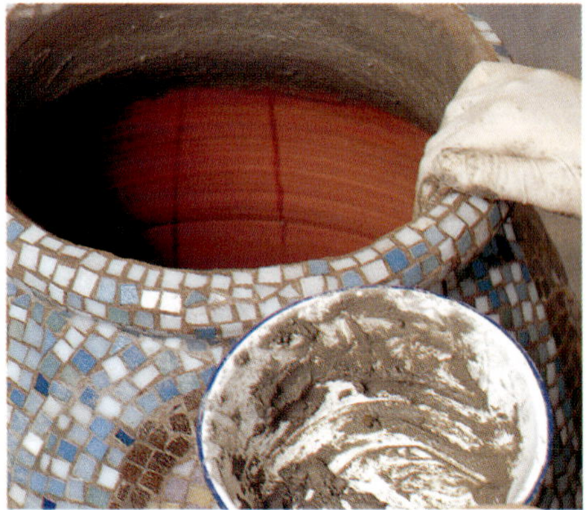

10 Finish by rubbing tile adhesive over the lip and down inside the pot. This prevents the mosaic from ending abruptly and gives the urn and mosaic a more unified and professional appearance.

In this piece, mosaic adds intense colour, and a contrasting effect, to a three-dimensional object. The colours and laying techniques convey an intensity of expression as well as a striking aesthetic effect.

Sculptural Head

You will need

Plaster head
Fine aluminium mesh
Wire
Tile adhesive
Small plasterer's trowel
Vitreous glass mosaic tiles in various colours
Tile nippers
Black tile grout
Tiler's sponge
Small screwdriver
Fine wet-and-dry (silicon carbide) paper
Soft cloth

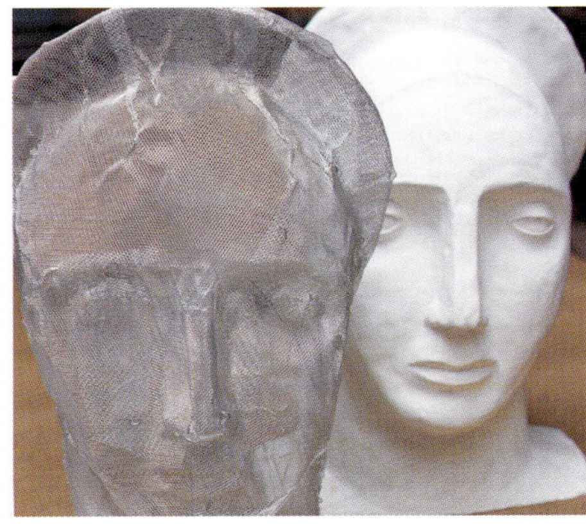

1 In this example, the base has been made from an original plaster head. Press a fine aluminium mesh against the surface of a plaster head and fold and mould it carefully to create the contours of the face and head. Do this in two halves, from the front around the contours of the face, and from the back, then remove them and join them together with twists of wire.

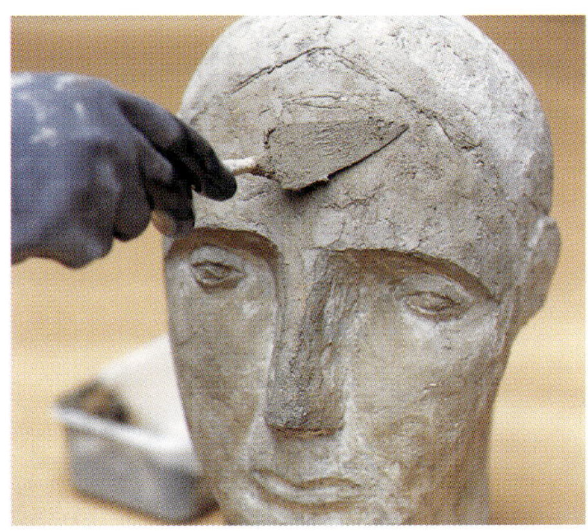

2 Create the form by applying a 12mm (½in) thick layer of tile adhesive over the mesh head with a small plasterer's trowel. Apply a thin layer first and work into the surface of the mesh, followed immediately (that is before it dries out) with a thicker layer. Some further modelling can be done at this stage, using the build-up of adhesive to refine the contours.

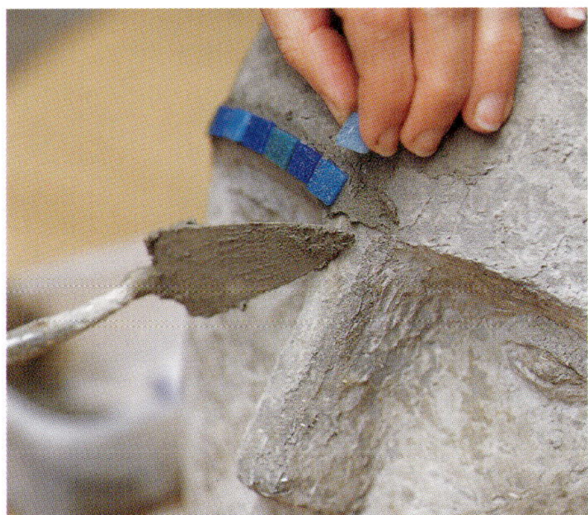

3 Cover the head in quarter-cut vitreous glass tesserae, sticking them to the base with a thin layer of tile adhesive. Apply this to small areas at a time with a small plasterer's trowel. The eyebrows would be a good place to start, as their curving lines generate the undulating lines of the forehead.

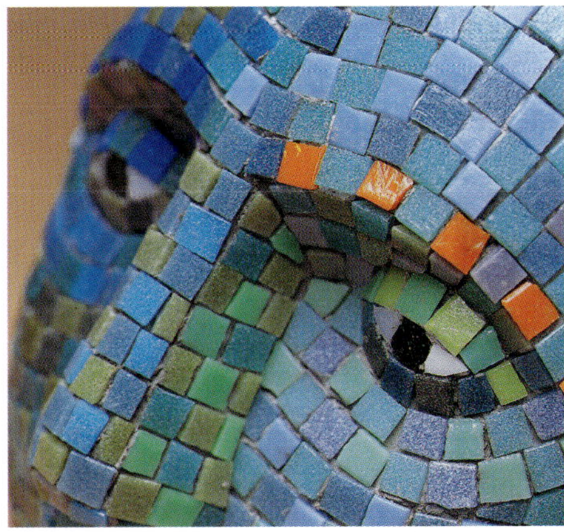

4 The eyes are very important in giving the piece definition and character and need to be tackled early in the process, as they will generate the laying lines of the cheeks. To maintain the even flow of mosaic, try to use full-quarter tiles where possible and avoid resorting to very small pieces, which will look clumsy and can be difficult to fix firmly.

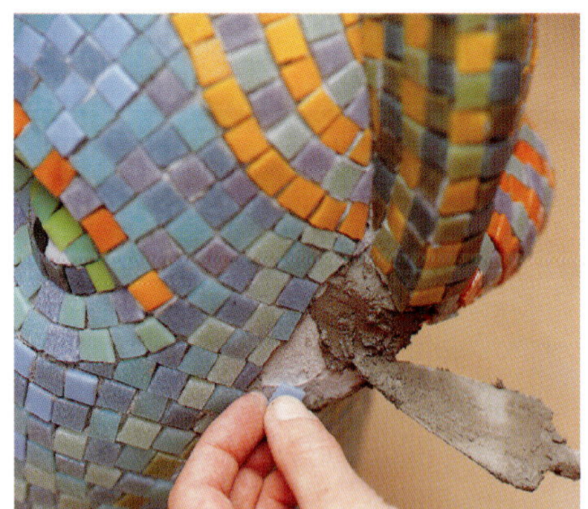

5 Where you are forming a sudden change in plane, such as over the eyebrows, around the top of the crown and at the edge of the ears, try to fix the pieces so that one bevelled edge joins up to another. This will keep the joint width as narrow as possible. These pieces will slightly overhang the base, and it is important to use enough adhesive to bond them firmly.

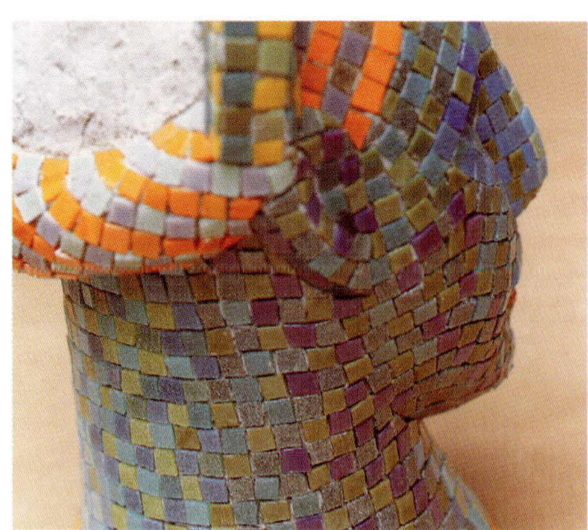

6 The lines of mosaic around the circumference of the neck have been carefully merged with the lines across the cheeks. Junctions of smaller cut tiles can be made where the line created relates to the form, such as around the eye socket and abutting the ear, but where the form requires a more gradual transition a blending of the lines will be less distracting and neater.

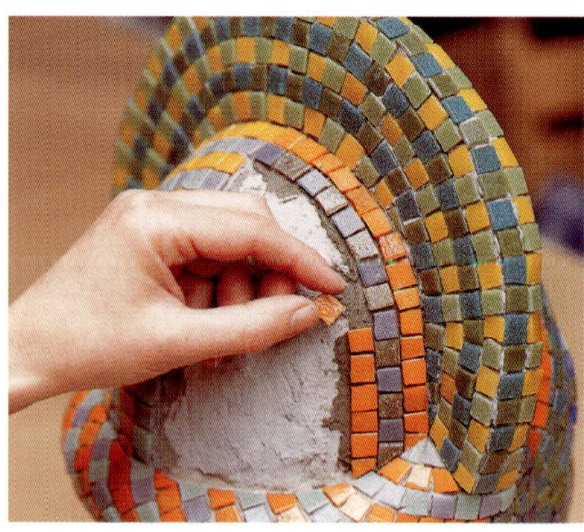

7 Cover the neck and face in a series of three-colour mixes that blend into each other by carrying one colour over into the next mix and avoiding harsh dividing lines. Lay the hair, crown and dress in two-colour stripes; the more organized patterns help to suggest a different texture from the areas of "skin". Make a contrast between the uniform treatment of the dress and crown across the piece and the asymmetry of the face and hair.

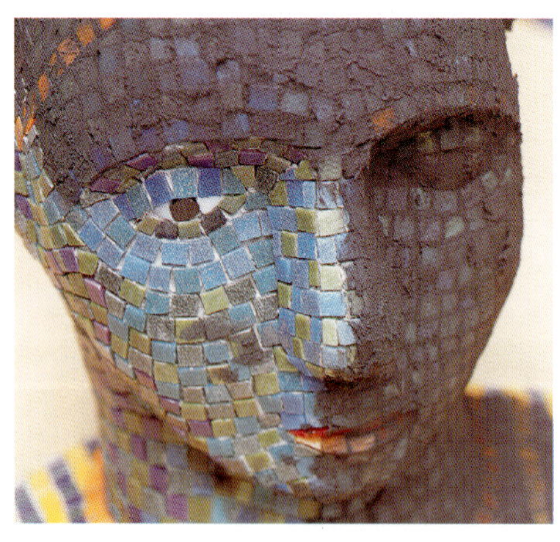

8 When the piece is covered and the adhesive is dry, apply black tile grout. Work the grout into the joints, curves and awkward corners with your fingers. Black grout gives extra intensity to the colours.

9 While the grout is still wet, wipe it clean using a densely textured tiler's sponge. Rinse the sponge often and avoid passing a dirty side back over the mosaic, as this will spread the grout rather than remove it. In fiddly areas, you may need to scrape away excess grout with a small screwdriver. Rub down any sharp edges with fine wet-and-dry (silicon carbide) paper, then leave to dry. Finally, polish the piece with a dry, soft cloth.

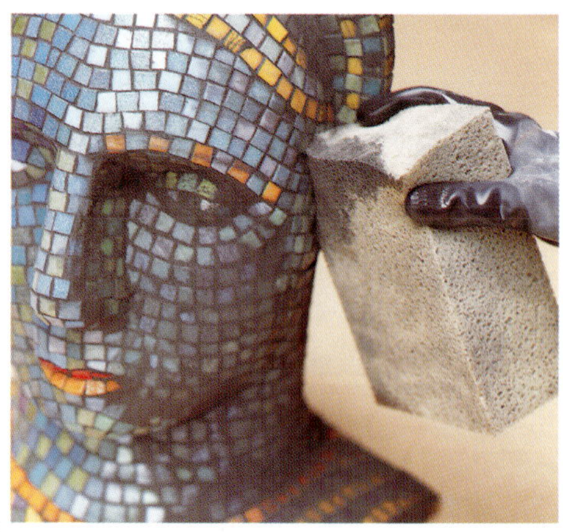

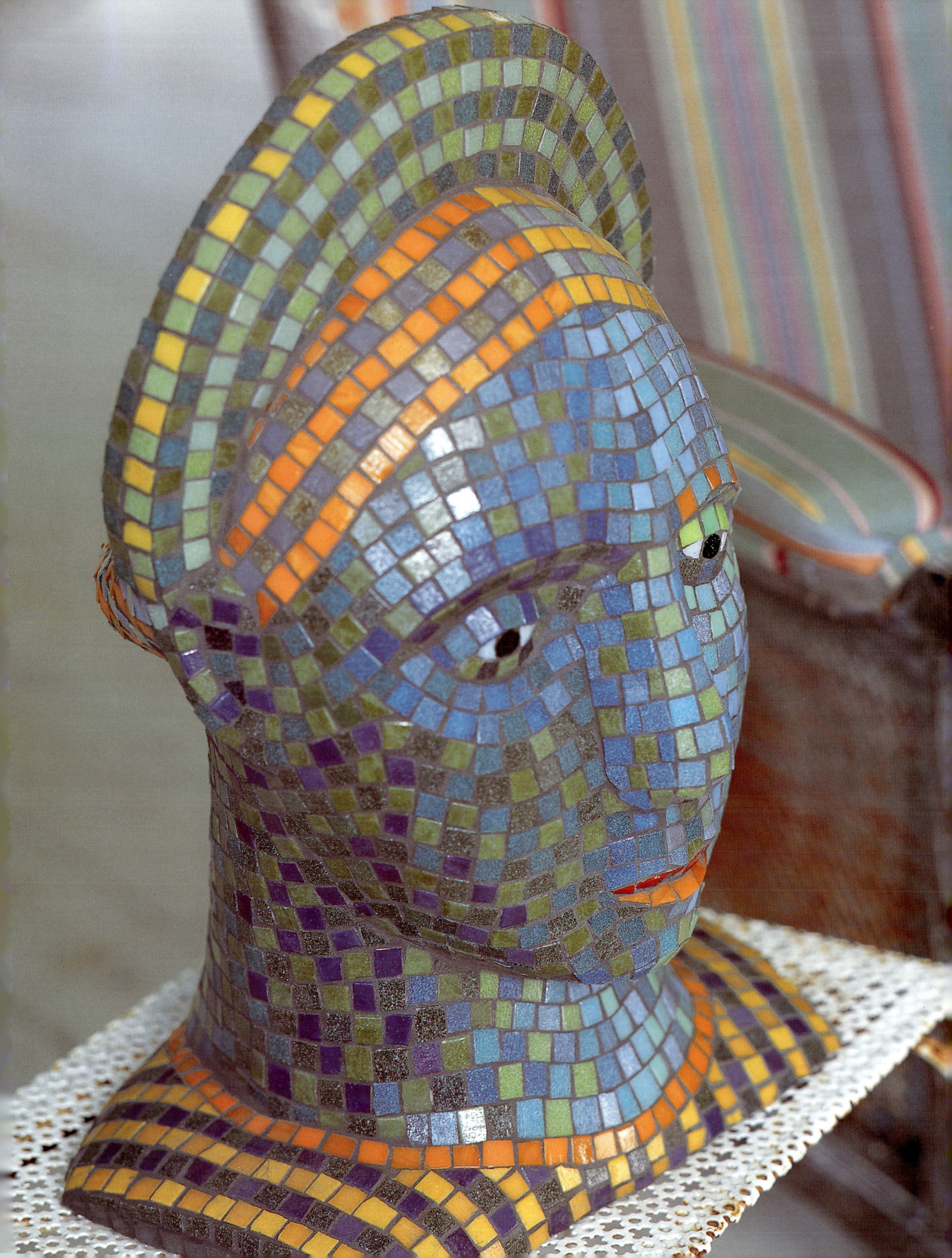

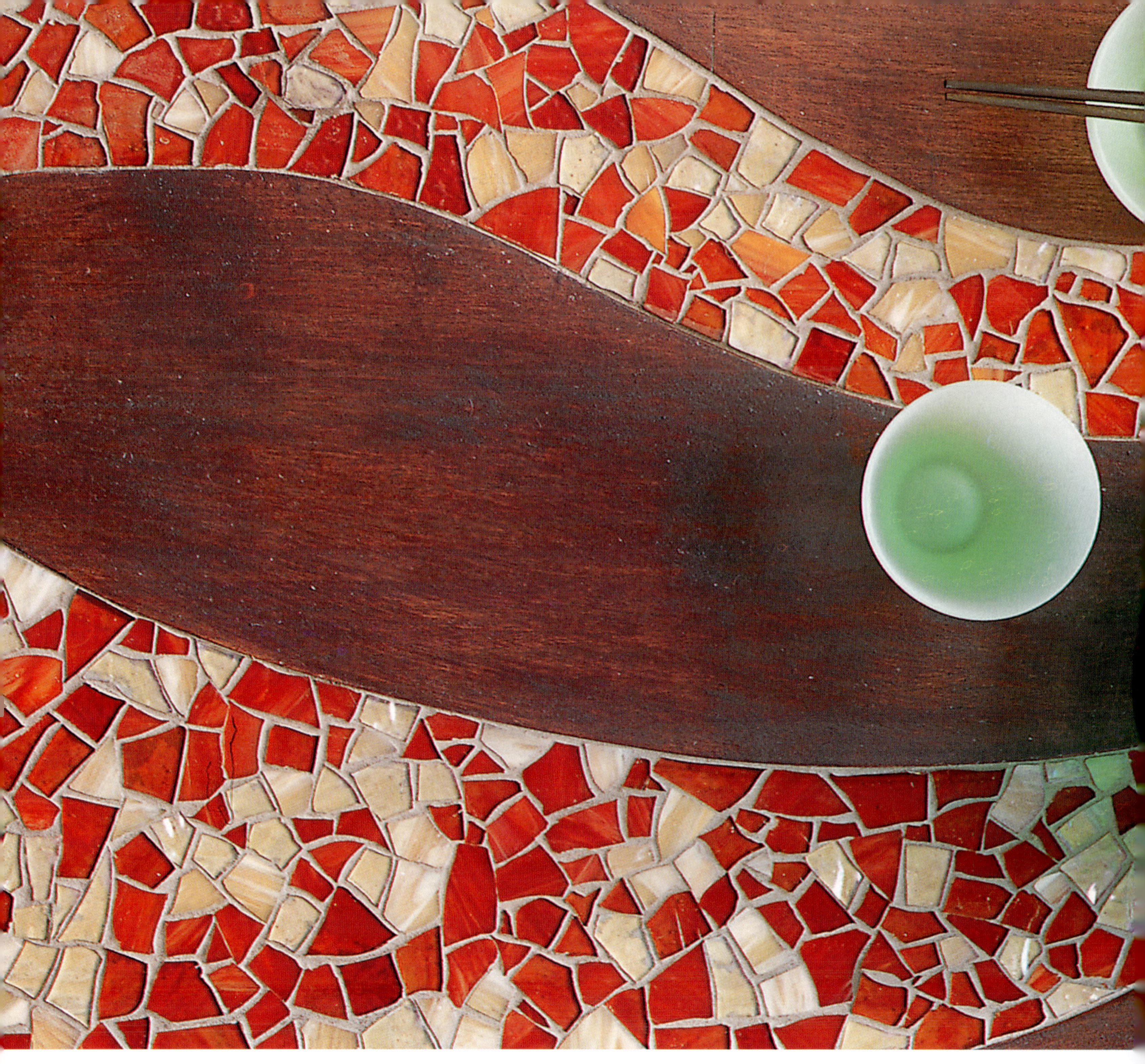

Furniture

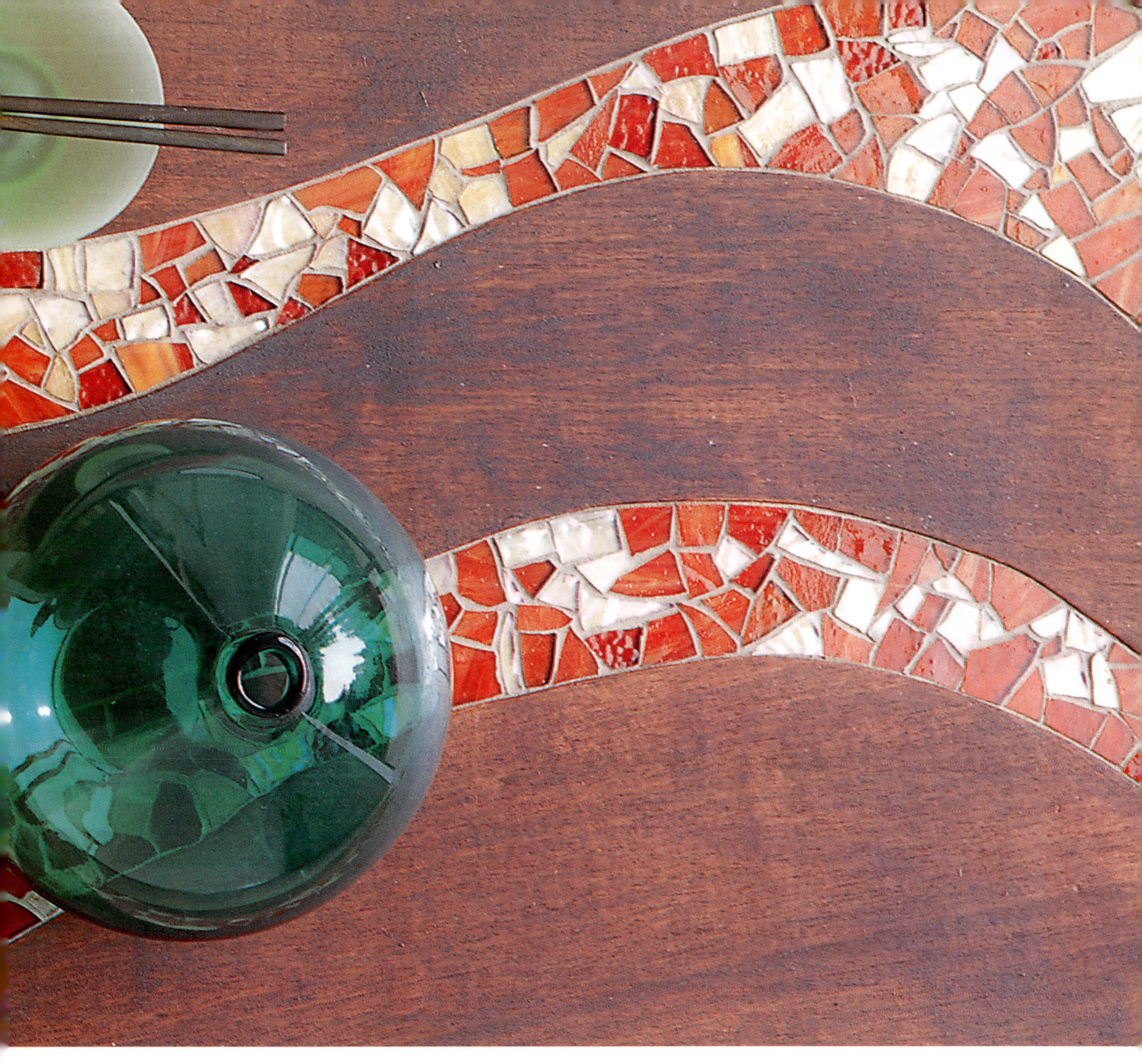

In this chapter there are plenty of ideas for creating and redecorating pieces of furniture, old or new. Revamp an old chest of drawers, or give a new lease of life to an ageing bedhead. The designs here are just the beginning – every project will have a unique angle, and every room or garden is different, so your finished result will be completely original. Use mosaic to customize your furniture with colour and texture.

Almost every room in the house contains an item of furniture that could be personalized by mosaic: from storage chests and chests of drawers to bedheads, home office furniture and screens.

Chests, beds and screens

Bedheads, chests, cupboards and screens are just some of the pieces of furniture that can be transformed by mosaic. Just a quick look around your house will give you plenty of inspiration.

Chests

Mosaic can turn both kinds of chests into highly unusual objects. A chest with a lifting lid can have panels of mosaic applied to the lid and front, while chests of drawers (bureaux) can have small matching or related motifs on each drawer. It is vital with such items that the tesserae do not impede the movement of drawers or doors.

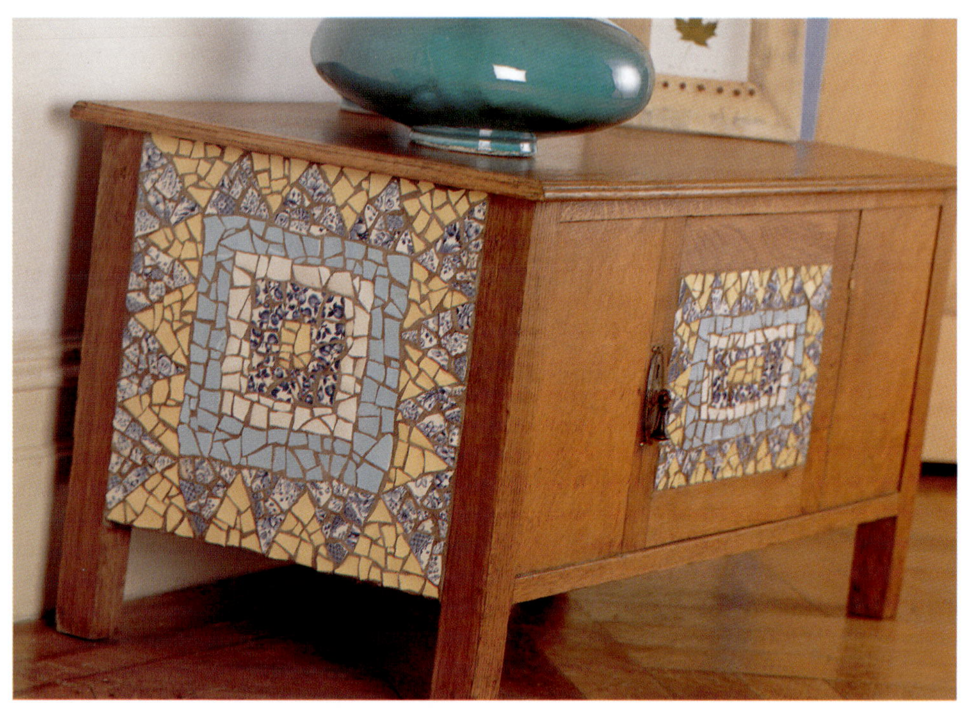

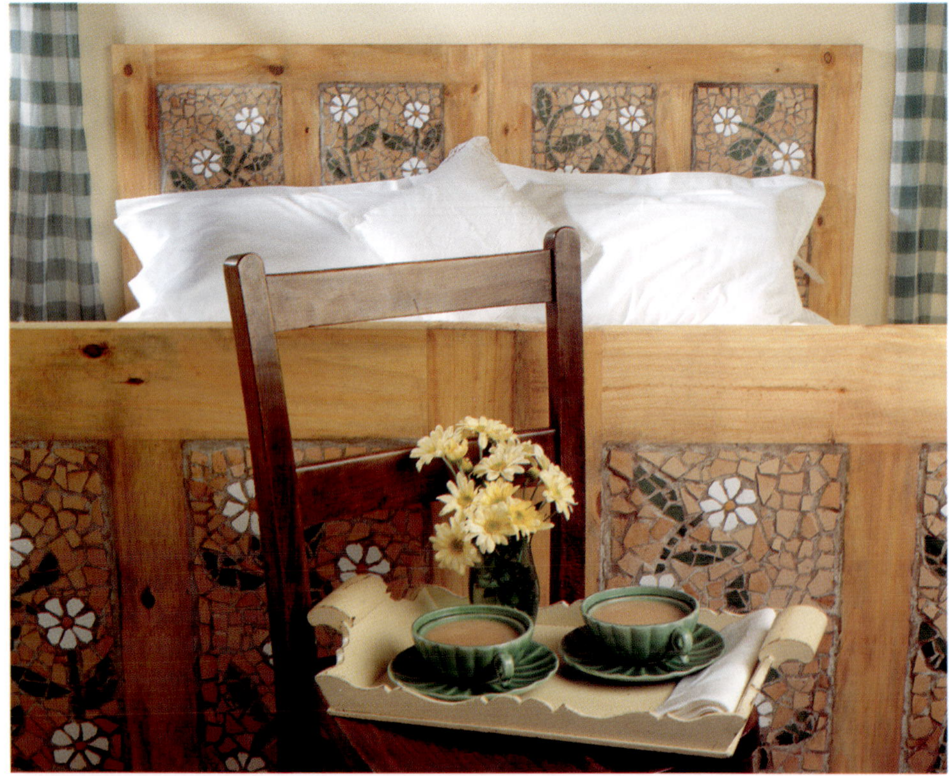

Above: Both end panels and a central panel on the door of this cupboard have been enlivened with mosaics using pieces of old china in a geometric design.

Left: The daisy-filled panels of this pine bedhead would look beautiful in a country-style bedroom.

Cupboards and dressers

Think about adding mosaic to the doors of cupboards or dressers. You do not have to cover the whole door; a small panel with perhaps a decorative border would suffice. Mosaic is an inventive way of reviving and personalizing mass-produced items of furniture or secondhand pieces.

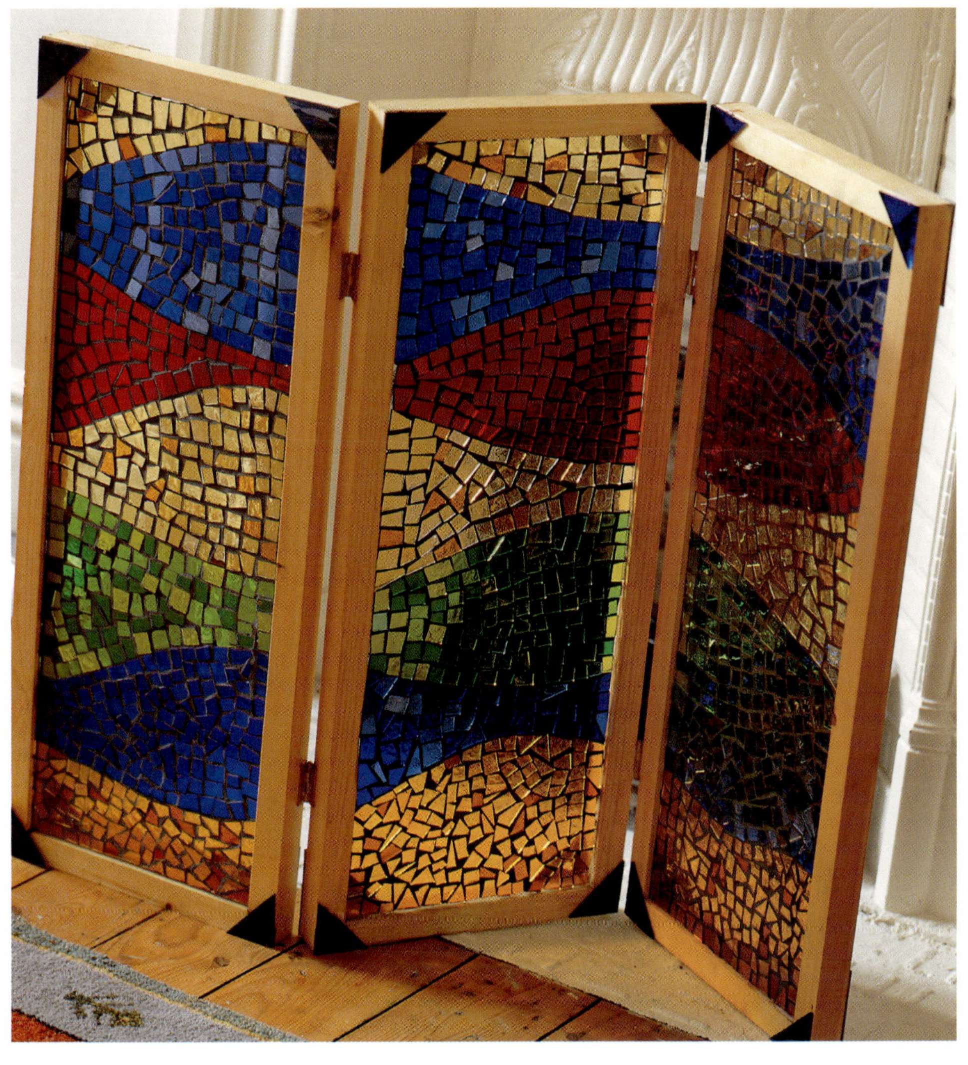

Above: Each drawer of this miniature wooden storage chest has its own striking motif, with just five colours of tiles used in the whole piece.

Left: In this golden stained-glass mosaic screen, the stained glass was laid on top of clear glass so that the light can still shine through. Bands of colour flow freely across the panels, giving a sense of movement.

Mosaic can be heavy, so you need to be sure that the furniture joints and any hinges, as well as the floor, will carry the extra weight. A cupboard with rather weak hinges could have its doors hanging under the extra weight.

When working on wood, a compound called admix may be added to tile adhesive to make it more flexible.

Beds

Wooden bedheads and footboards provide the opportunity for a bedroom transformation. The decorative theme could be carried on to other pieces of furniture in the bedroom, such as a bedside cabinet or chest of drawers, for a matching set.

Instead of the folk art flowers used on the opposite page, you could draw a modern, abstract design and fill it in with bold colours. Consider other themes for different areas of the house: a young child's bed, for example, could have a snakes and ladders design.

Home office

Desks, computer tables, filing cabinets and other home office furniture could benefit from mosaic panels or inserts. Remember that such pieces must do the job for which they are intended: computer tables should form a wobble-free base for the equipment; filing cabinets must have drawers that open and close; and it has to be possible to write and read easily at a desk. Adding personal touches in the form of mosaics – perhaps incorporating some symbol, logo or initials connected to the business – is a good way of making functional areas less intrusive in the rest of the living space.

Screens

A screen is the perfect solution for dividing a room into different areas, but a touch of lightness is needed to stop it becoming too slab-like. Mirror could be successful, as would gold, silver or other metallic materials in geometric and abstract designs. The play of light, natural or artificial, will add mystery, lightness and movement.

The humble table top is an ideal surface for a mosaicist, being flat and at a convenient height to be seen and admired. There are so many different kinds of table, that every room in the house can have one.

Tables

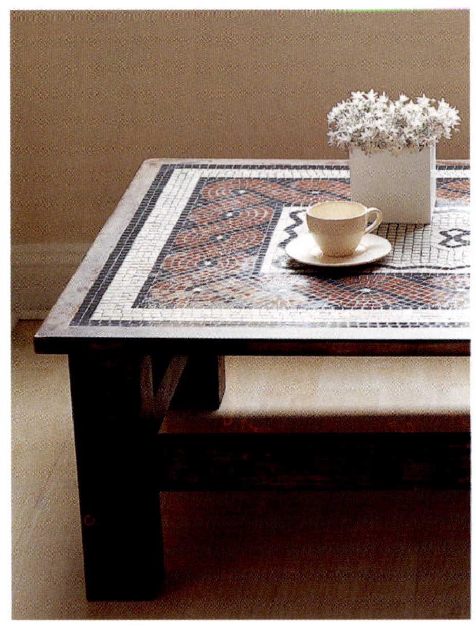

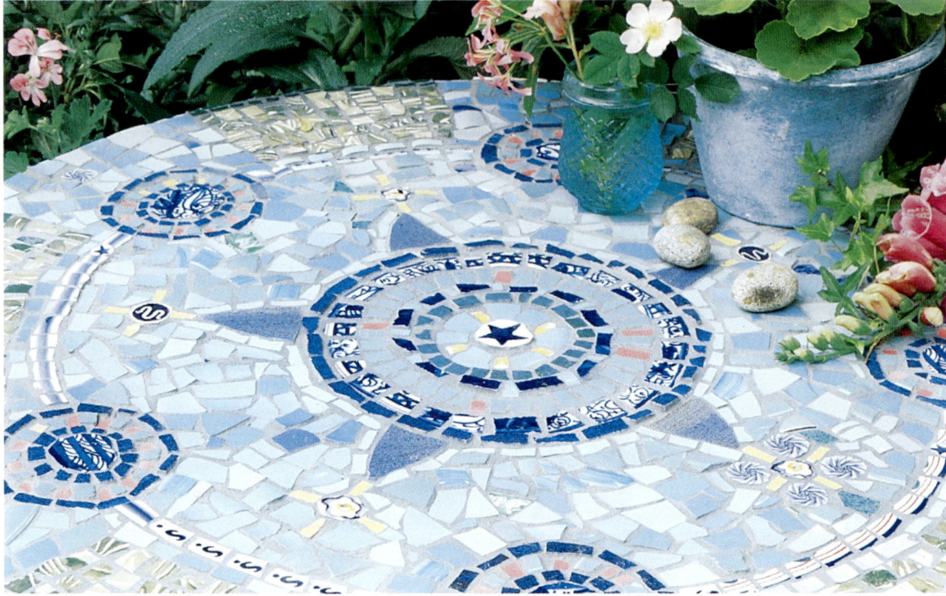

Above left: The strong rope design mosaic by Celia Gregory suits the square robustness of this coffee table.

Above: The robust nature of ceramic mosaic lends itself to garden furniture. Here the garden pots have been given a coat of paint to match the colour scheme.

A chess or games table, side, hall or bedside table, perhaps even a dressing table, would be perfect for mosaic. Garden tables are also ideal.

Finding or making a table

Relatively inexpensive tables are available from junk (curio) shops, and mosaic is an imaginative and fulfilling way of personalizing them.

Alternatively, you could easily make your own table tops from MDF (medium-density fiberboard), plywood or other manufactured boards, creating different shapes and sizes to suit your mosaic design by cutting them out with a jigsaw (saber saw) or circular saw.

The edge of the table can be finished in mosaic or have a stainless-steel rim or similar edging. Any sharp mosaic edges should be sanded down. You can buy simple metal bases or frames to support the table tops from second-hand stores; alternatively, you could commission one from a blacksmith or craftsperson, or just make your own from blocks of wood.

Table surfaces

You need to make sure that the finished result is smooth and even: people must be able to put drinks and vases on them with no danger of them toppling over or wobbling precariously.

You could mosaic the entire table top or you may prefer to insert a decorative panel into a part of it, often the centre. A mosaic border around the edge would also look attractive. Such panels or borders must be flush or level with (not above or below) the rest of the table top, and this needs to be taken into account at the design stage.

If you want to insert a mosaic panel or border, you will need to calculate what depth the finished work will be, then remove that amount from the depth of the table top and sink the mosaic into the prepared area. You should also use pieces of tile throughout with the same thickness.

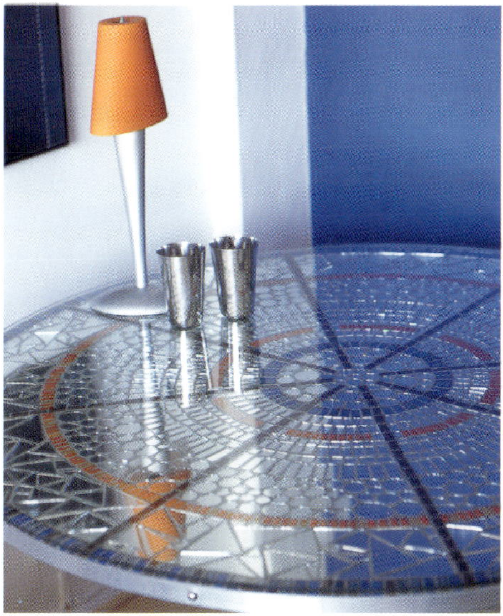

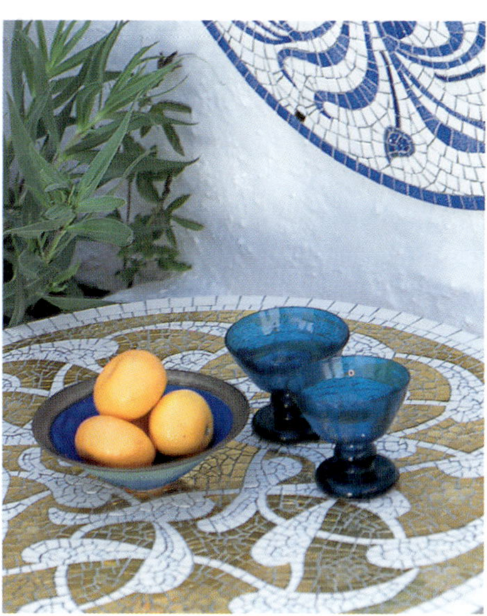

Non-porous materials, such as glazed clay, glass or a suitable stone, can be easily wiped dry without becoming stained. If the material you choose is porous, you could cover the entire surface of your design with a protective layer of glass. Ask a specialist to cut this to size.

Table-top designs

Your choice of design is, of course, personal, but it is worth noting that repeated patterns and continuous swirling or abstract designs work particularly well on circular tables. You could try a Celtic knot motif or an Islamic organic design. There are many pattern books available in craft shops to use for inspiration. The late Victorians were great pattern book makers, and in these you will find an abundance of choice for designs.

Above right: This table top by Elizabeth De'Ath is decorated with mosaic mirror, divided into sections and bands to create a distinct pattern.

Above far right: This Islamic-influenced table top and a roundel mosaic in similar patterns are by Elaine M. Goodwin.

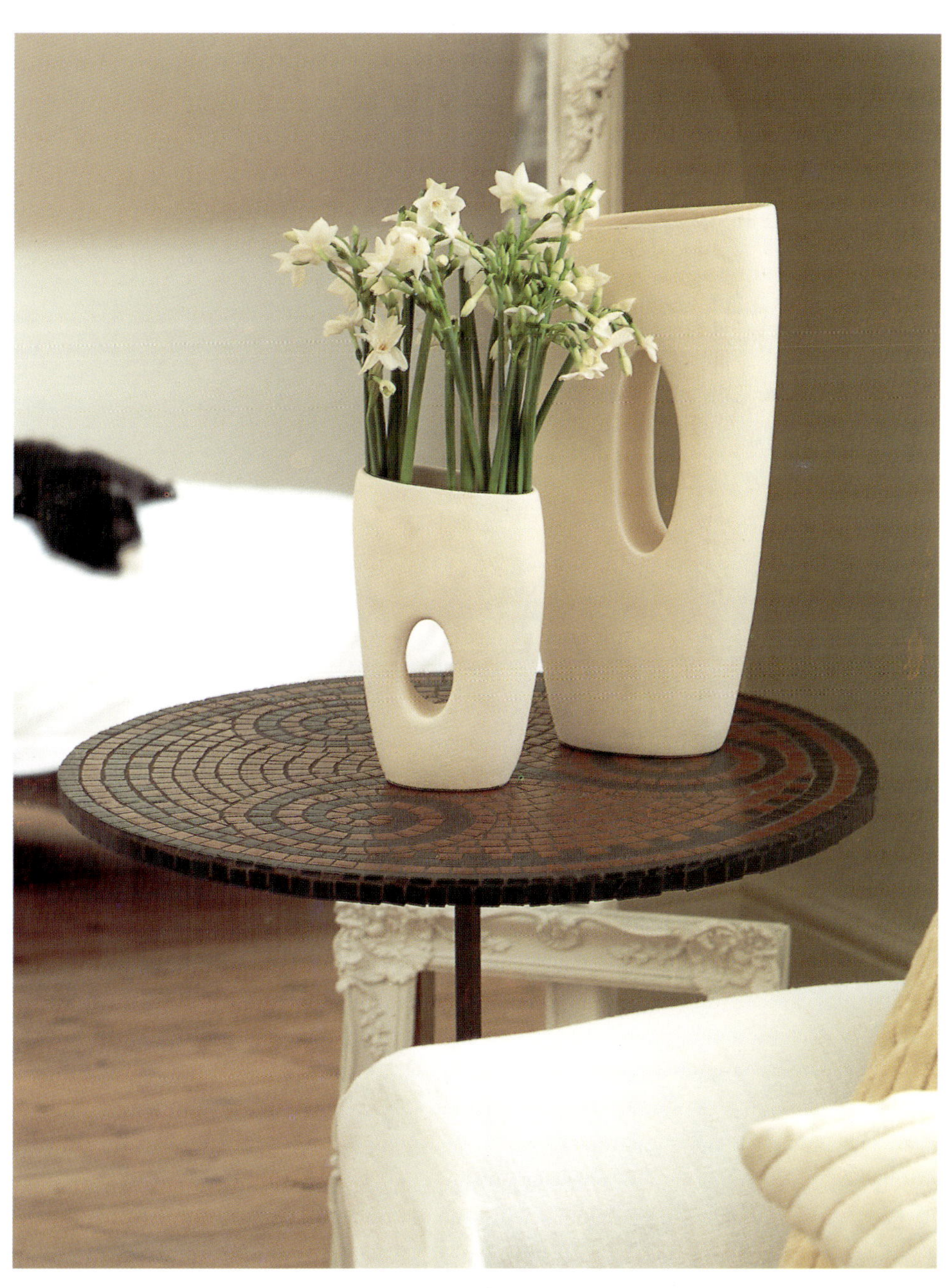

Right: Celtic designs have a timeless quality that suits both modern and traditional furniture.

Mosaic works extremely well on furniture in the garden. A chair is perhaps not the first item that you might think of applying mosaic to, but would make a real focal point for any patio area.

Garden Furniture

Adding mosaic is a wonderful way to revive tired or battered pieces of garden furniture, and it will also make pieces more weather-resistant.

Tables

A garden table is an ideal subject for mosaic. Not only is it a flat, horizontal surface, and therefore easy to work on, but it, and its surrounding chairs, will often be the centre of attention on the patio or lawn, making it the perfect place to create a dramatic design.

Geometric designs can make an impact by contrasting with the flowing lines of flowers and trees that surround them, while designs inspired more directly by nature can complement their surroundings. Whatever the design or colours used, a mosaic can transform the most humble garden table of any size or shape.

Chairs and benches

White plastic garden furniture cannot be made into works of art, but a simple kitchen-style chair or a standardized garden bench are both ideal candidates for the mosaic treatment.

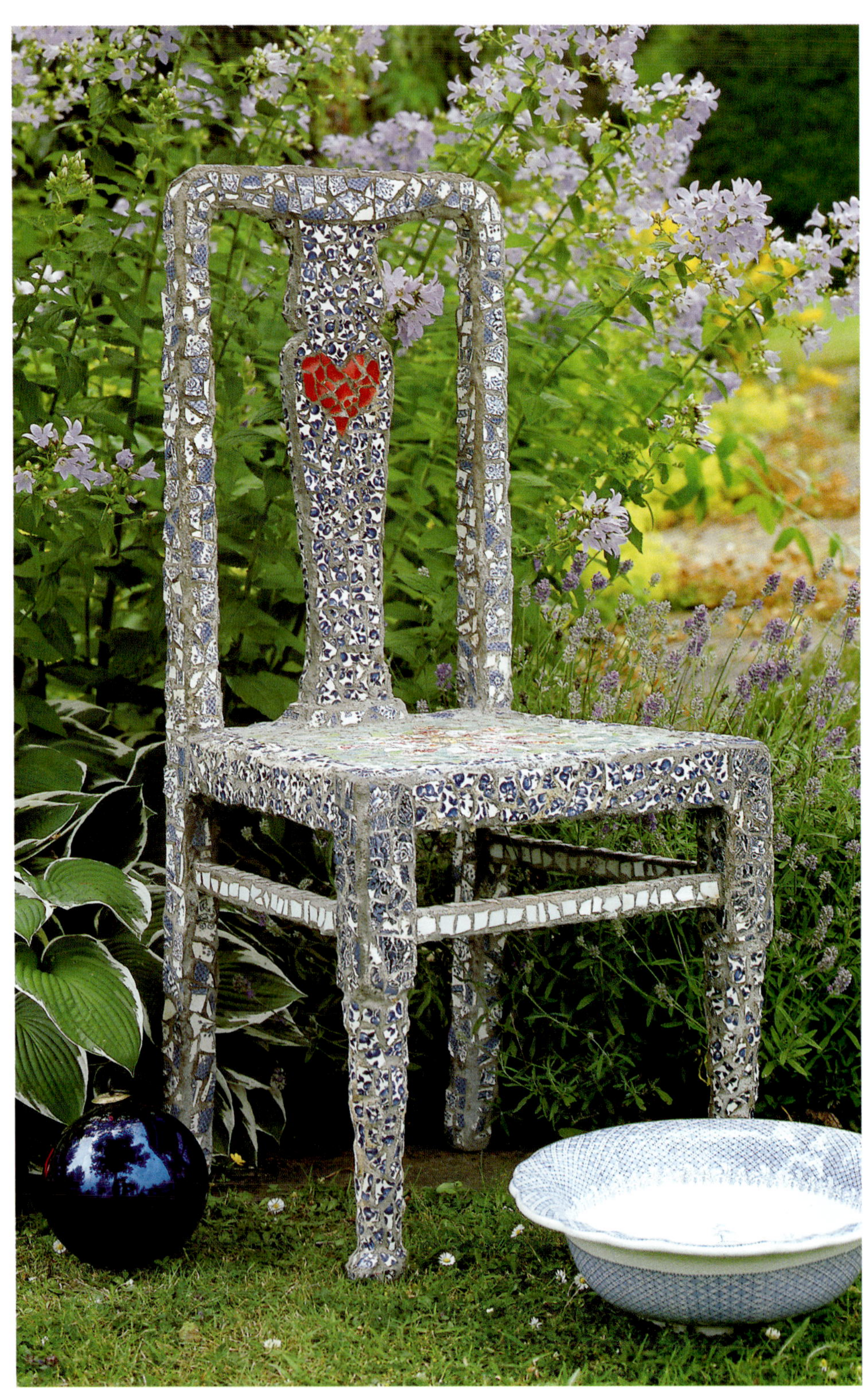

Right: An old chair is given a new lease of life by the addition of mosaic. A large, three-dimensional object such as this will require a deceptively large amount of tesserae to cover it.

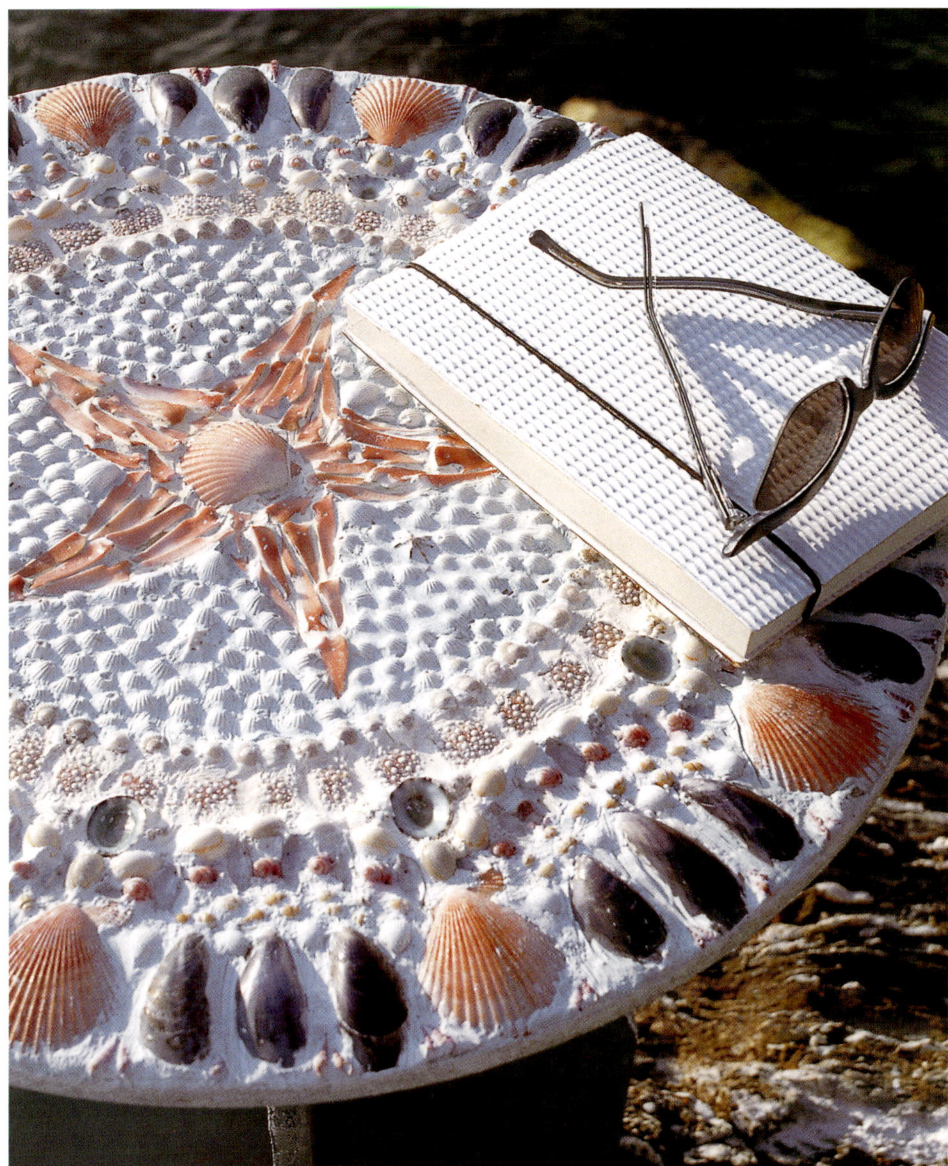

Almost any part of a chair or bench can take mosaic, though you must always remember that they are for sitting on and leaning against, so the mosaic must be flush, smooth and even.

Preparation

Think carefully about the amount of mosaic materials required: covering a large table top or an entire chair (or even a set of chairs) will take a large amount of tesserae.

The element of unity is also important. There should be continuity of pattern or colour to avoid the end result looking disjointed. Pieces do not need to be identical, but they must have some strong visual factor linking them, such as colour or pattern.

Below: A quirky sea urchin seat stands invitingly on the lawn. Vitreous glass tiles are suitable for outdoor use.

Above: This outstanding table is encrusted with scallop, cockle, cowrie, snail, mussel and limpet shells, plus a sea urchin.

Below: Ceramic floor tiles were used to create the star design on this table, and tiny gold tesserae were placed in the large gaps.

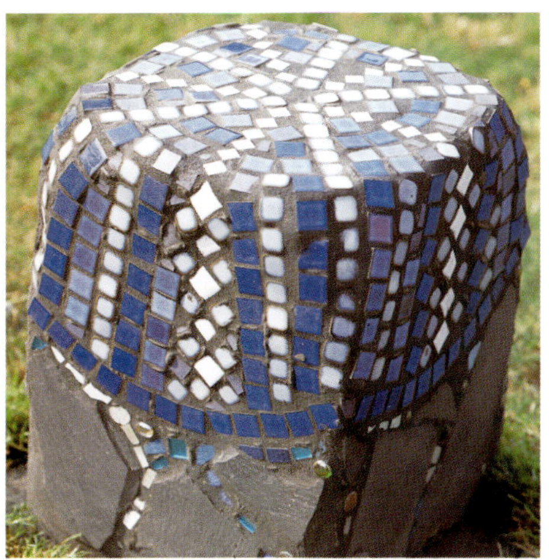

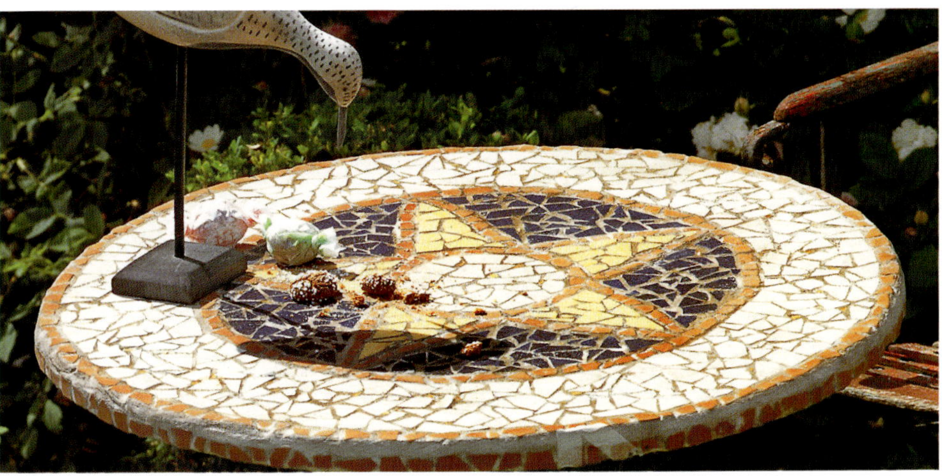

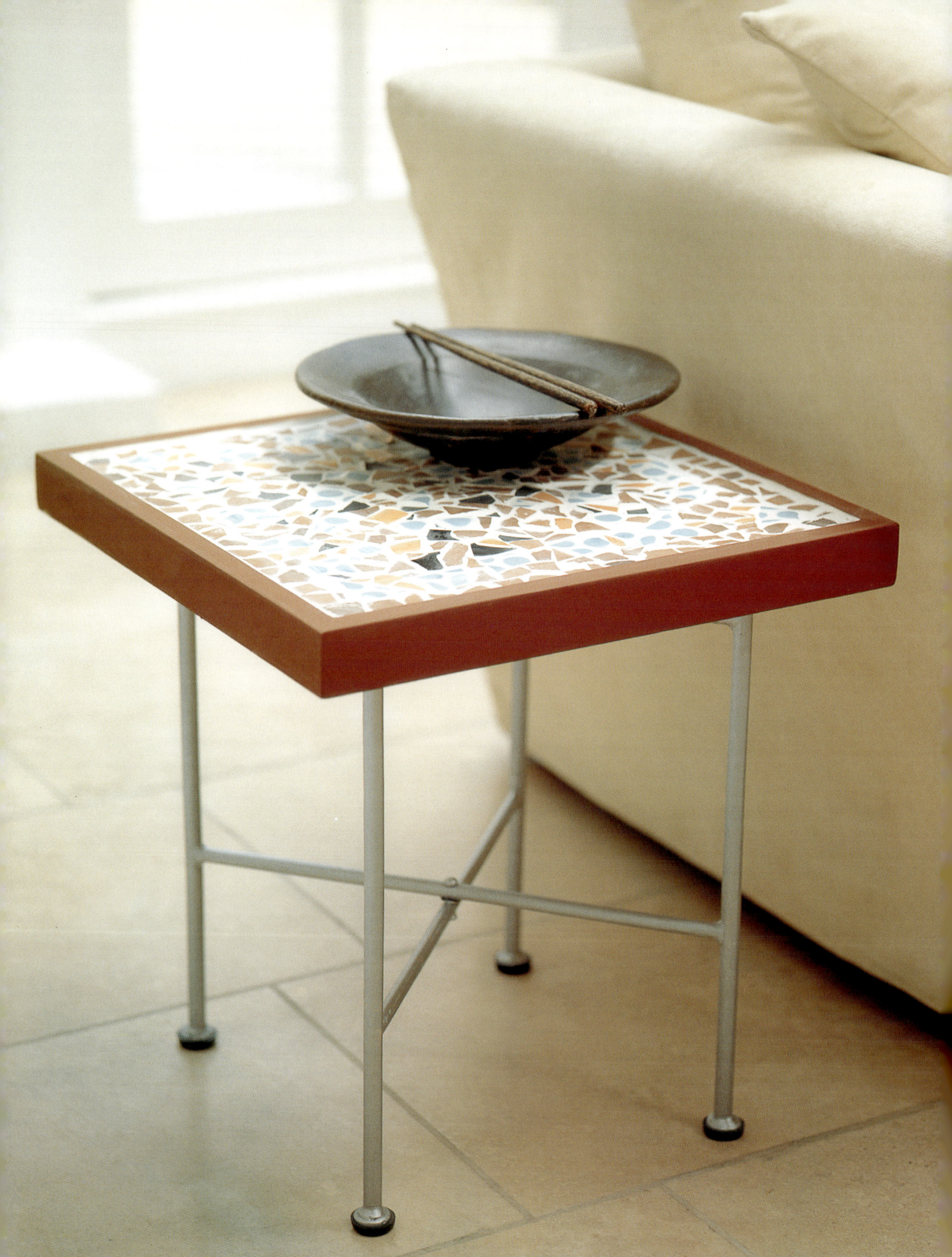

Never throw away your favourite china when it gets chipped or broken. Instead, give it another chance to shine as one of the patterns in a table-top mosaic. Unlike in a jigsaw, the pieces don't have to fit.

Mosaic Table Top

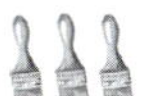

You will need

- 2cm (¾in) thick chipboard (particle board)
- Saw
- 5 x 2.5cm (2 x 1in) wood for frame
- Mitre saw
- Wood glue
- Panel pins (brads)
- Hammer
- Hardboard or thick card (stock)
- Metal ruler
- Craft (utility) knife
- Self-healing cutting mat
- PVA (white) glue
- Paintbrushes
- Old china and clay pots
- Old towels
- Tile adhesive
- Grout spreader
- Tile grout
- Sponge
- Soft cloth
- Paint
- Polyurethane varnish (optional)

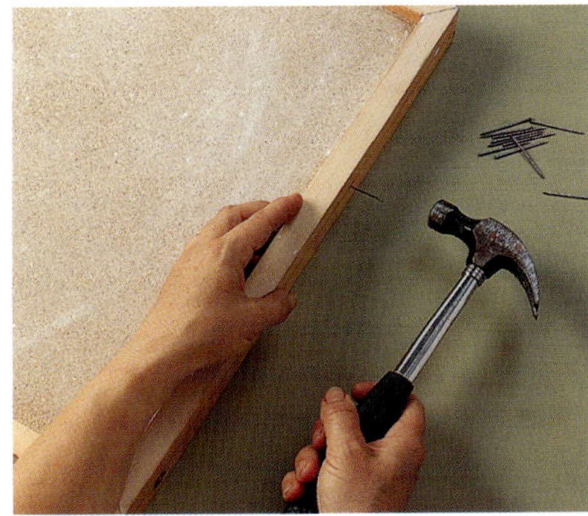

1 Cut the chipboard (particle board) to make a base of the required size for a table. Mitre the length of wood to make a frame to surround the base. Glue and pin the frame. There must be a recess of about 5cm (2in) depending on the depth of the material you are using for the mosaic.

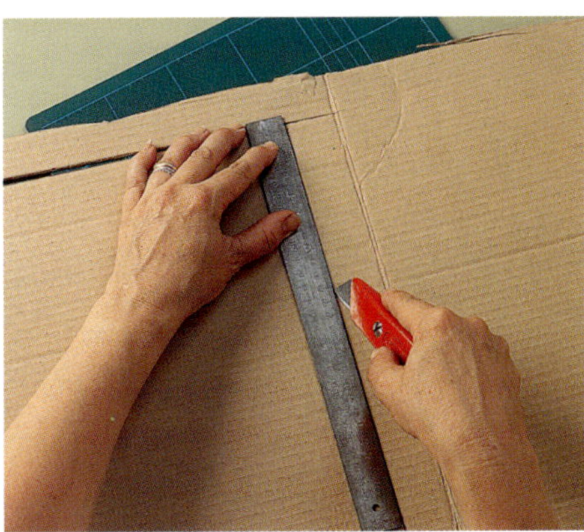

2 Cut a matching piece of thick card (stock) or hardboard to use for planning the design. Use a metal rule and a craft (utility) knife, being careful to press down onto a cut-resistant surface like a cutting mat.

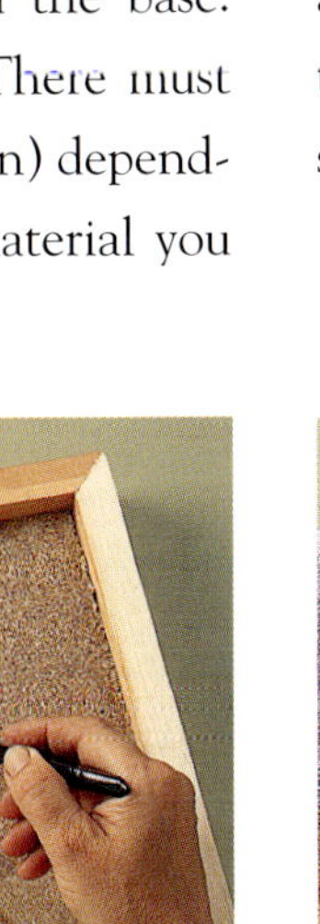

3 Paint the chipboard with diluted PVA (white) glue, to seal the base.

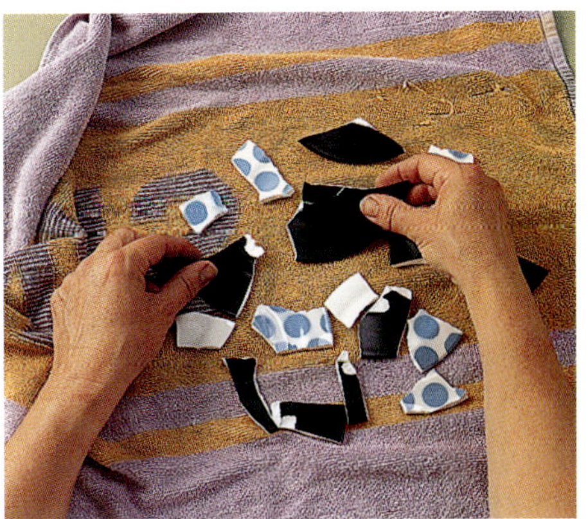

4 Place large pieces of china and pieces of clay pot between two old towels.

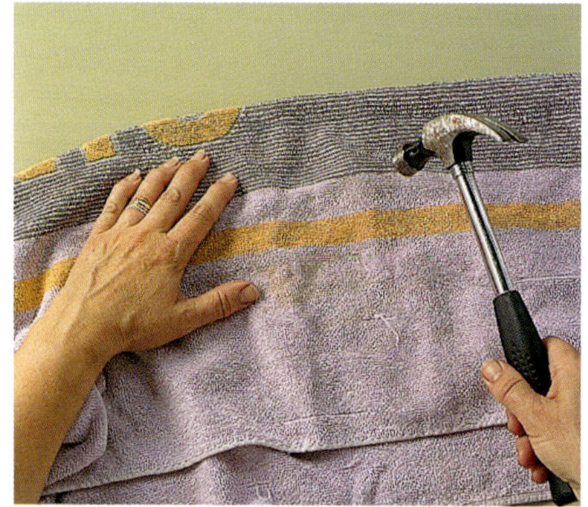

5 Smash the china and clay pot with a hammer. This can be done in a controlled way to get the shapes you need and to protect your eyes.

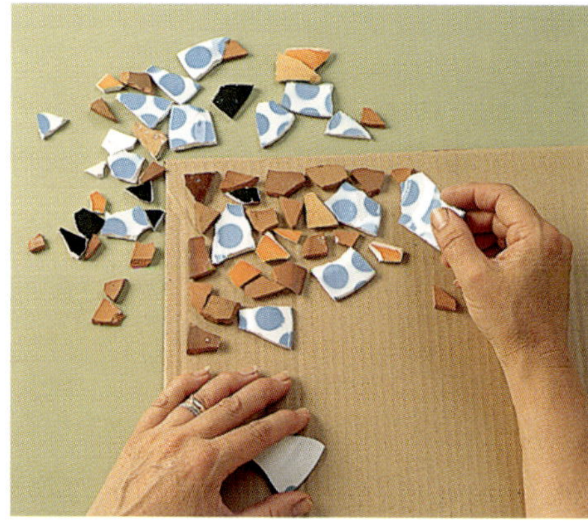

6 Plan the layout of your design on the hardboard or card (stock). The design can be whatever you want: random, geometric or representational.

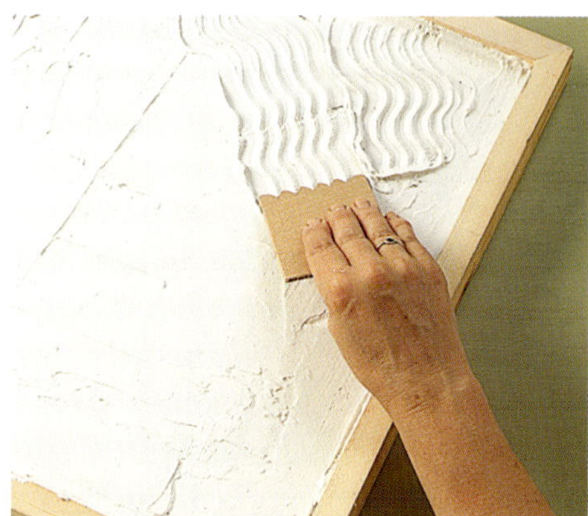

7 Using the notched side of a grout spreader coat the board with a layer of tile adhesive 5mm (¼in) deep. This spreader was made out of thick card.

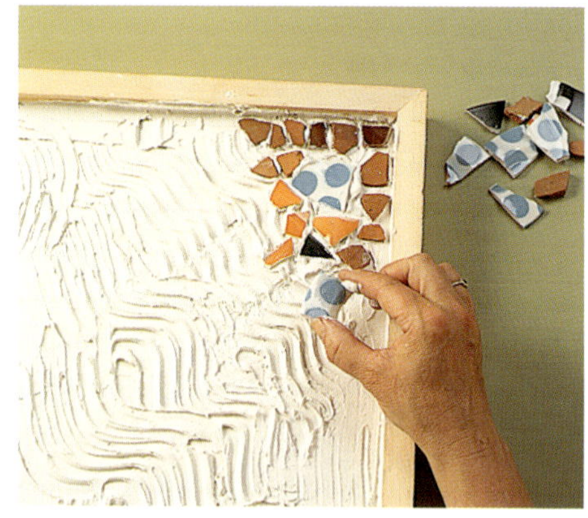

8 Transfer all the pieces, bedding them down in the adhesive to hide the different thicknesses and to make the surface as level as you can.

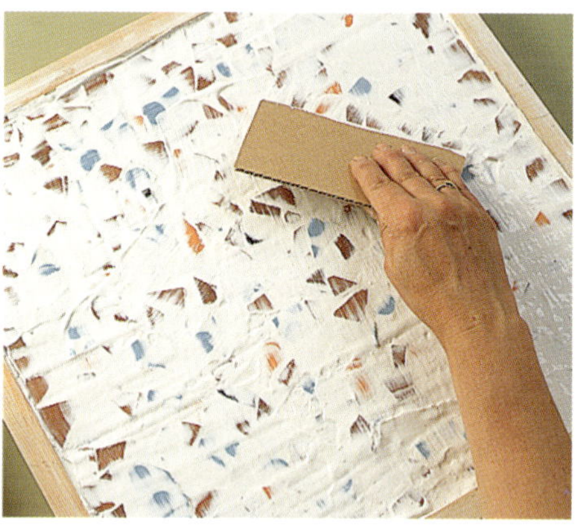

9 Leave to dry overnight, then apply the tile grout with a grout spreader. Ensure the grout is evenly distributed between the mosaic pieces.

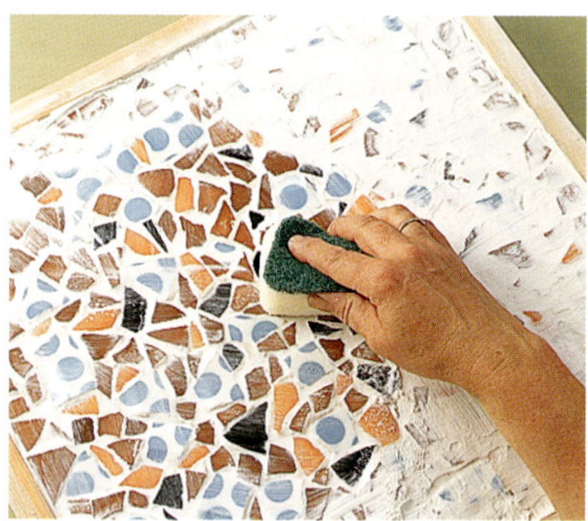

10 When the grout begins to dry, wipe off the excess with a damp sponge.

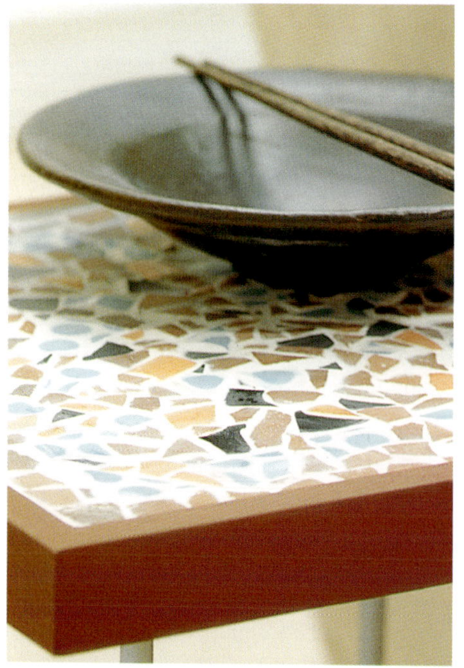

11 When the grout is dry, use a dry, soft cloth to buff up the shiny ceramic surface, so revealing all the colours.

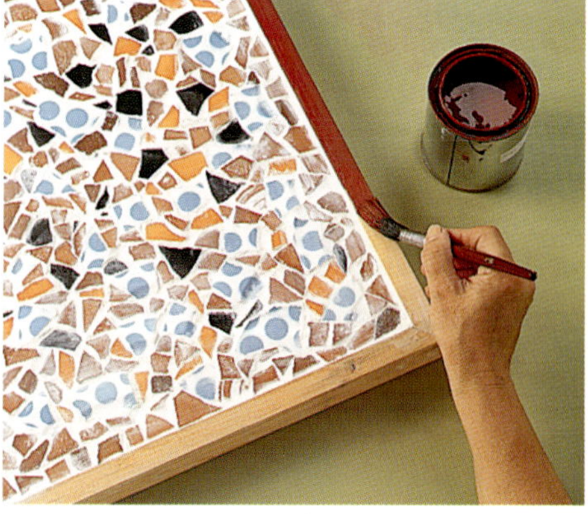

12 Paint the frame, using a colour that complements the mosaic, and apply two coats of polyurethane varnish if it is for outdoor use.

The bold design of this table top and the simplicity of its metal frame combine to create a table that would look good in the conservatory or garden. Tiny chips of gold-leaf smalti create glinting highlights.

Star Garden Table

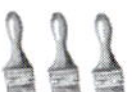

You will need

- 2cm (¾in) thick plywood
- Pencil
- String
- Drawing pin (thumb tack)
- Jigsaw (saber saw)
- Abrasive paper (sandpaper)
- PVA (white) glue
- Paintbrush
- Tape measure (optional)
- Selection of ceramic floor tiles
- Tile nippers
- Tile adhesive
- Flexible knife
- Sponge
- Piece of sacking (heavy cloth)
- Hammer
- Gold-leaf tiles
- Soft brush
- Plant mister
- Dilute hydrochloric acid, goggles and rubber (latex) gloves (optional)
- Metal table frame
- Screws
- Screwdriver
- Soft cloth

1 Follow the instructions for the Shades of Blue Garden Table to cut a circle from the plywood. Then prime with diluted PVA (white) glue, paying special attention to the edges.

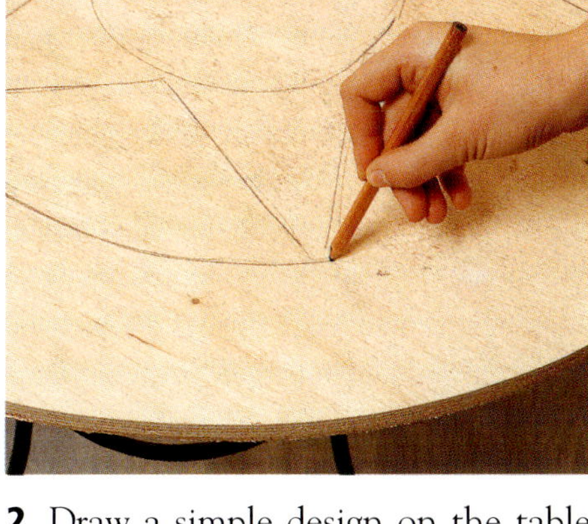

2 Draw a simple design on the table top. You may need to use a tape measure to get the proportions right, but don't be too rigid about the geometry, as a freehand approach suits this method of working.

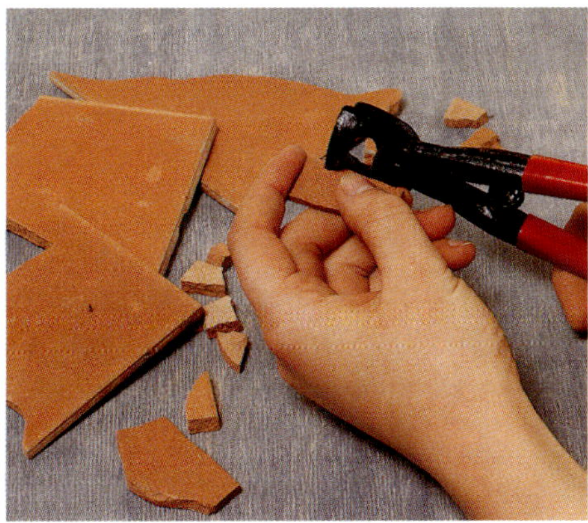

3 Cut the floor tiles that are in your outlining colour into small pieces using tile nippers. Try to cut them into a variety of shapes, as uniform shapes would jar with the crazy-paving effect of the smashed tesserae used for the rest of the table.

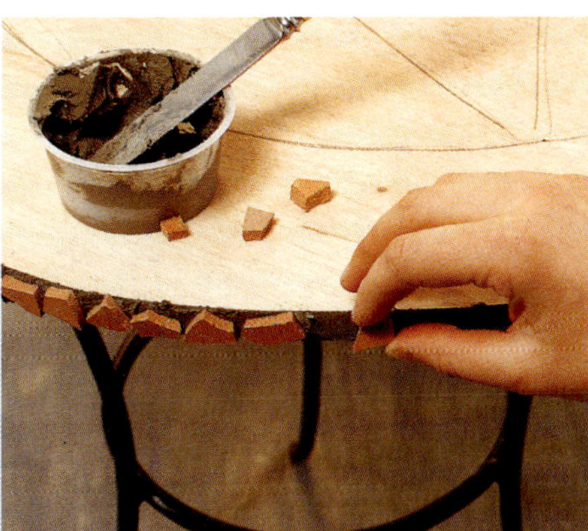

4 Using a flexible knife, spread tile adhesive around the edge of the table top. Firmly press the outlining tesserae into the adhesive, making sure they do not overlap the edges.

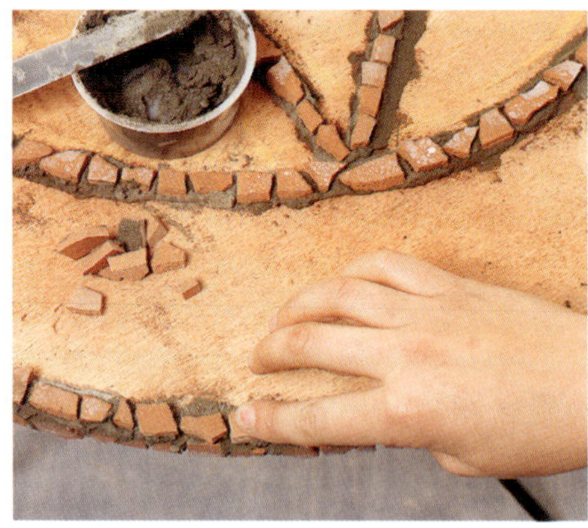

5 Apply tile adhesive to the lines of your drawing and press in the outlining tesserae. Use a sponge to wipe away any large bits of adhesive that have squashed out from under the edges of the tesserae, and leave to dry overnight.

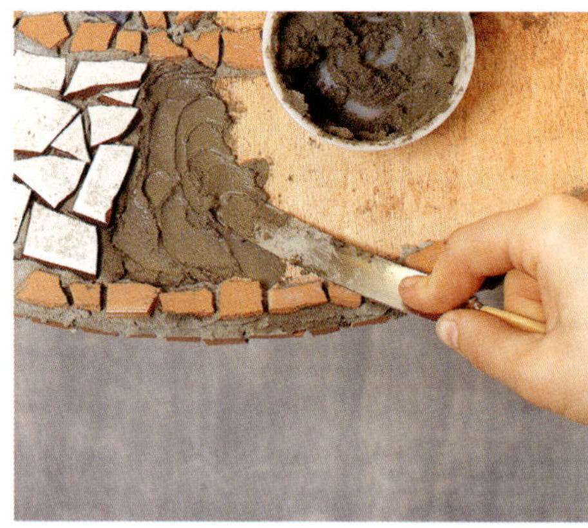

6 Cover the remaining tiles with a piece of sacking (heavy cloth) and smash them with a hammer. Apply tile adhesive to small areas at a time and press in the tile fragments between the outlines of the table top. Do this carefully, as the finished surface must be as flat as possible. Leave to dry overnight or while working on another area.

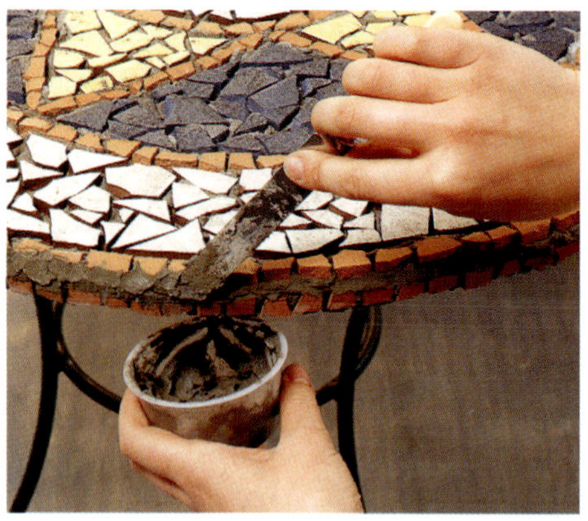

7 Using a flexible knife, smooth tile adhesive on to the edges of the table. Cut gold-leaf tiles into tiny, irregular tesserae using tile nippers. Place these in the larger gaps between the broken tiles on the table top. If necessary, first insert a blob of tile adhesive to ensure that the gold is at the same level as the tiles as the surface should be flat and smooth. Leave to dry overnight.

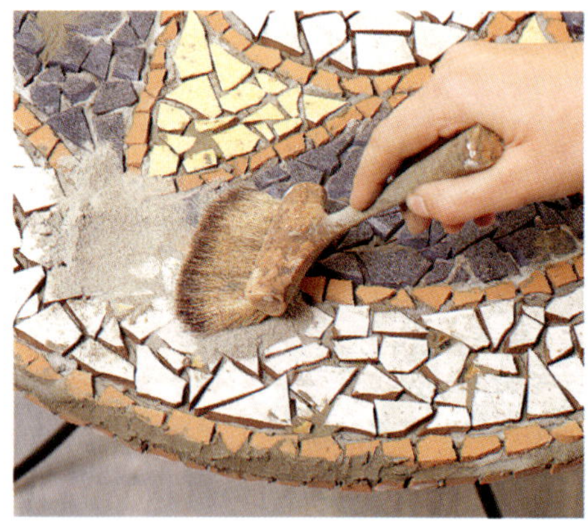

8 Spoon tile adhesive powder on to the surface of the table and smooth it into all the gaps with a soft brush. Spray water over the table. When the powder has absorbed enough water, wipe away any excess with a cloth. If the adhesive sinks when wetted, repeat this process. Leave to dry for 24 hours.

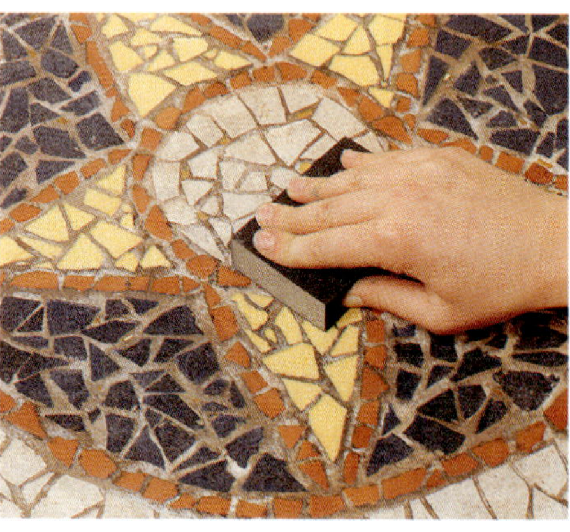

9 Turn the table top over and rub tile adhesive into the plywood on the underside with your fingers. Leave to dry overnight. Clean off excess adhesive with abrasive paper (sandpaper). Alternatively, use dilute hydrochloric acid, wearing goggles and rubber (latex) gloves, and apply it outside or where there is good ventilation. Wash any acid residue from the surface.

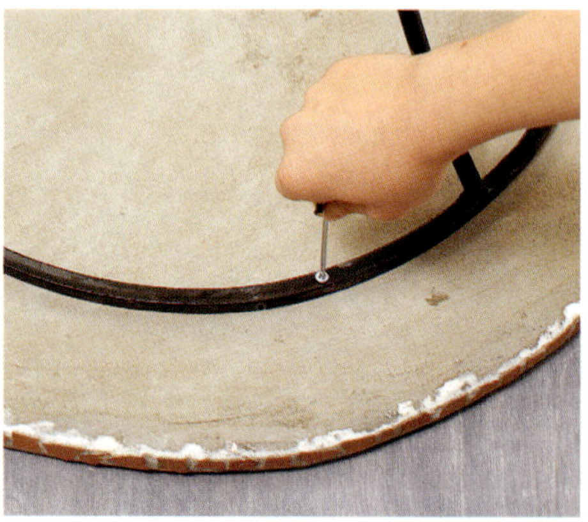

10 When clean, turn the table top face down on a protected surface and screw the metal frame in place using screws that are no longer than the thickness of the plywood. Finally, polish the table top with a dry, soft cloth.

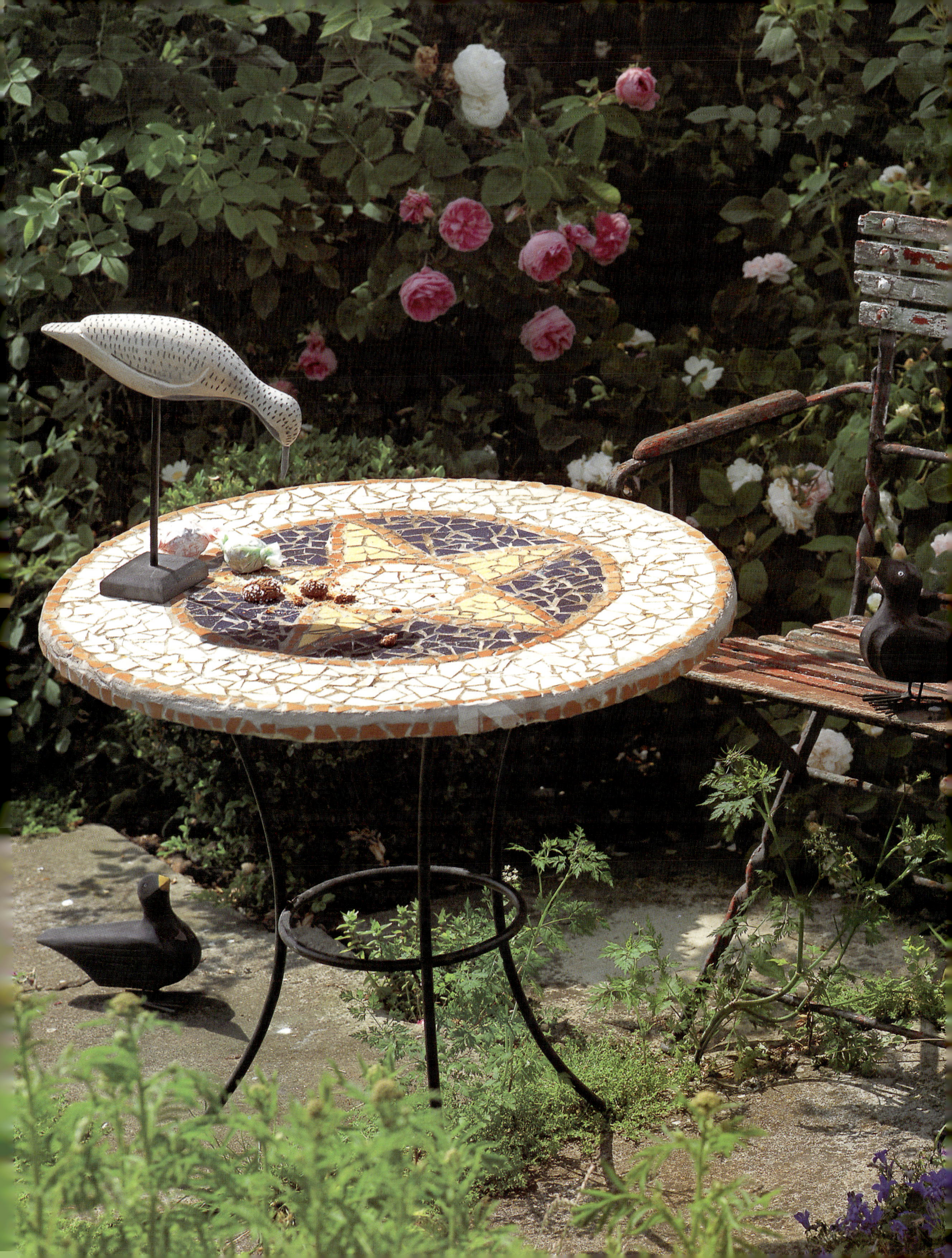

This simple shop-bought chest with drawers has been transformed by mosaic motifs into an individual, playful piece of furniture. The many white tesserae and the white adhesive give the shelf a fresh, clean look.

Storage Chest

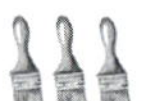

You will need

Shop-bought chest with drawers
Acrylic white undercoat paint
Paintbrush
Pencil
Thin ceramic household tiles in five colours, plus white
Tile nippers
Tile adhesive
Flexible knife
Sponge
Abrasive paper (sandpaper)
Paintscraper
Soft cloth

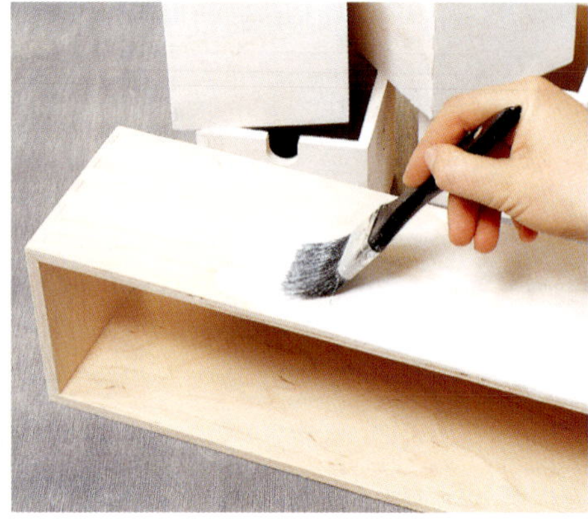

1 Paint the chest and drawers inside and out with watered-down white undercoat paint. Leave to dry.

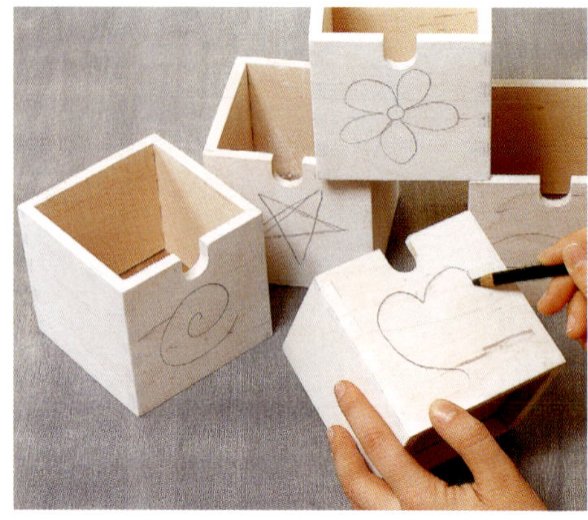

2 Draw a simple motif on the front of each drawer. Choose motifs that have a bold outline and are easily recognizable when executed in one colour, like a red heart, star, flower, spiral or fish.

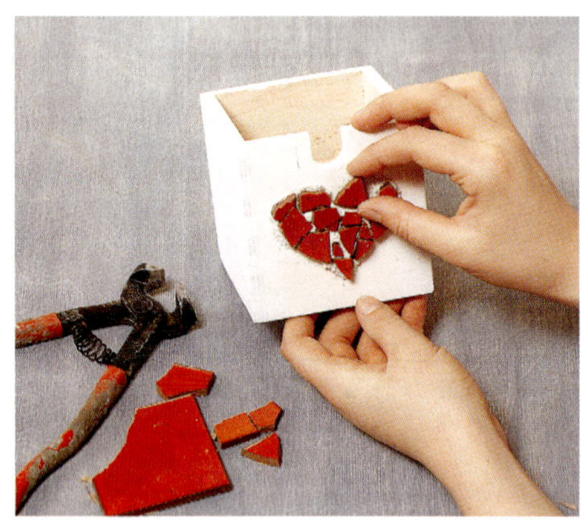

3 Cut the tiles into unevenly shaped tesserae using tile nippers. Using a flexible knife, spread some tile adhesive within the outline of one of the motifs, then firmly press single-coloured tesserae into it.

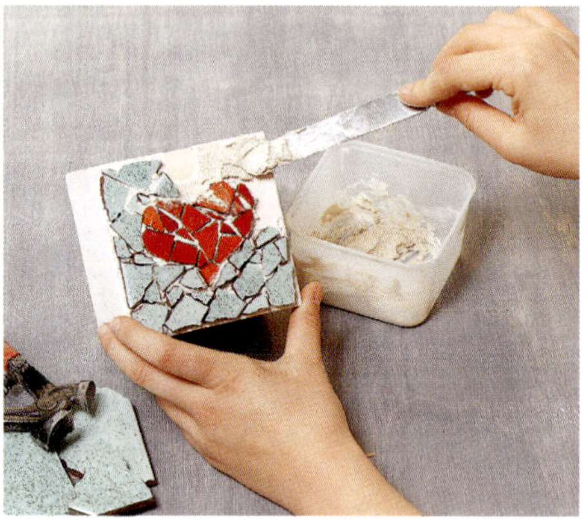

4 Spread tile adhesive on the rest of the drawer front, one area at a time, then surround the motif with tesserae of a different colour. Take care not to overlap the edges of the drawer. Cover the remaining drawer fronts using a different combination of two colours each time.

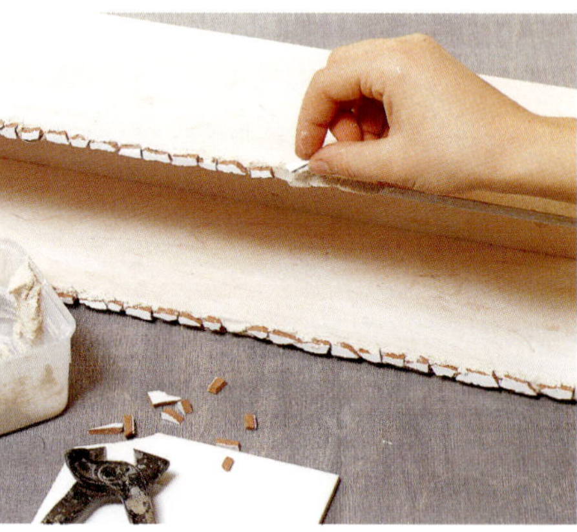

5 Cut tiny slivers of white tile. Stick these to the narrow front edges of the chest with tile adhesive. Do this very carefully so that none of the tesserae overlaps the edge.

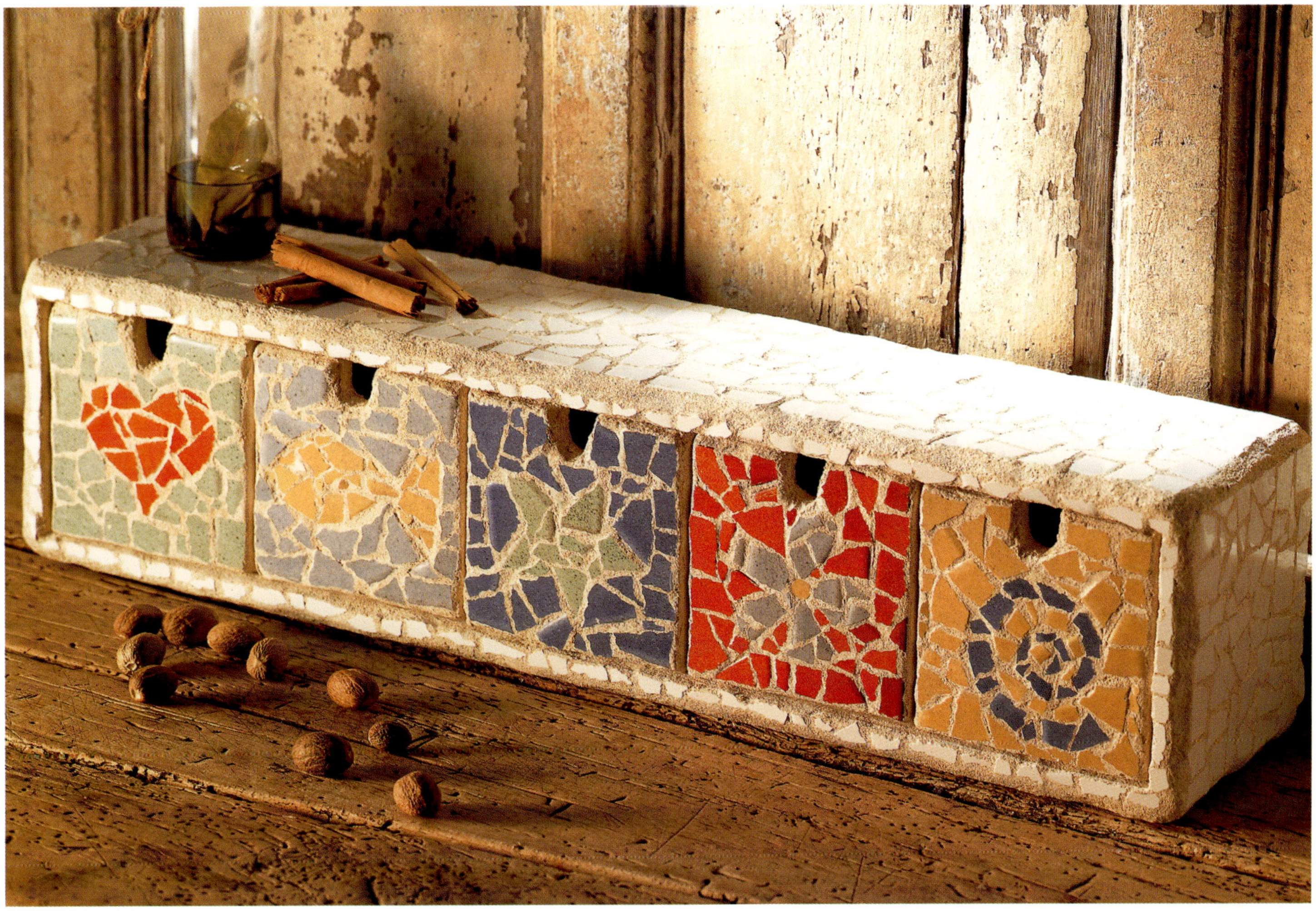

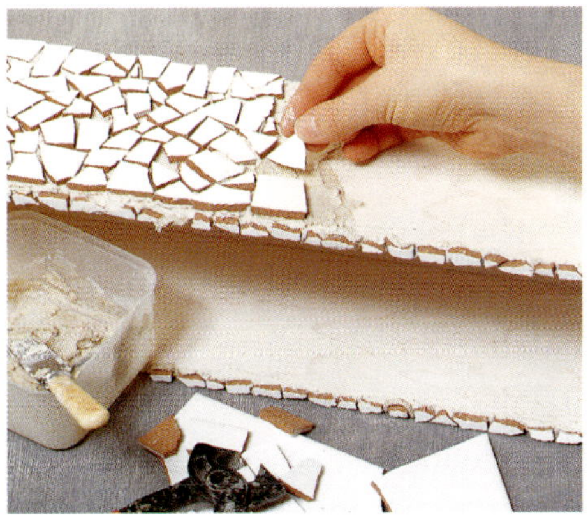

6 Cut more white tiles into various shapes and sizes, then stick these to the large, flat outside surfaces of the chest. When all four surfaces are covered, leave the chest and the drawers to dry overnight.

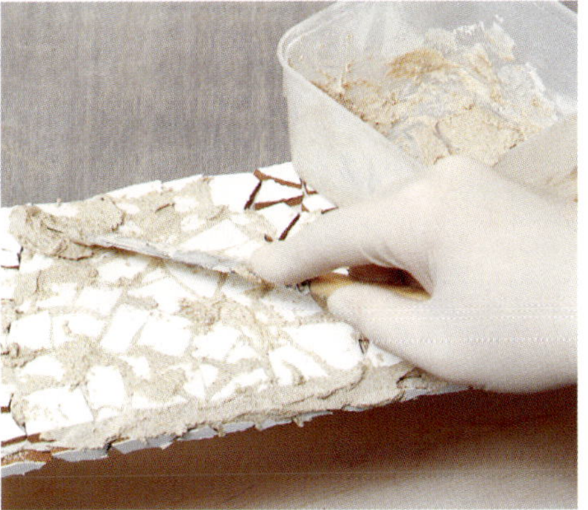

7 Spread tile adhesive over the surface of the chest and drawers with a flexible knife. Take special care when smoothing the adhesive into the thin edges of the chest and the edges of the drawer fronts, making sure it is flush with the edges. When all the gaps between the tesserae are filled, wipe off most of the excess adhesive with a damp sponge. Leave to dry for 24 hours.

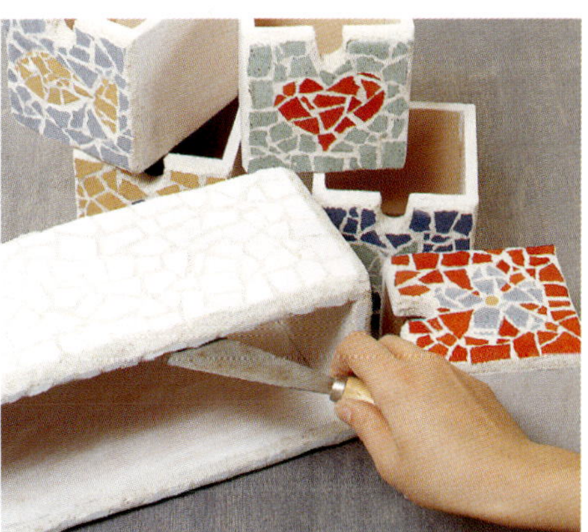

8 Sand off any remaining surface adhesive from the chest and drawers. Then use an implement with a sharp, flat edge, such as a paintscraper, to scrape along the inside edge of the chest and the sides of the drawers. Do this carefully to ensure there are no overlapping tesserae and that the action of the drawers is not impeded. Polish with a dry, soft cloth.

There is something immensely pleasing about the simple regularity of black-and-white patterns, whether the tiles are set chequerboard style or as diamonds. The border could be thicker or set in one colour only.

Black-and-white Tiled Table

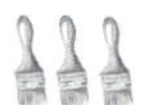

You will need

Small occasional table
PVA (white) glue
Paintbrushes
Craft (utility) knife
Pencil
Ruler
Thin wooden batten (furring strip)
Saw
Wood glue
Panel pins (brads)
Pin hammer
Small ceramic household tiles: black and white
Tile cutter
Notched spreader
Tile adhesive
Tile grout
Grout spreader
Sponge
Soft cloth
Acrylic paint (optional)

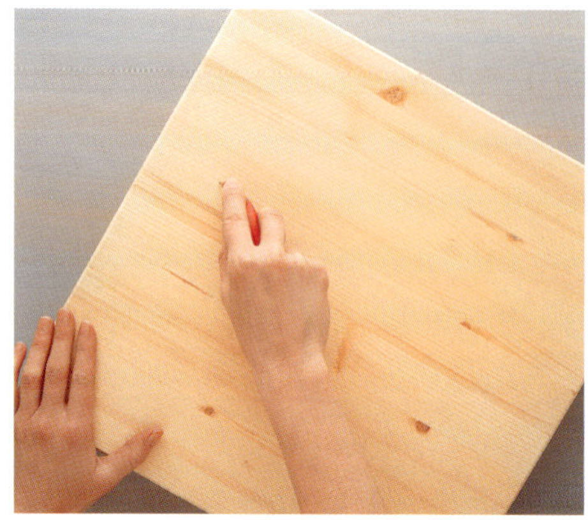

1 Remove the table top and seal with a coat of diluted PVA (white) glue. When the wood has dried, score the surface using a craft (utility) knife.

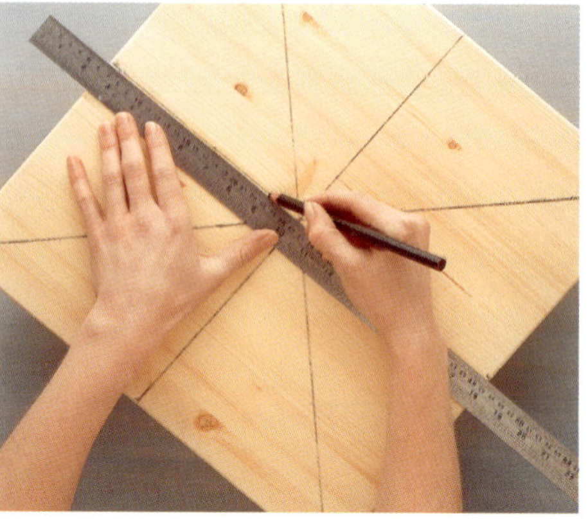

2 To help you to centre the tiles and work out how wide the borders will be, use a pencil and ruler to draw dividing lines (as shown) on the table top.

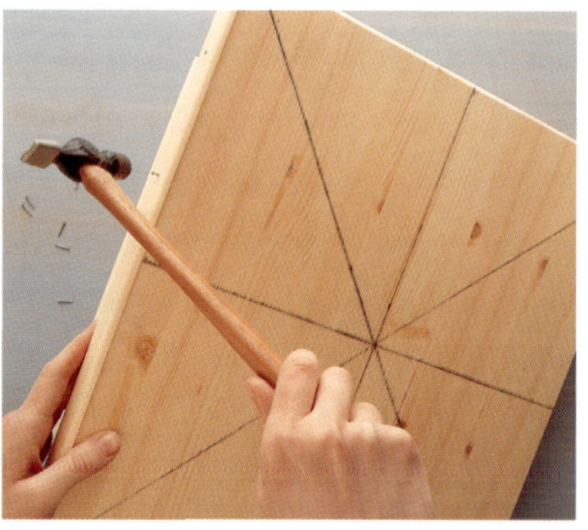

3 Cut four lengths of wooden batten (furring strip) to fit around the edges of the table. Attach with wood glue and panel pins (brads), leaving a lip around the top edge of exactly the depth of the tiles.

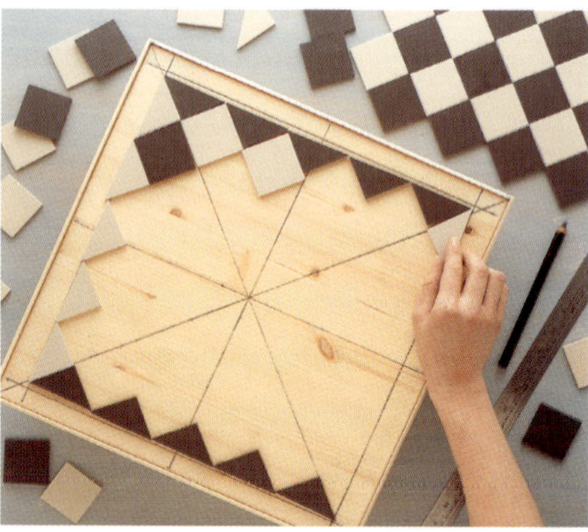

4 Cut a few tiles diagonally to make triangles. Lay these out as a border on the table top and fill in with whole tiles to see how many will fit. Draw border lines around the edges.

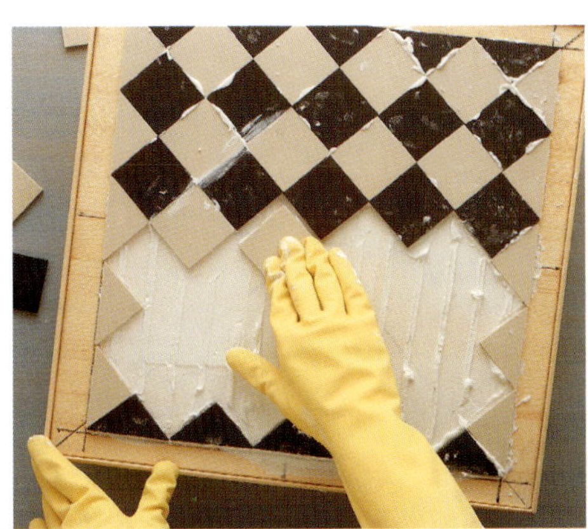

5 Spread tile adhesive over the surface of the table top, inside the border lines, using a notched spreader. Starting with the triangular border tiles, set out the pattern, butting the tiles together and leaving only very small gaps for the grouting.

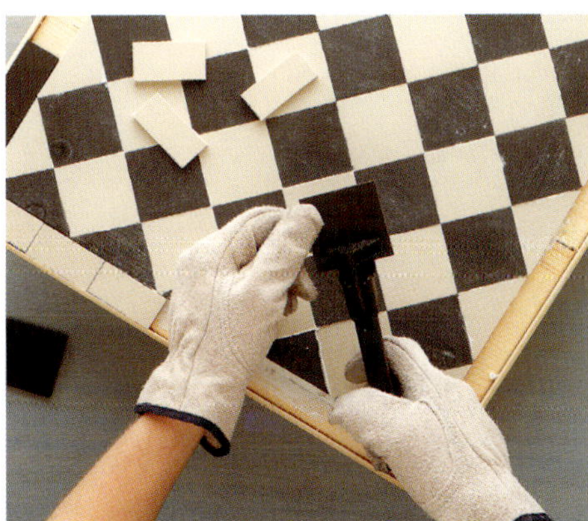

6 Cut strips of tile to fit around the borders, then fix in place as before. Once the tiles have dried, grout the surface, removing any excess with a damp sponge. When dry, polish the tiles with a dry, soft cloth. Attach the table top to the legs and seal and paint the table frame and legs if desired.

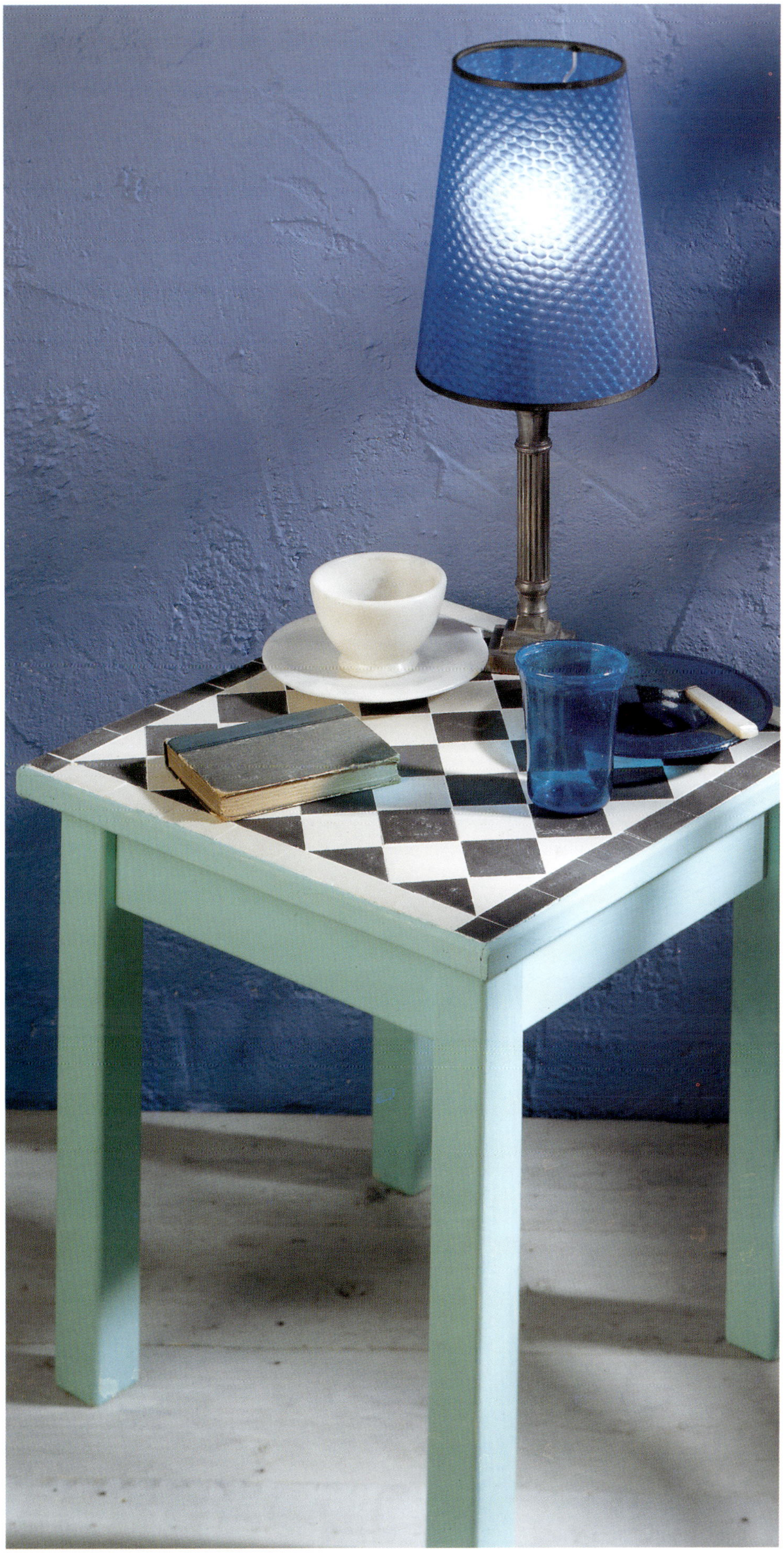

The daisy-filled panels of this pine bedhead, with matching footboard, would look beautiful in a country bedroom containing distressed wood furniture. The same design could be used on other panelled pieces.

Mosaic Bedhead

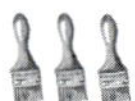

You will need

Unvarnished pine bedhead and footboard
PVA (white) glue
Paintbrush
Craft (utility) knife
Tile adhesive
Admix
Flexible knife
Soft pencil
Plain glazed ceramic tiles: white, orange, green and honey-coloured
Piece of sacking (heavy cloth)
Hammer
Tile nippers
Rubber spreader or cloth pad
Sponge
Abrasive paper (sandpaper)
Soft cloth

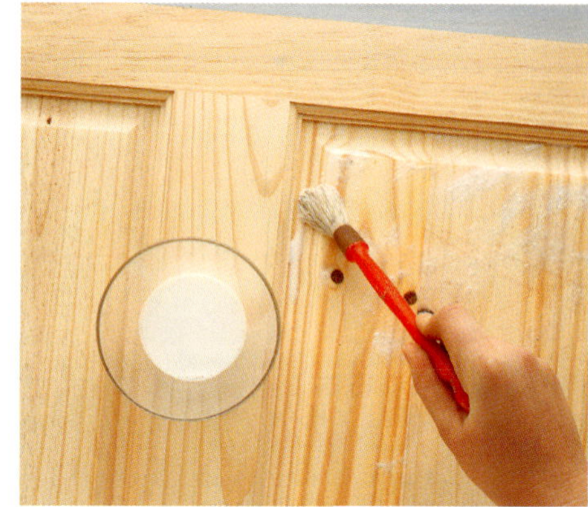

1 Seal the surface of the wood with diluted PVA (white) glue, then score the surface with a craft (utility) knife. Mix the tile adhesive with admix according to the instructions.

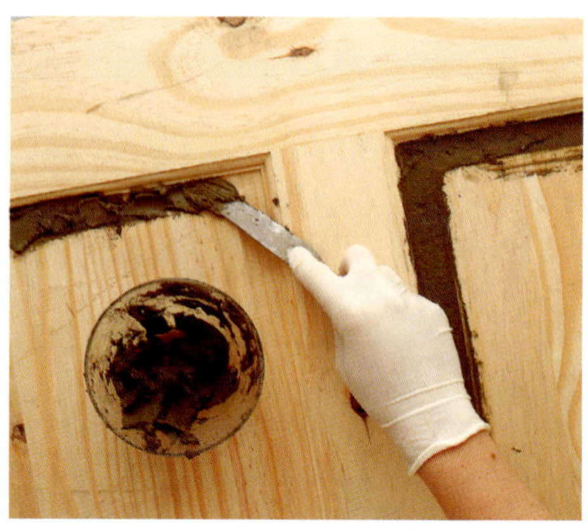

2 Using a flexible knife, fill any recesses in the areas to be decorated with the adhesive mixture. Leave for 24 hours to allow the adhesive to set.

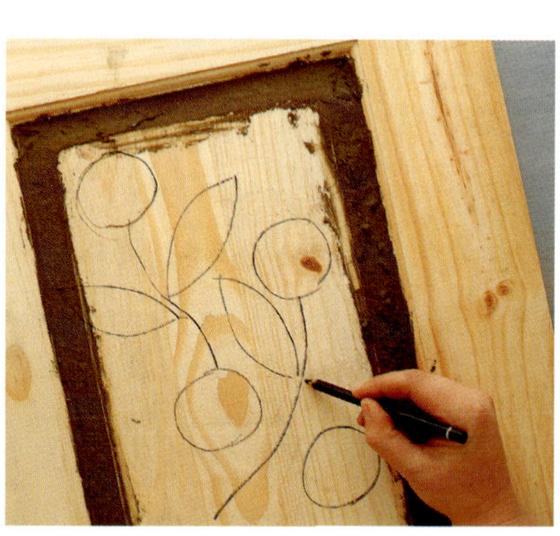

3 Draw a daisy design on the panels with a soft pencil.

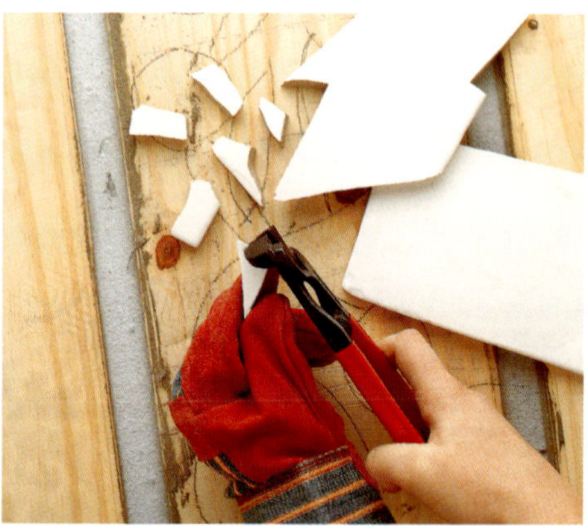

4 Wrap each white and orange tile separately in a piece of sacking (heavy cloth) and break them with a hammer. Trim the white tile pieces into petal shapes with mosaic nippers. Trim the orange tile pieces into round centres for the daisies.

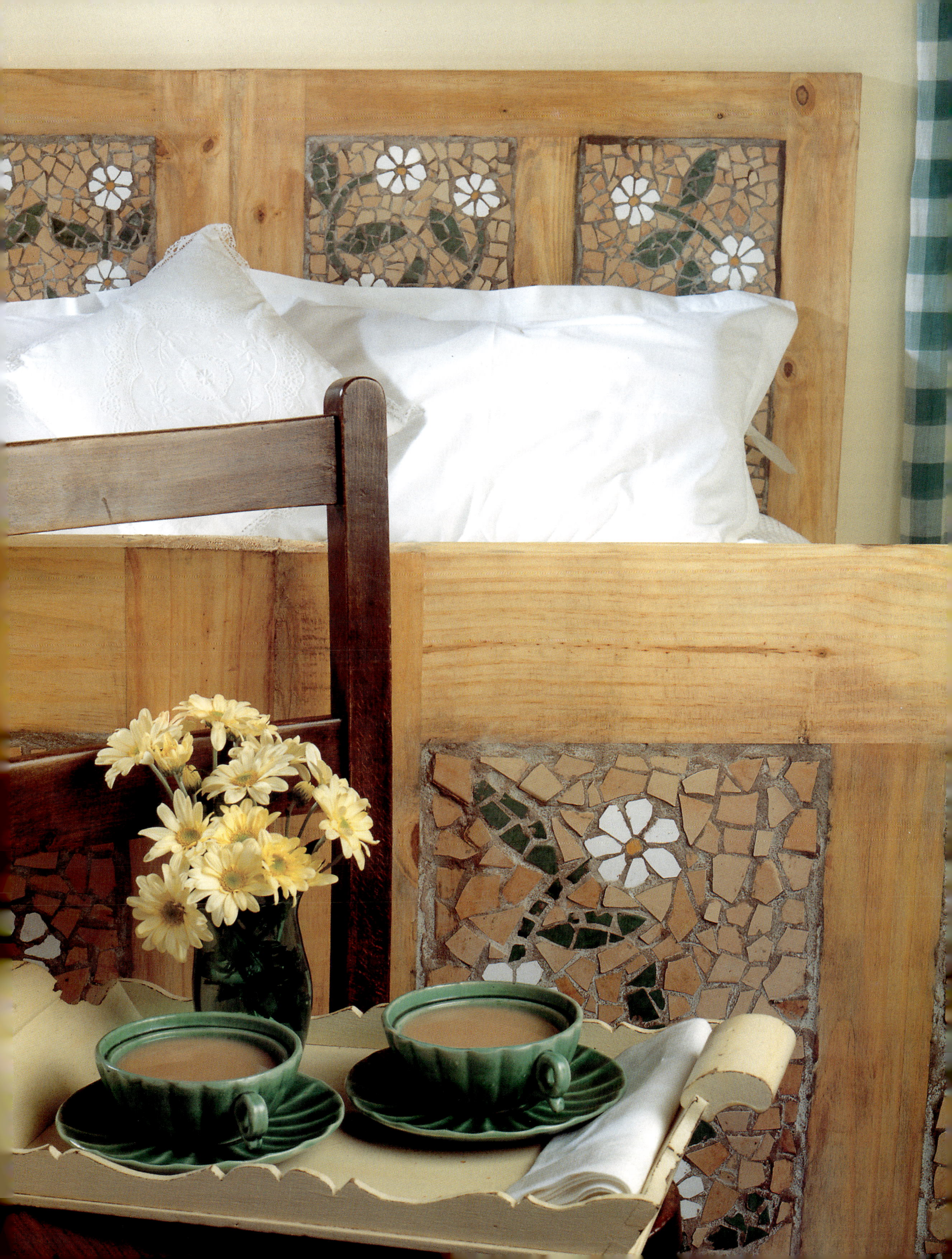

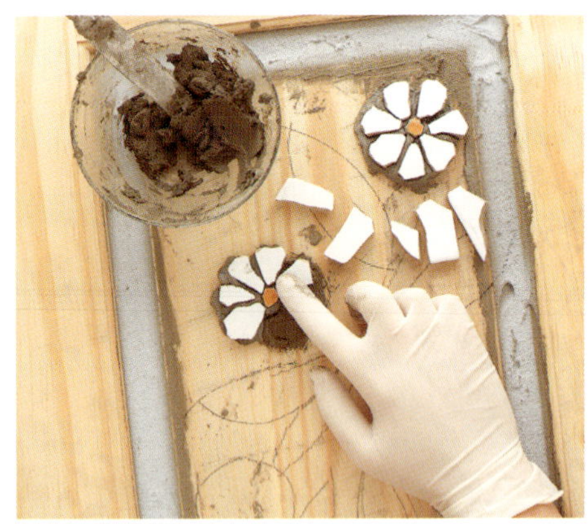

5 Spread the tile adhesive mixture over the daisy shapes on the panels. Press the white and orange tesserae in place to make the flowers.

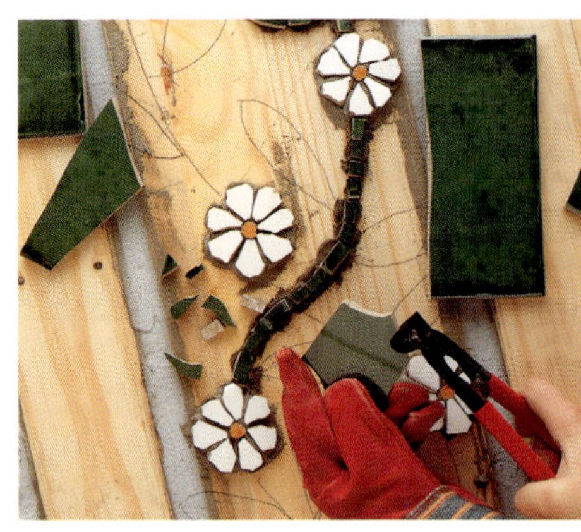

6 Smash the green tiles as before. Shape the pieces with tile nippers to make stems and leaves.

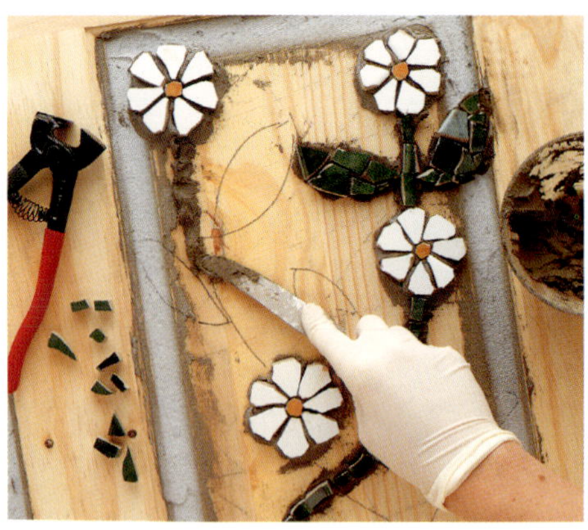

7 Spread the tile adhesive mixture over the appropriate areas of the design, then press the green tesserae into position to make leaves and stems. Leave to dry for 24 hours.

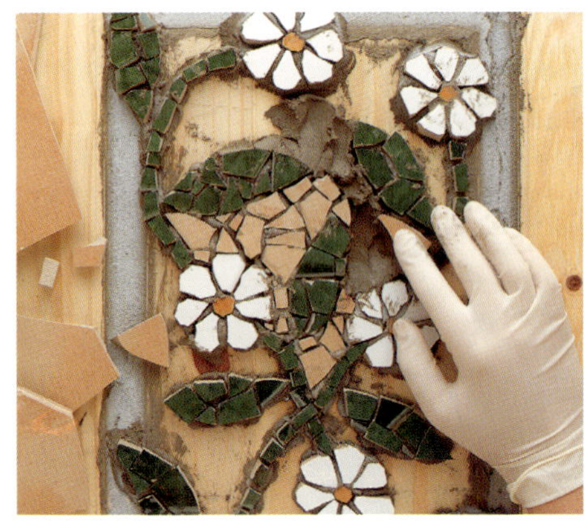

8 Finally, smash the honey-coloured tiles as before. Spread the tile adhesive mixture around the daisies and fill in the background, cutting the tesserae as necessary to fit.

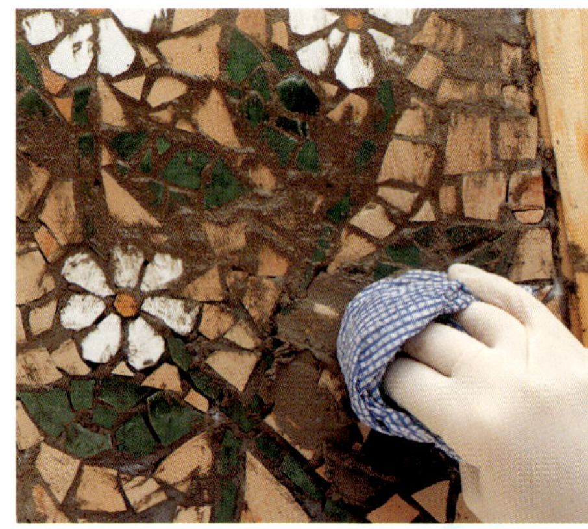

9 Using a rubber spreader or cloth pad, spread more adhesive over the mosaic. Push the adhesive well down into the spaces and make sure that all the sharp corners are covered. Remove any excess adhesive with a damp sponge, then leave to dry for 24 hours.

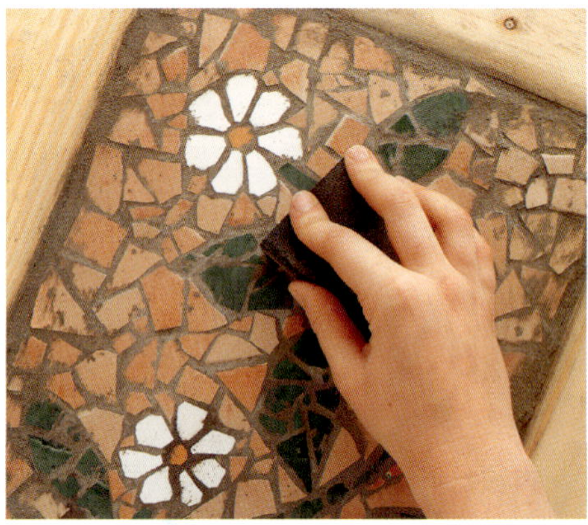

10 Lightly smooth the surface of the mosaic with abrasive paper (sandpaper). Polish with a dry, soft cloth.

A panelled piece of furniture is ideal for mosaic because it gives you a ready-made frame in which to work. This simple, geometric design is made with pieces of old china and is particularly effective.

Decorative Panel

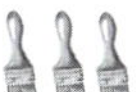

You will need

Piece of wooden furniture with a framed panel or panels
White spirit (paint thinner)
PVA (white) glue
Paintbrushes
Bradawl or awl
Soft dark pencil
Masking tape
Old china
Tile nippers
Tile adhesive
Admix
Flexible knife
Cloths
Abrasive paper (sandpaper)
Paintscraper

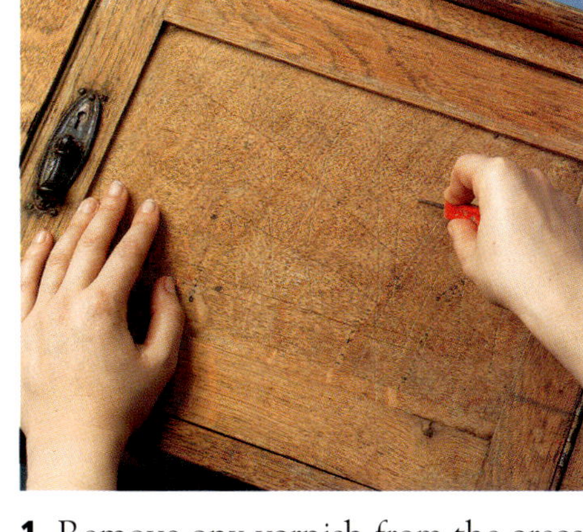

1 Remove any varnish from the areas of wood you wish to mosaic with white spirit (paint thinner). Prime with diluted PVA (white) glue and leave to dry. Score the surface with a bradawl or awl.

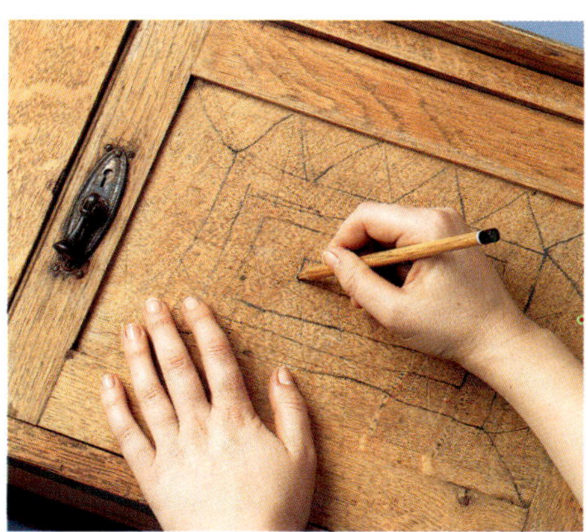

2 Draw a simple design on to the wood for the first panel. In this project we started with the cupboard door.

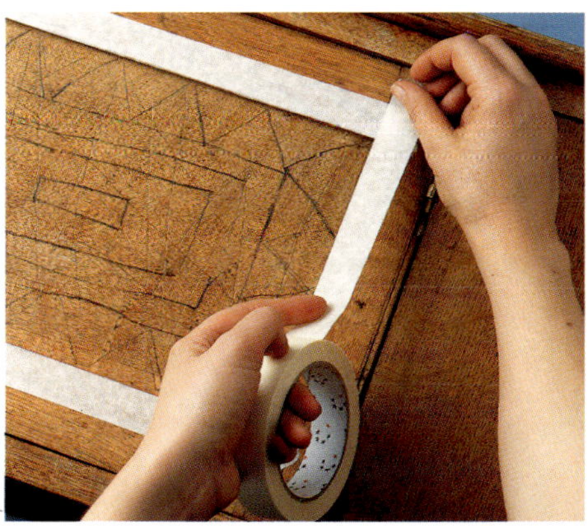

3 Stick masking tape around the raised edges of the panel(s) to protect the surrounding wood.

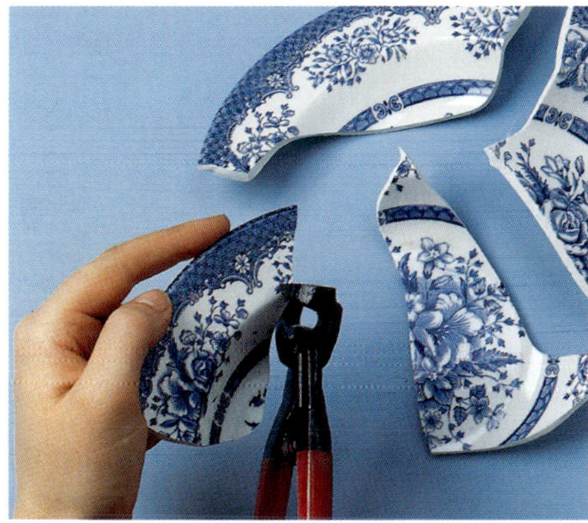

4 Using tile nippers, cut the old china into small, random shapes. Sort the pieces into colours or shades of particular colours. Test out the colour scheme by positioning the pieces on the design until you are satisfied.

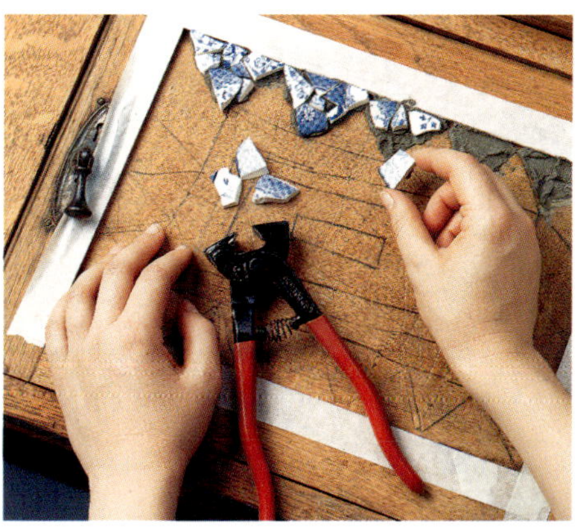

5 Mix the tile adhesive with admix according to the manufacturer's instructions. Working on a small area at a time, spread the mixture over each area of the pencil design with a flexible knife and press on the tesserae. Leave to dry.

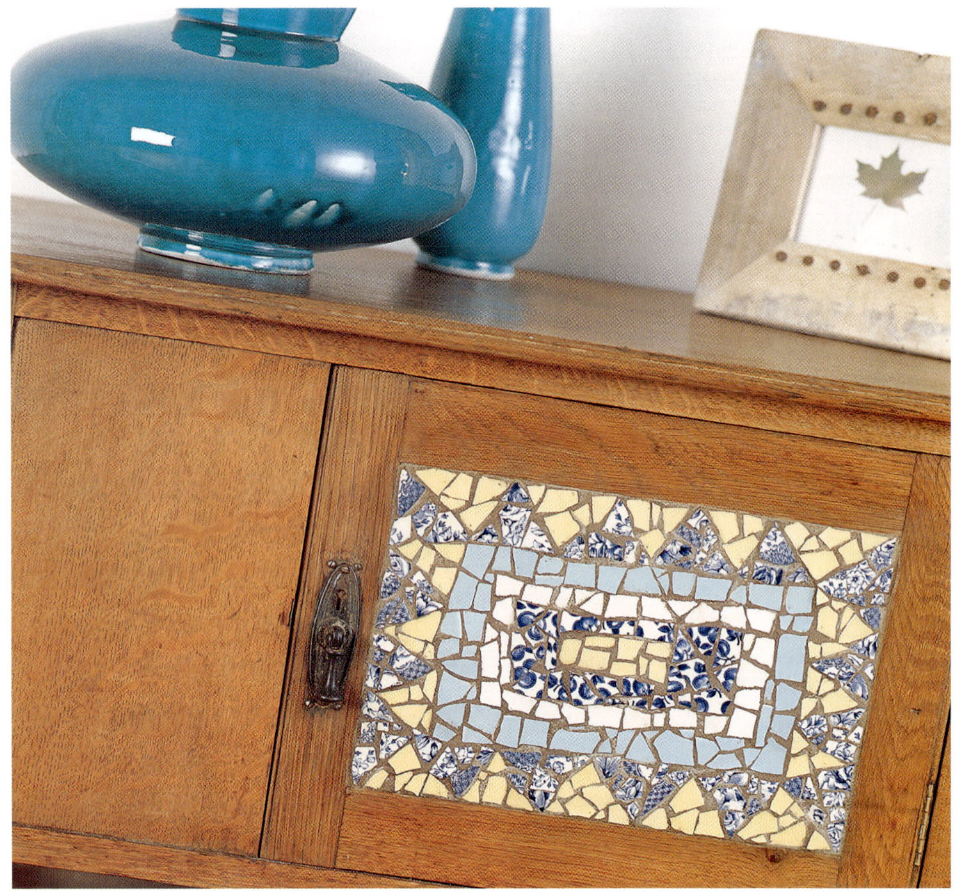

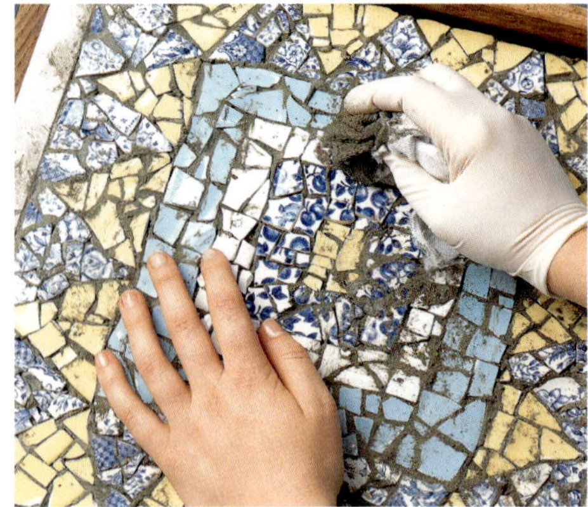

6 Grout the mosaic with more tile adhesive and admix mixture. The china pieces will make an uneven surface, so use a piece of cloth to reach into all the gaps. Wipe off the excess then leave to dry overnight.

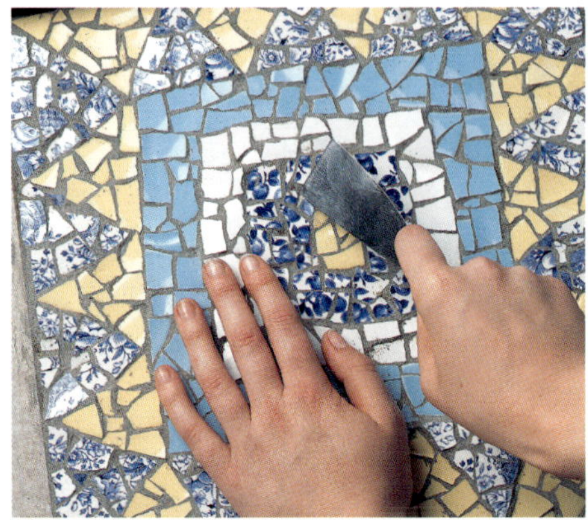

7 Carefully sand off any residual tile adhesive that may have dried on the surface of the mosaic, using fine abrasive paper (sandpaper). Use a paint-scraper to reach stubborn or awkward areas, such as those next to the wood.

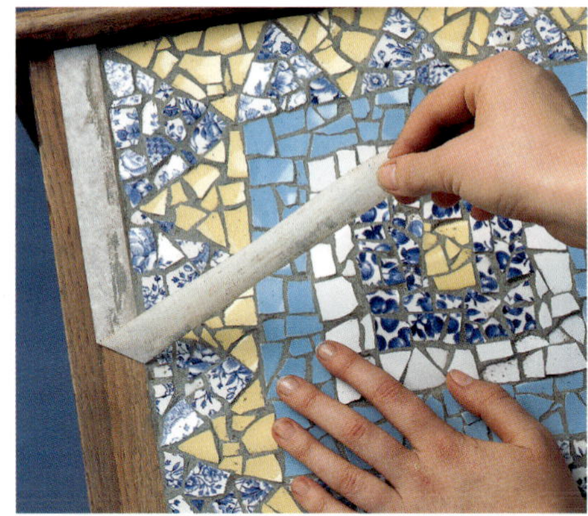

8 Once the residual adhesive is removed, carefully pull off the masking tape from around the edges of the mosaic panels.

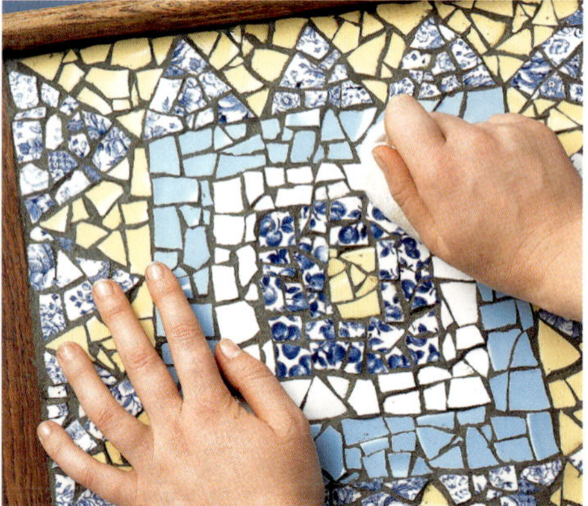

9 Finally, remove any remaining dried adhesive from the mosaic panels and polish the surface with a dry, soft cloth.

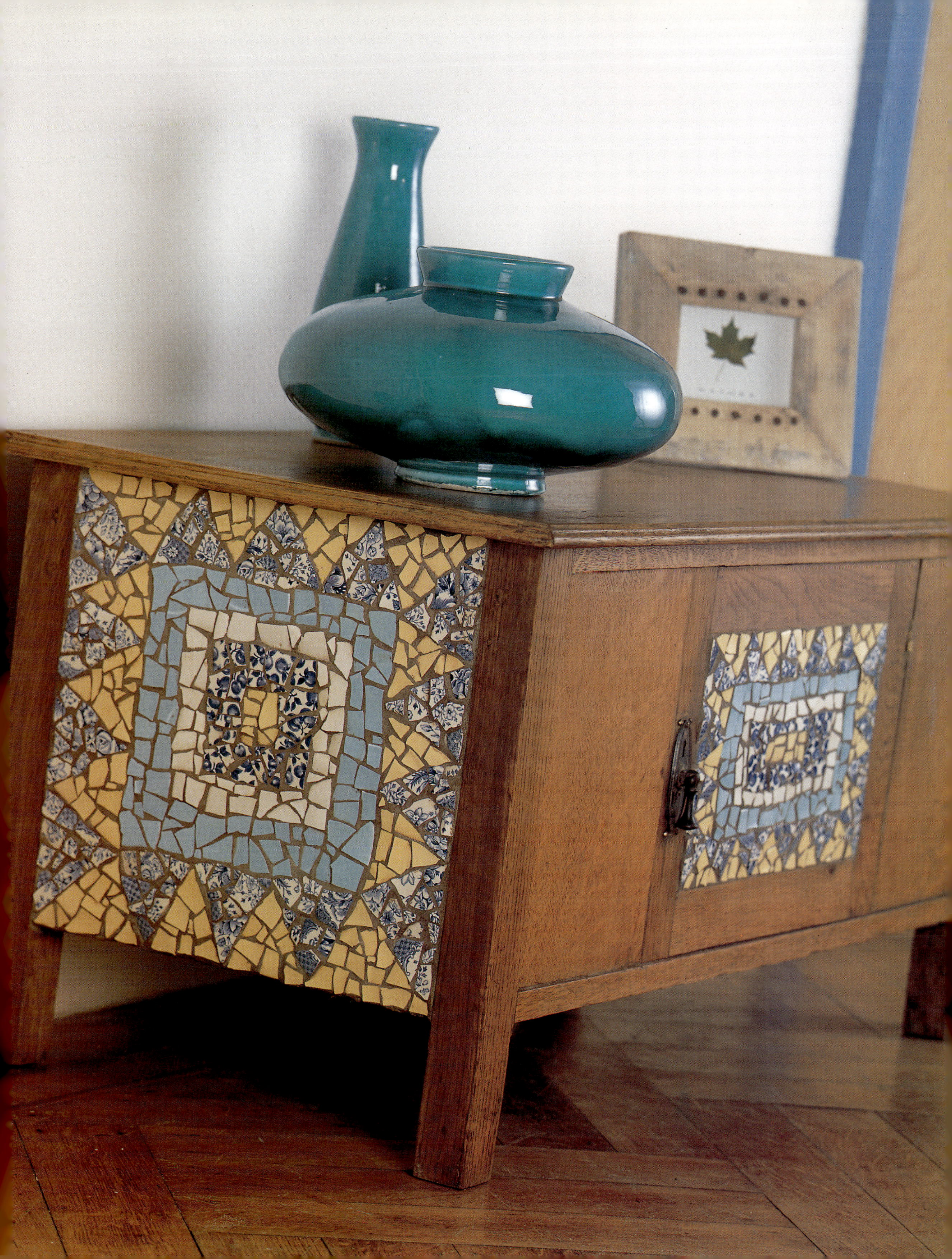

Sea urchins are found clinging to wild, rocky shorelines or nestling in rock pools. Their simple, pleasing shapes bring a taste of the ocean to your garden. They come in many colours, including these soft blues.

Sea Urchin Garden Seat

You will need

4 whole breezeblocks (cinderblocks) and 1 small cut piece
Sand
Cement
Hammer
Cold chisel
Charcoal
Vitreous glass mosaic tiles
Tile adhesive
Black cement stain
Notched trowel
Tile nippers
Slate
Piece of sacking (heavy cloth)
Glass baubles, silver and glass circles or stones

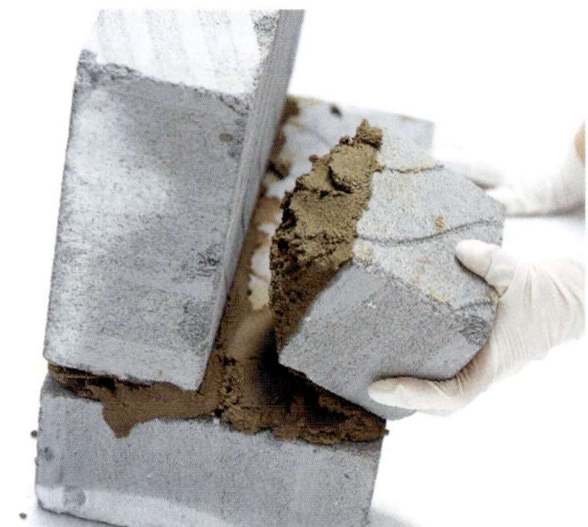

1 Mix 3 parts sand to 1 part cement with some water. Use this mortar to join the breezeblocks (cinderblocks) into a cube formed from two L shapes, with a cut block in the centre.

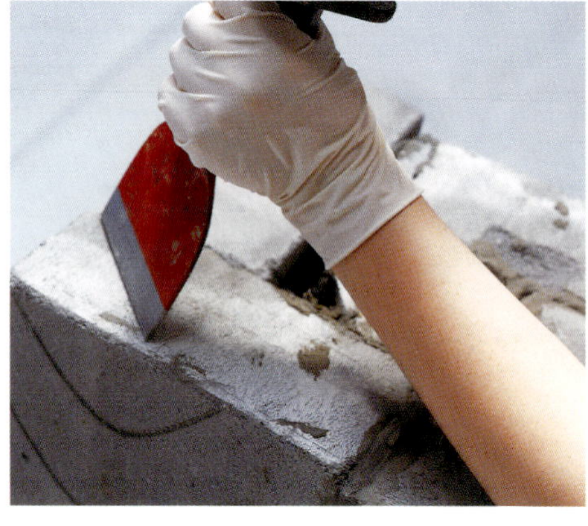

2 When the mortar is dry, knock off the corners of the blocks with a hammer and cold chisel. Continue to shape the blocks into a flat dome, with the cut block at the top.

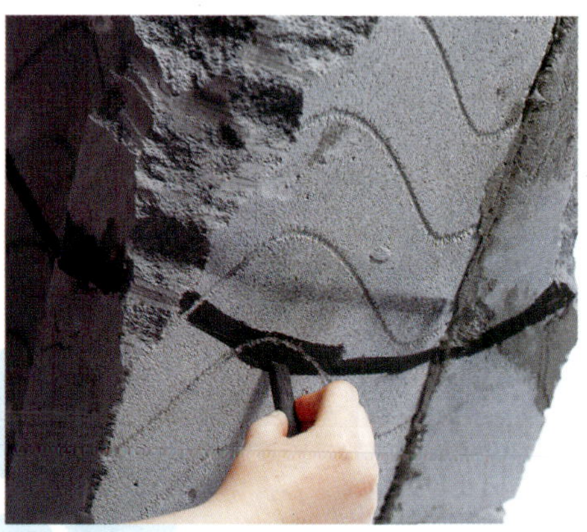

3 Using charcoal, draw a curved line on each side of the cube to give the impression of a rounded sea urchin. Draw lines radiating out from the centre. Keep your choice of colours simple and bold. Lay out the design before you start and apply the tiles to check the spacing. Vitreous glass tiles were chosen because of their suitability for outdoor work. Cut them into strips for easy lines or soak them off the mesh.

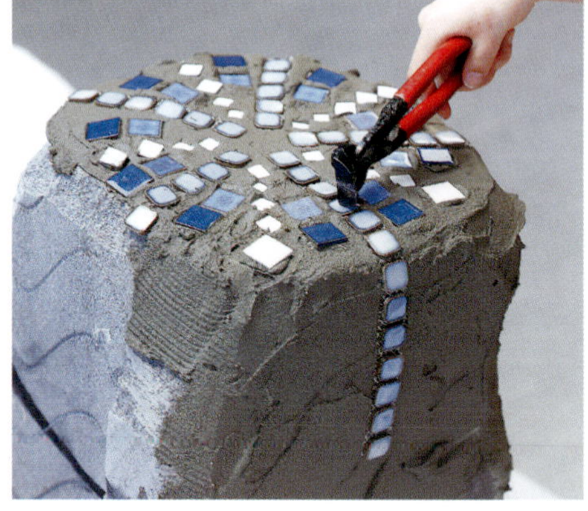

4 Add a small amount of black cement stain to the tile adhesive and trowel it directly on to the surface of the block, no more than 5mm (¼in) thick. Place each tile on the surface of the adhesive and tap it down sharply, once only, with the tile nippers. Do not adjust the tiles too much or they will lose their adhesion. Wrap the slate in a piece of sacking (heavy cloth) and break into pieces with a hammer.

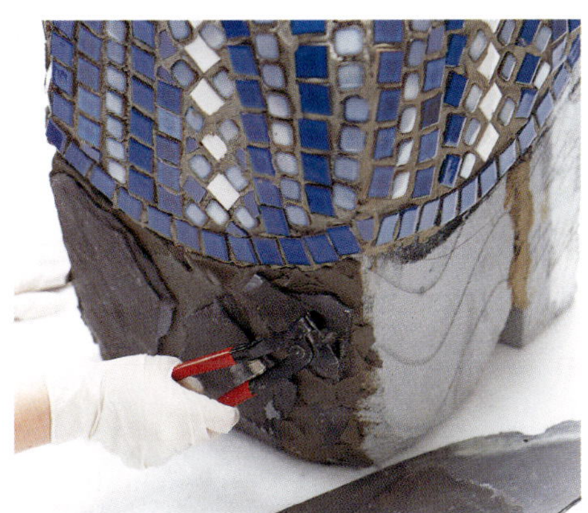

5 Avoid making any sharp edges, as these will have to be filed down afterwards. Use just one dark shade of tiles for the curved line marked in step 3 to give the design visual clarity. Place the broken slate pieces on the adhesive around the square base of the seat and tap them down with the tile nippers.

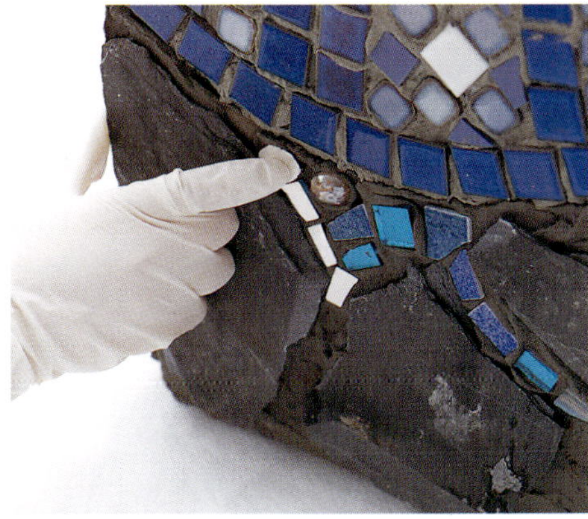

6 In between the gaps on the square base of the seat, place glass baubles, silver and glass circles, blue and white cut tiles or stones in the pattern of running water. Leave to dry completely. Grout the seat with sand, cement and black stain mixed with water. Allow to dry slowly but thoroughly. To secure the seat in position, dig out a shallow base for two breezeblocks, and then mortar the seat to them.

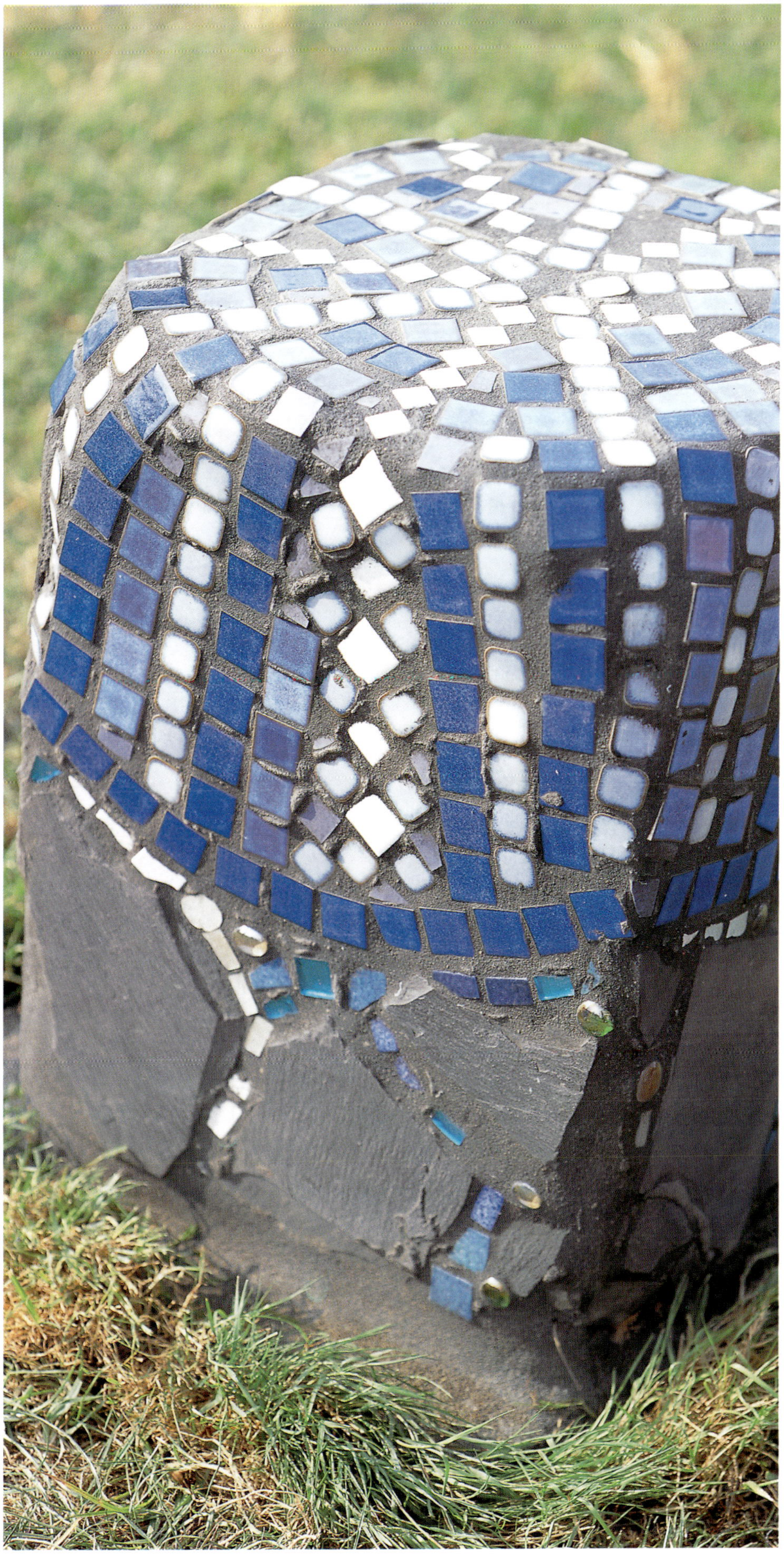

This striking table has been decorated with only bits of broken china and ceramic mosaic tiles, yet with clever colour coordination and a very simple design, it makes an attractive piece of garden furniture.

Shades of Blue Garden Table

You will need

2.5cm (1in) thick plywood
String
Drawing pin (thumb tack)
Pencil
Jigsaw (saber saw)
Abrasive paper (sandpaper)
Wood primer
Paintbrush
Broken china in various colours and patterns
Tile nippers
Tile adhesive
Flexible knife
Tile grout
Cement stain (optional)
Sponge
Soft cloth

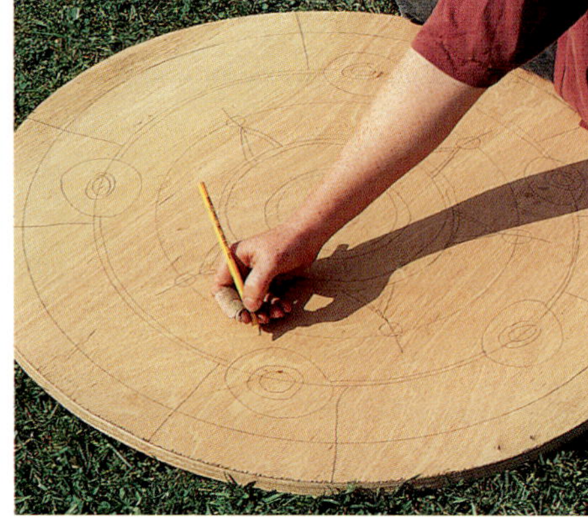

1 To mark a circle on the plywood, tie one end of a length of string, cut to the desired radius of the table top, to a drawing pin (thumb tack), and tie a pencil to the other end. Push the pin into the centre of the plywood, then draw the circle. Cut it out using a jigsaw (saber saw) and sand the edges. Draw your design, adjusting the string to draw concentric circles.

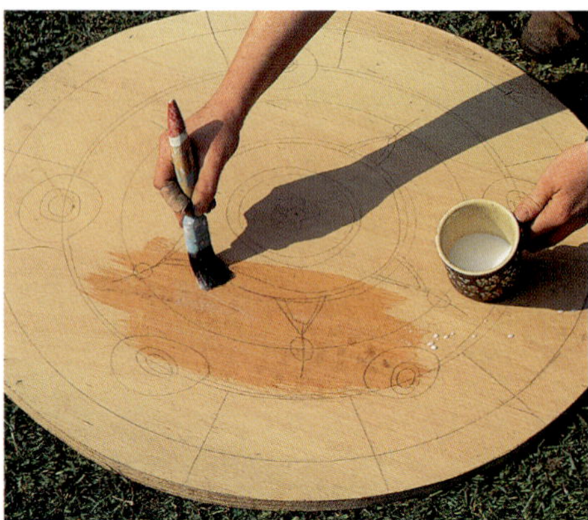

2 Prime the plywood circle with wood primer on the front, back and around the edge. Apply a thick and even coat, and allow each side to dry before proceeding with the next. Allow the primer to dry thoroughly according to the manufacturer's instructions before proceeding further.

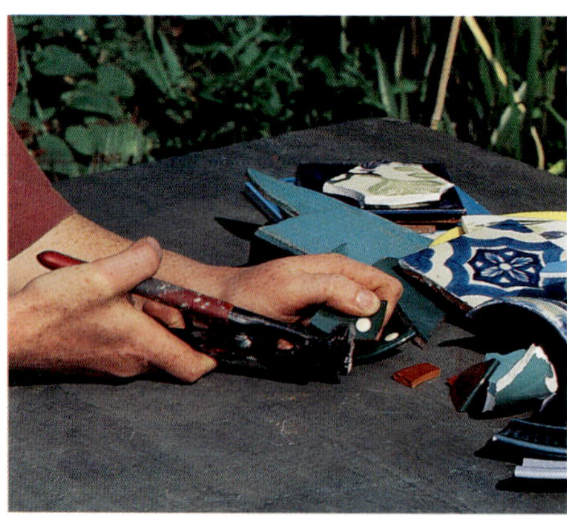

3 Using tile nippers, snip pieces of the china to fit your chosen design and arrange them on the table top. Also snip some more regularly shaped pieces, which will decorate the rim of the table.

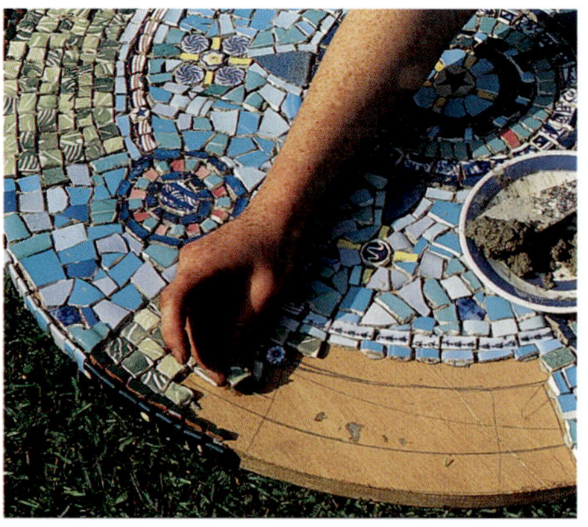

4 Spread tile adhesive on to the back of each piece of china with a flexible knife before fixing it in position. Cover the whole table with the design, then mosaic the rim.

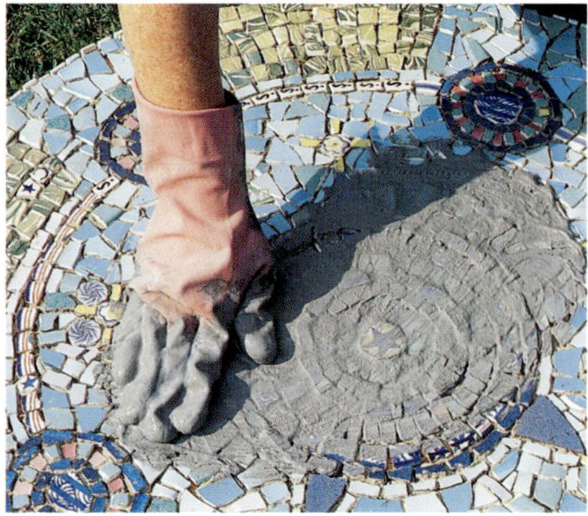

5 Mix up the grout, adding a stain if desired, then rub it into all the gaps with your fingers. Do not forget the rim. Clean off any excess with a damp sponge, then leave to dry. Polish with a dry, soft cloth.

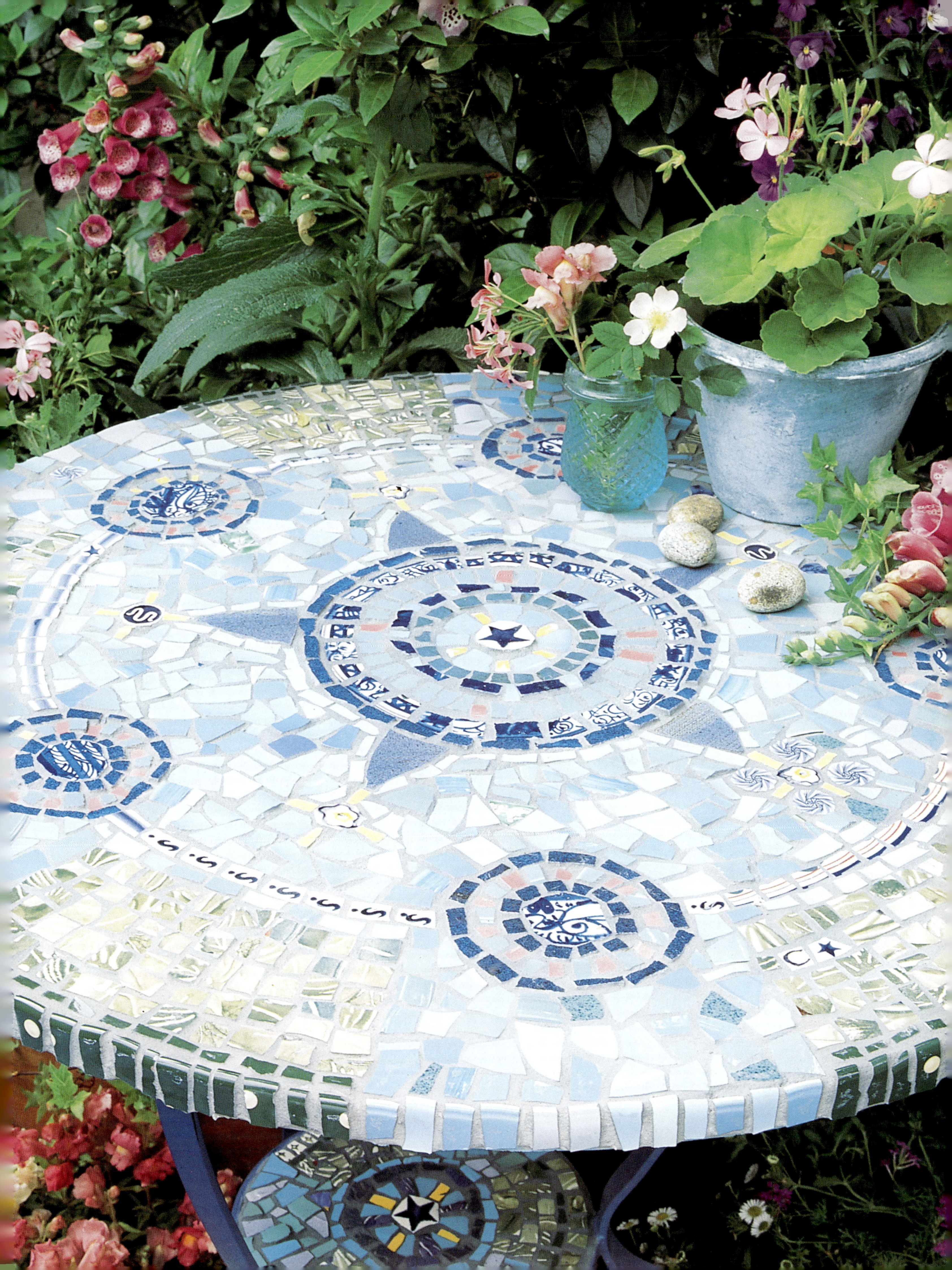

This traditional design uses the colours seen in ancient Roman mosaics to create a table top suitable for a simple metal base. Unglazed tiles are much easier than glazed tiles to cut and shape for this precise design.

Star Table

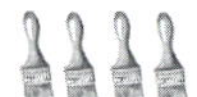

You will need

2cm (¾in) thick plywood sheet
String
Drawing pin (thumb tack)
Pencil
Jigsaw (saber saw)
Abrasive paper (sandpaper)
PVA (white) glue
Paintbrushes
Bradawl or awl
Pair of compasses
Pencil
Ruler
Black felt-tipped pen (optional)
Tile nippers
Unglazed ceramic mosaic tiles: white, beige, black and two shades of terracotta
Tile adhesive
Grout spreader
Sponge
Soft cloth

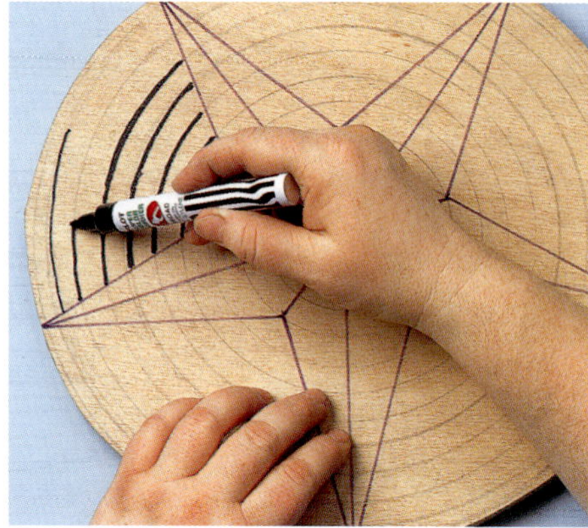

1 Follow the instructions for the Shades of Blue Garden Table to cut a circle from the plywood. Prime one side of the plywood with diluted PVA (white) glue and leave to dry. Score with a bradawl. Using a pair of compasses, draw circles 12mm (½in) apart, working out from the centre, then draw a large star on top. If you wish, go over the design in felt-tipped pen.

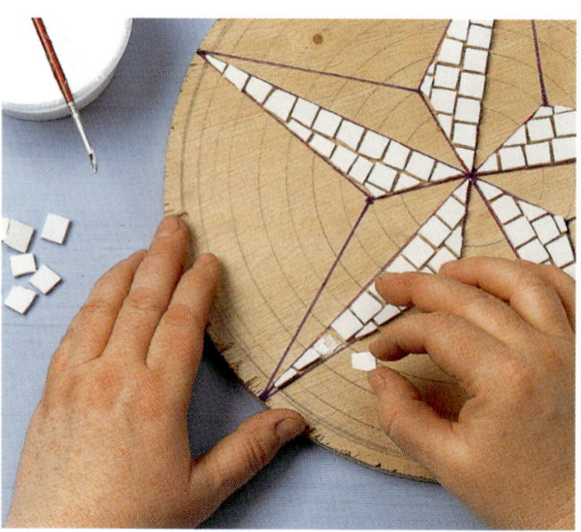

2 Using tile nippers, cut the white tiles into neat quarters. Apply PVA glue to the base in small sections, using a fine paintbrush. Stick the tesserae on to alternate sections of the star. Keep the rows straight and the gaps between the tesserae even and to a minimum. Trim the tesserae as necessary to fit. Continue laying the tesserae until all the white sections are complete.

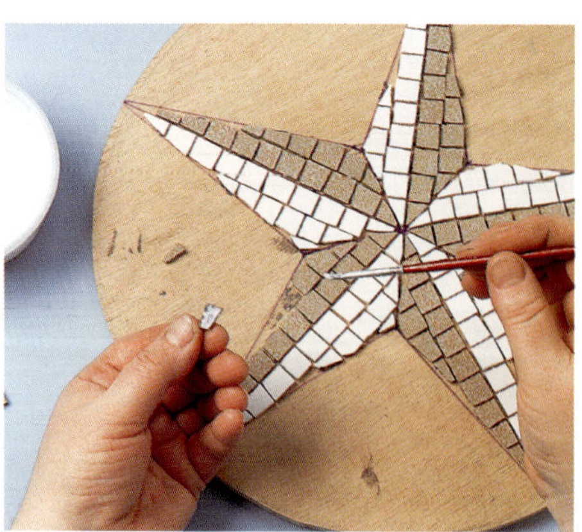

3 Cut up the beige tiles into neat quarters and fill in the other sections of the star in the same way as the white tiles in step 2.

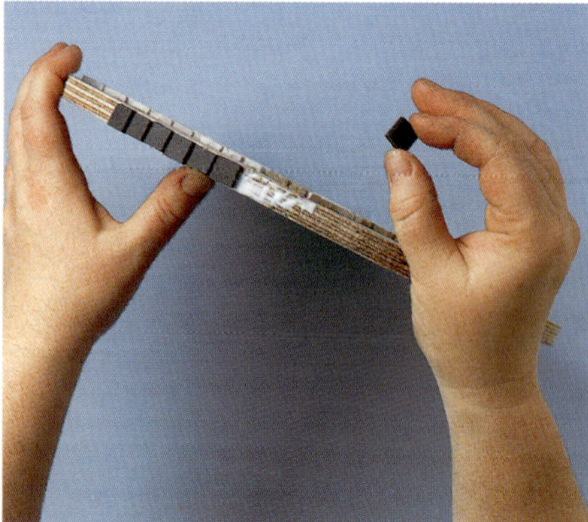

4 Cut the black tiles into neat quarters and glue around the edge of the plywood. Leave until it is completely dry.

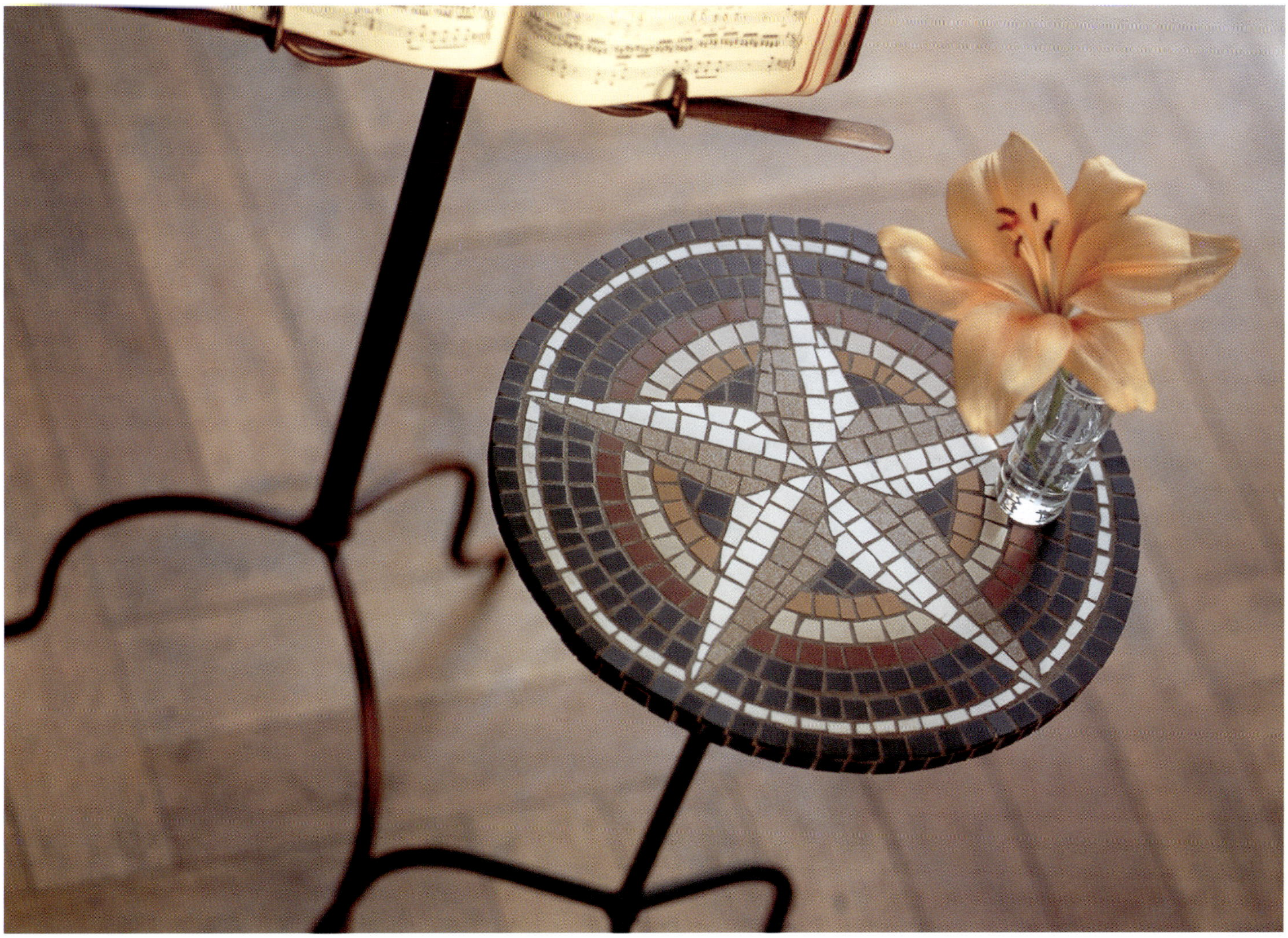

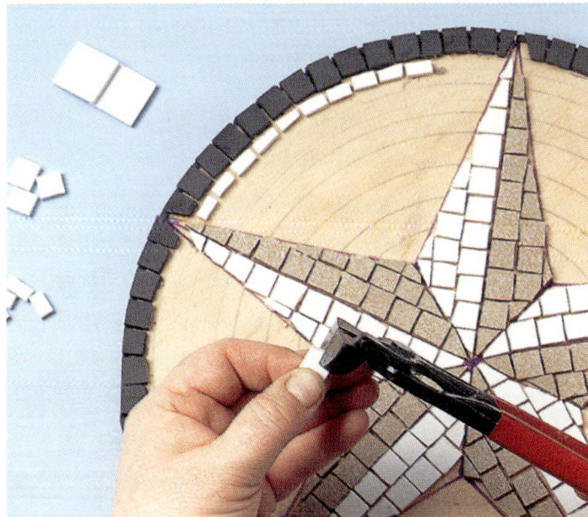

5 Glue a row of black quarter tiles around the outer edge of the table top. Cut some white quarter tiles in half and glue these inside the black circle, keeping the gaps to a minimum. Cut the terracotta tiles into quarters.

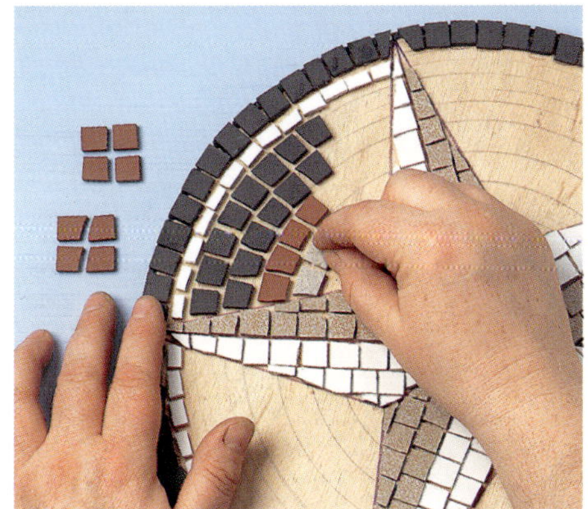

6 Using your drawn lines as a guide, fill in the rest of the background with alternating bands of colour. Lay out the tesserae before you glue them in place. Leave to dry overnight. Grout with tile adhesive, then clean the surface with a damp sponge. Leave to dry, then sand off any remaining adhesive and polish with a dry, soft cloth.

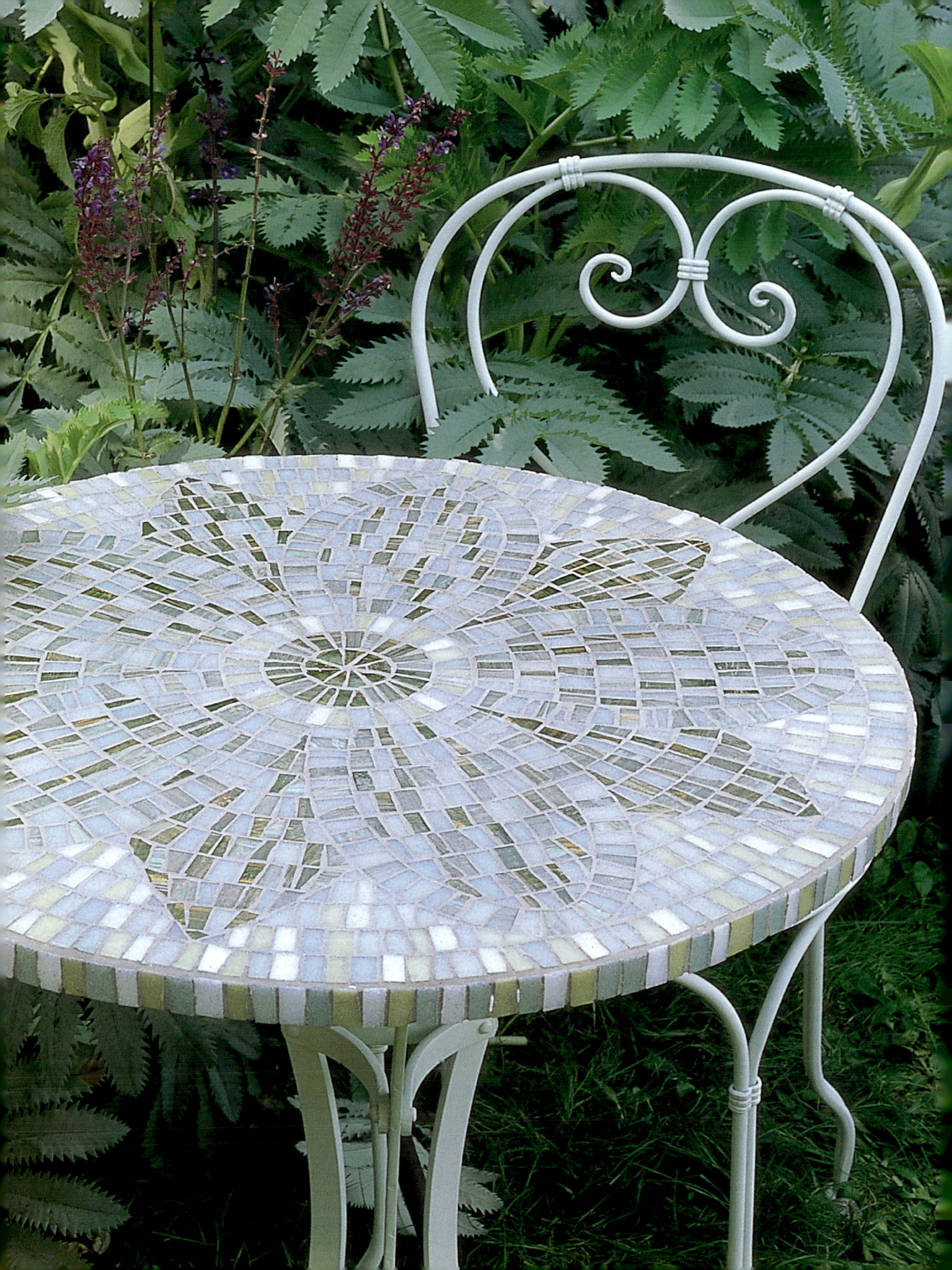

The combination of colours and the simple design of this mosaic table create a striking piece of furniture. The table can be used outdoors in good weather, but is not completely weatherproof.

Flower Garden Table

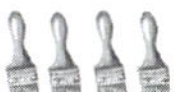

You will need

- 2.5cm (1in) thick plywood sheet
- String
- Drawing pin (thumb tack)
- Soft dark pencil
- Jigsaw (saber saw)
- Abrasive paper (sandpaper)
- Paper
- Masking tape
- Large sheet of tracing paper
- PVA (white) glue
- Paintbrush
- Vitreous glass mosaic tiles: off-white, light verdigris, dark verdigris, moss, gold-veined verdigris, gold-veined green
- Tile nippers
- Tile adhesive
- Flexible knife
- Soft cloth
- Tile grout
- Grout spreader
- Sponge

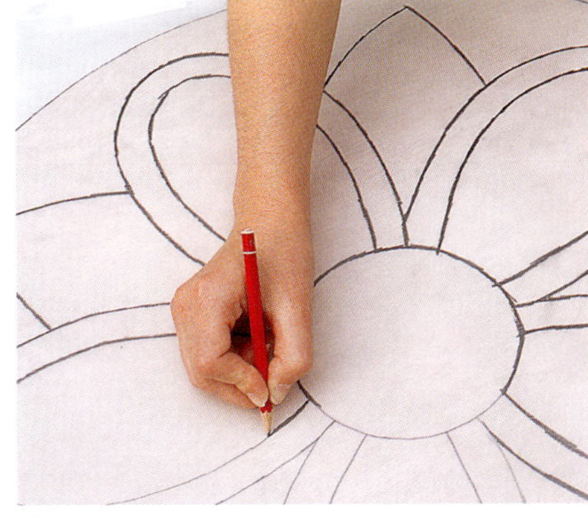

1 Follow the instructions for the Shades of Blue Garden Table to cut a circle from the plywood. Draw a large, rounded petal shape, with half a pointed petal on each side, on paper. Enlarge it on a photocopier until it is the right size for the table top. Then make four copies and stick them all together, so that you have five rounded and five pointed petals. Now trace the design on to tracing paper.

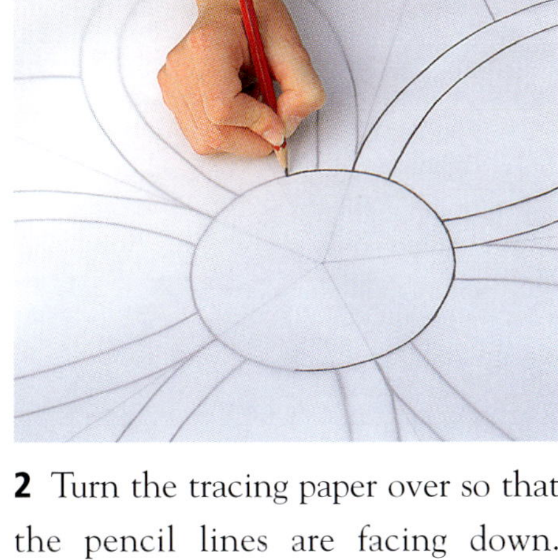

2 Turn the tracing paper over so that the pencil lines are facing down. Place the paper on top of the piece of plywood, and draw over the lines of the design with the pencil to transfer the marks to the plywood.

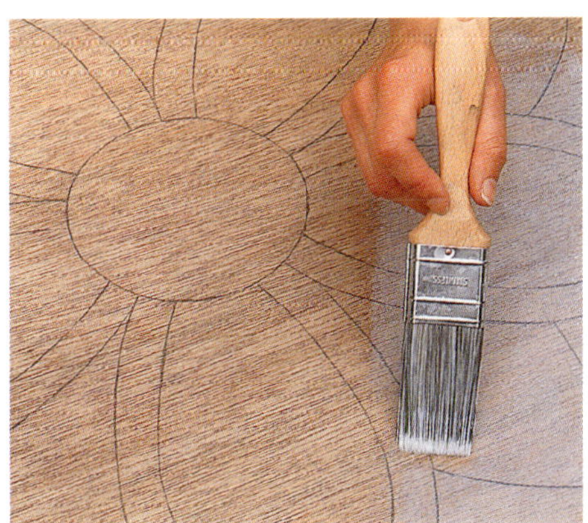

3 Seal the board with diluted PVA (white) glue, making sure you seal the edge of the plywood as well.

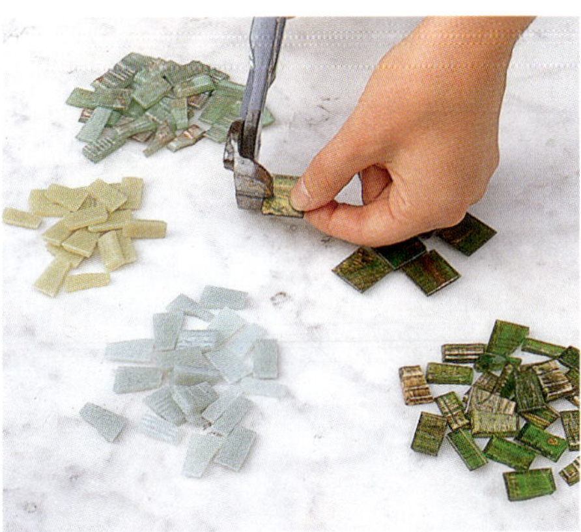

4 Using the tile nippers, cut the glass tiles into halves and thirds so you have a variety of widths. Make a small pile of each colour and save some whole tiles to cut into wedges later. ▶

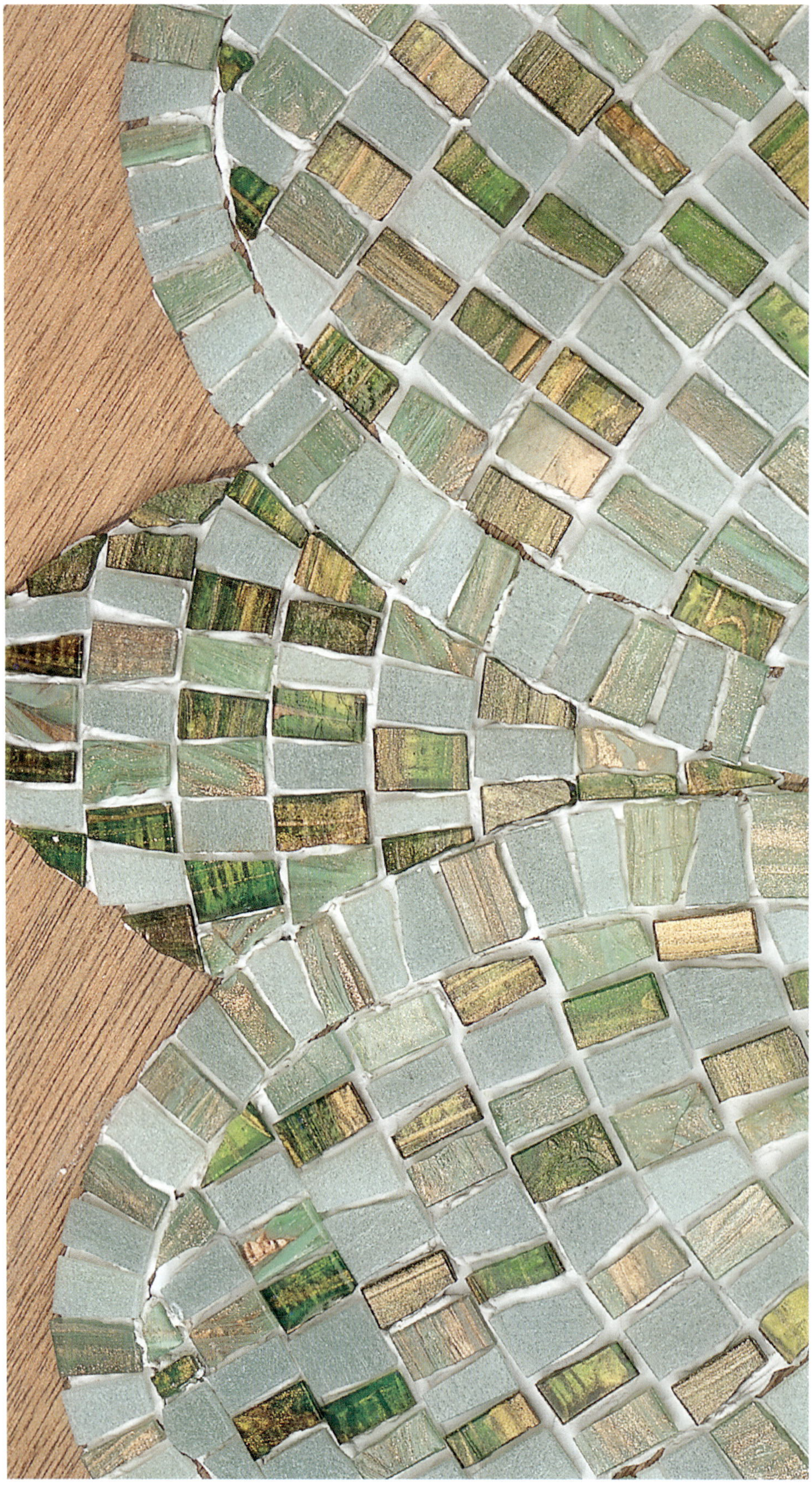

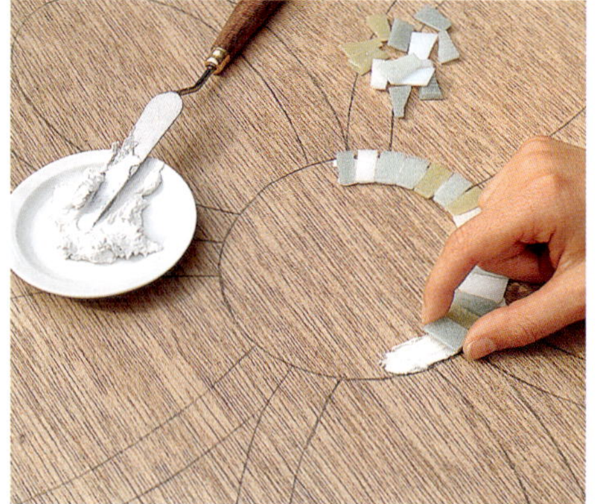

5 Using a flexible knife, spread tile adhesive over one area at a time, approximately 3mm (⅛in) deep. Select off-white, light verdigris, dark verdigris and moss-coloured tesserae, and press them into the tile adhesive, leaving a tiny gap between each piece for the grout to be applied later. Wipe away any adhesive spillages immediately with a cloth.

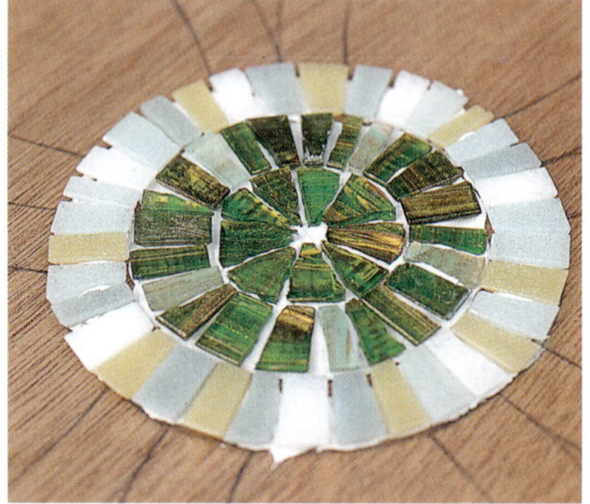

6 Fill in the area inside the ring with the gold-veined verdigris and gold-veined green tesserae. In order to achieve a neat finish in the centre of the design, nibble the tesserae into wedge shapes.

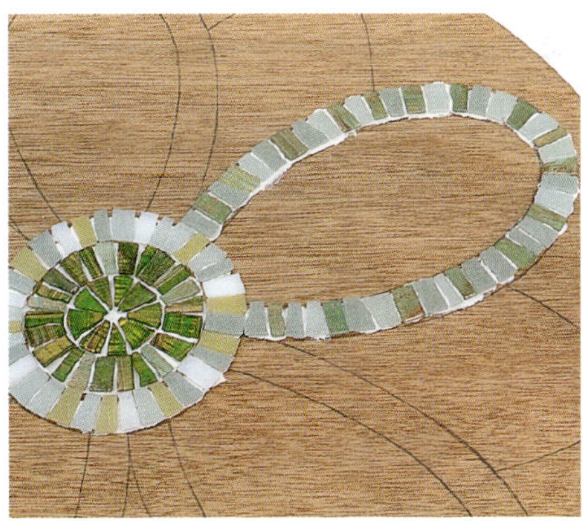

7 Stick down the outside rim of one of the rounded petals, using the light verdigris, dark verdigris and gold-veined verdigris tesserae.

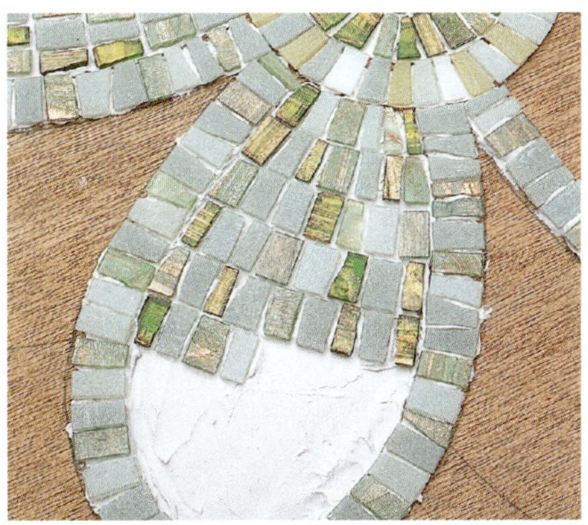

8 Fill in the rounded petal with the light verdigris, dark verdigris, gold-veined verdigris and gold-veined green tesserae, nibbling them to fit neatly within the rim of the petals. Repeat for the other rounded petals.

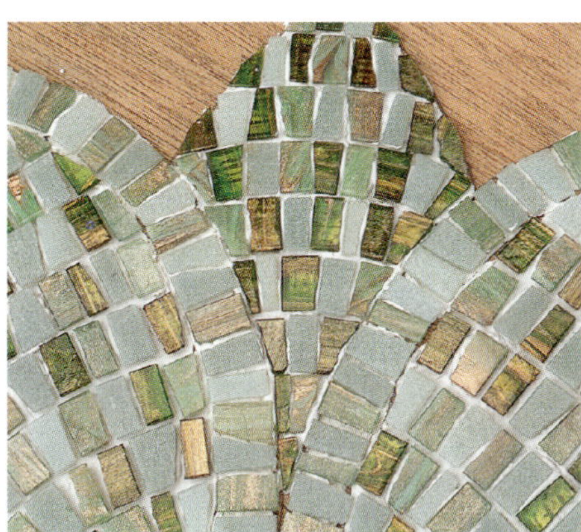

9 Fill in the pointed petals with the gold-veined verdigris, gold-veined green, light verdigris and dark verdigris tesserae.

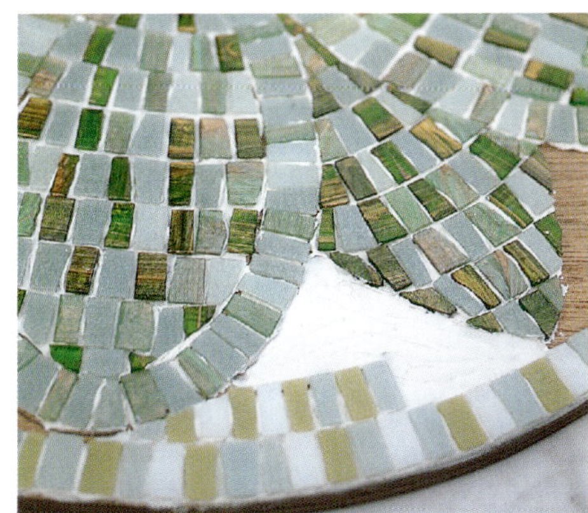

10 Fill in the area between the flower design and the edge of the plywood with the off-white, light verdigris and moss tesserae. Leave to dry for a day.

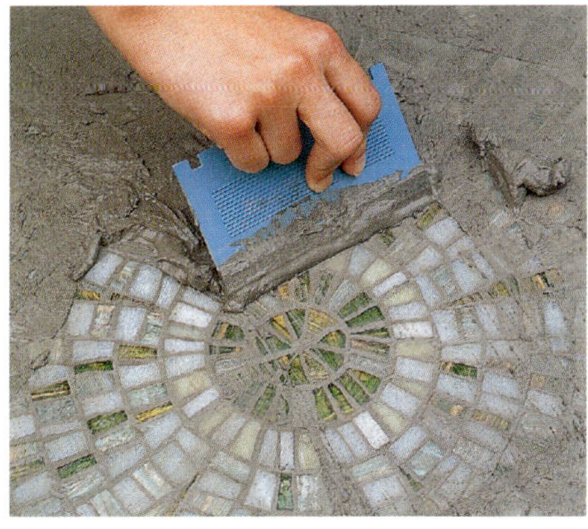

11 Push tile grout into all the cracks between the tesserae using a grout-spreader. Wipe any excess grout off the table top and edge with a damp sponge, then leave to dry.

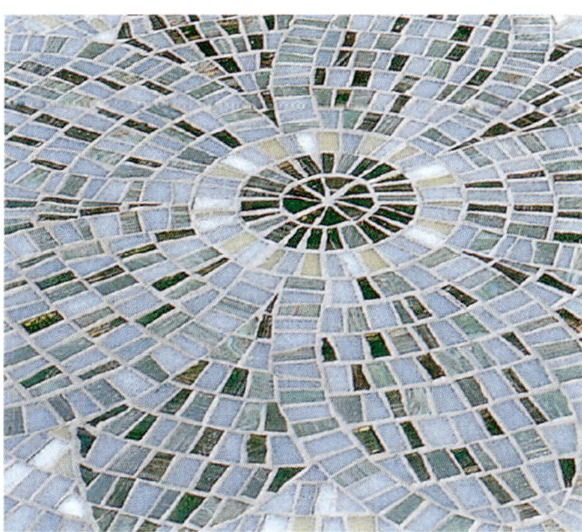

12 When the table top is dry, turn it over on to a protected surface and spread the base evenly with some tile adhesive in order to seal it. When it is dry, turn the table back again and polish the surface with a dry, soft cloth.

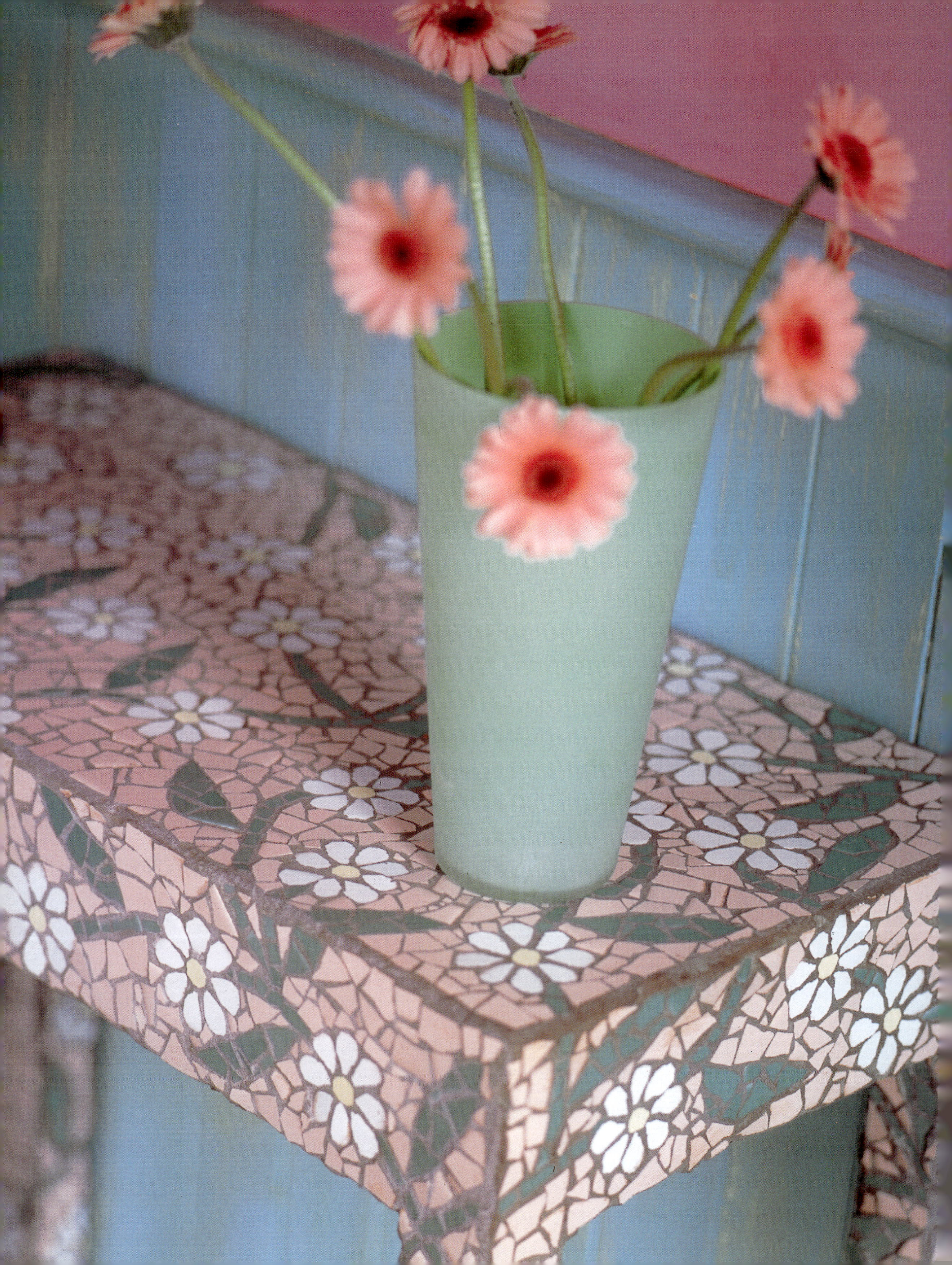

This wonderful table is literally strewn with daisies – green stems twine around the legs and a carpet of pretty white flowers spreads over the top. If the table has a rim, saw it off first to make the shape easier to mosaic.

Daisy-covered Table

You will need
Small table
White spirit (paint thinner)
Abrasive paper (sandpaper)
PVA (white) glue
Paintbrush
Bradawl or awl
Soft dark pencil
Thin-glazed ceramic household tiles: yellow, white, green, pale pink
Tile nippers
Tile adhesive
Admix
Flexible knife
Hammer
Piece of sacking (heavy cloth)
Rubber spreader
Sponge
Soft cloth

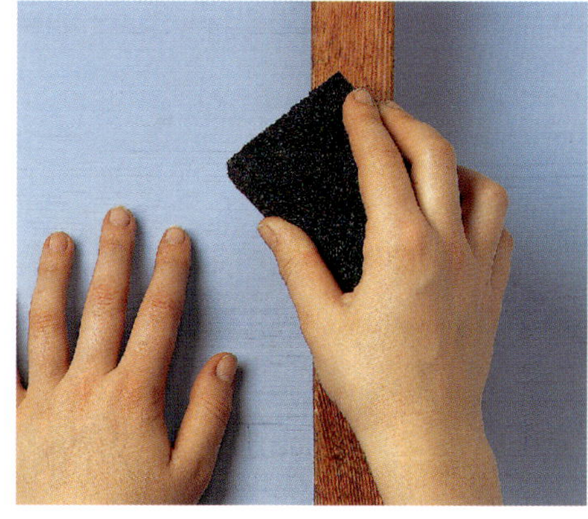

1 Remove any old wax, dirt, paint or varnish from the table using white spirit (paint thinner), then sand and prime with diluted PVA (white) glue. Leave to dry, then score all the surfaces with a bradawl or awl.

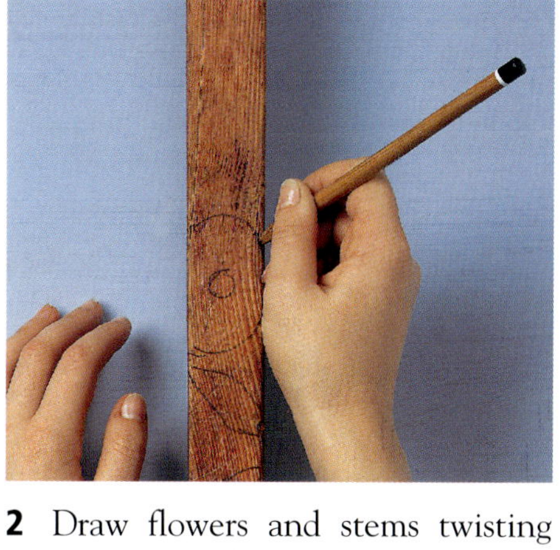

2 Draw flowers and stems twisting around the legs and spreading over the table top. Take care with your design where the legs join the table top.

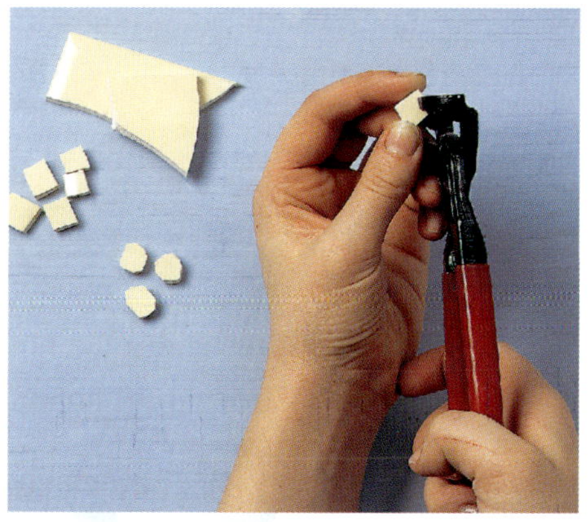

3 Using tile nippers, cut the yellow tiles into small squares, then nip off the corners to make circles for the centres of the flowers.

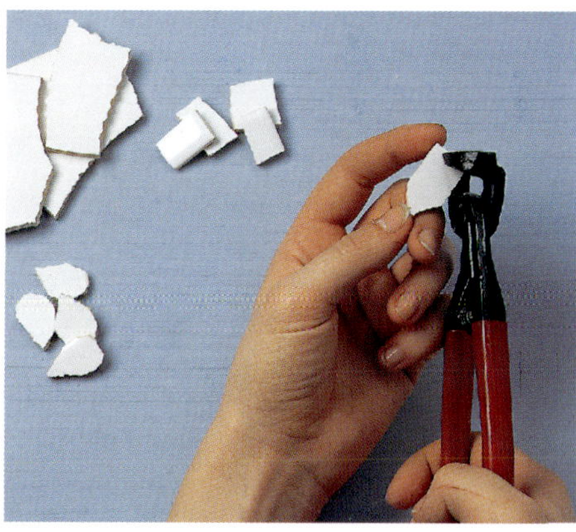

4 Cut the white tiles into small, equal size oblongs. Make these into petal shapes by nipping off the corners of each oblong.

▶

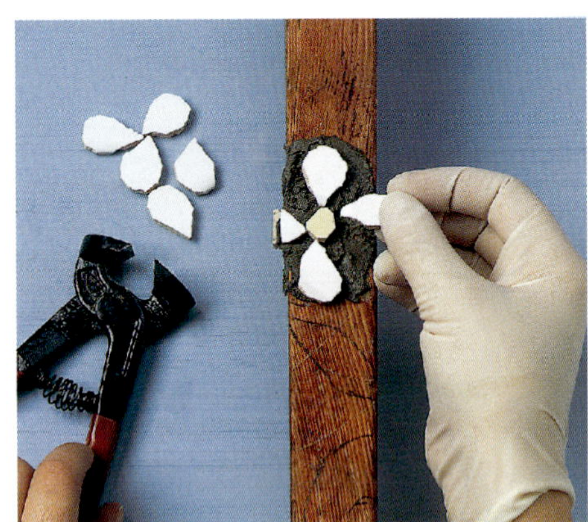

5 Mix the tile adhesive and admix together. Using a flexible knife, spread the mixture over a pencilled flower outline. Press in a yellow flower centre and the white petals – you may need to cut some petals on the legs in half. Complete all the flowers in this way.

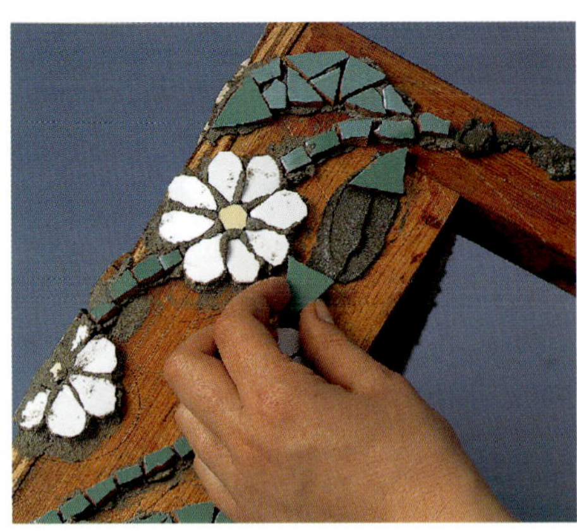

6 Spread a thin coat of the adhesive mixture along the pencil outlines of the stems and leaves. Cut the green tiles into appropriate stem and leaf shapes and press them in place. Leave to dry overnight.

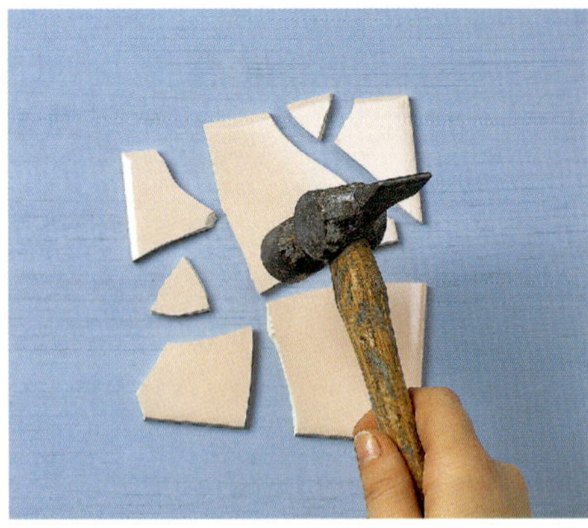

7 Using a hammer, break up the pale pink tiles. It is advisable to wrap each tile in a piece of sacking (heavy cloth) to prevent splintering and shattering.

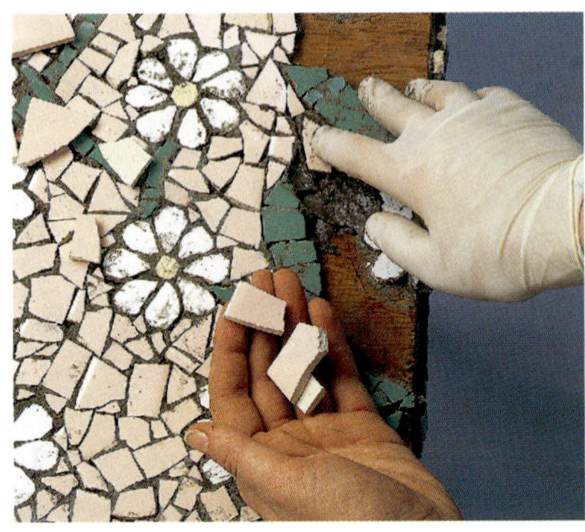

8 Working on a small area at a time, spread the adhesive mixture over the background areas. Press in the pale pink tile pieces to fit. Leave to dry overnight.

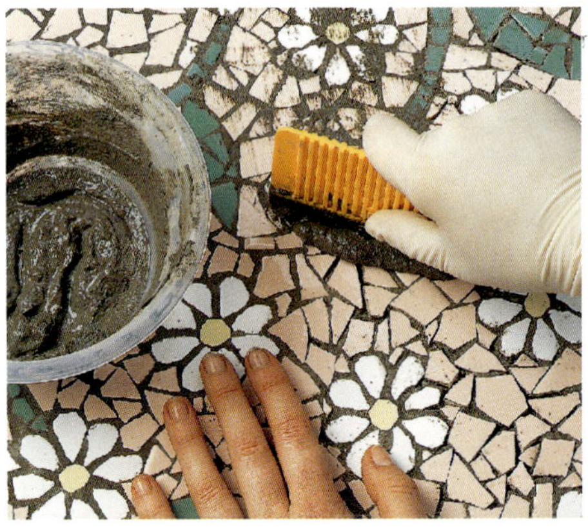

9 Grout the mosaic with tile adhesive, using a rubber spreader for the large flat areas and your fingers for the smaller areas. Wipe off the excess adhesive with a damp sponge and leave to dry overnight.

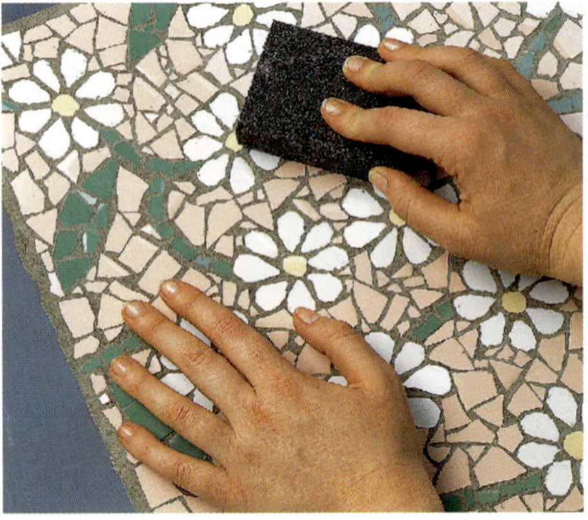

10 Carefully sand the surface of the table top and legs to remove any lumps of dried adhesive still remaining. Wipe with a damp sponge, if necessary, and polish with a dry, soft cloth.

In this project, the mosaics are laid in shapes inset on a surface, rather than over the entire area, and the intervening veneer forms are equally important. The lines give the table a sensual and dynamic feeling.

Stained-glass Table

You will need

110 x 70cm (43 x 28in) MDF (medium-density fiberboard) 18mm (¾in) thick
Soft pencil
Tracing paper
Scissors
Iron
3mm (⅛in) thick oak veneer
Craft (utility) knife
3mm (⅛in) thick stained-glass tiles: red, iridescent pink and rippled clear glass
Red chestnut wood stain
Paintbrushes
Clear polyurethane varnish
PVA (white) glue
Contact adhesive
G-clamps
Softwood blocks
Tile grout
Red cement stain
Sponge
Glass cleaner
21mm (⅞in) thick stainless-steel edging to cover edge of MDF and tiles

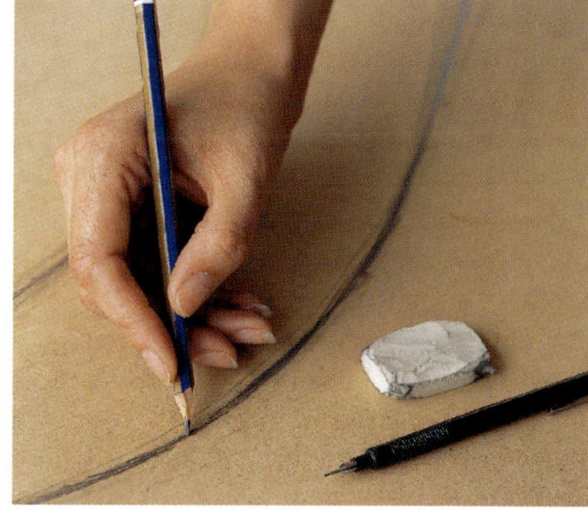

1 On the piece of MDF (medium-density fiberboard) draw six wavy lines with a soft pencil down the length of the board. These define the three bands that will be filled with the stained-glass and the four bands for the wooden veneer.

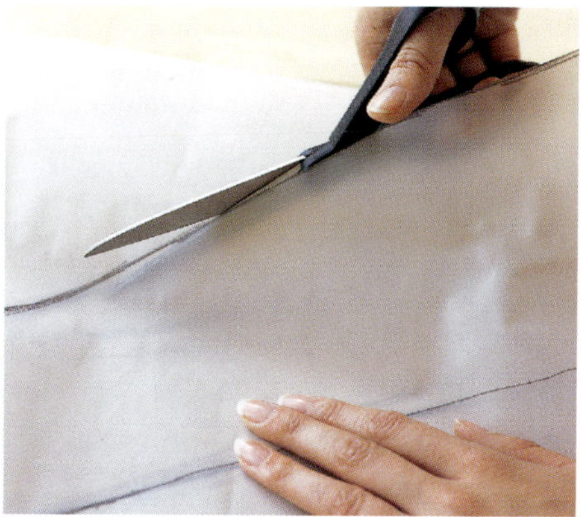

2 Trace the lines on to tracing paper. Then cut out templates of the four bands for the veneer. The wooden veneer should be 3mm (⅛in) thick, or the same thickness as the glass tiles to be used for the mosaic, so that they create a flat surface.

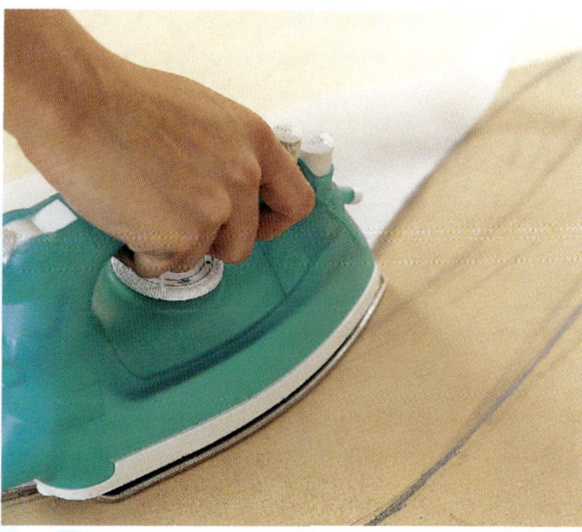

3 Iron the cut-out templates flat, using a warm, not hot, heat, as the tracing paper tends to crinkle and fold.

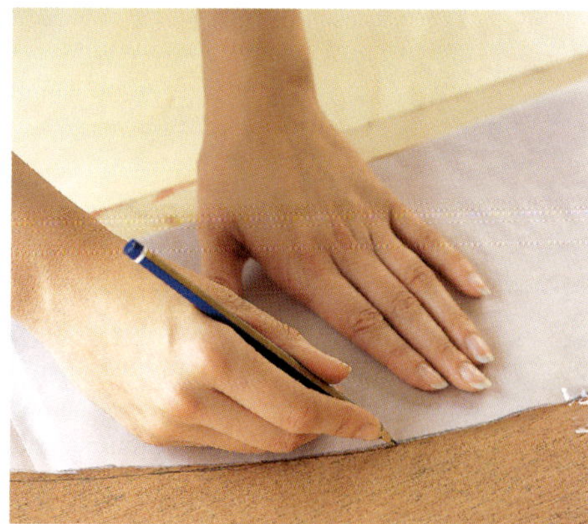

4 Place the templates on to the oak veneer. Using a soft pencil, carefully draw a line around the edge of each template. Placing any straight lines along the straight edge of the veneer makes it easier for cutting.

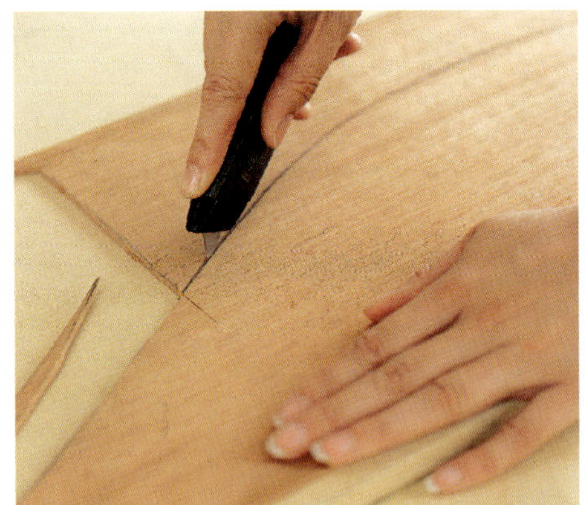

5 With the sharp blade of a craft (utility) knife, and working on a protected surface, score a strong line along the pencil marks. Work the curved lines in sections, removing excess veneer as you go.

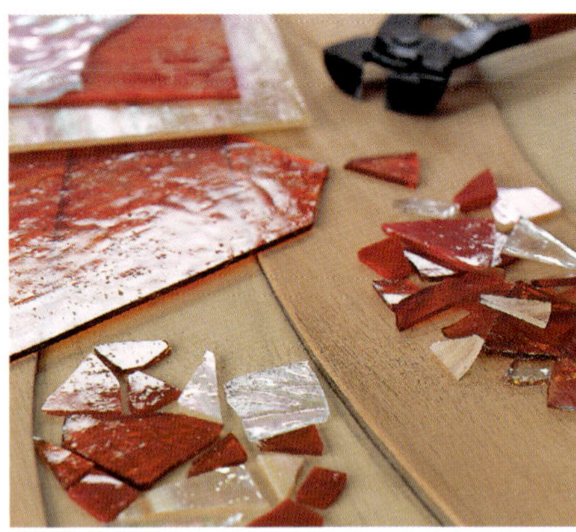

6 Place the four cut-out sections of veneer in their correct positions on the table. Using tile nippers, snip the stained-glass tiles into small pieces, laying them in position until the desired effect is achieved. In the planning, be aware of the balance of different coloured and rippled glass.

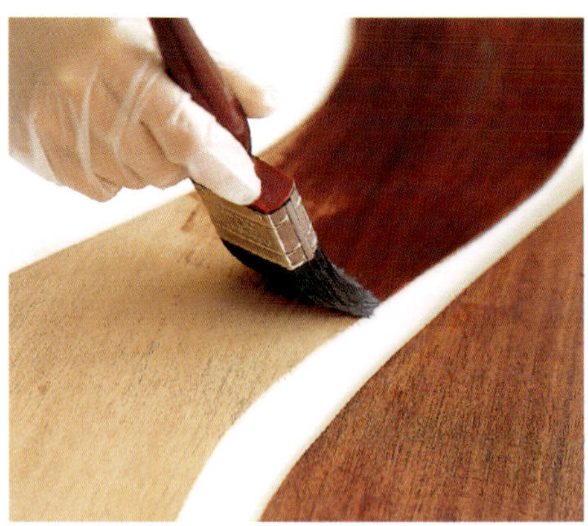

7 Lay the pieces of veneer on a protected surface and apply two thin coats of red chestnut wood stain. Allow to dry. Apply several coats of clear varnish to each piece, allowing each coat to dry before applying the next.

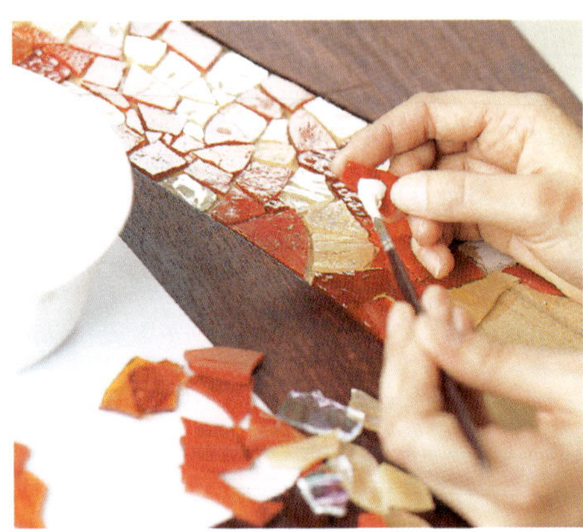

8 Place the veneer panels back in position on the table. Cover the back of the stained-glass tesserae evenly with PVA (white) glue, using a small paintbrush. Lay the pieces in a random arrangement on the table in a ratio of four red tiles to every two pink and one clear.

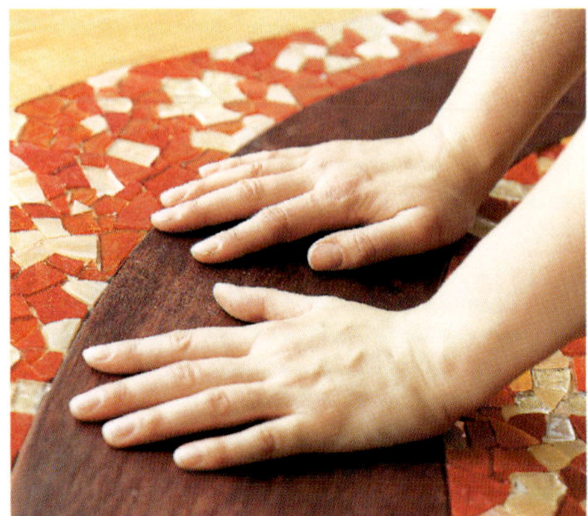

9 To stick the veneer down, use contact adhesive, following the manufacturer's instructions carefully. Apply a thin film of this glue on to both the back of the veneer and the surface of the table. After about 10 minutes, or when the glue is tacky, bring the two surfaces together and press down hard, clamp (using softwood blocks to protect the veneer) and leave to dry. Note that once the two surfaces have made contact, no repositioning is possible.

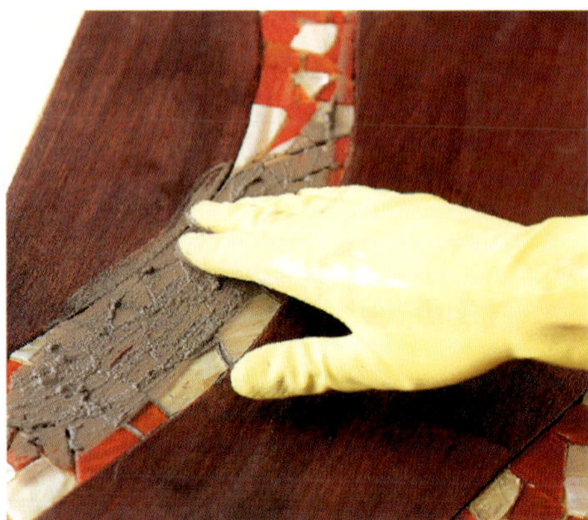

10 Carefully grout the mosaic bands with a grey tile grout mixed with red cement stain. Clean off the excess trying not to get any grout on the veneer. When it is nearly dry, go over the mosaic areas with a sponge dipped in glass cleaner to remove excess grout. When the grout is completely dry, glue the stainless-steel edging in position around the table using contact adhesive.

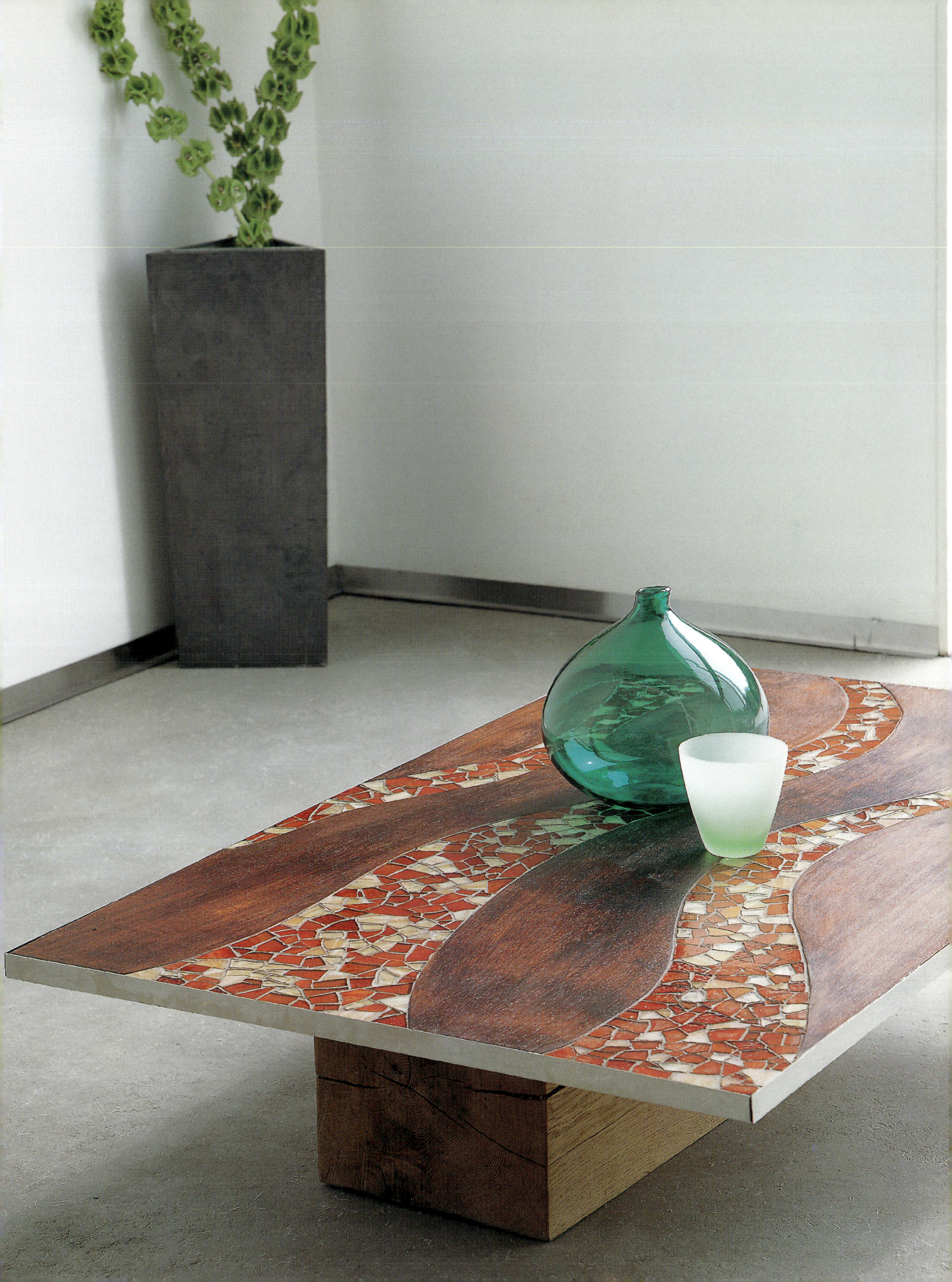

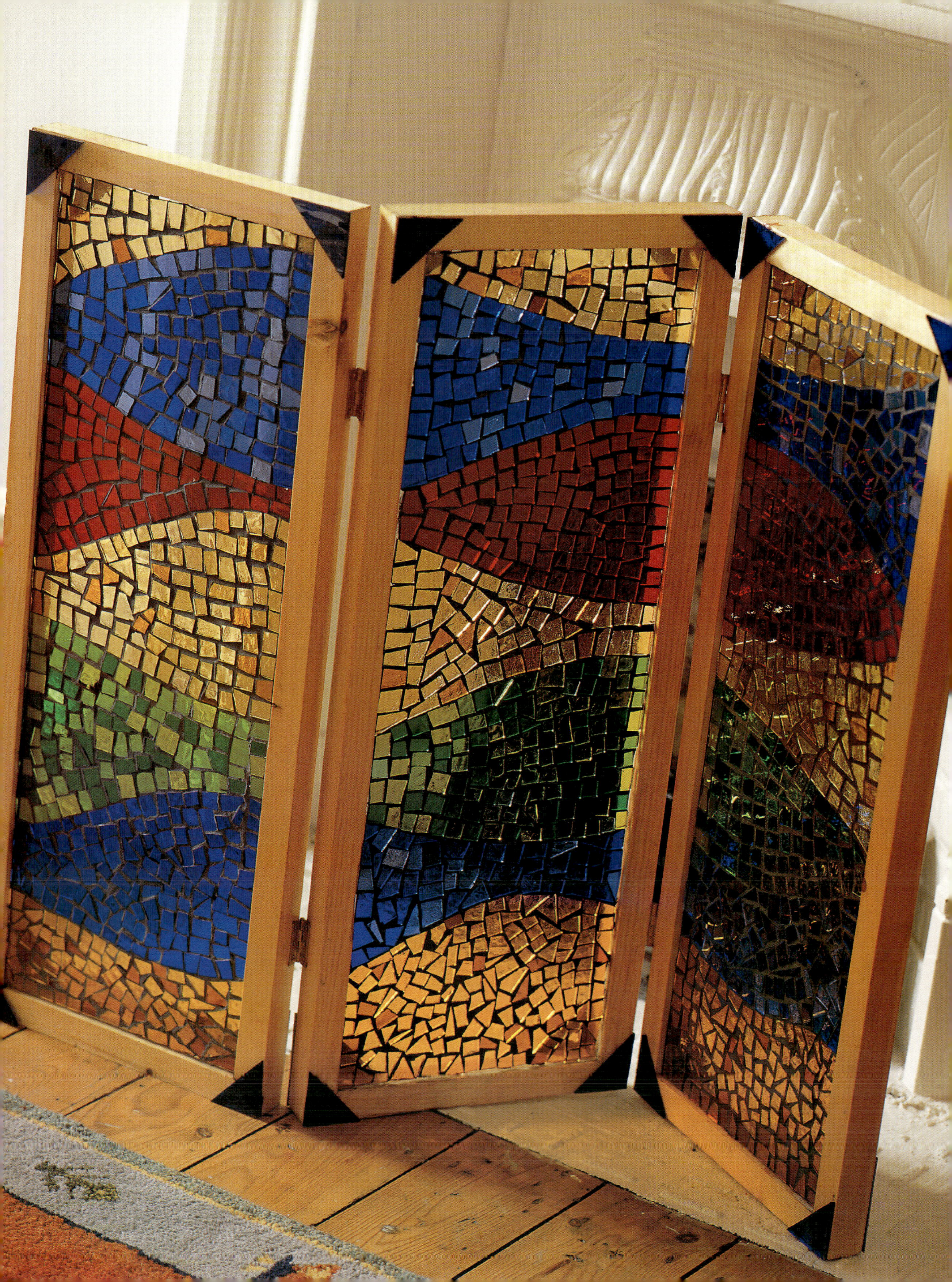

In this project, the coloured glass tesserae are laid on top of pieces of clear glass. Placing the screen in front of a window by day or a glowing fire at night means that light can shine through it.

Stained-glass Screen

You will need

Mitre block
Tape measure
Hacksaw
3 pieces of 2.5 x 4cm (1 x 1½in) wood, each 206cm (81in) long, with a 12mm (½in) rebate (rabbet)
Wood glue
Hammer
12 corner staples
Dark pencil
Drill
4 small hinges and screws
Screwdriver
Large sheet of paper
Black felt-tipped pen
3 pieces of clear glass, each 70 x 25cm (28 x 10in)
Permanent felt-tipped pen
Glass cutter
7 pieces of coloured glass, 27cm (10½in) square
Clear all-purpose adhesive
Tile grout
Black cement stain
Toothbrush
Paint scraper
Soft cloth
3 pieces of rectangular moulding, each 186cm (74in) long
Panel pins (brads)
12 metal corner plates and screws

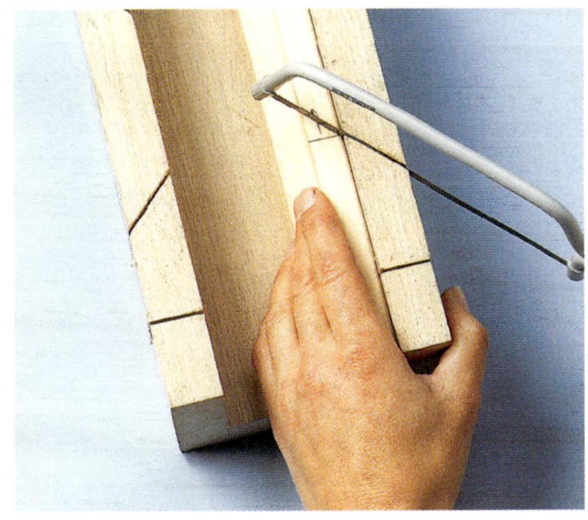

1 Using a mitre block and a hacksaw, cut each piece of rebated (rabbeted) wood into two 74cm (29in) long pieces and two 29cm (11½in) long pieces. These will form the wooden frame for the screen.

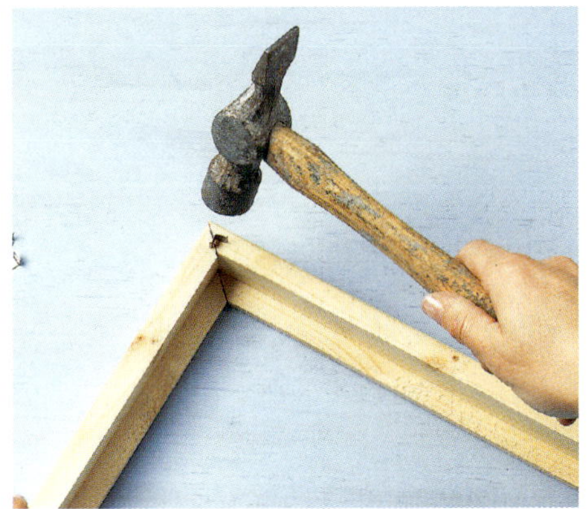

2 Lay the pieces of wood out on a flat surface to make three oblong frames. Glue the mitred ends together with wood glue, checking they are at right angles. Leave to dry, then hammer in a corner staple at each corner.

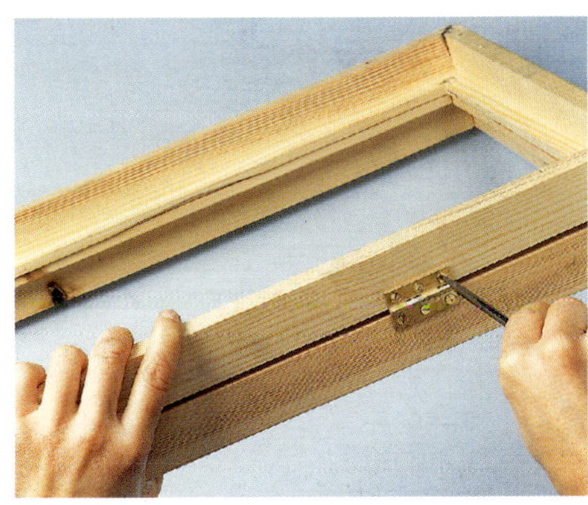

3 Place one frame on top of another, with the rebates facing outwards. With a dark pencil, mark the position of two hinges and their screw holes, as shown. Using a drill, make a shallow guidehole for each screw, then screw in the hinges. Attach the third wooden frame in the same way to form a three-piece screen.

▶

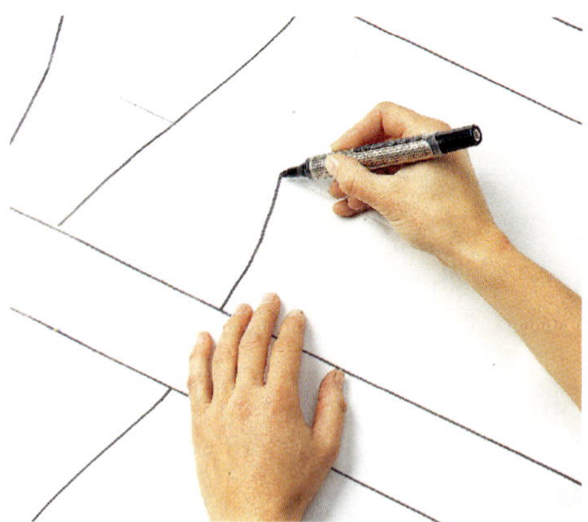

4 Place the three frames face down on a large sheet of paper. Using a black felt-tipped pen, draw around the inner edge of each frame. Then draw a simple design that flows in bands of colour from one frame to the next.

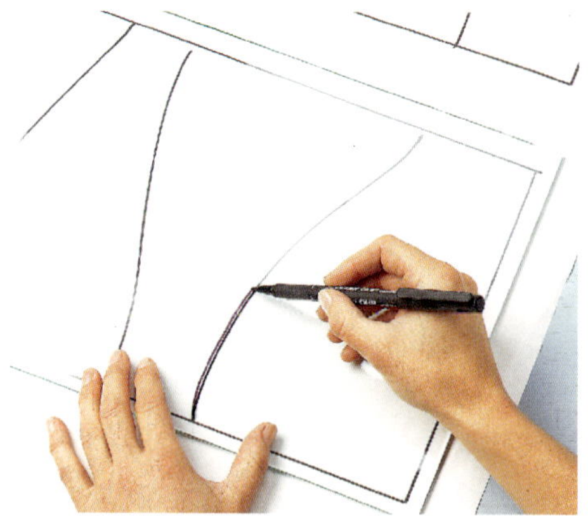

5 Place the pieces of clear glass over the paper drawings – the glass will be slightly larger. Using a permanent felt-tipped pen, trace your design on to the pieces of glass, taking care not to press too hard against them.

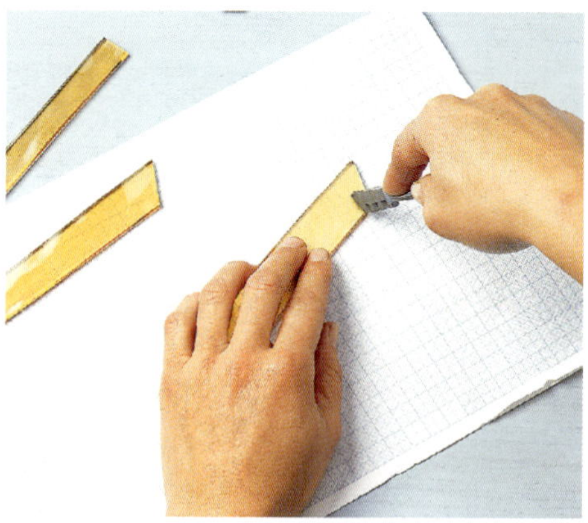

6 Using a glass cutter, cut 12 right-angled triangles of coloured glass for the corners of the screen. Reserve them on one side. Cut the rest of the coloured glass into random shaped pieces of roughly similar size.

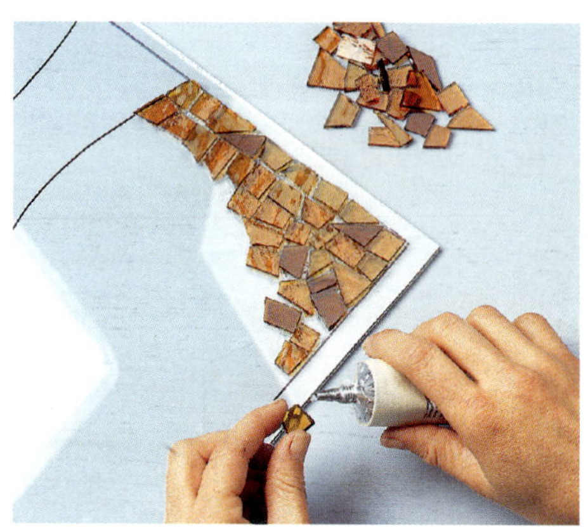

7 Using clear adhesive, glue the coloured pieces on to the clear glass panels. Work on a section of your design at a time, following each band across to the other panels. Leave to dry for 2 hours.

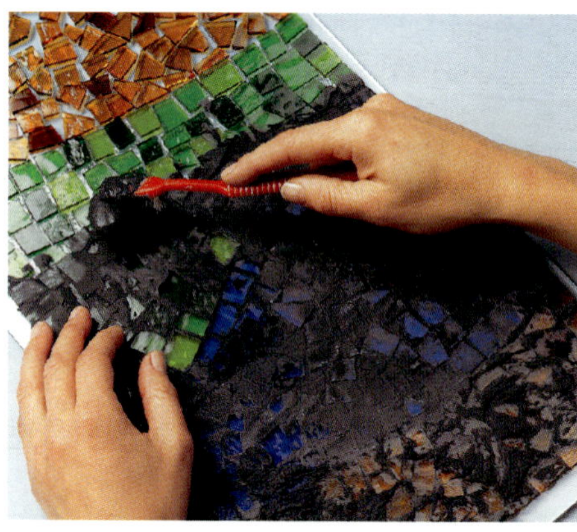

8 Mix the tile grout with the black cement stain and rub it over the surface of the mosaic. Use a toothbrush to make sure all the gaps are filled. Leave to dry for 1 hour.

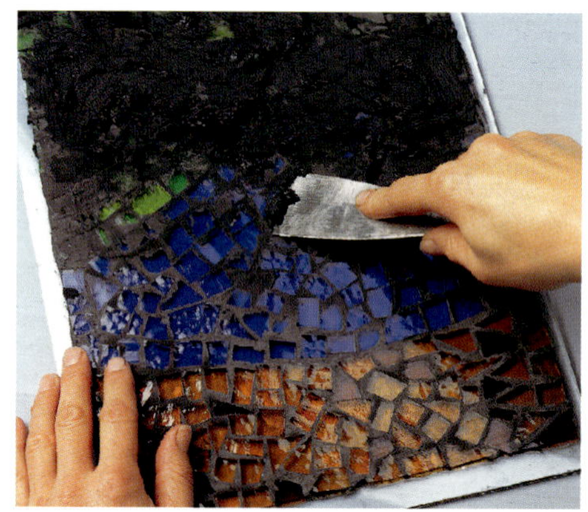

9 When completely dry, clean off any smaller areas of excess grout with a soft cloth. Residual, stubborn grout can be carefully removed with a paint scraper.

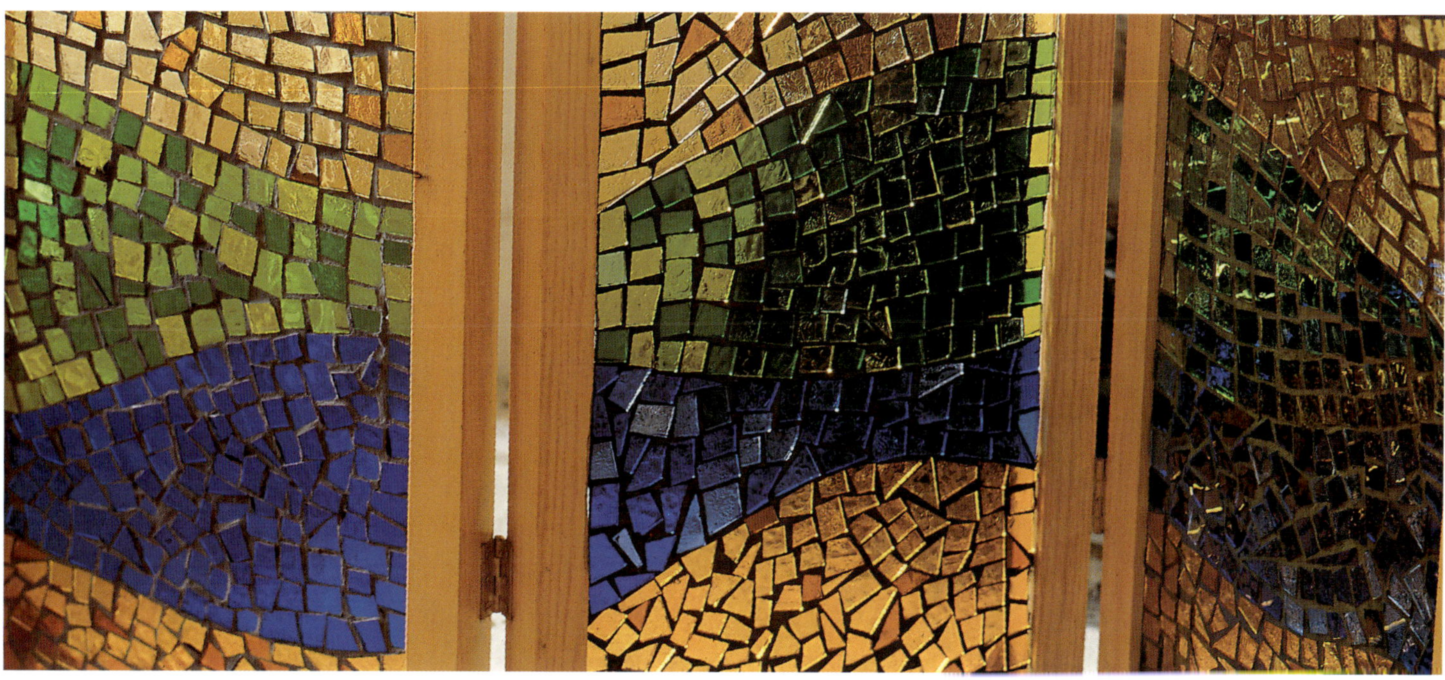

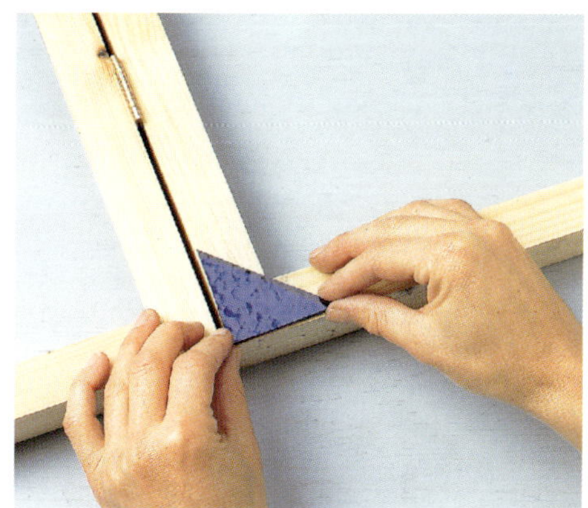

10 Glue one of the reserved right-angled triangles of coloured glass over the corner of the frames, at the front. Repeat with the other triangles, on each corner of the frame.

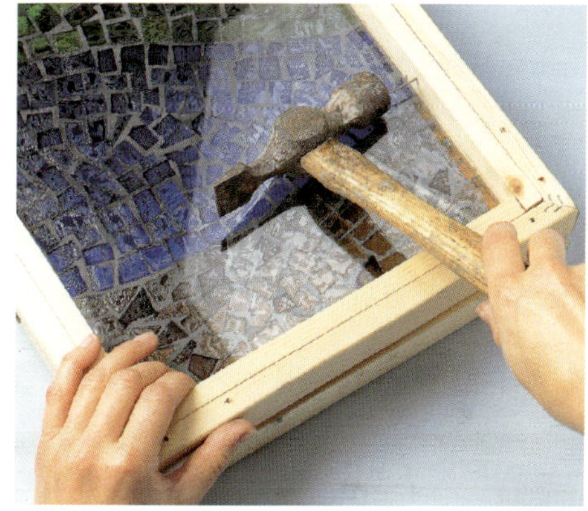

11 Cut each length of moulding into two 70cm (28in) lengths and two 23cm (9in) lengths. Place the glass panels within their frames, ensuring that they are the right way up, and slot the beading behind them. Fix them in place with panel pins (brads), being very careful as you use the hammer.

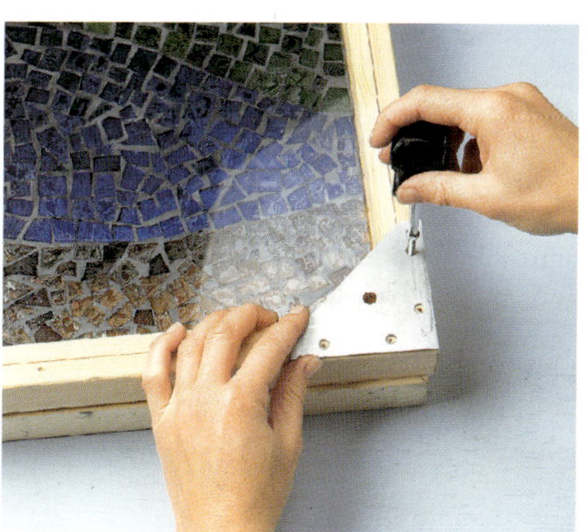

12 Make shallow guideholes with a drill, then screw the corner plates to the back of each corner of the frame. Finally, polish the surface of each of the mosaic panels with a dry, soft cloth.

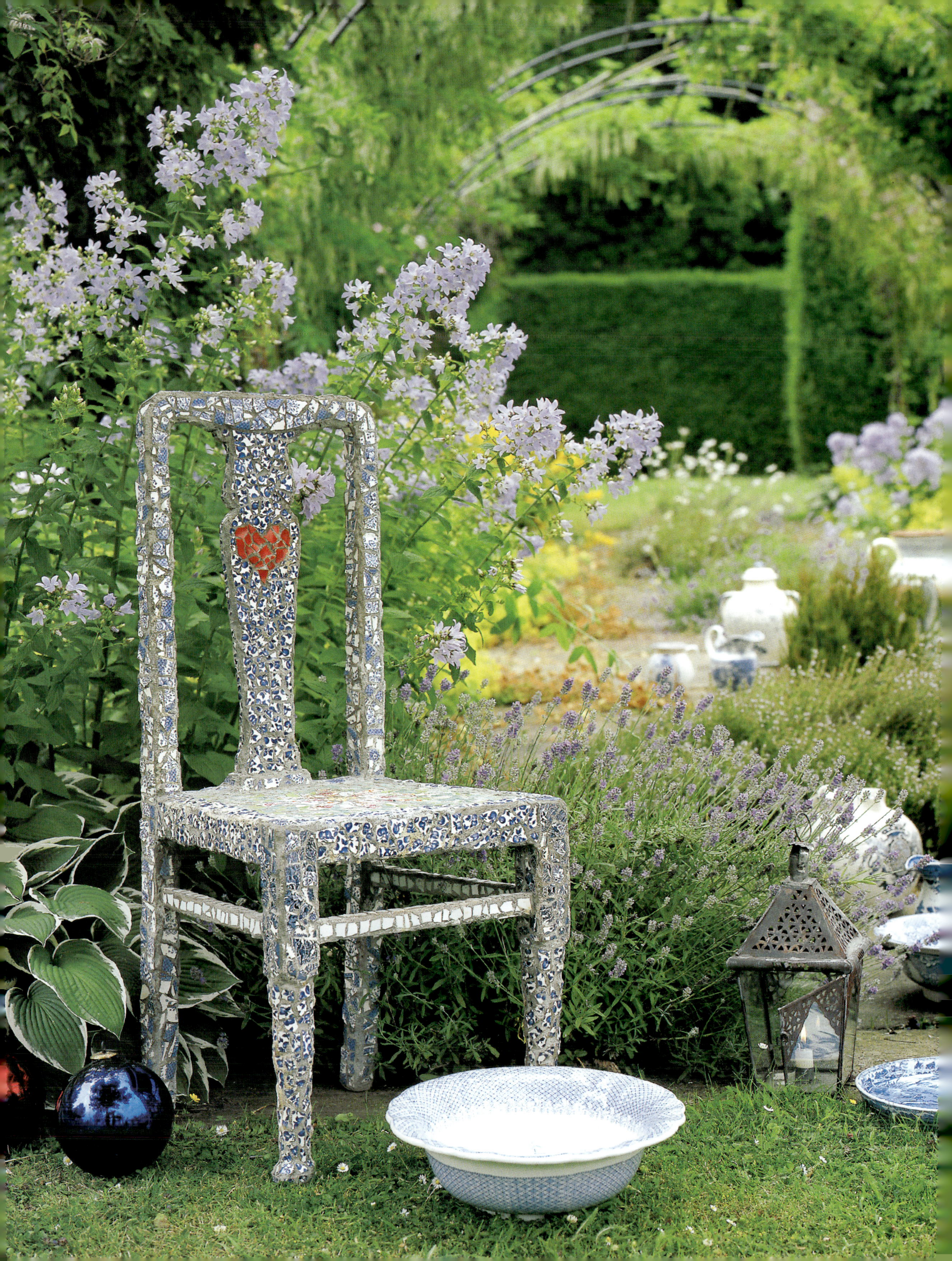

With a little work and imagination, this battered old chair has been transformed into an unusual, exciting piece of furniture. This example shows the extremes to which mosaic can successfully be taken.

Crazy Paving Chair

You will need

Wooden chair
2cm (¾in) thick plywood sheet and jigsaw (saber saw) (optional)
White spirit (paint thinner)
Abrasive paper (sandpaper)
PVA (white) glue
Paintbrush
Wood glue
Tile adhesive
Admix
Flexible knife
Pencil or chalk
Large selection of china
Tile nippers
Dilute hydrochloric acid, goggles and rubber (latex) gloves (optional)
Soft cloth

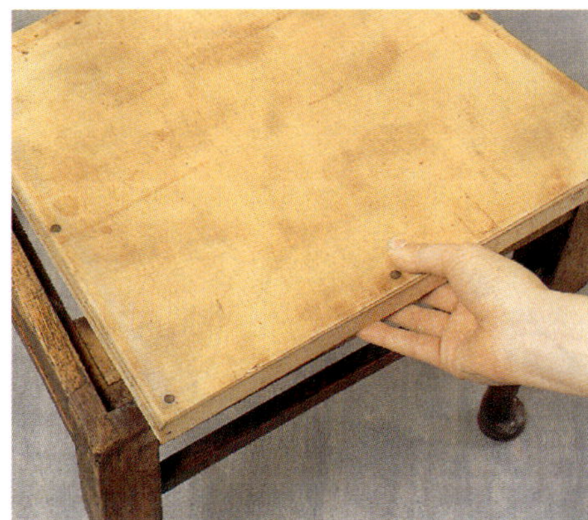

1 If the chair you have chosen has a padded seat, remove it. There may be a wooden pallet beneath the padding that you can use as a base for the mosaic. If not, cut a piece of plywood to fit in its place.

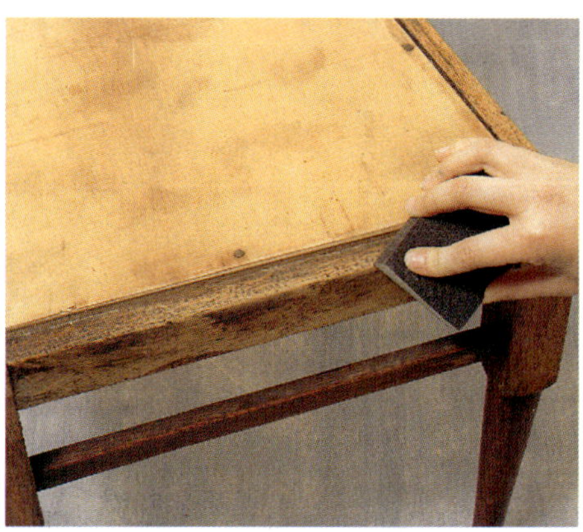

2 Strip the chair of any paint or varnish with white spirit (paint thinner) and sand down with coarse-grade abrasive paper (sandpaper). Then paint the whole chair with diluted PVA (white) glue to seal it.

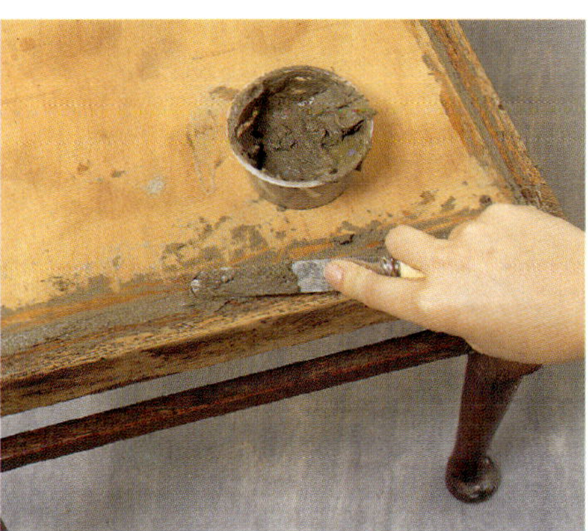

3 When the surface is dry, stick the seat in place with a strong wood glue. Use tile adhesive and admix (mixed to the manufacturer's instructions) to fill any gaps around the edge. This will give extra strength and flexibility.

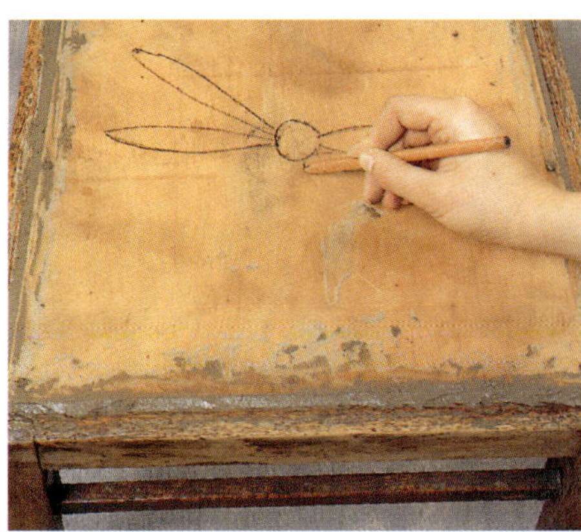

4 Draw a design or motifs on any large flat surfaces of the chair with a pencil or chalk. Use simple shapes that are easy to work with.

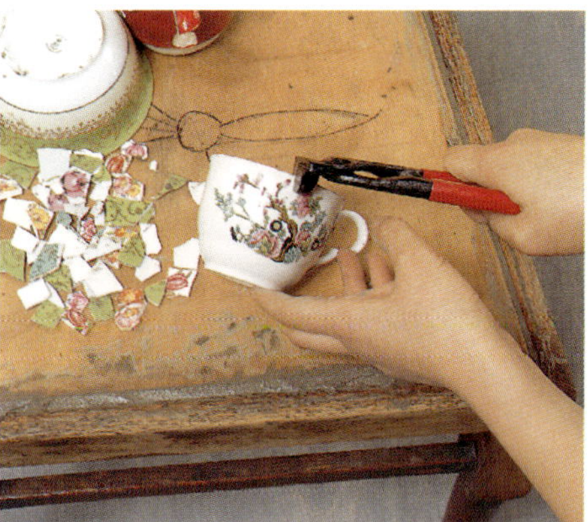

5 Select china that has colours and patterns to suit the motifs you have drawn. Using tile nippers, cut the china into the appropriate shapes and sizes for your design.

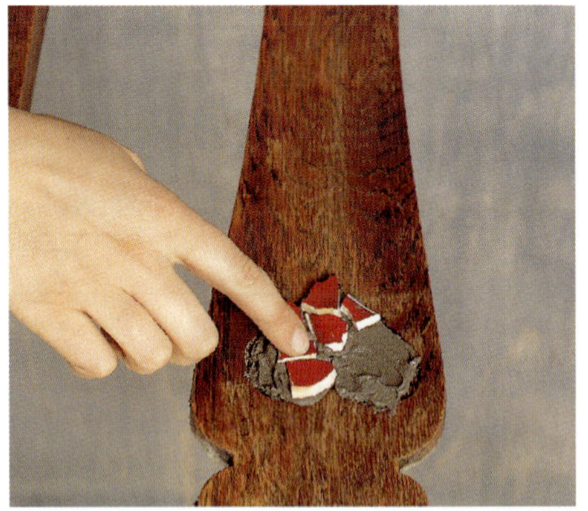

6 Spread the adhesive mixture within the areas of your design and press the cut china firmly into it. Select china to cover the rest of the chair. As you are unlikely to have enough of the same pattern to cover the whole chair, choose two or three patterns that look good together.

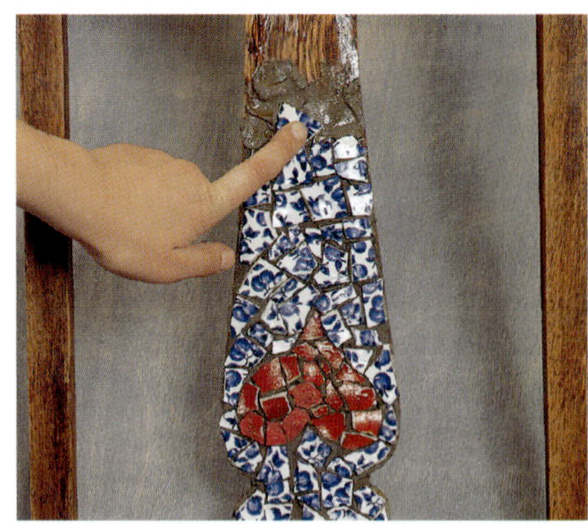

7 Cut the china into small, varied shapes. Working on small areas at a time, begin to tile the rest of the chair. Start with the back of the chair first, moving on to the legs, and finally the seat.

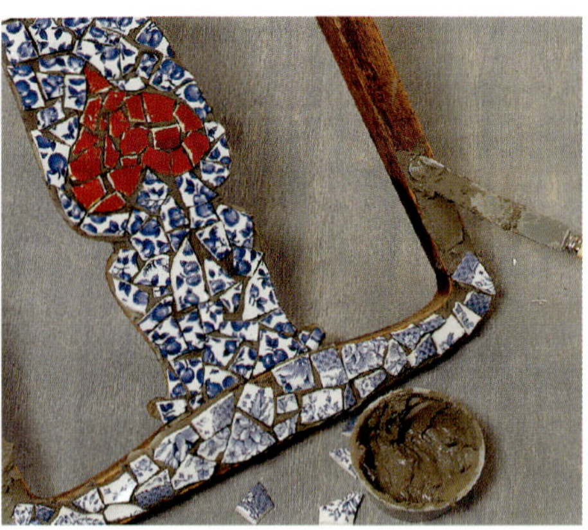

8 Where one section of wood meets another, change the pattern of the china you are using.

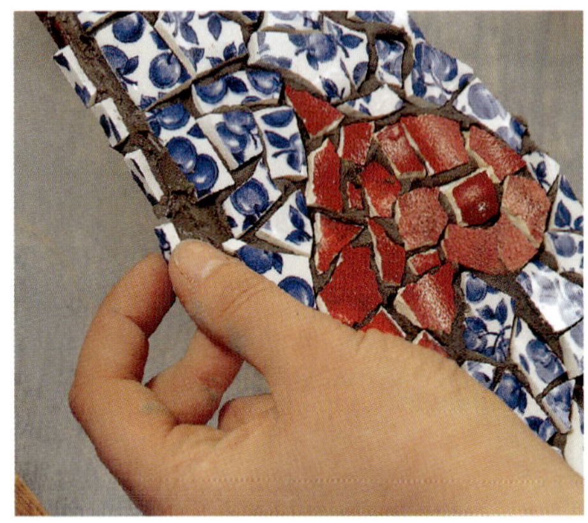

9 Cut appropriately patterned china into thin slivers and use these to tile the edges of any thin sections of wood. Here, the edges of the back rest are covered. Leave for at least 24 hours to dry completely.

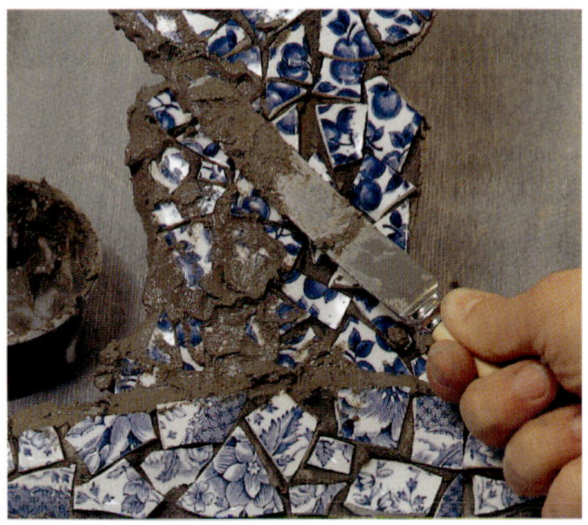

10 Mix up some more tile adhesive and admix. Using a flexible knife, smooth this into the four corners of every piece of wood. Use your fingers to rub it over the flat surfaces. Work on a small area at a time and try to clean off most of the excess as you go. Leave overnight to dry.

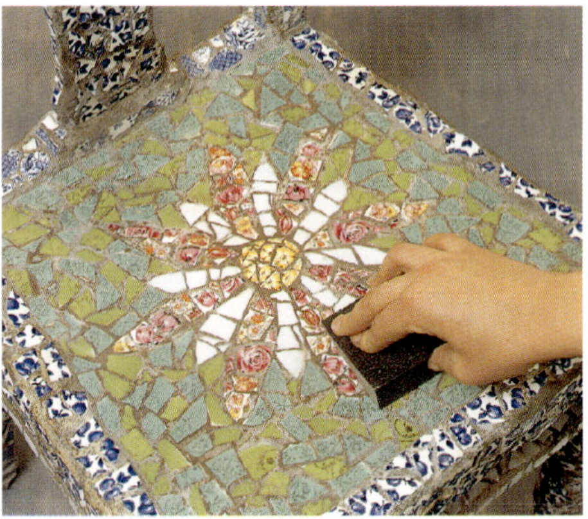

11 Sand off the excess adhesive. This can be quite a difficult job, as there are many awkward angles. Alternatively, dilute hydrochloric acid can be used, but you must wear goggles and rubber (latex) gloves and apply it either outside or where there is good ventilation. Wash any residue from the surface with plenty of water and, when dry, polish with a dry, soft cloth.

This simple table top has been transformed with a shell mosaic to make a piece of furniture that would be perfect for a patio or conservatory. The symmetrical arrangement of the shells makes an eye-catching design.

Shell Table

You will need

50cm (20in) diameter chipboard (particle board) table top
Ruler
Pencil
Protractor
Pair of compasses
PVA (white) glue
Paintbrushes
Assortment of shells from old necklaces or from the beach
Tile nippers
Tile grout
Grout spreader or small palette knife
Flannel (washcloth)
Drill and mop attachment or soft cloth
Emulsion (latex) or watercolour paint: pale blue-green and pale ochre
Pale blue-green colourwash

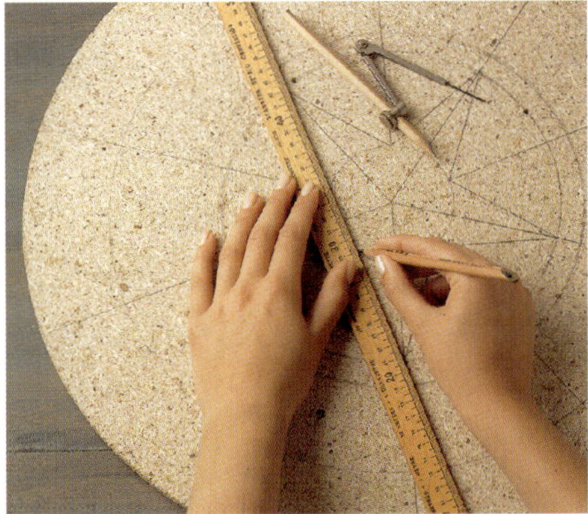

1 Using a ruler, pencil, protractor and a pair of compasses, draw a geometric pattern on the table top, following the one shown here or using a design of your own.

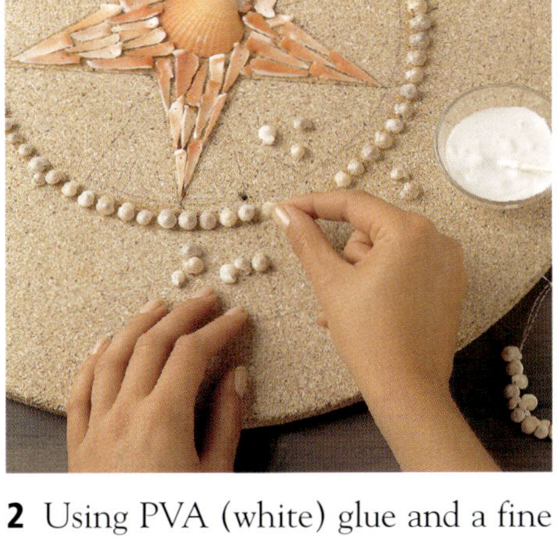

2 Using PVA (white) glue and a fine paintbrush, stick a scallop shell to the centre of the table. Glue pink shell pieces from an old necklace inside the starfish shape and surround the starfish with a circle of small snail shells.

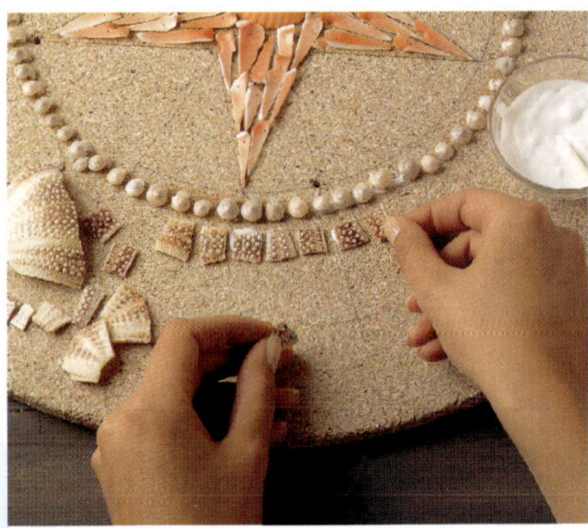

3 Break up a sea urchin into tesserae using tile nippers, and glue them in a circle outside the snail shells.

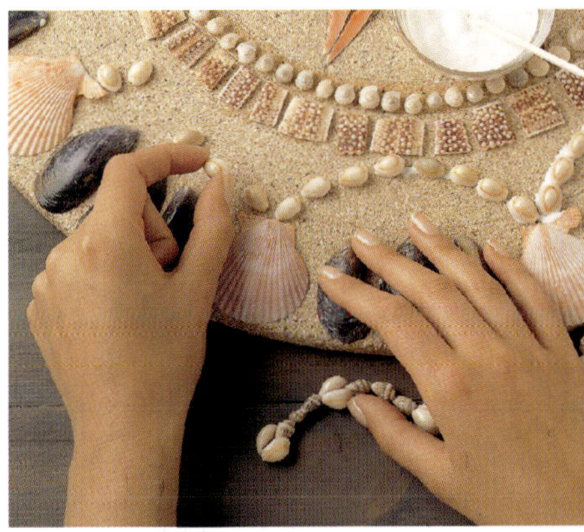

4 Glue ten scallop shells around the edge of the table top, spacing them evenly. Fill in the gaps between the them with mussel shells. Glue cowrie shells in arches between the scallops.

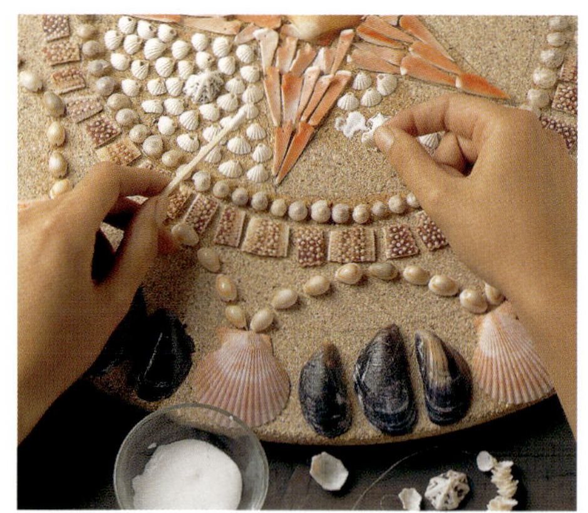

5 Glue a limpet shell in the middle of each space in the inner circle. Fill in the spaces around the limpet shells in between the legs of the starfish with small cockle shells.

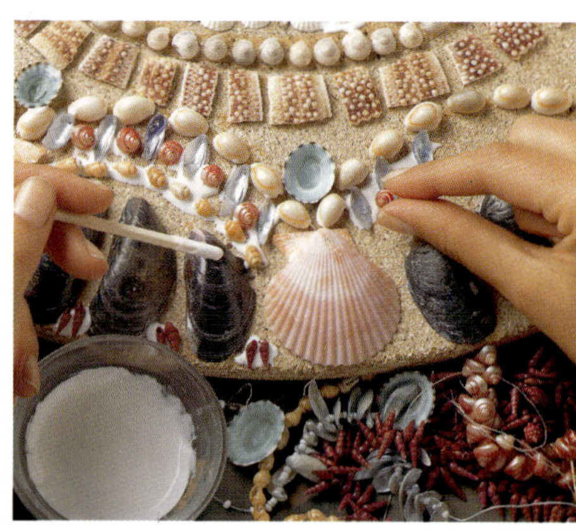

6 Fill in the remaining spaces on the table top with an assortment of small shells arranged in a regular pattern.

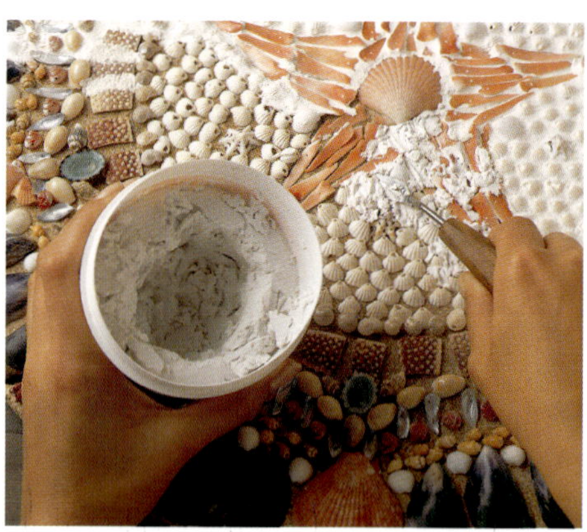

7 Starting in the centre and working on only a small area at a time, spread tile grout over the surface of the mosaic. Use a grout spreader or small palette knife to press the grout into the gaps.

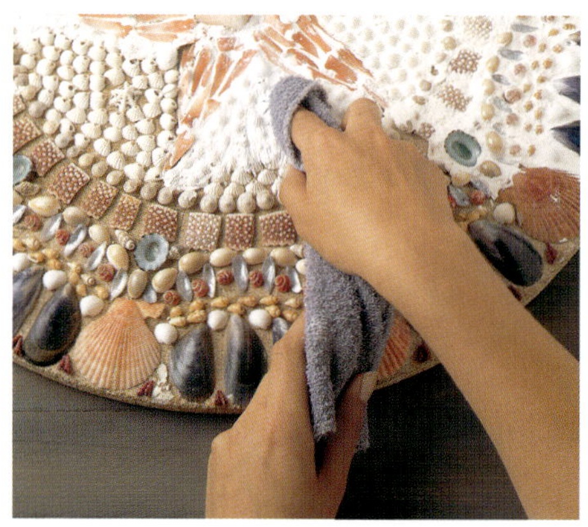

8 Use a paintbrush to work the grout into the gaps and smooth the surface with a little water. Press firmly with a damp flannel (washcloth) to impact the grout around the shells. Rub the flannel over the shells in an outward direction to remove any grout from the surface of the shells.

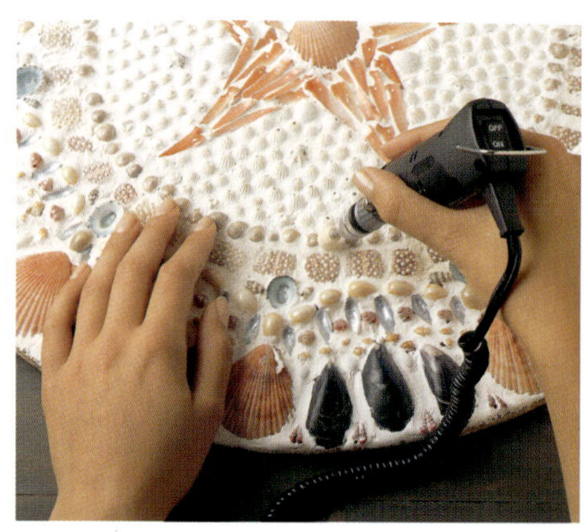

9 Repeat steps 7–8 until you have grouted the whole mosaic. Leave to dry for several hours, then polish with a mop attachment on your drill or with a soft cloth.

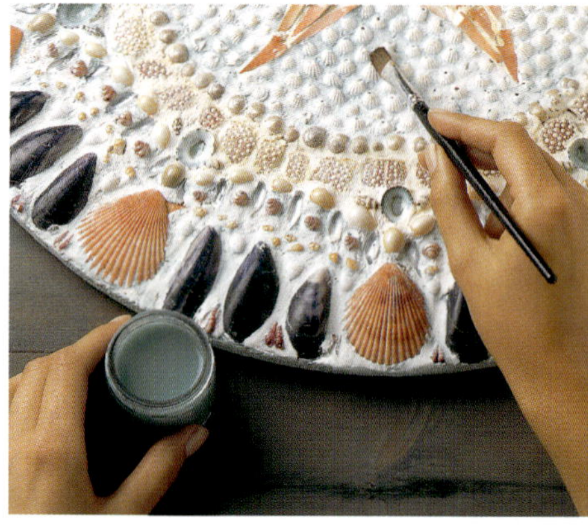

10 Paint the grouting with diluted emulsion (latex) or watercolour paints: pale blue-green for the inner circle and outer edge, and pale ochre for the midway band. Finally, apply several coats of pale blue-green colourwash to the edge of the table top.

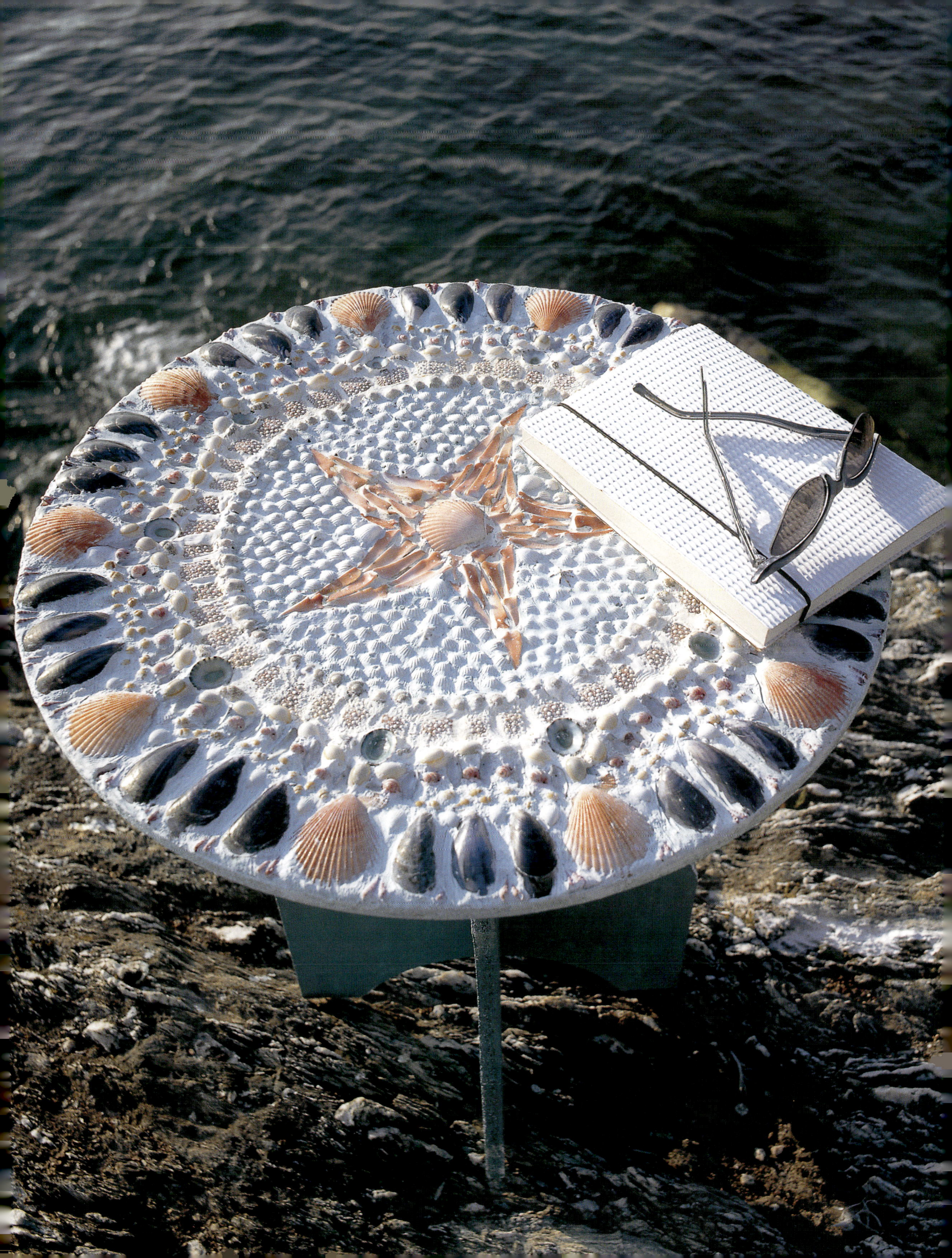

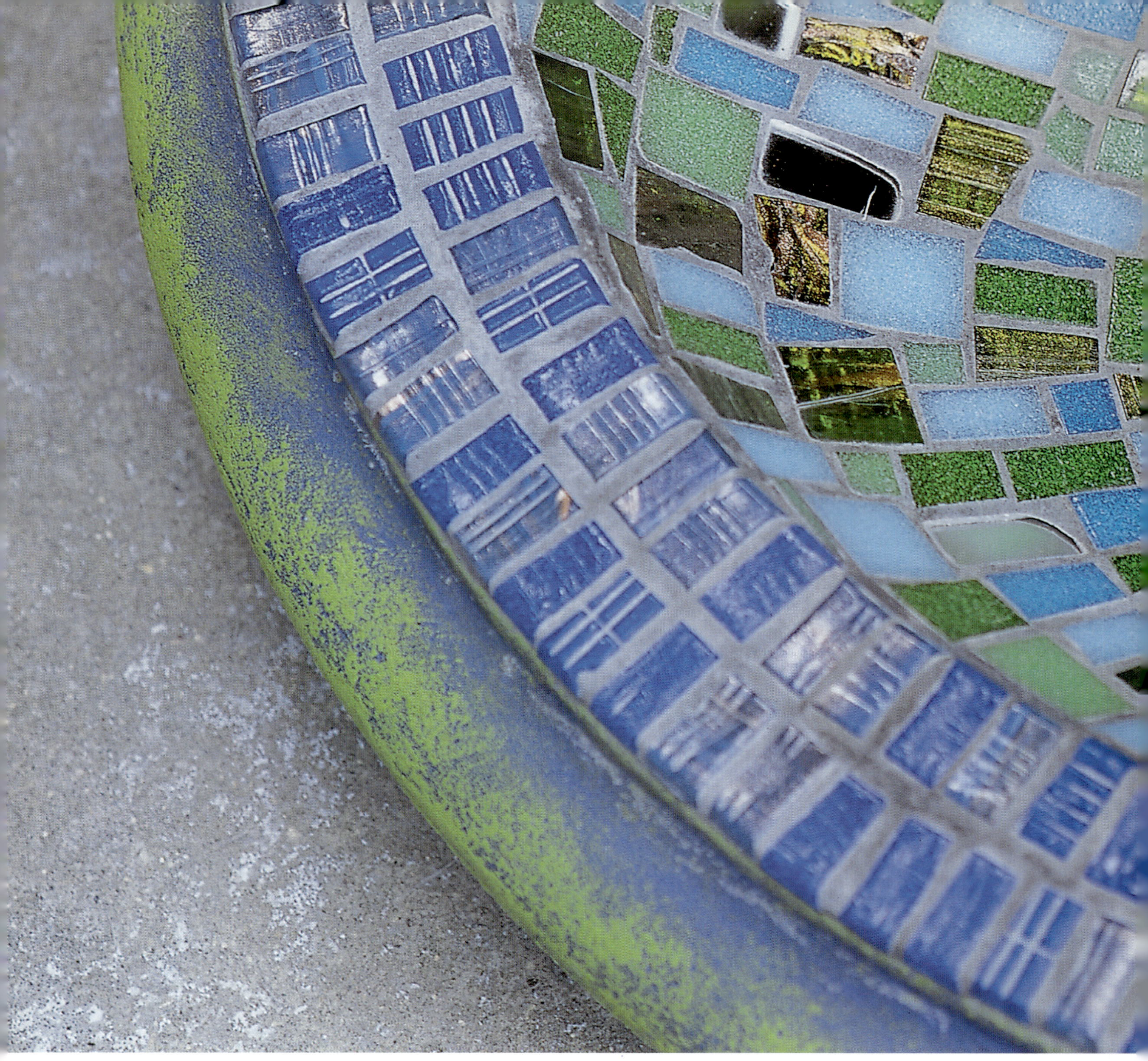

In Situ

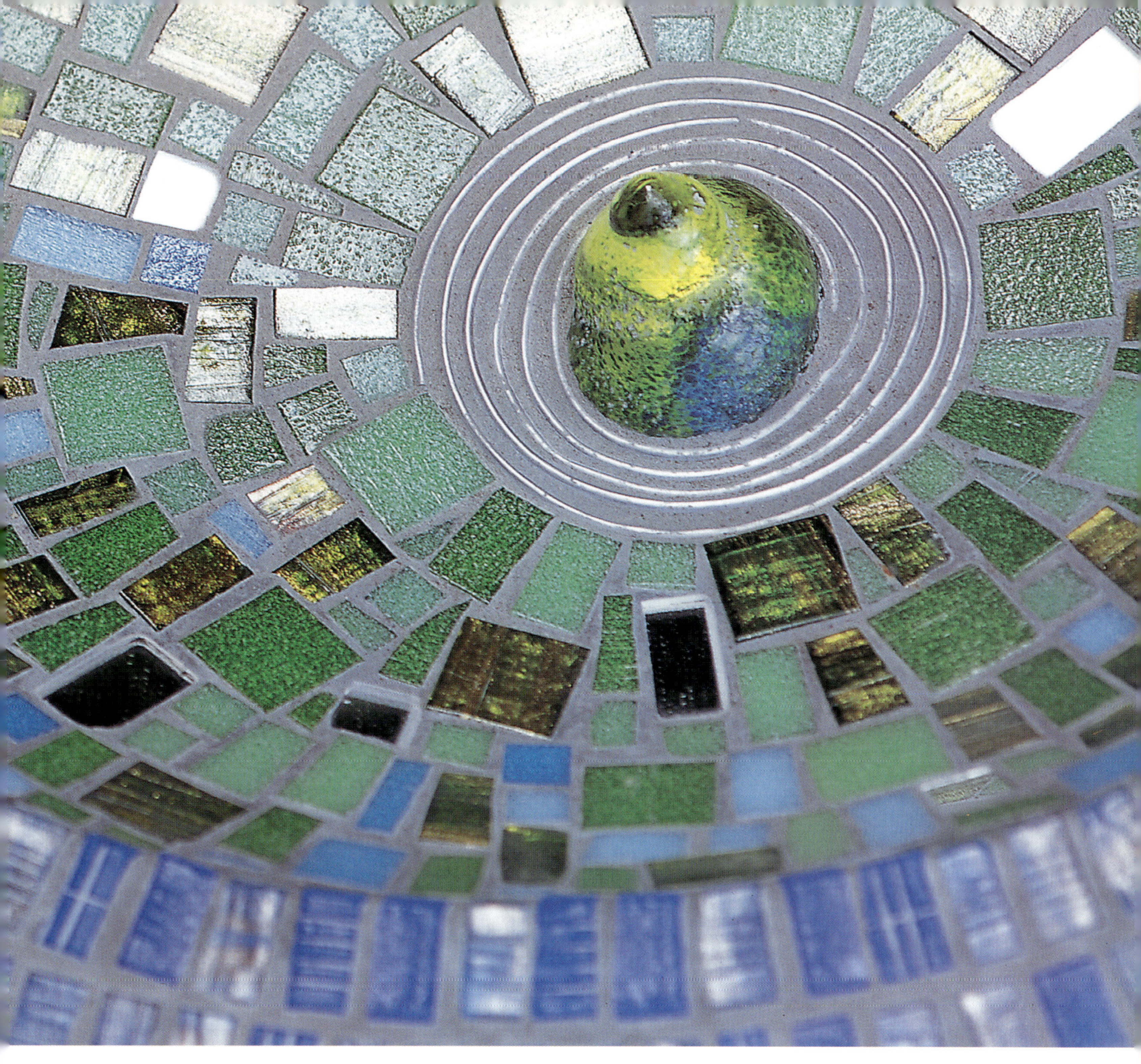

Some objects are freestanding, but some are bound to be affected by their position in a room or garden. Even loose tiles are often designed with a particular situation in mind, and this will influence the shape, colour and texture of the chosen design. Mosaics for use as a floor in a minimalist bathroom will have different criteria than a purely decorative feature. Projects that are destined for the outdoors will need particular consideration.

Walls in the home are perfect as settings for mosaic. It can cover a whole wall or be used in the form of insets or panels. Mosaic is ideal in hardworking areas such as the hall, utility room, kitchen or bathroom.

Interior Walls

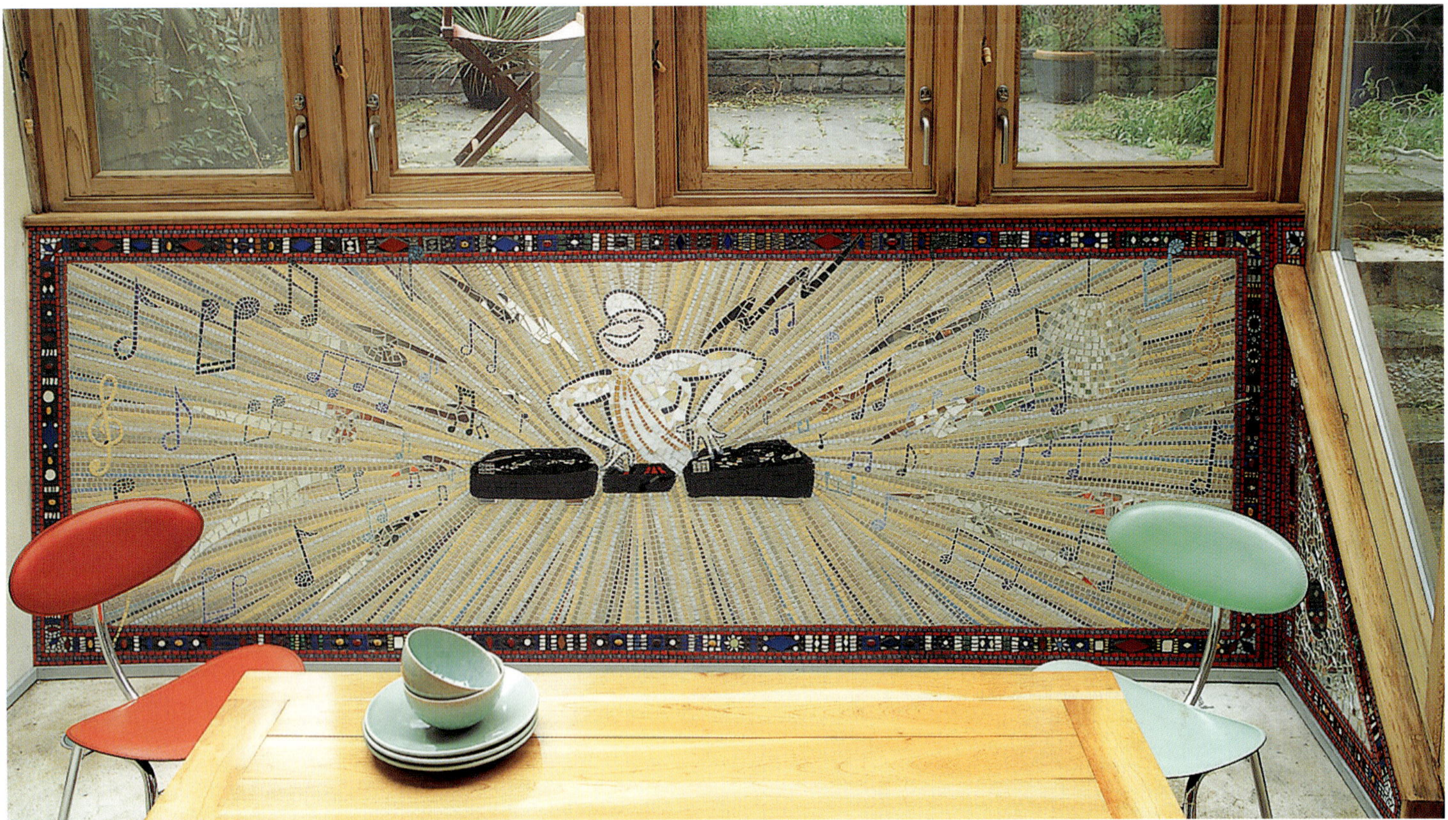

Entire walls of mosaic can look stunning, though they are ambitious projects that should not be undertaken by the inexperienced mosaicist. When planning such a feature, the elements of the design should be kept in scale with their setting: on the wall pictured opposite, the design as an entirety is composed of smaller patterns that can be absorbed by the eye at close quarters – there is no need to step back to try and see the whole. Different decorative schemes can be achieved with mosaic inside the home, from restful and intimate to bold and striking.

Practicalities

If you want to apply mosaic directly to an interior wall, you need to check first that the wall is strong enough to take the size and weight of mosaic and grout that you have in mind. Second, the wall's surface must be even. A strong torch beam shone across the wall will show up areas of unevenness.

Mirror

In some houses or apartments space is at a premium, especially in the bathroom. Using mirror is a good way to create the illusion of a room being much larger than it really is, and while a whole mirrored wall might be a little daunting, a fragmented wall of mirror mosaic is less revealing yet achieves the same illusion of space.

Above: This wall piece by Celia Gregory appears to be exploding with sound and transforms the conservatory in which it has been built.

Opposite: The Sublime Wall, *created by Robert Grace from various sizes of mosaic sheets has a large overall pattern along with detail to hold interest close up.*

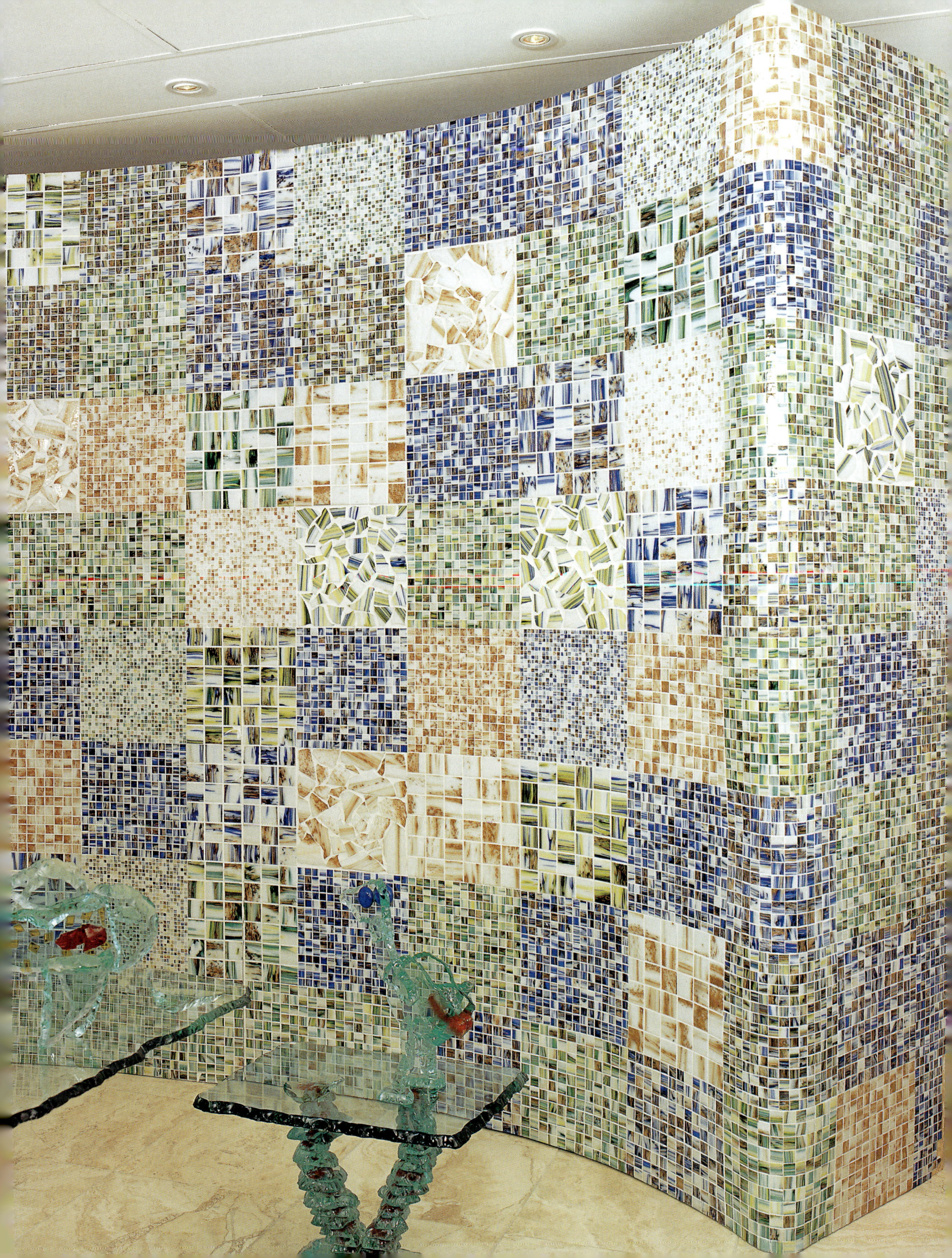

More manageable in size than complete murals, and more realistic projects for someone new to mosaic, decorative splashbacks, wall panels and shelves will brighten any room in the house.

Splashbacks, Panels and Shelves

Since the great strength of mosaic is its impact, an entire wall covered in it may be more than you want. In such cases, the ideal solution is a small area, such as a splashback or decorative panel, or even a shelf, specifically designed to suit its surroundings or its owner, or both.

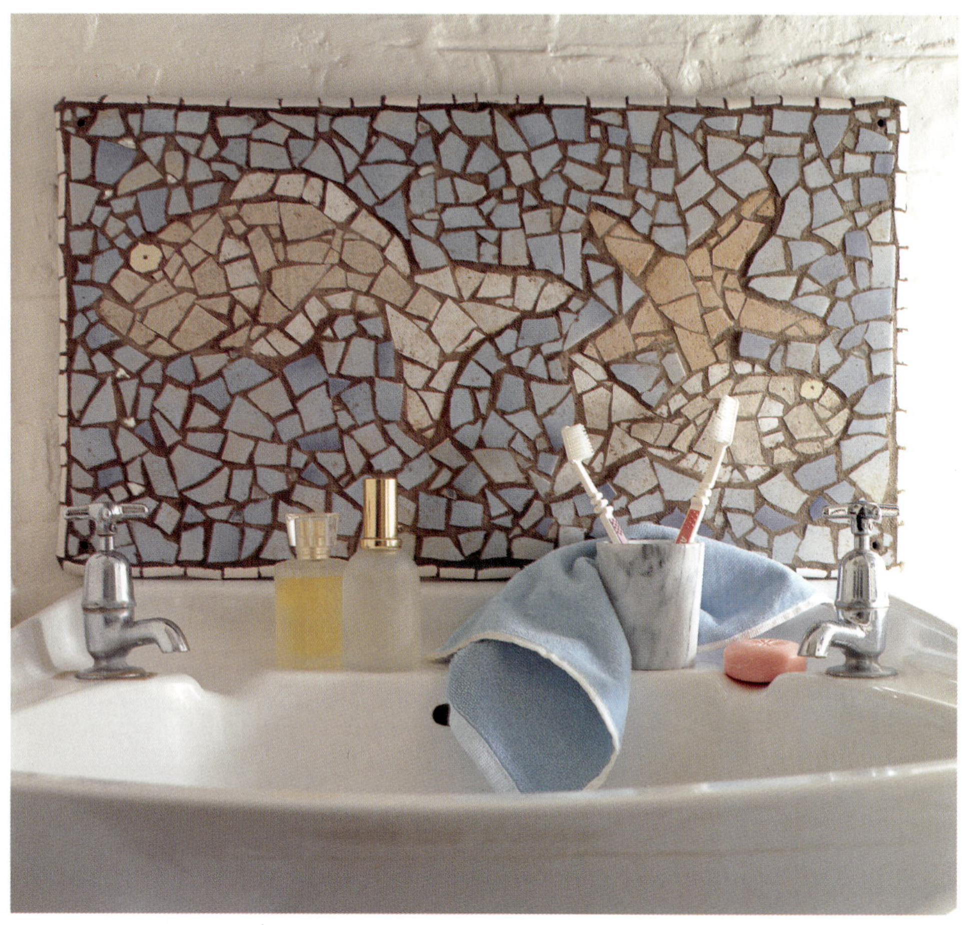

Splashbacks

Mosaic makes perfect splashbacks for cookers (stoves), kitchen sinks and bathroom basins, transforming such items into something unique to you. The design must be practical, as it will receive much wear and tear. A splash-back can be formed of a single panel or tiles grouped together.

In a kitchen, simple checks or plain colours with borders work well, while in a bathroom you might like to suggest the movement of waves and water. If you are aiming for something more personal, here is the opportunity to devise an image that picks up on the room's colour scheme but also incorporates elements that are individual to you and your family, such as your initials, a favourite flower or a family crest.

Friezes

Somewhere between splashbacks and wall panels come friezes. There are occasions when a minimal amount of decoration is all that is needed to transform an area of the house. A frieze, or similar narrow band or border, may be more effective than a larger element in small spaces such as a downstairs cloakroom or a shower room, or in busy areas such as a porch or hallway, where too much elaboration tends to be overlooked amid the bustle of people coming and going.

A small mosaic could also outline a window (perfect to highlight a porthole-style opening), a fire surround or mantelpiece to great effect.

Above: Watery themes suit mosaic panel splashbacks in kitchens and bathrooms.

Wall panels

A hanging wall panel makes a wonderful picture with depth and impact, and a plainly decorated room can be transformed by a well-executed mosaic panel. Including a border into its design finishes off any mosaic, but if you want to heighten the impression of a work of art, the mosaic panel could be framed before it is hung in position.

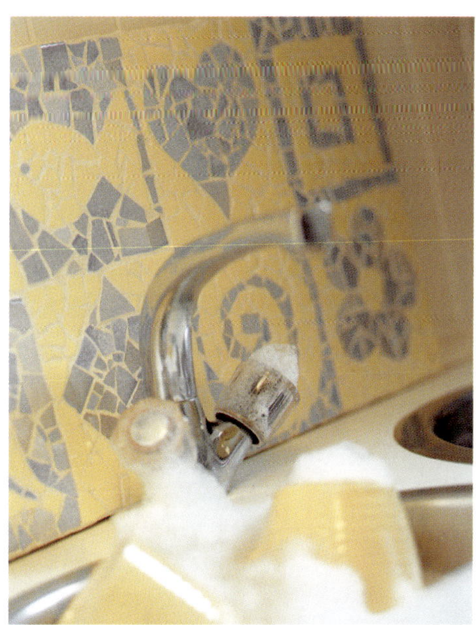

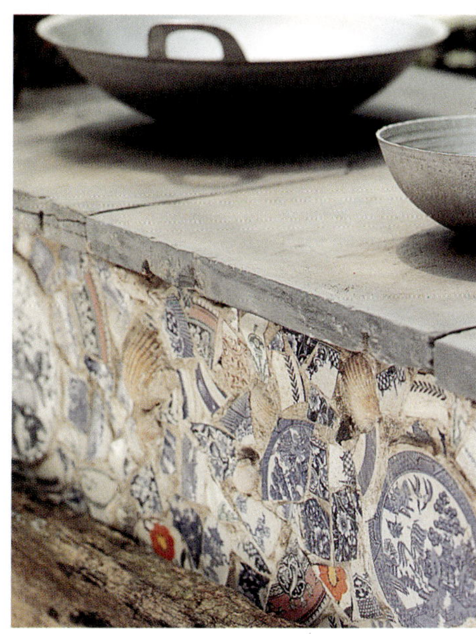

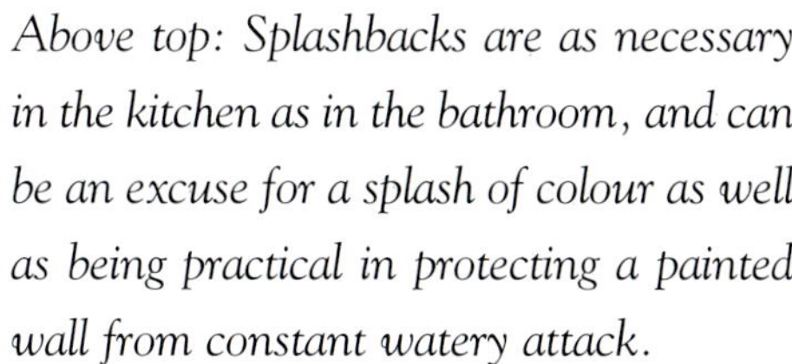

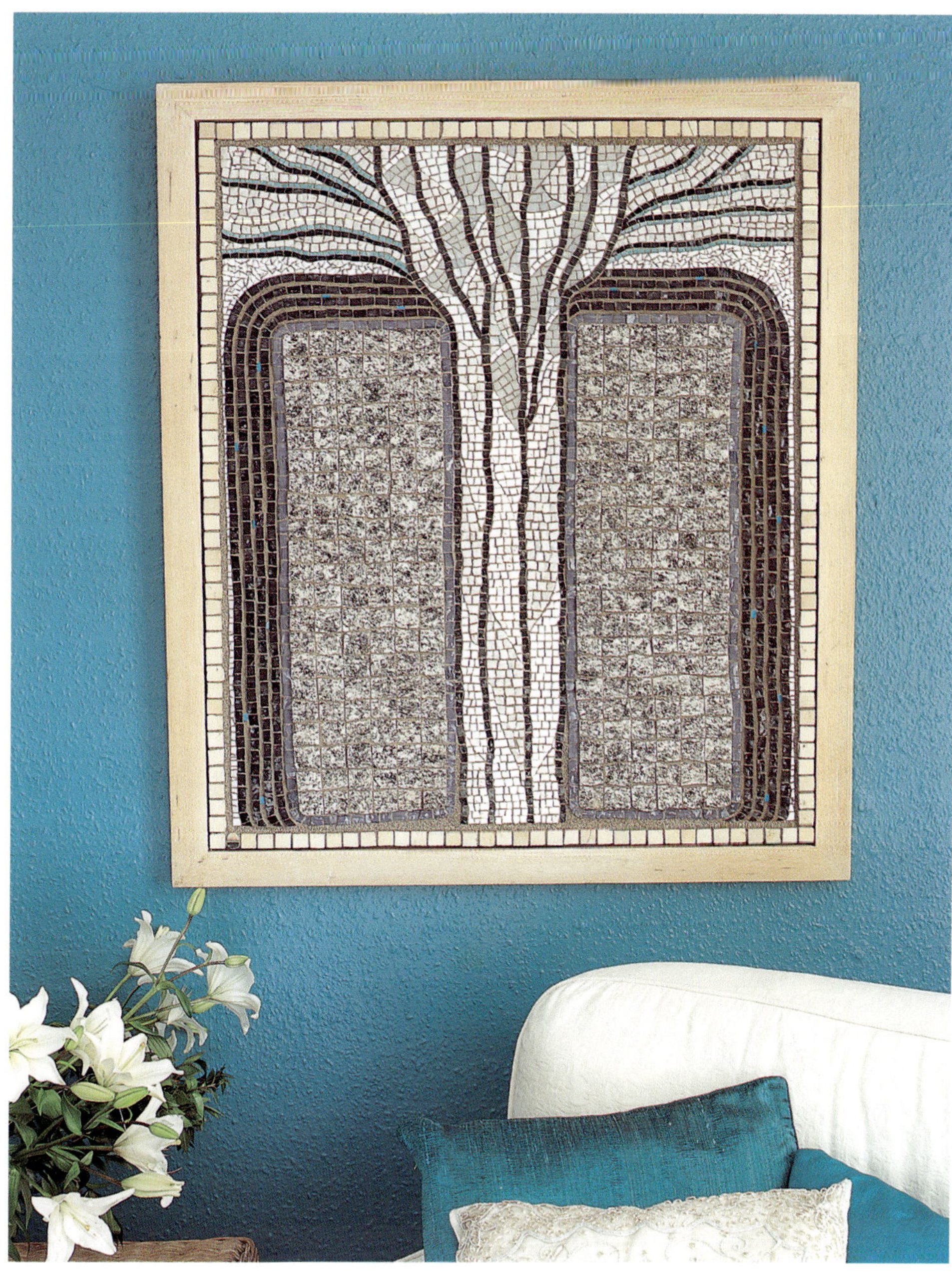

Above top: Splashbacks are as necessary in the kitchen as in the bathroom, and can be an excuse for a splash of colour as well as being practical in protecting a painted wall from constant watery attack.

Above: A mosaiced wall around the side of a garden pond. The broken china with the odd sea shell is set into a waterproof combined adhesive and grout, which was rubbed with a mixture of garden soil and pond water to age the mosaic and so successfully blends the new with the old.

Above: Gates of the Living – *maximum impact with minimum elaboration in this elegant panel by Elaine M. Goodwin.*

Wall panels can come in all shapes and sizes. A large panel could cover almost an entire wall, dominating the room, while a small one could demand attention by its bold colouring or eye-catching design.

Shelves

A further method of adding mosaic to walls is by way of a shelf or decorated rail. A shelf is an ideal project for a beginner, especially if a simple, all-over design is chosen rather than anything too complicated. Whether the mosaic is bright and colourful, made from pieces of old china, or calm and restful, made from broken slate, the result is still the introduction of a stunning design element into a room in a functional, yet decorative way. The same applies to a mosaiced rack or rail – adding a unique touch of colour.

Hallways, garden rooms, kitchens, utility rooms and bathrooms are obvious choices for mosaic, but it can also furnish living rooms without seeming too cold or hard to walk on.

Interior Flooring

Mosaic is a practical flooring choice for most areas, being versatile and durable – several examples around 2,000 years old are still in very good condition. Most mosaic materials are tough: they resist marks, spills, scuffs and stains, and are not inclined to fade over time. With the right preparation, they will stick to most surfaces and be comfortable underfoot. Any floor finish must be able to withstand feet, shoes, paws, claws and perhaps wheels as well.

A mosaic, whether covering the whole floor or just part of it, may be all the decoration a floor needs. Ornamentation does not always need to be at eye level to be effective, and treating your room scheme in this way can make a refreshing change.

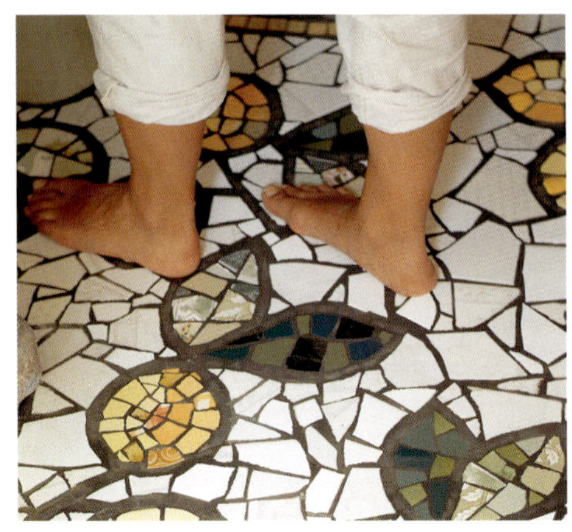

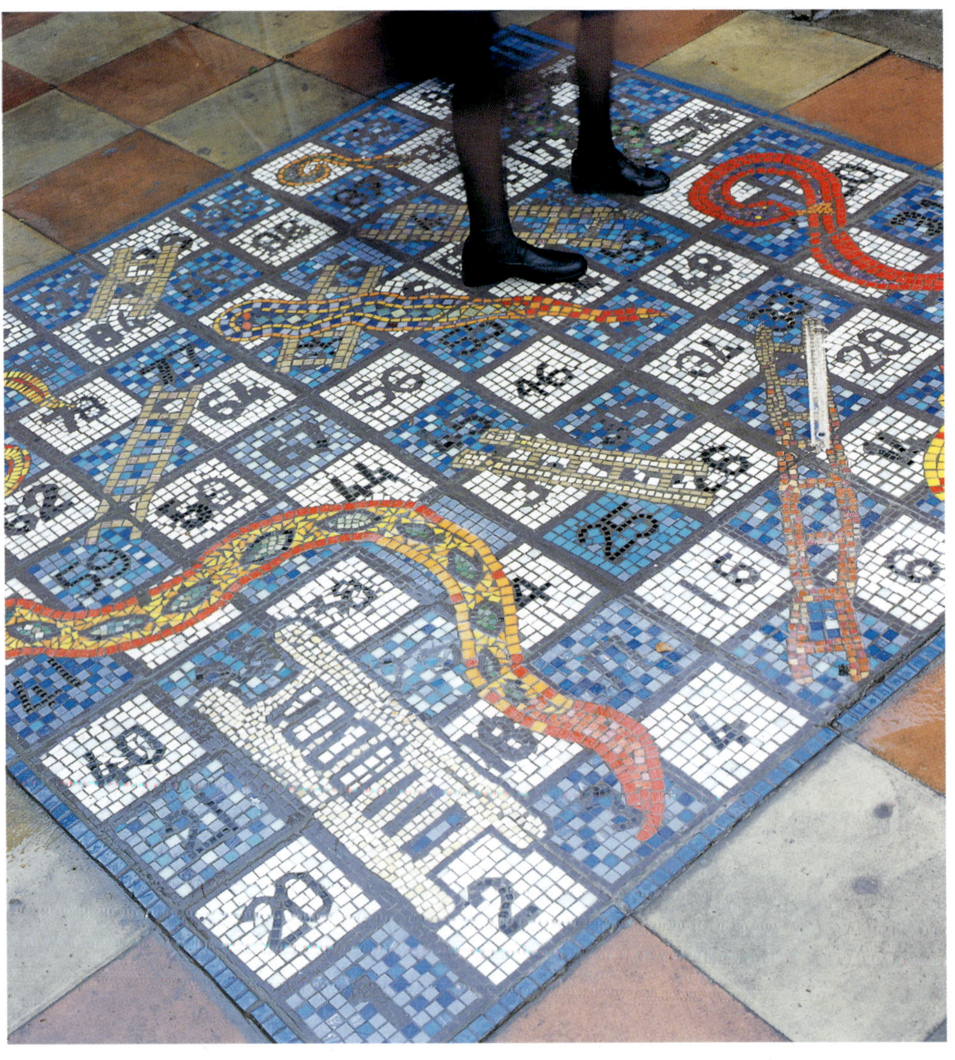

Above: Mosaic flooring is practical and hard-wearing in a bathroom but must be smooth to protect bare feet.

Left: Children can actually play on this fun and practical mosaic patio floor. Climb the ladders, but if you land on a snake, you slip back down.

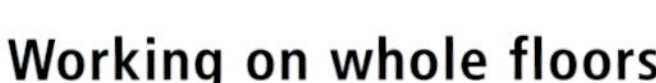

Working on whole floors

There is no reason at all why you should not mosaic a whole floor, but this is a major undertaking, requiring many hours of patient and skilled work. Alternatively, an inset is an effective way of achieving almost the same result with a fraction of the work.

Choose good, hard-wearing materials that are proof against the risk of damage. Stone and suitably glazed clay are ideal; glass is less so but can be used with care. The floor must be level and even before you lay the mosaic, otherwise it never will be.

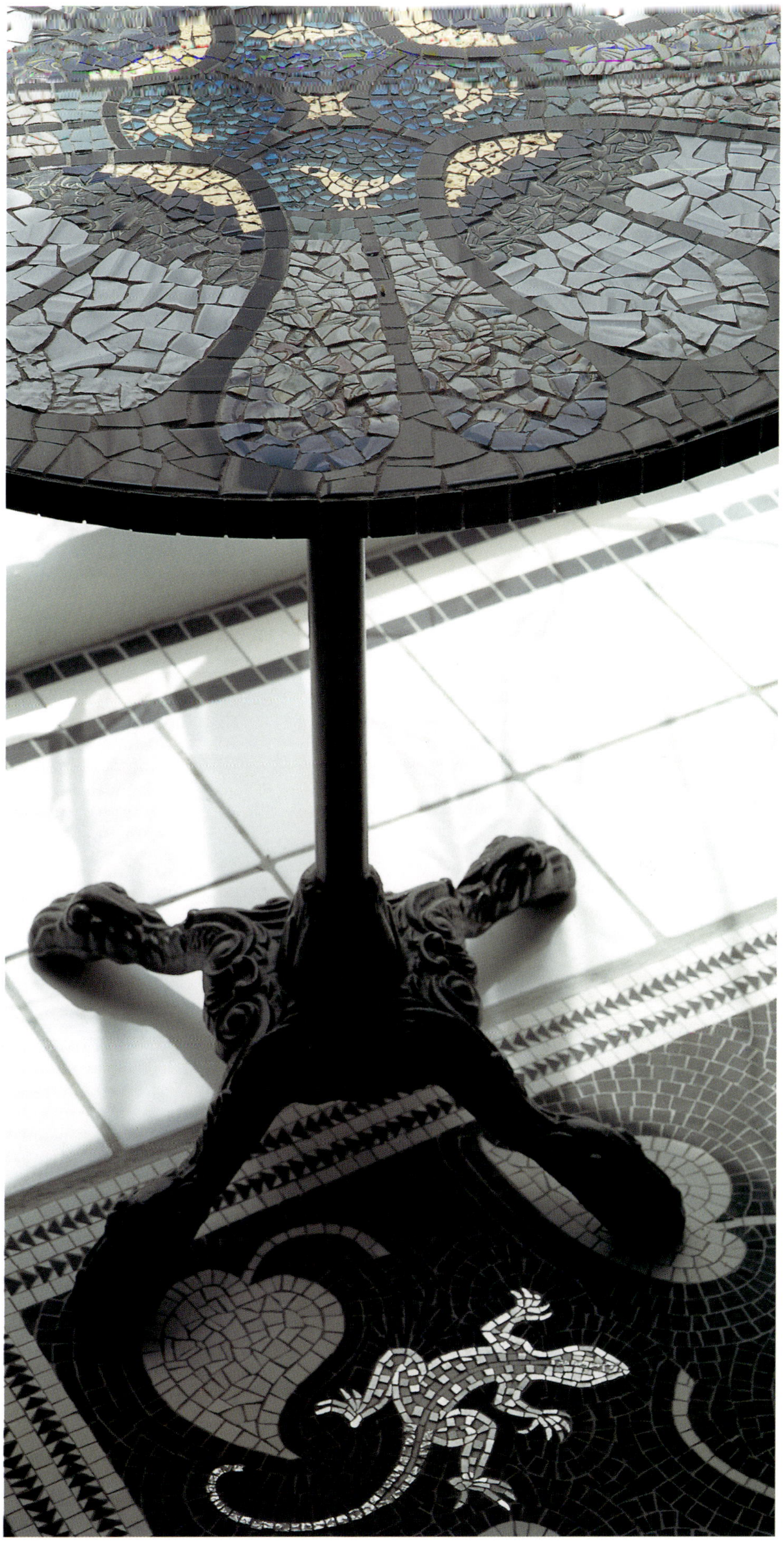

Right: Classic black and white tiles are enlivened by a floor inset with mosaic in a stylized reptile and ivy leaf design by Elaine M. Goodwin.

Below: Diamonds of stone and rough-textured pebbles would be perfect in a cottage or farmhouse.

It is important to remember scale when designing for floors. The eye will not want so much detail at this distance, either in the design itself or in the size of stone or tesserae: ensure they are not too small, or the overall result will appear too fussy. Large sections of colour with bold elements such as central motifs and borders work well.

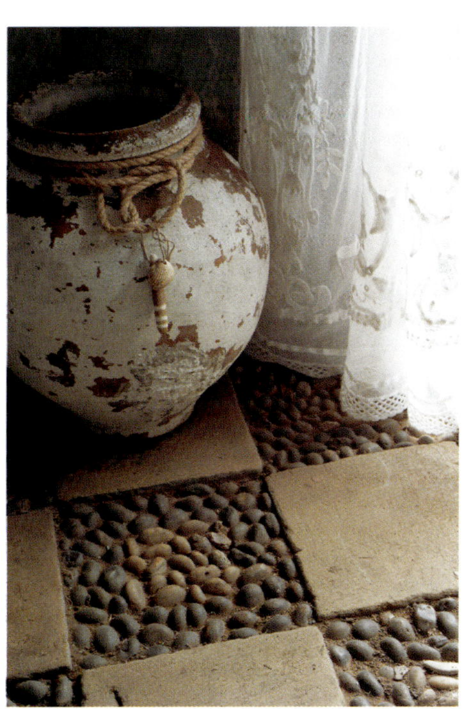

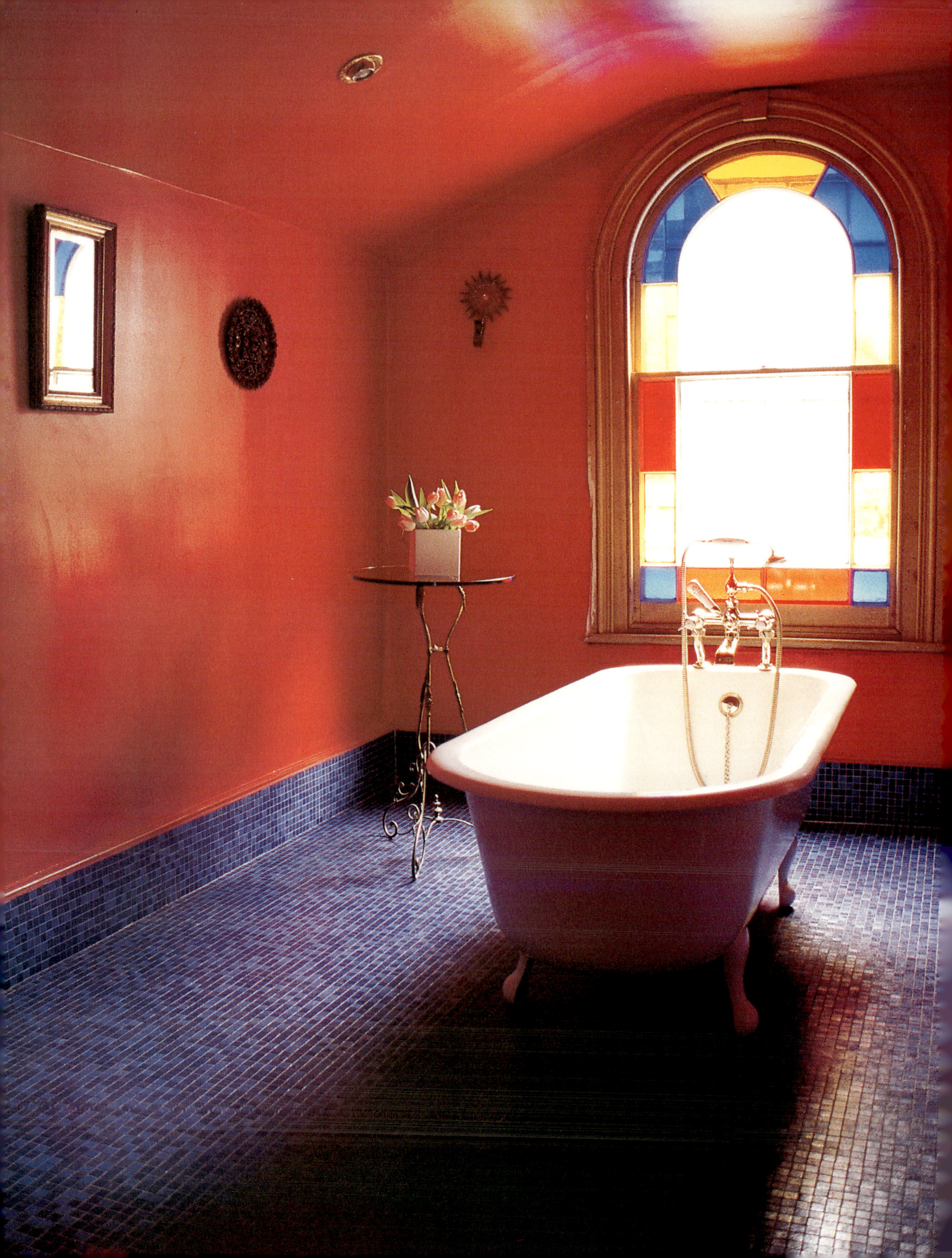

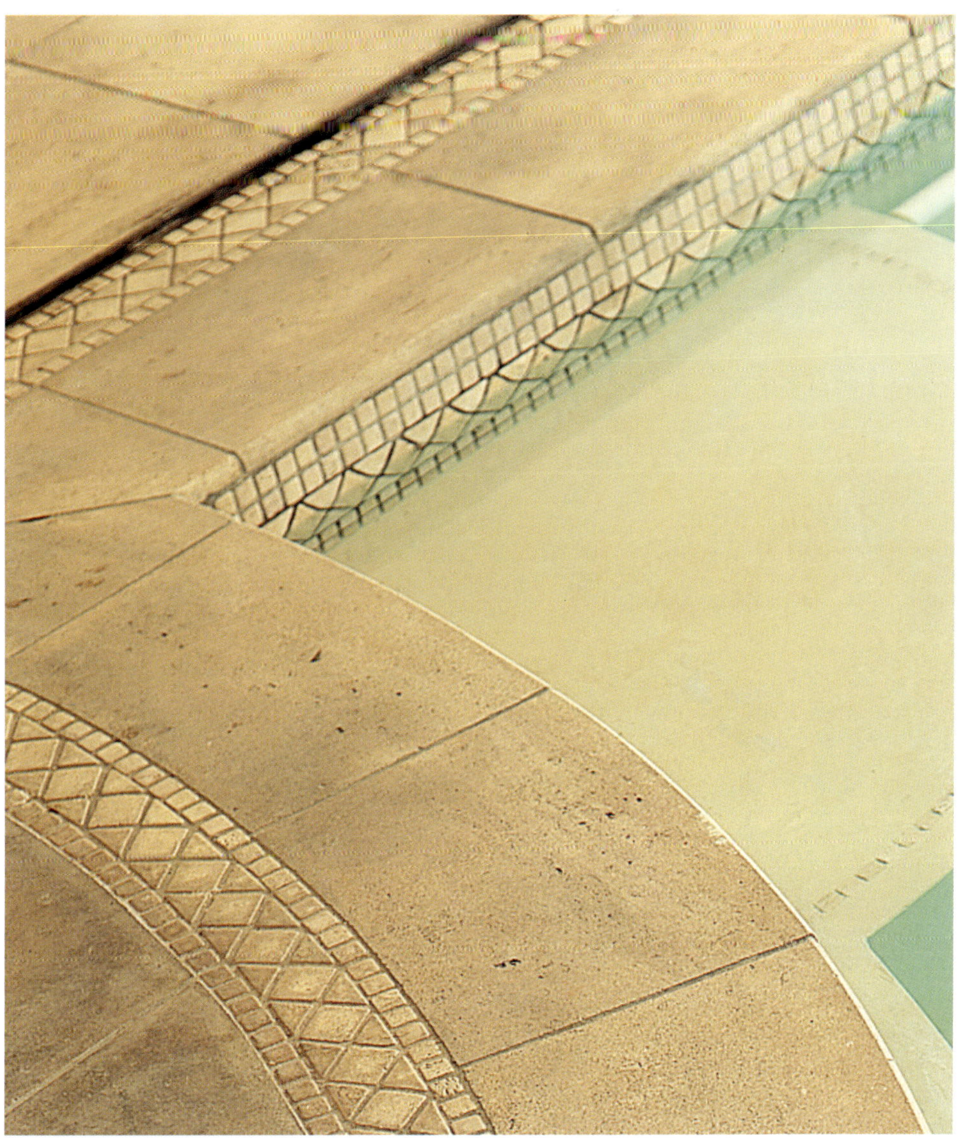

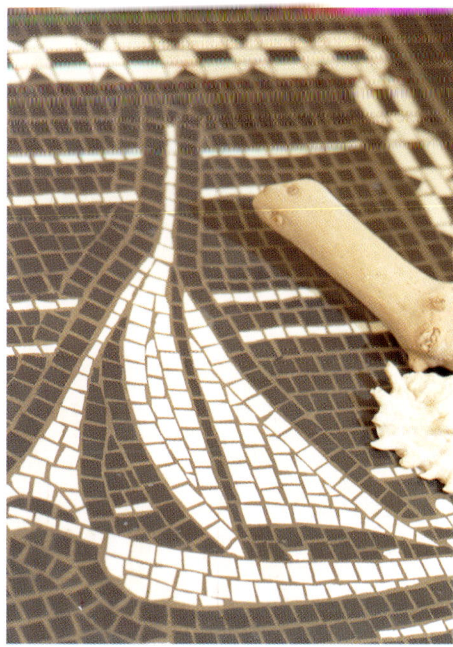

Above: This simple mosaic border is inserted into marble stone flooring. Designed by Celia Gregory, the pattern follows the edge of the pool, enhancing the shape without competing with the main tiles of the floor design.

Above right: Sea-inspired designs, such as sailing boats, shells or fish, are naturally at home in the bathroom as long as they are waterproof enough to withstand wear.

Opposite: The colours are allowed to speak for themselves in this unfussy, but boldly decorated bathroom with its dramatic stained-glass window.

Creative effects

Mosaic can be used on a large scale in a domestic setting. In the bathroom, whole floors and walls can be covered, or you can be less dramatic and cover just the floor. You could also cover the skirting (base) board to link the floor to the walls, or create a contrast.

The colour palette available is vast, especially if you use vitreous glass mosaic sheets. You could choose to echo interior details, such as stained glass in a window, or to co-ordinate the mosaic with other features in the room, such as the colour of the curtains or the bathroom suite.

For hallways, you might choose to work within a more muted colour palette, such as a soft green to balance a rich terracotta mosaic floor. On a porch, a warm shade also creates a welcoming feel.

Dividing a large floor area into sub-sections with the use of decorative borders helps to lead the eye through from the door along the corridors to the foot of the stairs.

Mosaic has a natural affinity with bathrooms. Soft, creamy colours and an elegant border will create a restful decorative scheme and a room to relax in. Marine life and nautical themes fit well into a bathroom scheme.

Living areas are suitable for mosaics, too. A small mosaic, such as a hearth, can be laid to give a sophisticated, smooth surface and create a focal point in a room. Black and white is a classic colour combination for tiled kitchen floors and can be livened up with a smart mosaic inset. If you have a quarry tile floor, a warm, terracotta mosaic would suit best.

Water features, such as fountains and ponds, or outdoor wall panels, are ideal ways of giving mosaic a more prominent role in the garden. The reflective qualities of many tiles make them highly suited to water.

Garden Installations

With the natural affinity between mosaic and water, fountains and other water features are ideal opportunities for the mosaicist to display their skill and imagination. The robustness and strength of colour of mosaic proves an effective counterbalance to the clear, fleeting nature of water.

Mosaic is ideally suited to gardens: it can be varied to suit any setting, its resistance to water means that rain or fountains cannot harm it or dim its vibrancy, and the play of ever-changing outdoor light adds constant interest.

It is best to keep any water feature in proportion. In a small courtyard, it can be tucked into a corner, mounted on a wall or even set in a container.

For a natural look, a mosaic of shells, stone or pebble can form a subtle framework for a pool or fountain, which darkens and gleams where the water moistens the stones. In a formal garden, you might choose to line the floor or the edge of a pool or pond with a suitable motif, while in an urban garden, a square or rectangular feature with geometric decoration looks good. In a cool, green or white garden, you could install a fountain to create delicate dappled reflections.

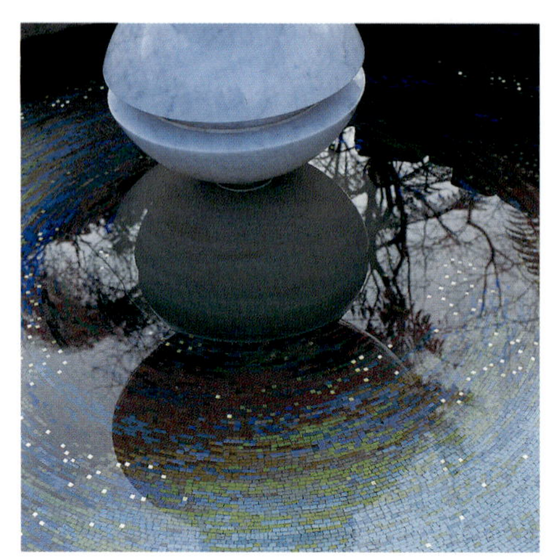

Above: Circles of oblong mosaics in blues and sea greens grow darker towards the centre of this pond by Trevor Caley, creating an illusion of depth, while random gold splashes add intriguing glitter.

Left: An elegant mirrored fountain by Rebecca Newnham.

Opposite: For richness, nothing beats gold, whether on its own or as part of a design for a bowl. A collection of water features by Elaine M. Goodwin.

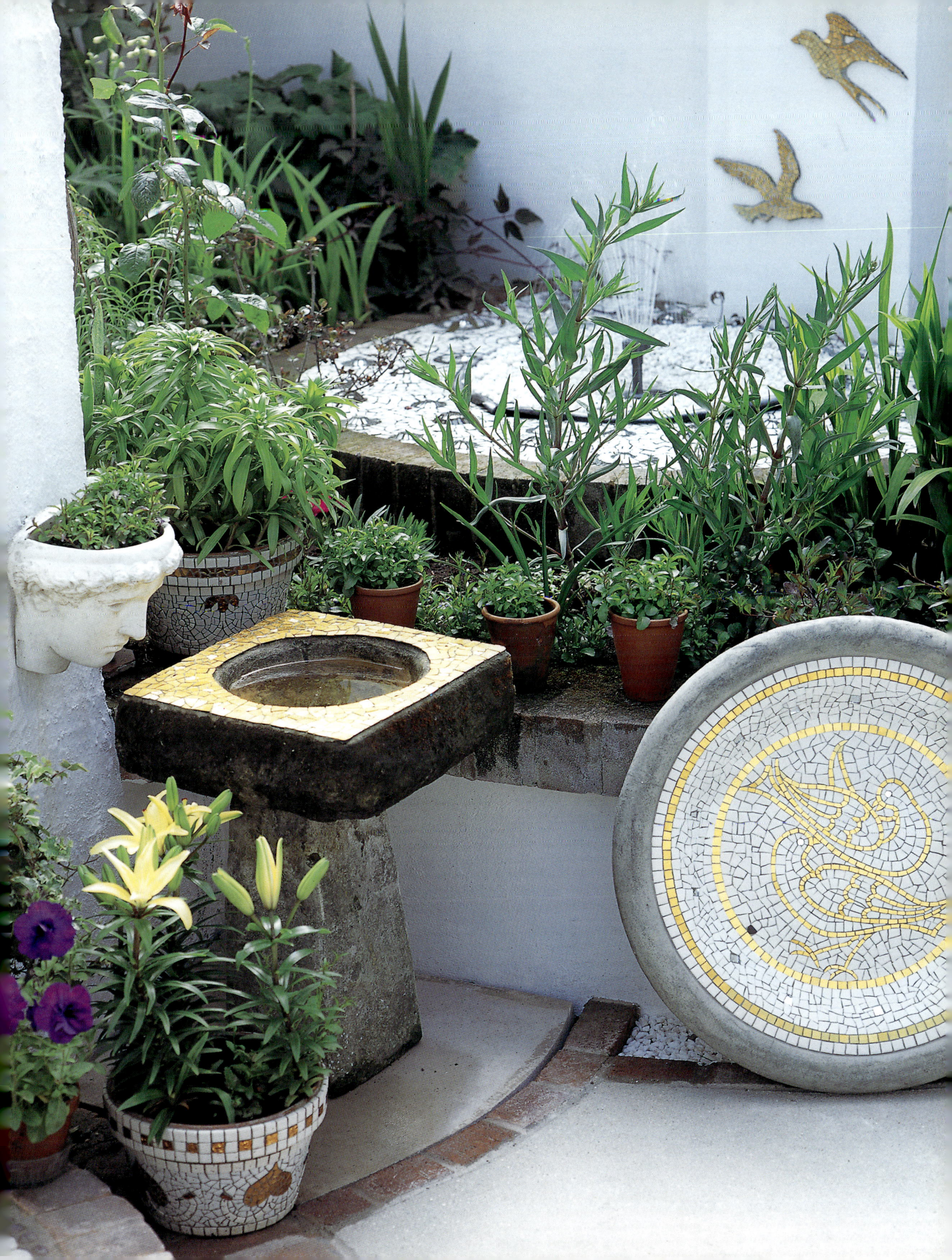

In this panel, the tiles have been laid very close together to avoid the need for grout. This allows the range of tones used here to relate to one another as directly as possible, giving a luminous, glowing appearance.

Abstract Colour Panel

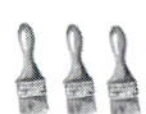

You will need

Vitreous glass mosaic tiles in various colours
Coloured pencils to match the tiles
Paper
Tracing paper
Tile nippers
MDF (medium-density fiberboard) 50 x 50cm (20 x 20in) with frame
Different coloured felt-tipped pens
Wood stain
Paintbrushes
PVA (white) glue
Soft cloth

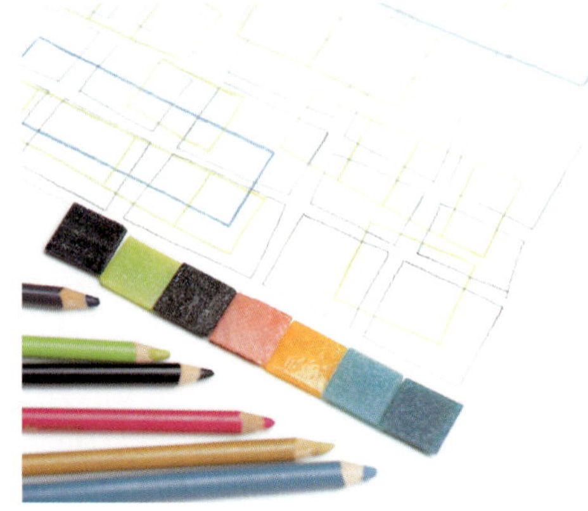

1 Match the proposed tile colours to the pencils to enable you to produce an accurate coloured drawing. As this scheme is fairly complex, involving boxes within boxes, and tonal colour changes, a line drawing was produced as a plan for the coloured sketch.

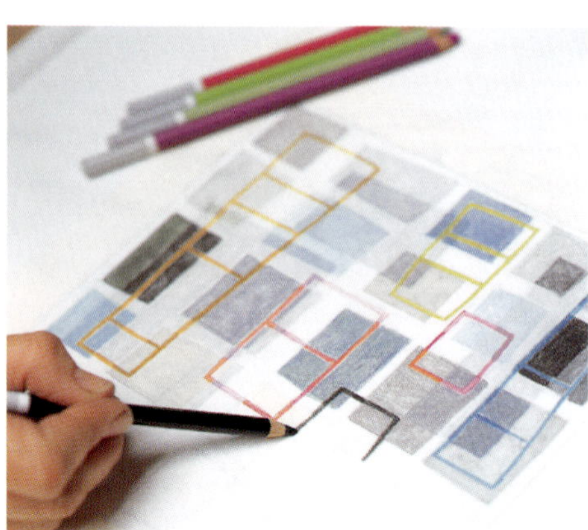

2 Draw an accurate coloured sketch. To get a good idea of how the different blocks of tones and shading will work, put a layer of tracing paper over the line drawing and fill in the coloured areas. Use the tile nippers to cut the mosaic tiles in your chosen colours.

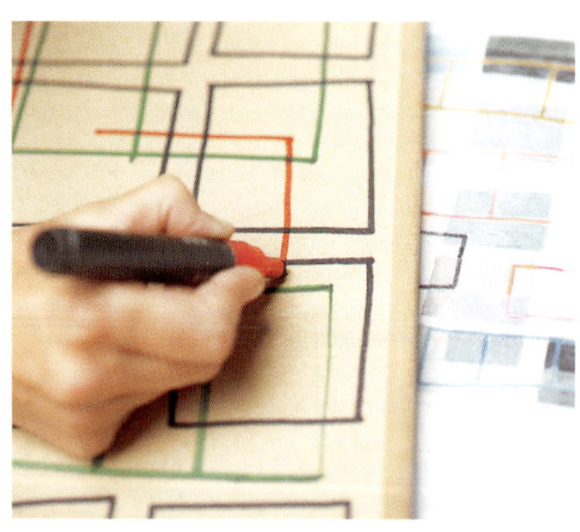

3 Draw the fundamentals of the design on to the board using felt-tipped pens. It is not necessary to mark up any more detail than you see here. The segmented pattern is sketched in black, and the ladder lines in different colours. Stain the frame of the board before starting to stick down the tiles.

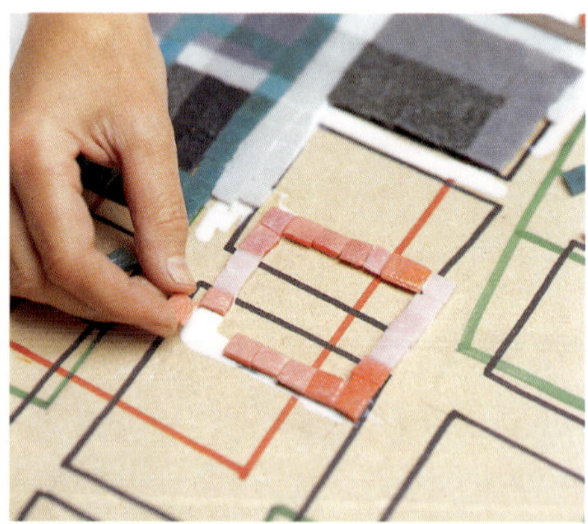

4 Sort your tiles into tones of greater or lesser intensity. Paint each area of the board that you are working on with a good layer of PVA (white) glue. If the layer is too thin, the tiles will fail to adhere; if it is too thick, the glue will squeeze between the joints on to the tile face. Start by laying the coloured ladder shapes.

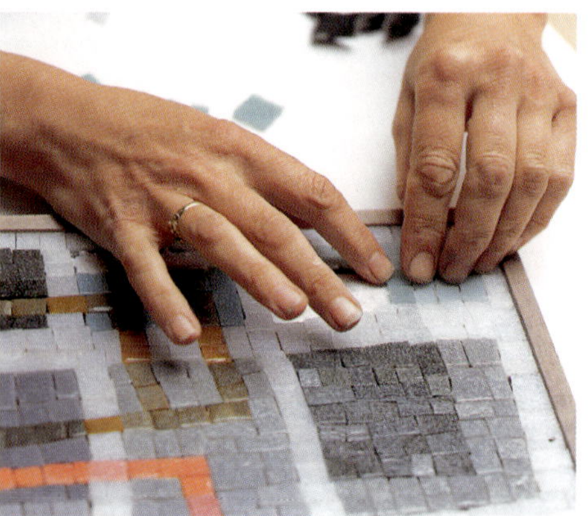

5 Continue working around the board, filling in the different coloured areas as you go. Wipe off any blobs of glue as you work, then wipe over the whole thing with a cloth when you have finished to remove any residual adhesive. Finally, polish with a dry, soft cloth.

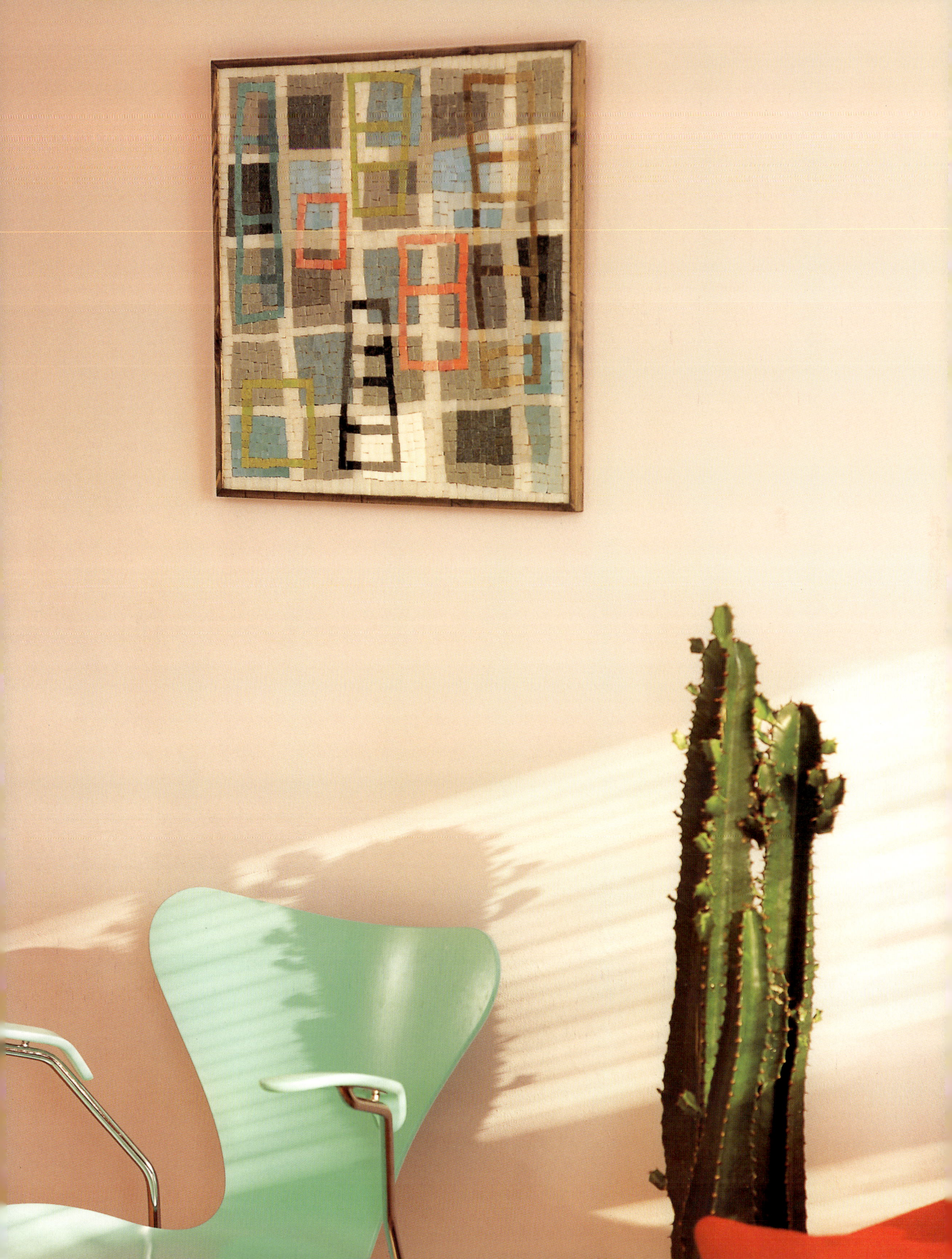

Norma Vondee has decorated the door of this bathroom cabinet with a witty *trompe-l'œil* mosaic. The shadows and highlights give the bottle, glass and pot the illusion of being three-dimensional.

Bathroom Cabinet

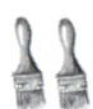

You will need

Wall-mounted cabinet with door
3mm (⅛in) thick plywood sheet
Saw
Bradawl or awl
Pencil
Ceramic mosaic tiles
Tile nippers
PVA (white) glue
Paintbrush
Masking tape
Sand
Cement
Red cement stain
Grout spreader
Sponge
Soft cloth

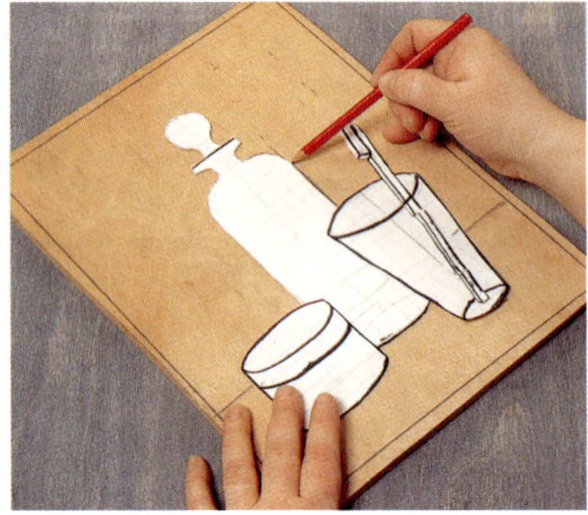

1 Remove the wooden or glass panel in the door of the bathroom cabinet. Cut a piece of plywood to the same size and score the surface with a bradawl or awl. Draw your design on the plywood. Mark in the ellipses and areas of shadow.

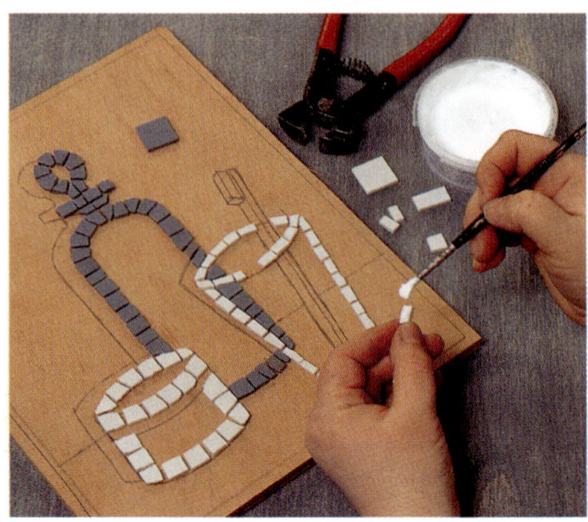

2 Cut the ceramic mosaic tiles into precise shapes using the tile nippers. Apply these tesserae to the main outlines of the shapes, fixing them in place with PVA (white) glue applied with a fine paintbrush. Take extra care when tiling curved areas, snipping the tiles into wedge shapes to ensure they fit.

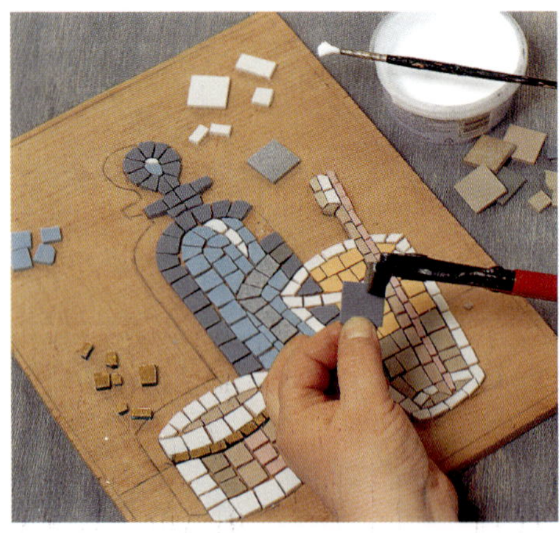

3 Fill the areas inside the outlines in contrasting colours. Here, reflections and highlights are depicted using different shades of tesserae to create the illusion of a three-dimensional scene.

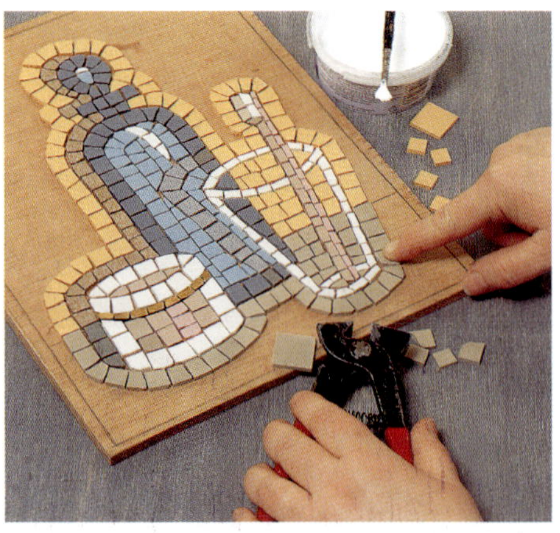

4 Outline the shapes with a row of tesserae in the background colour. If making a larger design, you could use a double row of tesserae to outline the subjects of the mosaic.

5 Fill in the background colour with tesserae arranged in straight lines, and leave overnight to dry. Secure the panel in position on the cabinet door and mask the frame with tape. Mix 3 parts sand and 1 part cement with water and a little red cement stain. Grout the mosaic with this mixture using a grout spreader. Clean the surface carefully with a damp sponge and leave to dry as slowly as possible, then polish with a dry, soft cloth.

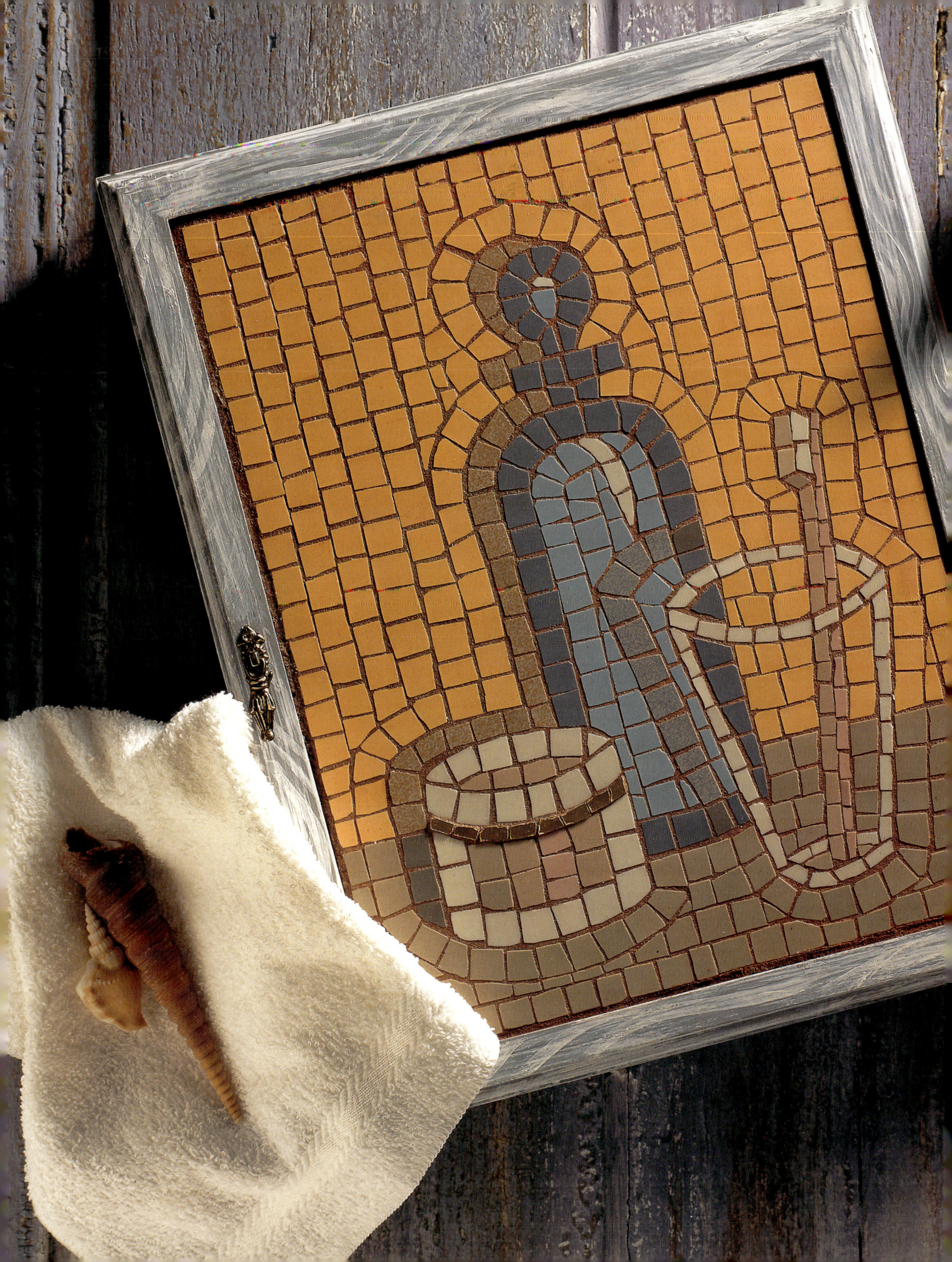

This dramatic mosaic creates the invigorating effect of rocks sparkling with drops of water in a mountain stream. This project is quick to complete, as it does not need to be grouted.

Slate Shelf

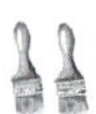

You will need

- 2cm (¾in) thick plywood sheet
- Saw
- Bradawl or awl
- PVA (white) glue
- Paintbrush
- Hammer
- Slate
- Piece of sacking (heavy cloth)
- Tile adhesive
- Black cement stain
- Flexible knife
- Pebbles
- Glass globules: blue, grey, white
- Silver smalti
- Tile nippers

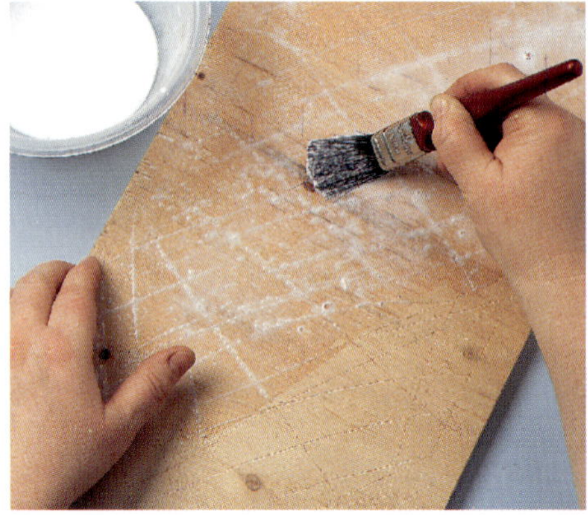

1 Cut the piece of thick plywood to the desired size with a saw. Lightly score one side with a bradawl or awl, then prime with diluted PVA (white) glue.

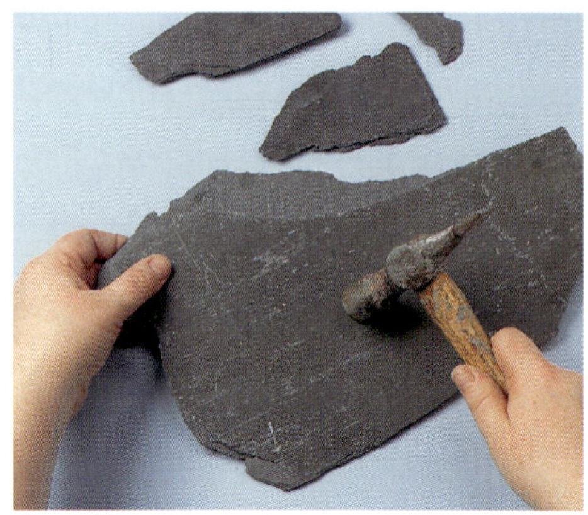

2 Using a hammer, break the slate into large chunks. It is advisable to wrap the slate in a piece of sacking (heavy cloth) to prevent injury.

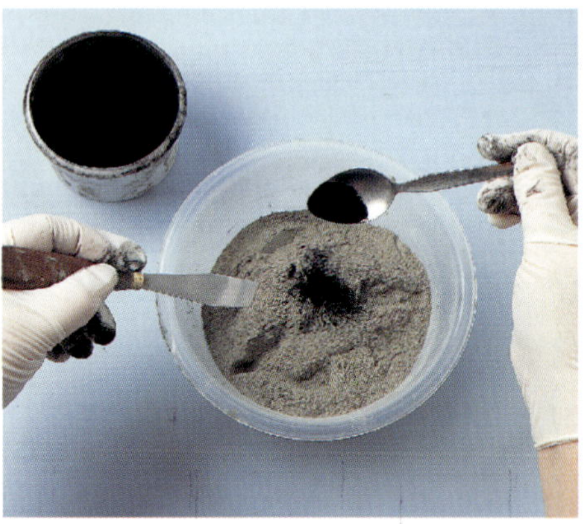

3 Mix the tile adhesive with half a teaspoon of black cement stain. Mix to a thick paste with cold water.

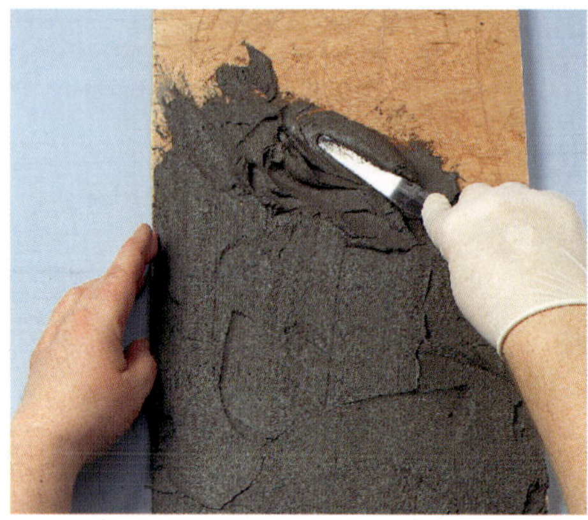

4 Using a flexible knife, spread the tile adhesive in a thick, even layer over the scored side of the plywood. Smooth it over the front to conceal the edge.

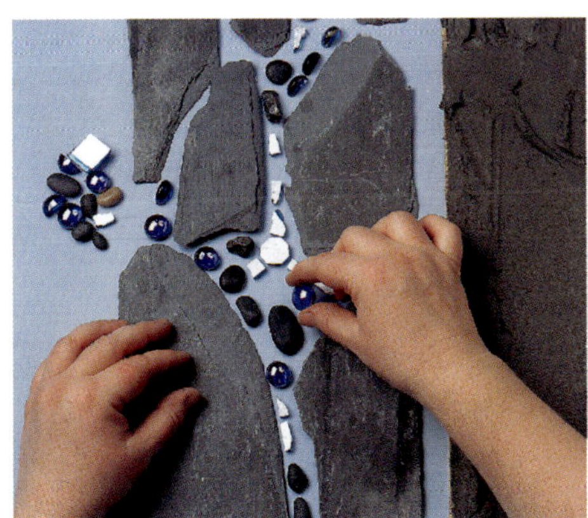

5 Arrange the broken slate, pebbles, glass globules and silver smalti on a flat surface next to the board in your chosen design, making any adjustments until you are satisfied.

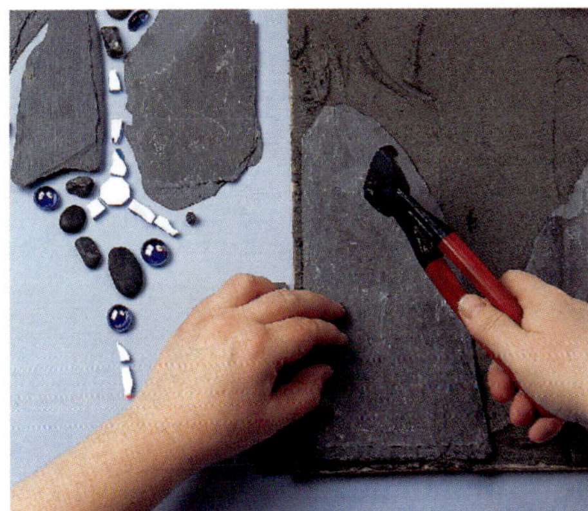

6 Transfer the design, piece by piece, to the board. Tap the slate with the side of the tile nippers to settle it, but do not move any pieces once firmly positioned. Leave to dry overnight.

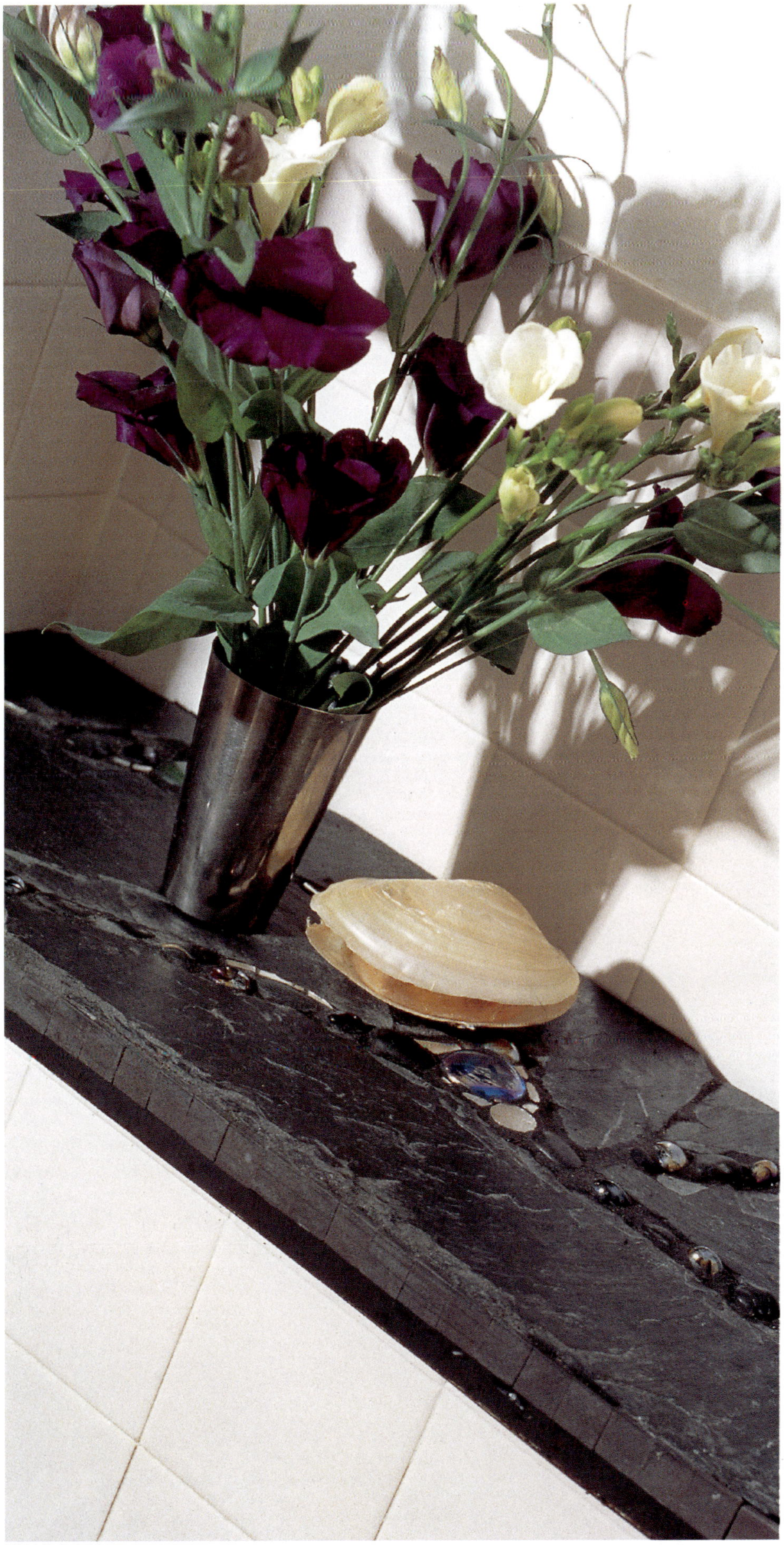

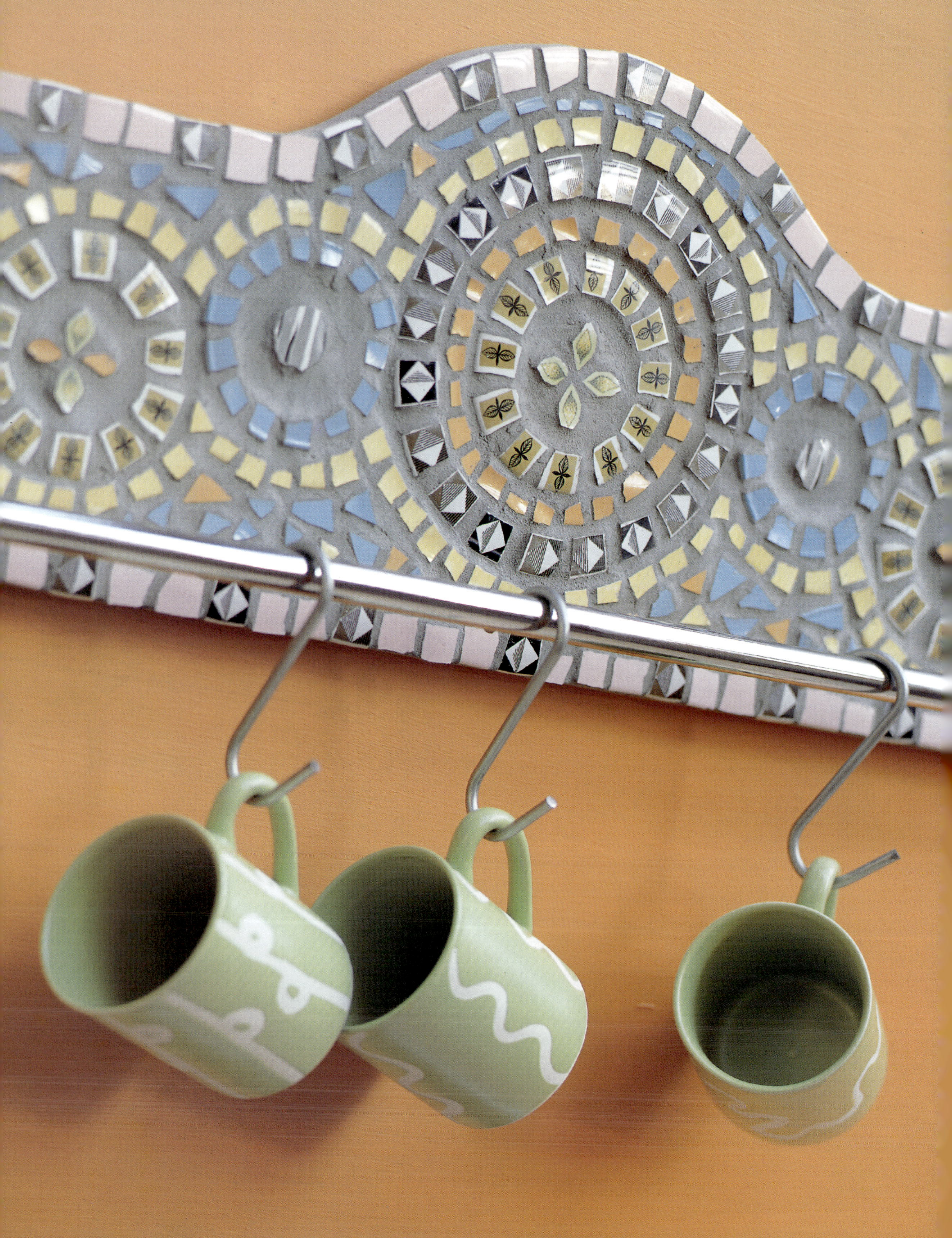

This useful and colourful kitchen rail is made out of old patterned china. The kitchen theme can be carried through by drawing around cups, plates and jars to create the circular designs.

China Rail

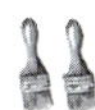

You will need

12mm (½in) thick MDF (medium-density fiberboard), cut to 60 x 25cm (24 x 10in)
Jigsaw (saber saw)
Abrasive paper (sandpaper)
PVA (white) glue
Paintbrush
Dark pencil
60cm (24in) long metal rail, with struts
Screws
Screwdriver
Plates, cups and jars, in different sizes
Hammer
Old patterned china
Piece of sacking (heavy cloth)
Tile nippers
Soft cloths
Tile grout
Rubber spreader
Paint scraper
S-shaped metal hooks
2 protruding mirror plates

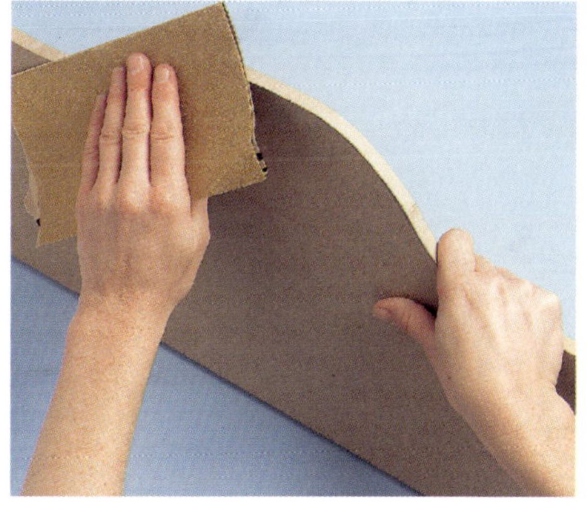

1 Using a jigsaw (saber saw), cut the MDF (medium-density fiberboard) so that it is 15cm (6in) high on either side, rising to a smooth curve in the centre. Sand the edges with abrasive paper (sandpaper) until smooth. Prime both sides of the board with diluted PVA (white) glue.

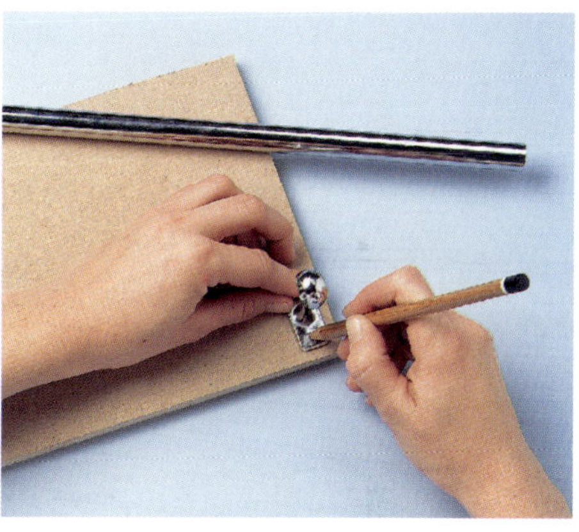

2 Using a dark pencil, mark the position of the rail fittings and screw holes clearly on the front of the board, one at either end.

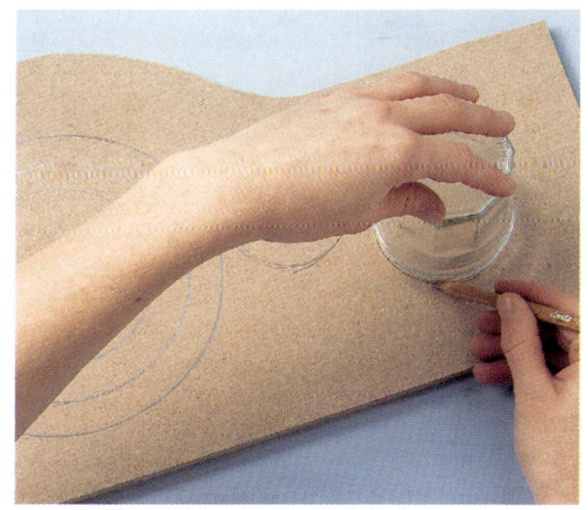

3 Draw around upturned plates, cups and jars to create a design of circles in different sizes.

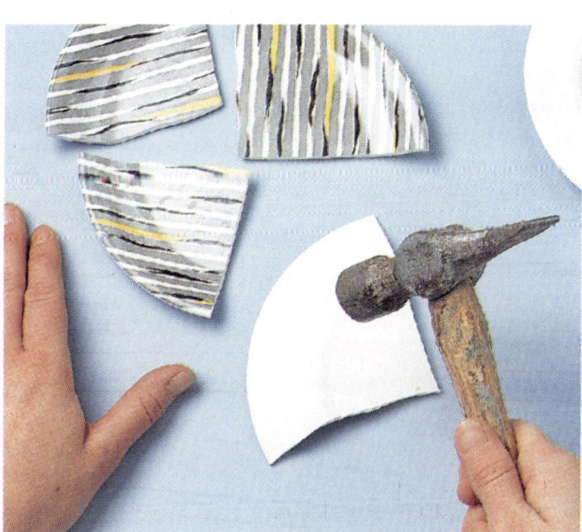

4 Using a hammer, break up the old patterned china. It is advisable to wrap each piece in sacking (heavy cloth) first to prevent injuries.

▶

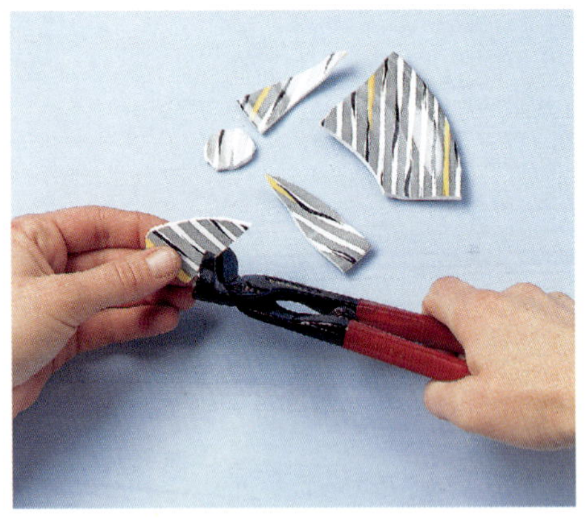

5 Using tile nippers, trim the pieces of china into neat squares, making the best use of the existing patterns on the china. Cut up all the china in this way. Try to arrange to have a mixture of patterned and colourful plain china to create contrast in the finished design. The patterned pieces might have a theme such as being black and white or having a recurring colour throughout the tesserae.

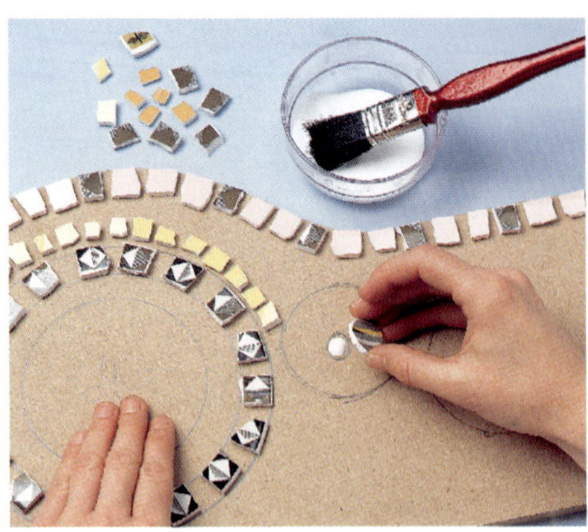

6 Working from the outside top layer first, stick the tesserae to the board with PVA (white) glue, following the lines of your pencil design. Build up the pattern, leaving a slight space in between each tile for the grout to fill. You may find it easier to work from the outside pattern inwards. Avoid laying tesserae over the marked screwholes. Remove any excess glue with a cloth as you work, and when the design is complete, leave to dry thoroughly, preferably overnight.

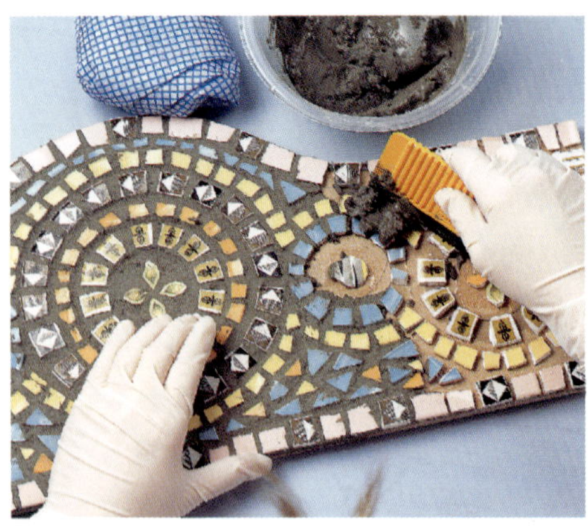

7 Rub your hands over the surface of the mosaic to check for any loose tesserae. If any pieces have worked their way loose, glue these down again and leave to dry. Then, using a rubber spreader, spread tile grout over the surface of the mosaic, filling all the gaps between the tesserae. Leave to dry for one hour.

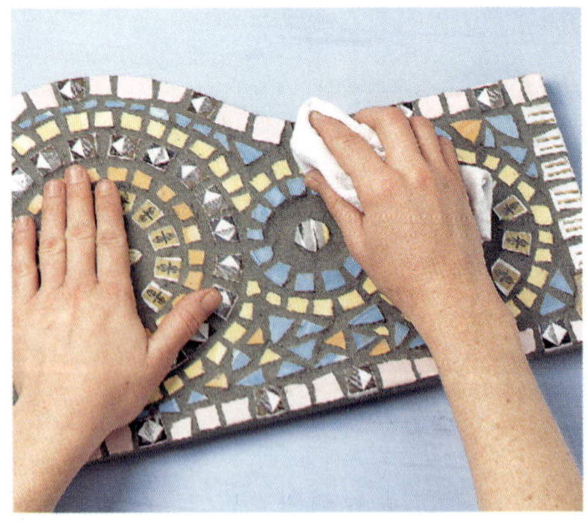

8 Polish the mosaic with a soft cloth, removing any grout that may have dried on the surface. Scrape off any stubborn grout with a paint scraper if necessary. Turn the board over and screw a protruding mirror plate in the centre of each side edge.

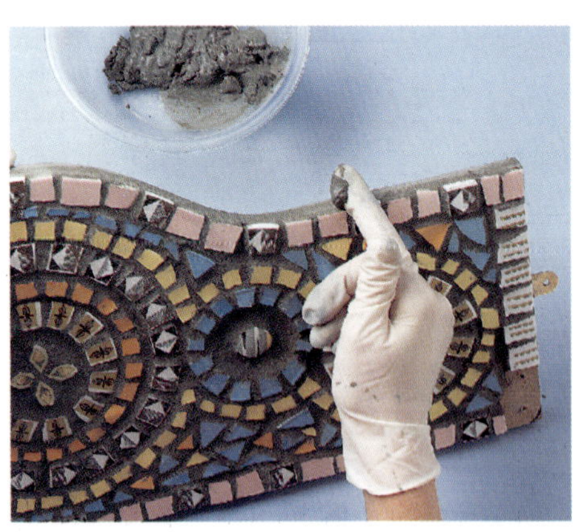

9 Smooth tile grout along all the edges of the board for a smooth finish. Leave to dry overnight, then sand smooth.

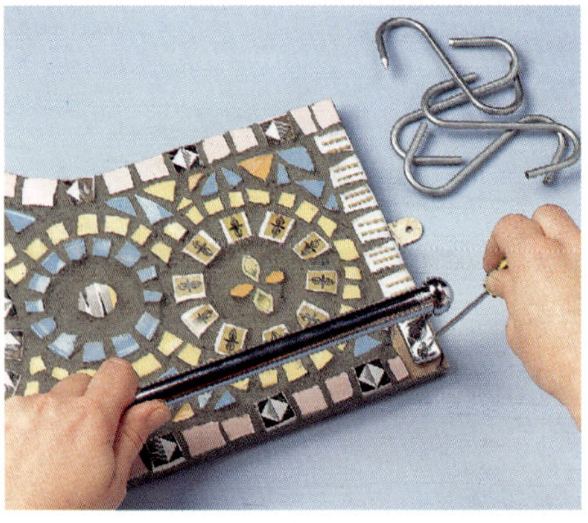

10 Screw the rail and struts to the front of the board, then screw the board firmly to the wall, using the mirror plates. Hang the S-shaped hooks on the rail.

The top of this kitchen shelf is exuberantly decorated in random colours, reminiscent of Antonio Gaudí's garden mosaics in Barcelona. You can achieve a quite different effect by using shades of one colour.

Crazy Paving Shelf

You will need

Ready-made wooden shelf, with brackets
Tape measure
2cm (3/4in) thick MDF (medium-density fiberboard) or pine
Saw
Metal cup hooks
Pencil
Clamps
Drill
Wood glue
Screwdriver
Screws
Plain glazed ceramic household tiles: oranges, reds, pinks, blues
Piece of sacking (heavy cloth)
Hammer
Tile nippers
Tile adhesive
Notched trowel
Tile grout
Cement stain
Rubber spreader
Sponge
Soft cloth

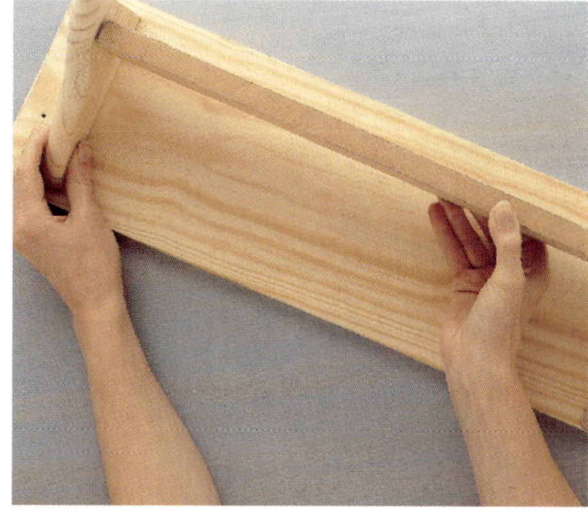

1 Measure the distance between the shelf brackets. Cut a backing strip of MDF (medium-density fiberboard) or pine to fit, allowing a border all the way around the edges wide enough to accomodate your design.

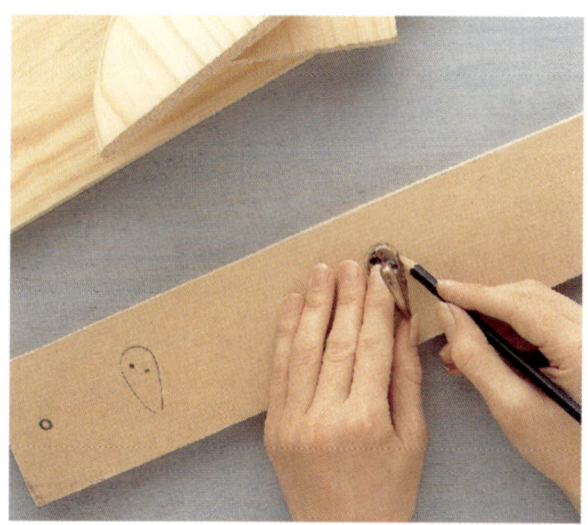

2 Space the cup hooks at equal distances on the backing strip and draw around them. Clamp the backing strip, then drill screw holes for the cup hooks. Drill a hole at either end as extra fixing for the finished shelf.

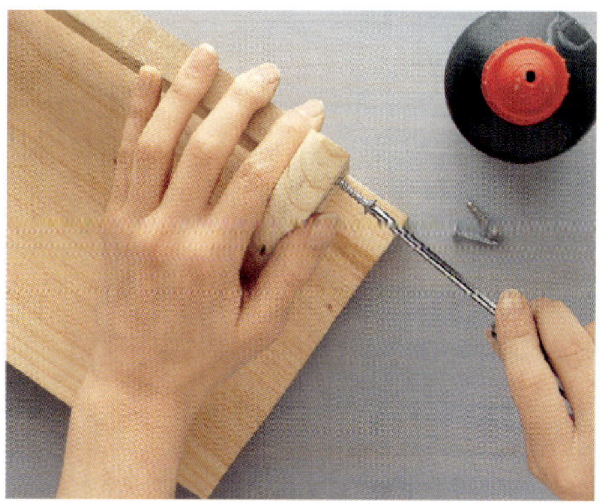

3 Mark the position of the backing strip between the shelf brackets. Using clamps, drill a hole in each bracket, then drill a hole at either end of the backing strip to match. Glue the backing strip in place with wood glue, then screw firmly together.

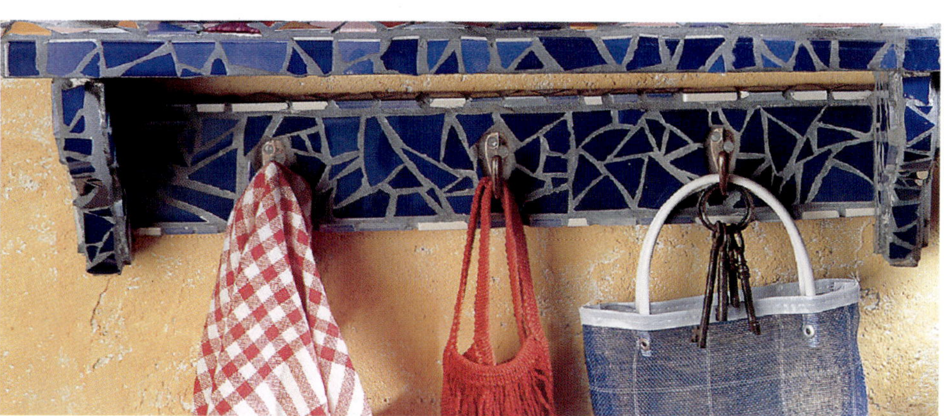

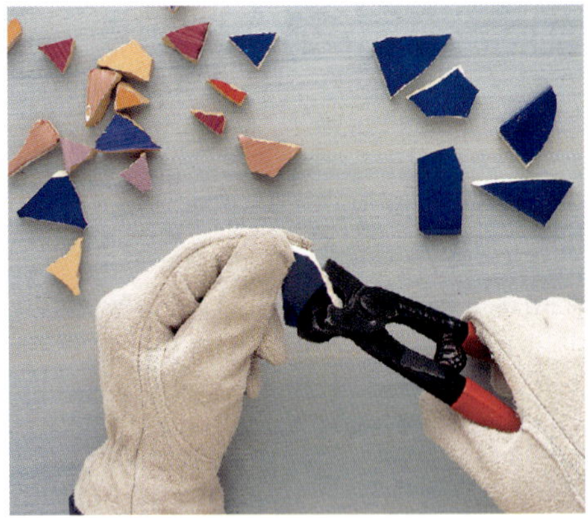

4 Wrap each tile separately in a piece of sacking (heavy cloth) and break it with a hammer. Trim the pieces into triangles with tile nippers, keeping some edge pieces to one side.

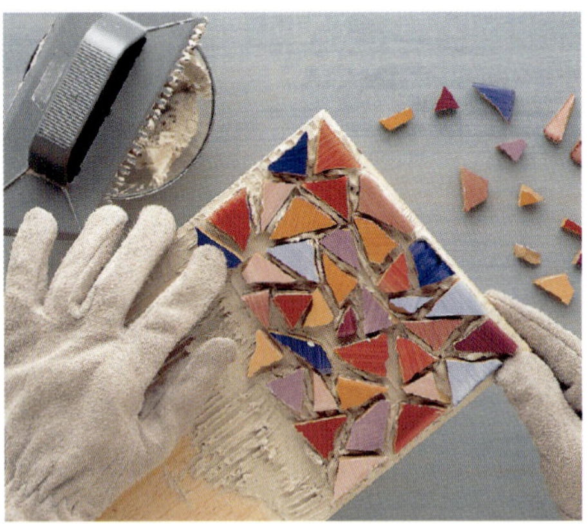

5 Using a notched trowel, spread a thick layer of tile adhesive over one-third of the shelf top, then press different coloured tesserae into the adhesive.

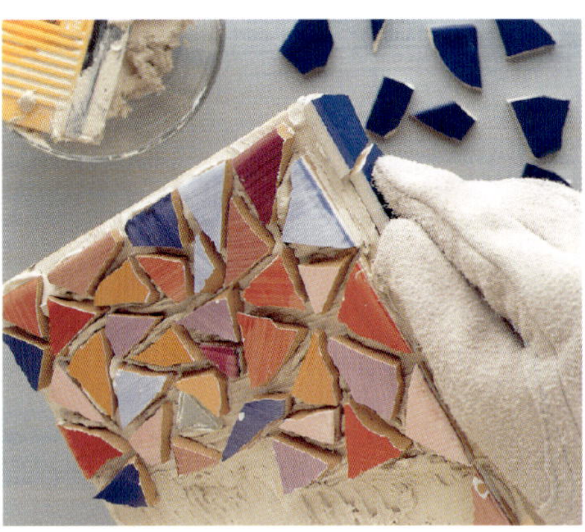

6 Cut square and rectangular pieces from the original edges of the dark blue tiles. Remove any sharp pieces. Apply the tile pieces to the shelf edges as before, to give them a smooth, safe finish. Complete the rest of the shelf top with the brightly coloured tiles.

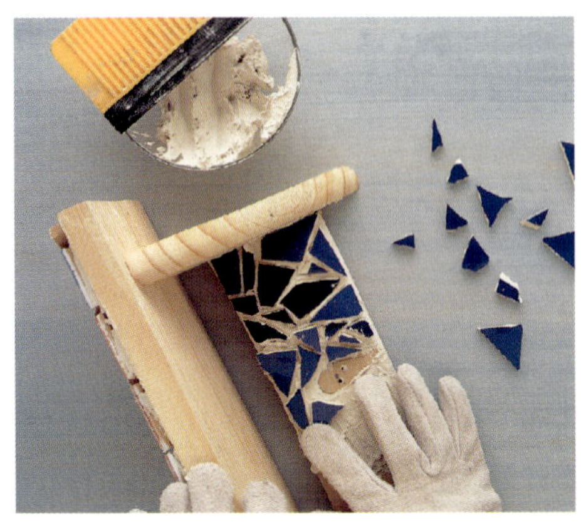

7 Apply adhesive to the backing strip as before, leaving spaces for the cup hooks and avoiding the end screw holes. Break the dark blue tiles and cut into triangles as before, then cover the backing strip and brackets with blue mosaic. Leave to dry thoroughly.

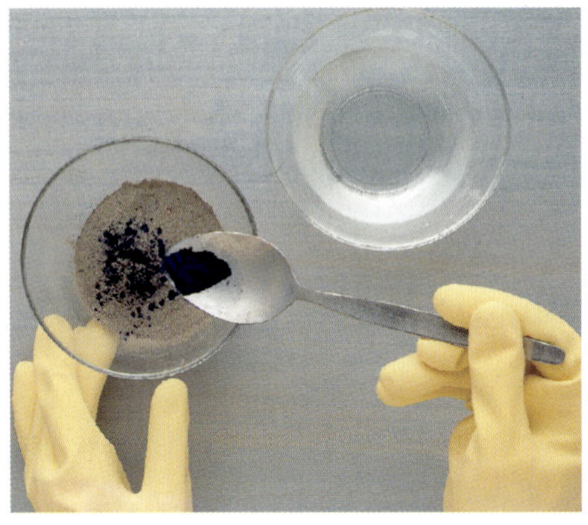

8 Mix the tile grout with some cement stain, following the manufacturer's instructions. Add water and mix thoroughly to a firm consistency.

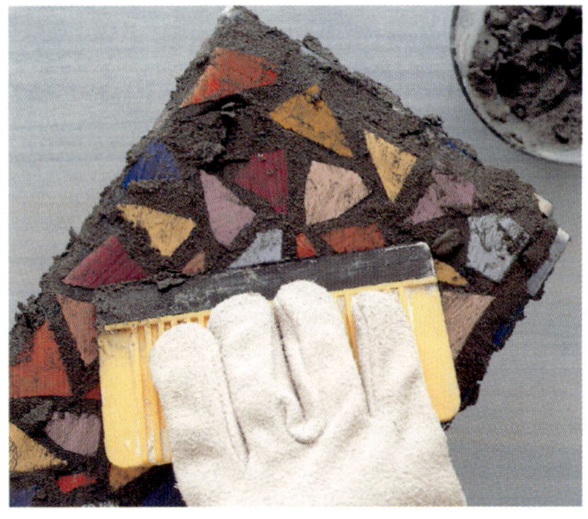

9 Spread the grout over the shelf with a rubber spreader, pushing it well down into the spaces between the tesserae and making sure that any sharp edges are covered. Remove excess grout with a damp sponge. Leave to dry completely, then polish the surface with a dry, soft cloth. Screw the shelf to the wall, using the shelf fixings and the holes drilled through the backing strip.

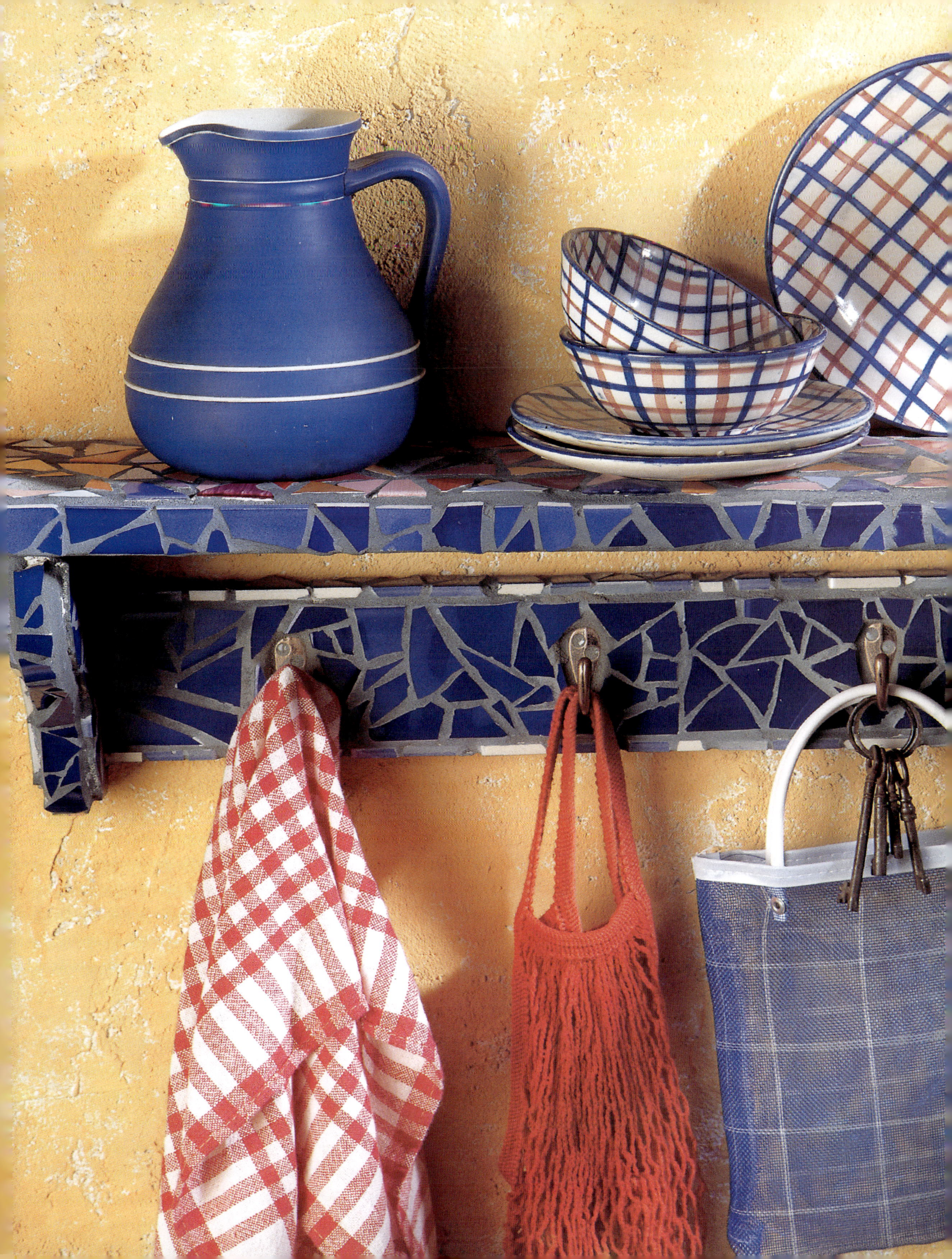

Mosaic is an ideal surface for decorating bathrooms and kitchens since it is waterproof and easy to wipe clean. This simple design is made of tiles in two colours, alternated to give a chequerboard effect.

Splashback Squares

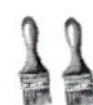

You will need

12mm (½in) thick plywood sheet, cut to fit along the top of your basin or sink and half as deep
PVA (white) glue
Paintbrushes
Bradawl or awl
Soft dark pencil
Thin-glazed ceramic household tiles in two contrasting colours
Tile nippers
Flexible knife
Tile adhesive
Damp sponge
Grout spreader or cloth pad
Abrasive paper (sandpaper)
Yacht varnish
4 domed mirror screws
Screwdriver

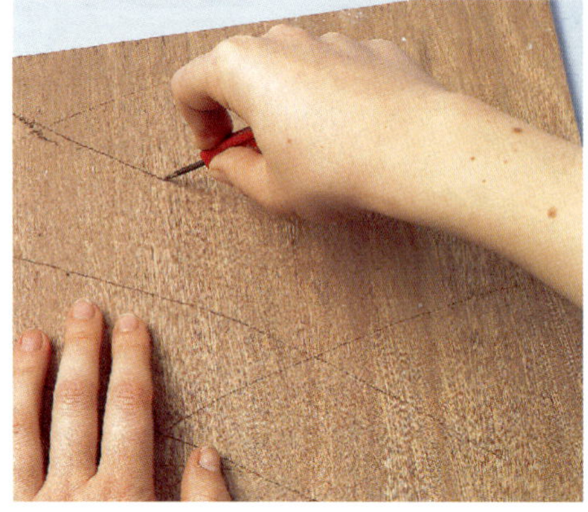

1 Prime both sides of the plywood with diluted PVA (white) glue. Leave to dry, then score across one side with a bradawl or awl to create a key for the tile to adhere to.

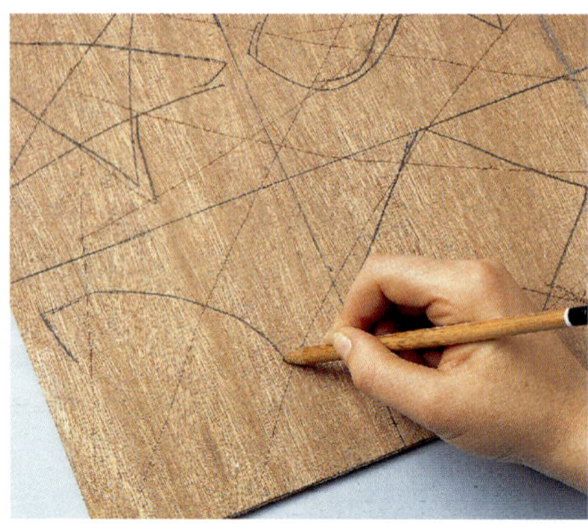

2 Divide the scored side of the plywood into eight squares. Draw a simple and easily recognisable motif of your choice into each square.

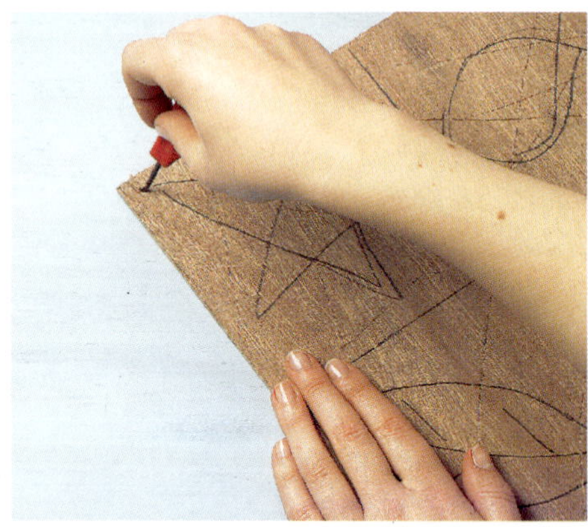

3 Make a hole in each corner of the plywood, using a bradawl or awl. These will form the holes for the screws to fix the splashback to the wall in its final position behind the sink.

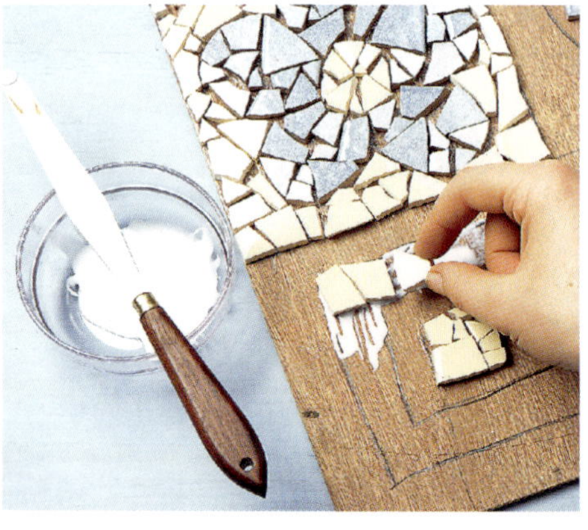

4 Using tile nippers, cut the tiles into random shapes. Following your drawn designs, and using a flexible knife, stick the tiles in place with PVA glue over the pencil markings on each square. Position the tiles carefully around the holes made for hanging. Wipe off any excess glue with a damp sponge before it dries. Leave until completely dry, preferably overnight.

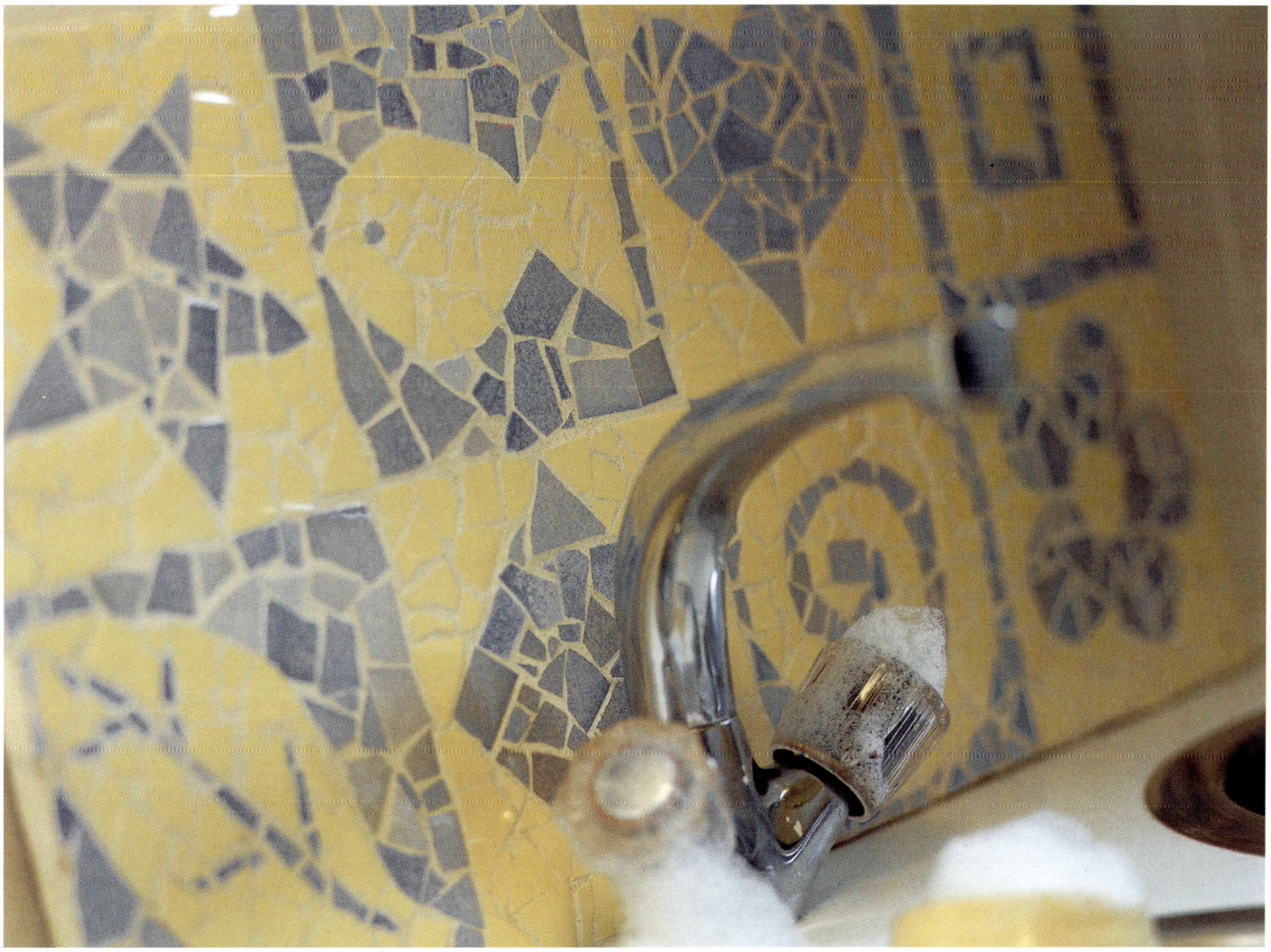

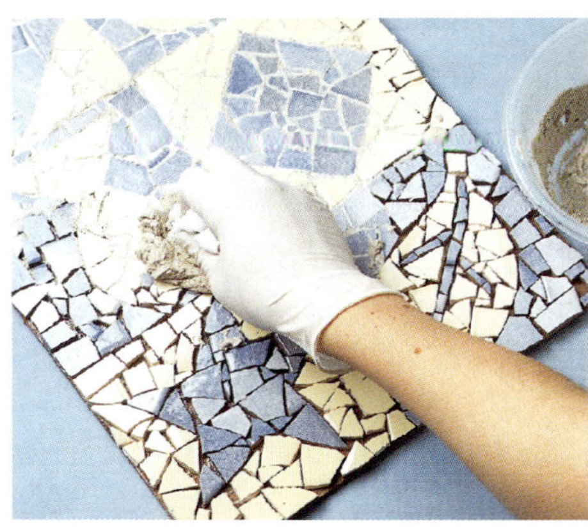

5 Spread tile adhesive over the surface of the mosaic with a grout spreader or cloth pad, smoothing around the edges with your fingers. Wipe off any excess adhesive and re-open the hanging holes. Leave to dry overnight.

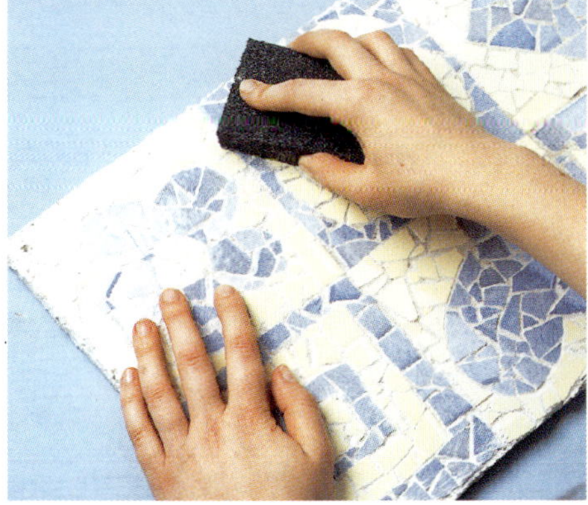

6 Carefully sand off any remaining dried adhesive on the surface of the mosaic. Paint the back of the plywood with yacht varnish to seal it and make it waterproof, and leave to dry for 1–2 hours. Fasten the splashback to the wall with domed mirror screws inserted through the holes at each corner.

A skirting board or step riser is an unusual and discreet way of introducing mosaic into your home. You can use a repeated design (such as this daisy), a succession of motifs, or a combination of the two.

Daisy Skirting Board

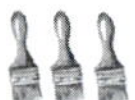

You will need

Skirting (base) board to fit the room
Abrasive paper (sandpaper)
PVA (white) glue
Paintbrush
Dark pencil
Ruler
Piece of sacking (heavy cloth)
Selection of marble tiles
Hammer
Tile adhesive
Flexible knife
Sponge
Soft cloth

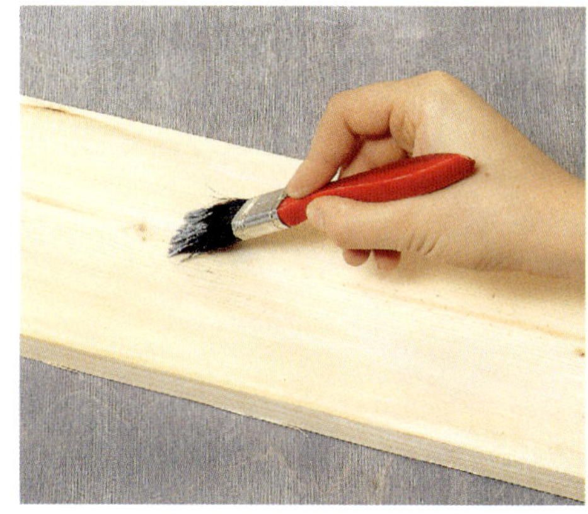

1 Roughen the surface of the skirting (base) board with coarse-grade abrasive paper (sandpaper), then prime with diluted PVA (white) glue. Leave to dry.

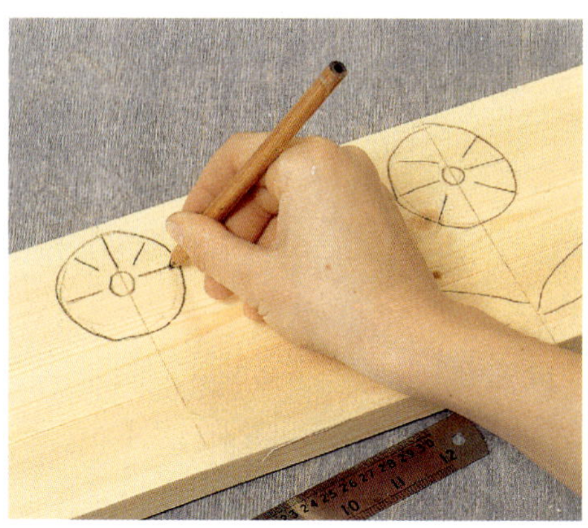

2 Mark the skirting board into small, equally spaced sections. Using a dark pencil, draw a simple motif in each section. Here, the motif is a daisy.

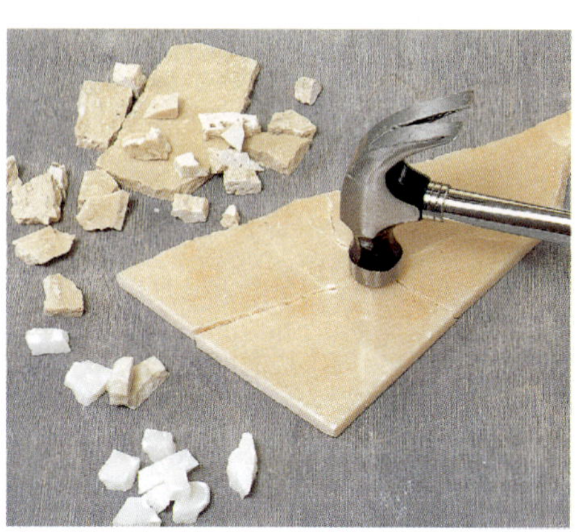

3 Smash the marble tiles for the daisies into small pieces with a hammer. It is advisable to wrap the tiles in a piece of sacking (heavy cloth).

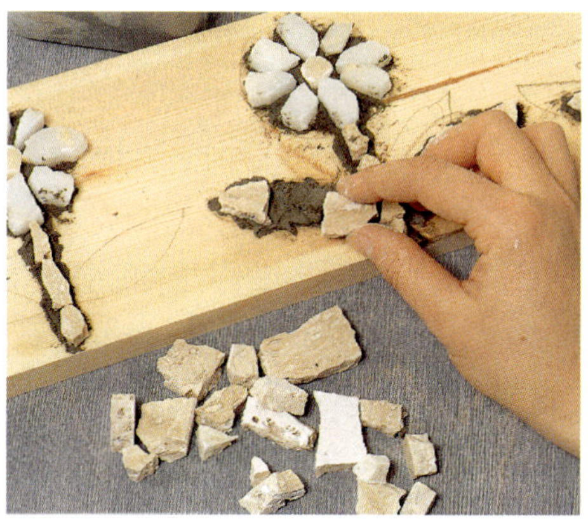

4 Using a flexible knife and working on a small area at a time, spread tile adhesive along the lines of your drawing. Press the broken pieces of marble firmly into the adhesive. Choose tesserae in shapes that echo those of the design. The marble can be roughly shaped by tapping the edges of larger tesserae with a hammer. When each motif is tiled, wipe off any excess adhesive with a sponge and leave to dry overnight.

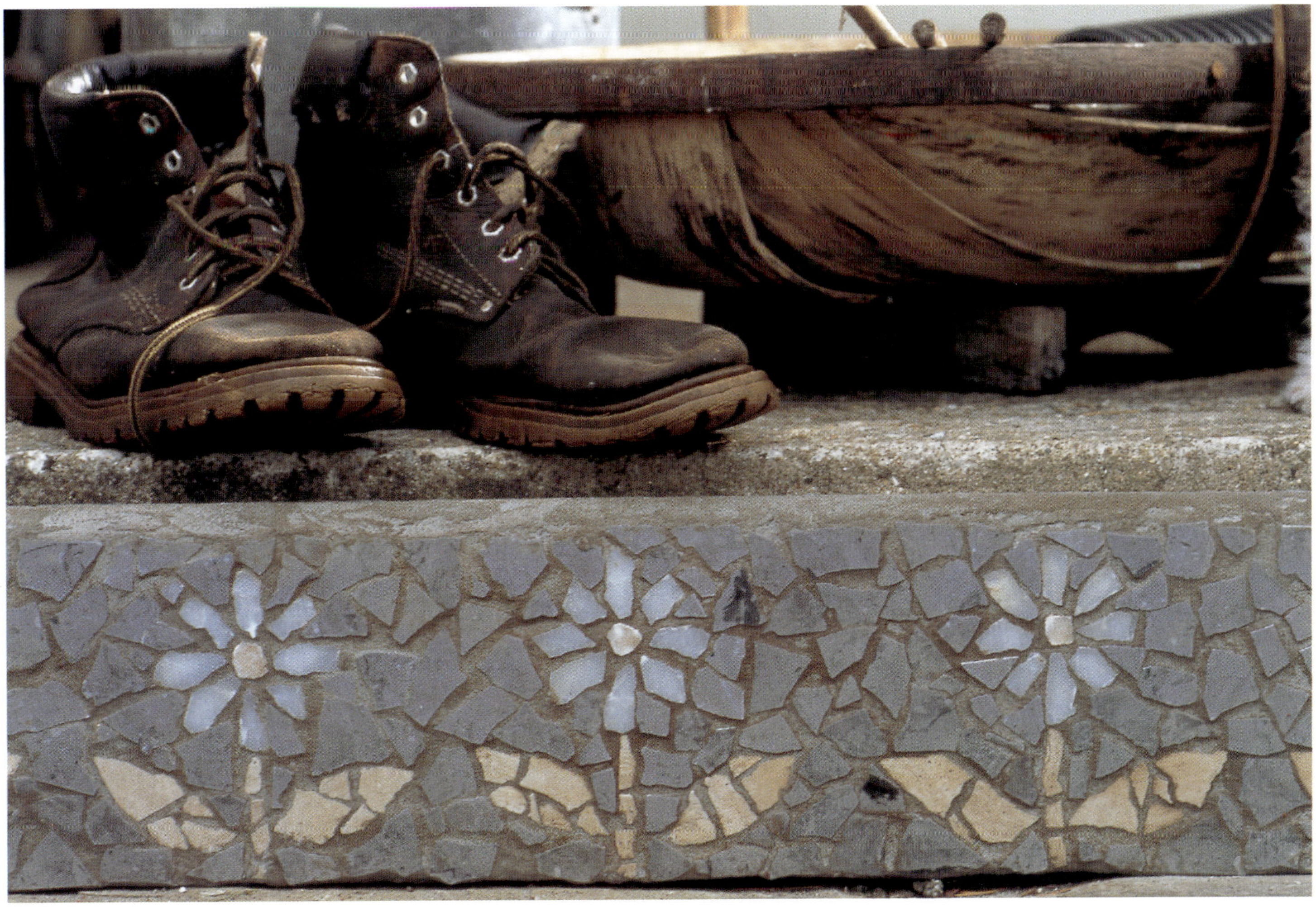

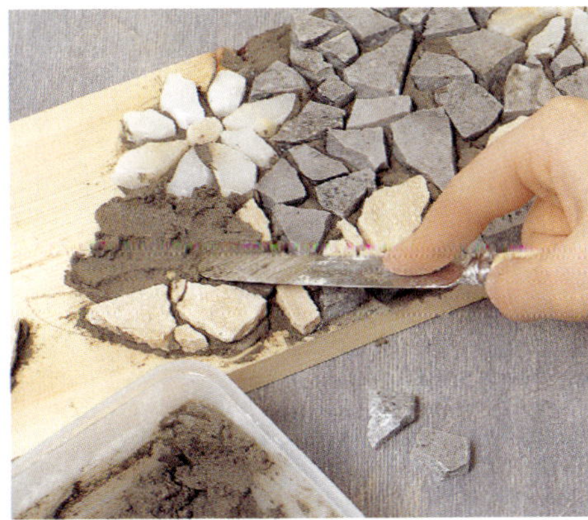

5 Break up the tiles in the background colour with a hammer. Working on a small area at a time, spread adhesive on to the untiled sections of skirting board and press the tesserae into it. When the surface is covered, use small pieces of the background colour to tile along the top edge of the skirting, ensuring that the tesserae do not overlap the edge. Leave to dry for 24 hours.

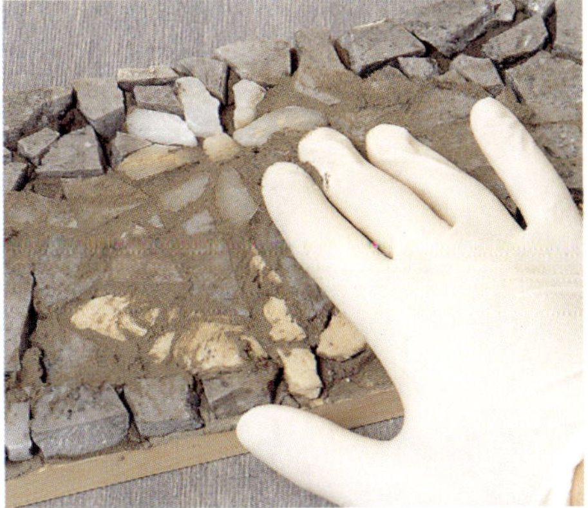

6 Rub more tile adhesive into the surface of the mosaic with your fingers, filling all the gaps between the tesserae. Use a flexible knife to spread the adhesive into the edge. Wipe off any excess with a damp sponge and leave overnight to dry.

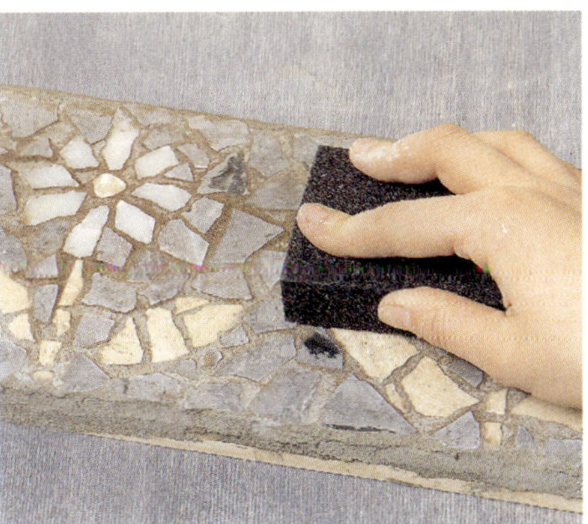

7 Sand off any adhesive that has dried on the surface of the mosaic and polish the surface with a dry, soft cloth. Fix the skirting board in position.

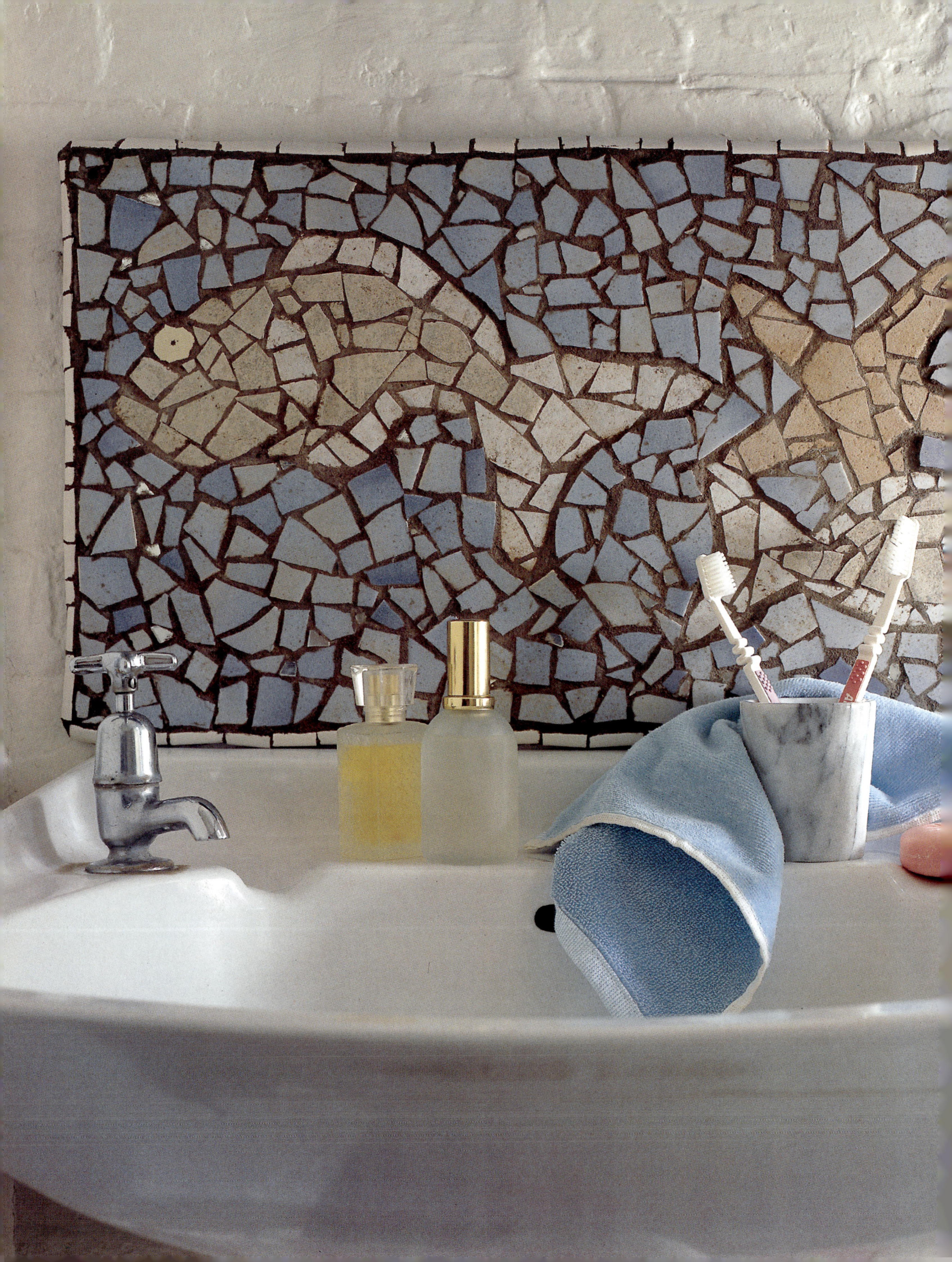

Mosaic is an ideal decorative surface or wall cladding for areas in which water is present, such as this splashback for a bathroom basin. It is made from roughly broken tiles, with chips of mirror to catch the light.

Fish Splashback

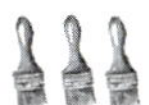

You will need

Tape measure
4mm (⅛in) thick plywood sheet
Saw
PVA (white) glue
Paintbrush
Soft dark pencil
Bradawl or awl
Ceramic household tiles: light grey, dark grey, soft pink, cream, and soft blue
Hammer
Piece of sacking (heavy cloth)
Tile nippers
Tile adhesive
Flexible knife
Thin edging tiles
Mirror
Soft brush
Plant mister
Drinking straw
Scissors
Abrasive paper (sandpaper)
Soft cloth
Drill
Wall plugs (plastic anchors)
4 domed mirror screws
Screwdriver

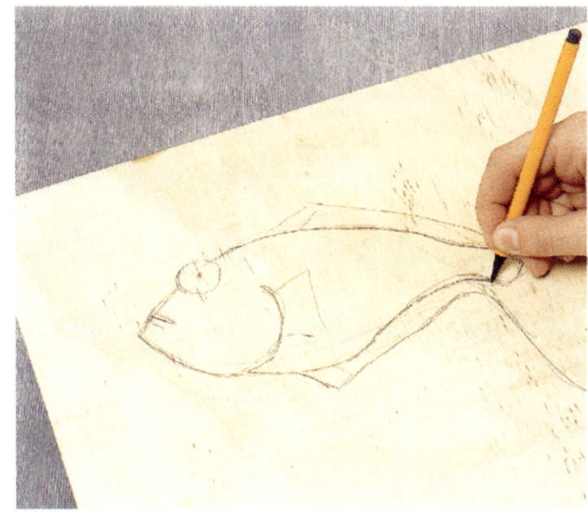

1 Measure the width of your basin and cut the plywood to size. Prime the surface with diluted PVA (white) glue. When it is dry, draw a simple fish design on the plywood.

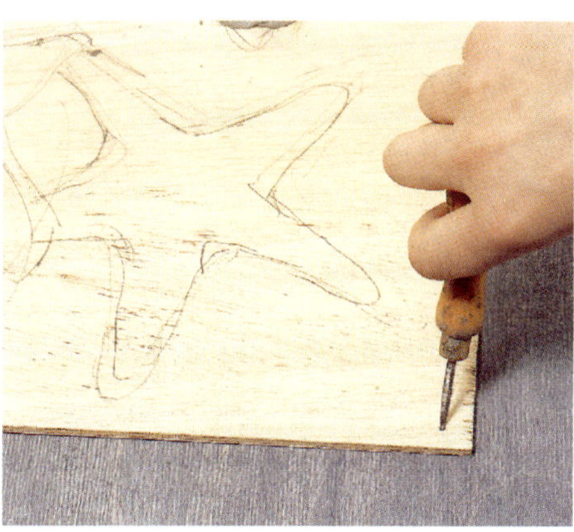

2 Using a bradawl or awl, make a hole through the plywood in each corner.

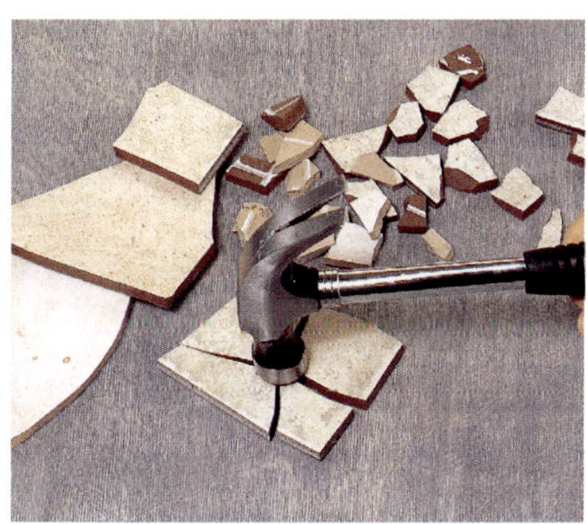

3 Select the colours of the tiles to be used for tesserae; here, two similar greys are used for the fish and a muted pink for the starfish. Smash the tiles into a variety of shapes using the hammer. It is advisable to wrap the tiles in a piece of sacking (heavy cloth) for this procedure.

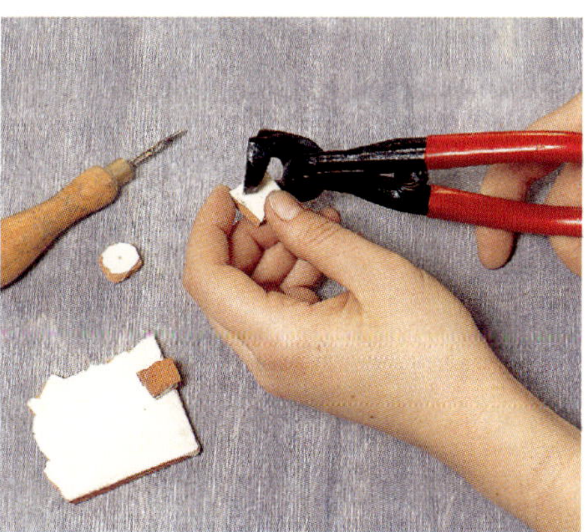

4 Select a suitable tile that has a soft base with a thin glaze, such as a Mexican tile. Using the tile nippers, nibble two circles for the eyes of the fish. Then use a bradawl or awl to carefully make a hole in the centre of each.

▶

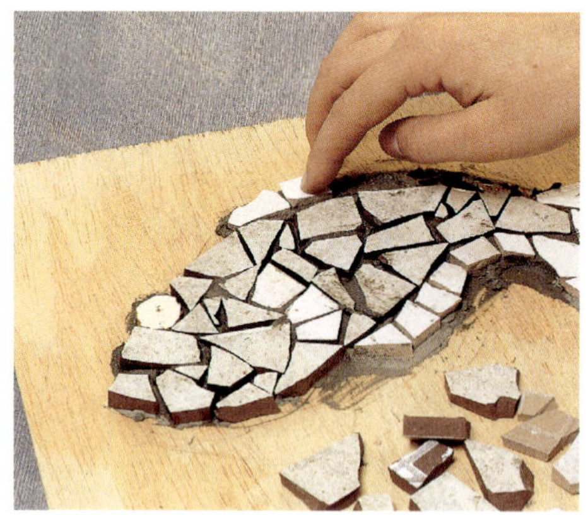

5 Spread some tile adhesive on to the base within the outlines of your drawing. Fix the tesserae within the drawn lines, using a lighter grey for the fins and tail and a darker grey for the body of the fish. Try to find tesserae in shapes that will fit within the drawing and suggest the movement of the fish. Use the pinkish tiles to fill in the starfish outline.

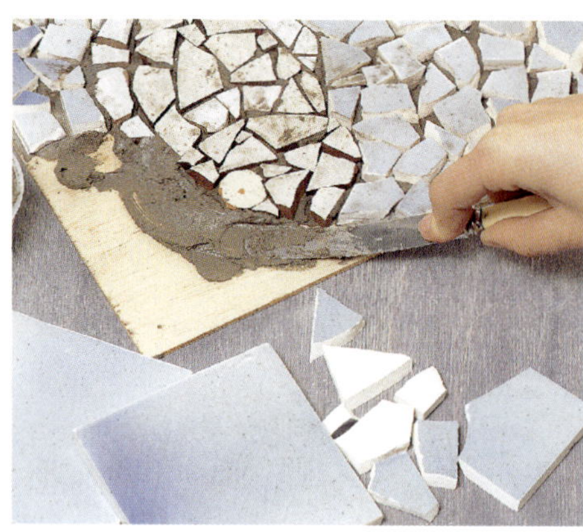

6 When the fish and starfish are complete, smash tiles of the background colour, in this case a soft blue. Spread some tile adhesive on to the base, a small area at a time. Press the background tesserae firmly into the adhesive. Be careful not to tile over the hanging holes in the corners.

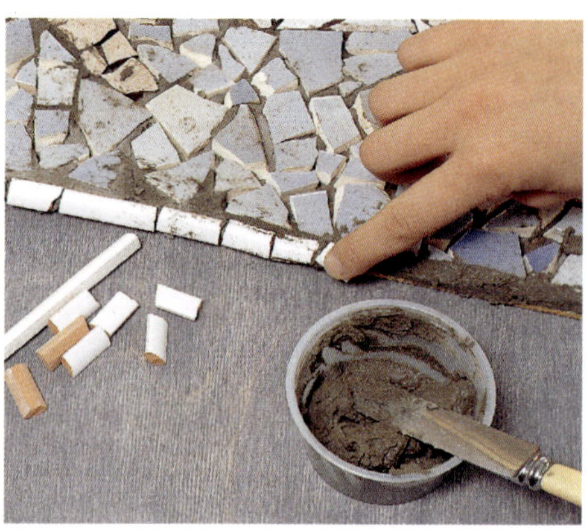

7 Cut thin edging tiles into short segments and fix them around the edge of the mosaic. Using tile nippers, cut the mirror into small pieces. Press these tesserae into the larger gaps in the design, on top of a blob of adhesive to keep them level with the other tesserae. Leave to dry for 24 hours.

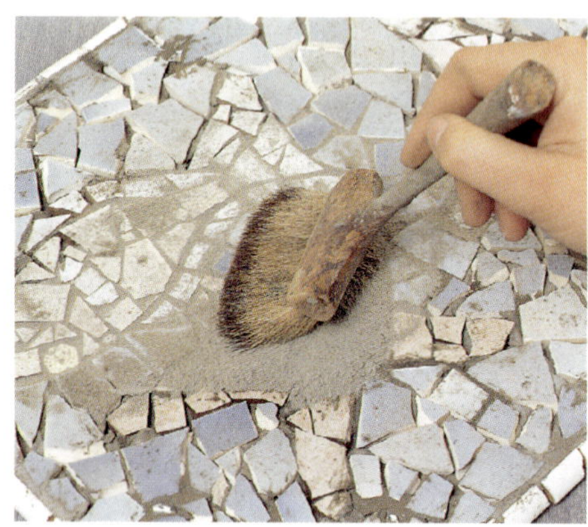

8 Spoon dry tile adhesive on to the surface of the splashback and brush it into the cracks using a soft brush. Avoid the area around the hanging holes. Spray the surface with plenty of water using a plant mister.

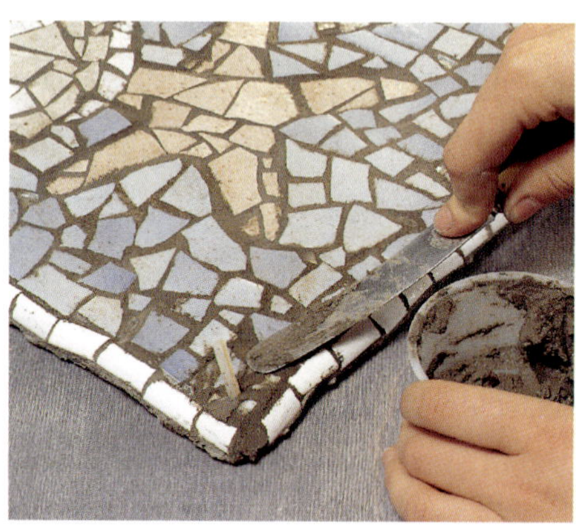

9 Cut a drinking straw into four pieces and stand one over the hole in each corner. Use some tile adhesive to grout around the straws. Leave to dry for 12 hours.

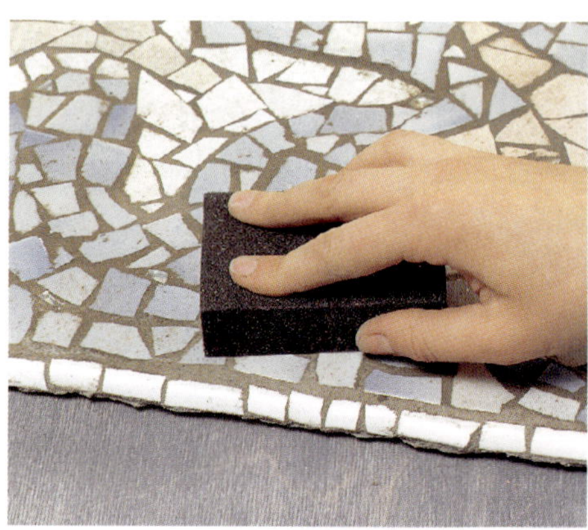

10 Remove the straws and sand off any adhesive remaining on the surface of the splashback, then polish with a dry, soft cloth. Place the splashback against the wall and mark the positions of the screw holes. Drill the holes and insert wall plugs (plastic anchors). Use mirror screws with domed heads to screw the splashback in position.

Storage of coats is always a problem, but if they have to be hung in a hall or room, a coat rack made of brightly coloured vitreous glass tiles will make this an interesting feature rather than a necessary evil.

Coat Rack

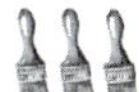

You will need

12mm (½in) thick MDF (medium-density fiberboard) or plywood sheet, cut to desired size
Pencil
Ruler
Jigsaw (saber saw)
Abrasive paper (sandpaper)
2 mirror plates
2 x 12mm (½in) screws
Screwdriver
3 coat hooks
Sharp knife
PVA (white) glue
Paintbrushes
Vitreous glass mosaic tiles: blue, yellow, green, red
Tile nippers
Tile grout
Rubber spreader
Soft cloths
Nailbrush

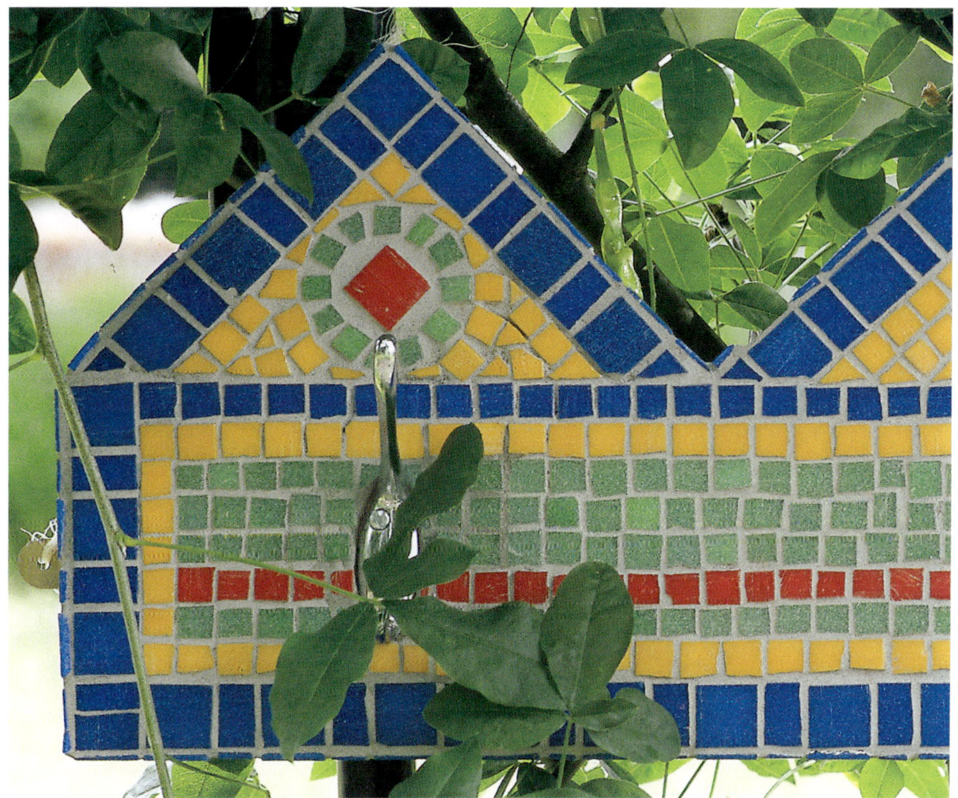

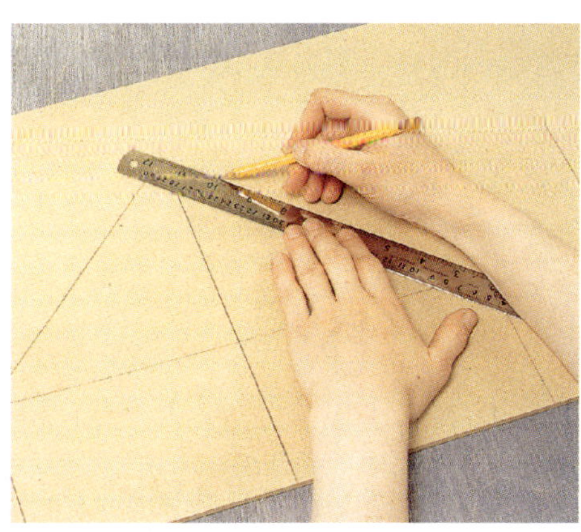

1 Draw the outline of the top on to the MDF (medium-density fiber-board) or plywood, using a pencil and ruler to make sure the proportions of the three triangles are correct. Cut around the outline using a jigsaw (saber saw). Sand down any rough edges.

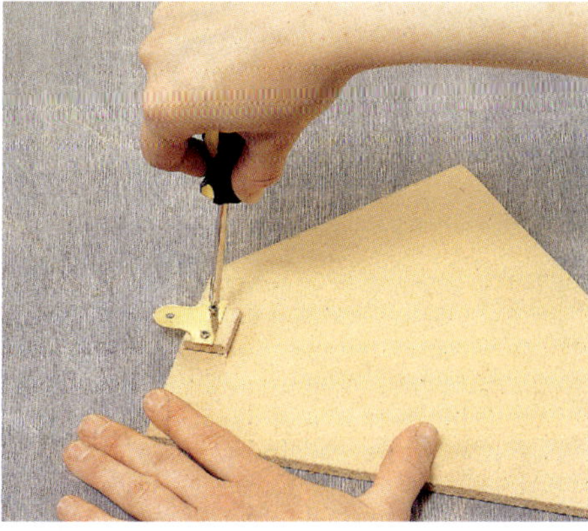

2 Attach two mirror plates to the back of the base, one at each end. Make sure the hanging screw holes stick out far enough from the sides of the base, so that when the sides are tiled with the tesserae the holes will remain uncovered.

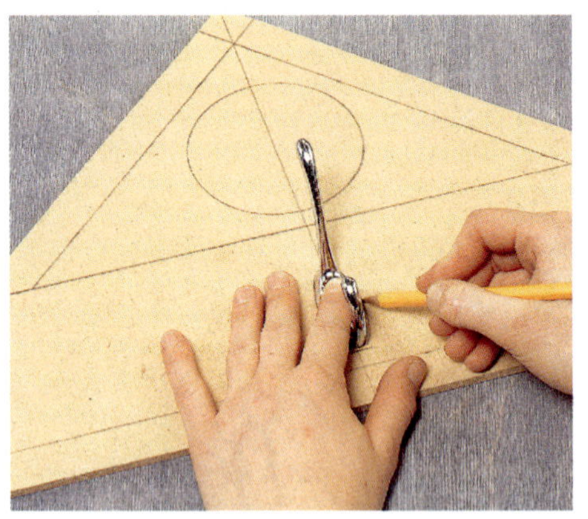

3 Draw the mosaic design on the surface of the base. Place the coat hooks in position and draw around them.

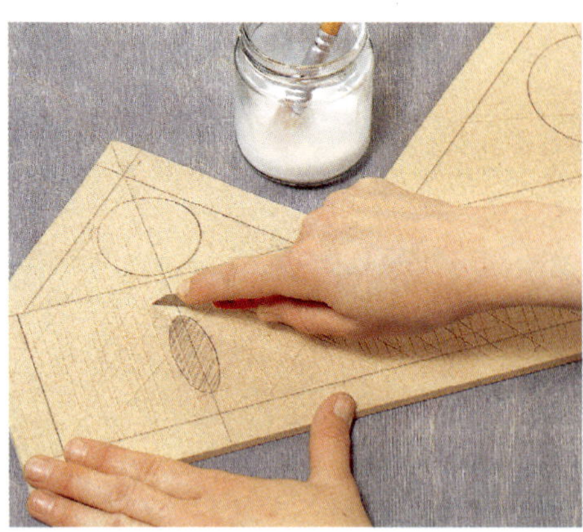

4 Score the base with a sharp knife and prime the front, back and sides with diluted PVA (white) glue.

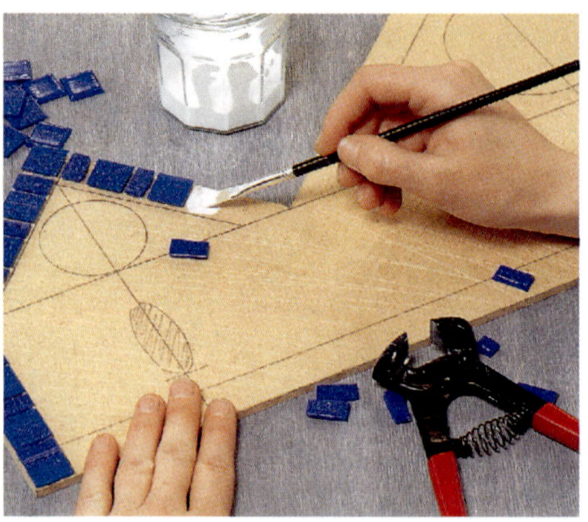

5 Cut some blue vitreous glass tiles in half with tile nippers. Fix these half tiles alternated with whole tiles all around the edge of the base with PVA glue applied carefully with a fine paintbrush.

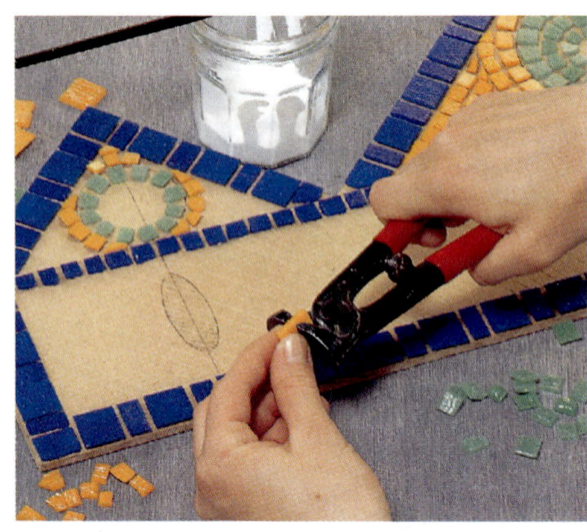

6 Stick tesserae to the areas between the main outlines in the other colours. Cover the entire surface, except for the areas where the hooks will be screwed in. Cut more blue tiles in half and carefully stick them along the sides of the base. Leave to dry for 24 hours.

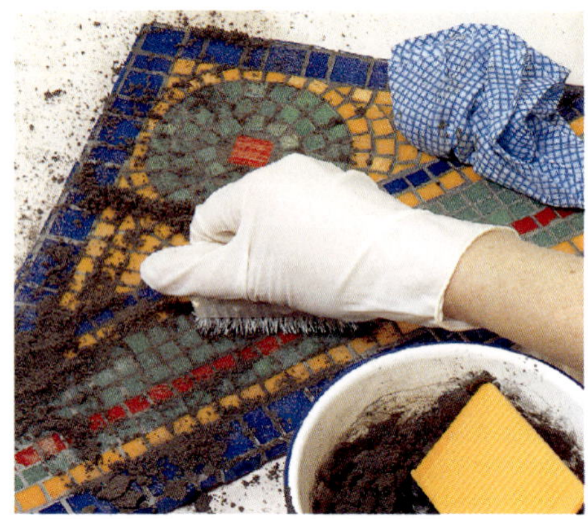

7 Using a rubber spreader, spread tile grout over the surface of the mosaic, pushing it into the gaps between the tesserae. Wipe off the excess grout with a damp cloth and leave for about 10 minutes, so that the surface dries. Then use a nailbrush to scrub off any grout that has dried on the surface of the mosaic. Leave to dry for 24 hours.

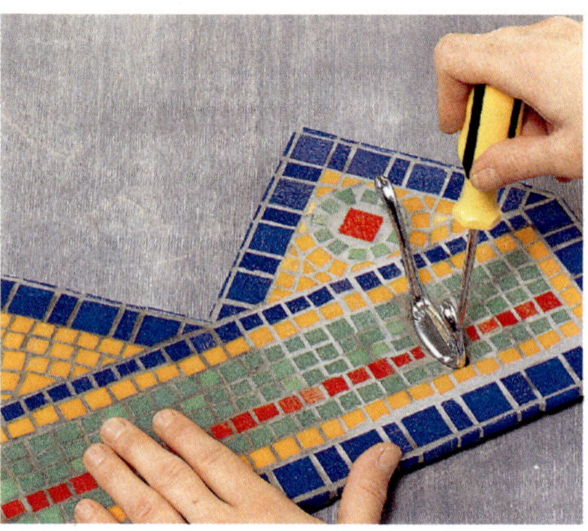

8 Sand off any remaining grout on the surface of the mosaic, then polish with a dry, soft cloth. Screw the coat hooks into position, and hang in place.

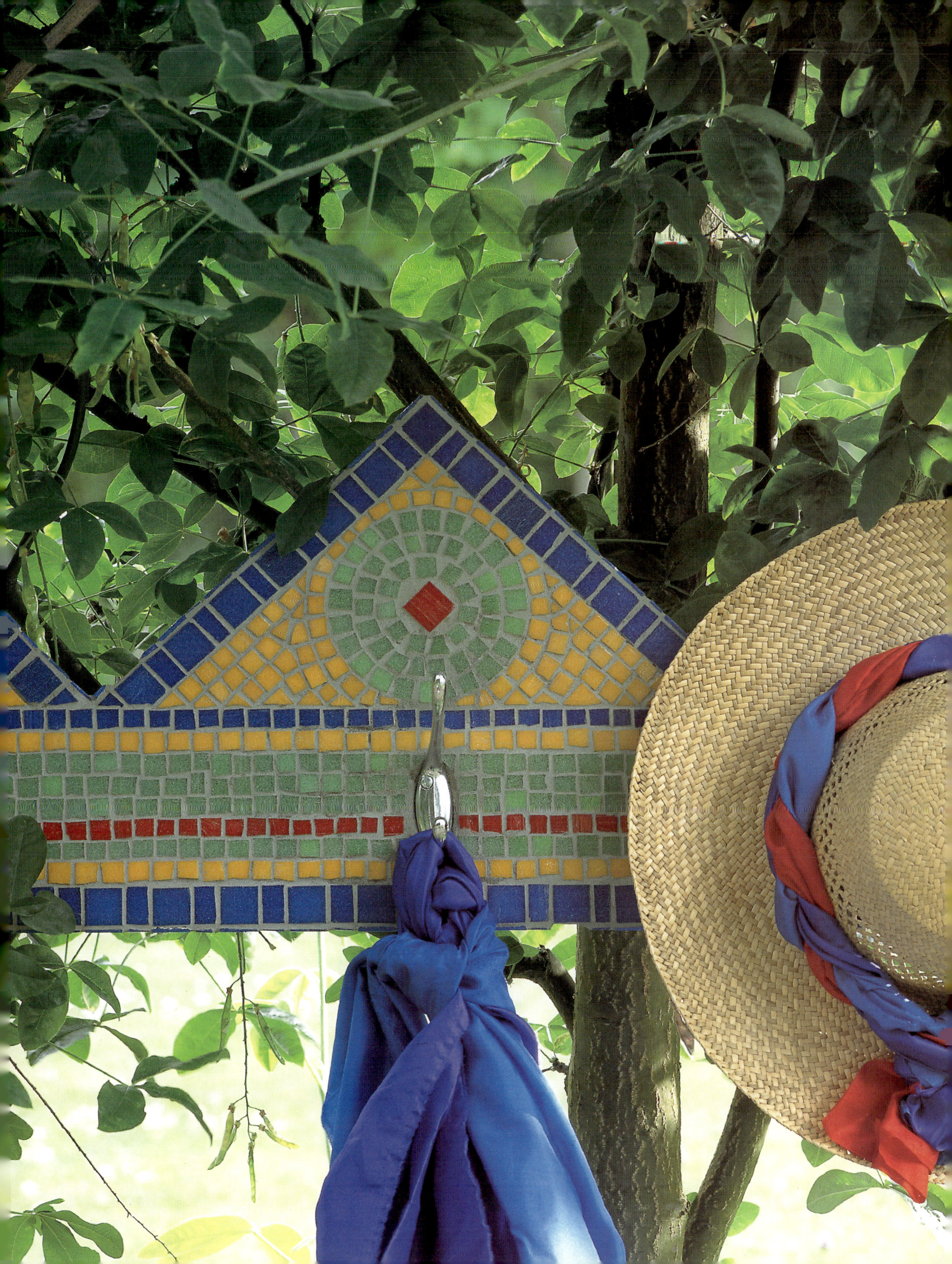

This hearth mosaic has a simple, contemporary feel with a strong use of colour, bringing a new lease of life to this old fireplace. It has been laid using a semi-indirect technique to ensure a smooth finish.

Mosaic Hearth

You will need

Chisel
Hammer
Brown paper
Craft (utility) knife
Scissors
PVA (white) glue
Sponge
Wooden board
Adhesive tape
Pencil
Ruler
Vitreous glass mosaic tiles: dark purple, light purple, and contrasting colours for the border infill
Tile nippers
Matt (flat) cream porcelain tiles
Paintbrush
Tile adhesive
Notched trowel and bucket
Wire (steel) wool
Screwdriver
Tile grout
Abrasive paper (sandpaper)
Soft cloth

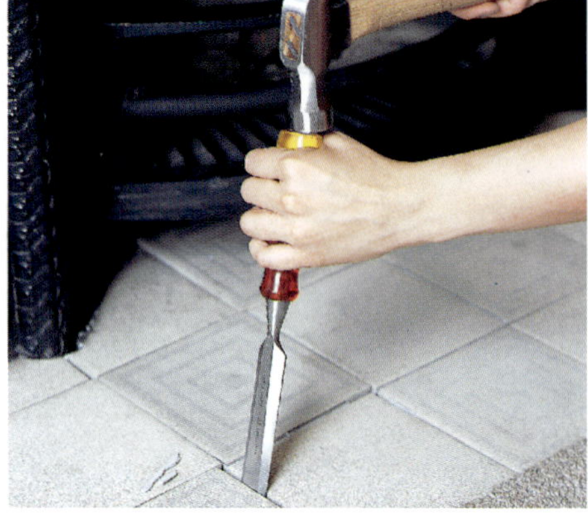

1 Using a chisel and hammer, remove any old tiles from the fireplace.

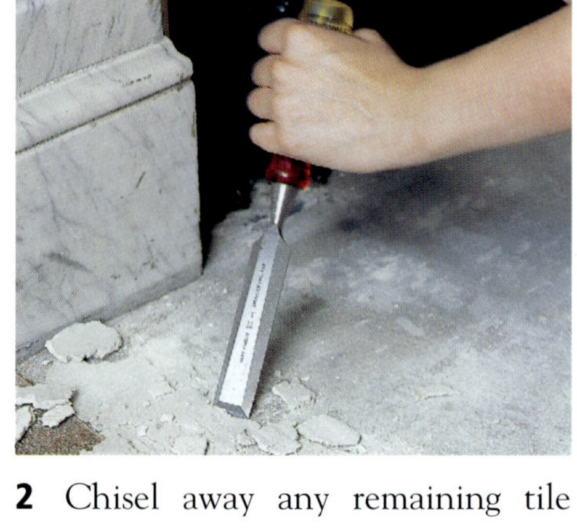

2 Chisel away any remaining tile adhesive. It is essential to have a very smooth surface on which to lay the mosaic if you are to get a good result.

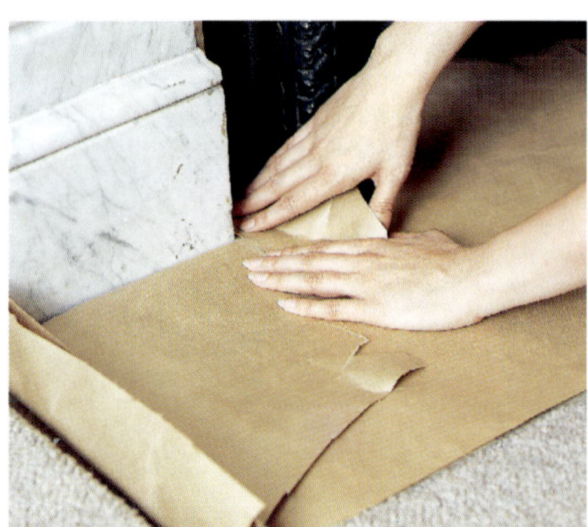

3 To make a template, take a piece of brown paper, larger than the area to be mosaiced, and fold over the edges to fit the space exactly. It can be tricky around the more detailed areas. Using a craft (utility) knife and scissors, cut out the shape accurately. Check it by placing it back into the hearth.

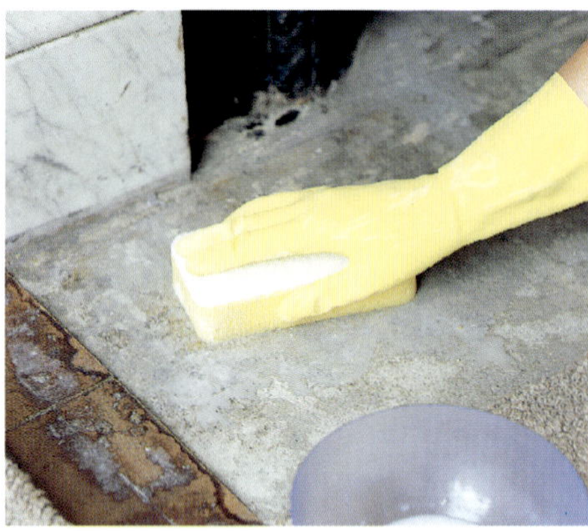

4 Brush away any loose debris from the fireplace. Seal the concrete by sponging some diluted PVA (white) glue all over it. Allow to dry.

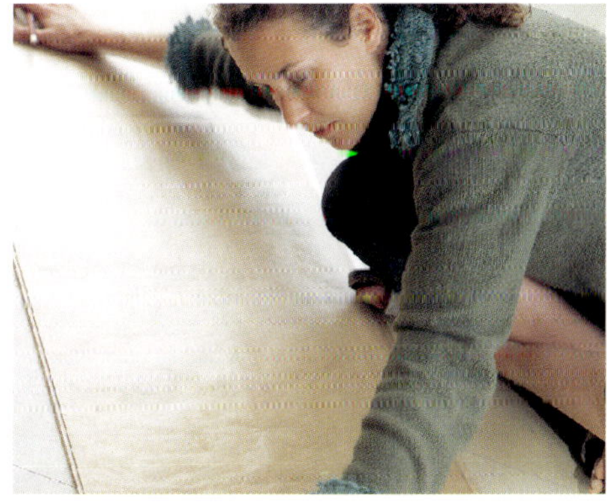

5 This technique works in reverse, so turn the template upside down. Place the template on a piece of wooden board and stick it down with adhesive tape to ensure that the paper does not move around.

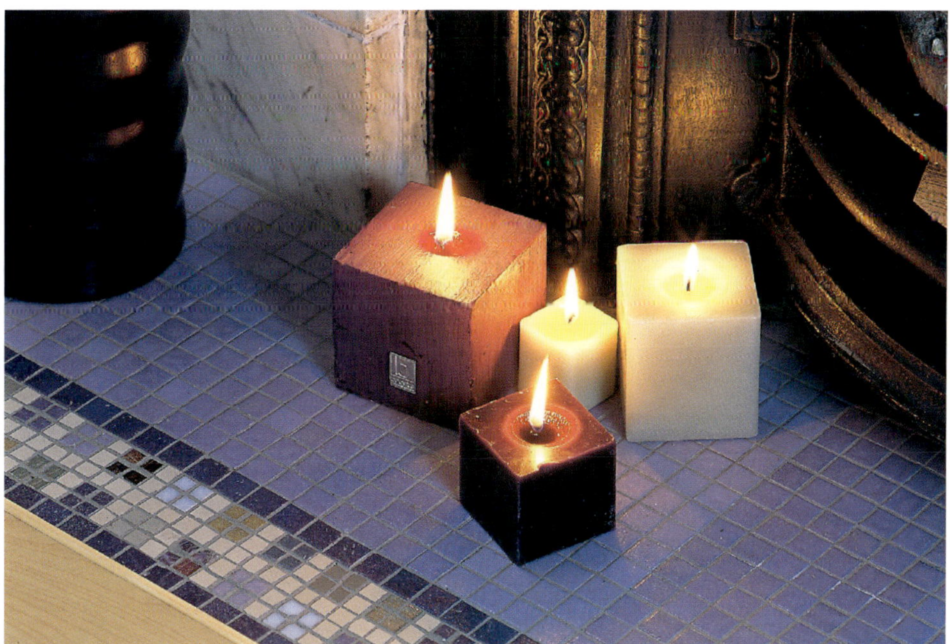

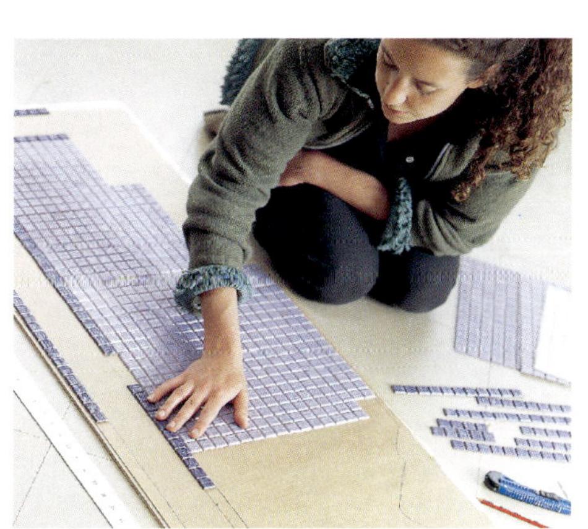

6 Mark the base line of the border edging at 2mm (1/16in) in from the edge (this allows a margin of error when fitting). Measuring from this line, mark three more lines: one at 2cm (3/4in), the second at 7cm (2¾in) and the third at 9cm (3½in). Stick strips of dark purple border tiles with PVA glue along the two narrow bands, paper side down, leaving a 5cm (2in) gap for the detail (see step 7). The bulk of the design is made up of sheets of pale purple vitreous glass, cut with a craft knife and laid in position, paper side down. Fill as much of the space as possible with whole tiles. Clip tiles to fit any gaps left at the back and sides of the mosaic, and stick them in place later.

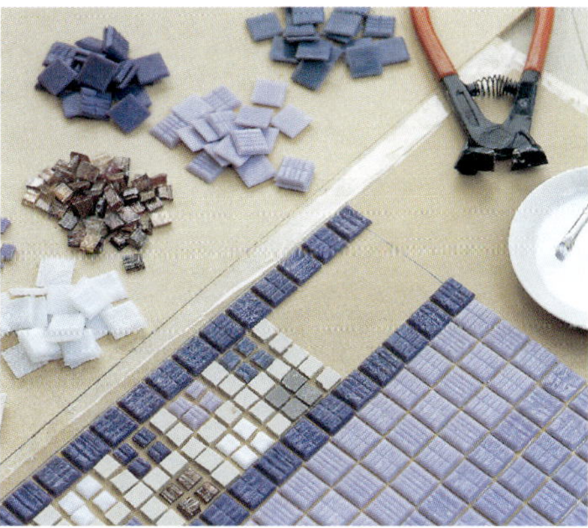

7 The detail of the border is made from matt (flat) cream porcelain tiles clipped into quarters with the tile nippers. Position these in a central line that runs between and parallel to the two strips of dark purple vitreous glass. Take care that the lines meet neatly at their corners. Then, starting in one corner, make a grid with cut quarters of cream tile at 2.5cm (1in) intervals inside the two dark purple bands. Fill in the gaps with a variety of colours from the vitreous glass range, clipped into quarters. To ensure the correct spacing, lay the tiles down before you stick them in position. Adjust the spacing so that the uniformed design works, taking particular care in the corners.

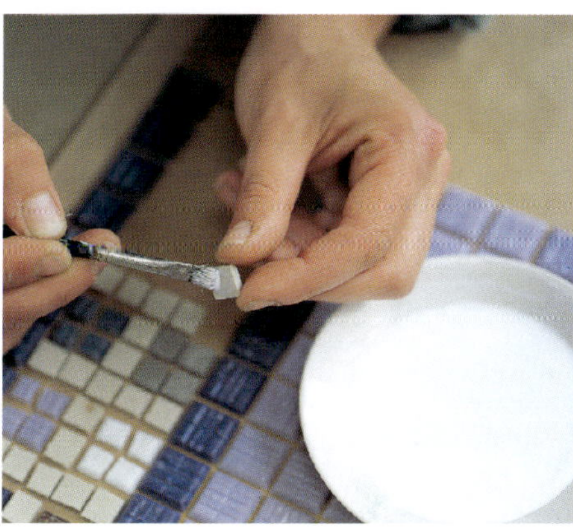

8 Using a small paintbrush, apply PVA glue to the front of the small tiles, and stick them on to the paper.

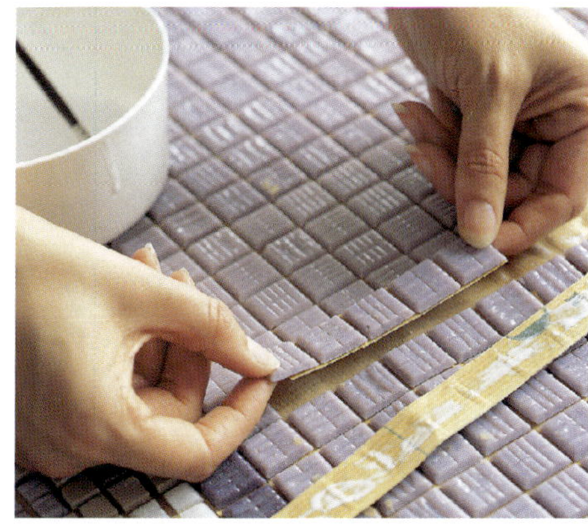

9 Apply PVA glue to the paper backing on the light purple tiles and stick them in position on the brown paper, filling in the gaps with the clipped tiles. Leave to dry for several hours. ▶

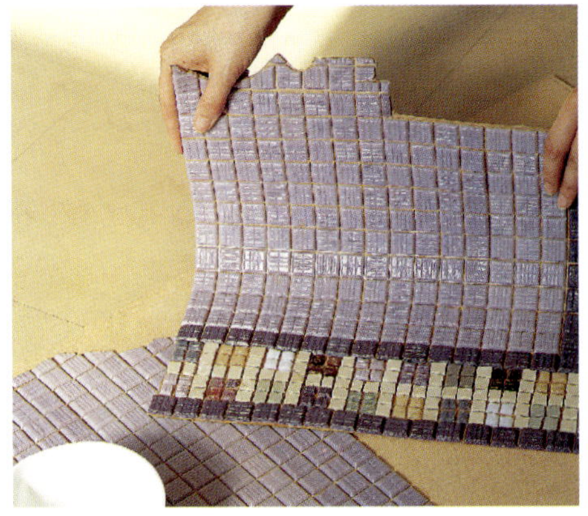

10 Cut up the mosaic into manageable pieces. Lift them up, shaking gently to remove tile fragments and any loose tiles. Stick these back in place.

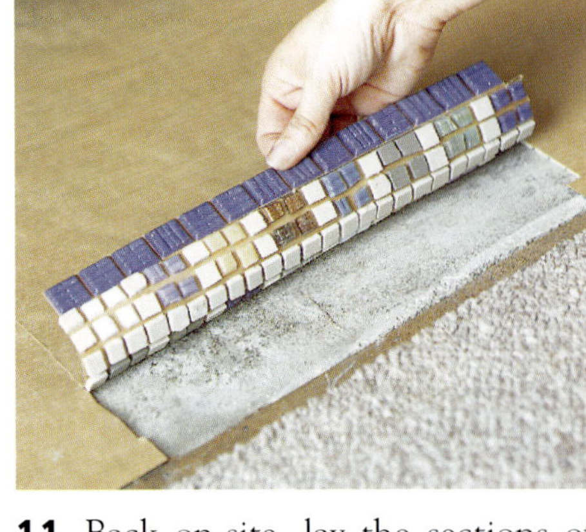

11 Back on-site, lay the sections of the mosaic, tile-side down. It should fit, and all you will see is brown paper.

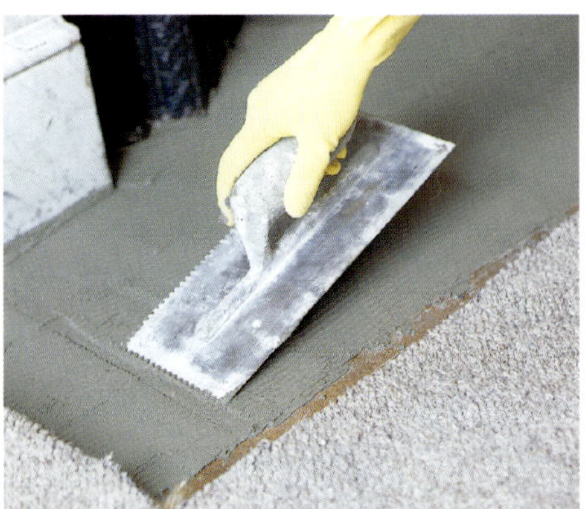

12 Lay the sheets carefully to one side, so that the order in which they need to be laid is obvious. Apply some grey tile adhesive to the concrete surface with a notched trowel, ensuring you lay a good even bed. Carefully lay down the sheets, tile-side down. Once you are happy with the positioning of the sheets, press them into the adhesive and rub over the surface with a damp sponge. Leave to dry for 24 hours.

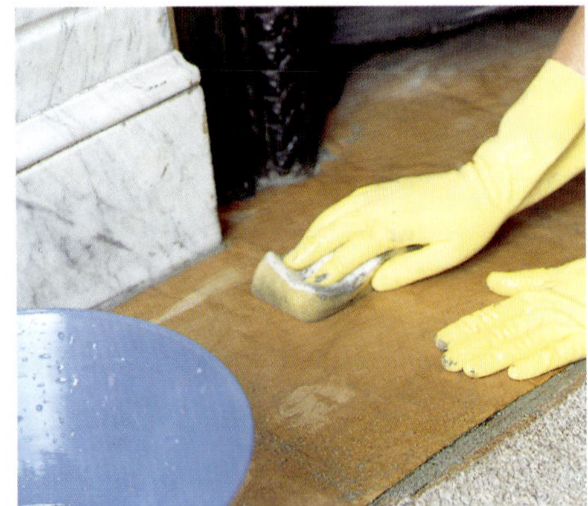

13 Fill a bucket with warm water and dampen the brown paper with a wet sponge. Leave for 5 minutes, then dampen again.

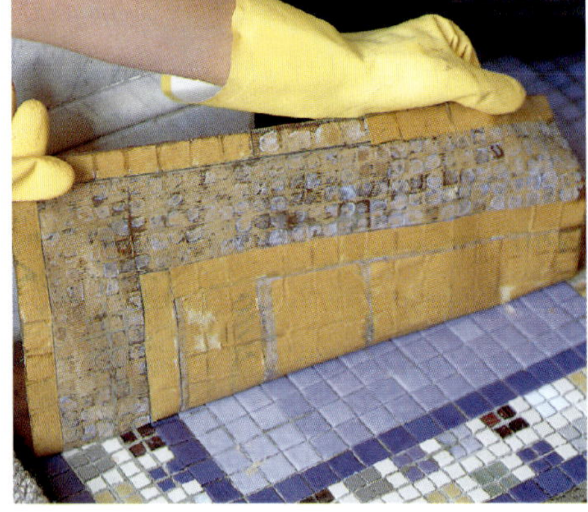

14 When the paper is ready it should peel off easily. Some bits will stick, but these can be cleaned off with wire (steel) wool. Wash the mosaic and glue back any pieces that have come loose.

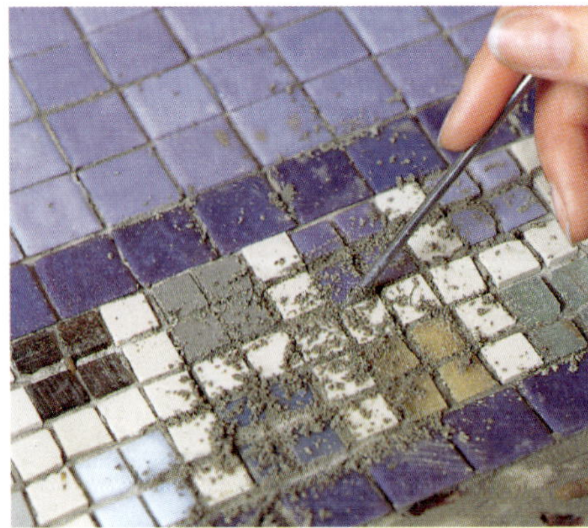

15 There is a tendency with this technique for adhesive to squeeze up between the gaps, and it tends to be a different colour from the grout. Clear this excess away with a screwdriver.

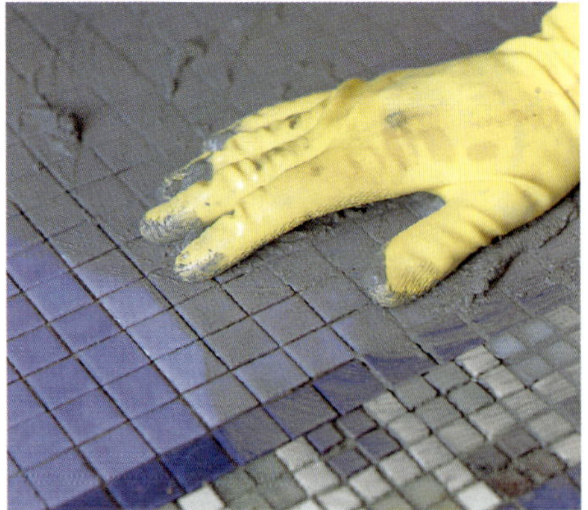

16 Grout the mosaic with a grey tile grout. Remove any excess grout with a damp sponge, then leave it to dry. Sand off any dried-on grout, then polish with a dry, soft cloth.

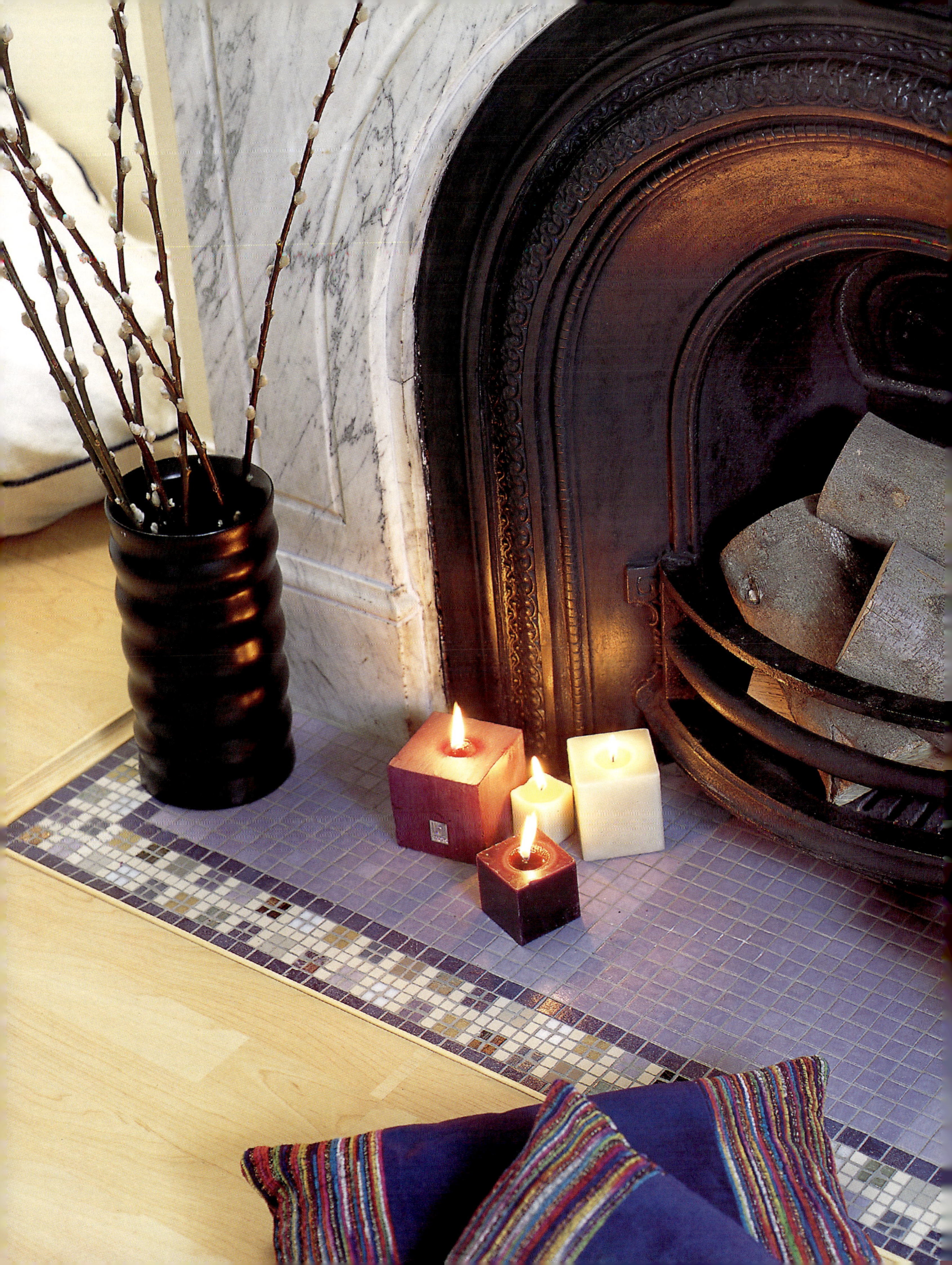

This decorative work is made with handpainted Mexican tiles, which are widely available. The blue-and-white patterned tesserae make a lively background, and the tree trunk is simply the back of the tiles.

Tree of Life Wall Panel

You will need

2cm (¾in) thick plywood sheet, cut to the size required (adjust your measurements to fit a row of whole border tiles in each direction)
Pencil
Drill and rebate (rabbet) bit
Mirror plate, with keyhole opening
Screwdriver
2 x 12mm (½in) screws
PVA (white) glue
Paintbrush
Bradawl or awl
Small handpainted glazed ceramic tiles, for the border
Tape measure
Soft dark pencil
Blue-and-white handpainted glazed ceramic tiles
Plain glazed ceramic household tiles: green, brown and beige
Tile nippers
Tile adhesive
Soft brush
Plant mister
Sponge
Soft cloth

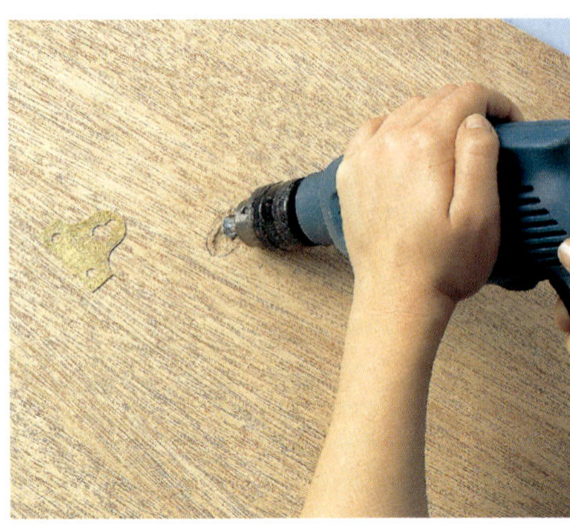

1 On the back of the plywood, mark a point halfway across the width and a third from the top. Drill a rebate (rabbet) to fit under the keyhole of the mirror plate. Screw the plate in place and prime both sides and the edge of the board with diluted PVA (white) glue. Leave to dry, then score the front with a bradawl or awl.

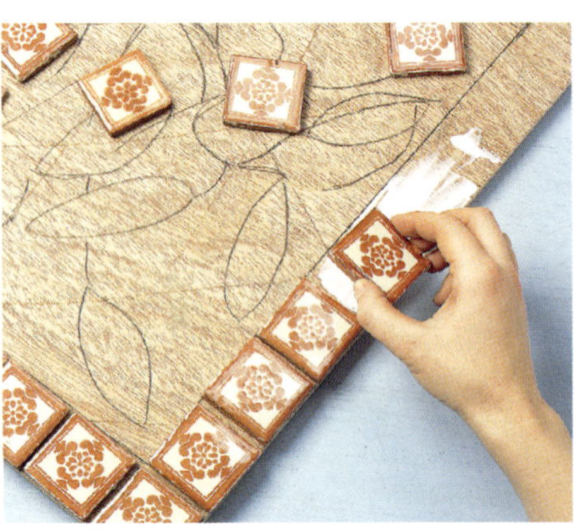

2 Measure the border tiles and draw a frame to match this size on the front of the board. Draw a simple tree in the centre. Cover the border of the board with PVA glue and stick the border tiles in position, placing them closely together and following the frame line.

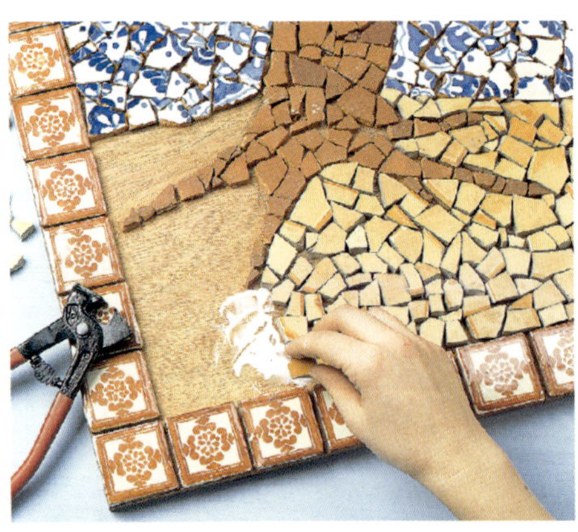

3 Use tile nippers to cut the blue-and-white tiles into small, irregular shapes. Glue into place for the sky. Cut brown tiles for the trunk; glue them face down on the board and prime with diluted glue. Cut and glue tiles for the leaves and earth. Leave to dry overnight.

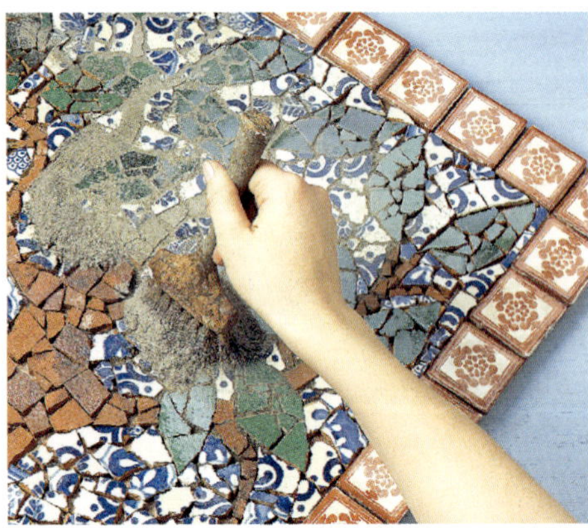

4 Brush dry tile adhesive over the panel, filling all the gaps. Spray with water until saturated. When dry, repeat if necessary, then rub adhesive into the crevices, wiping off the excess with a damp sponge. Dry overnight, then polish with a dry, soft cloth.

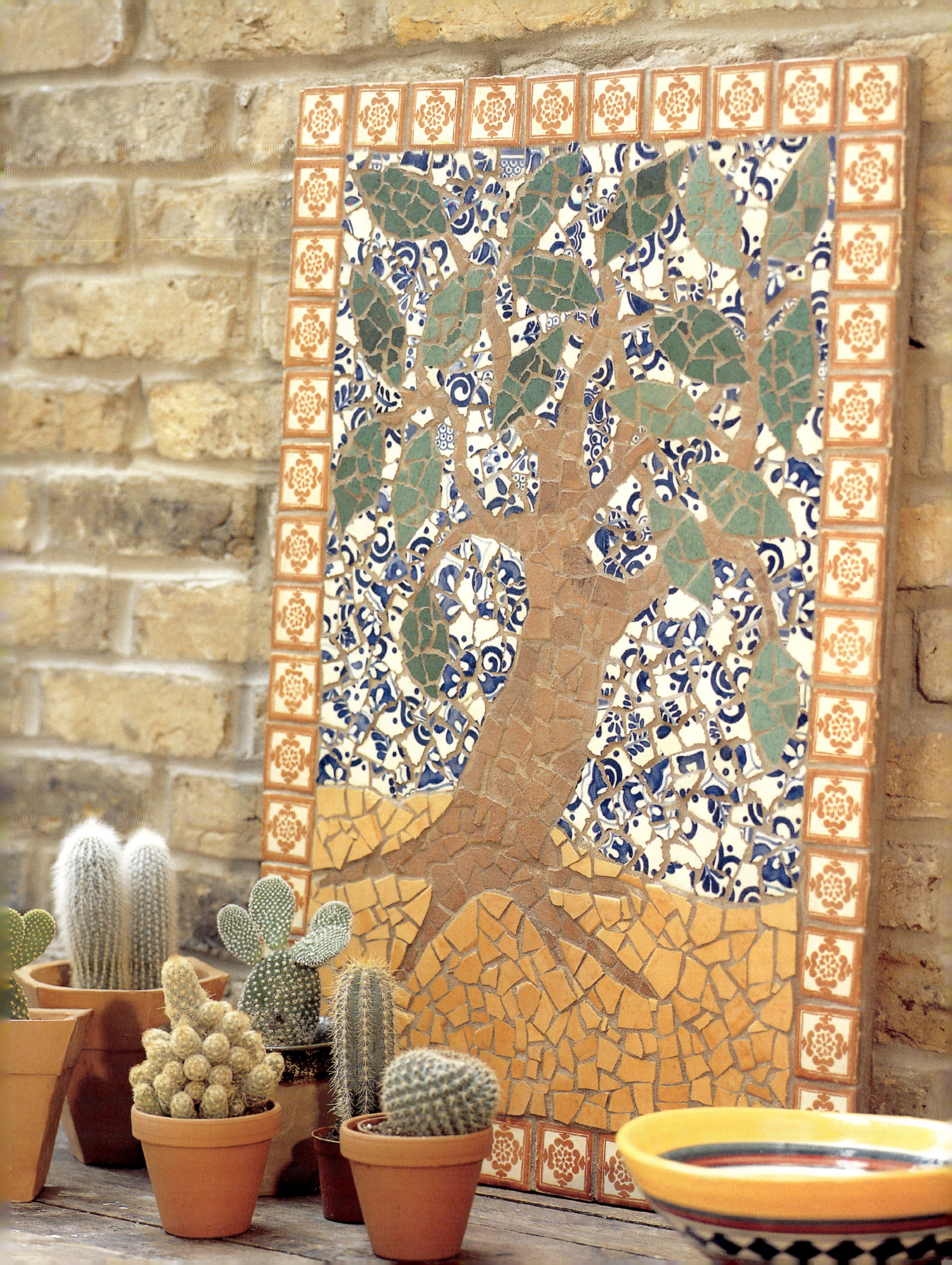

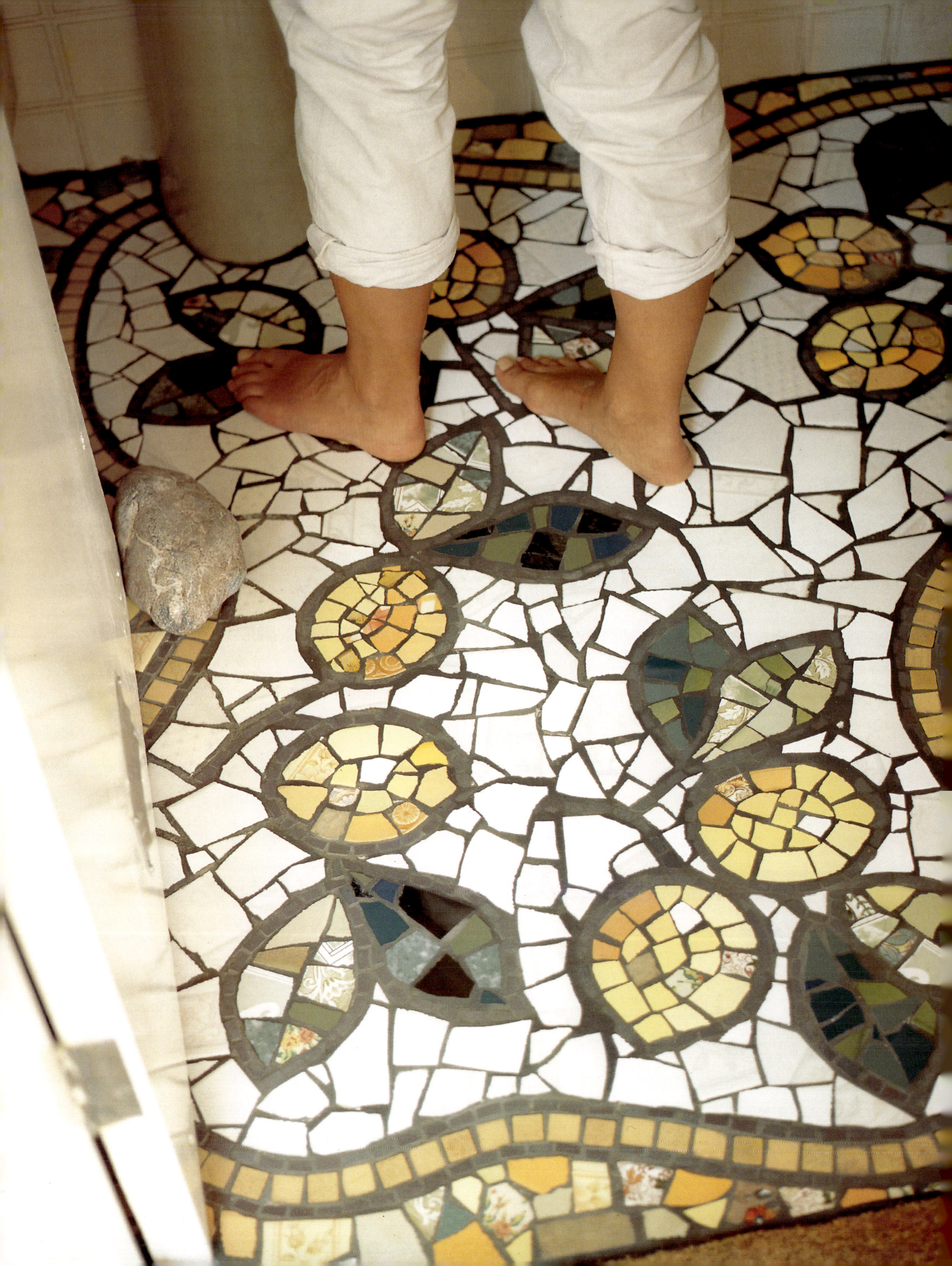

This lovely design is inspired by the cool tiled floors in Mediterranean countries. The finished mosaic is covered with a sheet of sticky back plastic and lowered on to the floor in sections.

Lemon Tree Floor

You will need

Pencil
Coloured paper
Scissors
Large sheet of white paper
Black felt-tipped pen
Glazed ceramic household tiles: various shades of yellow, green and grey, and white
Tile cutter
Tile nippers
Old plain and patterned china
Black ceramic mosaic tiles
White glazed ceramic tiles
Large sheet of sticky back plastic (contact paper)
Craft (utility) knife
Tile adhesive
Notched and rubber spreaders
Sponge
Soft cloth

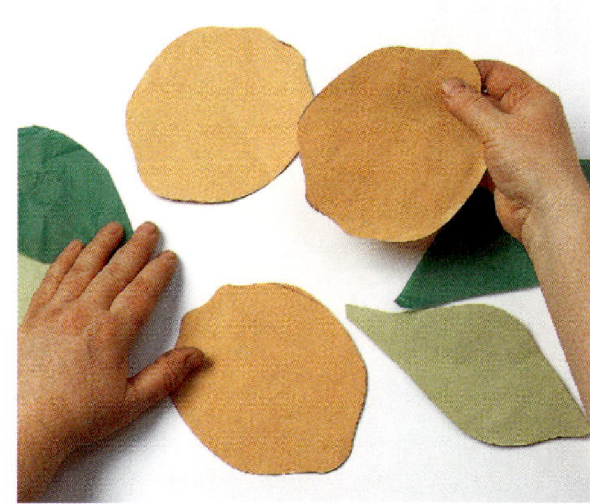

1 Draw sufficient lemon and leaf shapes on sheets of different coloured papers to cover the area of floor you wish to mosaic.

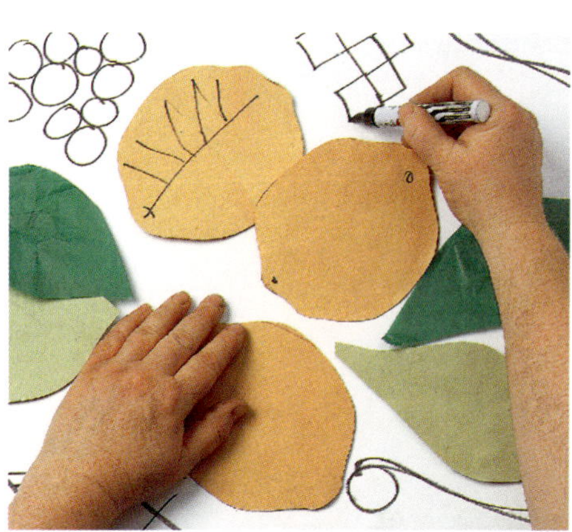

2 Cut the leaves and lemons out and arrange them on the large sheet of white paper. When you are happy with the design, draw in details such as stems and a decorative border around the edge of the design, using a felt-tipped pen.

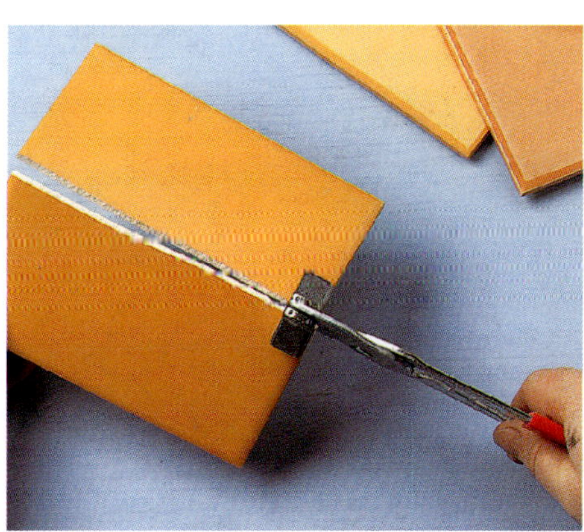

3 Using a tile cutter, score all the coloured ceramic household tiles down the centre. You may need to practise on some spares to get a straight line. Break each tile into neat halves by applying equal pressure on either side of the scored line with the tile cutter. This will result in a clean break.

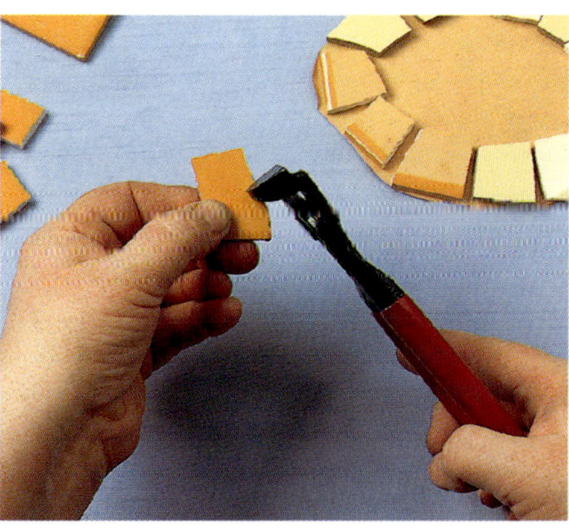

4 Using tile nippers, cut these tile pieces into small, equal-size tesserae. Cut up the china in the same way. Also cut up some of the black mosaic tiles, enough to outline each lemon, again into equal-size pieces.

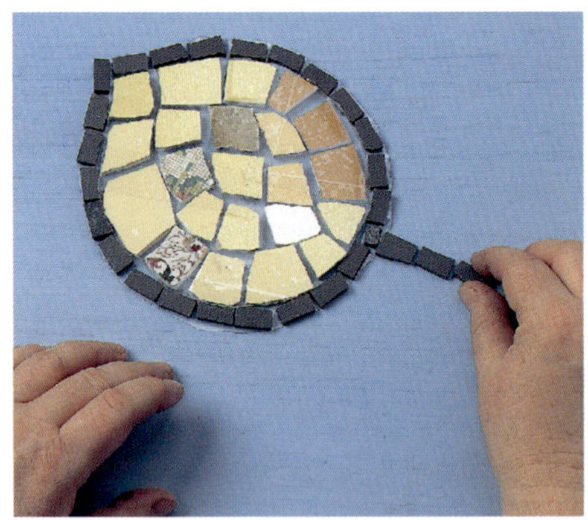

5 Following your paper design, arrange the pieces on a flat surface. To make the lemons appear three-dimensional, place the darker shades on one side. Outline each shape with black mosaic tiles and extend to make a stem.

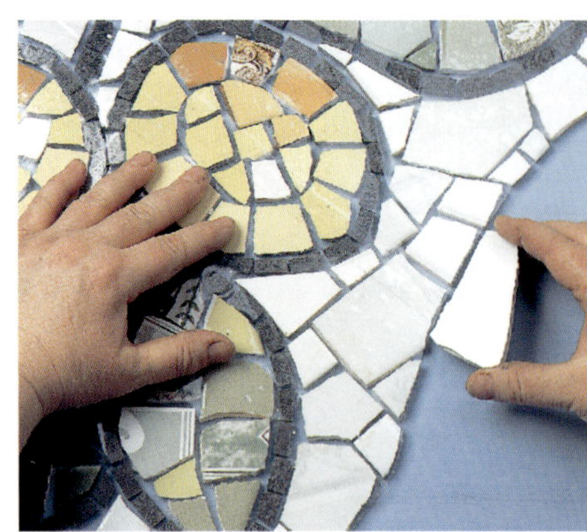

6 Using tile nippers, cut the white glazed tiles into random shapes. Fill in the background with a mosaic of large and small pieces. When a section is complete, hold the pieces together with a sheet of sticky back plastic.

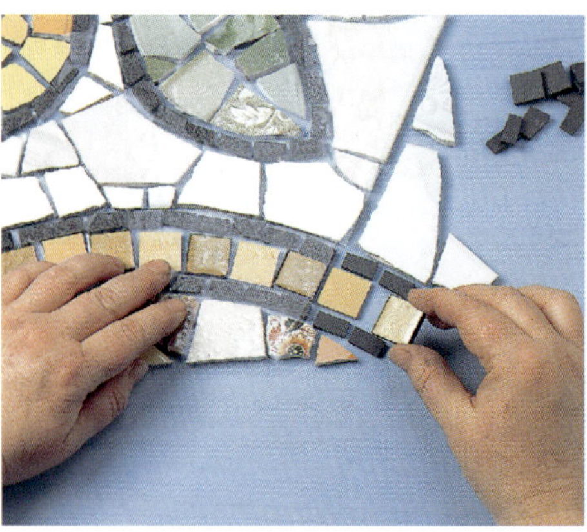

7 Finish with a border. This undulating border is made of square, yellow-toned tesserae, outlined with rectangular black tiles.

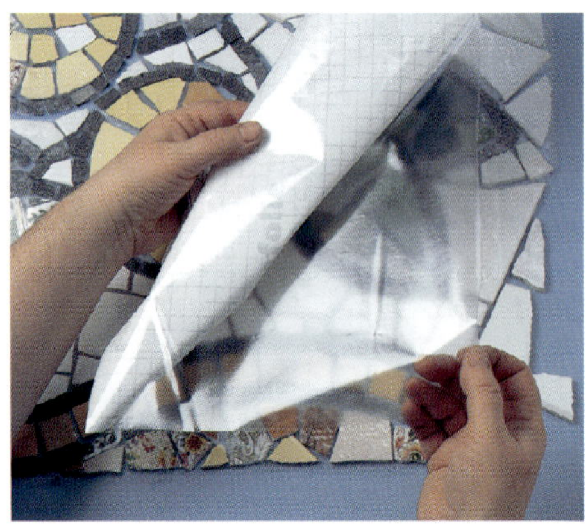

8 Peel the backing paper off the sticky back plastic (contact paper) and lay it carefully over the loose mosaic. You may have to work in sections.

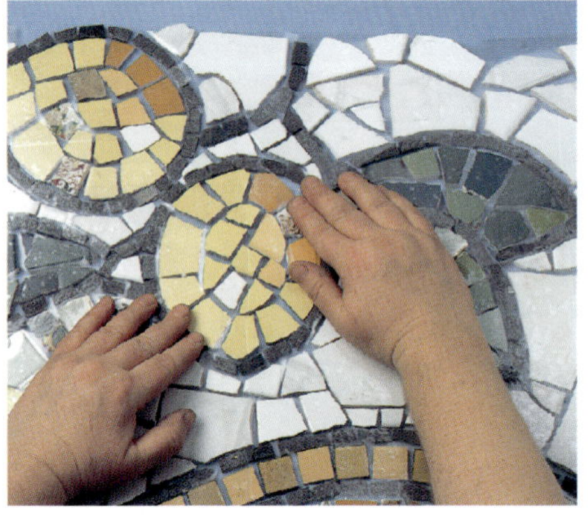

9 Smooth your hands over the plastic to make sure it has adhered to all the tesserae and that any air bubbles are eliminated.

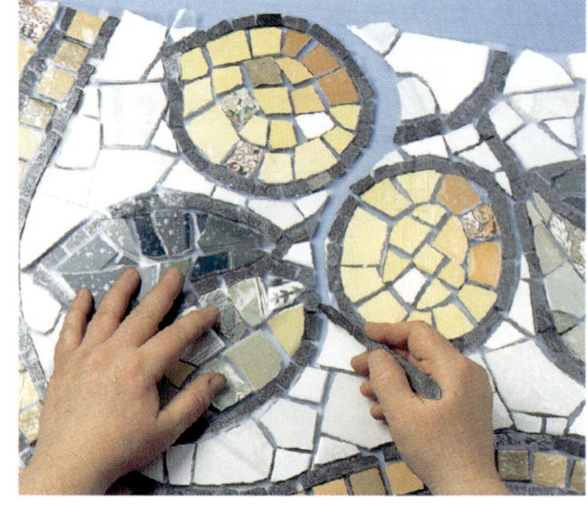

10 Using a craft (utility) knife, cut through the plastic to separate the mosaic into manageable sections.

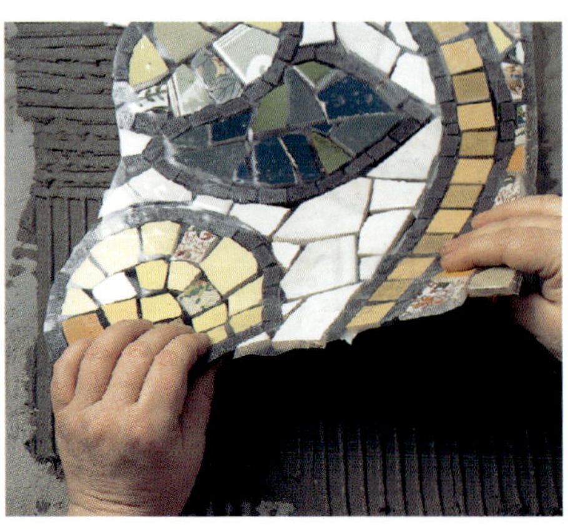

11 Spread tile adhesive over the floor area, using a notched spreader. Lower the mosaic carefully into the tile adhesive, section by section. Press down and leave to dry overnight. Peel off the plastic then grout the mosaic with more tile adhesive. Wipe off any excess adhesive with a damp sponge, leave to to dry, then polish with a dry, soft cloth.

Gardens offer mosaic artists the opportunity to experiment with more playful wall mosaics. This rather tongue-in-cheek princess design uses tesserae of vitreous glass in vibrant colours that will not fade.

Princess Wall Mosaic

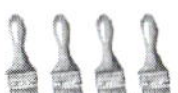

You will need

- Brown paper
- Pencil
- Tracing paper
- Scissors
- Vitreous glass mosaic tiles in various colours: pink, gold, blue and red
- Tile nippers
- PVA (white) glue
- Mirror
- Large wooden board
- Tile adhesive
- Notched trowel
- Grout spreader
- Sponge
- Abrasive paper (sandpaper)
- Dilute hydrochloric acid, goggles and rubber (latex) gloves (optional)
- Soft cloth

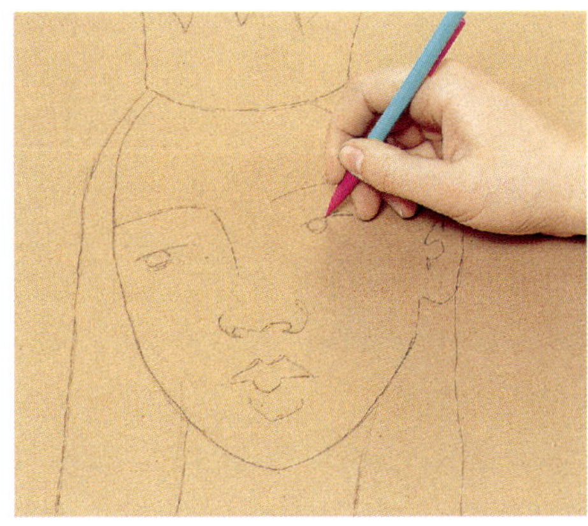

1 Draw a simple design for a princess on brown paper. Remember that this reverse method means that your mosaic will be worked in reverse, so plan your picture accordingly.

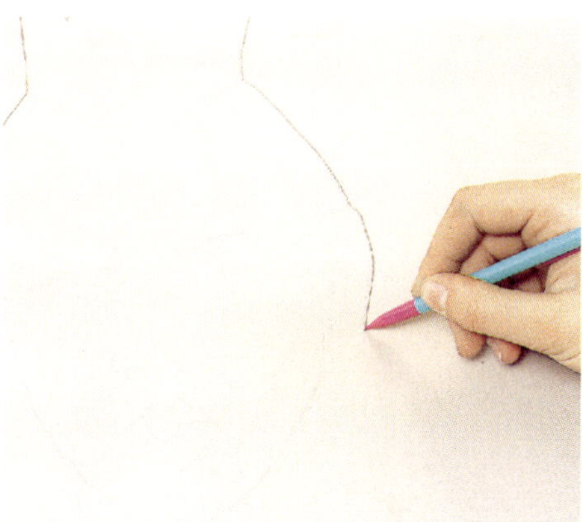

2 Make a tracing of the outline of your drawing and cut this out. You will use this later as a template to mark the area of the wall to be covered with tile adhesive.

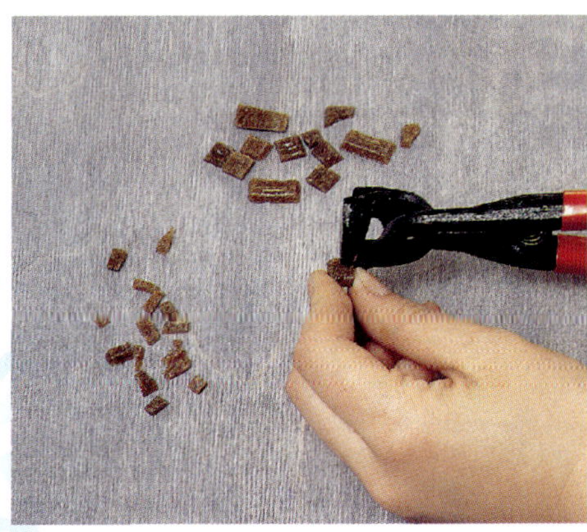

3 Using tile nippers, cut vitreous glass mosaic tiles in the chosen outlining colour into eighths.

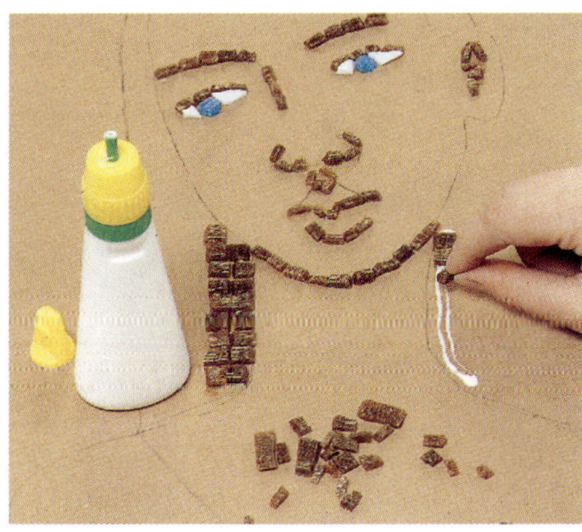

4 Stick these tesserae face down on to the main lines of your drawing using PVA (white) glue. Stick down any key features, such as the eyes and lips, in contrasting colours.

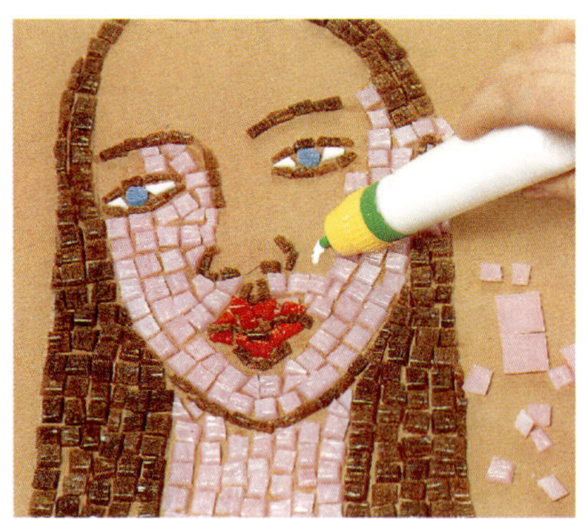

5 Cut pink vitreous glass tiles into quarters. Glue these face down to fill in the areas of skin between the outlines.

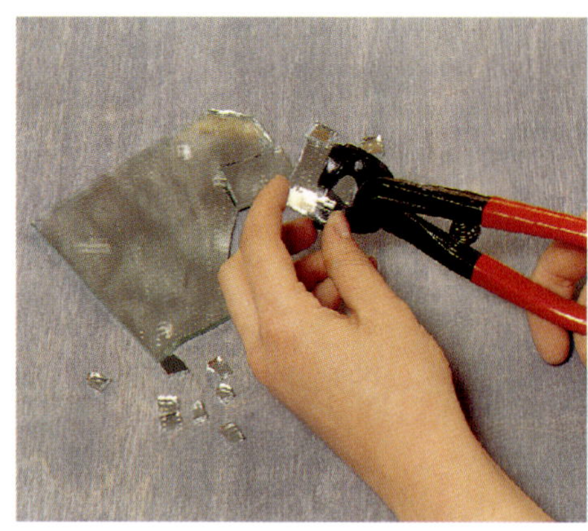

6 Cut the mirror into small pieces about the same size as the quartered vitreous glass tesserae.

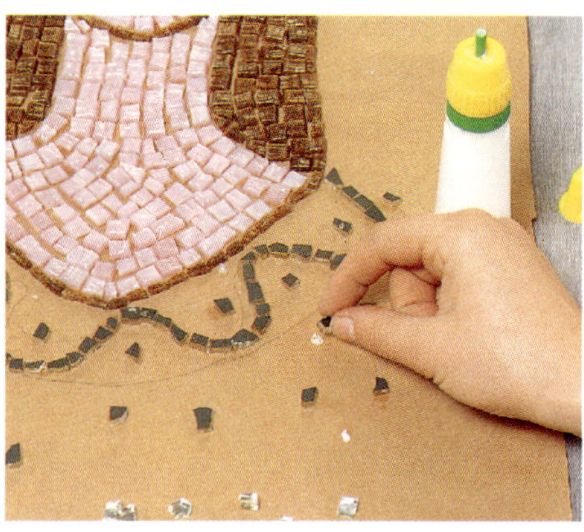

7 Stick the pieces of mirror face down on to the dress and in the crown.

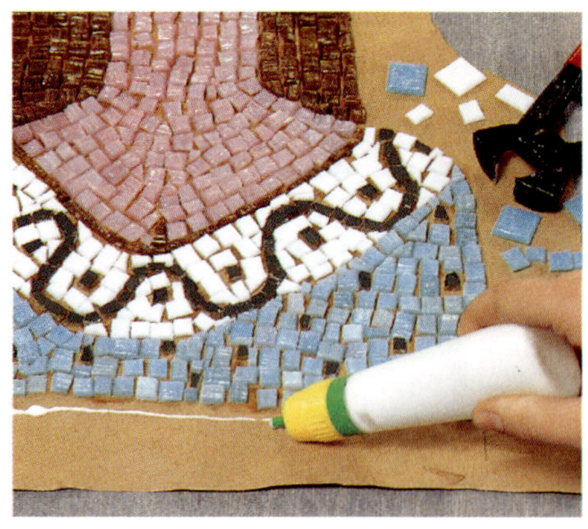

8 Cut the tiles for the dress and the crown into quarters and glue them face down between the pieces of mirror. Leave the paper-backed mosaic to dry securely in position.

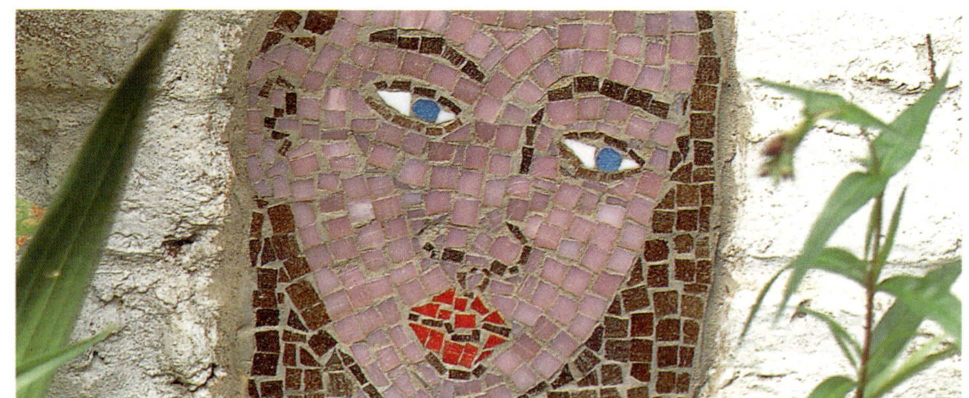

9 Transfer the mosaic to its final location, carrying it on a large wooden board to prevent any tesserae coming loose. Draw around the tracing paper template on the wall or floor. Spread tile adhesive over this area using a notched trowel, then press the mosaic into it, paper side up. Leave to dry for about 2 hours, then dampen the paper with a sponge and gently peel it away. Leave to dry overnight.

10 Grout the mosaic with more tile adhesive, using a grout spreader. Clean off any excess adhesive with a damp sponge and leave the mosaic to dry overnight. Remove any remaining cement with abrasive paper (sandpaper). Alternatively, dilute hydrochloric acid can be used, but you must wear goggles and rubber (latex) gloves and apply it outside or where there is good ventilation. Wash any acid residue from the surface with plenty of water. Finish by polishing the mosaic with a dry, soft cloth.

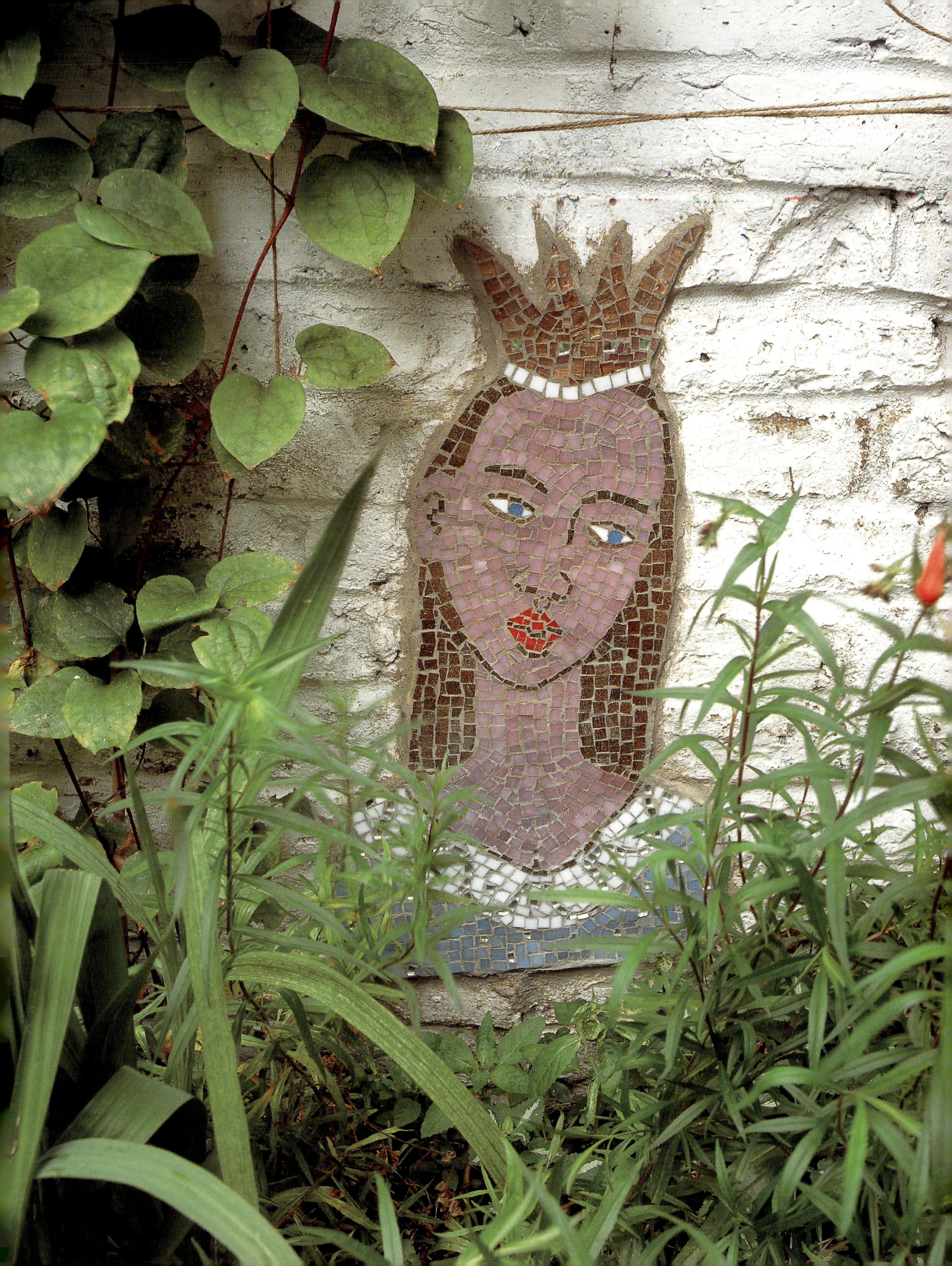

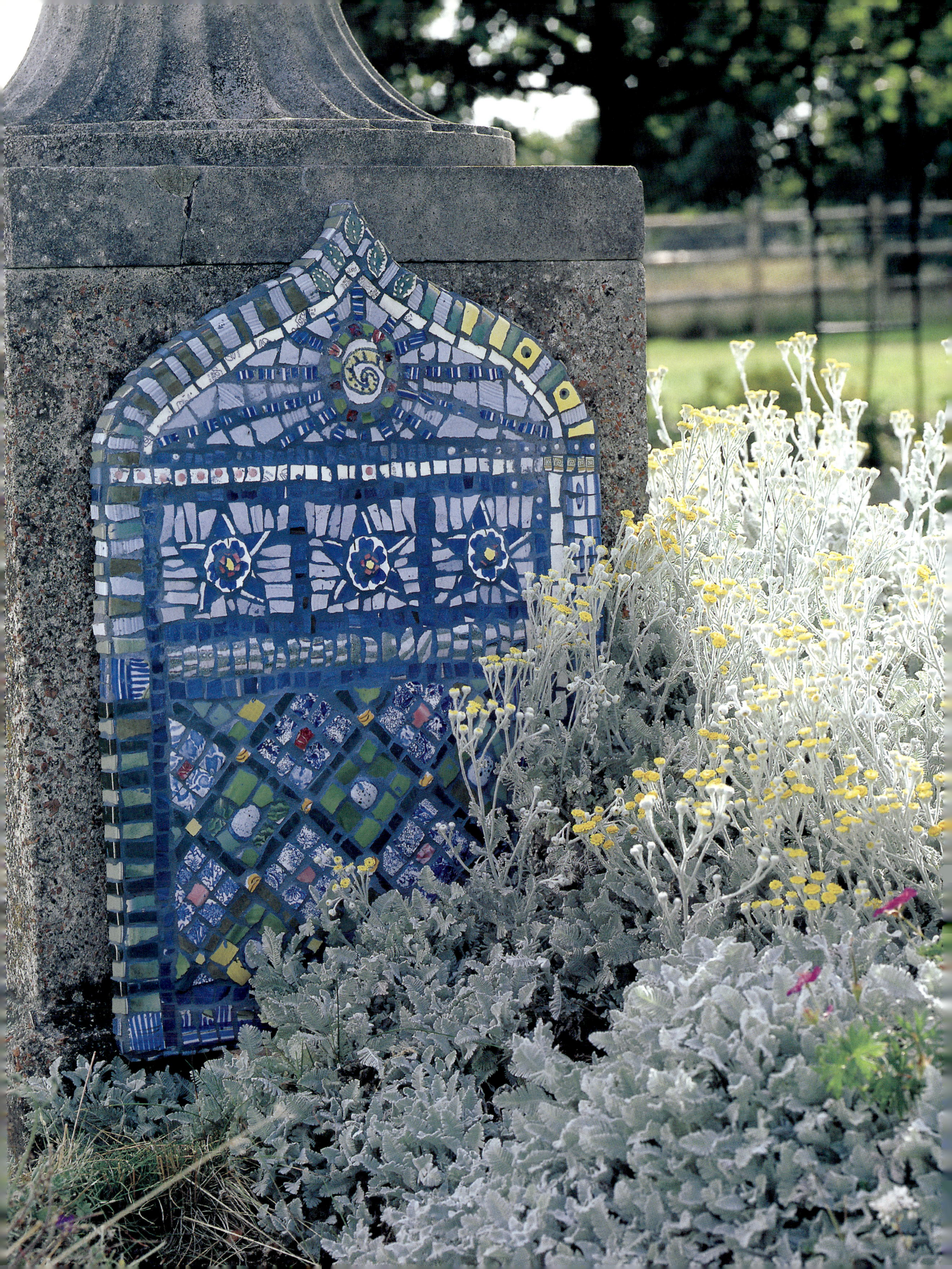

This richly textured panel is composed of tesserae cut from a variety of patterned china. Motifs are cut out and used as focal points for the patterns; some are raised to give them extra emphasis.

Mosaic Panel

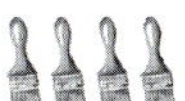

You will need

- 2cm (¾in) thick plywood sheet
- Pencil
- Thick card (stock) (optional)
- Jigsaw (saber saw)
- Abrasive paper (sandpaper)
- PVA (white) glue
- Paintbrushes
- Wood primer
- White undercoat paint
- Gloss paint
- Mirror plate, with keyhole opening
- Drill and rebate (rabbet) bit
- 2 x 2cm (¾in) screws
- Screwdriver
- Tracing paper (optional)
- Ruler, set square (triangle) and pair of compasses (optional)
- Selection of china
- Tile nippers
- Tile adhesive
- Tile grout
- Cement stain, vinyl matt emulsion (flat latex) or acrylic paint (optional)
- Grout spreader
- Nailbrush
- Soft cloth

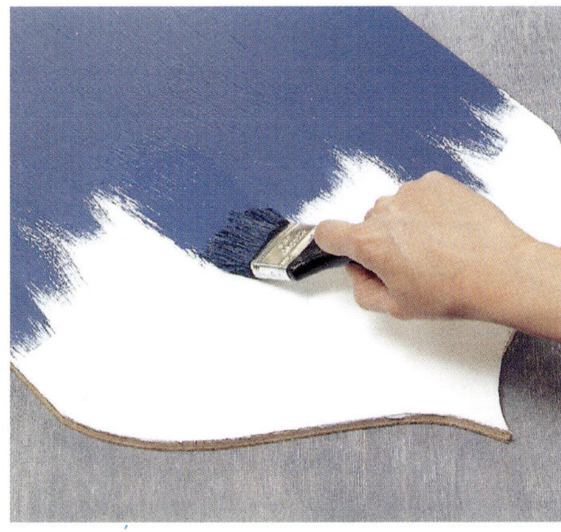

1 Draw the outer shape of the panel on to the sheet of plywood. (If you are unsure about drawing directly on to the surface, make a stencil from thick card.) Cut out around this shape using a jigsaw (saber saw) and sand down the rough edges. Seal one side and the edges with diluted PVA (white) glue. Paint the unsealed side with wood primer, undercoat paint and then gloss paint, allowing each coat to dry before applying the next.

2 Mark the position of the mirror plate on the unsealed back of the panel. Using a drill, rebate (rabbet) the area that will be under the key-hole-shaped opening so that it is large enough to take a screw head. Screw the mirror plate in position.

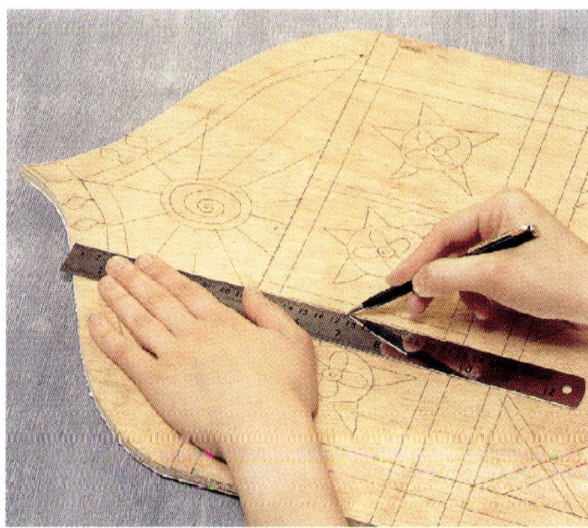

3 Draw your design on the sealed top surface. If necessary, trace and transfer your original design. Tools such as a ruler, set square and pair of compasses are helpful if your design has geometric elements.

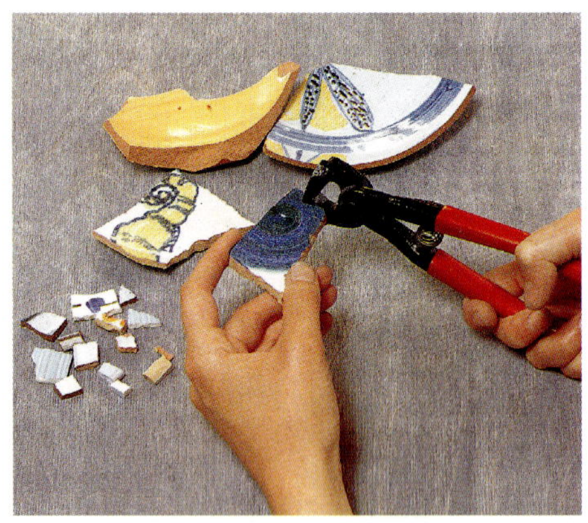

4 Sort the china into groups according to colour and pattern, and select interesting motifs that could be used to form the centrepieces of designs. Using the tile nippers, cut the china into the desired shapes.

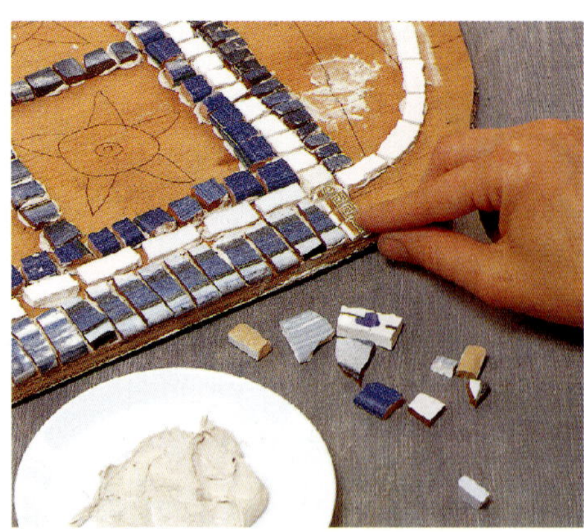

5 Using smooth edges cut from cups and plates, press the pieces into the tile adhesive first, then use them to tile the edges of the panel. Use small, regular-shaped tesserae to tile the structural lines of the design.

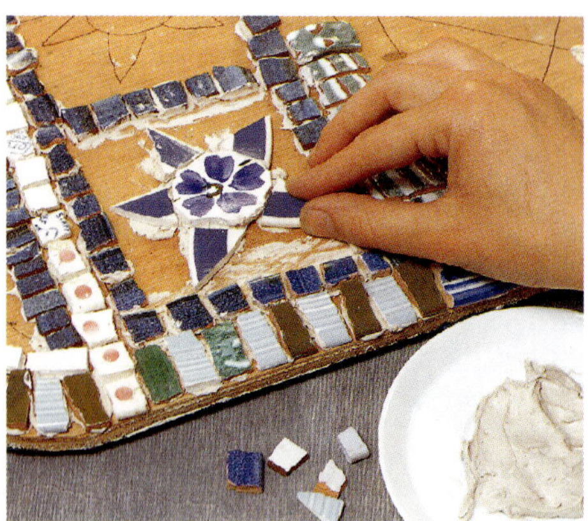

6 Raise small areas of the mosaic to give greater emphasis to sections of the design by setting the tesserae on a larger mound of tile adhesive. Cut more china and use it to form the patterns between the structural lines. Leave the panel to dry for 24 hours.

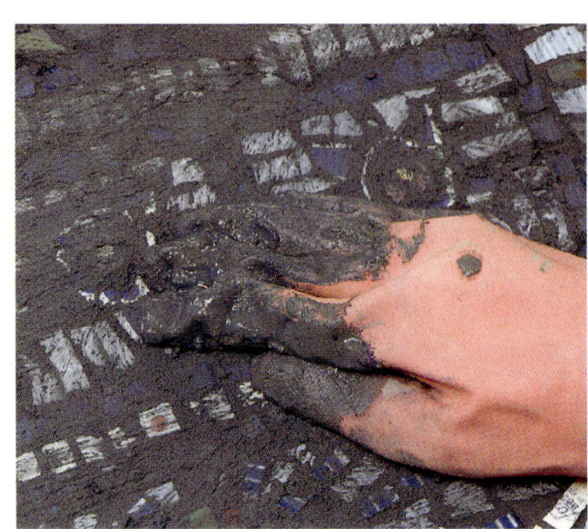

7 If you want the tile grout to be coloured, add cement stain, vinyl matt emulsion (flat latex) or acrylic paint to it. (If this is to be used indoors, cement stain is not essential.) Spread the grout over the surface using a grout spreader. Rub it into the gaps with your fingers.

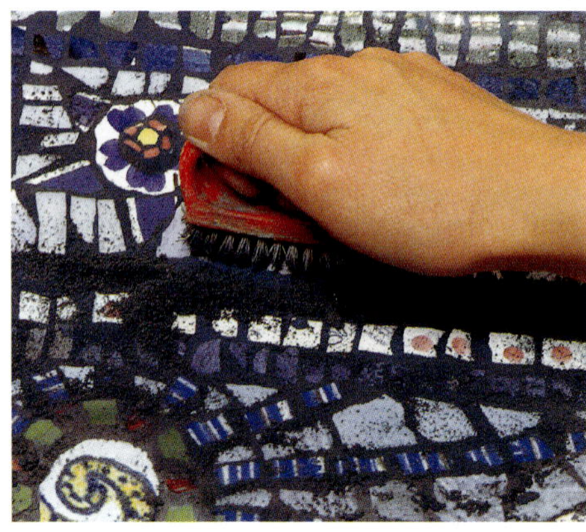

8 Allow the surface to dry for a few minutes, then scrub off any excess grout using a stiff nailbrush.

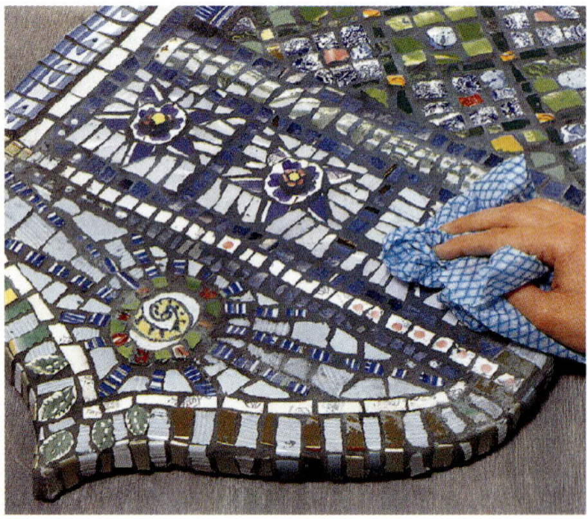

9 Leave to dry for 24 hours, then polish the surface with a dry, soft cloth.

This stunning pond is perfect for a small town garden, especially if it is sited near to a patio so that you can admire it while entertaining or dining alfresco on long summer evenings.

Mosaic Pond

You will need

Paper
Pencil
Outdoor tiles in a selection of greens and blues
Hammer
Piece of sacking (heavy cloth)
Spade
Galvanized metal pond, 1.2m (4ft) in diameter and 60cm (2ft) deep
Sand
Spirit (carpenter's) level
Piece of chalk
Wooden decking
Nails
Jigsaw (saber saw)
Tile adhesive
Adhesive spreader
Tile nippers
Mirror
Glue and glue gun
Tile grout
Flat trowel
Sponge

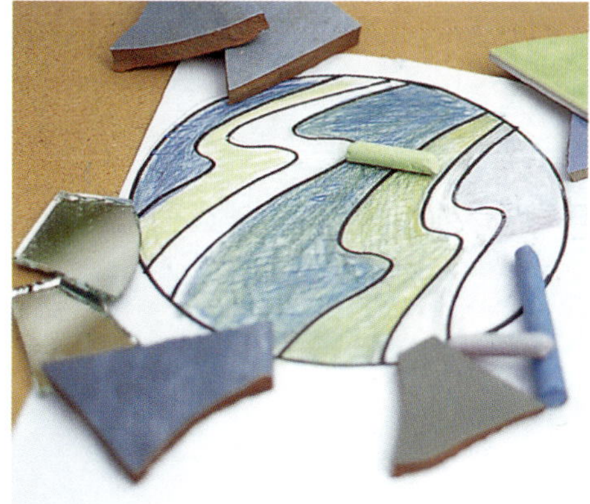

1 Mark out the design on a piece of paper. This does not have to be to scale, but it will give you some idea of the pattern and colour arrangement.

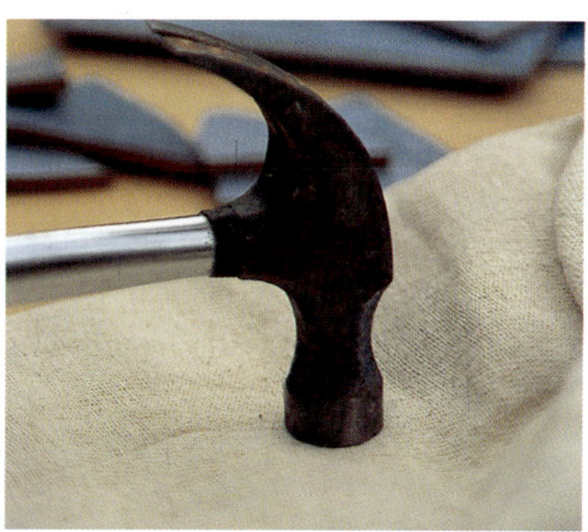

2 Smash the tiles using a hammer and some sacking (heavy cloth). Smash each colour of tile separately and keep the pieces in separate piles.

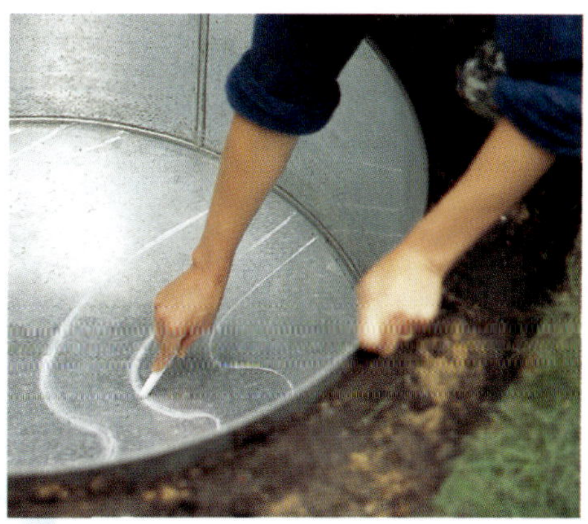

3 Dig a hole in the ground to accommodate the pond. Bed the pond in with a layer of sand. You will probably have to try the pond in the hole a few times until you get a good fit. Check that it is level with a spirit (carpenter's) level. Using a piece of chalk, mark out the design on the bottom of the pond.

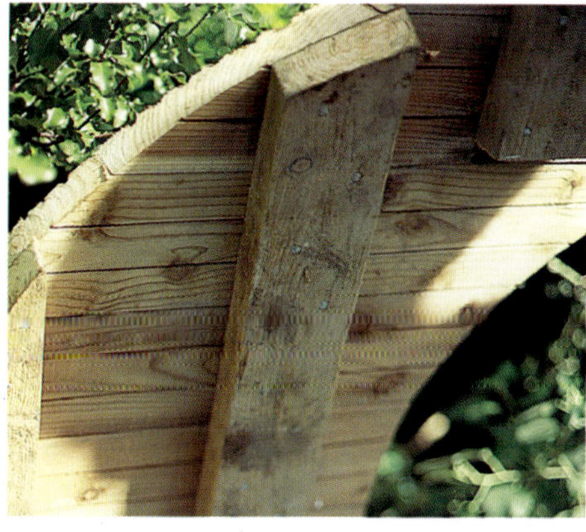

4 Construct the decking by nailing the wooden planks to two cross supports to create a rectangular shape, and then cut out the oval shape with a jigsaw (saber saw). (The picture shows the decking viewed from below.) Lay the oval-shaped piece of decking over the pond, and check that it is level using a spirit level.

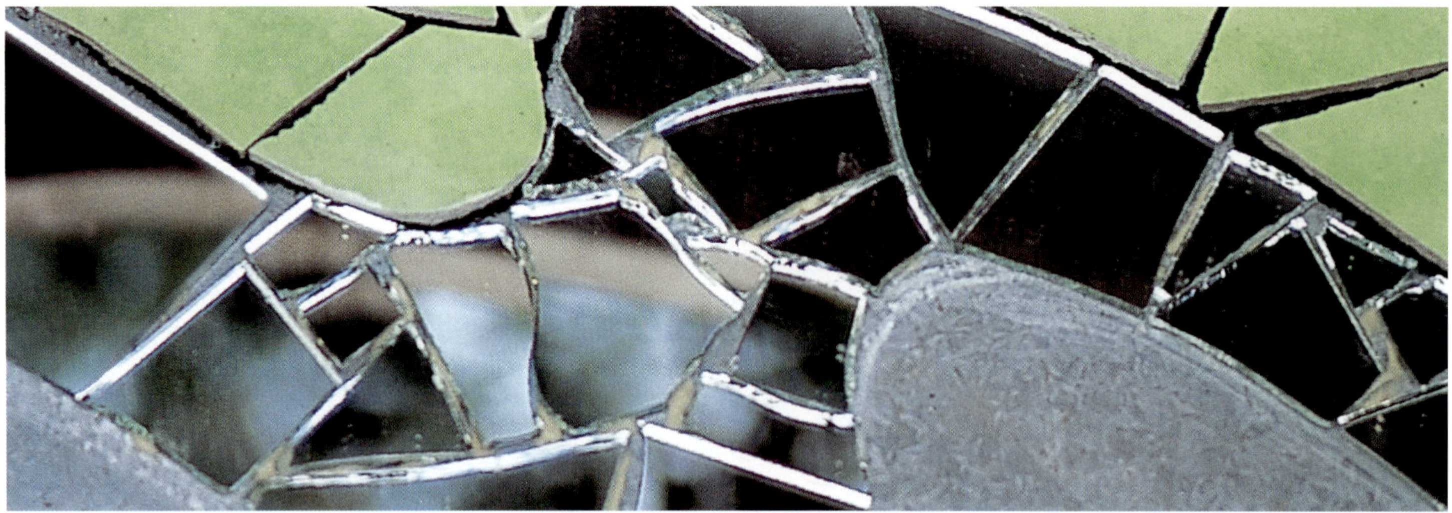

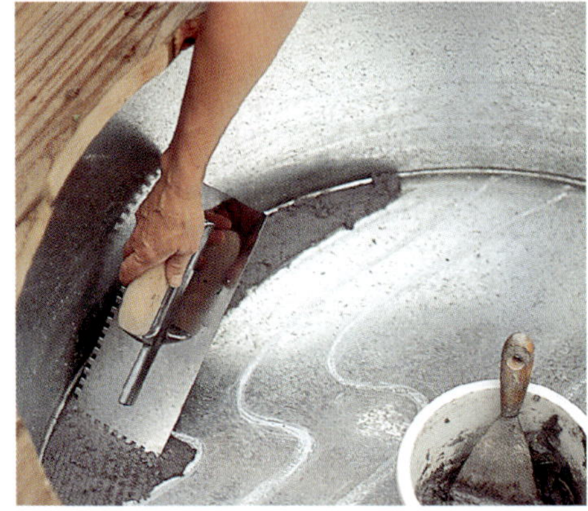

5 Spread a layer of tile adhesive over the first part of the design using an adhesive spreader.

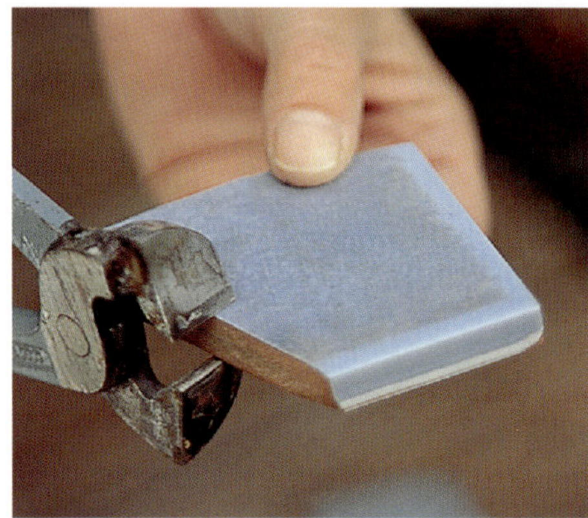

6 Stick the broken pieces of tile along the edge, but within the chalk line. Fill in the inside area. Use tile nippers to get the perfect shape. Finish this colour band.

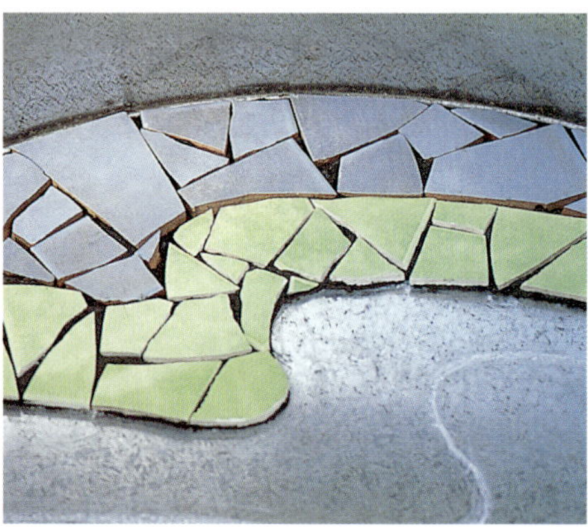

7 Start on the next colour, sticking down the tiles around the edge inside the chalk line as before. Finish this colour band.

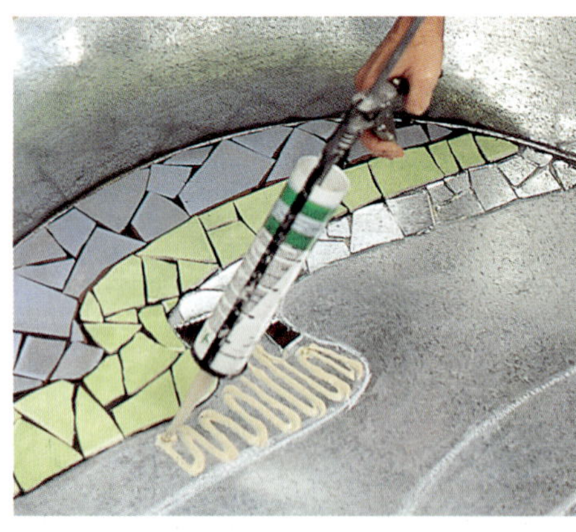

8 Cut up the mirror using the tile nippers. Cover the area for the pieces of mirror with glue from a glue gun, and stick down the mirror pieces as for the tile pieces. Finally, stick down the last colour of tile.

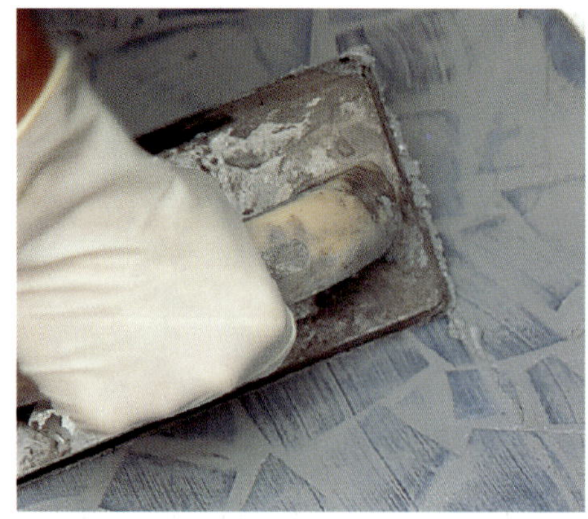

9 Allow the mosaic work to dry for three days. Grout the bottom of the pond with the tile grout, using a flat trowel.

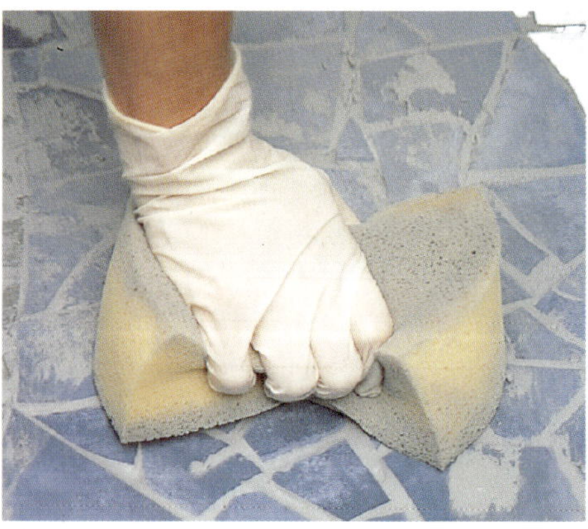

10 Clean with a damp sponge, then fill the pond with water.

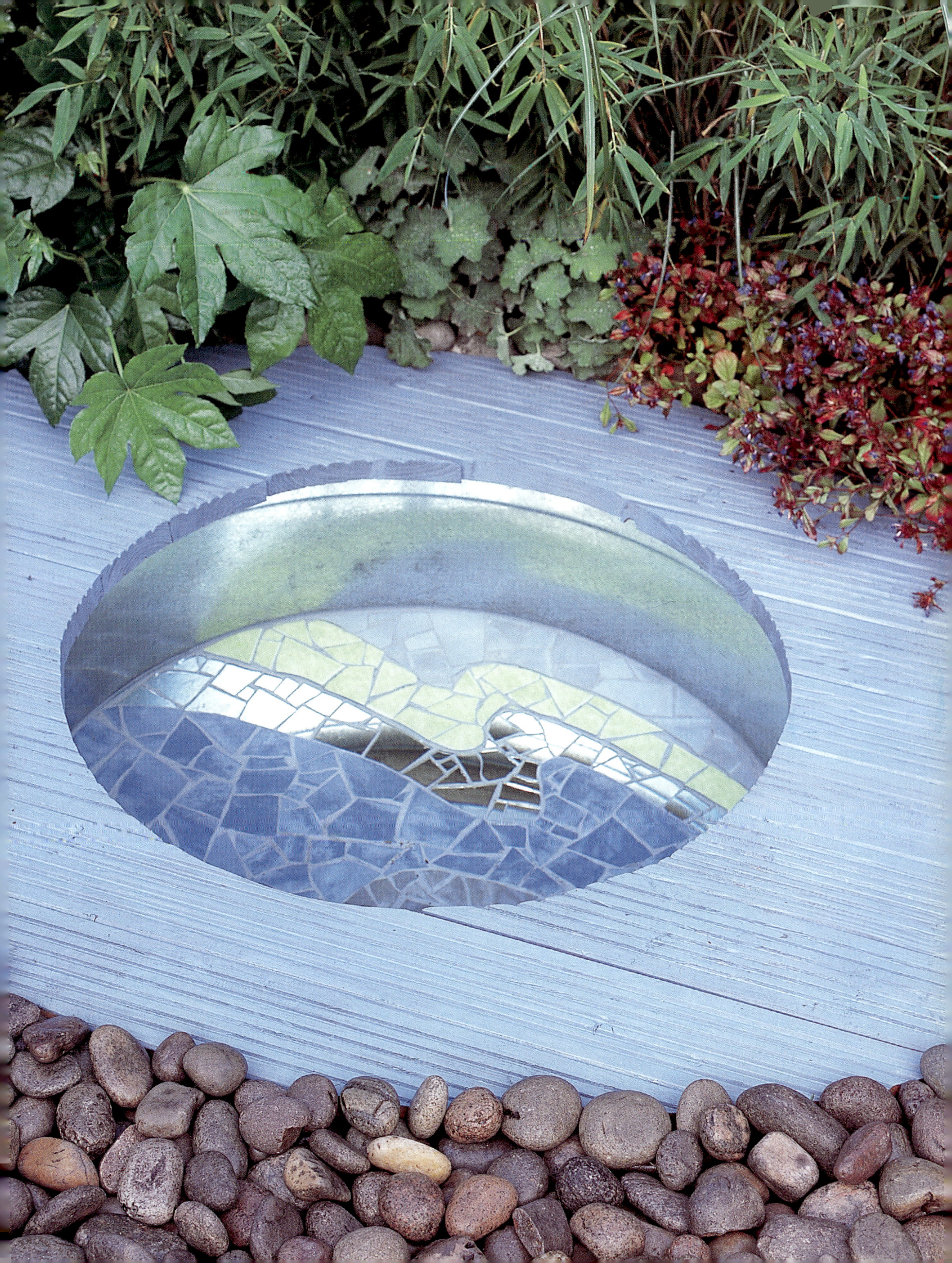

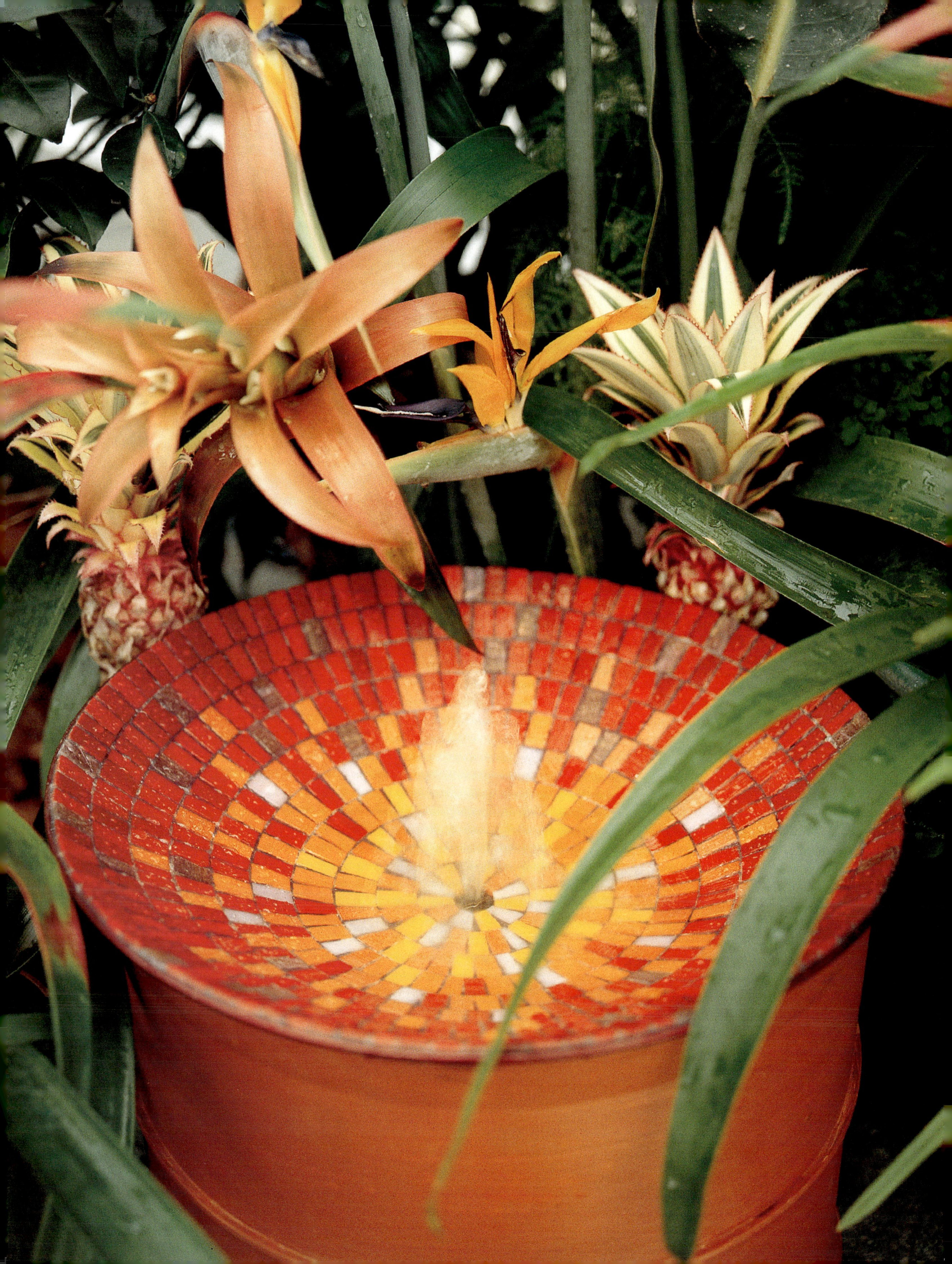

This striking water feature is perfect for use outdoors on a patio or indoors in a conservatory. Being portable, it can be brought in and out of the garden and would make a perfect centrepiece.

Fountain Bowl

Circular wooden panel, slightly smaller than the reservoir
Small dustbin (trash can) to act as a reservoir, about 60cm (24in) in diameter and 75cm (30in) deep
Screws
Screwdriver
4 wheeled feet
4 wooden blocks
Drill
5cm (2in) length of copper pipe, 2cm (¾in) in diameter
Hammer
White plastic container
Small pump (4 litres/1 gallon per minute)
Selection of vitreous glass mosaic tiles in a range of rich tropical colours
Paper
Tile nippers
Fibreglass bowl with a 2cm (¾in) hole drilled in the centre
Copper spraypaint (optional)
Glue and glue gun
Tile grout
Grout spreader
Sponge

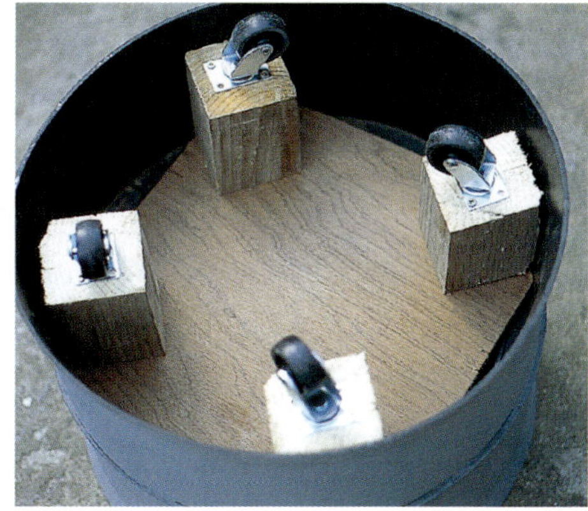

1 Fix the wooden panel inside the reservoir by screwing through from the outside of the dustbin. Attach the wheeled feet to the blocks of wood and screw them to the underside of the wooden panel. Drill a hole near the base of the reservoir for the pump cable.

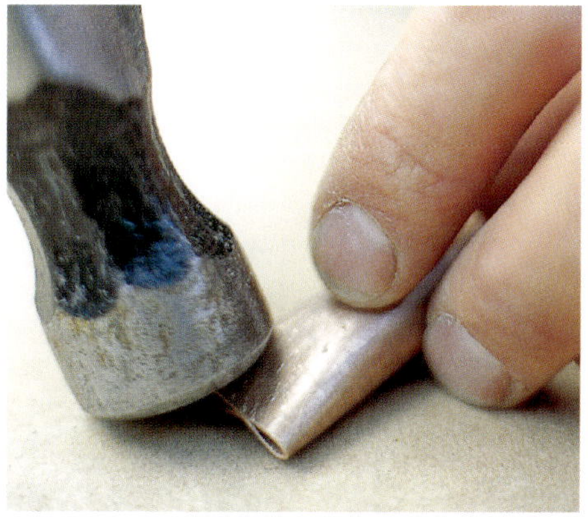

2 Using a hammer, flatten the piece of copper pipe at one end in order to create a narrow jet of water. Using the tip of a screwdriver, open up the flattened end of the copper pipe slightly to ensure that the water will flow freely.

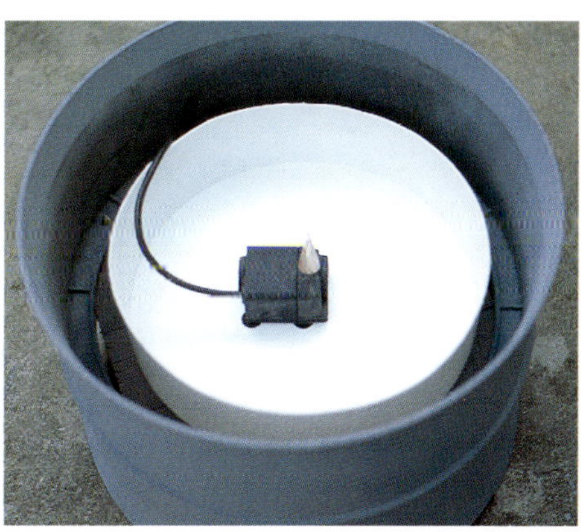

3 Position the white container in the centre of the reservoir, resting on the wooden panel. Add the pump, threading the cable through the hole drilled near the base of the reservoir in step 1.

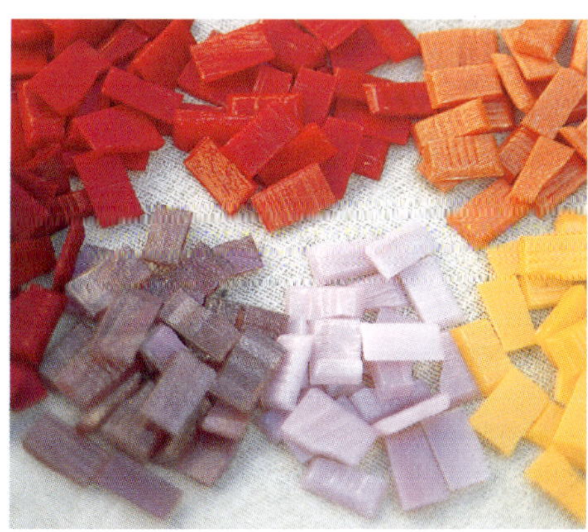

4 Select the glass tiles in a range of colours to achieve a bold, brightly coloured effect.

▶

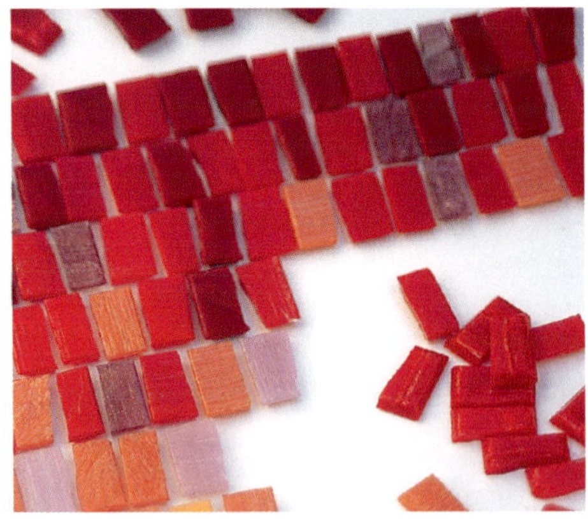

5 It is a good idea to test out the mosaic design on a piece of paper first. Arrange the tiles in concentric circles to achieve a pleasing blend of colours.

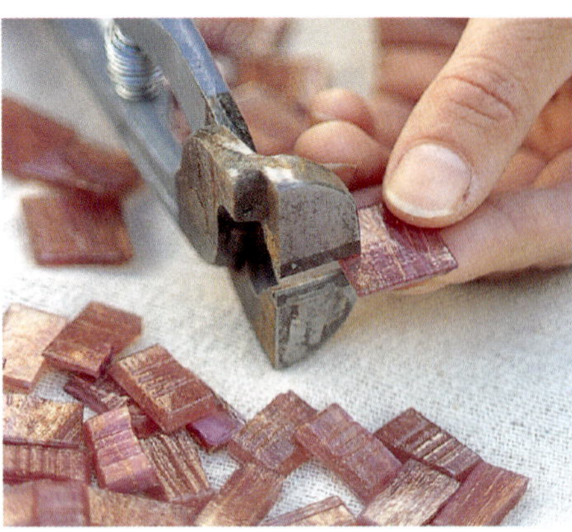

6 If necessary, cut the tiles into halves using the tile nippers.

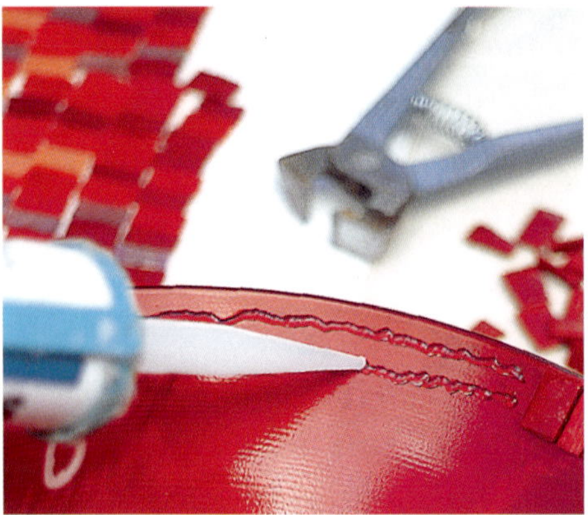

7 Spray the outside of the fibreglass bowl with copper paint if desired. Starting at the rim of the bowl, apply two lines of glue from a glue gun, keeping a small gap between the lines.

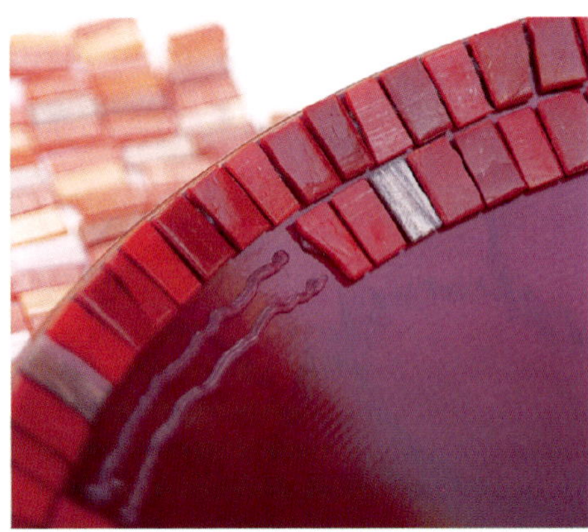

8 Press each tile firmly on to the adhesive. When the first row of tiles is in place, follow the same procedure for the second row, and continue with each row until you reach the centre.

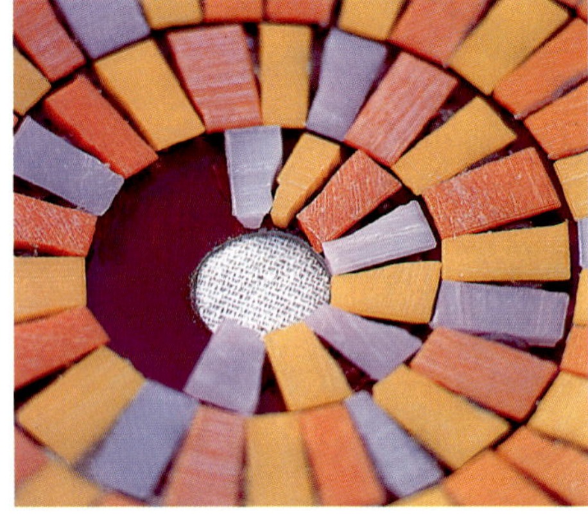

9 Finish by laying the final circle of tiles around the hole in the centre of the dish. You may have to cut the tiles to fit the final row. Allow to dry. Spread tile grout between the tiles using the grout spreader. Allow to dry, then wipe clean with a damp sponge. Fill the white container with water and place the bowl over the copper pipe.

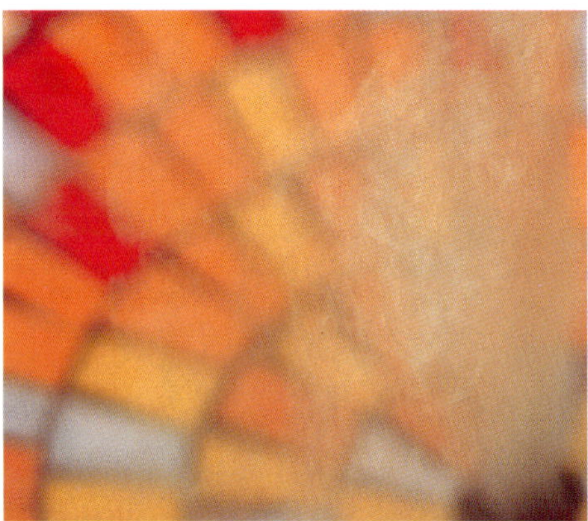

10 Plug in the pump, then adjust its flow rate to create a range of different sounds, from gushing fountain to gentle trickle, depending on your mood.

No artistic skills are required for this stunning mosaic, as the picture is simply an old etching enlarged on a photocopier. The tesserae are glued on to fibreglass mesh, then lowered into position on the floor.

Black-and-white Floor

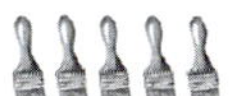

You will need

- Black-and-white image
- Clear film (plastic wrap)
- Masking tape
- Fibreglass mesh
- Unglazed ceramic mosaic tiles: black and white
- Tile nippers
- PVA (white) glue
- Paintbrush
- Craft (utility) knife
- Tile adhesive
- Notched spreader
- Flat wooden board
- Hammer
- Grout spreader
- Sponge
- Soft cloth

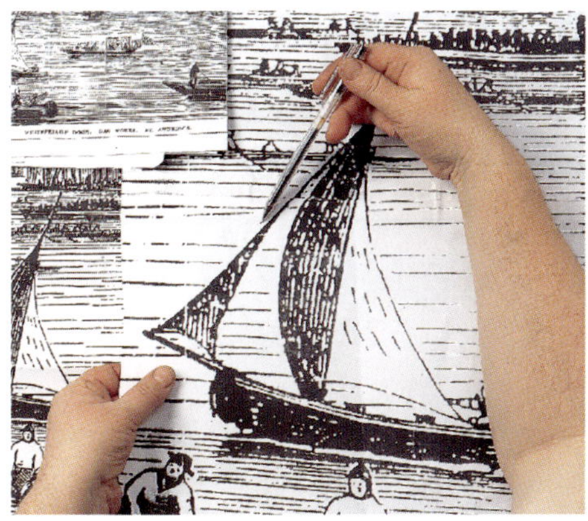

1 Decide on the image you wish to use, or you may wish to build up a picture from various elements. Enlarge on a photocopier to the required size.

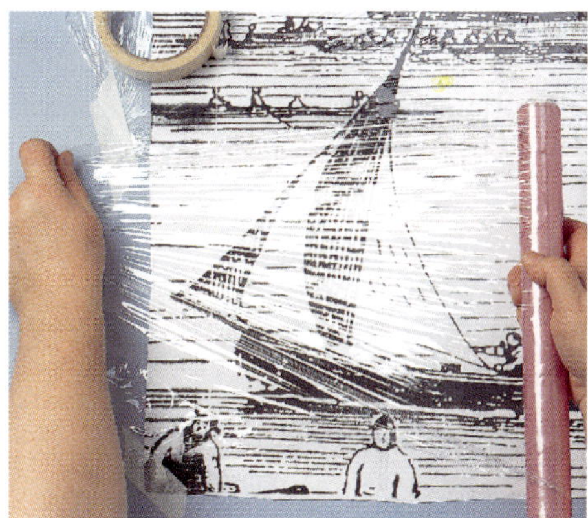

2 Working on a large work surface, cover the photocopy with clear film (plastic wrap) and secure the edges with masking tape. If your picture is built up from more than one image, repeat this process for all the sections.

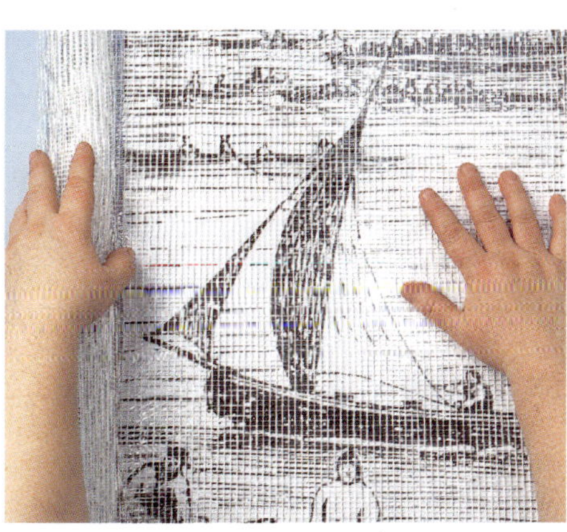

3 Position a piece of fibreglass mesh over the clear film, and tape it down to the work surface with masking tape. Using tile nippers, cut the tiles into quarters.

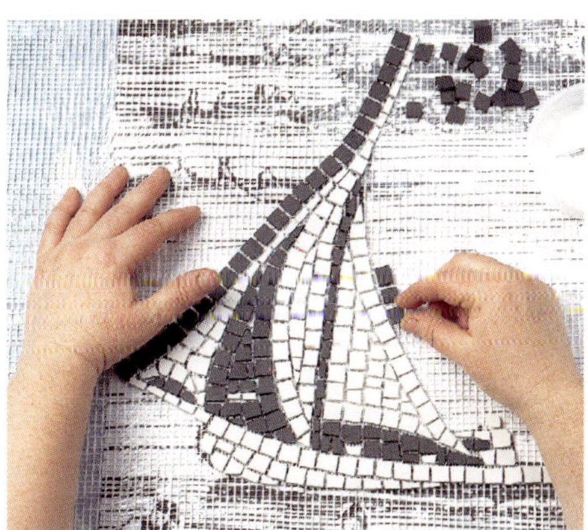

4 Beginning with the main features, such as the boat, glue the tesserae to the fibreglass mesh using PVA (white) glue and a fine paintbrush. Build up the picture, using the light and shade of the photocopy as a guide.

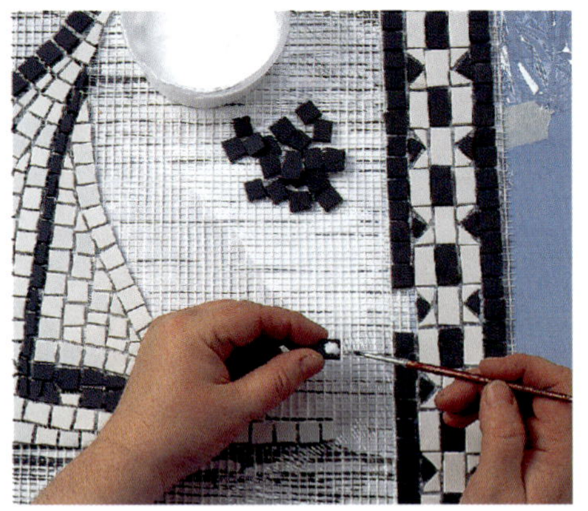

5 Outline the panel with a geometric border in black and white, cutting some of the tesserae in half to make triangular shapes.

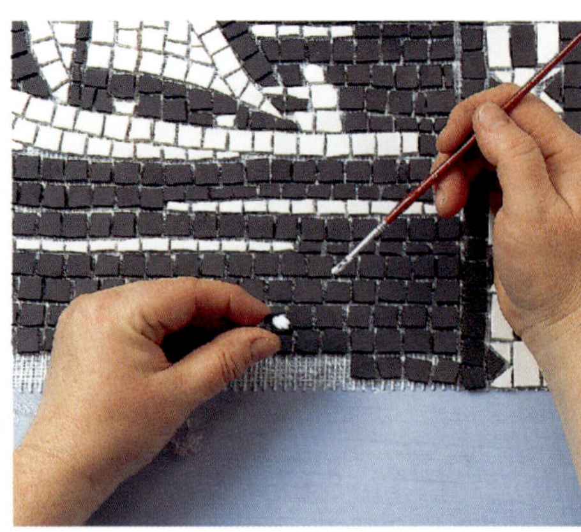

6 Fill in the background of the design, simplifying and accentuating the black and white areas, until the photocopy is completely covered. Leave to dry.

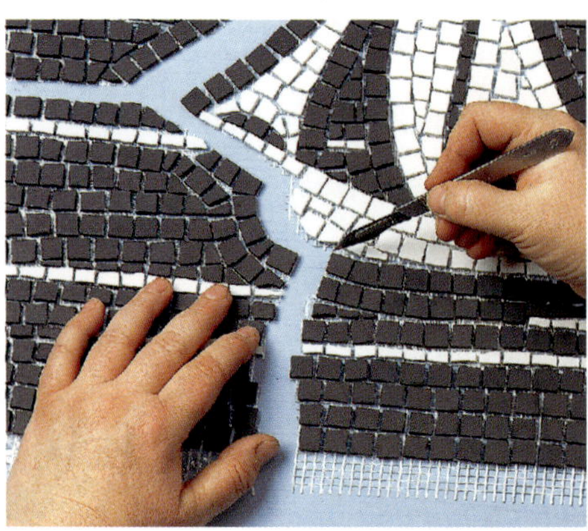

7 Using a craft (utility) knife, cut through the mesh and clear film, chopping the mosaic into manageable sections. You may find it helpful to cut around the boat shape, as shown.

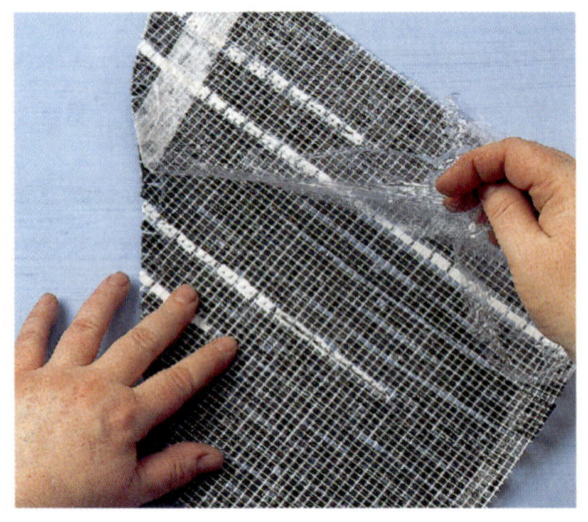

8 Turn the sections over and peel off the clear film. Using the craft knife, pierce any holes in the mesh that are clogged with glue.

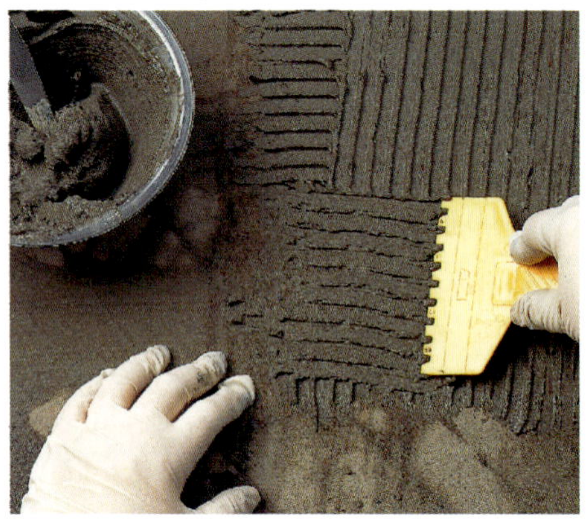

9 Spread tile adhesive over the bathroom floor, using a notched spreader. Work from the part of the floor furthest away from the door.

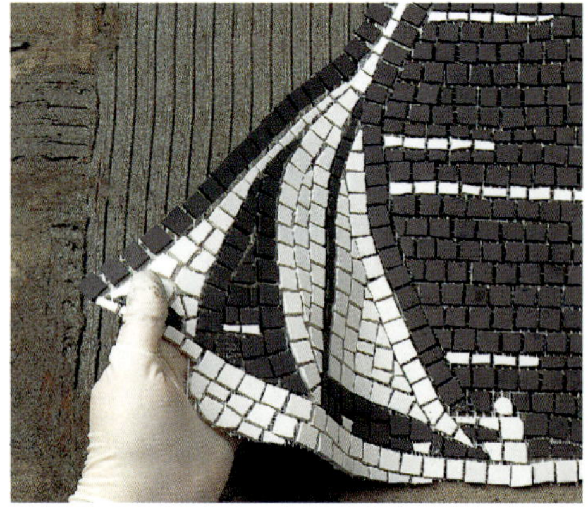

10 Carefully lay each section of the mosaic on the tile adhesive, mesh side down.

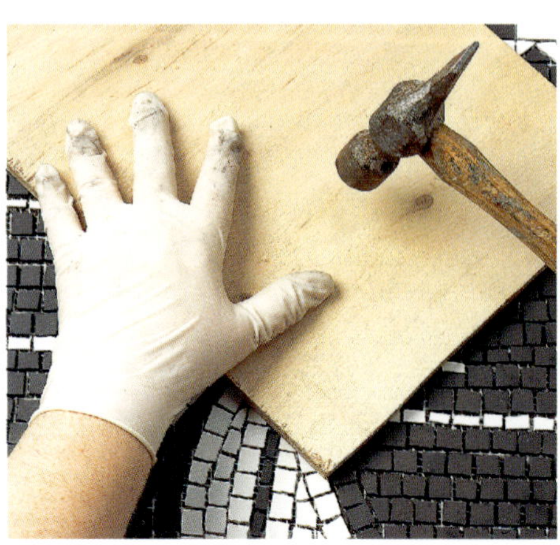

11 Place a flat wooden board over each part of the mosaic and tap with a hammer to make sure the tesserae are firmly embedded into the adhesive. Leave to dry overnight, then grout with more tile adhesive, using a grout spreader. Wipe away any excess with a damp sponge, then leave to dry. Finally, polish with a dry, soft cloth.

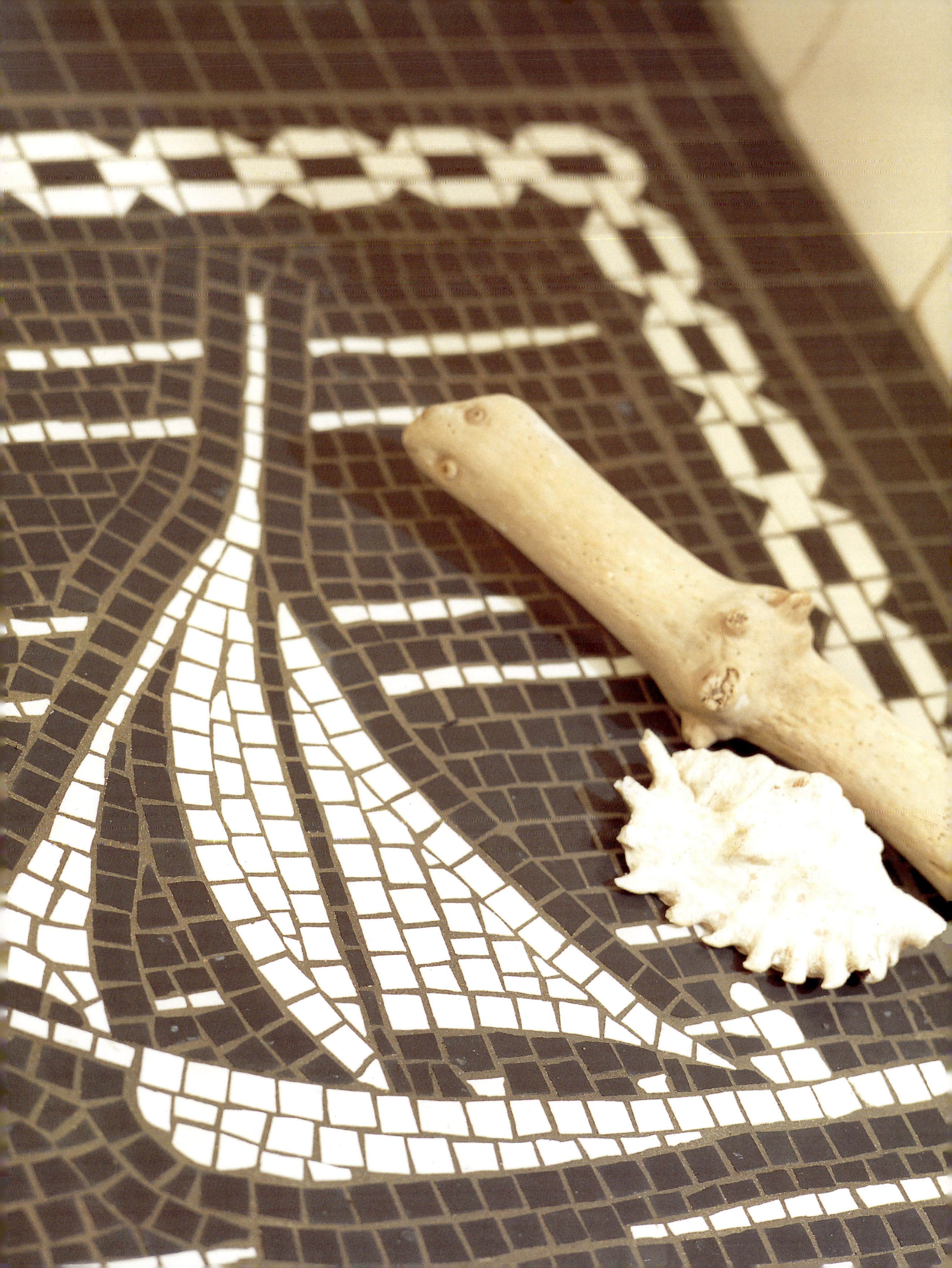

The ancient tradition of games, paths and puzzles in mosaic gives this simple, strong design an ageless appeal. The background is quick and easy to do, and the swirling design of the snakes uses vibrant colours.

Snakes and Ladders Floor

You will need

- Paper
- Felt-tipped pens
- Tape measure
- Scissors
- Clear film (plastic wrap)
- Fibreglass mesh
- Vitreous glass mosaic tiles in various colours and matt (flat) black
- Tile nippers
- PVA (white) glue
- Paintbrush
- Patio cleaner
- Black cement stain
- Tile adhesive
- Notched trowel
- Sand
- Cement
- Sponge

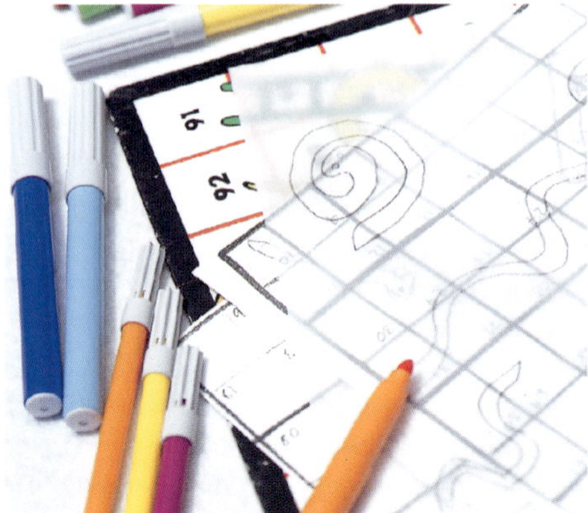

1 Draw up a masterplan for the whole board. Play a game on it to make sure that it works. Measure out one of the outside paving slabs to be covered. Cut out 25 pieces of paper to fit the slab.

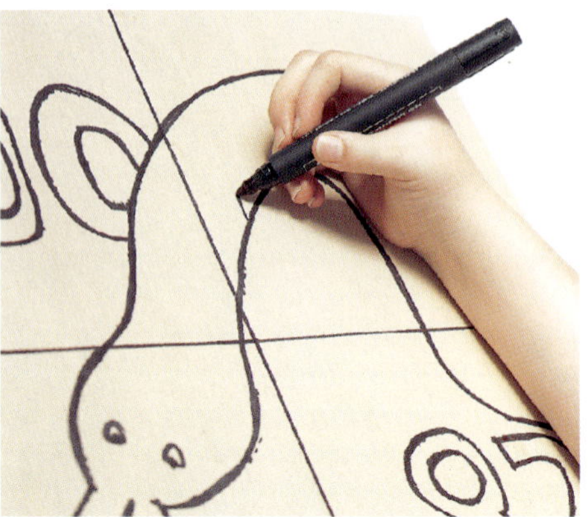

2 Fold them into quarters and mark out the sections. These are the 100 squares needed for your game. Copy out your design on to the 25 squares of paper using a thick felt-tipped pen.

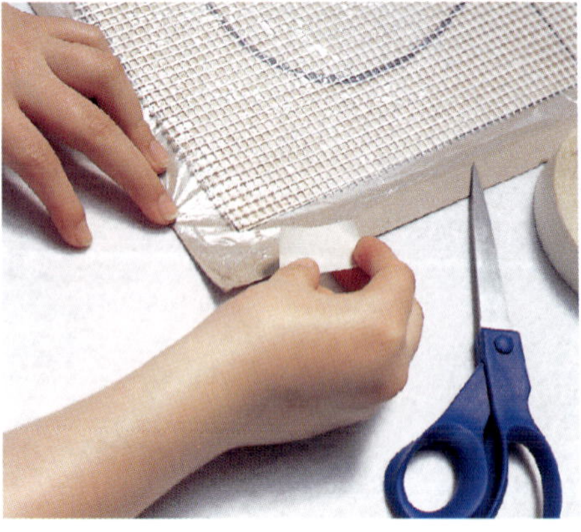

3 Cover the front of each of the 25 squares with clear film (plastic wrap) and then a piece of mesh, cut to size.

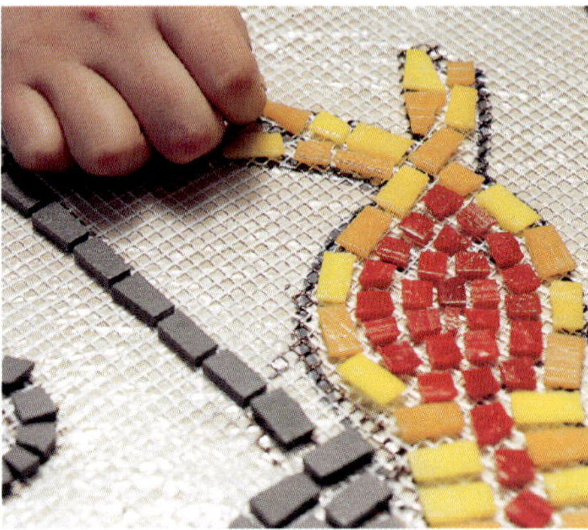

4 Outline each of the 100 squares with matt (flat) black tiles, cut in half. Use PVA (white) glue and a fine paintbrush to stick them to the mesh. Outline the numbers with quarter tiles and the snakes with both half and quarter tiles. Fill in the snakes and ladders with glossy, brightly coloured glass tiles.

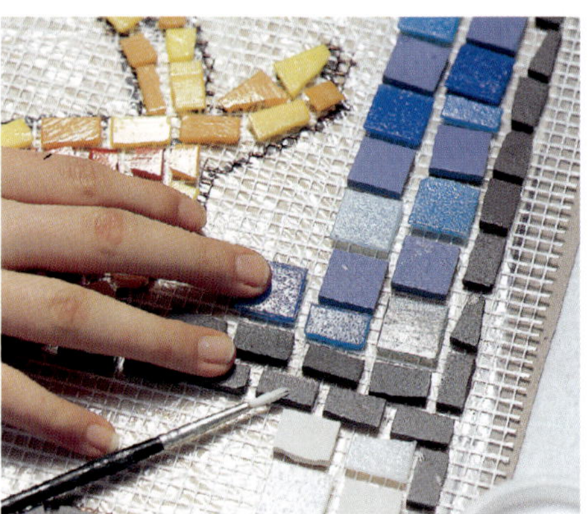

5 Fill in the background squares with different colours for even and odd squares. Leave the squares to dry overnight, then turn them over, peel off the paper and the plastic film (used to prevent the tiles and mesh sticking to the paper) and leave until totally dry. Make sure all the tiles are stuck on to the fibreglass mesh, and restick any that fall off.

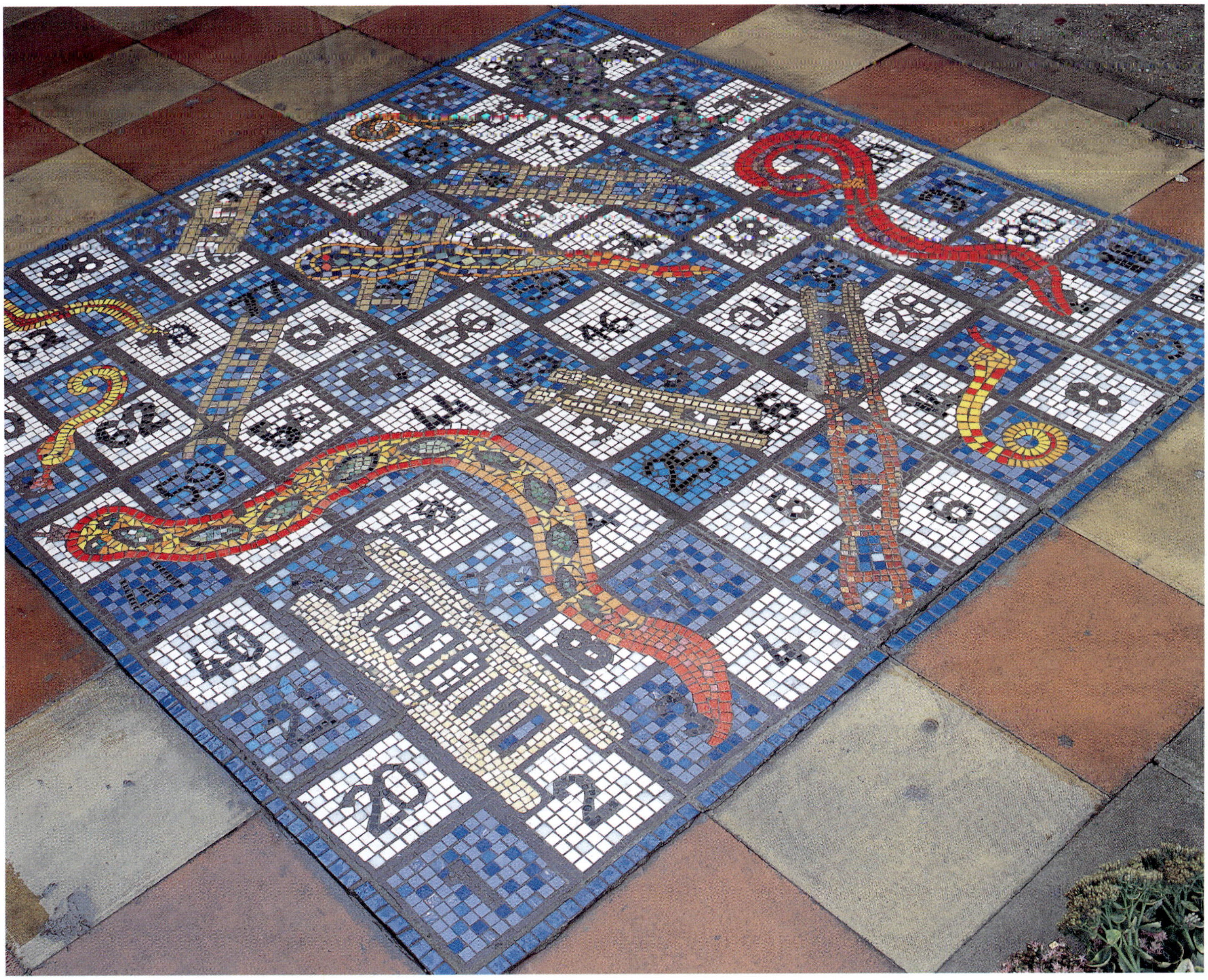

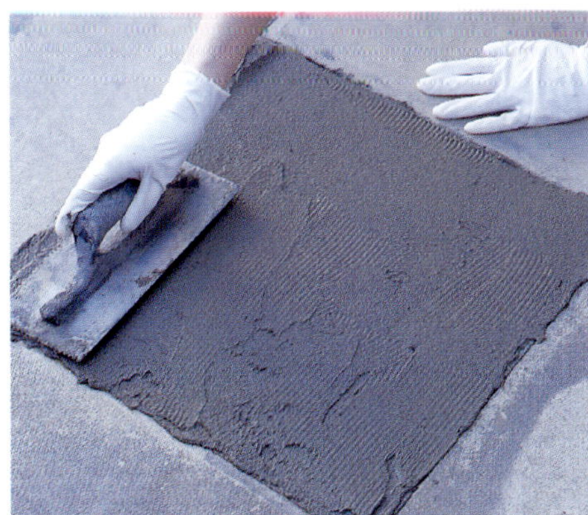

6 Clean all the paving slabs with patio cleaner and rinse well. Add a black cement stain to the tile adhesive, following the manufacturer's instructions, and apply a thin, even layer to each square with a notched trowel.

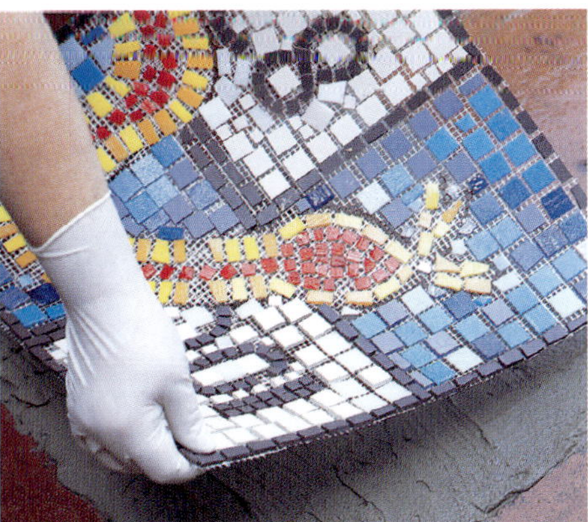

7 Lay on the design, one section at a time, allowing for gaps between the slabs. Mark all the pieces clearly and refer to the plan often as you work. Tamp down the squares gently and evenly. Leave to dry completely.

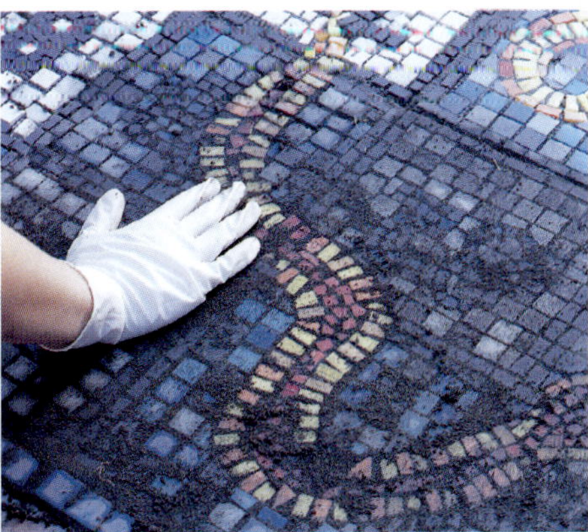

8 Grout the mosaic, using a mixture of sand, cement and water, with an added black stain. Wipe off the excess with a damp sponge and allow to dry slowly.

Acknowledgements

The projects were created by Helen Baird, with the following exceptions:

Emma Biggs, Mosaic Workshop: abstract mirror (pp. 130–2); abstract colour panel (pp. 204–5)

Tessa Brown: love letter rack (pp. 80–1)

Victoria Brown: Mediterranean mirror (pp. 102–3)

Marion Elliot: black-and-white tiled table (pp. 158–9)

Celia and Cohen Gregory: candle sconce (pp. 116–18); stained-glass table (pp. 179–81); hearth (pp. 226–9)

Sandra Hadfield: decorative planter (pp. 90–1); funky fruit bowl (pp. 97–9); mosaic fire screen (pp. 122–3); china rail (pp. 210–12); crazy paving shelf (pp. 213–5); coat rack (pp. 223–5)

Lesley Harle with Susan Conder: squiggle frame (pp. 100–1)

Simon Harman: fountain bowl (pp. 244–6)

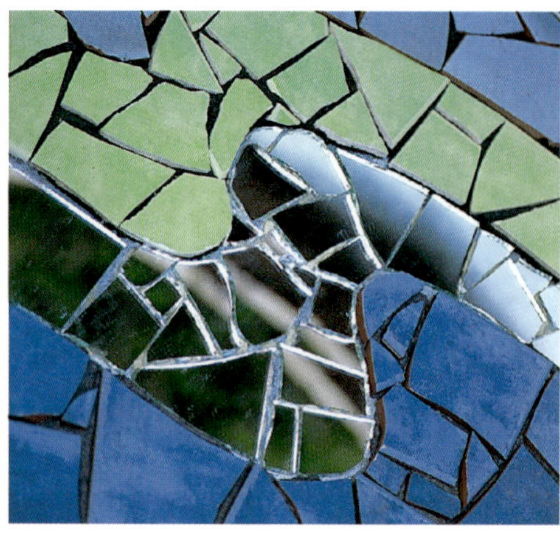

Tessa Hunkin, Mosaic Workshop: cosmic clock (pp. 114–15); sculptural head (pp. 139–41)

Mary Maguire: shell table (pp. 189–91)

Cleo Mussi: china tiles (pp. 78–9); plant pots (pp. 82–3); decorative spheres (pp. 86–7); part-tiled flowerpot (p. 92); sunflower mosaic (p. 93); star wall motifs (pp. 94–6); bathroom mirror (pp. 127–9); shades of blue garden table (pp. 168–9); mosaic panel (pp. 238–40)

Joanna Nevin: stained-glass candle-holder (pp. 84–5); stained-glass screen (pp. 182–5)

Tabby Riley: mirror mosaic (pp. 111–13); flower garden table (pp. 172–5); mosaic pond (pp. 241–3)

Sarah Round: house number plaque (p. 76); pot stand (p. 77)

Norma Vondee: sea urchin garden seat (pp. 166–7); star table (pp. 170–1); bathroom cabinet (pp. 206–7); slate shelf (pp. 208–9); lemon tree floor (pp. 232–4); black-and-white floor (pp. 247–9); snakes and ladders floor (pp. 250–1)

Stewart and Sally Walton: mosaic table top (pp. 150–2)

The publishers would like to thank the following for the use of images (t = top, b = bottom, l = left): pp. 8–9 The Art Archive/Dagli Orti; p. 10 The Travelsite; p. 11t The Art Archive/British Museum/Eileen Tweedy; p. 11b The Art Archive/Red-Head; p. 12tl The Art Archive/Byzantine Mosaic Museum Istanbul/Dagli Orti; p. 12–13 The Nek Chand Foundation/Henry Wilson/Raw Vision

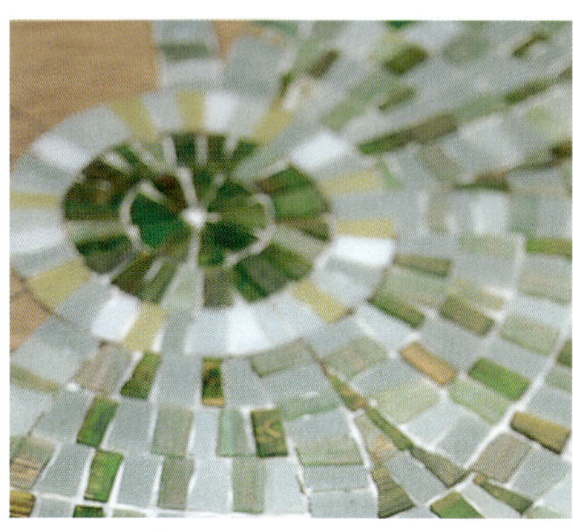

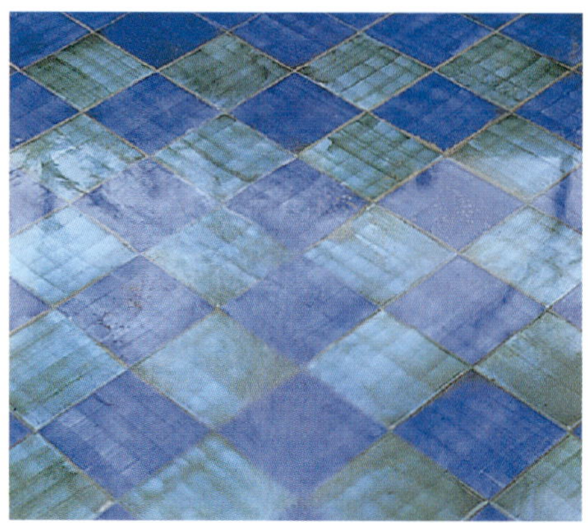

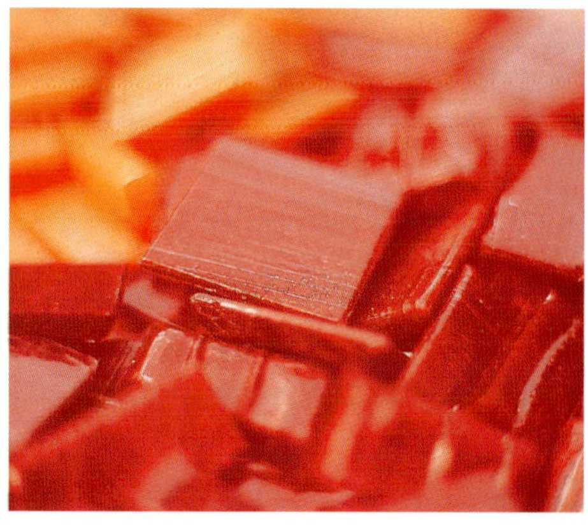

Useful Addresses

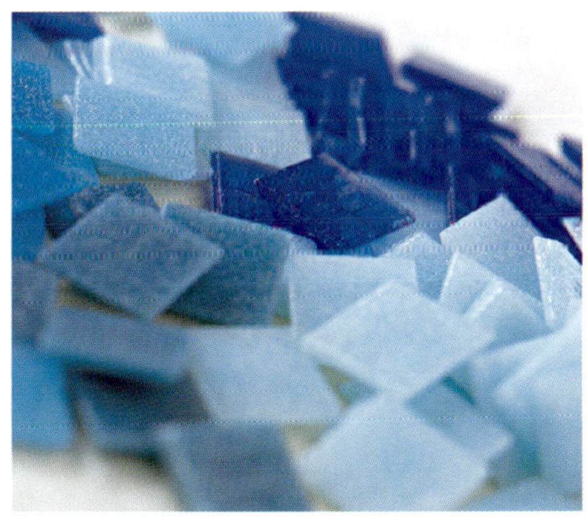

The equipment you will need can be found in most do-it-yourself, craft or hardware stores. The adresses listed here include speciality suppliers that may be useful when making the projects in this book.

Australia

Alan Patrick Pty Ltd
11 Agnes Street
Jolimont, Victoria 3002
Tel: (61) 3 9654 8288

The Crafts and Gifts Gallery
306 Hay Street
Subiaco, WA, 6088
craftgallery@optusnet.com.au
Tel: (61) 8 9381 8215

Finn's Stained Glass
129 Boundary Road
Peakhurst, NSW, 2210
www.finnsglass.com.au
Tel: (61) 2 9533 4333

France

Mosaik Atelier
17, rue Foucault
92110 Clichy
Tel: (33) 47 30 98 10

Italy

Angelo Orsoni
Cannergio 1045, 30121 Venezia
Tel: (39) 41 244 0002

Mario Dona e Figli Snc
Via Marchetti Guiseppe 6
33097 Spilimbergo (PN),Friuli

North America & Canada

Alice's Stained Glass
7015 N. 58th Avenue
Glendale, AZ 85301
Tel: (602) 939-7260

Brian's Crafts Unlimited
PO Box 731046
Ormond Beach, FL 32173-046
Tel: (904) 672-2726

Deco Tile
362 Davenport Road
Toronto, Canada M5R 1K6
Tel: (416) 413 7985

Dick Blick
PO Box 1267
Galesburg, IL 61402
Tel: (309) 343-6181

Eastern Art Glass
PO Box 341
Wcykoff, NJ 07481
Tel: (201) 847-0001

Hudson Glass Co., Inc.
219 N. Division St.,
Peekshill, NY 10566
Tel: (914) 737-2124

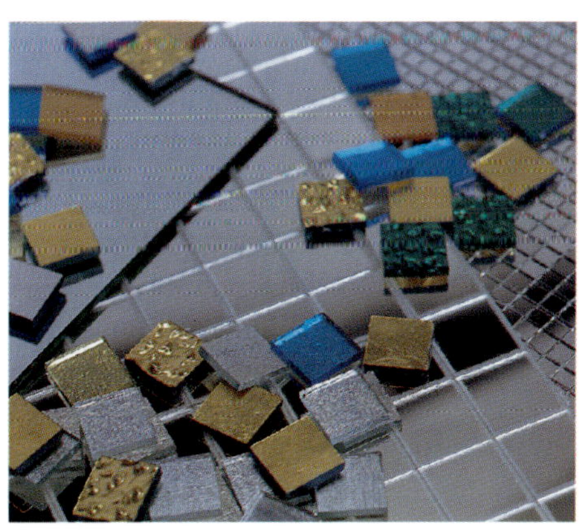

United Kingdom

Edgar Udney and Co Ltd
314 Balham High Road
London SW17 7AA
Tel: (44) 020 8767 8181
Ceramic glass and smalti. Fixing materials. Mail-order service.

Fired Earth
Twyford Mill
Oxford Road, Adderbury
Oxfordshire OX17 3HP
Tel: (44) 01295 812088

James Hetley & Co
Glasshouse Fields
London E1 9JA
Tel: (44) 020 7780 2345

Mosaic Workshop
1a Princeton Street
London W1R 4AX
www.mosaicworkshop.com
Tel: (44) 020 7404 9249

Reed Harris
Riverside House
27 Carnworth Road
London SW6 3HR
Tel: (44) 020 7736 7511

Index

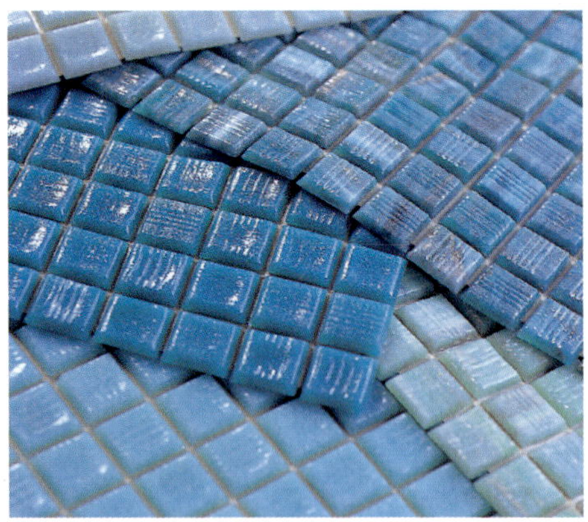
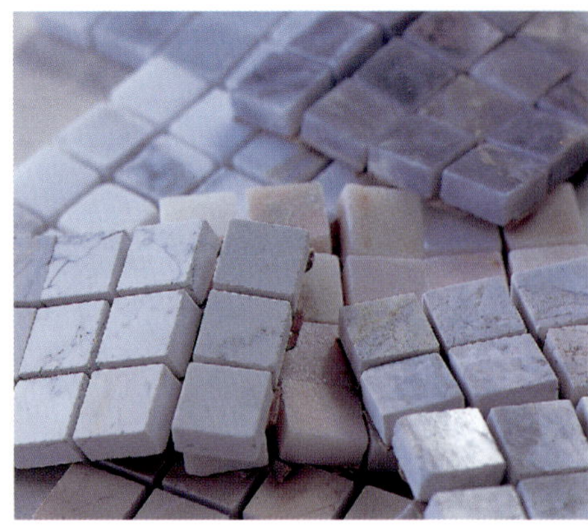
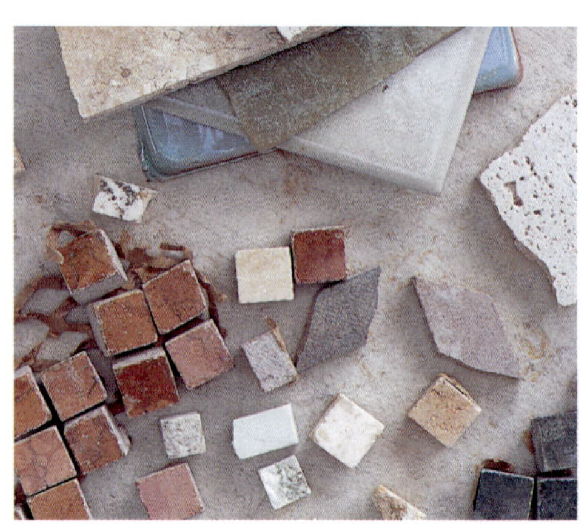

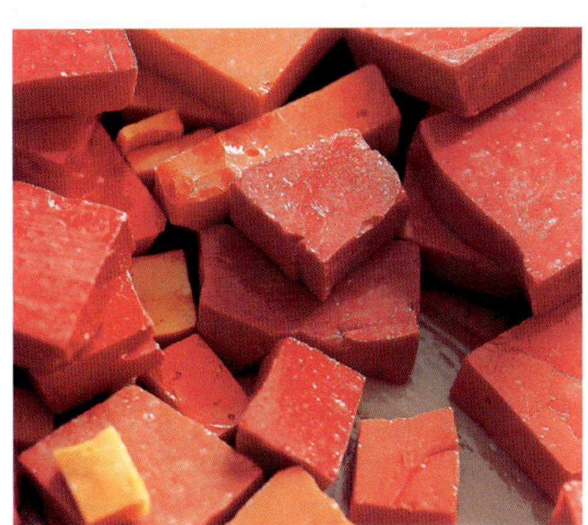
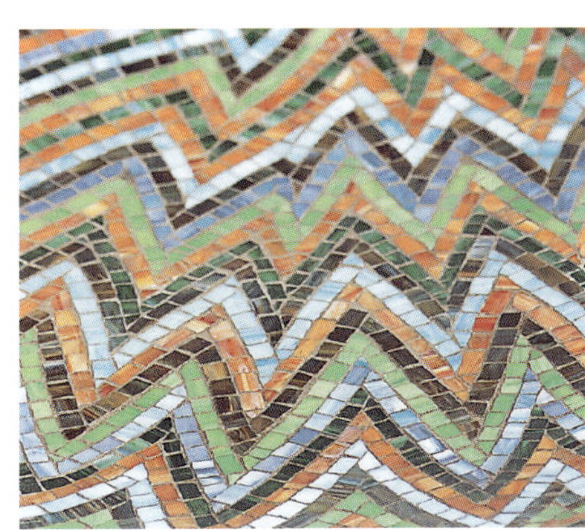
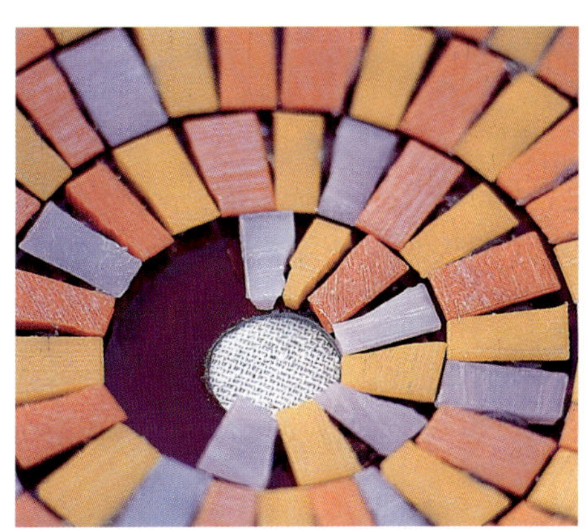

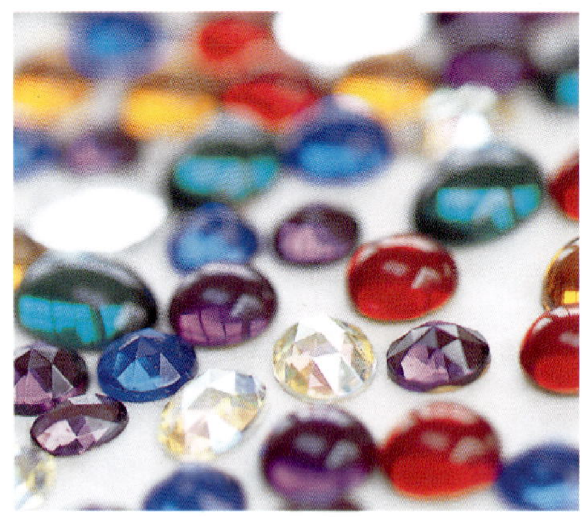
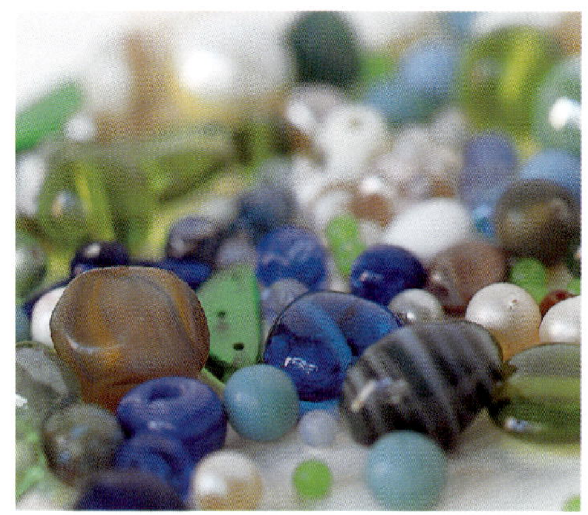
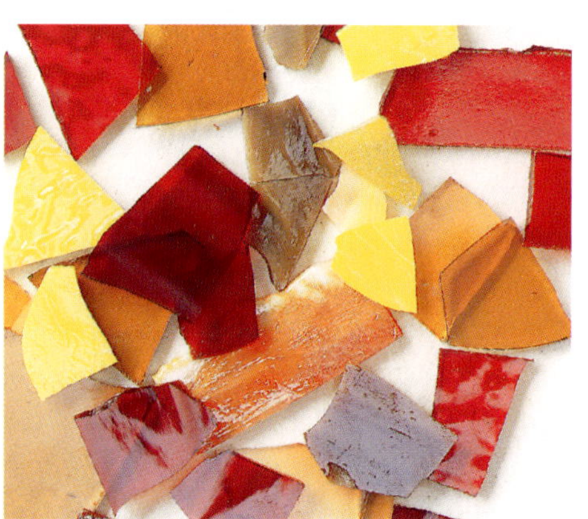